INTRODUCTION TO LEGAL METHOD AND PROCESS

CASES AND MATERIALS

Third Edition

By

Michael A. Berch
Professor of Law,
Arizona State University

Rebecca White Berch
Justice, Supreme Court of Arizona

Ralph S. Spritzer
Professor of Law Emeritus,
University of Pennsylvania,
Visiting Professor of Law, Arizona State University

AMERICAN CASEBOOK SERIES®

WEST
GROUP

A THOMSON COMPANY

Mat #18477661

American Casebook Series, and the West Group symbol
are registered trademarks used herein under license.

COPYRIGHT © 1984, 1992 WEST PUBLISHING CO.
COPYRIGHT © 2002 By WEST GROUP
            610 Opperman Drive
            P.O. Box 64526
            St. Paul, MN 55164–0526
            1–800–328–9352

ISBN 0–314–26002–1 (hard cover)
ISBN 0–314–26477–9 (soft cover)

TEXT IS PRINTED ON 10% POST
CONSUMER RECYCLED PAPER

For Sonna
and for our daughter, Jessica Jeanne,
with love.

M.A.B.
R.W.B.

For Lorraine, who shares with me our
autumn years in Arizona.

R.S.S.

*

Preface to the Third Edition

The core of legal method and process involves reading, analyzing and synthesizing judicial opinions and interpreting legislation. Chapters I, III, and V include these traditional materials in what we hope is an interesting and instructional format. Chapter II, the Anatomy of a Legal Dispute, is innovative for a legal method casebook. It follows a typical automobile accident through various legal processes leading to a civil lawsuit and culminating in a judgment. After digesting Chapter II, students should more fully appreciate the later materials on case analysis, legislation and the role of the courts. Indeed, several themes first introduced in Chapter II reemerge in later chapters of the book. Chapter VI analyzes the role of the courts in conflict resolution. We believe this subject matter is well suited to this course, although some schools may prefer to defer these materials to a course in constitutional law. We have also included discussion on the criminal justice system in Chapter IV.

A change in focus occurs in Chapter V. Just as early legal method casebooks erred in containing too little discussion of legislation, we believe more recent efforts err in the other direction. An intensive study of the legislative process—that is, analysis of what actually happens to a bill—is, in our opinion, not terribly important to the beginning law student.

The book does not purport to state the law regarding any substantive or procedural field. Rather, its purpose is to teach the methods of the study of law. For that reason, editing of the cases has been done sparingly. Our purpose is not to present the students with an ordered collection of rules and legal principles, but rather to acquaint them with the legal process in formulating common law and in interpreting statutory provisions. Extensive editing would have impeded this process. So too would have an excessive use of note cases. The subtle flavor of the cases and the evolution of their reasoning, so important to an understanding of the legal process, could easily have been sacrificed in the interests of brevity. Thus, in order to achieve the goal of understanding the way the law progresses, we have reproduced opinions rather fully and have included dissenting and concurring opinions insofar as they shed light on our objective. The same footnote numbering appears in the casebook as appears in the original sources; editors' footnotes are typically indicated by letters. To improve readability, deletions of materials in the cases have occasionally not been noted with asterisks.

Several factors prompted the preparation of this third edition. First has been the continued encouragement and suggestions of the professors who have adopted and students who have used the book. Second, since the publication of the second edition ten years ago, there have been significant judicial and legislative developments related to legal method and process. These developments have been integrated into the book. By way of illustration, we now discuss the impact of the Internet on concepts of personal jurisdiction, allude to *Bush v. Gore* and its impact on the role of the courts on principles of federalism, incorporate additional insights into the ever-challenging area of statutory construction, and incorporate several changes to the Model Rules of Professional Conduct.

We should like to thank the various publishers and authors who have permitted the use of copyrighted material. Appropriate references are included in the text of the book. We are deeply grateful to a number of people, without whom this book would not have been possible. First and foremost, we thank the more than 10,000 students who served, perhaps not with their informed consent, as our testing ground. Successive waves of classes over the past thirty-five years have contributed to this effort. Among those deserving our special thanks in the preparation of this third edition are Dean Patricia White of Arizona State University College of Law, who has encouraged and supported the undertaking; Caroline Larsen, a second-year student, who provided research assistance; and Jodi R. Miller, whose sharp eye for detail and cheerful good will even during rush periods made this third edition possible.

M.A.B.
R.W.B.
R.S.S.

Tempe, Arizona
February, 2002

Introduction

Introduction to Legal Method and Process embodies our belief that understanding process and procedures is as important as understanding substantive law. Substantive arrangements, whether voluntarily adopted through contractual undertakings or imposed by law as in the fields of torts and criminal law, cannot be learned in a vacuum; or to express the concept differently, procedure must inform the study of substantive law. Legal realists, skeptics, and postmodernists cannot dispute that the vast majority of the 1,000,000 American lawyers share the common heritage that the resolution of legal disputes depends upon method and process and that the evolution of law, statutory and judge-made, requires comprehension of the functions of and interrelationships among institutional methods and processes. This book attempts to clear the mist surrounding this tremendously important, but all too often arcane, subject. And it attempts to clear the mist before, or contemporaneously with, the students' study in law school of the substantive fields.

This book provides the analytical skills necessary for success in the study of law. Because mastery in law is acquired only by practice, the book also contains questions and exercises that allow students to apply and develop those skills. Chapter I provides general background on law school, such as information about law school classes, case briefs, and final examinations, and broad overviews of the common law and court systems in the United States. Chapter II chronicles a legal dispute and discusses the concerns that may arise between the occurrence of a typical automobile accident and its resolution in court. Chapter III illustrates the development of the common law and provides students an opportunity to analyze and synthesize four series of cases on different legal issues. Chapter IV describes the criminal process and guides students through some of the basic concepts in criminal procedure. Chapter V discusses interpretation and application of statutes. Chapter VI is devoted to the role of the federal courts in the American Legal System.

This course will introduce you to the skills that, according to the American Bar Association, are vital for any lawyer. See Rule 1.1 of the Model Rules of Professional Conduct (2002). These skills include "analysis of precedent, the evaluation of evidence and legal drafting, and determining what kind of legal problems a situation may involve." Comment 2 to Rule 1.1. This book also teaches how to interpret statutes, rules, and regulations.

In the study of law you will undoubtedly experience many frustrations. Classroom sessions may seem to breed only confusion. At times you will feel that you have not learned anything in the process. You will be aware of the growing pains; yet not be able to observe the accompanying growth. Progress in comprehending the materials does not occur in linear fashion. It may lie dormant for long periods. Do not be dismayed. If the experience of former generations of students teaches us anything, it is that with continued effort and hard work, you can reach the full potential of your skill and abilities by the end of this course.

Summary of Contents

Table of Contents

*

Table of Cases

The principal cases are in bold type. Cases cited or discussed in the text are roman type. References are to pages. Cases cited in principal cases and within other quoted materials are not included.

INTRODUCTION TO LEGAL METHOD AND PROCESS

CASES AND MATERIALS

Third Edition

*

Chapter I

MATERIALS AND METHODS
OF THE STUDY OF LAW

A. THE STUDY OF LAW

The Language of the Law

The study of law may fairly be compared to the study of a foreign language. It proceeds in an orderly fashion, one step at a time. When studying a language, the student must first master the alphabet, then proceed to acquire a rudimentary vocabulary. Combining the vocabulary with basic rules of grammar, the student learns to express thoughts in the foreign language. Similarly, in the law school setting the student must first learn to read, analyze, and brief judicial opinions before mastering other skills.

When you first read an opinion, the language may appear strange. Entire sentences may at first glance be incomprehensible. For example, *Hamer v. Sidway*,[a] a foundational case in many classes on the law of contracts, a traditional first semester course, begins as follows:

> Appeal [to the Court of Appeals] from an order of the general term of the supreme court in the fourth judicial department, reversing a judgment entered on the decision of the court at special term in the county clerk's office of Chemung County * * *.

What does this mean? What is a general term? A special term? Is it significant that the case is in the fourth judicial department rather than in another? What is the effect of a reversal? Once these mysteries are solved, the statement still makes no sense to the student who does not know that the Court of Appeals of New York is the highest court of the state and reviews cases decided by the state supreme court. The legal vocabulary still renders comprehension difficult even for those who understand the judicial hierarchy.

It is often helpful to understand how a case progresses through the judicial system. Many students impatiently skim over procedural material, searching for the real heart of the case, the rule of law. This is a

---

a.   124 N.Y. 538, 27 N.E. 256 (1891).

1

cardinal error. The factual and procedural context of a case often explains or constrains the rule of law emerging from it. Moreover, this background provides useful context and clues to the breadth and significance of the rule of law.

In addition, it can sometimes be difficult simply to figure out who said what. Consider the following note:

> BLACKMUN, J., announced the judgment of the Court and delivered the opinion of the Court with respect to Parts I, II, III–B, III–C, IV–B (except for the final paragraph), IV–D, IV–E, and IV–F, in which REHNQUIST, C.J., and WHITE, MARSHALL, and STEVENS, JJ., joined, and an opinion with respect to Parts III–A and IV–A, the final paragraph of Part IV–B, and Parts IV–C and V, in which REHNQUIST, C.J., and WHITE and STEVENS, JJ., joined. MARSHALL, J., filed an opinion concurring in part and dissenting in part. SCALIA, J., filed an opinion concurring in the judgment in part and dissenting in part, in which O'CONNOR and SOUTER, JJ., joined, and in all but Part III–C of which KENNEDY, J., joined. KENNEDY, J., filed an opinion concurring in the judgment in part and dissenting in part.

Lehnert v. Ferris Faculty Ass'n, 500 U.S. 507, 111 S. Ct. 1950 (1991). What would be the precedential effect of such a fragmented decision?

The Classroom

Law school classes are quite different from undergraduate classes. You will hear far fewer lectures. After the first few weeks of class, the professor will assume that you have mastered the facts and perhaps even the narrow rules of law of the cases. The professor will pose questions designed to make you analyze the applicability of the rule of law or a modified version of the rule to a hypothetical fact situation. Frequently, the questions will expose your lack of understanding of the materials assigned. Do not be alarmed. It is part of the process. Listen and learn.

The first semester student should make every effort to dispel confusion as quickly as possible. The most beneficial educational experience is to clarify matters on your own, but do not hesitate to ask the professor or other students for assistance if your efforts prove fruitless. For example, the statement in *Hamer v. Sidway, supra,* p. 1 regarding an appeal from the supreme court to the court of appeals seems nonsensical until you realize that the court of appeals is higher in New York's judicial structure than the supreme court. Why become frustrated? Ask the question. Confusion only begets further confusion as the semester advances.

So that you may begin to bring into focus the objectives of law school class procedures, an excerpt from an article by Professor Warren L. Shattuck, which appeared as part of a series on law school teaching methods, is reproduced below. You should reread this excerpt after a week or two of classes or any time you begin to feel that there is no object to the unanswered and, at times, seemingly unanswerable questions that will be your class fare for the months ahead.

Ideally, a law teacher would be a guide, leading students through the maze of problems, rules, techniques, arguments, and ideas which comprise the course. He would provide the organization necessary to an orderly progression and the discipline requisite to profitable class discussion. He would indicate and suggest, and resolve nothing. He would ask lots of questions and answer none. He would insist on precise thinking, analysis, and exposition. He would constantly stress the problem-solving function of the attorney. He would expend most of his energy on endeavors to stimulate student interest in the social and business conditions which produce legal problems and in the solutions which have been found in the past and are likely to be found in the future. He would maintain the pressure and pace which would produce the maximum student output. He would never lose sight of two basic facts—what he knows does not count; what the student takes away from the course is the payoff. Above all he would never be an animated and articulate textbook.

I suspect that an "ideal" law teacher, one who operated strictly in accordance with these standards, would not be popular with some of his students. Their resentment would focus on his refusal to divulge "what the law is" (students yearn to be told "the law on this point is * * * "), and his insistence on precision in analysis and exposition (students tend to use generalizations, the more vague the better). Investigation into the origins of their resentment would probably disclose some significant attitudes and deficiencies, developed in their pre-law-school experience. The variety of "education" which consists of exposure to pre-digested factual information, the student's role being a passive one, with success attending faithful note-taking and a retentive memory, can produce some strange results. One is the notion that education is a spectator sport, the student's basic approach being, "Here I am. Educate me." Certainly, too many of the men and women who come to law school have the erroneous notion that they are here to be educated by the faculty. Another result is inability to read accurately and critically, to speak or write clearly, or to reason closely. That too many law students suffer from these deficiencies can be testified to, with feeling, by any teacher.

Now let us appraise the goals of the "ideal" law teacher—that students shall educate themselves, dig information from its sources, be precise, discuss in class and be tested on the techniques by which lawyers solve problems. For the law graduate a working knowledge of many basic legal propositions and techniques is essential equipment. He must have it for analysis of the problems he encounters in practice. With it he can sometimes find solutions without extended research, and can in other instances get with assurance to the research necessary to a solution. The key idea here is the phrase "working knowledge." The graduate must be able to use his knowledge, to recognize a consideration problem when he encounters one, to draft a sound mortgage, to advise a client whether he can safely (in legal sense) do this or that.

How shall this relationship to information, this ability to use knowledge, this capacity to discharge the responsibilities of a lawyer, be acquired? Surely not from listening to lectures nor from reading with the intensity of attention one devotes to a novel. The student must locate and extricate relevant facts, observe at first hand the refinements of argument and reasoning which have moved courts and legislatures, ponder the analyses of text and periodical writers, think and reason closely, argue, explain, write. He must participate to the limits of his abilities in the education process. He must constantly keep in mind the environment in which he will operate as a graduate. That environment will consist of the legal problems of clients, a mass of statutes, cases and texts from which solutions must be excavated, and relentless pressure for correct solutions plus the argumentation, explanation or drafting which will implement them. Many of the problems are complex. The sources of solutions are often far from clear. Is a student equipped for the practice by any teaching method which simplifies or makes superficially easy his progress through law school, or is he just defrauded by such a method? Ought he not bitterly resent any teaching method which enables him to pursue a course without being cajoled, prodded or exasperated into doing all the work himself?

––––––––––

Study Methods

Students employ various aids to understand class material. Because law school is qualitatively different from undergraduate study, law students should not merely rely on methods that proved successful in the past. Virtually everyone in your class has achieved varying degrees of success in the undergraduate world; yet many will fail to achieve their full potential in law school, perhaps, in part, because of their inability to adapt to the changing requirements of law school. Several of the more frequently used study techniques employed by law students are described below:

Tape Recording. Some professors allow tape recording. Be careful, however, lest the use of a recorder cause inattentiveness. Because time is a critical factor to most first year students, you may not have the luxury of repeating each class. Use a recorder sparingly, if at all, and then only one having calibrations. Jot down in your notes the calibrations corresponding to areas you find confusing or that, for other reasons, you may wish to replay.

Note Taking by Computer or by Hand. Most students are not trained stenographers. If you were, you would appreciate that even the most gifted court reporters do not always comprehend what they record.

To attempt to simply transcribe a lecture can be disastrous if you miss key words or phrases. Be aware, too, that professors employing the Socratic method may intentionally lead students down false paths, only to clear up matters later in the period or even the next day. Why burden yourself by transcribing these deliberately sown inaccuracies?

It is difficult to record classroom information for later use. In this task the student faces the dilemma of the trial lawyer preparing for cross examination: Taking extensive notes during direct examination could mean failing to discern the subtleties that can only come from close scrutiny of the witness. Failing to take notes at all could result in forgetting an important area of inquiry. The wisest course is to listen to the class discussion and jot down the important questions posed and comments made by the professor. If you do not record these highlights, they will be lost to you within a few hours. Should the professor sum up an area, record the summary with precision.

When the bell rings at the end of a session, too many students literally bolt from the classroom. Some, however, spend not more than five or ten minutes, in pairs or in small groups, discussing the class, revising notes, or recording highlights of the session on a tape recorder or laptop computer. What point was the professor trying to make? What good points did your classmates make? What bad points? This process has the advantage of forcing the students to put into their own words the key elements of the day's class session.

Outside Reading. Students should not be too quick in the first semester to read materials other than the assigned course materials. Again, subject to the particular known wishes of your professor, it seems unnecessary at best and at times harmful to delve in great depth into any subject. The purpose of the first semester is to sharpen your legal analysis and application skills. By reading additional cases or outside authorities, you may actually be stifling those skills by relying instead on someone else's analysis of a case or an issue. The additional information gleaned from outside sources will probably be of little use on examinations. Even if the outside source is directly on point, you will get little credit for remembering it. Worse yet, the professor may disagree with the source's analysis. Rely on your own skills and analysis. You should however, carefully read the assigned material; then, if you have time, you may resort to hornbooks—but only after you have first read, reread, and digested the assigned materials.

Law Dictionaries. To students untrained in Latin and the technical legal terms and phrases employed by lawyers, many of the cases will not be comprehensible without reference to a law dictionary. Keep your legal dictionary by your side during your first semester and use it!

Review

You will usually be examined only once in each of your law school courses. The absence of quizzes and mid-term examinations requires that you assume the initiative to review periodically. Examination schedules do not always allow time for cramming; you may have only a few days to review each course. Quite apart from this practical consideration, realize that you are building knowledge in each of your courses: What you learn today will often be the basis for understanding the new material that you will be covering three weeks or three months in the future. Hence, what you learn today cannot be stored away in your notes to be reviewed just before exams; you must keep it stored in your mind by systematic review. Further, everything that you learn in law school can be multiplied by additional study; ideas that are fuzzy today may become clear next month with a little additional thought and increased knowledge. Thus, review expands your knowledge and understanding and fixes in your mind what you have learned.

You will find that class preparation seems to take all your study time. It is easy to put off review until Thanksgiving, Winter break,[b] or spring vacation and to devote your time to the seemingly more pressing job of preparing for classes. Be forewarned that these vacation periods are inadequate for any useful review unless you have refreshed your recollection as the weeks go by. Rather than cramming, set aside a three-, four-, or five-hour period each week for review. Individual review may be most effective for you, or you may find that group review with some of your classmates is more productive. During the first month, reviewing the week's work in all courses will probably be most useful; thereafter, you might review a single course each week. Do not be discouraged if your early review leaves unresolved questions. You are acquiring a foundation, which necessarily grows in increments.

Some students find it helpful to condense their notes and briefs into comprehensive written summaries as the final step in this periodic review. Others find it more useful to outline each course. Many keep a running outline in the margins of their notebooks. Each method is a mechanical means of recording syntheses of opinions and evaluative summaries of problem areas. You may find it helpful to talk to second- and third-year students to learn what review methods they use and whether they find them useful and efficient. Experiment with suggested methods to determine which ones suit you. In selecting and using your review method, keep in mind the objectives of review: (1) to keep the knowledge you acquire current; (2) to expand your knowledge; and (3) to get your notes and briefs into some form that will make effective final review possible.

Do not rely on someone else's outline. The value of the outline lies principally in its creation.

Law School Examinations

Success in law school is determined by grades on essay examinations.

b. Winter break may be too late, as many schools finish the first semester in advance of the holiday season.

The typical law school exam is far different from the examination process to which you were exposed as an undergraduate. Most are patterned after the types of legal problems you will encounter in practice. They will not simply require that you memorize and repeat information. Rather, they will require that you apply information you have learned to solve a problem posed by a given fact situation. For illustration, suppose your class in constitutional law had been assigned the celebrated case of *Marbury v. Madison*.[c] That case established the principle of judicial review—the power of federal courts, more particularly the Supreme Court of the United States, to declare congressional enactments unconstitutional. In a typical undergraduate course, an essay examination would simply require regurgitation of your understanding of *Marbury*—or, more likely, of your professor's understanding. In a law school examination, however, a hypothetical fact situation would be presented that differs from *Marbury,* and you would be required to explain the relevance of *Marbury* and its logical extension to the solution of the problem. For example, suppose *Marbury* were the only case you read that semester on the right of courts to declare statutes unconstitutional. A typical law school examination question might present a factual situation in which a *state* court is asked to nullify the application of a *federal* statute. A suggested answer to the exam would first analyze *Marbury,* pointing out that the United States Supreme Court has already declared that federal courts have the power to declare acts of Congress void. The student should then indicate that *Marbury* did not consider the propriety of a state court voiding a federal legislative act. The student should attempt to resolve the issue presented—that is, the power of the state courts to declare federal legislative enactments unconstitutional.[d] This requires the student to examine the policy considerations underlying *Marbury* and to extend, or decline to extend, these policies to the new set of facts. For example, a basic policy underlying *Marbury* is to require courts to follow the paramount authority of the United States Constitution. It would impair that principle for the state court to adhere to an unconstitutional statute—in other words to follow the statute despite its offensiveness to the United States Constitution. State judges too take an oath to uphold the Constitution of the United States. On the other hand, after noting that *Marbury* is not controlling on its facts,[e] the student might urge that the principle of judicial review should not be extended to allow state courts to invalidate federal legislative enactments. Perhaps the state courts should grant greater deference to federal statutes than federal courts owe. Such deference prevents unseemly confrontations with Congress and inconsistent rules of law among the fifty states that might result if each state had the power to invalidate federal statutes. These arguments are offered for illustrative purposes only—to demonstrate that plausible alternative positions may be successfully advanced in an examination.

c. 5 U.S. (1 Cranch) 137 (1803). See *infra* Chapter VI, Section C.

d. Even though the state court has the power to render the declaration, the stu-

dent should inquire whether it has the *duty* to do so.

e. For further elaboration of this concept, see *infra* Chapter I, Sections D and E.

The student should perceive the issues and be able to present plausible arguments on each side. The "correctness" of an answer is less significant than a demonstrated understanding of the issue, critical analysis of the law, and application of the law to the hypothetical facts presented in the examination.

The foregoing example highlights the way in which many students may actually be misled by professors' well-intentioned claims that students need not memorize the law. Analysis of the law can only proceed on a foundation of legal principles—and these principles must be known in advance of the test. Without knowing the principles of law, an Einstein would fare poorly on a law school examination. The art of exam taking, then, boils down to a basic knowledge of the law, an analysis of the law as it applies to the hypothetical case presented on the exam, and, finally, the ability to write the answer clearly and precisely.

The following observations are pertinent not only to exam-answer writing, but to problem solving and legal writing generally:

Be sure of your facts. Under the pressure of examination writing, many students attempt to gain additional time by reading the problems too quickly. Nothing could be more foolhardy. Misreading a single word or improperly identifying one of the parties involved can send you into a brilliant discussion of an issue not presented by the facts given. Most professors give no credit for discussion not invited by the facts. Some even penalize for irrelevant discussion.

Even after a careful reading, some students go astray by assuming facts or by drawing inferences not justified by the facts provided. Be sure that the facts upon which you rely in your analysis are expressly given. If they are not, ask yourself whether logic justifies assuming the existence of an unstated fact because of the existence of stated facts. If you decide that an assumption is warranted, state your assumption.

Students, like judges, frequently indulge in writing *dicta* (conclusions or opinions not necessary to determine the rights of the parties in the issue under discussion). On examination answers, they will say: "If such and such were true instead of such and such [thus changing the facts given them] then * * *," whereupon they detail rules that they know in lieu of the analysis sought by the professor. You are expected to solve the problems and issues presented in a factual pattern, not to engage in creating problems for which you know the answer. You may recognize this process by another name.

Be sure of the question(s) asked. In reading the facts given for a problem, you may assume that you know the ultimate question that will be asked. Don't assume. Read carefully the ultimate question posed, and direct your thinking toward answering that question. Some students prefer to read the ultimate question first, so that they can read the problem-facts with that question in mind.

Identify the issues. You cannot solve a problem until you know what the problem is; therefore, your first task is to isolate specific issues.

Some issues will contain sub-issues that must be resolved before the major issue can be answered. The more carefully and narrowly you define your issues, the more intelligently you will be able to reason to an ultimate conclusion.

Organize your thoughts before you begin writing. Outline your answer before you begin to write. For simple problems, you may be able to do this in your head, but it is better examination practice to write a logical or chronological word outline of the issues that you intend to discuss.

Give reasons for your conclusions. Merely stating an issue and its resolution is like an empty shell. You must also analyze the issue; explain why it creates a problem and how the facts and law relate to your ultimate conclusion. Give reasons for resolving the issue as you do, indicate possible alternative resolutions, and explain why you reject them.

Reach an ultimate conclusion. Be certain that you answer the exact ultimate question asked. Do not become so involved in discussing the intricacies of narrow issues that you omit the answer requested.

A wise approach is to begin any answer to a legal problem by stating your conclusion or a broad summary of your advice. This method has several advantages. First, this will point your professor's thinking in the direction you are heading in the ensuing discussion, making it easier for the professor to understand your discussion. Second, it will force you to reduce your scattered considerations to a direct answer before you start writing. Because of the problem of flipflopping, with its attendant erasures and cross-outs, you may prefer to leave a blank space at the beginning of the answer for the ultimate conclusion, which may be inserted after you have finished the analysis.

Some students straddle the fence on all issues: They recognize alternative possibilities without finally choosing one of them. Of course, evenly balanced issues exist, but the exigencies of life frequently require that you advise clients to take one course or another; the exigencies of exam writing frequently require that you choose between alternatives and arrive at some solution to the overall problem. If you are dealing with an evenly balanced issue, you can contrast the consequences of a choice of the rejected alternative.

Know your professor. One other very simple though often overlooked factor determining success in law school is awareness of each professor's peculiarities and predilections. If you have a reliable indication of the professor's desires derived from reviewing model examination answers on file in your school or from conversing with other students, you should follow such insights. Some professors concentrate on the basic law or rule; others, on policy considerations. Certain professors penalize "shotgun" answers, which hit all issues but fail to discuss any in depth; others give credit for spotting issues and do not penalize for incorrect or irrelevant issues. You must know and take into account the professor's desires. In an objective examination, for example, would you not insist upon knowing in advance whether there are penalties for incorrect answers?

Write clearly. Professors are not mind readers. They do not presume that you know the material. To the contrary, the presumption is that you are unknowledgeable until you prove otherwise. For that reason, you must write clearly.[f] From your brief-writing experience, you will have acquired the skill of precise analysis. Execute this skill on the examination. Once an examination has been turned in, you will have no further opportunity to explain your answers.

Observe the examination schedule. Typically, law school examinations are scheduled months in advance. Observe the schedule. Note the time between each exam (usually a day or two), and plan your study sessions accordingly.

Review old exams. Many law libraries maintain files of previous examinations. Early in your studies you may find it instructive to look at one or more of these files. Ascertain from each professor whether sample questions with model or representative student answers are available. Even a cursory review of answers may remove some of the concern created by uncertainty as to what is ultimately expected from you.

Practice. Part of the problem students face when they sit for their first set of law school exams is that they know the subject, but may not know how to state precisely what they mean. The examinations on file in the law school library provide examples of the types of questions that may be asked on your examinations. Practice *writing* responses to several of them. It is not enough simply to "think through" your responses or outline them. Practice writing your answers as you want them to appear in response to examination questions. Use introductory sentences, clear statements of the issues, precise statements of applicable legal principles, effective transitions, appropriate headings, and logical conclusions. You may find it more difficult than you might have anticipated to build an effective legal argument, even though your essential thought processes might have been correct. The students who receive the highest scores will be those who have learned not only how to think like lawyers, but those who have learned to write like lawyers.

If you have the ability to do so and your law school allows it, consider taking your examinations on a typewriter or computer. Most people can type considerably faster—and more neatly—than they can write by hand. A mediocre keyboarder can type 50 to 60 words per minute, while a fast handwriter writes only approximately 30 words per minute, many of which may be illegible. Consider the time and psychological advantages that accrue to the keyboarder. Remember that corrections and edits are more easily and neatly made on a typewriter or computer. Professors may also feel more kindly disposed toward grading a neatly typed essay than an answer hastily scrawled in a bluebook. If

---

f. Unclear, ambiguous, or illegible answers may on occasion aid the student who does not understand the problem or issue. That technique, however, will at best earn the student a low "C" rather than the deserved lower grade.

you feel uneasy using a typewriter or computer, begin using one at the beginning of the semester so that you become comfortable thinking while writing on a keyboard by exam time.

In short, although law school exams may differ from those you encountered in your earlier education, they should not needlessly intimidate you if you devote the time now to develop your legal analysis skills. Diligence now will stand you in good stead at exam time. And the skills you use to resolve exam answers are those you ultimately will apply to resolve your clients' disputes.

B. ON READING AND BRIEFING CASES

Most of your law study will center on reading and analyzing appellate decisions. To enable you to predict how future cases are likely to be resolved, you study how similar cases have been resolved in the past.

You will soon learn that the outcome of any particular case is, for your purposes, less important than the reasoning upon which it rests. For that reason, you must quickly learn to focus on the court's analysis of the problem before it. One way to focus your study is to brief each case.

A "brief" of a case is a short written summary of the important facts, issues, reasoning, and points of law discussed in an appellate decision.[g] Mastery of brief-writing skills is imperative for success in law school.

The key to writing a functional brief lies in first determining its purpose. There are several different reasons for briefing cases, each calling for a different type of brief. Students often prepare written briefs solely for use in class recitation. Rather than resort to memory when called upon to discuss the case in class, a student may rely upon the brief—sometimes to the point of reading it aloud. Briefs written for this purpose are not usually very helpful, largely because most instructors will not permit the reading exercise. In addition, when first writing briefs, many students will fail to anticipate most of the questions that the professor will ask. On a more practical level, the chances of being called upon in class are slim, the probabilities obviously varying with class size, the professor's teaching method, and other considerations. Briefing cases for classroom recitation may avoid a momentarily embarrassing classroom experience, but the effort and time consumed in preparing a brief solely for this purpose generally outweigh its benefits.

Preparation for final examinations is another standard justification for briefing. Yet early in your law studies it is difficult to write briefs that will accomplish this purpose. You may find that briefs prepared during the first few months of law school are of minimal assistance once your ability to analyze legal opinions has developed. You should not rely

---

g. Distinguish this from a lawyer's brief to the court, a memorandum of law ad- dressing legal issues involved in a case.

too heavily on briefs prepared in the early days of law school when you are preparing for final examinations and grades are at stake.

Thus we reach the real objective of brief writing: to aid in the comprehension of cases.

Francis Bacon once said, "Reading maketh a full man; conference a ready man; writing, an exact man."[h] Brief writing requires precise analysis. The process of distilling information into the brief forces the reader to think about what is being decided and to follow the court's reasoning. The brief should reveal those areas in which comprehension is less than adequate. Appreciating what you do not know is a necessary stage in the learning process.

Train yourself, from the first day of law school, to be precise in your analysis of legal material. Perusal of randomly selected law school examinations will illustrate the need for this precision. You will master this skill by carefully briefing cases from the outset.

You will use the same skills that you acquire in briefing cases when you take final examinations and write research memoranda and other legal documents. Only after you understand an opinion as the sum of its component parts can you use it to predict or support a similar result in an undecided case.[i] With practice, you will learn to brief skillfully and develop a briefing format and style that suit your particular purpose.

The process of briefing is as important as the end result. Committing your impression of a case to paper forces you to learn legal terminology and to begin thinking critically. Briefing cases thus refines legal analysis and writing skills and, like a dress rehearsal, prepares you for writing exams and practicing law.

There is no single right way to brief cases. You must develop the style and format that suit your purpose. Most legal briefs contain at least six sections: the heading, the facts, the procedure, the issue, the holding, and the rationale. In addition, many briefs contain "rule," evaluation, and synthesis sections. A short description of each of these sections and a sample case brief follow.[j]

Elements of a Case Brief

a. *Identification of the Case*

At a minimum, each brief should include the case name, the deciding court, and the year of the decision. Knowing the case name allows you to refer to the case easily; the deciding court provides insight into

---

h. Francis Bacon, an essay entitled *Of Studies.* Author Rebecca Berch protests the outdated sexist tone of the quote and moves to include women, too.

i. This section uses the words "case," "opinion," and "decision" interchangeably to refer to a court's published disposition of a particular controversy.

j. Other sources discuss briefing cases in more detail. *See, e.g.,* M. Rombauer, LEGAL PROBLEM SOLVING: ANALYSIS, RESEARCH AND WRITING 15–82 (5th ed. 1991), a classic in the field. We thank Professor Rombauer for sharing her thoughts on the brief-writing process.

the precedential value of the decision; the year tells you the historical context of the case and the opportunity of subsequent courts to limit, expand, or overrule the decision. You also may want to include the page of your casebook on which the case appears, so that you may refer to it easily when you review, or the volume number of the reporter and the page on which the case begins (its citation), so that you may find the full reported decision.

b. Facts

Your brief should include all the legally significant facts on which the court relied in deciding the case. The factual circumstances of a dispute are essential to understanding a court's opinion and to predicting the outcomes of future disputes. You must read the entire opinion and understand the issue and the court's rationale before you can select which facts were necessary for its result. For this reason, some students find it easier to write the facts section of a brief after they have written the issue and rationale sections.

Appellate courts typically do not decide what the facts are; rather, they determine the legal significance of the facts found by the trial court. If the appellate court decides that the trial court inadequately determined the facts, it will remand the case for a new determination. Rarely will the appellate court substitute its factual determination for that of the trial court. Nonetheless, the appellate court will include in its opinion the facts it considers relevant to its holding. Thus, the trial and appellate courts already have culled those facts they deem significant from the pleadings and evidence that the parties presented to them. If the appellate court did not consider a particular fact important enough to include in its opinion, you should not ordinarily second-guess the court's selection. But, just as the court may not include all arguably relevant facts, it may include facts that are not necessary to its result. For example, specific amounts, dates, and similar details rarely are essential to a court's rationale or to the outcome of a case. The court may include other facts because they add drama or narrative continuity to an opinion.

Thus, although your brief may include fewer facts than the court's opinion, you should include all facts necessary to explain the opinion. At a minimum, you should identify the parties, their relationship to each other or "status," and the nature of their dispute. Your briefs will be easier to understand if you always use the trial court designations for the parties (plaintiff, defendant), rather than switching from trial court to appellate court designations. At first glance, you cannot know whether the appellant was the plaintiff or defendant below. Using appellate labels can also be confusing because appellate labels may differ from jurisdiction to jurisdiction. Some jurisdictions call the party bringing the appeal the appellant; others use the terms plaintiff-in-error or petitioner. Correspondingly, some jurisdictions call the party that prevailed at trial the appellee, while others use the terms defendant-in-error or respondent.[k] Eliminate confusion by consistently using the trial court labels.

You also may find it helpful to refer to parties by their role in the drama, for example "seller" or "buyer," "landlord" or "tenant." This role may reveal something about the nature of the dispute, especially if you also include information about the status of the parties, for example "plaintiff tenant." Employees usually bring certain kinds of suits against employers; pedestrians or bicyclists bring certain kinds of suits against automobile drivers; tenants bring certain kinds of suits against landlords.

Include the nature of the dispute in your brief, for example, whether it is a contract or tort case or a criminal proceeding, and the facts on which the claim is based—that is, who did what to whom, with what result.

First-year law students frequently underestimate the importance of the facts section of the brief because it seems less "legal" than other sections of the brief and closer to the kind of literary narrative they encountered as undergraduates. For this reason, they sometimes skim over the facts when reading cases and recount them in a cursory manner in briefs. Because the first-year courses emphasize the common law, however, the facts of cases are extremely important. They may be the only factor upon which to distinguish later cases. Moreover, the facts, or "story," personalize a dispute and can provide a good mnemonic device for remembering other elements of the case.

c. Procedure or Procedural History

The procedure section of your brief should explain what happened in the trial court and in any intermediate appellate court. It contains the legal history of the case. You should include who sued whom, the legal theory or kind of action, the relief sought, and the outcome in the trial court. Pay particular attention to the procedural device through which the trial court decided the case. Was it decided on a motion to dismiss? a motion for summary judgment? after a trial to a jury? The answers to these questions determine how deferentially appellate courts will view the trial court's result.

In the procedure section, you should also include the result of any intermediate appeals. For example, if one of the parties appealed to an intermediate appellate court and that court reversed the judgment of the trial court, the court of last resort will review the intermediate appellate court's, not the trial court's, result. The court of last resort may reverse the intermediate appellate court and reinstate the trial court's verdict. You therefore should summarize the bases on which the trial and intermediate appellate courts rendered their judgments. The bases on

k. In most jurisdictions, the party who lost below and pursues a mandatory appeal is called the appellant and the opposing party, the appellee. The party who requests discretionary review ordinarily is called the petitioner; the party opposing discretionary review, the respondent.

which the court of last resort renders its opinion may differ from those of both lower courts.

This section will be more important in some contexts than in others. For example, the procedure may be less important in a Contracts class than in a Civil Procedure class. In any context, however, the procedural posture of a case often can explain what otherwise appears to be an anomalous result. An appellate court may uphold a jury's verdict, but reverse and remand for further proceedings a suit that reaches a similar result if the trial court reached the result on a motion to dismiss or for summary judgment.

The importance of the procedural context in understanding the ruling of the court cannot be overstated. Reprinted below is the excerpt of *Gibbons v. Pepper* and the accompanying authors' note that appeared in the casebook, *Materials for Legal Method*.[1] Note the importance of understanding the procedural context of the case.

GIBBONS v. PEPPER

1 Lord Raymond 38, Easter Term, 7 William III (1695).

Trespass, assault and battery. The defendant pleads that he rode upon a horse in the King's highway, and that his horse being affrighted ran away with him, so that he could not stop the horse; that there were several persons standing in the way, among whom the plaintiff stood; and that he called to them to take care, but that notwithstanding, the plaintiff did not go out of the way, but continued there; so that the defendant's horse ran over the plaintiff against the will of the defendant; quae est eadem transgressio, & c. The plaintiff demurred. And Serjeant Darnell for the defendant argued, that if the defendant in his justification shews that the accident was inevitable, and that the negligence of the defendant did not cause it, judgment shall be given for him. To prove which he cited Hob. 344, Weaver vers. Ward, Mo. 864, pl. 1192. 2 Roll.Abr. 548. 1 Brownl.Prec. 188.

Northey for the plaintiff said that in all these cases the defendant confessed a battery, which he afterwards justified; but in this case he justified a battery, which is no battery. Of which opinion was the whole Court, for if I ride upon a horse, and J.S. whips the horse, so that he runs away with me and runs over any other person, he who whipped the horse is guilty of the battery, and not me. But if I by spurring was the cause of such accident, then I am guilty. In the same manner, if A. takes the hand of B. and with it strikes C., A. is the trespasser, and not B. And, per Curiam, the defendant might have given this justification in evidence, upon the general issue pleaded. And therefore judgment was given for the plaintiff.

1. N. Dowling, E. Patterson & R. Powell, Materials for Legal Method 79–81 (H. Jones 2d ed. 1952).

Note

What does *Gibbons v. Pepper* DECIDE? That is, for what proposition of law can this case be taken as authority? Does *Gibbons v. Pepper* decide—or, as lawyers say, "hold"—that the rider of a runaway horse is liable in damages to an injured pedestrian even though the conceded facts are that the accident was unavoidable and in no way due to fault or negligence on the rider's part? At first reading, that would seem to be the decision, since judgment was given for the plaintiff in *Gibbons v. Pepper*.

But put on your procedural spectacles and read the case again. What was the exact question the court had before it for decision? Was the court called upon to decide whether unavoidable accident would be a good defense if properly pleaded and proved? Or was the court merely called upon to decide the narrower, more technical, question whether the defendant had entered a proper pleading in the case? As to the scope of the issue presented, note the court's care to point out that "the defendant might have given this *justification* in evidence upon the general issue pleaded." (Italics added.)

This difficult old case provides a dramatic illustration of the determinative control of procedure upon the breadth or narrowness of a judicial decision. About two hundred years after the decision in *Gibbons v. Pepper*, the case was cited as a precedent by the plaintiff in an action to recover damages for personal injuries caused by an act of the defendant but without any fault or negligence on the defendant's part. Here is what the later court had to say about the scope of the decision in *Gibbons v. Pepper:*

> The case of *Gibbons v. Pepper* (4 Mod. 404), decided in 1695, merely decided that a plea shewing that an accident caused by a runaway horse was *inevitable* was a bad plea in an action of trespass, because, if inevitable, that was a defense under the general issue. It was a mere decision on the pleading, and laid down nothing as regards the point raised in the present case.

Stanley v. Powell, L.R. [1891] 1 Q.B. 86, 90 (1890).

d. *Issue*

The issue is the question that the appellate court must answer to resolve the dispute before it. Many opinions address several issues; casebook authors, however, usually edit opinions so that they contain only one or two issues on which students should focus. If the case addresses more than one issue, you should have separate issue, rationale, holding, synthesis, and evaluation sections for each.

Write the issue in question form, tailoring it to the case by including the legally significant facts of the case. Frame your issue as narrowly as possible because courts usually attempt to resolve the disputes before them on the narrowest possible grounds. If your issue statement can apply to other cases, your statement may be too general.[m] See whether

---

m. Compare the issue statement in *Hess v. Pawloski, infra* p. 164 ("The question is whether the Massachusetts enactment contravenes the due process clause of the Fourteenth Amendment") with the issue statement in *International Shoe Co. v. Washington, infra* p. 173 ("The question for decision [is] whether, within the limitations of the due process clause of the Fourteenth Amendment, appellant, a Delaware corpora-

you have missed any legally significant facts that make this case differ from others.

The interplay between the facts and the applicable law creates the issue in a case. Legal principles regulate the relationships among parties, their respective rights and responsibilities, and their remedies if a dispute develops. The facts of a case thus determine whether a particular legal principle will apply. For example, the plaintiff in a civil case must establish all the elements of her cause of action; the absence of a single element may bar the plaintiff from obtaining relief. If, on appeal, the defendant disputes whether the plaintiff demonstrated a particular element of the action, the appellate court will focus its analysis on the proof surrounding that element. In other cases, the court may focus on a procedural defect (for example, lack of personal or subject matter jurisdiction or an improper jury instruction) or an affirmative defense (such as statute of limitations or payment). Liability, guilt, or innocence are less important in issue questions than the legal theory and facts on which the outcome is premised.

Courts often state issues in broad terms that do not describe the case before them very well. For example, a statement that "we must decide whether the trial court erred in entering summary judgment for the defendant" tells little about the case before the court. You must glean the precise issue from the facts and the court's evaluation of their significance. Remember that the law does not exist in a vacuum: Without the specific facts of the dispute, the court cannot determine the appropriate application of law. Thus, the issue asks what law appropriately applies to the facts of a case.

e. *Holding*

The holding is the court's response to the issue question. The holding may be stated as a single word ("yes" or "no") following the issue, or as an affirmative or negative restatement of the issue question. If you restate the issue as a declarative sentence incorporating the holding, you state the "rule" of the case. For example, suppose that the issue in the case you are reading is, "Should a 16–year old driver of a motor vehicle be held to an adult standard of care because he is engaged in an adult activity, rather than the 'child's standard of care'?"[n] If the holding is "yes," you can form the "rule" from the case by combining the issue and the holding into an affirmative declarative sentence: A 16–year old driver of a motor vehicle should be held to an adult standard of care rather than a child's standard because the driver is engaged in an adult activity.

tion, has by its activities in the State of Washington rendered itself amenable to proceedings in the courts of that state to recover unpaid contributions to the state unemployment compensation fund enacted by state statutes."). The issue statement in

Hess could apply to any of several cases. The issue statement in *International Shoe* clearly sets forth precisely the question the Court must answer to resolve the dispute.

n. *See Baxter v. Fugett, infra* p. 23.

Often courts call the specific result of a case its holding, for example, "We hold that defendant is liable to plaintiff." Because the purpose of a case brief is to understand the court's decision and to predict the outcomes of future cases, such a statement is of little concern to anyone except the immediate parties.

f. Reasoning or Rationale

This section should be the heart of your brief. Use it to explain why the appellate court decided the controversy as it did. The court's reasoning provides the grounds on which future litigants or courts will predict or defend similar results. Courts usually rely upon precedent, principle, or policy to justify decisions. To the extent you are able to identify these rationales, you should note them in this section of your brief.

Sometimes more than one reason justifies the result in a particular case. These reasons usually are not equally important to the result, however, and you should attempt to discern on which the court relied most heavily. Sometimes the relative importance of the court's justifications will become clear only in later opinions. Moreover, sometimes courts make remarks that do not directly support their result. Such remarks are called *"dicta"* or, when singular, *"dictum."* Statements that stray too far from the disputed matters may be called *"obiter dictum."* The court may address in *dicta* hypothetical facts or issues that are not before it. Because the *dictum* was said in passing and therefore was not necessary to the court's decision, it will not bind lower courts in future cases, although it may have strong persuasive value. Thus, *dicta* may be more important in resolving future disputes than in explaining the decision in which they occur. But *dicta* may be useful in distinguishing which rationales a court did find compelling.

You may at times have to read between the lines to discern the court's rationale. Appellate judges do not have to state their reasoning, although most judges usually do to guide litigants and lower courts. If the court does not consider its decision controversial—for example, if strong precedent supported the result—the court may not discuss its rationale. It may simply cite the case on which it relies. In addition, appellate decisions often result from a committee process; the final result may reflect less the real reasons of the various judges on the panel than the reasons that garnered majority support. Individual judges may sometimes be reluctant to state their real reasons for supporting a result.

Courts also employ legal principles such as canons of statutory construction[o] and common-law doctrines to resolve cases. For example, statutory text should be construed according to its plain meaning and ambiguous contracts should be construed against the drafters. Most legal principles originate in common sense. In the examples above, we assume that legislators mean what they say and that contract drafters are in a better position to protect their interests by drafting contracts clearly

----

o. *See infra* Chapter V.

than those who merely sign documents they did not write. Courts' rationales often reflect these commonsense understandings.

g. *Judgment*

The judgment is the result or outcome of the case. This optional section tells who won and what relief the court ordered, for example, "Judgment for defendant is reversed." It probably is of more interest to the immediate parties, however, than it is to future litigants or law students. You may want to include this section for class recitation purposes or as a mnemonic device, remembering who won may trigger the more important consideration of why she won.

h. *Synthesis*

In this section, you should attempt to tie the case you are briefing to others you have studied and briefed on the same issue. How does this case fit in with the others? Does this case follow the rules other cases have established? extend them? limit them? reverse them? disregard them?

At the end of the semester you will be examined on the way cases fit together to establish a body of law, not on the content of a single case. Analyzing the relationship between the assigned case and those preceding and following it prepares you more effectively for final examinations than studying each case in isolation. In addition, analyzing real-life legal problems requires incorporating and harmonizing disparate elements from many opinions. You will be better prepared to make this analysis in practice if, in law school, you have acquired the habit of seeing the "big picture," rather than focusing on its isolated parts.

i. *Evaluation*

Here you might consider whether the court has articulated valid reasons for its decision. Is the court's reasoning logical? Is it consistent with earlier cases? If not, did the court articulate satisfactory reasons for the change? Is the decision internally consistent? Does the reasoning support the result? Is the court's solution to the problem practical? Can it be implemented? Is the result fair? How will this decision affect future litigants? Was a better alternative available to the court? Did the court fairly face the issue before it or did it sidestep a difficult question? Has the court used unnecessarily broad language or unnecessarily vague terminology?

Many first-year students are reluctant to evaluate courts' decisions because criticism seems presumptuous and disrespectful. Usually, however, this reluctance quickly evaporates after exposure to professors' and second-and third-year students' criticisms of opinions. Remember that most of the cases you will be reading presented close questions or introduced novel legal theories, which is why they were included in the casebook. Moreover, some of these theories later were abandoned or ignored. Ask yourself how you would have reacted to the court's decision if you were the losing party. Also ask yourself how the decision will affect future litigants. Will they be better able to vindicate their legal rights? Is society better off because of the court's decision?

One approach that may help you identify shortcomings in an opinion is to consider how you would have decided the case had you been the judge or how you would have argued the case had you been counsel for one of the parties.

Law, unlike some other disciplines, contains few absolute rules or "right" answers. Skill in evaluating decisions will develop your ability to make persuasive arguments, an ability that will serve you well in law school and, later, in legal practice. Use the evaluation section to develop your ability to judge arguments and rationales.

There is no required form for a brief, and each student will acquire some distinctive elements of briefing style. A good form for a brief, however, is patterned after the sections set forth above, and accordingly has headings entitled Facts, Procedure, Issue(s), Holding, Reasoning, Judgment, Synthesis, and Evaluation.

A reported negligence case and a sample brief in the suggested form follow:

BAXTER v. FUGETT

Supreme Court of Oklahoma, 1967.
425 P.2d 462.

McINERNEY, JUSTICE.

This is an appeal by plaintiff from verdict and judgment for defendant in a negligence action arising out of a collision, at an Oklahoma City street intersection, between a bicycle ridden by a 12 year old plaintiff and an automobile driven by a 16 year old defendant. The mothers of the two boys were made parties plaintiff and defendant respectively, but in view of the single proposition argued on appeal, it will not be necessary to notice their respective interests in the case.

In the petition, the 16 year old defendant was charged with specific acts of negligence; in the answer, defendant pleaded contributory negligence, unavoidable accident, and the defense of sudden emergency.

No detailed summary of the evidence is necessary to an understanding of the single question raised on appeal. Plaintiff was riding his bicycle north on a through street. He could not recall any facts pertaining to the cause of the accident. Defendant testified, as a witness for plaintiff, that he was driving his automobile west toward an intersection where the through street was protected by a stop sign. After stopping and observing plaintiff about fifty feet away, defendant proceeded into the intersection and his automobile was struck at a point just behind the driver's seat on the left side by plaintiff's bicycle.

In his "statement of the case and pleadings" the trial judge informed the jury that plaintiff alleged that the defendant automobile driver was negligent in two particulars: (1) failure to keep a proper lookout, and (2) failure to yield the right of way. From the language in the petition, and from uncontradicted circumstances shown in evidence, it is clear that the allegation of failure to yield the right of way was based upon the requirement of 47 O.S.1961, § 11–403(b) that "every driver" approaching an intersection protected by a stop sign shall stop, and "after having stopped shall yield the right of way to any vehicle which * * * is approaching so closely on said highway as to constitute an immediate hazard." The trial judge also told the jury, among other things, that the defendant alleged that the 12 year old plaintiff was guilty of contributory negligence. No objection to the court's statement of the issues and pleadings was made by either party.

From verdict and judgment for defendant, plaintiff appeals.

The precise argument made on appeal, and the only one, is that the court erred in giving the following instruction:

> You are instructed that the plaintiff Robert Baxter at the time of this accident was 12 years of age and the defendant William M. Fugett was 16 years of age. In determining whether or not the defendant William M. Fugett was guilty of negligence and whether or not the plaintiff Robert Baxter was guilty of contributory negligence as heretofore defined in these instructions, you are instructed that by the term "ordinary care" as applied to children is meant that degree of care and caution which would usually and ordinarily be exercised by children of the age of 12 and 16 years under the same or similar circumstances. The conduct of children 12 years of age and 16 years of age is not necessarily to be judged by the same rules which would apply to an adult. The degree of care and caution required of a child is according to and commensurate with his age and mental capacity and his power to exercise such degree of care as a child of his age may be fairly presumed capable of exercising. Insofar as Robert Baxter and William M. Fugett may be presumed to do so it was their duty to take into consideration the fact that each was attempting to cross a public street upon which vehicular traffic could ordinarily be expected and in crossing the street to exercise ordinary care for his own safety and to watch out for traffic proceeding along the street.

> It was the duty of each to take into consideration all the circumstances and conditions surrounding the place of the accident and the possibility of injury which might result in crossing or attempting to cross the street at the time and place in question.

This instruction follows the general rule that when a minor is charged with common law negligence, his conduct is to be measured by a "child's standard of care" under which consideration is given to his age, mental capacity, judgment, etc. *Davis v. Bailey,* 162 Okl. 86, 19 P.2d 147; *Witt v. Houston,* 207 Okl. 25, 246 P.2d 753; *Morris v. White,* 177 Okl.

489, 60 P.2d 1031; *Bready v. Tipton,* Okl., 407 P.2d 194. These cases, however, involve the standard of care required of a child while engaged in activities commensurate with his age.

We are asked to approve the above standard of care for a 16 year old minor engaged in an adult activity. We decline to do so. The better reasoning is expressed in *Dellwo v. Pearson,* 259 Minn. 452, 107 N.W.2d 859, 97 A.L.R.2d 866. The Minnesota Supreme Court, in disapproving a similar instruction, and distinguishing between the contributory negligence and primary negligence of minors, said as follows:

> However, this court has previously recognized that there may be a difference between the standard of care that is required of a child *in protecting himself against hazards and the standard that may be applicable when these activities expose others to hazards.* (Emphasis supplied.)

The instruction complained of permits a minor to engage in adult activities which expose others to hazards, while imposing only a child's standard of care on the minor so engaged. This legal sanction is impractical and contrary to the circumstances of modern life. We hold that a minor, when operating an automobile, must exercise the same standard of care as an adult. Jurisdictions surrounding Oklahoma generally follow the rule announced in this case. *See Harrelson v. Whitehead,* 236 Ark. 325, 365 S.W.2d 868; *Allen v. Ellis,* 191 Kan. 311, 380 P.2d 408; *Wilson v. Shumate,* Mo., 296 S.W.2d 72; *Renegar v. Cramer,* Tex.Civ.App., 354 S.W.2d 663.

The Highway Safety Code, Title 47, Motor Vehicles, makes no distinction between minors and adults in defining "person", § 1–144, "driver", § 1–114, and "operator", § 1–140. No statute or rule of the road prescribing the operation of a motor vehicle makes any such distinction, but refers to "every person," when reference is made to the person, operating a vehicle and the duties required in the operation of a vehicle. It is the announced legislative policy of this state to prescribe only one standard of care upon a person operating a motor vehicle, regardless of the age of the person, and that is an adult standard of care. There is no reason to apply a different standard of care to negligent acts committed by a minor while driving an automobile, even though the negligent act is not a specific violation of a statute, since the activity of operating a motor vehicle on a public highway is the basis for imposing the standard of care, rather than the age of the person, and that is an adult standard.

Having determined that the giving of the instruction was error, and being of the opinion that this error was prejudicial to the plaintiff, the judgment of the trial court is reversed and the cause is remanded with directions to grant a new trial.

Suggested Brief

BAXTER v. FUGETT[p]

Supreme Court of Oklahoma, 1967.
425 P.2d 462.

Facts

Action for damages—negligence. Plaintiff, a 12–year old, was riding a bicycle on a through street. Defendant, a 16–year old driver, approached from a side street in his car. Defendant came to a full stop at the stop sign, then pulled out. Plaintiff ran into the driver's side of Defendant's car, injuring himself. Plaintiff claims that Defendant negligently failed to keep proper lookout and failed to yield the right of way. Defendant claims contributory negligence.

The court instructed the jurors that in considering whether both Plaintiff and Defendant used ordinary care, they should apply the standard of "care ordinarily exercised by children" 12 and 16 years old, respectively, and that the parties should not necessarily be judged by standard of care of an adult.

Procedure

Verdict and judgment for Defendant. Plaintiff appeals, urging error in the jury instruction.

Issue

Should a 16–year–old automobile driver be judged by the standard of care applicable to a 16 year–old child, rather than that applicable to an adult?

Holding

No.

Judgment

Judgment for Defendant is reversed and the case is remanded for a new trial.

Reasoning

1. The general rule is to hold children to the standard of care of others their age, but this rule applies if they are engaged in activity commensurate with their age. The child's standard is appropriate to require of a child in protecting himself, but a different standard may apply to protect others from harm. In dealing with driving automobiles, an adult activity, society must hold minors to the adult standard of care to protect the public.

---

p. This brief exemplifies a student form suitable for recitation or review purposes. Its writing style would not earn its author a high grade in a writing class, but is well-suited to its intended uses.

2.   Highway safety codes and other rules of the road do not distinguish between minors and adults. The code refers only to "every person," indicating a legislative policy to apply one standard of care to all drivers.

This brief contains no Synthesis section because no cases with which to synthesize *Baxter* have been provided. In the Evaluation section, the student might note that in the new trial the jury will be instructed that the minor driver should be held to the standards of an adult, whereas the contributory negligence of the bicyclist may be judged by standards relating to children. Can a jury properly make the distinction? Would the same be true if the bicyclist were 17 years of age? Suppose the plaintiff were a 17–year-old automobile driver—what standard of care is required of him in protecting himself against hazards?

On the retrial, should the trial judge iterate the instruction that he rendered at the first trial? "[I]t was their duty to take into consideration the fact that each was attempting to cross a public street upon which vehicular traffic could ordinarily be expected. . . ." Does this instruction limit the jury too much? Or do you believe we give juries too much discretion in deciding whether certain conduct constitutes negligence?

Note too that the case could have been decided in a manner that would render harmless the jury instruction on the standard of care for children. Suppose the jury had rendered a special finding that the bicyclist had been contributorily negligent. If such negligence were a complete defense to the action, an appellate court would not decide the question of the driver's standard of care since the judgment would be unimpaired by any such decision. In other words the defendant would still prevail. In *Baxter*, on the other hand, the jury rendered a general verdict in defendant's favor. The general verdict masks the basis of the decision and therefore the appellate court did properly reach the issue of the proper standard of care.

C. READINGS ON THE CASE METHOD

THE CASE METHOD IN AMERICAN LEGAL EDUCATION: ITS ORIGINS AND OBJECTIVES[q]

Edwin W. Patterson

* * *

II.

ESSENTIAL DEVICES OF THE CASE METHOD

While the case method of instruction has varied considerably in different courses under different teachers and in different law schools,

q. 4 Journal of Legal Education 1 (1951).

three devices have generally been deemed essential: (1) the casebook. (2) the participation of students in the class discussion. (3) the problem type of examination. Each of these has its variations.

1. *The casebook.* Langdell was driven to the preparation of his first casebook by the physical impossibility of providing for all the students in the class ready and convenient access to the original reports in the library. The casebook saves wear and tear on the library, and on the student, too. The casebook still fulfills this minimum function.

* * *

2. *The class discussion.* Student participation in the class discussion is still, I believe, an essential feature of the case method, and one which ought to be preserved at the sacrifice of some other values, such as additional information or a more orderly and explicit presentation of the teacher's ideas about the subject matter. The "Socratic dialogue" was the early ideal of class discussion. A student was asked to summarize orally a case in the book, the teacher asked him questions about it or put to him a hypothetical case; the student was called upon to defend his decision in relation to the case in the book or other cases. The hypothetical case, skillfully chosen by the teacher, thus became one of the chief instruments for pulling out the significance of the main case and for extending or limiting its doctrine or principle. The teacher, like Socrates, should ask more questions than either he or the student can answer. This process can be intellectually stimulating to the entire class and can give the students clues to what they should investigate further. The creation of doubt followed by its resolution is one of the important steps in the process of learning. Yet the Socratic method calls for great skill on the part of the teacher and considerable quick-wittedness on the part of the student. When protracted to the point where interest lags, it becomes tiresome and wasteful of time.

* * *

One corollary of the basic principles of the case method was that the teacher ought never to lecture, or to summarize the conclusions to be derived from the cases and the class discussion. The student was supposed to work out the conclusions from the questions of the teacher. I doubt if it is strictly applied by most teachers today. It does not seem to be necessary to the attainment of the aims of the case method. One can lead students to "think for themselves" by bringing out the arguments for and against a particular legal doctrine, and yet give them some conclusions as to which arguments seem preferable to the teacher, and which ones are more likely to prevail with the courts. The teacher should at least help the student acquire a consistent terminology, to replace the inconsistent terminologies used by courts in different cases. Moreover, after the student's doubts have been raised, he should eventually have the benefit of the teacher's mature conclusions.

Another variation in class discussion is the student's "statement of the case." The orthodox tradition is that the student called upon is asked to summarize the facts, legal issues, rulings or orders of the court, and the reasons given in the opinion, as a preliminary to further discussion. I find this still a useful technique for beginning students. I can often detect in the student's omission of some material fact that he has not correctly understood the legal issue in the reported case. A perception of how the legal issue was raised, procedurally, is often necessary in order to understand the difference between holding and dictum. Yet too much time can easily be spent on these details, and once the routine analysis is learned, many students become bored with the formal statement of cases. Hence the tendency is to dispense with it in the third year, or even in the second year. The chief difficulty here is to make the student read the cases carefully and be prepared to state them, without going through that formality. Unless he is so prepared, he is likely to have only a fumbling notion of the significance of the case. The casebook is a rather wasteful method of merely imparting the information contained in the opinion. Its value depends upon the student's doing some hard work on his own before he comes to the class.

The use of the case method in large classes is another paradox of legal education. The Socratic discourse of the case method would seem to require a small group of hearers and questioners. To place a legal Socrates in a room with 200 or even 250 questioners and victims seems like a travesty on Socratic dialogue. Yet the victim of the moment suffers vicariously for the others, who can perceive his errors and confusions better than he can. Besides, the ordeal of hypothetical questioning by a skillful teacher is good preparation for similar ordeals in the courtroom.

Three features of a good casebook can contribute to the interest and the orderliness of class discussion. One is the inclusion of cases whose facts provide some dramatic interest. Another is the choice and arrangement of cases so as to raise the question of conflicts between decisions. Economy of time may require that some topics be relegated to a note in order to permit the presentation of a series of divergent or conflicting cases on others. Conflict sharpens the edge of casuistry. A third feature is the editorial matter which enables the student to discover in advance of the class discussion the general significance of the case, and thus saves some of the victim's impromptu groping for answers to hypothetical questions.

3. *The examination.* The case method course calls for a hypothetical-case type of examination. The student has to give not only the decisions of a limited number of controversies, but also the reasons for his decision, in terms of analysis of the facts and statements of legal propositions. Beyond this the better student may give more basic reasons of social ethics or political principle, or may criticize the present legal rules because of the absence of such reasons. However, the examination period is not a very good time to do a careful job of constructive legal criticism. The best skill required for the hypothetical-case-essay examination is the ability to analyze the facts and to see all of the "points" or legal issues involved. The examinations with which I am familiar accomplish this by making the statements of facts rather complicated, so that a

half-hour per question is allowed for answering. In grading this type of question the mere decision (e.g., for the plaintiff) is usually unimportant and the grade depends on the quality of the essay.

Although the hypothetical-case-essay examination was much superior to the older type which called for definitions or explanations of legal terms, the grading of it called for a considerable latitude of discretion (since the answers could and did properly vary in analysis) and required the judgment of the man in charge of the course. In most, if not all, law schools it is a settled tradition that examination grading is not to be delegated to assistants. In large classes the delay in grading not only leaves the students in suspense but also creates some risks that the professor's standard of grading may change between the first papers he reads and the last. These and other arguments led to the introduction of the objective-type of examination in larger classes—75 or more. As far as I know this type of examination was first used, in law classes, at Columbia in 1923. When carefully prepared and expertly tested, such an examination can test most of the qualities or skills that the case method is intended to develop; that is, the analysis of a hypothetical case and the recognition of accurate or inaccurate use of terms. It measures diligence in preparation (a virtue not to be overlooked) more thoroughly because of the much larger number of questions than on the essay examination, and the corresponding lessening of the influence of Lady Luck.

* * *

III.

Ten Merits of the Case Method

Some of the advantages and disadvantages of the case method and its by-products have been referred to above. Here I list ten of its merits, relative to instruction by means of lectures or text-books.

1.   The case method conforms to the methods of the lawyer and the judge in our case-law system. It refers the student to some of the same sources that they use, it leads to professionally cautious reliance only on narrow generalizations and to distrust of broad generalizations, which is characteristic of Anglo–American case-law thinking. On the whole this tendency is a valuable trait of American culture; it is to be hoped that no amount of rhetoric and sentimentality will wholly discredit it, even though it needs (and finds) suitable correctives. The study of a set of problematic facts in relation to one or more legal generalizations gives the latter clarity of existential reference, more commonly called "concreteness of meaning." The student learns to "break down a case," to analyze a narrative into legal and factual issues.

2.   It requires the student to make his own synthesis of the subject matter, and makes him independent, to a large extent, of treatises and encyclopedias.

3.   It is pedagogically stimulating. The cases usually have some dramatic interest. Significantly, the Harvard Graduate School of Busi-

ness Administration has at considerable labor and expense introduced the study of selected current problems or "cases" of business men.

4. Terminology is learned from context rather than from formal definition. This is important especially because there is no common official terminology for most of the legal systems of the forty-eight states.

5. The critical powers of the student are developed by studying conflicting cases from different jurisdictions. When a "New York rule" and a "Massachusetts rule" are incompatible, students become interested in the relative merits of each.

6. The student gains slowly a trained intuition with respect to controversies and their legal consequences, which is useful in gap-filling. This is perhaps what Holmes referred to when he said that "nearly all the education which men can get from others is moral, not intellectual."

7. Reported cases are frequently good evidence of contemporary American culture, of the way people do business normally (the controversy arising from a deviation), of family arrangements, of police practices, etc. The rules or doctrines of older cases can be appraised by considering the cultural changes that have intervened since they were decided.

8. From the court's opinion the student often gets some understanding of the factors other than traditional doctrine that influenced the decision, such as the economic or political beliefs of judges. However, this advantage is exceptional.

9. The case method keeps the law teacher working; he cannot mumble last year's stale lecture notes (as professors in other departments are reputed to do); he has always the incentive to be more thoroughly prepared on the cases than his students, and to keep his notes up to date.

10. The law teacher often gains insight from the questions and discussions of the students. This would not be true of a straight lecture.

IV.

TEN DEMERITS OF THE CASE METHOD

Some of the disadvantages of the case method, or of certain versions of it, have been mentioned above. Here I list ten demerits, some of which can be reduced or eliminated.

1. The case method is a wasteful method of imparting information to students. Many law teachers of an earlier generation thought it fashionable to say that they taught "legal reasoning" and left the students to get "mere" information from reading in the law library. However, reasoning without information about the premises is pretty empty-headed. The law library is rarely equal to the strain, and adequate short texts are still relatively scarce. Some of the more recent casebooks contain a good deal of textual material. The editor can often write a better summary, for his purposes, than can be found elsewhere.

2.   The students are frequently too immature, especially in the first year, to make a good synthesis of legal doctrines or concepts, based upon case material. The instructor should give example and guidance; but one of the chief merits of the method is that the student is called upon to make up his own summary. The peddling of "canned" summaries should be strictly repressed.

3.   The impromptu gropings of the student who is called upon in class to answer hypothetical questions are of little value either to him or to the others. This demerit can be partly corrected by editorial notes and problems, in the casebook, which the student is asked to read in advance of the class discussion.

4.   The case method is an inadequate way of teaching legal history, either of English law or of the law of any American jurisdiction. Supplementary excerpts and notes in the casebook can partly serve this purpose. A separate course in legal history and in the method of tracing an historical line of development has its advantages.

5.   The case method is inadequate to present extra-legal materials which are relevant to legal doctrines, decisions and statutes. The accidental ways in which cases happen to be litigated and happen to be carried to appellate courts on significant issues make the reported cases at best a patchwork of relevant social and economic practices. However, this kind of material can best be presented in excerpts from nonlegal treatises or periodicals, in forms of documents, and in editorial notes.

6.   The case method is inadequate for the study of legislation. This is, in my judgment, the most serious demerit of the case method as originally conceived. The student needs training in the interpretation of statutory provisions that have not yet been judicially construed. This can be partly accomplished by well constructed hypothetical cases, used as the basis for class discussion.

7.   The case method absorbs so much time in analysis of meanings and logical application to hypothetical cases that no time is left for the study and discussion of the fundamental philosophy or ethical bases of the law. This tendency can be counteracted by a teacher who is determined to lead his students, sometimes, away from the earthiness of case study. The casebook can contain material appropriate for such a discussion.

8.   The preparation of casebooks has taken too many able legal scholars away from creative legal scholarship of permanent value. For example, Professor James Barr Ames, a brilliant and inspiring teacher, produced many annotated casebooks and only a single volume of essays. Fortunately the number of scholarly treatises is increasing.

9.   The student learns to evaluate authorities in a mythical legal system, The Law of This Course, and does not learn thoroughly the law of any one jurisdiction. To the extent that this is a disadvantage it is outweighed, I believe, by the merits of the comparative law technique.

10. The case method leaves untouched in the curriculum some practical legal problems which are not susceptible to litigation. For example, the proper organization of courts, the duties of the bar with respect to the needs for legal services of the indigent and of persons of moderate means, and the like. No doubt law students should receive an introduction to this reconstructive type of thinking. Yet there is a limit to what one can teach—and learn—in three academic years.

THE BRAMBLE BUSH[r]

Karl Llewellyn

* * *

III.   THIS CASE SYSTEM: WHAT TO DO WITH THE CASES

I have now sketched for you in charcoal outline—an unkind critic might remark, in bastard caricature—the part that law and law's minions play in our society, and the general history of a case at law. All this, for your ordained affairs, is background; you will be getting restive. Indeed, in delivering these lectures orally, I have felt the need, before the second hour, of setting to work to dynamite the foreground stumps: cases in casebooks have been assigned to you; what, then, are you to do with them?

Now the first thing you are to do with an opinion is to read it. Does this sound commonplace? Does this amuse you? There is no reason why it should amuse you. You have already read past seventeen expressions of whose meaning you have no conception. So hopeless is your ignorance of their meaning that you have no hard-edged memory of having seen unmeaning symbols on the page. You have applied to the court's opinion the reading technique that you use upon the Satevepost. Is a word unfamiliar? Read on that much more quickly! Onward and upward—we must not hold up the story.

That will not do. It is a pity, but you must learn to *read*. To read each word. To understand *each* word. You are outlanders in this country of the law. You do not know the speech. It must be learned. Like any other foreign tongue, it must be learned: by seeing words, by using them until they are familiar; meantime, by constant reference to the dictionary. What, dictionary? Tort, trespass, trover, plea, assumpsit, nisi prius, venire de novo, demurrer, joinder, traverse, abatement, general issue, tender, mandamus, certiorari, adverse possession, dependent relative revocation, and the rest. Law Latin, law French, aye, or law English— what do these strange terms mean to you? Can you rely upon the crumbs of language that remain from school? Does *cattle levant and couchant* mean *cows getting up and lying down*? Does *nisi prius* mean *unless before*? Or *traverse* mean an upper gallery in a church? I fear a dictionary is your only hope—a law dictionary—the one-volume kind you can keep ready on your desk. Can you trust the dictionary, is it accurate, does it

r.   Oceana Publications 41–43 (1951).

give you what you want? Of course not. No dictionary does. The life of words is in the using of them, in the wide network of their long associations, in the intangible something we denominate their feel. But the bare bones to work with the dictionary offers; and without those bare bones you may be sure the feel will never come.

The first thing to do with an opinion, then, is read it. The next thing is to get clear the actual decision, the judgment rendered. Who won, the plaintiff or defendant? And watch your step here. You are after in first instance the plaintiff and defendant *below,* in the trial court. In order to follow through what happened you must therefore first know the outcome *below*; else you do not see what was appealed from, nor by whom. You now follow through in order to see exactly what *further* judgment has been rendered on appeal. The stage is then cleared of form— although of course you do not yet know all that these forms mean, that they imply. You can turn now to what you want peculiarly to know. Given the actual judgments below and above as your indispensable framework—what has the case decided, and what can you derive from it as to what will be decided later?

You will be looking, in the opinion, or in the preliminary matter plus the opinion, for the following: a statement of the facts the court assumes; a statement of the precise way the question has come before the court—which includes what the plaintiff wanted below, and what the defendant did about it, the judgment below, and what the trial court did that is complained of; then the outcome on appeal, the judgment; and, finally the reasons this court gives for doing what it did. This does not look so bad. But it is much worse than it looks.

For all our cases are decided, all our opinions are written, all our predictions, all our arguments are made, on certain four assumptions. They are the first presuppositions of our study. They must be rutted into you till you can juggle with them standing on your head and in your sleep.

1) *The court must decide the dispute that is before it.* It cannot refuse because the job is hard, or dubious, or dangerous.

2) *The court can decide* only *the particular dispute which is before it.* When it speaks to that question it speaks ex cathedra, with authority, with finality, with an almost magic power. When it speaks to the question before, it announces *law,* and if what it announces is new, it legislates, it *makes* the law. But when it speaks to any other question at all, it says mere words, which no man needs to follow. Are such words worthless? They are not. We know them as judicial *dicta;* when they are wholly off the point at issue we call them *obiter dicta*—words dropped along the road, wayside remarks. Yet even wayside remarks shed light on the remarker. They may be very useful in the future to him, or to us. But he will not feel bound to them, as to his ex cathedra utterance. They came not hallowed by a Delphic frenzy. He may be slow to change them; but not so slow as in the other case.

3) *The court can decide the particular dispute only according to a* general *rule which covers a whole class of like disputes.* Our legal theory does not admit of single decisions standing on their own. If judges are free, are indeed forced, to decide new cases for which there is no rule, they must at least make a new rule as they decide. So far, good. But how wide, or how narrow, is the general rule in this particular case? That is a troublesome matter. The practice of our case–law, however, is I think fairly stated thus: it pays to be suspicious of general rules which look too wide; it pays to go slow in feeling *certain* that a wide rule has been laid down at all, or that, if seemingly laid down, it will be followed. For there is a fourth accepted canon:

4) *Everything, everything, everything, big or small, a judge may say in an opinion, is to be read with primary reference to the particular dispute, the particular question before him.* You are not to think that the words mean what they might if they stood alone. You are to have your eye on the case in hand, and to learn how to interpret all that has been said *merely* as a reason for deciding *that* case *that* way. At need.

THE MORAL RESPONSIBILITY OF LAW SCHOOLS[s]
Terrance Sandalow

* * *

The idea has arisen recently that the skills of "thinking like a lawyer," both those mentioned above and others, are easily acquired and that, having learned them in the first year, students might more profitably spend their subsequent years in law school learning something else. At least in part, the idea grows out of dissatisfaction with emphasis on the case method throughout law school. I hold no brief for the case method—indeed, I agree that it overused—but the notion that the skills it seeks to impart can be learned "once and for all" in the first year reflects inadequate understanding of those skills, of the means by which they are developed, and of the uses of the case method. At some mechanical and elementary level, no doubt, an able student can reasonably quickly learn to comprehend an appellate opinion and the techniques by which other cases are distinguished from it. But the development of these skills is not, after all, the real aim of the case method. The abilities to read imaginatively and with attention to the subtleties of language, to frame and test suitable hypotheses for synthesis, and to detect premises of thought and errors of logic, all of which the case method is aimed at developing, are not capacities that we either have or do not have, in the way that one either does or does not possess a law school degree. Capacities such as these are the product of continuous struggle to wrest meaning from disorder. They are developed and maintained only by continually undertaking and sustaining the activities pertaining to them.

s.   34 Journal of Legal Education 170–72 (June 1984).

The notion that the skills of critical inquiry, having been learned in the first year, can be set aside thereafter so that students may devote attention to other matters suffers from yet another vice, a failure to recognize the interdependence of these skills and of knowledge. Skill in reading and in analysis and synthesis is broadened and deepened as it comes into contact with new subject matter. Similarly, knowledge of a subject, except at a very superficial level, depends upon its having been acquired through the tools of critical inquiry. These considerations suggest that the real failing of legal education is not that it overemphasizes developing the skills of "thinking like a lawyer," but that it gives inadequate attention to the use of those skills in dealing with materials and issues that are not formally legal. The consequence of that inattention is the curious disjunction that too many lawyers display, careful craftsmanship in the performance of professional responsibilities and a lack of concern for the skills of craft in dealing with political and social issues. Increased attention to such issues, which are hardly irrelevant to the study of law, might lead students to an understanding that the skills of critical inquiry have uses that extend beyond the performance of professional tasks.

Obviously a good deal more might be said about these intellectual capacities and the role of legal education in developing them, but I want to turn to some other intellectual qualities with which law schools should also be concerned. A traditional aim of education, from which legal education has no exemption, is to strengthen the capacity of students to avoid common hazards to clear thought, such hazards as self-interest, provincialism of time and place, overdependence on familiar categories of thought, the inability to tolerate uncertainty, and sentimentality. The last of these may be used to illustrate the opportunities that legal education affords to overcoming these hazards.

* * *

Since the case method has taken such a beating in recent years, it is worth saying that appellate opinions can serve as an especially useful vehicle for the education of sentiment as well as to teach the importance of approaching abstract principles skeptically. The latter point is too familiar to require elaboration, but many will greet the former with astonishment. Appellate opinions, it will be said, report only carefully selected facts, and even those are often stated in highly abstract fashion; they are, for that reason, implausible vehicles for conveying a sense of the variousness and complexity of life. But though it is true that the opinions are written in that way, it does not follow that they must be read in the same way. A skillful teacher will lead students to read opinions imaginatively, with attention to the human possibilities that lie beneath their abstract language. The exploration of these possibilities, conjoined with consideration of their implications for judgment, offers opportunity for developing that fusion of feeling and intellect we call sensibility.

* * *

D. THE COMMON LAW SYSTEM

1. THE ROLE OF PRECEDENT IN JUDICIAL DECISIONS

Judicial opinions[t] will be the focus of much of your early study in law school. Your basic study tool for most of your first year courses will be a casebook that excerpts appellate court opinions and other materials. The collected materials should lead you to conclusions regarding the status of the law in the subject and to an understanding of the development of the law in that area.

The study of judicial opinions predominantly centers around that portion of our legal system known as the Common Law System, under which law is derived from judicial decisions. In our system, a judge faced with a controversy first determines the facts of the case, either by herself, if on a motion or trial to the bench, or with the aid of a jury. The trial judge must also decide what the law is or, if no law exists, what it should be. To determine the law, a judge will look to see whether the courts in the jurisdiction have resolved a similar controversy. If so, the judge may be bound by the doctrine of *stare decisis*[u] to follow the *precedent*. If the facts of the cases differ, the court must determine whether it should follow the rule announced in the earlier case. If so, it will extend the precedent. If, however, the judge decides that the earlier rule does not produce the best result in the present case, the judge may limit the application of the rule or decline to apply it. Whether the judge decides to apply the earlier rule may depend upon such factors as social policy and the logical and consistent development of the law.

When you, as an attorney, seek to solve a legal problem, to advise a client on a future course of action, or to advise a client regarding rights or liabilities arising from past events, you will frequently follow the same course as does a judge: You will look for similar factual situations in decided cases, ascertain the rules developed in those cases, and attempt to predict how a judge might resolve your client's problem. Because the conclusion you reach and the advice you give will frequently be based on analysis of judicial opinions, it follows that the best preparation for your work in the legal field is practice in analyzing opinions. Moreover, opinions represent resolutions of problems; understanding how courts resolve problems will help you to analyze and solve new problems.

In the common law system, courts are supposed to decide only those cases before them, not give opinions on hypothetical cases. Sometimes, however, in deciding cases, judges will provide illustrations or examples of the application of a rule. If the court's language is not necessary to the

t. A judicial *opinion* is the court's written decision in a case. The *decision* is the result the court reaches in a dispute. These terms are frequently used interchangeably with the term *case*, which refers to the entire controversy before a court. Law students should be aware of the meanings of these terms and should use them precisely.

u. *Stare decisis* means "to adhere to decided cases." We will return to this concept in our discussion of the structure of the court system, *infra,* p. 40.

disposition of the case, it is *"dictum."*[v] Even lower courts in the same jurisdiction are not bound to follow *dicta*, although well-reasoned *dicta* can be persuasive and may guide a trial court as to the probable resolution of the matter on appeal. Law students should note persuasive *dicta*. They may prove helpful in predicting the outcomes of future cases.

As you are probably aware, disputes are initially resolved in trial courts, and the party who loses in trial court typically has a right to appeal to a higher court. The function of an appellate court is to review lower court cases to determine the propriety of the proceedings in the trial court. Within narrow limits, an appellate court may also examine whether factual determinations are supported by the evidence introduced in the trial court, but it does not receive evidence for the purpose of making factual determinations.[w] When an appellate court has reached its decision in a case on appeal, it reports its decision in an opinion. The opinions of appellate courts are generally printed,[x] and it is these opinions that you will encounter in law school.

2. THE NATURE OF CASE LAW[y]

Case law in some form and to some extent is found wherever there is law. A mere series of decisions of individual cases does not of course in itself constitute a system of law. But in any judicial system rules of law arise sooner or later out of such decisions of cases, as rules of action arise out of the solution of practical problems, whether or not such formulations are desired, intended or consciously recognized. These generalizations contained in, or built upon, past decisions, when taken as normative for future disputes, create a legal system of precedent. Precedent, however, is operative before it is recognized. Toward its operation drive all those phases of human make-up which build habit in the individual and institutions in the group: laziness as to the reworking of a problem once solved; the time and energy saved by routine, especially under any pressure of business; the values of routine as a curb on arbitrariness and as a prop of weakness, inexperience and instability; the social values of predictability; the power of whatever exists to produce expectations and the power of expectations to become normative. The force of precedent in the law is heightened by an additional factor: that curious, almost universal, sense of justice which urges that all men are properly to be treated alike in like circumstances. As the social system varies we meet infinite variations as to what men or treatments or

v. *Dicta* is plural; *dictum* is singular. Providing the definition is easier than determining when the nonessential statements taken together state one idea, and hence should be called *dictum*, or whether they state more than one idea, and thus are properly called *dicta*.

w. There are exceptions to this principle. See West's Ann. Cal. Civ. Code P. § 909.

x. Today, courts resort frequently to unpublished opinions. For problems related to the use of unpublished opinions, see *Unreported Decisions in the United States Court of Appeals*, 63 Corn. L. Rev. 128 (1977).

y. The following paragraph appears in Karl N. Llewellyn "Caselaw," 3 Encyclopedia of the Social Sciences 249 (1930).

circumstances are to be classed as "like"; but the pressure to accept the views of the time and place remains.

———

Case law is made up of decisions that resolve one or more legal or factual issues presented to the court by litigants in a legal proceeding. A decision may terminate the legal dispute. Recall the case of *Baxter v. Fugett, supra* p. 23. Had the court in *Baxter* affirmed the judgment of the lower court in favor of the defendant or had no appeal been taken, the legal dispute would have been finally resolved. Often, however, the lower court decision is but a step toward the final resolution. In *Baxter,* the appellate court reversed the lower court's judgment and remanded the case for a new trial. The appellate court decided an important legal issue: What standard of care is owed by minors while operating motor vehicles? The jury on retrial will review the facts in light of the proper legal standard. Eventually, a final resolution of the controversy will be rendered, although perhaps after further appeals and retrials. This resolution, referred to as a final judgment, will bind the litigants. This binding effect is embraced by the doctrine of *res judicata.*[z]

The appellate decision in *Baxter,* however, did more than merely decide an aspect of a legal controversy between the parties before the court. It also settled a rule of law concerning the standard of care owed by minors when operating vehicles. This decision is now binding on all future litigants presenting the same or similar issues within the same legal system. *Baxter* will be cited as precedent, or binding authority, for the resolution of that issue in that particular jurisdiction. This binding effect is what we referred to earlier by the Latin term *stare decisis.*[aa]

Baxter may also be cited as persuasive authority in other jurisdictions. Whether the courts of other jurisdictions will accept the *Baxter* rule regarding the standard of care owed by minor automobile drivers will depend on a host of considerations. Can you identify some of them?

As noted, a significant limitation on the doctrine of *stare decisis,* or precedent, is that its binding force pertains only to factually similar cases. When the facts in a subsequent case differ materially, the cases are said to be distinguishable, and the rule of law announced in the former case need not be applied. You will spend countless hours in the first year of law school learning to distinguish the facts contained in judicial opinions from hypotheticals posed by professors. There is no easy test for determining to what extent a legal rule is tied to the specific facts of the case in which it is set forth, or even for ascertaining what

z. *Res judicata* encompasses the notion that a matter once decided should not ordinarily be relitigated, that the social and economic wastefulness of relitigation, based solely on the belief that the tribunal may have reached an incorrect result, should not be countenanced. There must be an end to litigation.

aa. *See supra.* Justice Brandeis once commented that "[s]*tare decisis* is usually the wise policy, because in most matters it is more important that the applicable rule of law is settled than that it be settled right." *Burnet v. Coronado Oil & Gas Co.,* 285 U.S. 393, 406–08 (1932) (Brandeis, J., dissenting).

facts are material to the resolution of the case. The determination is largely one of careful reasoning, experience, and acquired instinct, developed through years of practice.

Upon what facts is the decision based? The "real" facts or the facts reported in the opinion? Suppose in *Baxter* the court had erroneously found the operator of the vehicle to be a minor. Would the mistake in the age of the defendant render the decision of any less precedential force in subsequent cases actually dealing with minor drivers? For the rule of law to be binding as precedent, there must be unity between the facts as perceived by the court, even if mistakenly, and the rule announced in the case.

The extent to which a decision is binding in the jurisdiction in which it is decided also depends upon the position the rendering court occupies the judicial hierarchy. In the federal system, as in many state systems, there are three levels of courts: (1) trial courts, known as lower or inferior courts, (2) intermediate appellate courts, and (3) the highest court or court of last resort, referred to in the federal and most state court systems as the Supreme Court. A decision of the highest court is binding upon the two lower levels. A decision of an intermediate court does not bind the Supreme Court although, as you would expect, it does bind the trial courts in the appellate court's district. Trial court opinions are usually unreported and do not bind any level.

Appellate courts retain the power to overrule their own precedents. To fully appreciate the effect of overruling a precedent, recall the distinct functions of a case: (1) to resolve a particular controversy between actual litigants and (2) to establish a rule of law for future cases. In other words, the case is *res judicata* for the parties and *stare decisis* for all future litigants. The overruling process affects only the latter function.

Let us examine this concept. Suppose the Supreme Court of Oklahoma, the court that decided *Baxter,* faced with the same issue in a subsequent case, decides either that *Baxter* had been incorrectly decided or that its rationale is no longer persuasive. Should the decision be perpetuated? Or should the court remedy the perceived defect by applying a doctrine now thought to be correct?

The legal system has earned something of a bad reputation in the literature for its alleged blind adherence to outmoded precedent. Jonathan Swift, in a satire on English jurisprudence had Gulliver say to one of the Houyhnhnms:

> It is a maxim among these men [lawyers], that whatever has been done before may legally be done again; and therefore they take special care to record all the decisions formerly made, even those which have through ignorance or corruption contradicted the rule of common justice and the general reason of mankind. These, under the name of precedents, they produce as authorities and thereby endeavor to justify the most iniquitous opinions; and they are so

lucky in this practice that it rarely fails of decrees answering to their intent and expectation.[bb]

Perhaps the system owes a duty to society to periodically review and revise the decisions upon which it relies. What are the countervailing principles?

Whatever might have been historically true, courts seem to feel less constrained to follow their own precedent in the field of constitutional law than in other fields. Is it more important to the development of constitutional law than to other fields of law that the Supreme Court of the United States retain the right to overrule precedent? Does your answer depend to any extent on the inability of other political branches to effect a change in constitutional interpretation without a constitutional amendment? Is the power to overrule cases as important in other areas of the law where legislative bodies may effect change? If the rule of law announced in *Baxter* is unwise, should resort to the legislature be the exclusive avenue of change? What are the competing considerations?

While the overruling process is a deviation from application of the doctrine of *stare decisis,* its utility can easily be recognized, especially in the field of constitutional law. Yet courts often stop short of directly overruling precedent. They often apply more covert measures of neutralizing undesired authority, such as distinguishing and limiting prior decisions to their precise facts. By limiting the rule to the specific facts of a prior case, the court virtually overrules the precedent. The precedent becomes a derelict on the judicial waterway. Is there anything to be said for retaining the derelict?

The doctrine of *stare decisis* permits the lower courts less latitude in disregarding precedent. Lower courts do not ordinarily indulge in deciding whether a higher court's decision is correct. If changes in socio-economic conditions have rendered a precedent unsound, however, lower courts have refused, albeit rarely, to follow the earlier case, even when it is indistinguishable from a pending case. Should lower courts be permitted this discretion? If lower courts are permitted to disregard precedent, is there a danger that discretion may turn into license? Should not the doctrine of *stare decisis* mandate adherence to higher court authority, right or wrong? If not, where should the line be drawn? *See Barnette v. West Virginia State Board of Education,* 47 F. Supp. 251 (S.D.W. Va.1942).

Development of the common law depends to some extent upon the way in which cases are presented to the courts. The judiciary ordinarily occupies a passive role in the selection of cases. Even where the appellate court retains unbridled discretion to accept review, the aggrieved party would ordinarily have had to petition the court in the first instance.

Institutional organizations, either as litigants or as resources for litigation, may be vitally concerned with the development of doctrinal principles. The Sierra Club, ACLU, NAACP, and National Association of

bb. J. Swift, GULLIVER'S TRAVELS: Houyhnhnms, ch. 5.

Attorneys General are examples of the diverse organizations that litigate in the courts. Special ethical concerns are encountered where the non-client retains the lawyer to represent a litigant and the interests of the client and non-client materially diverge. The Rules of Professional Conduct allow the payment of compensation to the lawyer from the non-client as along as the client consents and there is no interference with the lawyer's independent professional judgment or with the client-lawyer relationship. *See* Rule 1.8(f), ABA Model Rules of Professional Conduct (2002).

Claims are presented by litigants through the adversary process. It is the litigants who decide whether to institute suit and, even more importantly for law-making purposes, whether to perfect appeals. Litigants generally are not concerned whether their cases will have salutory effects on the development of doctrinal principles. Lon L. Fuller discusses the issue of fortuity in the presentation and resolution of cases on the common law system in the following excerpt:

AMERICAN LEGAL REALISM[cc]
Lon L. Fuller

* * *

Often a whole field of law is influenced permanently by the particular turn taken by the first case arising in the field. This case may have carried a certain factual and ethical complexion which was actually the determinative element in its decision. The court in deciding it, however, may lay down a categorical rule which subsequently becomes divorced from the particular circumstances of its first utterance and controls perhaps hundreds of cases which from an ethical or "factual" viewpoint are quite different from the first and "critical" case. There is an even more sinister possibility. Organized interest groups, aware of the importance of such critical cases, may see to it that these cases "come up in the right way." Thus by the expenditure of a little money and effort at the right time the whole future development of a field of law may be influenced.

* * * Just as a whole field of law may be influenced by the accidental *presence* of a particular case at a particular stage of its development, so a whole field of law may be influenced by the accidental *absence* of a decision which might serve as a sort of *doctrinal bridge* between existing rules and needed new law.

The case of *Shuey v. United States* decided that the published offer of a reward might be effectively revoked by an announcement given equal publicity. Pollock in his treatise on contracts admits the reasonableness of the decision but adds the remark that it "seems a rather strong piece of judicial legislation." Why this? Because previous decisions had declared that a revocation takes effect only when "communicated." This revocation had not been "communicated" since it had never come

cc. 82 U. Pa. L. Rev. 429, 440–42 (1934).

to the knowledge of the claimant of the reward. Now suppose that there had intervened between these previous decisions and the case of *Shuey v. United States* a case in which a letter of revocation had been promptly delivered at the place of business of the offeree and had been allowed to remain unopened on his desk. Without much question a court would have held that such a revocation was "communicated" so soon as the offeree had had a fair opportunity to become familiar with it. And had such a case existed before the *Shuey* case is it likely that anyone would have regarded that decision as a "strong piece of judicial legislation"? Pollock's attitude was influenced by the purely fortuitous circumstance that there did not exist a case which could operate to carry his mind, without shock, from the older cases to the decision in the *Shuey* case.

The possibility that a doctrinal bridge may be lacking represents, then, an additional element of fortuity in the development of case law, operating to make the litigant's rights depend on the chronological order in which his case comes up. Furthermore it is an element which is especially likely to be operative in fields where social practice is changing rapidly. Social practice may change so rapidly that by the time cases actually get into litigation they are so far removed from what the court is familiar with that the court is left without any intellectual conduit to carry it from the old to the new.

* * *

Incidentally this whole discussion gives point to a statement once made by Ihering. * * * The statement was that Roman law was great because it was built upon a system of "case law" which did not discriminate between real and hypothetical cases. The jurisconsults gave answer to all cases put to them, without inquiring whether they were real. This gave a continuity to the body of doctrine which they developed which cannot exist where only "real" cases are dealt with.

E.   THE TWO FUNCTIONS OF JUDICIAL DECISIONS: *STARE DECISIS* AND *RES JUDICATA*

As a law student, you will be less concerned with the results of a published opinion than with the reasoning supporting the result. Those reasons will help you predict the outcome of future cases. Law study involves reading and analyzing appellate decisions. In many situations, the parties are unconcerned with the precise reasoning of the court. All they want to know is the result. At other times, the parties, as well as strangers to the litigation, may wish to explore the reasoning of the court as a guide to future behavior. Thus, as you can see, appellate decisions serve two separate and distinct functions.

The following hypothetical fact situation illustrates these different functions. Able sues Baker for injuries resulting from an automobile intersection collision in the forum state. Able claims that Baker ran a red light and was under the influence of alcohol at the time of the accident. A final decision for the plaintiff, Able, decides the controversy. Able has a legally enforceable judgment against Baker as a result of the accident. Should the case not be appealed to a higher court, it usually makes little difference to the parties involved whether the decision was based on the red light violation or intoxication. But let us now suppose that Baker appeals from the adverse judgment.

Suppose the trial court instructed the jury:

> If you find that at the time of the accident in question the defendant's blood contained a blood-alcohol level of .10 or greater, you must find that the defendant's ability to control his vehicle was impaired by virtue of his consumption of alcoholic beverages. You must make this finding even if you could have believed, based upon other competent evidence presented at this trial, that the defendant's ability to control his vehicle was not impaired by virtue of his consumption of alcoholic beverages.

Under the applicable statute, a blood alcohol level of .10 or greater creates a presumption of "driving under the influence." The statute, however, does not expressly prohibit the jury from considering contrary evidence on the defendant's state of intoxication. The opinion of the Supreme Court of the State, reversing the judgment in favor of Able, might read as follows:

> Under the statutes of this State, a blood alcohol level of .10 or more establishes that the ability of a driver to control his vehicle is impaired. This presumption is rebuttable. The defendant may introduce and have the jury consider competent evidence to the contrary. The jury may, in its discretion, weigh all the evidence in determining whether the driver was under the influence of intoxicating beverages. Reversed and remanded for further proceedings not inconsistent with this opinion.[dd]

The court has made a significant statement on the meaning of the statute. It has made clear that even where a blood alcohol level of .10 is shown, the jury may still find that the defendant's ability to control his or her motor vehicle was not impaired. Under the doctrine of *stare decisis,* this legal proposition will bind judges in all courts of the state in all pending and future proceedings.[ee] But what about cases in which final judgments had been rendered under the erroneous instruction? If the case is not presently on review and the time for appeal has expired, the

---

dd. Had the jury specifically found for the plaintiff based upon the alternative ground, the red light infraction, the case would have been affirmed unless the appellate court found insufficient evidence to support the decision or some other error or irregularity. A general verdict—one that merely finds for one of the parties without any particularization of the ground—may mask the basis of the decision. The appellate court normally has no choice other than to reverse the judgment should it disavow the legal validity of one alternative, although it would have approved the other ground. A few jurisdictions may affirm a general verdict if any alternative ground supports the verdict.

ee. *See supra* Chapter I, Section D.

judgment stands. The doctrine of *res judicata* does not ordinarily allow vacating the judgment under these circumstances.

In some cases it may be difficult to discriminate between a rule of law, which is binding under the doctrine of *stare decisis,* and *"dictum"*— a statement in a case that is not necessary to the decision and therefore does not have controlling force in subsequent adjudications. To distinguish holding from *dictum,* you must digest the facts and understand the procedural context in which each case arises. Even after painstaking analysis, however, it may not be possible to do more than make an educated guess as to the ruling of the case. Even if you correctly distinguish the holding from the *dictum,* the wheat from the chaff, later decisions may embrace the *dictum* as a rule of law, turning chaff into wheat. This is the stuff upon which first year law study is based.

A case may also present alternative grounds for decision, each of which is independently sufficient to support the court's ruling. Either or both of the grounds may become rules of law binding in future cases. To the extent a holding is an alternative basis for deciding a case, a future court may have additional latitude in refusing to apply it. For example, let us return to *Able v. Baker.* Suppose the trial court judgment for Able is appealed by Baker and affirmed by the court.[ff] In marshalling the evidence regarding the signal infraction, the appellate court refers to the defendant's admission that he entered the intersection on a yellow light. In a later case, directly presenting the question of a defendant's liability for entering an intersection against a yellow light, a lower court might assert that the relevant passage in the opinion was not essential to the result and therefore is not binding.

While you cannot know with litmus-test precision what courts will do in future situations, lawyers (and law students) are frequently called upon to make such predictions. It is an exciting and challenging process, to which you will be exposed for the rest of your legal careers.

We have already briefly examined the two functions of a judicial decision. *Rush v. Maple Heights,* reprinted below, illustrates these functions.

RUSH v. MAPLE HEIGHTS

Supreme Court of Ohio, 1958.
167 Ohio St. 221, 147 N.E.2d 599.

STATEMENT OF THE CASE

* * *

This cause was commenced in the Court of Common Pleas of Cuyahoga County as an action to recover damages for personal injuries resulting from a fall while plaintiff, appellee herein, was riding on a

---

ff. In this circumstance, we may assume that the court agreed with the lower court's instruction regarding intoxication, and that the jury predicated liability on both bases set forth in the complaint.

motorcycle over a street in defendant city of Maple Heights, appellant herein.

In her second amended petition, plaintiff alleges that on or about September 20, 1951, she was a passenger on a motorcycle operated by her husband and proceeding in an easterly direction on Schreiber Road within the limits of Maple Heights at a speed of not more than 20 miles per hour, when she was thrown to the ground and injured.

She alleges further that the defendant was negligent in failing to keep Schreiber Road in good repair and free from nuisance, in suffering large holes, "bumps" and "dips" to exist in the regularly traveled portion of the street, and in failing to erect warning signs giving notice of the unsafe and dangerous condition of Schreiber Road; that the city had notice; and that her injuries were caused directly and proximately by the negligence of the defendant city.

She then alleges:

Thereafter the plaintiff herein, Lenore Rush, duly filed an action for damage to personal property in the Municipal Court of Cleveland, Ohio, being cause number A 241 307 on the docket of said court, against the defendant herein, the city of Maple Heights. The cause proceeded to trial on or about the 23rd day of March 1954, the Municipal Court of Cleveland rendered its judgment in favor of the plaintiff therein, Lenore Rush, and against the defendant therein, the city of Maple Heights. Thereafter upon the motion of the defendant, the city of Maple Heights the Municipal Court of Cleveland rendered its findings of fact and conclusions of law as follows:

The court finds that the city of Maple Heights had actual notice of the condition of Schreiber Road.

That the city was negligent in not repairing the hole complained of in plaintiff's petition.

That such negligence on the part of the city was the proximate cause of the damages sustained by plaintiff in the amount of $100.

CONCLUSIONS OF LAW

Judgment for plaintiff in the amount of $100.

Thereafter on April 19, 1954, the Municipal Court of Cleveland duly overruled the motion of the defendant the city of Maple Heights for a new trial, whereupon the defendant therein filed its notice of appeal to the Court of Appeals in and for Cuyahoga County, Ohio. After the filing of briefs therein and oral argument thereto, the Court of Appeals on or about the 17th day of December 1954 affirmed the judgment of the Municipal Court of Cleveland in favor of the plaintiff, Lenore Rush, and against the defendant therein, the city of Maple Heights and directed that a special mandate issue to the Municipal Court of Cleveland in order to carry the judgment into execution.

Thereafter the defendant therein, the city of Maple Heights filed its motion to certify the proceedings to the Supreme Court of Ohio. After the filing of briefs therein and oral argument thereto, the Supreme Court of Ohio on or about the 21st day of February 1955 denied the motion to certify and affirmed the judgment of the Court of Appeals and the Municipal Court of Cleveland in favor of the plaintiff, Lenore Rush, and against the defendant the city of Maple Heights.

* * *

The plaintiff in cause number A 241 307 in the Municipal Court of Cleveland is the same Lenore Rush who is the plaintiff herein; the defendant in cause number A 241 307 in the Municipal Court of Cleveland is the same city of Maple Heights, defendant herein. The allegations of negligence in cause number A 241 307 in the Municipal Court of Cleveland are the same as the allegations of negligence hereinbefore set forth. The issue of negligence is therefore *res judicata* between the parties hereto.

Plaintiff then filed a motion for an order setting the cause for trial "on the issue of damages alone for the reason that the liability of the defendant has been determined heretofore by the Supreme Court in case number A 241 307 on the docket of the Municipal Court of Cleveland."

In its answer, defendant denies plaintiff's allegations charging it with negligence.

Relative to the effect of the previous action between the parties in the Cleveland Municipal Court, the defendant answers as follows:

[D]efendant admits the filing of a lawsuit by plaintiff against defendant in Cleveland Municipal Court and that plaintiff obtained judgment therein, but this defendant denies that said Cleveland Municipal Court judgment is controlling herein.

Defendant further denies for want of knowledge that the damage sued for in the Cleveland Municipal Court case and the injuries sued for herein allegedly arise out of the same incident, *i.e.*, a fall from a motorcycle striking a hole in the street.

Defendant's answer admits further that it appealed from the judgment of the Municipal Court to the Court of Appeals and to the Supreme Court as alleged by plaintiff and denies for want of knowledge that plaintiff was injured at the time and place or in the manner and to the extent described in plaintiff's petition.

After a pretrial conference, the motion of plaintiff for an order setting this cause for trial on the issue of damages only was sustained, and the case was assigned for trial. A jury was empanelled, and the case submitted.

The court charged the jury that it was not to be "concerned with the issues of defendant's negligence, proximate cause or plaintiff's contributory negligence," because those issues were resolved favorably to the plaintiff and against the defendant in another action between the same parties in the Cleveland Municipal Court, and that the action in that court did not involve a claim for bodily injury, and under the law plaintiff had the right to bring her separate action for personal injuries in the Court of Common Pleas.

The court charged that, as a matter of law, if the plaintiff was involved in this accident on September 20, 1951, and suffered injuries as the proximate result thereof, the defendant would be legally responsible to the plaintiff for whatever injuries she sustained in that accident; that she was required to prove affirmatively, by the preponderance of the evidence, "that she was a passenger upon a motorcycle, operated by her husband on Schreiber Road, in the city of Maple Heights, Ohio, on or about September 20, 1951, and that such motorcycle was involved in an accident by striking a hole in said street, and she must further prove that she was injured in said accident and, if so, the extent of such injury; and that such injuries, if any, were the direct and proximate result of such accident."

The jury returned a verdict for the plaintiff in the amount of $12,000.

An appeal was perfected to the Court of Appeals, which affirmed the judgment.

The cause is in this court upon the allowance of a motion to certify the record.

HERBERT, JUDGE.

The eighth error assigned by the defendant is that "the trial and appellate courts committed error in permitting plaintiff to split her cause of action and to file a separate action in the Cleveland Municipal Court for her property damage and reduce same to judgment, and, thereafter, to proceed, in the Cuyahoga County Common Pleas Court, with a separate action for personal injuries, both claims arising out of a single accident."

Other facets of this question have been before the court before.

In the case of *Vasu v. Kohlers, Inc.,* 145 Ohio St. 321, 61 N.E.2d 707, 709, 166 A.L.R. 855, plaintiff operating an automobile came into collision with defendant's truck, in which collision he suffered personal injuries and also damage to his automobile. At the time of collision, plaintiff had coverage of a $50 deductible collision policy on his automobile. The insurance company paid the plaintiff a sum covering the damage to his automobile, whereupon, in accordance with a provision of the policy, the plaintiff assigned to the insurer his claim for such damage.

In February 1942, the insurance company commenced an action in the Common Pleas Court of Mahoning County against Kohlers, Inc., the defendant in the reported case to recoup the money paid by it to cover the damage to Vasu's automobile.

In August 1942, Vasu commenced an action in the same court against Kohlers, Inc., to recover for personal injuries which he suffered in the same collision.

In March 1943, in the insurance company's action, a verdict was rendered in favor of the defendant, followed by judgment.

Two months later an amended answer was filed in the *Vasu* case, setting out as a bar to the action for recovery of damages for the personal injuries suffered by plaintiff the judgment rendered in favor of defendant in the insurance company case. A motion to strike that defense having been sustained, a second amended answer was filed omitting allegations as to such judgment. A trial of the action resulted in a verdict for plaintiff, upon which judgment was entered.

On appeal to the Court of Appeals the defendant claimed that the Court of Common Pleas erred in sustaining plaintiff's motion to strike from the defendant's answer the defense of *res judicata* claimed to have arisen by reason of the judgment in favor of the defendant in the action by the insurance company.

The Court of Appeals reversed the judgment of the Court of Common Pleas and entered final judgment in favor of defendant.

This court reversed the judgment of the Court of Appeals, holding in the syllabus, in part, as follows:

* * *

4. Injuries to both person and property suffered by the same person as a result of the same wrongful act are infringements of different rights and give rise to distinct causes of action, with the result that the recovery or denial of recovery of compensation for damages to the property is no bar to an action subsequently prosecuted for the personal injury, unless by an adverse judgment in the first action issues are determined against the plaintiff which operate as an estoppel against him in the second action.

* * *

6. Where an injury to person and to property through a single wrongful act causes a prior contract of indemnity and subrogation as to the injury to property, to come into operation for the benefit of the person injured, the indemnitor may prosecute a separate action against the party causing such injury for reimbursement for indemnity monies paid under such contract.

7. Parties in privy, in the sense that they are bound by a judgment, are those who acquired an interest in the subject matter after the beginning of the action or the rendition of the judgment; and if their title or interest attached before that fact, they are not bound unless made parties.

8. A grantor or assignor is not bound, as to third persons, by any judgment which such third persons may obtain against his

grantee or assignee adjudicating the title to or claim for the interest transferred unless he participated in the action in such manner as to become, in effect, a party.

* * * The sixth, seventh and eighth paragraphs deal with the factual situation which existed in the *Vasu* case, *i.e.,* a prior contract of indemnity and subrogation. Although, as discussed *infra,* it was not actually necessary to the determination of the issue in that case, attention centers on the fourth paragraph.

* * *

[Subsequent] cases, distinguishing and explaining the *Vasu* case, have not changed the rule established in paragraph four of the syllabus of the latter case, holding that injuries to both person and property suffered by the same person as a result of the same wrongful act are infringements of different rights and give rise to distinct causes of action.

However, it is contended here that that rule is in conflict with the great weight of authority in this country and has caused vexatious litigation. * * *

Upon examination of decisions of courts of last resort, we find that the majority rule is followed in the following cases in each of which the action was between the person suffering injury and the person committing the tort, and where insurers were not involved, as in the case here. [Citations omitted.]

* * *

The minority rule would seem to stem from the English case of *Brunsden v. Humphrey* (1884), 14 Q.B. 141. The facts in that case are set forth in the opinion in the *Vasu* case, concluding with the statement:

> The Master of the Rolls, in his opinion, stated that the test is "whether the same sort of evidence would prove the plaintiff's case in the two actions," and that, in the action relating to the cab, "it would be necessary to give evidence of the damage done to the plaintiff's vehicle. In the present action it would be necessary to give evidence of the bodily injury occasioned to the plaintiff, and of the sufferings which he has undergone, and for this purpose to call medical witnesses. This one test shows that the causes of action as to the damage done to the plaintiff's cab, and as to the injury occasioned to the plaintiff's person, are distinct."

The fallacy of the reasoning in the English court is best portrayed in the dissenting opinion of Lord Coleridge, as follows:

> It appears to me that whether the negligence of the servant, or the impact of the vehicle which the servant drove, be the technical cause of action, equally the cause is one and the same: that the injury done to the plaintiff is injury done to him at one and the same moment by one and the same act in respect of different *rights,* i.e. his person and his goods, I do not in the least deny; but it seems to

me a subtlety not warranted by law to hold that a man cannot bring two actions, if he is injured in his arm and in his leg, but can bring two, if besides his arm and leg being injured, his trousers which contain his leg, and his coatsleeve which contains his arm, have been torn.

There appears to be no valid reason in these days of code pleading to adhere to the old English rule as to distinctions between injuries to the person and damages to the person's property resulting from a single tort. It would seem that the minority rule is bottomed on the proposition that the right of bodily security is fundamentally different from the right of security of property and, also, that, in actions predicated upon a negligent act, damages are a necessary element of each independent cause of action and no recovery may be had unless and until actual consequential damages are shown.

Whether or not injuries to both person and property resulting from the same wrongful act are to be treated as injuries to separate rights or as separate items of damage, a plaintiff may maintain only one action to enforce his rights existing at the time such action is commenced.

The decision of the question actually in issue in the *Vasu* case is found in paragraphs six, seven and eight of the syllabus, as it is quite apparent from the facts there that the first judgment, claimed to be *res judicata* in Vasu's action against the defendant, was rendered against Vasu's insurer in an action initiated by it after having paid Vasu for the damages to his automobile.

Upon further examination of the cases from other jurisdictions, it appears that in those instances where the courts have held to the majority rule, a separation of causes of action is almost universally recognized where an insurer has acquired by an assignment or by subrogation the right to recover for money it has advanced to pay for property damage.

In some instances those jurisdictions recognize the right of the insurer to become a party to the action and recover in the single action that part of the damages to which it has become subrogated.

In other states, and particularly in those having statutes requiring actions to be brought by the real party in interest, the courts have recognized the right of the insurer to bring a separate action to recover in its own name for that part of a single cause of action to which it has become entitled by payment of damages.

* * *

The reason why the exception is recognized that, where the plaintiff has recovered from an insurance company a part of his damage, he is not estopped from prosecuting his own action, is well stated in the North Carolina case of *Underwood v. Dooley, supra* [197 N.C. 100, 147 S.E. 690], as follows:

It cannot be held as law in this state that the owner of an automobile, who, as the result of the wrong or tort of another, has sustained damages both to his automobile and to his person, and whose automobile is insured against the loss or damage which he has sustained because of injuries to his automobile, is put to an election whether or not he shall, in order to maintain an action against the wrongdoer to recover damages for injuries to [his] person, release the insurance company from all liability to him under its policy. He does not lose his right of action to recover for the injuries to his person, by accepting from the insurance company the amount for which it is liable to him * * *.

Coming again to the defendant's eighth assignment of error, it is noted that the rule attributed to the Ohio courts is based primarily on the *Vasu* case, as it is stated in 1 Ohio Jurisprudence (2d), 360, although prior lower court decisions reaching a different conclusion are cited and recognized therein with the statement that "these cases are impliedly overruled."

Apparently, much of the vexatious litigation, with its attendant confusion, which has resulted in recent years from the filing of separate petitions by the same plaintiff, one for personal injuries and one for property damage although sustained simultaneously, has grown from that one decision, this case presenting a good example.

In the light of the foregoing, it is the view of this court that the so-called majority rule conforms much more properly to modern practice, and that the rule declared in the fourth paragraph of the syllabus in the *Vasu* case, on a point not actually at issue therein, should not be followed.

We, therefore, conclude and hold that, where a person suffers both personal injuries and property damage as a result of the same wrongful act, only a single cause of action arises, the different injuries occasioned thereby being separate items of damage from such act. It follows that paragraph four of the syllabus in the *Vasu* case must be overruled.

Judgment reversed and final judgment for defendant.

WEYGANDT, C.J., and STEWART, TAFT, MATTHIAS and BELL, JJ., concur.

ZIMMERMAN, J., dissents.

STEWART, JUDGE (concurring).

In [*Vasu*] Judge Hart stated in part:

The rule at common law and in a majority of the states of the union is that damages resulting from a single wrongful act, even though they include both property and personal injury damages, are, when suffered by the same person, the subject of only one action against the wrongdoer.

However, he referred to the fact that there were a number of state jurisdictions which followed the English rule, and known as the two-causes-of-action rule, and then proceeded to announce that rule as the

Ohio rule, and it was written into the fourth paragraph of the syllabus of the *Vasu* case. If it had been necessary to decide the question whether a single tort gives rise to two causes of action as to the one injured by such tort, I would be reluctant to disturb that holding. However, neither the discussion in the *Vasu* case as to whether a single or double cause of action arises from one tort nor the language of the fourth paragraph of the syllabus was necessary to decide the issue presented in the case, and obviously both such language and such paragraph are *obiter dicta* and, therefore, are not as persuasive an authority as if they had been appropriate to the question presented.

As to the [English] case, which is the basis for the minority rule in this country, it seems to me that the dissenting opinion of Lord Coleridge, as quoted in the majority opinion in the present case, is not only highly persuasive but logically unanswerable, and that this court is justified in departing from the *obiter dicta* of the *Vasu* case.

ZIMMERMAN, JUDGE (dissenting).

I am not unalterably opposed to upsetting prior decisions of this court where changing conditions and the lessons of experience clearly indicate the desirability of such course, but, where those considerations do not obtain, established law should remain undisturbed in order to insure a stability on which the lower courts and the legal profession generally may rely with some degree of confidence.

There is abundant and respectable authority for [the majority and minority rule]. Ohio has deliberately adopted one of them, and I can find no impelling reason for changing the rule at the present time.

Notes and Questions

1. Brief the *Rush* case. Briefing should assist you in understanding the opinion.

2. *Rush* illustrates the two functions of a judicial decision. We will first examine the doctrine of *stare decisis* and then briefly examine *res judicata*.

The parties in *Rush* were not involved in the *Vasu* litigation. Yet their destiny was inextricably tied to the application of its principles of law. The lower courts felt constrained under the doctrine of *stare decisis* to follow that precedent in later controversies involving the same legal question between different parties. In lawyers' terminology, *Vasu* is referred to as controlling authority. The more difficult task is to identify with precision the controlling statement or rule in *Vasu* to which lower courts must adhere. Both the municipal court and the court of appeals believed the language in the *Vasu* opinion permitting a plaintiff to split a cause of action arising from a single tort and sue separately for personal injuries and property damages was controlling. Note that once it had determined the controlling force of the precedent, a lower court would not be free to examine anew the merits or desirability of the rule of law. But questions remain: Why was the rule in paragraph 4 of the syllabus controlling? Was it necessary to the decision in *Vasu?* Recall that *Vasu* involved separate suits by distinct parties, one by Vasu's insurer for property damage and the other by Vasu in his own right for personal injuries. If you agree with the supreme court in *Rush* that the language regarding splitting the cause of action was *dictum*, why did the lower courts blindly adhere to the ruling?

The supreme court, on the other hand, did not feel constrained under the doctrine of *stare decisis* to follow the *Vasu* ruling. It embraced an exception to the doctrine allowing a court to refuse to follow its own precedents and declare them no longer the law. Under what circumstances may (or should) a court overrule precedent?

Rush supplies certain clues. First, the court examined subsequent cases to determine whether the precedent had been undermined or eroded. After searching the Ohio law for grounds justifying departure from the precedent and finding none, the court then analyzed the law of other jurisdictions. Having made this survey, the court found that the *Vasu* rule caused vexatious litigation and conflicted with the weight of authority in other jurisdictions. The court therefore specifically held "that the rule declared in the fourth paragraph of the syllabus in the *Vasu* case *on a point not actually at issue therein * * ** must be overruled." (Emphasis supplied.) Absent judicial decisions questioning the soundness of a precedent, are there other permissible sources a court may examine when deciding to overrule a precedent?

If the language of *Vasu* that permitted splitting the cause of action is *dicta,* as the court implied, why was it necessary to overrule it? Does the opinion or the concurring opinion cast doubt on the right of a court to overrule prior holdings, as contrasted to *dicta?* If not on the right, then on the exercise of discretion whether to overrule?

Courts usually reserve the overruling process for repudiating the narrow holdings of cases when they have no other principled ways to discard them. Whether the court overrules a rule contained in a case or uses another method to limit its application in future cases may be important to lower courts. If the precedent is overruled, it has no continuing vitality whatsoever; if merely distinguished, it may have some continuing force.

3. Judge Stewart wrote a separate concurring opinion. He would have been reluctant to disturb the *Vasu* rule had it been necessary to the result in the case. Having found, however, that the statement was *obiter dictum,* he believed the court was justified in overruling it. Why the greater reluctance if the rule had been necessary to the decision? What other factors are relevant to the decision whether to overrule a particular precedent? What factors in addition to the "logically unanswerable" dissenting opinion of Lord Coleridge? And what happened to the justifiable expectations of the parties and their lawyers? Assume that Mrs. Rush's lawyers deliberately split the actions in reliance upon the rule of law announced in *Vasu.* Was the result in *Rush,* giving retroactive effect to the overruling of *Vasu* and dismissing the plaintiff's claim for personal injuries, fair? What alternatives does the court have if it determines that a precedent is unsound, but believes that parties may have acted in reliance upon it?

4. Judge Zimmerman, in dissent, appeared concerned with the stability of our system of law and believed that the legal profession should be able to rely with some degree of certainty upon the status of the law. He believed the *Vasu* rule was a firmly established precedent, not to be discarded

without an "impelling reason." What factors are relevant to whether there exists an impelling reason? What about fairness to the litigants?

5.   When a court has decided a controversy, the judgment has *stare decisis* consequences affecting the parties and others who were not parties to the litigation. But the judgment has particular binding force on the parties. This force is embraced under the doctrine of *res judicata*. Simply stated, *res judicata* underscores the notion that an action between the litigants must eventually come to an end—whether rightly or wrongly decided. *Res judicata* binds the parties in two different ways: It prevents (a) litigation of claims that should have been brought in the former proceeding (claims preclusion) and (b) relitigation, usually in separate and distinct lawsuits, of matters that were actually determined in the first litigation (issue preclusion).

Rush exemplifies how each party relied upon a different facet of the doctrine of *res judicata*. The plaintiff, relying on issue preclusion, contended that the city's liability already had been determined in the first suit. *Vasu* held that injuries to person and property suffered by the same person in the same accident gave rise to distinct causes of action and that separate suits stemming from one accident might be brought. The plaintiff in *Rush* contended that the city should be estopped from disclaiming liability in the second suit because liability had been established in the first suit. The lower courts in *Rush* approved the use of issue preclusion and foreclosed inquiry into the question of the city's liability. The city, on the other hand, relying on the doctrine of claims preclusion, contended that separate actions for property damage and personal injuries arising from the same accident were impermissible. The supreme court, in overruling *Vasu*, embraced the doctrine of claims preclusion and dismissed the plaintiff's lawsuit.

6.   You should now carefully note the distinction between "reversing" a judgment and "overruling" a precedent. In *Rush,* the lower court judgment in favor of the plaintiff was reversed—that is, judgment was entered for the defendant, dismissing the plaintiff's claim. The principle of law stated in *Vasu* was overruled. The overruling process did not affect the judgment or claims involved in the earlier case; only the propositions of law were affected. Thus, the status of the parties in *Vasu* was not altered by *Rush;* in other words, *Vasu* still had *res judicata* consequences (claims and issue preclusion) to its parties.

F.   OVERVIEW OF THE JUDICIAL SYSTEMS

A general understanding of the organization of the court systems in this country is important to the beginning law student. Too many entering students remain unaware that two basic court systems operate simultaneously in the United States, and this initial misunderstanding breeds confusion when important legal concepts such as jurisdiction and venue are discussed. Even the materials on *stare decisis* in the previous section cannot be fully appreciated without knowledge of our dual system because precedent is binding in the legal system that announced the rule.[gg]

gg.   In various situations precedent may be binding in other systems. For example,

The following section is intended only as an overview of the systems. Other courses in your law school and other sections of this book will delve more deeply into the intricacies of this subject. The following materials, however, should assist in dispelling some initial confusion and should aid in understanding the legal method materials in the remainder of this book.

1. THE STATE COURT SYSTEMS

Each of the fifty states has a court system. Although the structure differs from state to state, a few general observations may be made.

Court systems are created to adjudicate controversies. Whether a case is fit for judicial resolution depends primarily upon the laws of the state, which are embodied in its constitution, statutes, rules, and common law. Some controversies are immediately cognizable in the judicial system. Others must be deferred until termination of proceedings brought before other dispute-resolution bodies, such as administrative agencies or arbitration panels. Still others, by their nature, are not fit for judicial resolution. In most cases lawyers have little difficulty fitting disputes into one of the former categories. For example, automobile collision cases are immediately cognizable in court; cases involving granting, suspension, or revocation of licenses are usually committed to administrative agencies before judicial proceedings may be instituted; and many squabbles fall outside the ambit of the court system. The latter category includes matters that do not present legally sufficient claims. Can you think of any examples that fall into this category?

All court systems are hierarchical—that is, lower trial court decisions may be reviewed by a higher court. There may even be more than one appellate court level within the system.

Each state has created "petty" tribunals to handle civil matters involving small amounts of money or property of minimal value. Each state has also established courts of general jurisdiction, which are empowered to try cases without regard to subject matter or monetary limitations. Even courts of general jurisdiction, however, may be somewhat restricted in the kinds of cases they can hear. Federal law has on occasion limited state court subject matter jurisdiction and has placed selected subjects solely within the competence of the federal system. State law may also carve out subjects from the jurisdiction of state courts of general jurisdiction. Yet the nomenclature, courts of general jurisdiction, is still used, although "general" may be somewhat more restricted than the term implies.

A state may invest a particular court system with exclusive jurisdiction over specific classes of cases. If a plaintiff wishes to institute a case

United States Supreme Court decisions regarding federal law are binding on all courts within the United States, federal and state. Similarly, state court appellate decisions on state substantive law are binding on federal courts sitting in diversity cases— that is, cases in which federal jurisdiction is founded on the diverse state citizenship of the parties. *See infra* p. 57.

falling within one of these exclusive categories in a state court, she must commence the action in the court designated by state law as having exclusive jurisdiction. Other times, a plaintiff has a choice between two or more court systems. Such overlapping jurisdiction is termed "concurrent."

In addition to petty courts and courts of general jurisdiction, some states have established specialized courts to hear limited or technical subjects. Areas of the law traditionally accorded such treatment include probate and juvenile proceedings.

Extreme caution must be taken in analyzing state laws relating to jurisdiction, for if a plaintiff proceeds in the wrong court system, the case may be dismissed or the judgment set aside. This is true even if the jurisdictional defect is not raised until the time of the appeal or perhaps years later in a collateral proceeding. A judgment rendered by a court not having jurisdiction over the subject matter is, according to traditional doctrine, void. Courses in civil procedure recount in lurid detail the plight of litigants who made the egregious error of proceeding in the wrong court.

Every state has a court of last resort, the tribunal at the top of the tier of the state court system. Most states also have intermediate appellate courts which, as the student might expect, are placed between the trial court and the court of last resort. Appellate courts generally review the "record" of the trial court proceedings to determine whether any error materially affected the judgment. If so, and the point was properly raised, the case will be reversed and remanded for retrial, if necessary. If no material error is found, the case will be affirmed. The function of the appellate court is not to retry the case, to hear witnesses, or to substitute its findings of fact for those of the lower court. Its review is limited to determining whether any legal error, procedural or substantive, occurred and whether that error substantially and adversely affected an aggrieved party.

State law determines the procedural steps for reviewing state trial court judgments. It designates the court to which the appeal should be taken, the time within which the appellant must appeal, the method of perfecting an appeal, and the steps to be taken after perfection. State law also dictates whether the appeal is "as of right"—that is, automatic—or whether the appellate court has discretion not to accept the appeal. A litigant usually has at least one appeal as of right to the intermediate appellate court, as long as he follows the procedural requirements designated by statute or rules of court. Appeal to the highest court is often discretionary.

The highest state court settles the law of the state. If a case presents a federal question (an issue regarding the construction, interpretation and application of federal law), the case may in certain circumstances be reviewed by the United States Supreme Court.

2. THE FEDERAL COURT SYSTEM[hh]

Article III of the United States Constitution provides for the establishment of a federal court system. It declares that the judicial power shall be vested in the Supreme Court and in "such inferior courts as the Congress may ordain and establish." Congress wasted no time in creating the lower federal court system. In the Act of September 24, 1789, known as the Great Judiciary Act, Congress established federal trial courts. The resolve of the first Congress to establish inferior federal trial courts has never wavered.

In general, the system contains a three-tier hierarchy: (1) District Courts. There are currently ninety-four federal judicial districts, including at least one in each state, the District of Columbia, and Puerto Rico. This number includes the district courts in the territories of Guam, the Virgin Islands, and the Northern Mariana Islands. (2) Courts of Appeals. There are thirteen courts of appeals: one for the District of Columbia, the Court of Appeals for the Federal Circuit, and eleven for the numbered circuits. The number of judges varies from circuit to circuit. (3) The Supreme Court. This court of last resort consists of nine justices. There are also a few specialized courts.

The subject matter jurisdiction of the federal court system is restricted by Article III of the Constitution and congressional statutes enacted pursuant to the Constitution:

> The judicial Power shall extend to all Cases, in Law and Equity, arising under this Constitution, the Laws of the United States, and Treaties made, or which shall be made, under their Authority; * * * to controversies * * * between Citizens of different States; * * * U.S. CONST. art. III, § 2.

The jurisdiction of the federal courts rests upon the nature of the dispute (for example, federal courts have jurisdiction over cases arising under the Constitution, laws, and treaties of the United States), or on the character of the parties (for example, federal courts have jurisdiction over controversies between citizens of different states). Moreover, the judicial power extends only to "cases" and "controversies," words that have for two centuries limited the matters fit for judicial resolution.[ii]

Article III of the Constitution designates the cases in which the Supreme Court has original jurisdiction—that is, jurisdiction to hear the case in the first instance and to finally decide it. In all other cases, the Supreme Court has appellate jurisdiction—that is, jurisdiction to hear appeals from other courts, subject to such exceptions and regulations as Congress makes.

Congress has broad power to govern or to restrict the types of cases that may be brought originally into the federal court system. In fact except for a brief one-year period, Congress did not extend lower federal

hh. A more detailed discussion of this subject matter appears in Chapter VI, Section B, *infra*. The present section is intended to provide the beginning law student with an overview of the system.

ii. See *infra* Chapter VI, Section D.

court jurisdiction to cases arising under the Constitution, laws or treaties of United States until 1875. It presumably left these questions to be decided in the state court systems, subject in certain instances to appellate review by the United States Supreme Court.

Even when Congress has conferred original jurisdiction over a category of cases, it has often limited the jurisdiction to cases involving a minimum dollar amount. Thus, cases founded on diversity of citizenship may presently be brought in a federal district court only if the amount in controversy exceeds $75,000, exclusive of interest and costs.

Congress may designate federal court jurisdiction exclusive of or concurrent with state-court jurisdiction. If a federal statute is silent on this issue, a strong presumption favors concurrent jurisdiction.

If federal and state courts have concurrent jurisdiction over a controversy, the plaintiff has the option of selecting the forum in which to institute the lawsuit. If the plaintiff selects the state court system, the defendant may have the right to "remove" the action to the federal system. If the defendant does not remove the action, it remains in the state court system. If the case presents a federal question during the proceedings, it may be reviewed by the United States Supreme Court under conditions imposed by Congress.

It is not enough that a court have jurisdiction over the subject matter of a dispute. The action must also be brought in a court within the system having proper venue and jurisdiction over the defendant.[jj]

Venue refers to the place of trial. The rules and statutes that prescribe the particular court within the system where the action is to be brought regulate the venue. Generally speaking, considerations of convenience to the litigants govern venue criteria. To illustrate this concept, assume a California citizen has a legal dispute involving more than $75,000 with a citizen of New York. The federal district courts have subject matter jurisdiction of the controversy. The case involves a dispute between citizens of different states in excess of the minimum jurisdictional amount. In which particular district court may the plaintiff commence the lawsuit? The answer is dictated in part by a venue statute. In diversity cases, suit may usually be maintained in any district where a defendant resides or in the district in which the claim arose. As you can see, considerations of venue do restrict the plaintiff's choice of forum. Later we will examine another concept, *personal* jurisdiction, which also restricts forum selection. *See infra* Chapter III.

The foregoing discussion of the American court system is intended only as an overview to acquaint the beginning law student with the structure and jurisdiction of state and federal courts. It is hoped that this discussion may forestall some initial confusion. For a more in-depth discussion of this subject, see *infra* Chapter VI.

---

jj. These limitations also govern the allocation of cases within state court systems.

G. JURISTS' VIEWS OF THE JUDICIAL PROCESS AND FUNCTION

AN INTRODUCTION TO LEGAL REASONING[kk]
Dean Edward Levi

The basic pattern of legal reasoning is reasoning by example. It is reasoning from case to case. It is a three-step process described by the doctrine of precedent in which a proposition descriptive of the first case is made into a rule of law and then applied to a next similar situation. The steps are these: similarity is seen between cases; next the rule of law inherent in the first case is announced; then the rule of law is made applicable to the second case. This is a method of reasoning necessary for the law, but it has characteristics which under other circumstances might be considered imperfections.

These characteristics become evident if the legal process is approached as though it were a method of applying general rules of law to diverse facts—in short, as though the doctrine of precedent meant that general rules, once properly determined, remained unchanged, and then were applied, albeit imperfectly, in later cases. If this were the doctrine, it would be disturbing to find that the rules change from case to case and are remade with each case. Yet this change in the rules is the indispensable dynamic quality of law. It occurs because the scope of a rule of law, and therefore its meaning, depends upon a determination of what facts will be considered similar to those present when the rule was first announced. The finding of similarity or difference is the key step in the legal process.

The determination of similarity or difference is the function of each judge. Where case law is considered, and there is no statute, he is not bound by the statement of the rule of law made by the prior judge even in the controlling case. The statement is mere dictum, and this means that the judge in the present case may find irrelevant the existence or absence of facts which prior judges thought important. It is not what the prior judge intended that is of any importance; rather it is what the present judge, attempting to see the law as a fairly consistent whole, thinks should be the determining classification.

THE BRAMBLE BUSH[ll]
Karl N. Llewellyn

We turn first to what I may call the orthodox doctrine of precedent, with which, in its essence, you are already familiar. Every case lays down a rule, the rule of the case. The express ratio decidendi is prima facie the rule of the case, since it is the ground upon which the court chose to rest its decision. But a later court can reexamine the case and can invoke the canon that no judge has power to decide what is not before him, can, through examination of the facts or of the procedural issue, narrow the picture of what was actually before the court and can hold that the

kk. University of Chicago Press 1–2 (1948).

　ll. Oceana Publications 66–69 (1951).

ruling made requires to be understood as thus restricted. In the extreme form this results in what is known as expressly "confining the case to its particular facts." This rule holds only of redheaded Walpoles in pale magenta Buick cars. * * *

Now this orthodox view of the authority of precedent—which I shall call the *strict* view—is but one of two views which seem to me wholly contradictory to each other. It is in practice the dogma which is applied to *unwelcome* precedents. It is the recognized, legitimate, honorable technique for whittling precedents away, for making the lawyer, in his argument, and the court in its decision, free of them. It is a surgeon's knife.

It is orthodox, I think, because it has been more discussed than is the other. * * * The technique of arguing for a distinction has become systematized. And when men start talking of authority, or of the doctrine of precedent, they turn naturally to that part of their minds which has been *consciously* devoted to the problem; they call up the cases, the analyses, the arguments, which have been made under such conditions. * * * The strict doctrine, then, is the technique to be learned. *But not to be mistaken for the whole.*

For when you turn to the actual operations of the courts, or, indeed, to the arguments of lawyers, you will find a totally different view of precedent at work beside this first one. That I shall call, to give it a name, the *loose view* of precedent. That is the view that a court has decided, and decided authoritatively, *any* point or all points on which it chose, after due argument, to pass. No matter how broad the statement, no matter how unnecessary on the facts or the procedural issues, if that was the rule the court laid down, then that the court has held. Indeed, this view carries over often into dicta, and even into dicta which are grandly obiter. In its extreme form this results in thinking and arguing exclusively from *language* that is found in past opinions, and in citing and working with that language wholly without reference to the facts of the case which called the language forth.

Now it is obvious that this is a device not for cutting past opinions away from judges' feet, but for using them as a springboard when they are found convenient. This is a device for *capitalizing welcome precedents*. And both lawyers and the judges use it so. And judged by the practice of the most respected courts, as of the courts of ordinary stature, this doctrine of precedent is like the other, recognized, legitimate, honorable.

What I wish to sink deep into your minds about the doctrine of precedent, therefore, is that it is two-headed. It is Janus-faced. That it is not one doctrine, nor one line of doctrine, but two, and two which, *applied at the same time to the same precedent, are contradictory of each other*. That there is one doctrine for getting rid of precedents deemed troublesome and one doctrine for making use of precedents that seem helpful. That these two doctrines exist side by side. * * * Until you realize this you do not see how it is possible for law to change and to develop, and yet to stand on the past. You do not see how it is possible to avoid the past mistakes of courts, and yet to make use of every happy insight for which a judge in writing may have found expression. Indeed it seems to me that here we may have part of the answer to the problem as to whether precedent is not as bad as good—supporting a weak judge by the labors of strong predecessors, but binding a strong judge by the errors of the weak. For look again at this matter of the *difficulty* of the doctrine. The strict view—that view that cuts the past away—is *hard* to use. An ignorant, an unskilful judge will find it hard to use; the past will bind him. But the skilful judge—he whom we would make free—*is* thus made free. He has the knife in hand; and he can free himself.

* * *

People—and they are curiously many—who think that precedent produces or ever did produce a certainty that did not involve matters of judgment and of persuasion, or who think that what I have described involves improper equivocation by the courts or departure from the court-ways of some golden age—such people simply do not know our system of precedent in which they live.

THE NATURE OF THE JUDICIAL PROCESS[mm]

Benjamin N. Cardozo

* * * We are reminded by William James in a telling page of his lectures on Pragmatism that every one of us has in truth an underlying philosophy of life, even those of us to whom the names and the notions of philosophy are unknown or anathema. There is in each of us a stream of tendency, whether you choose to call it philosophy or not, which gives coherence and direction to thought and action. Judges cannot escape that current any more than other mortals. All their lives, forces which they do not recognize and cannot name, have been tugging at them— inherited instincts, traditional beliefs, acquired convictions; and the resultant is an outlook on life, a conception of social needs, a sense in James's phrase of "the total push and pressure of the cosmos," which, when reasons are nicely balanced, must determine where choice shall fall. In this mental background every problem finds its setting. We may try to see things as objectively as we please. None the less, we can never see them with any eyes except our own.

* * *

The first thing he [the judge] does is to compare the case before him with the precedents, whether stored in his mind or hidden in the books. I do not mean that precedents are ultimate sources of the law, supplying the sole equipment that is needed for the legal armory, the sole tools, to borrow Maitland's phrase, "in the legal smithy." Back of precedents are the basic juridical conceptions which are the postulates of judicial

mm. Pp. 12–13, 19–21, 29–32, 40–42, 51–52, 54–56, 58, 62–66, 71–73, 75, 98–99, 112–17, 124–26, 129, 167–69 (1921), copyright Yale University Press (1921).

reasoning, and farther back are the habits of life, the institutions of society, in which those conceptions had their origin, and which, by a process of interaction, they have modified in turn. None the less, in a system so highly developed as our own, precedents have so covered the ground that they fix the point of departure from which the labor of the judge begins. Almost invariably, his first step is to examine and compare them. If they are plain and to the point, there may be need of nothing more. *Stare decisis* is at least the everyday working rule of our law. * * * Some judges seldom get beyond that process in any case. Their notion of their duty is to match the colors of the case at hand against the colors of many sample cases spread out upon their desk. The sample nearest in shade supplies the applicable rule. But, of course, no system of living law can be evolved by such a process, and no judge of a high court, worthy of his office, views the function of his place so narrowly. If that were all there was to our calling, there would be little of intellectual interest about it. The man who had the best card index of the cases would also be the wisest judge. It is when the colors do not match, when the references in the index fail, when there is no decisive precedent, that the serious business of the judge begins.

* * *

There is the constant need, as every law student knows, to separate the accidental and the non-essential from the essential and inherent. Let us assume, however, that this task has been achieved, and that the precedent is known as it really is. Let us assume too that the principle, latent within it, has been skillfully extracted and accurately stated. Only half or less than half of the work has yet been done. The problem remains to fix the bounds and the tendencies of development and growth, to set the directive force in motion along the right path at the parting of the ways.

The directive force of a principle may be exerted along the line of logical progression; this I will call the rule of analogy or the method of philosophy; along the line of historical development; this I will call the method of evolution; along the line of the customs of the community; this I will call the method of tradition; along the lines of justice, morals and social welfare, the *mores* of the day; and this I will call the method of sociology.

I have put first among the principles of selection to guide our choice of paths, the rule of analogy or the method of philosophy. In putting it first, I do not mean to rate it as most important. On the contrary, it is often sacrificed to others. I have put it first because it has, I think, a certain presumption in its favor. Given a mass of particulars, a congeries of judgments on related topics, the principle that unifies and rationalizes them has a tendency, and a legitimate one, to project and extend itself to new cases within the limits of its capacity to unify and rationalize. It has the primacy that comes from natural and orderly and logical succession. Homage is due to it over every competing principle that is unable by appeal to history or tradition or policy or justice to make out a better right. All sorts of deflecting forces may appear to contest its sway and absorb its power. At least, it is the heir presumptive. A pretender to the title will have to fight his way.

* * *

The directive force of logic does not always exert itself, however, along a single and unobstructed path. One principle or precedent, pushed to the limit of its logic, may point to one conclusion; another principle or precedent, followed with like logic, may point with equal certainty to another. In this conflict, we must choose between the two paths, selecting one or other, or perhaps striking out upon a third, which will be the resultant of the two forces in combination, or will represent the mean between extremes. Let me take as an illustration of such conflict the famous case of *Riggs v. Palmer,* 115 N.Y. 506, 22 N.E. 188.[nn] That case decided that a legatee who had murdered his testator would not be permitted by a court of equity to enjoy the benefits of the will. Conflicting principles were there in competition for the mastery. One of them prevailed, and vanquished all the others. There was the principle of the binding force of a will disposing of the estate of a testator in conformity with law. That principle, pushed to the limit of its logic, seemed to uphold the title of the murderer. There was the principle that civil courts may not add to the pains and penalties of crimes. That, pushed to the limit of its logic, seemed again to uphold his title. But over against these was another principle, of greater generality, its roots deeply fastened in universal sentiments of justice, the principle that no man should profit from his own inequity or take advantage of his own wrong. The logic of this principle prevailed over the logic of the others. I say its logic prevailed. The thing which really interests us, however, is why and how the choice was made between one logic and another. In this instance, the reason is not obscure. One path was followed, another closed, because of the conviction in the judicial mind that the one selected led to justice. Analogies and precedents and the principles behind them were brought together as rivals for precedence; in the end, the principle that was thought to be most fundamental, to represent the larger and deeper social interests, put its competitors to flight.

* * *

The method of philosophy comes in competition, however, with other tendencies which find their outlet in other methods. One of these is the historical method, or the method of evolution. The tendency of a principle to expand itself to the limit of its logic may be counteracted by the tendency to confine itself within the limits of its history. I do not mean that even then the two methods are always in opposition. A classification which treats them as distinct is, doubtless, subject to the reproach that it involves a certain overlapping of the lines and principles of division. Very often, the effect of history is to make the path of logic clear. Growth may be logical whether it is shaped by the principle of

---

nn.   Reprinted *infra* at pp. 414–19.

consistency with the past or by that of consistency with some pre-established norm, some general conception, some "indwelling, and creative principle." The directive force of the precedent may be found either in the events that made it what it is, or in some principle which enables us to say of it that it is what it ought to be. Development may involve either an investigation of origins or an effort of pure reason. Both methods have their logic. For the moment, however, it will be convenient to identify the method of history with the one, and to confine the method of logic or philosophy to the other. Some conceptions of the law owe their existing form almost exclusively to history. They are not to be understood except as historical growths. In the development of such principles, history is likely to predominate over logic or pure reason. * * *

Let me speak first of those fields where there can be no progress without history. I think the law of real property supplies the readiest example. No lawgiver meditating a code of laws conceived the system of feudal tenures. History built up the system and the law that went with it. Never by a process of logical deduction from the idea of abstract ownership could we distinguish the incidents of an estate in fee simple from those of an estate for life, or those of an estate for life from those of an estate for years. Upon these points, "a page of history is worth a volume of logic." So it is wherever we turn in the forest of the law of the land. Restraints upon alienation, the suspension of absolute ownership, contingent remainders, executory devises, private trusts and trusts for charities, all these heads of the law are intelligible only in the light of history, and get from history the impetus which must shape their subsequent development. I do not mean that even in this field, the method of philosophy plays no part at all. Some of the conceptions of the land law, once fixed, are pushed to their logical conclusions with inexorable severity. The point is rather that the conceptions themselves have come to us from without and not from within, that they embody the thought, not so much of the present as of the past, that separated from the past their form and meaning are unintelligible and arbitrary, and hence that their development, in order to be truly logical, must be mindful of their origins. In a measure that is true of most of the conceptions of our law. * * * Often the two methods supplement each other. Which method will predominate in any case may depend at times upon intuitions of convenience or fitness too subtle to be formulated, too imponderable to be valued, too volatile to be localized or even fully apprehended. Sometimes the prevailing tendencies exhibited in the current writings of philosophical jurists may sway the balance. There are vogues and fashions in jurisprudence as in literature and art and dress. * * *

If history and philosophy do not serve to fix the direction of a principle, custom may step in.

* * *

It is, however, not so much in the making of new rules as in the application of old ones that the creative energy of custom most often manifests itself today. General standards of right and duty are established. Custom must determine whether there has been adherence or departure. My partner has the powers that are usual in the trade. They may be so well known that the courts will notice them judicially. Such for illustration is the power of a member of a trading firm to make or indorse negotiable paper in the course of the firm's business. They may be such that the court will require evidence of their existence. The master in the discharge of his duty to protect the servant against harm must exercise the degree of care that is commonly exercised in like circumstance by men of ordinary prudence. The triers of the facts in determining whether that standard has been attained must consult the habits of life, the everyday beliefs and practices, of the men and women about them. Innumerable, also, are the cases where the course of dealing to be followed is defined by the customs, or, more properly speaking, the usages of a particular trade or market or profession. The constant assumption runs throughout the law that the natural and spontaneous evolutions of habit fix the limits of right and wrong. A slight extension of custom identifies it with customary morality, the prevailing standard of right conduct, the *mores* of the time. * * *

Three of the directive forces of our law, philosophy, history and custom, have now been seen at work. * * * How are we to choose between them? Putting that question aside, how do we choose between them? Some concepts of the law have been in a peculiar sense historical growths. In such departments, history will tend to give direction to development. In other departments, certain large and fundamental concepts, which comparative jurisprudence shows to be common to other highly developed systems, loom up above all others. In these we shall give a larger scope to logic and symmetry. A broad field there also is in which rules may, with approximately the same convenience, be settled one way or the other. Here custom tends to assert itself as the controlling force in guiding the choice of paths. Finally, when the social needs demand one settlement rather than another, there are times when we must bend symmetry, ignore history and sacrifice custom in the pursuit of other and larger ends.

From history and philosophy and custom, we pass, therefore, to the force which in our day and generation is becoming the greatest of them all, the power of social justice which finds its outlet and expression in the method of sociology.

The final cause of law is the welfare of society. The rule that misses its aim cannot permanently justify its existence. "Ethical considerations can no more be excluded from the administration of justice which is the end and purpose of all civil laws than one can exclude the vital air from his room and live." Logic and history and custom have their place. We will shape the law to conform to them when we may; but only within bounds. The end which the law serves will dominate them all.

* * *

Social welfare is a broad term. I use it to cover many concepts more or less allied. It may mean what is commonly spoken of as public policy, the good of the collective body. In such cases, its demands are often those of mere expediency or prudence. It may mean on the other hand the social gain that is wrought by adherence to the standards of right conduct, which find expression in the *mores* of the community. In such cases, its demands are those of religion or of ethics or of the social sense of justice, whether formulated in creed or system, or imminent in the common mind. One does not readily find a single term to cover these and kindred aims which shade off into one another by imperceptible gradations. * * *

It is true, I think, today in every department of the law that the social value of a rule has become a test of growing power and importance. This truth is powerfully driven home to the lawyers of this country in the writings of Dean Pound. "Perhaps the most significant advance in the modern science of law is the change from the analytical to the functional attitude." "The emphasis has changed from the content of the precept and the existence of the remedy to the effect of the precept in action and the availability and efficiency of the remedy to attain the ends for which the precept was devised." * * *

All departments of the law have been touched and elevated by this spirit. In some, however, the method of sociology works in harmony with the method of philosophy or of evolution or of tradition. Those, therefore, are the fields where logic and coherence and consistency must still be sought as ends. In others, it seems to displace the methods that compete with it. Those are the fields where the virtues of consistency must yield within those interstitial limits where judicial power moves. In a sense it is true that we are applying the method of sociology when we pursue logic and coherence and consistency as the greater social values. I am concerned for the moment with the fields in which the method is an antagonism to others rather than with those in which their action is in unison.

* * *

I have chosen these branches of the law merely as conspicuous illustrations of the application by the courts of the method of sociology. But the truth is that there is no branch where the method is not fruitful. Even when it does not seem to dominate, it is always in reserve. It is the arbiter between other methods, determining in the last analysis the choice of each, weighing their competing claims, setting bounds to their pretensions, balancing and moderating and harmonizing them all. Few rules in our time are so well established that they may not be called upon any day to justify their existence as means adapted to an end.

* * *

We get a striking illustration of the force of logical consistency, then of its gradual breaking down before the demands of practical convenience in isolated or exceptional instances, and finally of the generative force of the exceptions as a new stock, in the cases that deal with the right of a beneficiary to recover on a contract. England has been logically consistent and has refused the right of action altogether. New York and most states yielded to the demands of convenience and enforced the right of action, but at first only exceptionally and subject to many restrictions. Gradually the exceptions broadened till today they have left little of the rule.

* * *

My analysis of the judicial process comes then to this, and little more: Logic, and history, and custom, and utility, and the accepted standards of right conduct, are the forces which singly or in combination shape the progress of the law. Which of these forces shall dominate in any case must depend largely upon the comparative importance or value of the social interests that will be thereby promoted or impaired. One of the most fundamental social interests is that law shall be uniform and impartial. There must be nothing in its action that savors of prejudice or favor or even arbitrary whim or fitfulness. Therefore in the main there shall be adherence to precedent. There shall be symmetrical development, consistently with history or custom when history or custom has been the motive force, or the chief one, in giving shape to existing rules, and with logic or philosophy when the motive power has been theirs. But symmetrical development may be bought at too high a price. Uniformity ceases to be a good when it becomes uniformity of oppression. The social interest served by symmetry or certainty must then be balanced against the social interest served by equity and fairness or other elements of social welfare. These may enjoin upon the judge the duty of drawing the line at another angle, of staking the path along new courses, of marking a new point of departure from which others who come after him will set out upon their journey.

If you ask how he is to know when one interest outweighs another, I can only answer that he must get his knowledge just as the legislator gets it, from experience and study and reflection; in brief, from life itself. Here, indeed, is the point of contact between the legislator's work and his. The choice of methods, the appraisement of values, must in the end be guided by like considerations for the one as for the other. Each indeed is legislating within the limits of his competence. No doubt the limits for the judge are narrower. He legislates only between gaps. He fills the open spaces in the law. How far he may go without traveling beyond the walls of the interstices cannot be staked out for him upon a chart. He must learn it for himself as he gains the sense of fitness and proportion that comes with years of habitude in the practice of an art. Even within the gaps, restrictions not easy to define, but felt, however impalpable they may be, by every judge and lawyer, hedge and circumscribe his action. They are established by the traditions of the centuries, by the example of other judges, his predecessors and his colleagues, by the collective judgment of the profession, and by the duty of adherence to the pervading spirit of the law.

* * *

There is in truth nothing revolutionary or even novel in this view of the judicial function. It is the way that courts have gone about their business for centuries in the development of the common law. The difference from age to age is not so much in the recognition of the need that law shall conform itself to an end. It is rather in the nature of the end to which there has been need to conform. There have been periods when uniformity, even rigidity, the elimination of the personal element, were felt to be the paramount needs. By a sort of paradox, the end was best served by disregarding it and thinking only of the means. Gradually the need of a more flexible system asserted itself. Often the gap between the old rule and the new was bridged by the pious fraud of a fiction. The thing which concerns us here is that it was bridged whenever the importance of the end was dominant. Today the use of fictions has declined; and the springs of action are disclosed where once they were concealed. Even now, they are not fully known, however, even to those whom they control. Much of the process has been unconscious or nearly so. The ends to which courts have addressed themselves, the reasons and motives that have guided them, have often been vaguely felt, intuitively or almost intuitively apprehended, seldom explicitly avowed.

* * *

In thus recognizing, as I do, that the power to declare the law carries with it the power, and within limits the duty, to make law when none exists, I do not mean to range myself with the jurists who seem to hold that in reality there is no law except the decisions of the courts. I think the truth is midway between the extremes that are represented at one end by Coke and Hale and Blackstone and at the other by such authors as Austin and Holland and Gray and Jethro Brown. The theory of the older writers was that judges did not legislate at all. A pre-existing rule was there, imbedded, if concealed, in the body of the customary law. All that the judges did, was to throw off the wrappings, and expose the statute to our view. Since the days of Bentham and Austin, no one, it is believed, has accepted this theory without deduction or reserve, though even in modern decisions we find traces of its lingering influence. Today there is rather danger of another though an opposite error. From holding that the law is never made by judges, the votaries of the Austinian analysis have been led at times to the conclusion that it is never made by anyone else. Customs, no matter how firmly established, are not law, they say, until adopted by the courts. Even statutes are not law because the courts must fix their meaning.

* * *

In countless litigations, the law is so clear that judges have no discretion. They have the right to legislate within gaps, but often there are no gaps. We shall have a false view of the landscape if we look at the waste spaces only, and refuse to see the acres already sown and fruitful. I think the difficulty has its origin in the failure to distinguish between right and power, between the command embodied in a judgment and the jural principle to which the obedience of the judge is due. Judges have, of course, the power, though not the right, to ignore the mandate of a statute, and render judgment in despite of it. They have the power, though not the right, to travel beyond the walls of the interstices, the bounds set to judicial innovation by precedent and custom.

* * *

I have spoken of the forces of which judges avowedly avail to shape the form and content of their judgments. Even these forces are seldom fully in consciousness. They lie so near the surface, however, that their existence and influence are not likely to be disclaimed. But the subject is not exhausted with the recognition of their power. Deep below consciousness are other forces, the likes and the dislikes, the predilections and the prejudices, the complex of instincts and emotions and habits and convictions, which make the man, whether he be litigant or judge. * * * The great tides and currents which engulf the rest of men do not turn aside in their course, and pass the judges by. We like to figure to ourselves the processes of justice as coldly objective and impersonal. The law, conceived of as a real existence, dwelling apart and alone, speaks, through the voices of priests and ministers, the words which they have no choice except to utter. That is an ideal of objective truth toward which every system of jurisprudence tends. It is an ideal of which great publicists and judges have spoken as of something possible to attain. * * * It has a lofty sound; it is well and finally said; but it can never be more than partly true.

A RETURN TO STARE DECISIS[oo]

Herman Oliphant

No identical case can arise. All other cases will differ in some circumstance,—in time, if in no other, and most of them will have some differences which are not trivial. *Decision* in the sense meant in *stare decisis* must, therefore, refer to a proposition of law covering a group of fact situations * * * as a minimum, the fact situation of the instant case and at least one other.

To bring together into one class even this minimum of two fact situations however similar they may be, always has required and always will require an abstraction. If Paul and Peter are to be thought of together at all, they must both be apostles or be thought of as having some other attribute in common. Classification is abstraction. An element or elements common to the two fact situations put into one class must be drawn out from each to become the content of the category and the subject of the proposition of law which is thus applied to the two cases.

oo. 14 A.B.A.J. 71 (1928). Reprinted with permission from the ABA Journal.

But such a grouping may include multitudes of fact situations so long as a single attribute common to them all can be found. Between these two extremes lies a gradation of groups of fact situations each with its corresponding proposition of law, ranging from a grouping subtending but two situations to those covering hosts of them. This series of groupings of fact situations gives us a parallel series of corresponding propositions of law, each more and more generalized as we recede farther and farther from the instant state of facts and include more and more fact situations in the successive groupings. It is a mounting and widening structure, each proposition including all that has gone before and becoming more general by embracing new states of fact. For example, A's father induces her not to marry B as she promised to do. On a holding that the father is not liable to B for so doing, a gradation of widening propositions can be built, a very few of which are:

1.   Fathers are privileged to induce daughters to break promises to marry.

2.   Parents are so privileged.

3.   Parents are so privileged as to both daughters and sons.

4.   All persons are so privileged as to promises to marry.

5.   Parents are so privileged as to all promises made by their children.

6.   All persons are so privileged as to all promises made by anyone.

There can be erected upon the action taken by a court in any case such a gradation of generalizations and this is commonly done in the opinion. Sometimes it is built up to dizzy heights by the court itself and at times, by law teachers and writers, it is reared to those lofty summits of the absolute and the infinite.

Where on that gradation of propositions are we to take our stand and say "This proposition is the decision of this case within the meaning of the doctrine of *stare decisis?*" Can a proposition of law of this * * * type ever become so broad that, as to any of the cases it would cover, it is mere dictum?

That would be difficult enough if it ended there. But just as one and the same apple can be thrown into any one of many groups of barrels according to its size, color, shape, etc., so also there stretches up and away from every single case in the books, not one possible gradation of widening generalizations, but many. Multitudes of radii shoot out from it, each pair enclosing one of an indefinite number of these gradations of broader and broader generalizations. * * *

A student is told to see the "doctrine" or "principle" of a case, but which of its welter of stairs shall he ascend and how high up shall he go? Is there some one step on some one stair which is *the* decision of the case within the meaning of the mandate *stare decisis?* That is the double difficulty. Each precedent considered by a judge and each case studied by a student rests at the center of a vast and empty stadium. The angle and distance from which that case is to be viewed involves the choice of a seat. Which shall be chosen? Neither judge nor student can escape the fact that he can and must choose. * * *

Chapter II

THE ANATOMY OF A
LEGAL DISPUTE

A. OUR STORY BEGINS[a]

The day was not like most other days for Kim Johnson. She was spending the weekend with her boyfriend, Curt Baker, in Las Vegas, Nevada. Kim sat in the passenger side of Curt's car, going north on Flamingo Drive. It was raining heavily and the roads were slick, but that did not dampen their enthusiasm.

Meanwhile, John Roscoe was heading south on Flamingo. He'd had a few beers to celebrate a successful day at the rodeo. The competition had been stiff but he had won several events. Because he felt tired, he decided to check into a nearby motel and wait until morning to start the long drive home to San Mateo, California. The motel was only a mile from the intersection of Flamingo Drive and Las Vegas Avenue. He reached the intersection, pulled into the left turn lane, and waited. The traffic light turned yellow. He looked ahead, saw no approaching cars and began making the left turn east on Las Vegas Avenue.

Within an instant there was heard the awful screech of brakes, a crash, the sound of metal on metal, glass shattering, and the moans of suffering. Curt's car hit John's truck broadside.

The following hour witnessed a flurry of activity. Some people ran to the scene of the accident to render aid and comfort. Many vehicles slowed and then continued down the road without stopping. Then sirens split the air. Police arrived. An ambulance whisked Kim to the hospital. She was unconscious.

Our story has begun. Let us go back in time to the scene of the accident and follow events as they unfold.

a. Any resemblance to an actual case is purely coincidental. Statements as to the law of a particular jurisdiction may be hypothetical assumptions made for pedagogical purposes.

B. THE LAW INTERVENES

Within fifteen minutes of the crash, the police question John and Curt at the scene. One officer, suspecting that John had been drinking, administers a field sobriety test. Concluding that John is under the influence of alcohol, the officer takes him to the station for further tests. A GCI[b] test is administered. It indicates a blood alcohol level of .09. The officer cites John for failing to yield to oncoming traffic and driving under the influence. He then releases John to one of his rodeo friends who has come to the station to post bail.

One of the functions of the police at the scene of an accident is to record witnesses' statements. In this case there are three disinterested witnesses—that is, witnesses other than the participants in the accident. Henry recalls that he was in the right hand lane proceeding north on Flamingo and had been stopped "for at least 10 seconds" when Curt's car passed him on his left and ran into John's vehicle. Sarah was driving south on Flamingo and had been braking as she observed the yellow light. She states emphatically that she heard the crash moments after the light had already turned red. Still another witness, Bill, who was walking east on Las Vegas Avenue at the time of impact recalls that, after hearing the crash, he turned around and saw that the light was red for east/west traffic and therefore "must have been green or yellow" for north/south traffic.

An accident reconstruction specialist takes various measurements to determine the speed of the two vehicles before and at the point of impact. Because of the wet pavement and other road conditions, the reconstructionist cannot satisfactorily determine the speed of either of the vehicles before the impact.

Police officers at the scene record statements from John and Curt. Because of Kim's physical condition, she is not questioned.

If you were the police officer at the scene of the accident, would you have also given Curt a citation? Does the police officer have discretion regarding issuance of citations? What facts should a police officer consider? What sources would you consult in answering these questions?

C. JOHN'S DILEMMA

Should John plead guilty to the traffic citation? Does your answer depend upon the amount of the anticipated fine? The inconvenience of returning to Las Vegas to defend the action? The effect the plea might have on John's right to drive? The effect it might have on any civil lawsuits arising from the accident? The effect it might have on John's insurer's duty to defend and indemnify him for monetary losses resulting from a civil lawsuit? Would John, as a lay person, be able to answer these questions without consulting an attorney? Should he consult an attorney at this stage? If he consults a California attorney, will the latter be able to assist him in Nevada? If not, what might he do? If consulted,

b. Gas chromatograph intoximeter—a device for measuring blood alcohol levels.

should the California attorney take any immediate steps to protect John? What steps?

John contacts an attorney who reads the relevant provisions of John's automobile insurance policy. The policy provides coverage of $100,000 per person and $300,000 per event for negligent infliction of personal injury and property damage coverage of $25,000. John does not have any insurance to cover the extensive damage to his truck. Significantly, the policy excludes from coverage any loss or damage caused by the insured while driving under the influence of alcohol. The policy also contains a standard provision: "The company will defend any suit against its insured for damages which if paid would be a loss under the terms of this policy with attorneys hired and paid by the company." If you were John's attorney, what would you advise him with respect to having the insurance company defend him in a lawsuit stemming from the accident? Would you negotiate with the insurance company? When? How?

The policy requires that the insured must notify the insurance company immediately of any accident for which a claim may be made. It also provides that the insured must make a sworn statement to the insurance company of the events leading to the accident. What problems might the insured encounter in preparing the sworn statement? Should he first discuss the content with the insurer? Could a statement under oath be used against John later? Perhaps even prejudice the insurer? Is there not an inherent conflict of interest between the insurer and John? To put it simply, John may not care too much whether a judgment is entered against him—as long as the company is responsible for paying it; on the other hand, the company might wish to establish that John was intoxicated to avoid any obligation to indemnify under the insurance policy. Can an attorney selected by the insurance company really defend John? Do you perceive any ethical problems?

The problems alluded to in the preceding paragraph have been studied by the organized bar, the insurance industry, and the courts. In 1972, the American Bar Association promulgated the following Guiding Principles:[c]

IV. CONFLICTS OF INTEREST—DUTIES OF ATTORNEY

In any claim or in any suit where the attorney selected by the company to defend the claim or action becomes aware of facts or information which indicate to him a question of coverage in the matter being defended or any other conflict of interest between the company and the insured with respect to the defense of the matter, *the attorney should promptly inform both the company and the insured, preferably in writing,* of the nature and extent of the conflicting interest. In any such suit, the company or its attorney should invite the insured to retain his own counsel at his own expense to represent his separate interest.

(Emphasis added.)

   c. The "Guiding Principles" cited above were rescinded in August 1980.

* * *

VI. Duty of Attorney Not to Disclose Certain Facts and Information

Where the attorney selected by the company to defend a claim or suit becomes aware of facts or information, imparted to him by the insured under circumstances indicating the insured's belief that such disclosure would not be revealed to the insurance company *but would be treated as a confidential communication* to the attorney, which indicate to the attorney a lack of coverage, then as to such matters, disclosures made directly to the attorney, *should not be revealed to the company by the attorney nor should the attorney discuss with the insured the legal significance of the disclosure or the nature of the coverage question.*

(Emphasis added.)

* * *

IX. Withdrawal

In any case where the company or the attorney selected by the company to defend the suit decides to withdraw from the defense of the action brought against the insured, *the insured should be fully advised of such decision and the reasons therefor;* and every reasonable effort should be made to avoid prejudice to or impairment of the rights of the insured.

(Emphasis added.)

In the course of investigating the accident, the attorney retained by the insurance company requests a copy of the police report, which shows John's citation for intoxication. The insurer-retained attorney then confers with John who states that he consumed four or five beers in the hour or two immediately preceding the accident. What should the attorney do? Are the Guiding Principles above helpful?

Most courts considering this issue have rejected the approach taken in the Guiding Principles. The principle espoused by the courts is that, although the insurer has a contractual obligation to pay for legal services, the retained lawyer's loyalty belongs solely to the insured. One court stated the duty of loyalty as follows:

When counsel, although paid by the casualty company, undertakes to represent the policyholder and files his notice of appearance, he owes to his client, the assured, an undeviating and single allegiance. His fealty embraces the requirement to produce in court all witnesses, fact and expert, who are available and necessary for the proper protection of the rights of his client. It is immaterial that such procedure increases the cost of the carrier beyond the policy coverage limit.

The attorney may not seek to reduce the company's loss by attempting to save a portion of the total indemnity in negotiations for the settlement of a negligence action, if by so doing he needlessly subjects the assured to judgment in excess of the policy limit. His duty to the assured is paramount. The Canons of Professional Ethics make it pellucid that there are not two standards, one applying to counsel privately retained by a client, and the other to counsel paid by an insurance carrier. * * * If the interests of the carrier and the assured are or are likely to become diverse, he cannot represent both.

American Employers Insurance Co. v. Goble Aircraft Specialties, 205 Misc. 1066, 1075, 131 N.Y.S.2d 393, 401–02 (1954). Does *Goble Aircraft* clarify or confuse the attorney's duties in this situation? Yet another question, and one to which we will return, see *infra* section G, is which law controls if the laws of California, Nevada and Arizona differ on this issue?

D. COLLATERAL CONSEQUENCES

John received a citation for driving while intoxicated. In most states this charge falls within the jurisdiction of the criminal courts. It may also have other serious ramifications for John, such as the loss or suspension of the privilege to drive an automobile. We shall briefly examine the criminal justice system and the administrative process.

1. THE CRIMINAL JUSTICE SYSTEM[d]

Study of the criminal justice system focuses on society's goals in categorizing conduct as criminal. The division of civil and criminal law may be best understood in relation to the ends served. The civil law generally attempts to compensate victims; the criminal law, to punish offenders. At times the attributes are blended; thus punitive damages, a form of punishment, may be awarded in civil cases, and restitution to the victim, a civil remedy, may be awarded as part of the sentencing process in criminal cases.

The criminal justice system is quite different from its civil counterpart in the same jurisdiction. It involves three separate yet interrelated parts—the police, the courts, and the corrections system. Courts deal with those whom the police arrest, and police activities are controlled in significant respects by the courts. Corrections involvement results from convictions.

Many laypersons perceive criminal court procedures as a confusing maze, the intricacies of which only those versed in the law can comprehend. In truth, anyone willing to take the time and effort to analyze statutes and rules can readily understand the system.

Each state defines standards of minimum competence for operating motor vehicles and specifies penalties for deviation from those standards.

d. Chapter IV examines the criminal system.

Most states classify driving while intoxicated as a misdemeanor or petty offense. In some states, a conviction results in the automatic suspension of one's driver's license for six months. In many states, John could face a jail sentence upon conviction for a first offense. A fine is also commonly imposed.

In serious criminal cases, federal law guarantees a trial by jury in the state court system. In minor cases, state law may guarantee trial by jury. In all criminal cases, serious and minor, all elements of the offense charged must be proved beyond a reasonable doubt. This standard differs from the civil standard which, according to the issue, may range from the preponderance of the evidence test (by the greater weight of the evidence) to the clear and convincing evidence test.

2. THE ADMINISTRATIVE PROCESS

Modern government carries on many functions: It collects taxes, disburses funds, distributes benefits, licenses private activities, and provides myriad services to the public. Many of these functions are carried out by administrative agencies. Modern government is preeminently administrative, exercising legal power through administrative agencies.

Licensing is one widely used administrative or regulatory technique to control access to an activity and to enforce minimum qualifications of competence. In the case of automobile licenses, the licensing functions are generally carried out by the motor vehicle department. This department has the power to suspend or revoke licenses or impose other sanctions for the failure to meet or maintain minimum standards. Although the sanctions may be imposed administratively, court proceedings may ultimately be used to punish violators or prevent them from engaging in the activity without a license.

E. KIM'S PREDICAMENT

Kim had not had the slightest acquaintance with the law in all her 21 years. This state of equipoise soon vanished. Within a few days of returning home to Phoenix, Kim received a bill for $600 from the ambulance company and another bill for $1600 from the hospital for emergency treatment. She simply does not have the money to pay these amounts. Is she obligated to do so? What if Curt signed the hospital admittance form that contained an agreement on his part to reimburse the hospital for Kim's treatment? Is he obligated? May a hospital legally deny admittance if no financially solvent person assumes responsibility for the bills?

Because she was unable to work for two weeks after the accident, Kim lost her job. Her boss regretted letting her go and said he would consider rehiring her if he needed another waitress.

Kim has been seeing a physical therapist for many weeks. The pain is subsiding and there is no sign of any permanent injury other than a rather obtrusive three–inch scar on her left cheek.

If you were Kim would you now seek the assistance of an attorney?

One of the premises of our legal system is that legal actions must be initiated by an aggrieved party. Historically, lawyers were forbidden from seeking out clients or calling legal problems to their attention for purposes of bringing lawsuits. In fact, many states subject certain forms of solicitation to criminal sanctions. Why?

Advertising for and soliciting clients are still among the most frequently debated issues confronting the profession. According to United States Supreme Court decisions, truthful and non-misleading advertising of legal services is protected under the First Amendment to the United States Constitution. That means that any state law to the contrary is unconstitutional and may not be enforced. Yet in-person solicitation to a layperson for the purpose of obtaining employment for the lawyer is still proscribed under the ethical rules. Why should truthful newspaper advertisements, television commercials, written communications, or prerecorded telephone messages be constitutionally protected while commercially oriented in-person solicitation is not?

The ambulance company or the hospital might commence legal proceedings against Kim and that may motivate her to retain an attorney. Even then, it is her choice whether to seek legal assistance.

How would you select an attorney? Would you look in the classified section of the telephone directory? Ask your friends? Call the bar association? Would you seek an attorney licensed in Arizona? Nevada?

In our case, Kim's mother has a friend named Jessica Hamilton who had been recently admitted to the Arizona bar. She told Jessica about Kim's problem and gave her a copy of the Nevada police reports and the witness statements that Curt had provided to Kim. Jessica suggests to Kim's mother that Kim give her a call if she desires legal assistance.

Even at this time, Jessica perceives some problems with the case. First, although Kim seems to have a good case against someone, Curt appears a likely defendant. Would Kim authorize suit against her boyfriend? A major consideration with personal injury cases is whether any potential defendant has sufficient resources to pay the damages. In this case, as in so many others, insurance is the only real source of payment. How would Jessica determine the relevant details of the insurance coverage, if any? Another problem is whether she can even represent Kim in a suit against John. After all, the accident happened in Nevada and John is a resident of California. From her courses in law school, she recalls that the Arizona courts might not be able to adjudicate the controversy against John. The state of the accident is generally the most convenient place in which to institute suit. It is the state whose substantive laws will apply and the state where the witnesses probably live. Jessica observes from the police report, however, that Bill and Sarah, two of the disinterested witnesses, listed Phoenix, Arizona as their place of residence.

Kim knows that she needs a lawyer. She decidedly does not want to handle these legal matters on her own, but she also does not have money to pay a lawyer. She has heard from friends that lawyers charge very high fees. Kim makes an appointment to see Jessica the following day and anxiously awaits the visit, hoping that the question of payment can be resolved later.

F. THE FIRST INTERVIEW

Conducting the initial interview is an art. It varies with the nature of the dispute and the sophistication of the client. The interview is usually the first step in the creation of the lawyer-client relationship.

The attorney need not agree to take a case. Many legitimate reasons may influence lawyers to refuse prospective clients or cases. One reason is lack of experience in an area of law. The lawyer may not have the time or feel it fair to bill the client for the time it takes to obtain sufficient expertise to handle a matter. Another legitimate reason to decline representation is the threat of an actual or potential conflict of interests. A lawyer may not represent parties who have conflicting interests. Why? At times a conflict is obvious; at other times it is difficult to perceive, especially during the first interview. Can you think of examples where conflicts might not reveal themselves at this early stage? May a lawyer represent Kim in a suit against Curt and represent Curt in a suit against John?

Occasionally a case is rejected because the attorney and client cannot come to an acceptable fee arrangement, or perhaps the press of business precludes acceptance of the case. Some lawyers will not handle a case because they fear economic, social, or political reprisals. Are these legitimate reasons for refusing cases?

At the initial interview, the lawyer should obtain full disclosure of the facts. Clients often hesitate to divulge damaging or embarrassing facts to a lawyer. Should the lawyer not obtain all relevant information in time to prepare for litigation, however, the result can be disastrous. Thus the lawyer must sometimes probe deeply into sensitive areas. This too is an art.

In Kim's case none of the foregoing problems immediately emerges. Jessica has read all accounts of the accident. There is little question that either John or Curt or both were responsible. Kim apparently did nothing wrong. At the initial interview, Kim confirms what Curt had reported to the police: Curt was driving approximately 40 miles an hour (the posted speed limit) and entered the intersection precisely as the light turned yellow. While in the intersection he applied his brakes, fishtailed, and then struck John's truck broadside. Kim blacked out and was revived at the hospital.

Upon further probing, Kim recalls that it was very difficult to see in the downpour, that they were late for a meeting with their friends, and that Curt had consumed two drinks in the hour or two before the collision. Upon further examination, she believes he may have had as many as four.

Kim states that she is still in pain and that medical treatment may have to continue for a year or more. She is paying $200 per week for therapy. She cannot return to her waitressing job because standing for extended periods causes pain. Furthermore, the scar on her cheek causes her considerable embarrassment.

Kim wants Jessica to bring an action against John. She believes that Curt would want Jessica to represent him, too. Indeed, she advises Jessica that Curt will be at the office shortly to participate in the interview. What should Jessica do about seeing Curt? Is there a problem in seeing Curt and obtaining his version of the accident? Would Kim's legal position be improved if Curt had run the red light? If so, may Jessica call this fact to Kim's attention? Must Jessica so advise Kim? What if Kim changes her statement to reflect that Curt went through a red light? Does a lawyer have an ethical obligation to prevent such a change? This subject has intrigued lawyers for centuries. The following article is an excellent account of the "Lawyer's Trilemma." The article focuses on criminal litigation, a context in which the dilemma is exacerbated.

PERJURY: THE LAWYER'S TRILEMMA[e]

Monroe H. Freedman

Is it ever proper for a lawyer to present perjured testimony?

One's instinctive response is in the negative. On analysis, however, it becomes apparent that the question is exceedingly perplexing. In at least one situation, that of the criminal defense lawyer, my own answer is in the affirmative.

At the outset, we should dispose of some common question-begging responses. The attorney, we are told, is an officer of the court participating in a search for truth. Those propositions, however, merely serve to state the problem in different words: As an officer of the court, participating in a search for truth, what is the attorney obligated to do when faced with perjured testimony? That question cannot be answered properly without an appreciation of the fact that the attorney functions in an adversary system of justice which imposes three conflicting obligations upon the advocate. The difficulties presented by these obligations are particularly acute in the criminal defense area because of the presumption of innocence, the burden on the state to prove its case beyond reasonable doubt, and the right to put the prosecution to its proof.

First, the ABA Standards Relating to the Defense Function require the lawyer to determine all relevant facts known to the accused, because "counsel cannot properly perform their duties without knowing the

e. 1 Litigation 26 (Winter, 1975). Professor Freedman's views are set forth more fully in his book, *Lawyers' Ethics in an* *Adversary System* (1975), and in "Personal Responsibility in a Professional System," 27 Cath. U.L. Rev. 191 (1978).

truth.'' The lawyer who is ignorant of any potentially relevant fact ''incapacitates himself to serve his client effectively,'' because ''an adequate defense cannot be framed if the lawyer does not know what is likely to develop at trial.''

Second, the lawyer must hold in strictest confidence the disclosures made by the client in the course of the professional relationship. The Standards admonish that ''nothing is more fundamental to the lawyer-client relationship than the establishment of trust and confidence,'' and that the ''first duty'' of an attorney is ''to keep the secrets of his clients.'' If this were not so, the client would not feel free to confide fully, and the lawyer would not be able to fulfill the obligation to ascertain all relevant facts. Accordingly, counsel is required to establish a relationship of trust and confidence, to explain the necessity of full disclosure of all facts, and to explain to the client the obligation of confidentiality which makes privileged the accused's disclosures.

Third, Canon 22 of the Canons of Professional Ethics tells us that the lawyer is an officer of the court, and his or her conduct before the court ''should be characterized by candor.''

Defining the Trilemma

As soon as one begins to think about those responsibilities, it becomes apparent that the conscientious attorney is faced with what we may call a trilemma—that is, the lawyer is required to know everything, to keep it in confidence, and to reveal it to the court.

* * *

Misleading First Reading

Where the lawyer has foreknowledge of perjury, * * * the Code appears, at first reading, to be unambiguous. According to DR 7–102(A)(4), a lawyer must not ''knowingly use perjured testimony or false evidence.'' The difficulty, however, is that the Code does not indicate how the lawyer is to go about fulfilling that obligation. What if the lawyer advises the client that perjury is unlawful and, perhaps, bad tactics as well, but the client nevertheless insists upon taking the stand and committing perjury? What steps, specifically, should the lawyer take? Just how difficult it is to answer that question becomes apparent if we review the relationship between lawyer and client as it develops, and consider the contexts in which the decision to commit perjury may arise.

If we recognize that professional responsibility requires that an advocate have full knowledge of every pertinent fact, then the lawyer must seek the truth from the client, not shun it. That means that the attorney will have to dig and pry and cajole, and, even then, the lawyer will not be successful without convincing the client that full disclosure to the lawyer will never result in prejudice to the client by any word or action of the attorney. That is particularly true in the case of the indigent criminal defendant, who meets the lawyer for the first time in the cell block or the rotunda of the jail. The client did not choose the lawyer, who comes as a stranger sent by the judge and who therefore appears to be part of the system that is attempting to punish the defendant. It is no easy task to persuade such a client to talk freely without fear of harm.

However, the inclination to mislead one's lawyer is not restricted to the indigent or even to the criminal defendant. Randolph Paul has observed a similar phenomenon among a wealthier class in a far more congenial atmosphere. The tax advisor, notes Mr. Paul, will sometimes have to "dynamite the facts of his case out of the unwilling witnesses on his own side—witnesses who are nervous, witnesses who are confused about their own interest, witnesses who try to be too smart for their own good, and witnesses who subconsciously do not want to understand what has happened despite the fact that they must if they are to testify coherently." Mr. Paul goes on to explain that the truth can be obtained only by persuading the client that it would be a violation of a sacred obligation for the lawyer ever to reveal a client's confidence. Of course, once the lawyer has thus persuaded the client of the obligation of confidentiality, that obligation must be respected scrupulously.

ILLUSTRATING THE TRILEMMA

Assume the following situation. Your client has been falsely accused of a robbery committed at 16th and P Streets at 11:00 p.m. He reveals to you that he was at 15th and P Streets at 10:55 that evening, but that he was walking east, away from the scene of the crime, and that by 11:00 p.m., he was six blocks away. At the trial, there are two prosecution witnesses. The first mistakenly, but with some degree of persuasiveness, identifies your client as the criminal. The second prosecution witness is an elderly woman who is somewhat nervous and who wears glasses. She testifies truthfully and accurately that she saw your client at 15th and P Streets at 10:55 p.m. She has corroborated the erroneous testimony of the first witness and made conviction extremely likely.

The client then insists upon taking the stand in his own defense, not only to deny the erroneous evidence identifying him as the criminal, but also to deny the truthful, but highly damaging, testimony of the corroborating witness who placed him one block away from the intersection five minutes prior to the crime. Of course, if he tells the truth and thus verifies the corroborating witness, the jury will be more inclined to accept the inaccurate testimony of the principal witness, who specifically identified him as the criminal.

In my opinion, the attorney's obligation in such a situation would be to advise the client that the proposed testimony is unlawful, but to proceed in the normal fashion in presenting the testimony and arguing the case to the jury if the client makes the decision to go forward. Any other course would be a betrayal of the assurances of confidentiality given by the attorney to induce the client to reveal everything, however damaging it might appear.

A frequent objection to the position that the attorney must go along with the client's decision to commit perjury is that the lawyer would be guilty of subornation of perjury. Subornation, however, consists of willfully procuring perjury, which is not the case when the attorney indicates to the client that the client's proposed course of conduct would be unlawful, but then accepts the client's decision. Beyond that, there is a point of view which has been expressed to me by a number of experienced attorneys, that the criminal defendant has a "right to tell his story." What that suggests is that it is simply too much to expect of a human being, caught up in the criminal process and facing loss of liberty and the horrors of imprisonment, not to attempt to lie to avoid that penalty. For that reason, criminal defendants in most European countries do not testify under oath, but simply "tell their stories." It is also noteworthy that subsequent perjury prosecutions against criminal defendants in this country are extremely rare, being used almost exclusively in cases in which the prosecutor's motive is questionable.

COLLATERAL WITNESSES

The discussion thus far has focused only on the lawyer's obligation when the perjury is presented by the client. Some authorities indicate a distinction between perjury by the criminal defendant who has a right to take the stand, and perjury by collateral witnesses. I agree that there is an important distinction, and that the case involving collateral witnesses is not at all as clear as that involving the client alone. In one criminal case, however, a new trial was ordered when the trial court discovered that the defendant's attorney had refused to put on the defendant's mother and sister because he was concerned about perjury. Certainly a spouse or parent would be acting under the same human compulsion as a defendant, and I find it difficult to imagine myself denouncing my client's spouse or parent as a perjurer, and, thereby, denouncing my client as well. I do not know, however, how much wider that circle of close identity might be drawn.

The most obvious way to avoid the ethical difficulty of the trilemma is for the lawyer to withdraw from the case, at least if there is sufficient time before trial for the client to retain another attorney. The client will then go to the nearest law office, realizing that the obligation of confidentiality is not what is has been represented to be and withhold incriminating information or the fact of guilt from the new attorney. And, of course, in a substantial number of cases, the courts will not permit counsel to withdraw.

In terms of professional ethics, the practice of withdrawing from a case under such circumstances is difficult to defend, since the identical perjured testimony will ultimately be presented. Moreover, the new attorney will be ignorant of the perjury and therefore will be in no position to attempt to discourage the client from presenting it. Only the original attorney, who knows the truth, has that opportunity but loses it in the very act of evading the ethical problem.

* * *

Since there are actually three obligations that create the difficulty—the third being the attorney's duty to learn all the facts—there is, of course, another way to resolve the difficulty. That is, by "selective ignorance." The attorney can make it clear to the client from the outset that the attorney does not want to hear an admission of guilt or incriminating information from the client. According to the Standards, that tactic is "most egregious" and constitutes "professional impropriety." On a practical level, it also puts an unreasonable burden on the unsophisticated client to select what to tell and what to hold back, and it can seriously impair the attorney's effectiveness in counseling the client and in trying the case.

The question remains: What should the lawyer do when faced with the client's insistence upon taking the stand and committing perjury? It is in response to that question in criminal cases that the Standards [Proposed Standard 4–7.7] present a most extraordinary solution, which, to my knowledge, has never been advocated by anyone other than Chief Justice Burger (who served as chairman in preparing the Standards): If the lawyer knows that the client intends to commit perjury, the lawyer "must confine his examination to identifying the witness as the defendant and permitting him to make his statement." The lawyer "may not engage in direct examination of the defendant * * * in the conventional manner" and, moreover, "may not later * * * recite or rely upon the false testimony in his closing argument."

It is difficult to imagine a more unprofessional and irresponsible proposal. The first objection is a purely practical one: The prosecutor might well object to testimony from the defendant in narrative form rather than in the conventional manner, because it would give the prosecutor no opportunity to object to inadmissible evidence prior to the jury's hearing it. The Standards provide no guidance as to what the defense attorney should do if the objection is sustained.

THE JURY'S ASSUMPTIONS

More importantly, experienced trial attorneys have often noted that jurors assume that the defendant's lawyer knows the truth about the case, and that the jury will frequently judge the defendant by drawing inferences from the attorney's conduct in the case. There is, of course, only one inference that can be drawn if the defendant's own attorney turns his or her back on the defendant at the most critical point in the trial, and then, in closing argument, sums up the case with no reference whatsoever to the fact that the defendant has testified or to the evidence presented in that testimony. Ironically, the Standards reject any solution that would involve informing the judge, but then propose a solution that, as a practical matter, succeeds in informing not only the judge but the jury as well.

It would appear that the ABA Standards have chosen to resolve the trilemma by maintaining the requirements of complete knowledge and of candor to the court, and sacrificing confidentiality. Interestingly, however, that may not in fact be the case. I say that because the Standards fail to answer a critically important question: Should the client be told about the obligation the Standards seek to impose on the attorney? That is, the Standards ignore the issue of whether the lawyer should say to the client at the outset of their relationship, "I think it's only fair that I warn you: If you should tell me anything incriminating and subsequently decide to deny the incriminating facts at trial, I would not be able to examine you in the ordinary manner or to argue your untrue testimony to the jury." The Canadian Bar Association, for example, takes an extremely hard line against the presentation of perjury by the client, but it also explicitly requires that the client be put on notice of that fact. Obviously, any other course would be a gross betrayal of the client's trust, since everything else said by the attorney in attempting to obtain complete information about the case would indicate to the client that no information thus obtained would be used to the client's disadvantage.

On the other hand, the inevitable result of the position taken by the Canadian Bar Association would be to caution the client not to be completely candid with the attorney. That, of course, returns us to resolving the trilemma by maintaining confidentiality and candor, but sacrificing complete knowledge—a solution which, as we have already seen, is denounced in criminal cases by the Standards as "unscrupulous," "most egregious," and "professional impropriety."

Thus, the Standards, by failing to face up to the question of whether to put the client on notice, take us out of the trilemma by one door only to lead us back by another.

Earlier we noted that the Code of Professional Responsibility appears to be unambiguous in proscribing the known use of perjured testimony, but that the Code does not indicate how the lawyer is to go about fulfilling that obligation. Analysis of the various alternatives that have been suggested shows that none of them is wholly satisfactory, and that some are impractical and violate basic rights of the client. In addition, the ABA Standards rely upon unsupported assertions of what lawyers "universally" think and do. It is therefore relevant and important to consider the actual practices of attorneys faced with the ethical issue in their daily work.

A survey conducted among lawyers in the District of Columbia is extremely revealing. The overall conclusion is that "less than five percent of practicing attorneys queried consistently acted in a manner the legal profession claims that members of the Bar act, and, under the new Code of Professional Responsibility, demands that they act." Specifically, when asked what to do when the client indicates an intention to commit perjury, ninety-five percent of the attorneys responding indicated that they would call the defendant and ninety percent stated that they would question the witness in the normal fashion.

That rather gross discrepancy between published standards and professional action is perhaps best explained by attorneys' reactions to being asked to participate in the survey. Virtually all of the attorneys personally interviewed refused to make an on-the-record statement, although without exception they eagerly cooperated and were willing to participate in an anonymous interview.

Senior partners of two of Washington's most prestigious law firms, after refusing to allow the circulation of the questionnaire among the firm's members, permitted personal interviews on the condition that neither their names, names of the other members in the firm interviewed, nor the name of their firm would be published. Both attorneys, after apologizing for their insistence upon anonymity, explained that many of the local judges with whom they dealt daily would not look favorably upon their true views about the role of the defense attorney in a criminal case, especially if aired publicly. Their reason for not complying with the ABA's rules relating to the presentation of perjury was that those standards would compromise their role as advocates in an adversary system.

* * *

I continue to stand with those lawyers who hold that the lawyer's obligation of confidentiality does not permit him to disclose the facts he has learned from his client which form the basis for his conclusion that the client intends to perjure himself. What that means—necessarily, it seems to me—is that, at least the criminal defense attorney, however unwillingly in terms of personal morality, has a professional responsibility as an advocate in an adversary system to examine the perjurious client in the ordinary way and to argue to the jury, as evidence in the case, the testimony presented by the defendant.

———

The American Bar Association adopted the Model Rules of Professional Conduct in 1983. By 2002, approximately forty states had adopted the substance of the rules' provisions. Rule 3.3 specifically addresses the tension between the duty of candor toward a tribunal and the duty to maintain client confidences. Pertinent portions of the rules and comments follow:

RULE 3.3 *Candor Toward the Tribunal*

(a) A lawyer shall not knowingly:

(1) make a false statement of material fact or law to a tribunal;

(2) fail to disclose a material fact to a tribunal when disclosure is necessary to avoid assisting a criminal or fraudulent act by the client;

* * *

(4) offer evidence that the lawyer knows to be false. If a lawyer has offered material evidence and comes to know of its falsity, the lawyer shall take reasonable remedial measures.

(b) The duties stated in paragraph (a) continue to the conclusion of the proceeding, and apply even if compliance requires disclosure of information otherwise protected by [rules covering client confidences and secrets].

* * *

The comments to the Model Rules of Professional Conduct provide guidance as to the proper interpretation of the rules. Consider the following comments concerning "Perjury by a Criminal Defendant" and "Remedial Measures."[f]

Perjury by a Criminal Defendant

[7]   Whether an advocate for a criminally accused has the same duty of disclosure has been intensely debated. While it is agreed that the lawyer should seek to persuade the client to refrain from the perjurious testimony, there has been dispute concerning the lawyer's duty when that persuasion fails. If the confrontation with the client occurs before trial, the lawyer ordinarily can withdraw. Withdrawal before trial may not be possible, however, either because trial is imminent, or because the confrontation with the client does not take place until the trial itself, or because no other counsel is available.

[8]   The most difficult situation, therefore, arises in a criminal case where the accused insists on testifying when the lawyer knows that the testimony is perjurious. The lawyer's effort to rectify the situation can increase the likelihood of the client's being convicted as well as opening the possibility of a prosecution for perjury. On the other hand, if the lawyer does not exercise control over the proof, the lawyer participates, although in a merely passive way, in deception of the court.

[9]   Three resolutions of this dilemma have been proposed. One is to permit the accused to testify by a narrative without guidance through the lawyer's questioning. This compromises both contending principles; it exempts the lawyer from the duty to disclose false evidence but subjects the client to an implicit disclosure of information imparted to counsel. Another suggested resolution, of relatively recent origin, is that the advocate be entirely excused from the duty to reveal perjury if the perjury is that of the client. This is a coherent solution but makes the advocate a knowing instrument of perjury.

[10]   The other resolution of the dilemma is that the lawyer must reveal the client's perjury if necessary to rectify the situation. A criminal accused has a right to the assistance of an advocate, a right to testify and a right of confidential communication with counsel. However, an accused should not have a right to assistance of counsel in committing perjury. Furthermore, an advocate has an

f.   In 2002, the ABA amended Rule 3.3   of this discussion.
in ways that are not relevant for purposes

obligation, not only in professional ethics but under the law as well, to avoid implication in the commission of perjury or other falsification of evidence.

Remedial Measures

[11]   If perjured testimony or false evidence has been offered, the advocate's proper course ordinarily is to remonstrate with the client confidentially. If that fails, the advocate should seek to withdraw if that will remedy the situation. If withdrawal will not remedy the situation or is impossible, the advocate should make disclosure to the court. It is for the court then to determine what should be done—making a statement about the matter to the trier of fact, ordering a mistrial or perhaps nothing. If the false testimony was that of the client, the client may controvert the lawyer's version of their communication when the lawyer discloses the situation to the court. If there is an issue whether the client has committed perjury, the lawyer cannot represent the client in resolution of the issue and a mistrial may be unavoidable. An unscrupulous client might in this way attempt to produce a series of mistrials and thus escape prosecution. However, a second such encounter could be construed as a deliberate abuse of the right to counsel and as such a waiver of the right to further representation.

The Model Rules reject Professor Freedman's approach. Do they provide a better solution? Note the alternatives open to the court once the perjury is disclosed. What do you think the court will do? Does your answer depend in part on whether the trial is before the court or before a jury? Why?

————

Jessica advises Kim that she cannot represent Curt. She relates that Kim has a cause of action against Curt, but reserves decision on whether to advise Kim to sue Curt. What additional information may Jessica desire before advising Kim? Jessica states that any suit between the two would be a "friendly suit." Is there any problem in bringing a lawsuit against a "friend" when the ultimate liability will be paid by an insurance carrier? Are there unique problems when the suit involves friends?

Kim is nervous about testifying as to the details of her relationship with Curt. Must these details come out at the trial? Can Kim be protected in any way? Can she testify that they took separate rooms when in fact they did not? Can Jessica take any action to prevent the inquiry into the matter? Is the relationship between Kim and Curt relevant to any of the issues of the case? Can any of these questions be answered by someone who is not skilled in trial practice?

Once a professional relationship is agreed upon, a retainer agreement should be drawn up. Kim is relieved that Jessica offers to represent her on a contingency fee basis; Jessica will take a percentage of any recovery, in this case twenty-five percent upon settlement or thirty-three and a third percent should the case proceed to trial. Jessica will be entitled to no fee if there is no recovery. Does such an agreement create a conflict between the economic interests of Kim and Jessica? Can you think of ways to avoid or mitigate the effects of these conflicts? Is reliance on Jessica's integrity sufficient protection for Kim? The ethical implications of contingency fees are discussed in the following article.

SOME ETHICAL QUESTIONS ABOUT PERCENTAGE FEES[g]

John F. Grady

* * *

I propose to analyze the typical automobile accident case. Let me emphasize that I am not referring to a complicated, multi-party type of case, but to the common case involving two cars or a car and a pedestrian. I choose this kind of case because it accounts for the vast majority of personal injury claims. The complicated case is exceptional.

I think it should take a competent lawyer no more than 15 hours to prepare this type of case for trial. * * *

The trial itself should not take more than two to two and one-half days, assuming it is a jury trial. Including time for preparation of jury instructions and any additional legal research, the trial should take no more than 15 hours of the lawyer's time. The usual breakdown would be about ten hours in court and five hours spent before and after court sessions at the office, including any time required for post-trial motions.

* * *

Let us assume that the lawyer has taken the case on a one-third contingent basis, which is typical. If plaintiff's injury was not very serious—assume he sustained soft tissue injuries with modest special damages—we might have a verdict of $4,500. This would certainly be in the low range of cases that would be thought worth trying to a jury verdict. On such a verdict, the lawyer would receive a fee of $1,500, which, divided by his 30 hours of effort, results in compensation at the rate of $50 per hour. I think the regular hourly rates of most lawyers do not exceed this amount. A $3,000 verdict would result in a fee of $33 per hour, an amount that would not be satisfactory compensation, but that would probably cover the lawyer's overhead.

Consider what happens as we go up the scale. A $15,000 verdict results in a $5,000 fee, which, divided by 30 hours, comes to $166 per hour. On a $45,000 verdict, the $15,000 fee compensates the attorney at a rate of $500 per hour.

g. 2 Litigation 20 (Summer, 1976). Copyright © 1976 by the American Bar Association. Reprinted by permission. The authors note that attorneys' fees have in-creased substantially since 1976, when the article was published. The points Grady makes, however, remain valid today.

What causes me to question the propriety of the ever-increasing fee in proportion to the size of the verdict is this: there is little, if any, relationship between the efforts of the lawyer and the size of the verdict, once we assume a verdict in favor of the plaintiff. The size of the verdict is determined by the nature and extent of the plaintiff's injury and resulting damages. Conceding that some lawyers are more brilliant and more eloquent than others, we flatter ourselves unduly if we think the performance of counsel is a large factor in the size of the verdict. Juries award money to compensate for injuries, and, as a general rule, the worse the injury the larger the verdict. To illustrate the point, the identical collision can cause a whiplash injury or result in an amputation of a leg. No more work is required to develop the medical aspects of an amputation case than is involved in a whiplash case. In fact, considering the skepticism that many people have about soft tissue injuries, the amputation case will probably take less persuasive ability. But even though the same amount of work is involved, the whiplash verdict might be $4,500, for a fee of $50 per hour, while the amputation verdict might be $200,000, providing a fee of more than $6,000 per hour.[h]

* * *

Another fortuitous circumstance affecting the fee is the number of claimants the lawyer represents in a particular case. Assume that a father, mother and two children are struck at an intersection and all of them sustain injuries. The liability evidence is the same for all. Frequently, they will have the same doctor, who simply brings four sets of records to court instead of one. His testimony takes longer, and I admit that there is some additional work required of the lawyer. However, in the typical case of four plaintiffs, the additional work is not at all proportionate to the additional fees the lawyer will realize when he charges each of the plaintiffs the same percentage, which—make no mistake about it—is what he ordinarily does.

* * *

Neither is there any appreciable difference in the amount of work each side must do in preparing and trying the case. Sometimes the defense lawyer actually does more work, since he has an insurance company to satisfy and frequently has to spend time writing formal reports to the company. In general, however, he will spend the same 30 hours in preparing and trying the simple accident case that the plaintiff's attorney will spend.

Assume the verdict comes in at $45,000. The plaintiff's attorney would receive a fee of $15,000 for his 30 hours of work. The attorney retained by the insurance company invariably charges on a time basis, with perhaps some allowance made for a good result. In the Chicago

---

h. Our calculations show that the attorney's fee in such a case would be $2,200 per hour, not the $6,000 reported in the article. We arrive at our conclusion as follows: $200,000 verdict, multiplied by .33 (the contingency fee) = $66,000. That sum divided by 30 (the number of hours worked by the attorney) yields an hourly rate of $2,200.

area, very few insurance defense attorneys charge more than $50 an hour for time prior to trial or more than $500 a day for trial. These ceilings exist because there is intense competition for insurance company business, and the companies know what they have to pay to engage competent counsel. In other words, on the defense side we have the two factors that are usually lacking on the plaintiff's side: a sophisticated client and price competition among the available attorneys. The result is that, for the case involving the $45,000 verdict, a defense attorney would probably receive a maximum fee of $2,500 [sic] (15 hours trial preparation at $50 an hour, plus three days on trial at $500 a day). So, for trying the same case, the plaintiff's attorney receives a fee that is more than six times that received by the defense attorney.

* * *

Thus far, I have been raising questions about the propriety of the fees charged in cases tried to verdict. As we all know, however, very few personal injury cases are actually tried to verdict. Roughly 90 percent of the cases filed are settled before trial commences. Thus, in 90 percent of the simple accident cases, the lawyer will spend no more than 15 hours of his time. The ethical questions presented in the settled cases are, I think, even more serious than those presented by the cases which are tried. In the case of the $45,000 settlement, for example, how can a $15,000 fee be justified? Such a fee amounts to $1,000 an hour, assuming the lawyer has completed his trial preparation and settles just as the trial is about to start. But it might not happen that way. The case may be settled before suit is even filed, or shortly after it is filed, or midway through discovery. In any of those situations (and, again, confining ourselves to the simple automobile accident case), the lawyer will spend less than 15 hours.

* * *

I now turn to the subject of why we have the percentage fee system in the first place. What justification is there for a lawyer charging a percentage of the verdict or settlement? The usual justification is that, since the fee is contingent, or uncertain, and the lawyer is taking a chance of receiving no fee at all, it is equitable to compensate him at a higher rate than if his compensation were certain. This willingness on the part of the lawyer to limit his source of compensation to the proceeds of any recovery is said to be salutary, since it enables persons who lack the funds for legal fees to obtain competent counsel. Thus, the system works to the advantage of the injured plaintiff.

It all sounds so reasonable. Surely there is much to be said for providing a means to permit indigent persons to engage counsel to press meritorious suits. There is no doubt that the contingent fee has made possible many suits that could not otherwise have been brought. But while one may approve the basic concept of contingent fees—and I do— one can still question how the concept is applied. The problem, it seems to me, is that we have regarded the "one-third contingent fee" arrangement as applicable to all cases involving personal injuries, without paying enough attention to the facts of the particular case and the needs of the particular client. Permit me to explain.

* * *

The vast majority of personal injury cases involve no uncertainty that the lawyer is going to be paid something. The only question is how much. Thus, the question is whether a mere uncertainty about the amount of compensation justifies a lawyer taking a large percentage of the recovery, such as one-third or one-fourth. Assume, for instance, the good liability case where the admitted special damages exceed the policy limit and the defendant has no assets worth pursuing. The only uncertainty here is whether the case will be settled for the full policy limit or at a discount of, say, 10 percent. The company may hold back payment for a vexatious length of time, but the case will never be tried because the company does not want to spend money on a loser and, in addition, cannot risk being held liable for an excess verdict on a negligence or bad faith theory. Such situations occur frequently and they usually involve policy limits of $10,000. How can a lawyer justify a fee of $3,300 or even $2,500 in such a situation? I submit that he cannot but I know that such fees are routinely charged.

One sometimes hears the argument that the attorney is entitled to collect his "third" in easy cases to make up for all the "losers" he handles. This explanation does not withstand analysis. Putting aside for a moment the question of whether one client can properly be surcharged to compensate for the deficiencies in another client's case, the fact of the matter is that there just are not very many "losers." As we have seen, at least 95 percent of the total claims handled by lawyers are settled before trial, and many of these settlements involve very little work on the part of the lawyer.

* * *

I think we must start determining our fee charges in personal injury cases on the same basis we determine fees in any other kind of litigation. We cannot continue with the unthinking assumption that every injured plaintiff should be charged one-third, or even that he is necessarily charged on a percentage basis at all.

Specifically, I think the lawyer must consider at least these three questions in each case:

1. Is there a genuine and substantial question on liability, or is the only real question the amount of damages?

2. Is the case likely to be settled or tried to verdict?

3. Is the amount of the recovery likely to be small or large—for example, is it a soft tissue injury or does it involve the death of the family breadwinner?

Until the lawyer knows the answers to these questions, he has insufficient basis for determining whether a percentage fee is proper and, if proper, what percentage would be fair.

—————

The agreement between Jessica and Kim provides that the client remains liable in all events for the costs and expenses incurred, including filing fees, photocopying costs, deposition fees, etc. Jessica should specifically advise Kim of her overall economic exposure. Why? Why should the lawyer insist upon burdening the client with these costs? May the lawyer advance these costs? Suppose there is no real prospect of reimbursement other than out of the recovery proceeds, if any? May the payment of expenses be contingent on the outcome?

The client should also be informed of the lawyer's role in the future conduct of the case. Specifically, the client should be advised that the lawyer retains some responsibility for decisions concerning the theory of the case, the court system in which suit is instituted, and the timing of negotiations. The client retains the ultimate right to choose whether to sue a particular defendant and whether to accept or reject a settlement offer. The client's decision should be informed. The lawyer must provide sufficient background information to enable the client to make an informed judgment. The American Bar Association Standards designate the respective roles of lawyers and client with respect to the control and direction of litigation[i] as follows:

Standard 4–5.2   Control and Direction of the Case

(a) Certain decisions relating to the conduct of the case are ultimately for the accused and others are ultimately for defense counsel. The decisions which are to be made by the accused after full consultation with counsel are: (i) what pleas to enter; (ii) whether to waive jury trial; and (iii) whether to testify in his or her own behalf.

(b) The decisions on what witnesses to call, whether and how to conduct cross-examination, what jurors to accept or strike, what trial motions should be made, and all other strategic and tactical decisions are the exclusive province of the lawyer after consultation with the client.

(c) If a disagreement on significant matters of tactics or strategy arises between the lawyer and the client, the lawyer should make a record of the circumstances, the lawyer's advice and reasons, and the conclusion reached. The record should be made in a manner which protects the confidentiality of the lawyer-client relationship.

Does the standard represent an utopian dream? Can an unsophisticated client truly make "informed" decisions? Will lawyers really take

i. The following ethical standard applies to criminal cases; it appears that the principles would be followed in civil cases.

the time to supply enough details for an informed decision? Will the lawyer's presentation be sufficiently objective to enhance the prospects of an informed decision by the client?

New Rule 1.0(e) of the ABA Model Rules of Professional Conduct provides as follows: " 'Informed consent' denotes the agreement by a person to a proposed course of conduct after the lawyer has communicated adequate information and explanation about the material risks of and reasonably available alternatives to the proposed course of conduct." Comment 6 clarifies the standards for determining what disclosures the lawyer must make to the client:

Informed Consent

Many of the Rules of Professional Conduct require the lawyer to obtain the informed consent of a client or other person (e.g., a former client or, under certain circumstances, a prospective client) before accepting or continuing representation or pursuing a course of conduct. See, e.g., Rules 1.2(c), 1.6(a) and 1.7(b). The communication necessary to obtain such consent will vary according to the Rule involved and the circumstances giving rise to the need to obtain informed consent. The lawyer must make reasonable efforts to ensure that the client or other person possesses information reasonably adequate to make an informed decision. Ordinarily, this will require communication that includes a disclosure of the facts and circumstances giving rise to the situation, any explanation reasonably necessary to inform the client or other person of the material advantages and disadvantages of the proposed course of conduct and a discussion of the client's or other person's options and alternatives. In some circumstances it may be appropriate for a lawyer to advise a client or other person to seek the advice of other counsel. A lawyer need not inform a client or other person of facts or implications already known to the client or other person; nevertheless, a lawyer who does not personally inform the client or other person assumes the risk that the client or other person is inadequately informed and the consent is invalid. In determining whether the information and explanation provided are reasonably adequate, relevant factors include whether the client or other person is experienced in legal matters generally and in making decisions of the type involved, and whether the client or other person is independently represented by other counsel in giving the consent. Normally, such persons need less information and explanation than others, and generally a client or other person who is independently represented by other counsel in giving the consent should be assumed to have given informed consent.

G. ANALYSIS OF THE CASE

Jessica must now identify the relevant legal principles and apply those principles to the facts of the case. She may also wish to interview prospective witnesses before the suit is filed, in order to solidify the facts before too much time lapses and before they are interviewed by adverse parties. Why? Is it important in Kim's case, where each of the known witnesses has already given a written statement? In your opinion, is there anything questionable or unseemly about witness interviews? May Jessica also interview John and Curt? Are there different considerations involved in interviewing prospective defendants as opposed to mere witnesses?

1. IDENTIFYING LEGAL PRINCIPLES

Some cases present novel questions of law. Most of the legal questions of liability in Kim's case, however, are routine. All states allow a civil remedy against a negligent motorist. Jessica knows that the law of Nevada would apply to determine the rights and duties of the drivers involved. Why? The more difficult issue is not one of law, but whether either of the prospective defendants was in fact negligent. Jessica knows enough about juries to conclude that if she sues both John and Curt in the same suit, the jury will probably find against one or both. On the other hand, if she is forced to bring separate lawsuits against John and Curt she may as a practical matter lose both, each jury believing that the fault lies exclusively with the non-named defendant. Jessica requests one of her law clerks to research the following points of Nevada law:

a) Does Nevada have what is commonly referred to as a guest statute—that is, a statute that restricts suits by passengers or "guests" against the "host" or driver of the car? After researching Nevada statutes, the clerk concludes that there is no guest statute.[j]

b) Does Nevada have a dramshop law that might render the owner of a bar liable for any motor vehicle injuries resulting from the consumption of alcoholic beverages on the premises? Research does not uncover a dramshop law, so Jessica does not pursue further investigation along these lines.

c) What is the status of the admissibility of the GCI (blood alcohol) test and the inference or presumption arising from a reading of .09? Does Nevada law control on this issue if the suit is brought in another state? Jessica believes that questions of evidence are determined by the law of the forum—that is, the state where the suit is instituted. How important are these evidence questions in selecting the place where suit is brought? Are these legitimate considerations?

d) Does Nevada statutory or common law make any of the activities of the parties negligence as a matter of law? In other words, is the failure to yield during a left turn negligence as a matter of law? If so, John cannot exculpate himself by attempting to show reasonable behavior under the circumstances. Does any of this matter?

---

j. Jessica knows the law of Arizona on most of these points. If the laws of Arizona and Nevada differ on any issue she will have to research which law applies. This inquiry entails identifying the forum in which the suit is instituted. *See infra* Chapter III, exercise III.

e) How does Nevada law allocate responsibility for compensating injury when two or more persons are responsible for causing the injury? If Nevada law follows the common law rule of joint and several liability, each wrongdoer is individually liable for the total judgment. Although the plaintiff cannot recover more than the total amount of her judgment, she can allocate the liability among jointly and severally liable defendants in any proportion she chooses. Thus, Kim could recover the total amount of her loss either from Curt or from John. Joint and several liability has the advantage of affording an injured plaintiff a full recovery. Opponents of joint and several liability feel that it operates unfairly in cases in which the largely responsible defendant is indigent but a minor actor has a "deep pocket."

If Nevada follows the rule of several liability, then each wrongdoer is responsible to pay only for the portion of the injury that he caused. Thus, to recover the full amount of her loss, Kim would probably have to sue both John and Curt. The jury (or the judge in a trial to the bench) decides the percentage of fault of each defendant, and each is then responsible to pay that portion of the judgment. Kim knows that Arizona has adopted a comparative fault statute. Would it apply in a suit brought in Arizona?

f) Kim confided to Jessica that she did not have the seat belt fastened prior to the accident. Does Nevada law permit or even require a finding of contributory negligence on her part? Would a finding of contributory negligence preclude recovery against John or Curt? In other words, has Nevada adopted the comparative negligence[k] doctrine or does it still bar any recovery for plaintiffs who were contributorily negligent?

Other legal issues will emerge during the lawsuit, some involving the merits of the suit, others dealing with peripheral matters. Jessica need not necessarily identify and resolve these other legal questions at this time.

2. IDENTIFYING THE SALIENT FACTS

The ultimate factual question on the liability issue concerns fault. Was anyone at fault in causing the accident? From the witness statements in the police reports, the accident reconstruction expert's report, and her discussions with Kim, Jessica is in command of the basic facts underlying the accident. She therefore decides not to interview any witnesses, but rather to concentrate on drafting a complaint. Before filing the complaint, Jessica must choose the proper court system and prepare the legal papers necessary to commence the lawsuit. But first she explores the feasibility of settlement.

k. Comparative negligence operates to reduce recovery in the proportion plaintiff's negligence bears to the defendants' negligence. The plaintiff's negligence does not bar all recovery, as it would under the contributory negligence doctrine.

H. NEGOTIATION

Most disputes are resolved without legal action.[1] Others are resolved only through the catalysis of the lawsuit. Jessica must decide whether to attempt to settle the matter at this stage. This involves identifying the insurers and deciding whether to give the defendants and their respective insurers advance notice of the impending lawsuit. What factors would you consider in making this decision? Can you think of any reason that would negatively dispose you toward negotiation at this time?

Jessica decides to contact the insurance companies directly. Curt's insurer brusquely turns down any request in excess of reimbursement of medical expenses. It appears that Curt has a policy that provides medical payment up to $15,000 regardless of fault. May Jessica obtain these funds and reserve Kim's right to sue for additional amounts? May the insurer refuse to make medical payments unless it obtains a release by Kim of any other claim against Curt?

John's insurance company is even more intractable. It asserts a complete defense based upon the "alcohol" exclusion clause. By this action, has the insurance company already prejudiced John in his defense of any forthcoming legal action? The company also reports that John had not paid his semi-annual premium when it was due, one month before the accident. The company returned the premium check tendered by John a few days after the accident. What additional problems do you see?

A favorable settlement appearing unlikely, Jessica now must decide whether to bring suit and where. The question of whether to sue may only be answered by Kim. Kim abides by Jessica's suggestion to sue both John and Curt. Curt has already been advised by Kim of the "friendly" nature of the suit against him and seems resigned, although he is concerned that the suit may affect future premium rates. Can Jessica properly advise him on how he should proceed in the event of a threatened premium increase?

I. ALTERNATIVE DISPUTE RESOLUTION

As already noted, most legal problems are resolved through negotiation. This is particularly true for commercial and contractual disputes. Negotiation permits the parties to control the process without the intervention of third parties. Where negotiation is not feasible or has already failed, however, the parties may involve a third party to assist in resolving the impasse. Mediation is the term that has been used for one form of third-party assistance in arriving at a resolution. The mediator may control the process, but has no power to impose a solution. Arbitration, on the other hand, is a method of adjudication that grants the arbitrator or arbitration panel the right to impose a solution. These three basic methods–negotiation, mediation and arbitration–are sometimes combined with other elements of dispute resolution to accommo-

---

1. During the past decade, many people have resolved disputes outside the confines of the traditional court system. *See* Section I, *infra*.

date the needs of complex cases and the parties' desire for a just and inexpensive resolution to legal disputes.

To avoid costly and time-consuming litigation, parties may insert arbitration clauses in their contracts. At one time, courts disfavored these provisions on the ground that they infringed on the jurisdiction of the courts. As such, they were held void and unenforceable. Since the enactment of the Federal Arbitration Act in the 1920s, however, the tide has slowly turned so that today these provisions are readily enforced. Indeed, the provisions of the Act extend to all contracts affecting commerce and, subject to limited exceptions, state courts, like their federal counterparts, are bound to enforce these arbitration clauses.

The arbitrability of federal statutory claims is also well established. For example, despite arguments that several of these statutes contained provisions that should have rendered the arbitration agreement void, the Supreme Court has enforced arbitration clauses in securities, anti-trust, and racketeering litigation. Of course, there are valid reasons why a court will not enforce an arbitration clause as, for example, where the clause had been incorporated into the agreement as a result of fraud or overreaching. The Supreme Court has enthusiastically embraced provisions that divest the federal courts of jurisdiction in deference to other judicial fora. The Court has reasoned that "[t]he expansion of American business and industry will hardly be encouraged if, notwithstanding solemn contracts, we insist on a parochial concept that all disputes must be resolved under our laws and in our courts." *Bremen v. Zapata Off-Shore Co.*, 407 U.S. 1, 15 (1972). It acknowledged the reality that disallowing methods of adjudication chosen by the parties "reflects something of a provincial attitude regarding the fairness of other tribunals" "in an era when all courts are overloaded and when businesses once essentially local now operate in world markets." *Id.* at 12. The *Bremen* reasoning and principles apply to all methods of conflict resolution outside the traditional court system, including arbitration. Indeed the use of these nontraditional means has exploded in the past thirty years and, given the expense and delay of traditional litigation, will undoubtedly continue to expand.

J. SELECTING THE COURT SYSTEM

1. JURISDICTION

Jessica must now determine the forum—that is, the court system in which the action will be commenced. She would like to choose a court, state or federal, that may properly adjudicate the case against both John and Curt. She does not want to be placed in the unenviable position of having to bring two separate lawsuits.[m] It would be too costly and might result in what lawyers refer to as "inconsistent verdicts": (1) each jury might find in favor of the named defendant by placing the blame on the absent defendant, or (2) in jurisdictions that have "several liability," the

---

m. Can you think of any reasons favoring the institution of separate suits?

jury might assess the percentage of liability very differently, each time benefitting the named defendant.

Jessica must identify the fora that have "jurisdiction" over the subject matter as well as over each defendant. If either subject matter or personal jurisdiction is lacking or the court lacks venue, the case may be dismissed, and she would have to file a new lawsuit in a court system that has both subject matter and personal jurisdiction and where proper venue lies. This entails additional time and expense. It may even jeopardize her client's chances of ever being heard on the merits.

A court system has subject matter jurisdiction of the case or controversy when the constitution and statutes have conferred upon the judiciary the right to hear that class of cases. All states have courts of general jurisdiction, and the presumption is that they have jurisdiction over a particular class of cases, unless a contrary showing is made. As noted, the contrary showing may be demonstrated by resort to state laws. Federal laws must also be analyzed for their effect on jurisdiction. Congress may withdraw classes of cases from the cognizance of the state judiciary. In Kim's case, state courts of general jurisdiction may hear this routine negligence case. For reasons unrelated to subject matter jurisdiction, Jessica narrows her choices to the state courts of California, Nevada, and Arizona.

Before discussing personal jurisdiction and venue in the state court system, a slight digression regarding the subject matter jurisdiction of the federal courts is appropriate. It is a cardinal principle that federal courts are courts of limited jurisdiction. They are empowered to hear only those cases and controversies that fall within the judicial power defined in the Constitution and that have been entrusted to them by Congress through a jurisdictional grant. This principle has a number of corollaries. First, unlike state courts of general jurisdiction, federal courts presumptively lack subject matter jurisdiction until a contrary demonstration is made. Second, subject matter jurisdiction may not be conferred by consent of the parties. The defect may even be raised for the first time on appeal. Most procedural defects are waived by the parties if not raised in a proper and timely fashion in accordance with the provisions of the applicable rules of civil procedure. Not so with subject matter jurisdiction defects: "Whenever it appears by suggestion of the parties or otherwise that the court lacks jurisdiction of the subject matter the court shall dismiss the actions."[n] Extreme care must be exercised before filing suit in the federal system.

Most lawsuits brought in the federal system either arise under the federal law or involve controversies between citizens of different states in which at least $75,000 is at issue. This automobile negligence case arises under the laws of the State of Nevada, not under federal law. Yet it does involve a dispute between citizens of Arizona and California. Does that satisfy the diversity requirement? Many years ago, Chief Justice Marshall announced the doctrine of "complete diversity." No plaintiff

n.   Fed. R. Civ. P. 12(h)(3).

may be a citizen of the same state as any named defendant. Because Kim, a citizen of Arizona, will name John and Curt, citizens of California and Arizona respectively, as defendants, the complete diversity doctrine has not been satisfied. Jessica could elect to sue only John and meet the diversity requirements, but for reasons previously mentioned, she has decided to sue both defendants in the same action. If Jessica joins Curt, the federal courts will not have subject matter jurisdiction of the automobile accident lawsuit; consequently Jessica turns to identifying the appropriate state forum.

As previously noted, in addition to subject matter jurisdiction, the court must also have jurisdiction over the person. Do not confuse these different kinds of jurisdiction. Jurisdiction over the person is a waivable defect—that is, a defendant must assert the objection in a proper and timely fashion in order to preserve it.

Jurisdiction over the person refers to the power of a court to require the defendant to defend the lawsuit or suffer the consequences of a default judgment. Keep in mind that a money judgment, whether entered after a full trial or upon default, may be enforced not only in the rendering state but in other states as well.

In the formative years of our country, jurisdiction over the person was equated with the power of the court to seize the defendant within the territory. Although actual arrest eventually gave way to the summons (a constructive arrest), jurisdiction over the person still focused on territorial concepts relating to seizure of the defendant. Seizure of the defendant has given way to the service upon the defendant of notice of the pendency of the lawsuit. Concepts of jurisdiction over the person born in an era of arrests have matured into quite a different concern— the fairness of subjecting the defendant to the adjudicatory powers of a particular court system. While territorial limitations are not totally discarded, jurisdiction over the person now focuses on the fairness of subjecting a defendant to a lawsuit in the particular forum. Chapter III contains an extended discussion of the judicial decisions in this area.

Jessica has mastered the materials relating to subject matter and personal jurisdiction. She knows that while California has personal jurisdiction over its citizen, John, it probably cannot obtain jurisdiction over Curt. She reaches the latter conclusion knowing that Curt neither lives in nor has contacts with California that would make it reasonable or fair for California to assert jurisdiction over him. May she bring the suit there anticipating that Curt will waive the defense of lack of personal jurisdiction? Would such a waiver, if made, have consequences for Curt under his insurance policy? If so, would it have consequences for Kim? Jessica believes it is wise not to file suit in the courts of California.

Because the accident occurred in Nevada, the Nevada nonresident motorist statute, reprinted below, permits the assertion of jurisdiction over both Curt and John.

The use and operation of a motor vehicle over the public roads, streets or highways, or in any other area open to the public and commonly used by motor vehicles, in the State of Nevada by any person, either as principal, master, agent or servant, shall be deemed an appointment by the operator, on behalf of himself and his principal or master, his executor, administrator or personal representative, of the director of the department of motor vehicles and public safety to be his true and lawful attorney upon whom may be served all legal process in any action or proceeding against him, his principal or master, his executor, administrator or personal representative, growing out of such use or resulting in damage or loss to person or property, and the use or operation signifies his agreement that any such process against him which is so served has the same legal force and validity as though served upon him personally within the State of Nevada.

Nev. Rev. Stat. § 14.070(1) (1998).

———

Should the suit be instituted in Nevada, however, Jessica might be compelled to associate with local counsel. Why? Moreover, the forum would not be convenient for Kim. Suing in Nevada might make it difficult to obtain the live testimony of the two Arizona witnesses. Would this difficulty be advantageous or disadvantageous for Kim? Note that the witnesses testimony may be taken before trial by a device called a deposition. Depositions are commonly recorded stenographically; the witness is placed under oath and the lawyer questions the witness much as would occur at a trial. One major difference is that there is no judge present during the deposition to rule on objections. If a witness is unavailable to testify at trial, the deposition may be read to the jury, subject to the court's ruling on objections. Are there any differences in impact upon the jury between listening to live testimony in open court and deposition testimony?

Jessica prefers to bring the suit in Arizona.

She recalls from the police report that John listed "rodeo rider" as his occupation. She calls an acquaintance in the rodeo business to learn more. She hits paydirt. It appears that John rides the rodeo circuit and is registered to participate in several events in a major Arizona rodeo within the next month.

Jessica researches the law to determine whether the Arizona judicial system may assert jurisdiction over a defendant who visits the state. She knows that 100 years ago there would have been no problem in asserting jurisdiction on the basis of mere physical presence. Later cases cast some doubt on that rule. Upon researching the law, however, Jessica decides there is a good chance that the state courts of Arizona may properly assert personal jurisdiction over John. *See infra* Chapter III, Section B.

Because John may be uninsured, Jessica would like to be able to seize any of John's assets in the State of Arizona. Although seizure, also known as attachment or garnishment, no longer provides a basis of jurisdiction (*see infra* Chapter III, Section B), it would provide leverage for settlement and guarantee the existence of property in Arizona should Kim obtain a favorable judgment. Are there any ethical considerations in tying up a person's property? His wages? His means of subsistence? An Arizona statute, reprinted below, permits seizure of property as a security measure in some cases.° Is Kim's case included in the statutory description?

A plaintiff * * * may in the following cases have the property of the defendant attached as security for satisfaction of any judgment which may be recovered, unless the defendant gives security to pay such judgment:

1. In an action upon a contract, express or implied, for payment of money which is not fully secured by real or personal property, or, if originally so secured, the value of such security has, without any act of the plaintiff or the person to whom the security was given, substantially diminished below the balance owed.

2. When an action is pending for damages and the defendant is about to dispose of or remove his property beyond the jurisdiction of the court in which the action is pending.

3. In an action for damages or upon contract, express or implied, against a defendant not residing in this state or a foreign corporation doing business in this state.

* * *

Ariz. Rev. Stat. § 12–1521 (1994).

2. VENUE

Another question Jessica must resolve before filing the action concerns venue—that is, in which particular court within the state court system may the action be brought? Each county in Arizona has its own court of "general jurisdiction" known as the superior court. Venue restrictions limit the choice of court to the one or ones that have some statutorily relevant connection with the case. Which provisions of the Arizona venue statute, reprinted below, would be relevant to Jessica's inquiry?

No person shall be sued out of the county in which such person resides, except:

1. When a defendant or all of several defendants reside without the state or their residence is unknown, the action may be brought in the county in which the plaintiff resides.

* * *

o. Note that Arizona, not Nevada, law would apply. The state law must always meet federal constitutional limitations. *See infra* Chapter III, Section B.

3. Transient persons may be sued in any county in which found.

4. Persons who have contracted a debt or obligation in one county and thereafter remove to another county may be sued in either county.

* * *

6. Persons who have contracted a debt or obligation without the state may be sued in any county in which found.

7. When there are several defendants residing in different counties, action may be brought in the county in which any of the defendants reside.

* * *

10. When the foundation of the action is a crime, offense or trespass for which an action in damages may lie, the action may be brought in the county in which the crime, offense or trespass was committed or in the county in which the defendant or any of the several defendants reside or may be found. . . .

* * *

Ariz. Rev. Stat. § 12–401 (1994).

K. PLEADINGS AND PRETRIAL MOTIONS

1. THE COMPLAINT

Now that Jessica has chosen the court in which to bring suit, the Superior Court of Arizona in Maricopa County,[p] she prepares a complaint. A complaint is a legal document setting forth the basis of the suit against the defendants. Much of the content of the complaint is dictated by the procedural rules of the state. There is latitude, however, for some originality. Drafting a complaint is an art, not a science.

How much information should Jessica include in the complaint? At one pole, Kim might summarily assert that the defendants owe her a sum of money, without including any specifics in the complaint. At the other pole, the complaint could set forth in detail every item of evidence that may be introduced at trial, together with a detailed statement of statutes, rules, and cases relied upon. Obviously, no sensible procedural system would adopt either of these extremes.

Historically, court systems have differed on the specificity required in a complaint. The degree of detail required by a jurisdiction generally depends upon the purposes intended to be served by the complaint. In some jurisdictions, the purpose of the pleadings is to identify the legal and factual contentions and disclose what the party intends to show at trial. In these jurisdictions Jessica would allege, for example, that John

---

p. Curt lives in Maricopa County; the rodeo will take place in Maricopa County.

owned and operated the vehicle in question, that he was inebriated, that he failed to yield to an oncoming vehicle, and that Curt went through a yellow (or red) light. She might also allege that John or Curt or both failed to proceed reasonably under the circumstances. A more modern objective of pleadings, adopted by the federal courts and many state systems, including Arizona's, is to give the adversary general notice of the claims and defenses. Specificity of the charge is not required. Jessica drafts the complaint to fulfill the notice pleading purpose.

The complaint follows the approved form for similar cases. After alleging the basis of jurisdiction, the complaint recites that Curt Baker or John Roscoe or both "willfully or recklessly or negligently drove or caused to be driven motor vehicles in such a manner as to cause injury to Plaintiff Kim Johnson, a passenger in the vehicle operated by Curt Baker." The complaint further alleges that as a result of the foregoing incident the plaintiff was injured, received lacerations and scars, was prevented from working, and had incurred and would continue to incur expenses for medical attention and hospitalization in the sum of $8,500. The *ad damnum* or "damages" clause requests judgment in the sum of $75,000.

Later stages of the lawsuit will develop the more detailed factual and legal contentions that other jurisdictions require to be asserted at the pleading stage. Can you identify some advantages of the modern system? Some disadvantages? Does the modern system encourage an attorney to file a complaint without giving much thought to the legal consequences? Would it be preferable to return to a more detailed statement of the case? How would a plaintiff know these details before instituting the suit? If a plaintiff pleads with specificity, are there any consequences for failing to prove the specific allegations of the complaint? Would it be fair to penalize a litigant if the facts established at trial differed from the allegations of the complaint?

When the complaint is filed with the court, the clerk of the court issues a summons. Statutes and rules provide the method of service of the summons and complaint upon the defendant. The body of the following summons is a standard form designed to bring the suit to the defendant's attention. What else does the summons accomplish?

YOU ARE HEREBY SUMMONED and required to appear and defend, within the time applicable, in this action in this Court. If served within Arizona, you shall appear and defend within 20 days after the service of the Summons and Complaint upon you, exclusive of the day of service. If served out of the State of Arizona— whether by direct service, by registered or certified mail, or by publication—you shall appear and defend within 30 days after the service of the Summons and Complaint upon you is complete, exclusive of the day of service. Service by registered or certified mail without the State of Arizona is complete 30 days after the date of filing the receipt and affidavit of service with the Court. Service by publication is complete 30 days after the date of first publication. Direct service is complete when made. * * *

YOU ARE HEREBY NOTIFIED that in case of your failure to appear and defend within the time applicable, judgment by default may be rendered against you for the relief demanded in the Complaint.

YOU ARE CAUTIONED that in order to appear and defend, you must file a proper response in writing with the Clerk of this Court, accompanied by the necessary filing fee, within the time required. You are required to serve a copy of any response upon Plaintiff's attorney.

Once served, the process server files in the court a document called the return or affidavit of service. This document indicates the method of service and provides a court record of the fact of service. After service it is incumbent upon the defendant to respond to the lawsuit within the period designated in the summons.

2. THE DEFENDANTS' RESPONSES

The defendants and their insurers anticipated the action, so it came as no surprise when service of the complaint was made upon Curt. The service upon John, however, presented a different situation. *See infra* pp. 209–18.

Indeed, in many cases, attorneys agree in advance to accept service on behalf of their clients. This consent reduces the cost of service that will ultimately be borne by the losing party to the litigation. Incidentally, this method also avoids embarrassment to the defendant. The most common method of service today is personal service of a summons and complaint upon the defendant, although courts have accepted other less expensive methods of service. There are rather amusing anecdotes involving attempts to evade service. Consider the following article:

PROFILES—PLACE AND LEAVE WITH[q]

St. Clair McKelway

* * * In a little frame house near the intersection of Rogers and Flatbush Avenues in Brooklyn there lived until a few years ago an old lady named Mrs. Katherina Schnible. She was seventy-two and a little lame. She owned the house and rented out the first two floors as apartments, but there were mortgages and she had not met the payments. She knew the bank that held the mortgages was about to foreclose * * *. Her son, who lived with her, went out to work at eight in the morning and did not return until six, so from eight till six every day, except Sunday, Mrs. Schnible stayed in her room on the third floor and refused to open the door, no matter who knocked. Came a day when she heard a heavy footfall on the first landing, heard somebody running frantically up the first flight of stairs, heard a man's voice shouting something. Then the footsteps came closer, up the second flight of stairs, and right outside her door she heard yelled the word "Fire!" Mrs. Schnible opened her door and hobbled hurriedly into the hall. "Hello,

q. Copyright 1935 by St. Clair McKelway. Reprinted from McKelway, *True Tales From the Annals of Crime and Rascality*, The New Yorker, Aug. 24, 1935, at 23–26. Reprinted by permission of Random House, Inc.

Mrs. Schnible,'' said a man standing there. ''Here's a summons for you.'' He handed her the papers, and the proceedings were begun which eventually put Mrs. Schnible out of her house.

Harry Grossman, who was the man in the hall, is regarded by those who employ him as the champion process-server of the day. He is an instrument of justice and his profession is a corner-stone of civil law, but not many of the people he serves appreciate that. * * * Grossman has been cursed by hundreds of defendants, many of them distinguished citizens. Defendants have thrown him down flights of stairs and shoved him off porches. He has been pinched, slapped, punched, and kicked by scores of individuals, and he was beaten up one time by a family of seven.

* * *

''Place and leave with'' is the legal phrase for what a process-server must do with a summons when he goes out to serve papers on a defendant, but the courts never have explained precisely what that means. Where the process-server must place the papers is still a nice legal question. A process-server once threw a summons-and-complaint at James Gordon Bennett and hit him in the chest with it, but the courts held that this was not a proper service. Another famous case in the lawbooks tells of a defendant named Martin, who in 1893 hid himself under his wife's petticoats and refused to receive the papers. The process-server saw him crouching there, so he put the papers on what seemed to be the defendant's shoulder, and went away. The Supreme Court rendered a decision which held that ''where a person, to avoid service of summons, shelters himself in his wife's petticoats, the laying of the papers on his shoulder will be a sufficient service.''

* * *

Tens of thousands of papers have to be served in the course of a year in this city, and the majority of them are handled for the law firms by process-serving agencies, which rely for their profits on quantity and a quick turnover. * * * Cases involving expert dodgers or stubborn hug-the-hearths usually are turned over to private detective agencies, and the detective agencies usually hire Grossman to serve the papers. When the Electrical Research Product Institute sued the Fox Film Corporation for $15,000,000 in 1930, the lawyers for the plaintiff, naturally, surmised that it would be difficult to ''place and leave with'' William Fox, Winfield Sheehan, and other defendants, the papers summoning them to come to court. Grossman received the assignment through a detective agency. He got in to see Fox by having a telegram sent from Boston saying that Mr. Grossman had ''closed the theatre deal'' and would call on Fox at eleven o'clock the next morning. When Grossman reached Fox's office, the film executive's secretary told him Mr. Fox had received the wire but was not sure what deal it was that had been closed. ''My God,'' said Grossman, ''the theatre deal—that's what deal! If this is the way I am to be received, never mind—to hell with it!'' He started out, and the secretary called him back. "Just wait one moment," she said. "I'll tell Mr. Fox." She opened a door marked "Private" and went into an inner office. Grossman followed her and handed Fox the subpoena. Fox started up from his desk indignantly, but Grossman's indignation expressed itself first. "You, a multi-millionaire!" Grossman shouted. "Is it decent, is it nice, for a multi-millionaire who can be sued for fifteen million dollars to hide from me? Why don't you take the papers like a man?" This so flabbergasted Fox that he sank back in his chair, and Grossman went through the corporation's offices unimpeded and served papers on Sheehan, two vice-presidents, the secretary, and the treasurer.

* * * Harry established a reputation as an adroit private detective before he was old enough to serve subpoenas. * * * But after he had passed his eighteenth birthday and had begun to serve summonses and subpoenas, it was evident to his employer, and to everybody else who knew him, that he had found a vocation in which he might expect to excel. During his first year he served Maude Adams by posing as a youthful adorer. When she came out of the stage entrance at the Empire Theatre after a performance one evening, Grossman stepped in front of her holding in his left hand a bouquet of jonquils. "Are you Maude Adams?" he asked. "Oh, are those really for me?" she exclaimed, reaching for the flowers, "No, but this is," said Grossman, jerking back the bouquet. With his right hand he served her with a summons. He still remembers that he had paid fifty cents for the jonquils and that he was able to sell them back to the florist for twenty.

———

Curt and John did not resist service of process. Indeed Curt's insurance company agreed to accept service on his behalf. John was served with the summons and complaint when he appeared at the rodeo. John and the rodeo sponsor were also served with several court orders. These orders effected a seizure of John's property (valuable horses and any winning rodeo purses), subject to the future disposition of the court. Note the problem of obtaining prejudgment seizure orders without having first given John notice and an opportunity to contest the issuance of the orders. *See infra* Chapter III, Section C. Why should the rodeo sponsor accede to the seizure orders? What penalties might be assessed if the sponsor, in violation of an order, handed over the winning purse to John? Might the attachment and garnishment force a prompt settlement of the case? Are you disturbed by the use of this type of leverage for settlement? Suppose John takes the horses to California. What sanctions may Kim employ? Would California assist the Arizona judicial system's efforts to "punish" John?

When John was served with the summons and complaint, he immediately called his insurance company and was soon contacted by an attorney retained by the company. John inquired whether the court orders prevented him from leaving the state with his property. Can you understand why an attorney, facing a problem such as this, would hesitate to counsel the client to flout the court orders? Isn't the safest course to seek judicial relief from the attachment and garnishment orders? Yet, note the time constraints. John wants his property immediately. If the lawyer, after balancing all the considerations, incorrectly advises John that he may go to California, is he aiding and abetting a contempt of the court? Is his license to practice law in jeopardy? Can you now appreciate why lawyers take conservative approaches in advising clients?

Look at the problem from a different perspective. If the attorney counsels acquiescence to an improper order, who but the client may complain? Even if the client could have gone to California with impunity, can he hold the attorney legally responsible for poor advice?[r] For taking a more restrictive position than was required under the circumstances? Would the bar association reprimand the attorney for giving conservative advice? Whom does the attorney represent anyway? John? The insurance company? Himself? Be aware of these conflicts in practice.

Suppose John's attorney discovers facts that would release the insurer from its obligation to indemnify. May he divulge this information to the insurer? Must he? *See supra* pp. 72–74. Keep in mind that the insurer may retain the attorney in many other cases. In light of this economic reality is it possible for him to give his undivided loyalty to John? Even to the disadvantage of the insurer? Should John retain his own attorney? If so, who should pay that attorney's legal fees?

The summons specifies the number of days within which the defendant must answer the complaint or take other appropriate action. If the defendant fails to act within that time period, the plaintiff may obtain a default judgment against the defendant. Default judgments, like other judgments of the court, may entail very serious consequences. Attorneys, conscious of the consequences of default judgments, have developed office procedures to prevent inadvertent default.

At this stage of the litigation, a number of options are available to the defendant. He may consider contacting the plaintiff's attorney to negotiate an amicable settlement. Many factors enter into the decision whether and when to discuss settlement. Can you think of any?

Few attorneys avail themselves of this opportunity at an early stage of a personal injury suit. One reason for this is a belief that the plaintiff, having just prepared and filed a complaint, is riding a psychological crest. Perhaps the defendant should turn the tide, even a little, before exploring settlement. If settlement is anticipated, the defendant's goal may be to expend as little money as possible defending the case. Yet this may not always be true. Why? The defendant must, of course, consider the cost of attorneys' fees in opposing the litigation. Can you identify any reasons why a defendant would risk the potential expenditure of greater sums in defense of litigation than in acceptance of a settlement?

r. And how would he discover the advice was poor?

John's and Curt's respective attorneys decide not to negotiate at this time. The insurance companies believe that there are meritorious defenses to the lawsuit. Moreover, even if a jury finds liability the damages might be minimal in view of the nature of the injuries and the lack of residual effects other than the minor scar on Kim's face. Even though substantial sums are claimed in the complaint, the insurance companies believe they have little to lose in litigating the matter.

An issue that often arises in negligence suits is the plaintiff's offer to settle for an amount just below the insurance policy limit. The policy limit is the maximum amount for which the insurance company could be liable under the policy. The issue arises when a defendant is sued for an amount that exceeds the policy limit and, during the course of litigation, the plaintiff offers to settle for a sum less than the policy limit. In the past, an insurance company would not settle if it believed that it bore only a slight risk of a judgment in excess of the plaintiff's offer. The basis of this "gamble" was the company's assumption that any amounts awarded in excess of the policy limit would be borne by the insured, not the insurer. This assumption proved incorrect. Recent cases have held that the insured should not be primarily responsible for paying amounts in excess of the limit, if the insurer should have reasonably settled within the policy limit. Many plaintiffs' attorneys now employ the strategy of offering to settle just within the policy limit, hoping to place the insurer in a dilemma. Can you describe this dilemma? How might the insurer handle it? In Kim's case, this strategy would not be used because the amount claimed in the complaint did not approach either policy limit.

Typically, defendants consider the following defenses and strategies in responding to the complaint:

i. Objections unrelated to the substantive merits of the case. For example, John should consider objecting to the jurisdiction of the Arizona courts. He may also object to the seizure of his property.

ii. Denial of the factual contentions and disagreement with the legal rules presented in the plaintiff's complaint. Each defendant may contend that he was driving in a reasonable and prudent manner. The defendants may charge Kim with contributory or comparative negligence, which, if established, would be either a complete bar to or a partial mitigation of recovery.[s] Can you think of ways in which a passenger might be negligent? In some cases, the defendant may even deny the underlying facts, including the occurrence of an accident or the identity of the parties involved. Can you think of other substantive defenses to Kim's suit that the defendants may wish to consider?

iii. Claims against a codefendant (crossclaims) or claims against the plaintiff (counterclaims). For example, Curt may wish to interpose a crossclaim against John for personal injuries and property damage arising from the accident. John may have similar claims against Curt.

---

s. Whether it is a bar or a reduction depends upon the applicability of the com-parative negligence doctrine. *See supra* p. 94.

The legal and tactical considerations involved in deciding whether to counterclaim and crossclaim are quite technical.

Another possible basis exists for a claim between Curt and John. Certain states permit contribution among persons who are found to be jointly and severally liable to the plaintiff. *See supra* p. 94. For example, should Kim obtain a jury verdict of $100,000 against Curt and John, either defendant could satisfy the entire judgment and then seek reimbursement from the other.

iv. Disagreement regarding the extent of damages. Many personal injury cases boil down to a dispute over the amount the plaintiff requests in damages. The defendants may contend that Kim need not have missed any work and should not be compensated for her lost earnings. The defendants may further claim that Kim has not suffered any permanent injury. They may also dispute the extent of Kim's pain and suffering. The art of advocacy reaches its zenith when fine advocates present jury arguments on the extent of the plaintiff's damages.

Theoretically, the issues of liability and damages are separate and distinct. In fact, the judge will instruct the jury to consider first the question of liability. Should the defendants not be found at fault, then damage issues need not be considered or resolved. On the other hand, a finding of liability will occasion inquiry into the issue of adequate compensation for the plaintiff. Regardless of the theoretical soundness of the separation doctrine, every trial attorney recognizes the close relationship between the two issues. In an ordinary negligence action, juries may award higher damages if they find from the evidence that the defendant's conduct was not merely negligent, but reckless or intentional. Likewise, to the dismay of many plaintiffs' lawyers, a meager jury verdict, barely covering the out-of-pocket expenses, may be the product of a compromise verdict. Some jurors are just not sufficiently convinced of a defendant's liability—so the jurors compromise with a reduced damage award.

The defendant may select the manner of raising the defenses. The most common mode of asserting defenses is by setting them forth in a pleading that responds to plaintiff's complaint. In most jurisdictions this pleading is called an answer. It may admit some allegations, deny others, and affirmatively assert still other allegations and defenses.

Many jurisdictions also allow the filing of pre-answer motions. A motion is a written request to the court for specified relief. Pre-answer motions are often based on technical matters, such as lack of jurisdiction over the subject matter or the defendant. These technical matters are called "pleas in abatement" or "matters in abatement." The disposition of the plea may affect the right to proceed in a particular court, but has nothing to do with the substantive merits of the case. A victory for the defendant on these motions does not necessarily end the litigation. The plaintiff may begin anew in the proper court system if time limits and other considerations allow.

Other pre-answer motions are not technical in nature. A common motion, referred to in the federal courts as a "motion to dismiss the complaint for failure to state a claim upon which relief may be granted," tests the plaintiff's legal theory. It is premised upon the assumption that even were the facts exactly as the plaintiff alleges, the law does not give a right to relief. If the defendant is correct in this assertion, a trial would be a waste of time. Thus, the law gives the defendant a right to obtain an early adjudication without going to trial. In Kim's case, if the facts are as Kim alleges there is a cause of action, so neither defendant moves to dismiss the complaint for failure to state a claim.

On the other hand, suppose that Jessica asserted in the complaint a claim against the owner of the bar that served beer to John. In defense, the owner could deny serving any liquor to John, or alternatively, claim that if liquor were served, it was served without knowledge or reason to believe that John was drunk. But suppose that under Nevada law, there is no right to impose liability against a bar owner under any circumstances. Should the bar owner not be permitted to test the legal sufficiency of the complaint before expending time, energy, and financial resources defending the case? The procedural vehicle by which the sufficiency of the complaint may be tested is the motion to dismiss for failure to state a claim.

John has two technical defenses: lack of jurisdiction over the person and illegality of the seizure of his assets. He may decide not to raise either defense, preferring instead to go to trial on the merits of the case, or he may raise these defenses before trial either in his answer or in a pre-answer motion. The former approach is not an effective way to raise the illegal seizure of property since John wants an early disposition of the matter so that he can take the property out of Arizona. John files a motion to dismiss for lack of personal jurisdiction and to lift the seizure orders. Sections B and C of Chapter III analyze the due process implications of personal jurisdiction and seizures of property under similar circumstances. We will return to the questions raised here after analyzing those cases. Suffice it to say that each attorney should thoroughly canvass the law on the subject and present written memoranda and perhaps even oral argument to the court. The court will then decide whether to grant or deny the motions. In a course on civil procedure you will study the alternatives available to the parties after the trial court's disposition of these motions.

After reviewing John's motion and Kim's response, the court denies the motion. John's counsel then files his answer to Kim's complaint. Curt had already filed an answer. Each answer admits the occurrence of the accident in question but denies any wrongdoing.

Each answer also asserts that the plaintiff and the other defendant were negligent and reserves the right to show the proper amount of damages to the jury. Do you believe there is any factual basis for the assertion of negligence against Kim? Does the attorney have an ethical obligation to inquire into the foundation of pleadings before asserting defenses? Consider the following rule of procedure, presently in effect in the federal system. Each state has the same or similar rules designed to assure honesty in pleadings.

> Every pleading, written motion, and other paper shall be signed by at least one attorney of record in the attorney's individual name, or, if the party is not represented by an attorney, shall be signed by the party. * * *

> By presenting to the court (whether by signing, filing, submitting, or later advocating) a pleading, written motion, or other paper, an attorney or unrepresented party is certifying that to the best of the person's knowledge, information, and belief, formed after an inquiry reasonable under the circumstances,—

> > (1) it is not being presented for any improper purpose, such as to harass or to cause unnecessary delay or needless increase in the cost of litigation;

> > (2) the claims, defenses, and other legal contentions therein are warranted by existing law or by a nonfrivolous argument for the extension, modification, or reversal of existing law or the establishment of new law;

> > (3) the allegations and other factual contentions have evidentiary support or, if specifically so identified, are likely to have evidentiary support after a reasonable opportunity for further investigation or discovery; and

> > (4) the details of factual contentions are warranted on the evidence or, if specifically so identified, are reasonably based on a lack of information or belief. * * *

Fed. R. Civ. P. 11(a), (b).

By admitting that the accident caused injury, the defendants' answers narrow the scope of the dispute. The issues remaining for resolution are who is at fault, and what are the damages.

L. PRETRIAL DISCLOSURE AND DISCOVERY

The pleadings set forth the parties' basic claims. Discovery and disclosure obligations clarify the legal and factual issues for trial, such as the color of the traffic light immediately preceding the accident, whether the participants acted reasonably and prudently under the circumstances, and the extent of the damages.

In a bygone era, after the pleading stage, the parties would simply await the trial of the matter. True, parties might have interviewed and obtained statements from willing witnesses, but there was no judicial procedure for obtaining witness statements. Similarly, there were only limited means by which one party could obtain information in the possession of another party.

All this has drastically changed in civil cases. Pretrial discovery of relevant nonprivileged facts is readily accessible to any litigant desiring the information. The surprise witness—entering dramatically into the court room in a last minute attempt to save the case—is a relic of the past. This theory of justice, pejoratively labeled the "sporting theory of justice," is moribund, if not completely dead.

Modern civil procedure rules contain a panoply of discovery devices for learning the facts of the case. You will undoubtedly spend many months early in your law career learning the mechanics of discovery. They include written interrogatories to adverse parties, oral questioning under oath to party and nonparty witnesses, notices to discover documents, and orders to produce a party for a physical or mental examination. Whatever device is employed, discovery is limited to relevant, nonprivileged matters.

These information-gathering techniques are designed to obtain information to eliminate surprise at trial, to narrow the scope of the controversy, to preserve testimony and evidence that might otherwise not be available at trial, and, incidentally, to enhance prospects for settlement. Some lawyers use discovery to bludgeon an adversary into submission. Is it proper to use discovery to harass or burden an opponent or to delay the ultimate resolution of the controversy? Consider the following provision of the Federal Rules of Civil Procedure:

* * *

The frequency or extent of use of the discovery methods * * * shall be limited by the court if it determines that: (i) the discovery sought is unreasonably cumulative or duplicative, or is obtainable from some other source that is more convenient, less burdensome, or less expensive; (ii) the party seeking discovery has had ample opportunity by discovery in the action to obtain the information sought; or (iii) the burden or expense of the proposed discovery outweighs its likely benefit, taking into account the needs of the case, the amount in controversy, the parties' resources, the importance of the issues at stake in the litigation, and the importance of the proposed discovery in resolving the issues. The court may act upon its own initiative after reasonable notice or pursuant to a motion. * * *

Fed. R. Civ. P. 26(b)(2).

The question of priority of discovery may be significant to the parties. Consider the presentation at trial. The plaintiff presents her case first, which typically means that she will call witnesses for examination and cross-examination. Upon completion of the plaintiff's presentation, the defendants elect whether to call any witnesses on their behalf. At trial it is usually advantageous to go first, to condition the trier of fact (jury); psychologists contend that such an opportunity is vital to the art of persuasion. Discovery, however, takes place outside the presence of the court or jury. Still, it is often as desirable to have priority in obtaining information in discovery as in presenting one's case before judge and jury. Why? Do not assume that only a dishonest party would want to know the adversary's position before testifying. In many cases honest witnesses get a chance to refresh their recollection with information obtained in the discovery process. In the typical automobile collision case where two parties take contrary views with respect to the same occurrence, lawyers generally desire priority in discovery. Discovery usually proceeds without court intervention. If the parties cannot agree on priority, scheduling, or other details, however, the judge may resolve the dispute.

In Kim's case the parties exchange sets of interrogatories. Interrogatories are written questions propounded to an opposing party to be answered in writing, under oath, within a designated time. In some jurisdictions these interrogatories are classified either as uniform or nonuniform. Because certain areas of inquiry are common to most automobile accident cases, the rules of procedure may provide a uniform set of questions. These questions may be compartmentalized into categories such as (a) general background and identification, (b) vehicles and drivers, (c) accident and investigation, (d) injuries and damages, (e) pre-existing and aggravated injuries, (f) impairment to employment, (g) permanency of injuries and future damages, (h) prior and subsequent accidents, and (i) witnesses and exhibits. The lawyer may not need to ask every question and may delete categories not relevant to the case. Moreover, uniform interrogatories may be supplemented with nonuniform interrogatories, questions that are specifically tailored to the facts of a case.

Interrogatories are a useful and inexpensive device for obtaining details concerning the background of a party, medical bills, names and addresses of witnesses, and descriptions of documents and other papers. They should not be relied upon to obtain admissions of fault, neglect, or wrongdoing. Why? The answering parties, although under oath, have considerable time to prepare answers and often do so with the aid of their attorneys. Few questions can be so phrased as to extract a major concession from an unwilling opponent.

Jessica needs additional time within which to marshal the information requested by the interrogatories served by John's lawyer. She requests a two-week extension of time to answer. This request is granted by defendant's attorney and a stipulation, an agreement between the attorneys subject to the approval of the court, is entered into between counsel. Under what circumstances may a lawyer properly refuse to grant an extension to an adversary?

The plaintiff's answers are subsequently served on John's attorney. They contain some important details concerning amounts expended for medical treatment and lost earnings but also much that is useless. Consider the following question and answer:

Q. "How did the accident occur?"

A. "John turned left and hit the vehicle in which I was riding."

Is this answer helpful? To whom? Note that at trial John may introduce the statement as an admission against *Kim*. Should he?

Each attorney must decide whether and to what extent to utilize the discovery process. Can you identify some of the relevant considerations? Would you attempt to balance the cost of discovery against the anticipated benefits? If documents in the possession of the adversary are essential to the preparation of the case, a request to produce these documents should be served. If the documents are in the possession of a nonparty, the documents can be obtained by serving the person with a subpoena "duces tecum" that describes with particularity the documents requested. Before trial, parties may take the testimony of any witnesses by deposition.

Kim's and Curt's attorneys have no problem with deposing Sarah and Bill, two of the occurrence witnesses, because they reside in Arizona and so are subject to the subpoena power of the Arizona judicial system. Henry, the other occurrence witness, however, lives in Nevada. Thus, unless the party desiring to take the deposition travels to Nevada and perhaps even offers to reimburse opposing counsels' expenses in attending, the deposition may be unavailable. Of course, parties like Kim, Curt, and John are subject to the jurisdiction of the court and must comply with all discovery requests seeking relevant, nonprivileged information.

Each party decides to depose each of the other parties. In this case the plaintiff, Kim, serves her notices first and the defendants do not contest priority. Is priority important in this case?

Jessica has taken many depositions in her years at the bar and knows that the method of questioning and the scope of the deposition depend entirely upon the objective. A deposition may serve several purposes: first, to obtain information that may provide the basis for further factual exploration; second, to obtain admissions for impeachment, a tactic through which a witness whose statement is different at the trial is confronted with the prior inconsistent statement under oath. The purpose of the confrontation is twofold: to credit the former version or to discredit the trustworthiness or reliability of the deponent. Impeachment is a major weapon of modern trial advocacy. A third reason for taking depositions is to preserve or perpetuate evidence for use at trial. Such use may become significant in the event the deponent will not be available as a witness at the trial.

There are other less obvious objectives of depositions. One may be to obtain facts to support a motion for summary judgment, a motion made before trial on the grounds that there is no genuine dispute as to any material fact and the moving party is entitled to judgment as a matter of law. This device is seldom used in car accident cases because the underlying facts (fault and damages) are usually in dispute. For illustrative purposes, assume the suit had been instituted against the owner of a bar, claiming service of liquor to John in violation of the dramshop act. The owner denies having served John any alcoholic beverages on the date in question. The owner's attorney may depose John to establish that he had been served alcoholic beverages in a different establishment. If the plaintiff does not produce evidence to rebut those facts, the bar owner's motion for summary judgment on the basis of the facts contained in the deposition probably would be granted.

Another purpose for taking depositions may be likened to the flexing of muscles in a sporting event—to exhibit to the opposition the strength of one's case and, incidentally, the prowess of one's attorney. This may lead to a favorable settlement.

The rules also provide that whenever the physical or mental condition of a party is in controversy, the court or the parties by agreement may require a medical examination. These examinations are commonplace in personal injury litigation. Although the rule requires a showing of good cause, the showing is perfunctory in personal injury cases. Kim agrees to a medical examination by a doctor of the defendants' choosing. Had Kim objected to the particular doctor, the court has the power to designate another.

One recurring issue in pretrial discovery is the extent to which materials prepared by one party or his agent in anticipation of litigation or for trial are subject to discovery by an adverse party. Such materials are called "work product." Whether these materials should be privileged, and therefore private, or subject to examination by opposing parties implicates the rights of attorneys as well as the rights of the respective litigants. For example, assume that defense counsel had obtained statements from each of the disinterested witnesses. Under what circumstances should Jessica be able to obtain production of these statements before the trial? Consider the majority opinion from the landmark case of *Hickman v. Taylor*, excerpted below.

HICKMAN v. TAYLOR

Supreme Court of the United States, 1947.
329 U.S. 495, 67 S.Ct. 385, 91 L.Ed. 451.

JUSTICE MURPHY delivered the opinion of the Court.

This case presents an important problem under the Federal Rules of Civil Procedure as to the extent to which a party may inquire into oral and written statements of witnesses, or other information, secured by an adverse party's counsel in the course of preparation for possible litigation after a claim has arisen. Examination into a person's files and records, including those resulting from the professional activities of an attorney, must be judged with care. It is not without reason that various safeguards have been established to preclude unwarranted excursions into the privacy of a man's work. At the same time, public policy supports reasonable and necessary inquiries. Properly to balance these competing interests is a delicate and difficult task.

On February 7, 1943, the tug "J.M. Taylor" sank while engaged in helping to tow a car float of the Baltimore & Ohio Railroad across the Delaware River at Philadelphia. The accident was apparently unusual in nature, the cause of it still being unknown. Five of the nine crew members were drowned. Three days later the tug owners and the underwriters employed a law firm, of which respondent Fortenbaugh is a member, to defend them against potential suits by representatives of the deceased crew members and to sue the railroad for damages to the tug.

A public hearing was held on March 4, 1943, before the United States Steamboat Inspectors, at which the four survivors were examined. This testimony was recorded and made available to all interested parties. Shortly thereafter, Fortenbaugh privately interviewed the survivors and took statements from them with an eye toward the anticipated litigation; the survivors signed these statements on March 29. Fortenbaugh also interviewed other persons believed to have some information relating to the accident and in some cases he made memoranda of what they told him. At the time when Fortenbaugh secured the statements of the survivors, representatives of two of the deceased crew members had been in communication with him. Ultimately claims were presented by representatives of all five of the deceased; four of the claims, however, were settled without litigation. The fifth claimant, petitioner herein, brought suit in a federal court under the Jones Act on November 26, 1943, naming as defendants the two tug owners, individually and as partners, and the railroad.

One year later, petitioner filed 39 interrogatories directed to the tug owners. The 38th interrogatory read: "State whether any statements of the members of the crews of the Tugs 'J.M. Taylor' and 'Philadelphia' or of any other vessel were taken in connection with the towing of the car float and the sinking of the Tug 'John M. Taylor.' Attach hereto exact copies of all such statements if in writing, and if oral, set forth in detail the exact provisions of any such oral statements or reports."

Supplemental interrogatories asked whether any oral or written statements, records, reports or other memoranda had been made concerning any matter relative to the towing operation, the sinking of the tug, the salvaging and repair of the tug, and the death of the deceased. If the answer was in the affirmative, the tug owners were then requested to set forth the nature of all such records, reports, statements or other memoranda.

The tug owners, through Fortenbaugh, answered all of the interrogatories except No. 38 and the supplemental ones just described. While admitting that statements of the survivors had been taken they declined to summarize or set forth the contents. They did so on the ground that such requests called "for privileged matter obtained in preparation for litigation" and constituted "an attempt to obtain indirectly counsel's private files." It was claimed that answering these requests "would involve practically turning over not only the complete files, but also the telephone records and, almost, the thoughts of counsel."

In connection with the hearing on these objections, Fortenbaugh made a written statement and gave an informal oral deposition explaining the circumstances under which he had taken the statements. But he was not expressly asked in the deposition to produce the statements. The District Court for the Eastern District of Pennsylvania, sitting *en banc,* held that the requested matters were not privileged. 4 F.R.D. 479. The court then decreed that the tug owners and Fortenbaugh, as counsel and agent for the tug owners, forthwith "answer Plaintiff's 38th interrogatory and supplementary interrogatories; produce all written statements of witnesses obtained by Mr. Fortenbaugh, as counsel and agent for Defendants; state in substance any fact concerning this case which Defendants learned through oral statements made by witnesses to Mr. Fortenbaugh whether or not included in his private memoranda and produce Mr. Fortenbaugh's memoranda containing statements of fact by witnesses or to submit these memoranda to the Court for determination of those portions which should be revealed to Plaintiff." Upon their refusal, the court adjudged them in contempt and ordered them imprisoned until they complied.

The Third Circuit Court of Appeals, also sitting *en banc,* reversed the judgment of the District Court. 153 F.2d 212. It held that the information here sought was part of the "work product of the lawyer" and hence privileged from discovery under the Federal Rules of Civil Procedure. The importance of the problem, which has engendered a great divergence of views among district courts, led us to grant certiorari. 328 U.S. 876, 66 S.Ct. 1337.

The pre-trial deposition-discovery mechanism established by Rules 26 to 37 is one of the most significant innovations of the Federal Rules of Civil Procedure. Under the prior federal practice, the pre-trial functions of notice-giving, issue-formulation and fact-revelation were performed primarily and inadequately by the pleadings. Inquiry into the issues and the facts before trial was narrowly confined and was often cumbersome in method. The new rules, however, restrict the pleadings to the task of general notice-giving and invest the deposition-discovery process with a vital role in the preparation for trial. The various instruments of discovery now serve (1) as a device, along with the pre-trial hearing under Rule 16, to narrow and clarify the basic issues between the parties, and (2) as a device for ascertaining the facts, or information as to the existence or whereabouts of facts, relative to those issues. Thus civil trials in the federal courts no longer need be carried on in the dark. The way is now clear, consistent with recognized privileges, for the parties to obtain the fullest possible knowledge of the issues and facts before trial.

* * *

We agree, of course, that the deposition-discovery rules are to be accorded a broad and liberal treatment. No longer can the time-honored cry of "fishing expedition" serve to preclude a party from inquiring into the facts underlying his opponent's case. Mutual knowledge of all the relevant facts gathered by both parties is essential to proper litigation. To that end, either party may compel the other to disgorge whatever facts he has in his possession. The deposition-discovery procedure simply advances the stage at which the disclosure can be compelled from the time of trial to the period preceding it, thus reducing the possibility of surprise. But discovery, like all matters of procedure, has ultimate and necessary boundaries. As indicated by [the] Rules, limitations inevitably arise when it can be shown that the examination is being conducted in bad faith or in such a manner as to annoy, embarrass or oppress the person subject to the inquiry. And as Rule 26(b) provides, further limitations come into existence when the inquiry touches upon the irrelevant or encroaches upon the recognized domains of privilege.

We also agree that the memoranda, statements and mental impressions in issue in this case fall outside the scope of the attorney-client privilege and hence are not protected from discovery on that basis. It is unnecessary here to delineate the content and scope of that privilege as recognized in the federal courts. For present purposes, it suffices to note that the protective cloak of this privilege does not extend to information which an attorney secures from a witness while acting for his client in anticipation of litigation. Nor does this privilege concern the memoranda, briefs, communications and other writings prepared by counsel for his own use in prosecuting his client's case; and it is equally unrelated to writings which reflect an attorney's mental impressions, conclusions, opinions or legal theories.

But the impropriety of invoking that privilege does not provide an answer to the problem before us. Petitioner has made more than an ordinary request for relevant, non-privileged facts in the possession of his adversaries or their counsel. He has sought discovery as of right of oral and written statements of witnesses whose identity is well known and whose availability to petitioner appears unimpaired. He has sought production of these matters after making the most searching inquiries of his opponents as to the circumstances surrounding the fatal accident, which inquiries were sworn to have been answered to the best of their information and belief. Interrogatories were directed toward all the events prior to, during and subsequent to the sinking of the tug. Full and honest answers to such broad inquiries would necessarily have included all pertinent information gleaned by Fortenbaugh through his interviews with the witnesses. Petitioner makes no suggestion, and we cannot assume, that the tug owners or Fortenbaugh were incomplete or dishonest in the framing of their answers. In addition, petitioner was free to examine the public testimony of the witnesses taken before the United States Steamboat Inspectors. We are thus dealing with an attempt to secure the production of written statements and mental impressions contained in the files and the mind of the attorney Fortenbaugh without any showing of necessity or any indication or claim that denial of such production would unduly prejudice the preparation of petitioner's case or cause him any hardship or injustice. For aught that appears, the essence of what petitioner seeks either has been revealed to him already through the interrogatories or is readily available to him direct from the witnesses for the asking.

* * *

We do not mean to say that all written materials obtained or prepared by an adversary's counsel with an eye toward litigation are necessarily free from discovery in all cases. Where relevant and nonprivileged facts remain hidden in an attorney's file and where production of those facts is essential to the preparation of one's case, discovery may properly be had. Such written statements and documents might, under certain circumstances, be admissible in evidence or give clues as to the existence or location of relevant facts. Or they might be useful for purposes of impeachment or corroboration. And production might be justified where the witnesses are no longer available or can be reached only with difficulty. Were production of written statements and documents to be precluded under such circumstances, the liberal ideals of the deposition-discovery portions of the Federal Rules of Civil Procedure would be stripped of much of their meaning. But the general policy against invading the privacy of an attorney's course of preparation is so well recognized and so essential to an orderly working of our system of legal procedure that a burden rests on the one who would invade that privacy to establish adequate reasons to justify production through a subpoena or court order. That burden, we believe, is necessarily implicit in the rules as now constituted.

* * * No attempt was made to establish any reason why Fortenbaugh should be forced to produce the written statements. There was only a naked, general demand for these materials as of right and a finding by the District Court that no recognizable privilege was involved. That was insufficient to justify discovery under these circumstances and the court should have sustained the refusal of the tug owners and Fortenbaugh to produce.

* * *

Petitioner's counsel frankly admits that he wants the oral statements only to help prepare himself to examine witnesses and to make sure that he has overlooked nothing. That is insufficient under the circumstances to permit him an exception to the policy underlying the privacy of Fortenbaugh's professional activities. If there should be a rare situation justifying production of these matters, petitioner's case is not of that type.

* * *

Affirmed.[t]

———

Discovery has now been completed. No one has moved for summary judgment. The case is now ready for a pretrial conference.

t. Rule 26(b)(3) of the Federal Rules of   the Rule from *Hickman*.
Civil Procedure now substantially codifies

M. THE PRETRIAL CONFERENCE

The pretrial conference may serve several functions. The foremost function is to facilitate the trial. It also provides an opportunity to explore settlement of the case. The applicable Arizona rule reprinted below embraces both purposes.

> In any action, the court may in its discretion direct the parties ... to participate, either in person or, with leave of court, by telephone, in a conference or conferences before trial for such purposes as:
>
> > (1) expediting the disposition of the action;
> >
> > (2) establishing early and continuing control so that the case will not be protracted because of lack of management;
> >
> > (3) discouraging wasteful pretrial activities; and
> >
> > (4) improving the quality of the trial through more thorough preparation.

Ariz. R. Civ. P. 16(a). Federal Rule 16(a) allows the court to use the pretrial conference to facilitate the settlement of the case.

The rule does not compel the court to hold pretrial conferences. It leaves the matter to the court's discretion. What factors may the court properly consider in the exercise of this discretion? Does it depend on the purpose for calling the conference? If streamlining the case for trial is the primary purpose, would mandatory conferences be productive in relatively simple cases?

The attorneys in *Johnson v. Roscoe & Baker* participate in the conference before Judge Barnes, who later presides at the trial. After the conference, the judge enters an order reciting the action taken by the court. In jurisdictions in which the judge who eventually presides at the trial also conducts the pretrial conference, might there be still another purpose to the conference?

Although most judges and attorneys generally agree on the benefits of the pretrial conference, these benefits are not achieved automatically and without hard work on the part of the participants. As one federal judge aptly stated:

> [Pretrial proceedings] require the diligent efforts of both court and counsel working in earnest co-operation to a common purpose. For success the leadership, direction, and stimulus of the judge are vital. True, he needs unusual qualities of tact, persistence, and patience to instruct lawyers in trial ways unlike the state practice to which they are accustomed, to still the emotional animosities of counsel who have allowed themselves to become too closely identified with their clients' causes, and generally to lead the parties and their attorneys to the frank and unforced concessions which alone justify the procedure. If a judge is not prepared to give the time and

effort thus required for successful pre-trial, it would seem that he should avail himself of the discretion still accorded him under F.R. 16 of not engaging in the attempt. But if he does undertake it and carry it through in the spirit of the rule, it is, as experience is now continually demonstrating, one of the most rewarding accomplishments to which a federal judge can aspire. He will deserve and receive public plaudits for his efficient dispatch of the public business; but even more, he will receive the grateful thanks of counsel and litigants for better justice more shortly and efficiently obtained.

Padovani v. Bruchhausen, 293 F.2d 546, 550 (2d Cir. 1961).

Do you believe that the adversary system, which lauds trial combativeness, can expect opposing counsel to cooperate for a common purpose? Suppose simplification of the issues is not in the best interest of one of the parties. Should the judge take an active role to foster cooperation in these cases as well?

Jessica believes settlement may be in Kim's best interests. Why? She also perceives the advantage of a pretrial conference before the judge who will also preside at the trial. The defendants, she hopes, will not be able to withstand the judge's entreaties. Why would any judge be disposed to assist in settlement efforts? Jessica carefully charts her strategy, with Kim's approval.

Should the plaintiff reach a settlement with one defendant, must the terms of the agreement be revealed to the jury? Suppose the plaintiff agrees to dismiss Curt at the end of the trial in exchange for Curt's agreement to offer no resistance at the trial? Would Kim be wise to enter into such an agreement? Is the perceived vice in the agreement eliminated by an offer to disclose it to the jury? One court opined that such disclosure would not prevent prejudice to the non-settling defendant's case "since the jurors might infer that all the parties to the agreement believed that the nonagreeing defendant was really the party at fault." Do you agree?

Each of the defendants refuses to settle the case. Neither offers any counter-settlement offer. Is this a wise strategy? If you had represented a defendant would you have offered something, anticipating that the plaintiff would accept the offer and proceed against the remaining defendant? Would you consider whether the remaining defendant has a right of action against the settling defendant? What, if anything, would be lost by making an offer since the offer is inadmissible at trial? Would it jeopardize or enhance your position before the judge? Would that matter if the determination of fault and damages will be made by a jury?

Since the pretrial conference did not terminate the case, it proceeds to trial before Judge Barnes and the jury.

N. JURY CONSIDERATIONS

In most lawsuits claiming money damages, the parties are guaranteed the right to a trial by jury. In the federal court the right is preserved by the seventh amendment to the United States Constitution. State constitutions contain similar guarantees. Where there is a right to a jury trial, any party may demand it and, once demanded, it may not be withdrawn without the consent of the adversary. The rules of procedure set forth specific requirements for the timing and method of the demand for trial by jury. One curious phenomenon of certain jurisdictions should be noted: An inadvertent failure to comply with the procedural rules for claiming trial by jury may not be excused by the court even though the right to jury trial is of constitutional dimension. Why?

Many factors influence a litigant's decision to request a jury trial. These factors range from considerations of delay and expense to issues of jury appeal. A jury trial may add months, even years, to the ultimate disposition of the case. Why? Why would delay benefit one of the parties? Would delay ever benefit a plaintiff? Reread Rule 11, reprinted p. 110, *supra.*

With respect to jury appeal, consider the argument that jurors tend to disregard court instructions that a plaintiff may not recover if she is even slightly contributorily negligent. Should the system permit the jury to ignore the law? Although the following statement refers to jury nullification in the criminal context, the phenomenon also occurs in civil cases.

> [J]uries commonly tend to disregard a fundamental axiom of our jurisprudence that the only parties to litigation in the criminal law are the state and the defendant. Thanks to this sloppy indifference, many jurors allow the contributory negligence or the viciousness of the victim of the crime to enter into their weighing of the culpability of the defendant. In other words, the jurors confound the clear distinction between the civil and the criminal law and look on the action charged to the defendant as a tort rather than a crime. "The cases," we are told, "show a bootlegging of tort concepts of contributory negligence and assumption of risk into the criminal law."
>
> * * * Many will ask the same question James Fenimore Cooper asked more than a century ago: In a society that has been foolish enough to establish an elective judiciary and wise enough to make judicial tenure subject to good behavior, does a jury serve any more useful purpose than that of a symbol of freedom? On Patriot's Day we celebrate the fortitude of the juries that set William Penn and John Peter Zenger free. On what days shall we celebrate the courage of those solid yeoman who, in our own day, saw fit to let * * * [those accused of killing civil rights activists] Medgar Evers, Mrs. Viola Liuzzo and Jonathan Daniels go free? There are surely occasions on which one is tempted to suggest that the time has come to amend our constitutions so as to allow the abolition of the jury even in criminal cases. * * *
>
> Before that happens, however, I hope that someone will undertake a study no less extensive than the Chicago–Ford jury project to

determine whether or not our judges are to be trusted with the power that would be theirs were they to go it alone. I confess *The American Jury* seems infected by an excessive respect for the vision, wisdom and integrity of American judges. I have too often heard practicing lawyers from our large cities insist that the one reason— and that a compelling one—for preserving jury trial is that it is our best safeguard against the corruption of judges.[u]

————

Jessica demands a trial by jury in a timely manner.

Studies indicate that jurors award greater monetary damages than judges, although juries are not as erratic as some believe.

The function of the jury in the trial process is to resolve the disputed issues of fact. The judge resolves issues of law. The jury is instructed that it should apply the rules of law to the facts. How can a jury comprehend difficult legal issues set forth in the jury instructions? Consider some of the more frequently used instructions in a negligence case, reprinted *infra* p. 145.

Are they comprehensible? Should the jury be given the instructions in written form? Can you perceive any danger to the fulfillment of the jury function if instructions are given in written form? Are you concerned that some jurors may attempt to analyze the language too carefully?

The procedures for jury selection differ from jurisdiction to jurisdiction and even among courtrooms in the same jurisdiction. The process is called the *voir dire*—literally "to say the truth." Textbooks often relate that *voir dire* is a process of selecting impartial jurors. Actually, *voir dire* may have quite a different function. Most lawyers attempt to obtain a jury sympathetic to the client's case. If the lawyer conducting the *voir dire* understands human nature, knows the details of the case, and projects a favorable image, she can benefit greatly from the opportunity to select the jurors. On the other hand, the lawyer who unthinkingly accepts any juror on a mistaken belief in the juror's innate fairness, or on the inherent strength of the lawyer's own case, courts disaster. So does any lawyer who misleads prospective jurors as to the facts of the case. One object of the *voir dire* is to give counsel sufficient information to enable her to intelligently challenge individual jurors. Discussion of the two kinds of challenges, "for cause" and "peremptory," and the manner of exercising each one, is beyond the scope of this chapter.

Following are some passages from the *voir dire* in *Johnson v. Roscoe & Baker*. Defense counsel is questioning prospective jurors. Consider why defense counsel would make these statements.

u. Professor Howe's review of Kalven & Zeisel, *The American Jury*, in 215 *Scientific American* 295, 298 (Sept. 1966).

Q. You folks understand that in a trial of a lawsuit there is a division of labor between the judge and the jury. You are to decide the facts, and the judge will instruct you on the law. You must follow the law. Can you do that?

As free Americans we have the right to disagree with the law—even to try to change it in the proper way—but if you accept your responsibility as jurors you are pledging to follow it. Can you do that?

Do you understand that if you do not follow the law our system has failed?

So if the judge instructs you that the mere fact that an accident has occurred does not cast fault on any defendant and that the plaintiff carries the burden of proving fault, you must follow that instruction even though your sympathies may be with the plaintiff. Can you do that?

The statements made and inquiries posed during *voir dire* may depend upon the nature of the case. For example, in personal injury litigation counsel may seek to elicit information concerning the driving habits of prospective jurors, whether the juror or a member of his family has been involved in an accident, whether a lawsuit had to be brought, and whether the outcome was favorable. Assume a prospective juror responds that she instituted a personal injury suit arising from an automobile accident. If the recovery was much less than the prospective juror had anticipated, would plaintiff's counsel necessarily wish to strike her from the panel? As plaintiff's attorney, would you risk having (or desire) her on the jury? If the juror did not bring suit, would that make her a poor choice for the plaintiff? On the other hand, suppose the juror received a very favorable jury award. Would that fact bias her for or against the plaintiff? Suppose the juror thought she did not merit that award? Suppose she had to stray from the "literal truth" to obtain that award? Or suppose the eventual award was less than Kim's request and yet the juror's injuries were more extensive? Can you understand why, if given the opportunity to conduct detailed *voir dire* of prospective jurors, counsel may be able to make more informed decisions regarding the acceptability of a juror?

Voir dire presents an excellent opportunity to condition the jury. The example set forth below is taken from the criminal law field, but aptly illustrates how a skillful advocate can use *voir dire* to condition prospective jurors. As you know, in a criminal case the government must establish a defendant's guilt beyond a reasonable doubt. This is a much more difficult standard to meet than the civil standard of preponderance of the evidence, which simply means by the greater weight of the evidence. A colloquy between defense counsel and a prospective juror in a criminal case might proceed along the following lines:

Q. Ms. Jones, as you sit there have you formed an opinion yet about the guilt or innocence of my client?

A. No, I haven't.

Q. In other words, without hearing the evidence you cannot say one way or the other whether my client is guilty of the crime or not?

A. That's right, without hearing the evidence.

Q. And that seems only fair, Ms. Jones?

A. Yes.

Q. Thank you, Ms. Jones. I know you will try to be fair. But I am going to tell you that your mind should be made up already. The judge will instruct you that Harry is presumed innocent; that is the American system.

A. I guess so.

Q. So when the judge tells you about the presumption, it means that you should have an opinion regarding guilt or innocence. At this stage, Harry is innocent unless proven guilty beyond a reasonable doubt. Can you abide by that Ms. Jones?

A. Sure.

Q. So if you were a defendant you would want someone like yourself who has the same frame of mind—who believes you are innocent until proven guilty beyond a reasonable doubt?

A. Yes.

Isn't this a more effective way to convey the presumption of innocence to the jury than a lecture by the defense counsel in the closing argument or a passing statement by the judge in his instructions to the jury?

————

In *Johnson v. Roscoe & Baker*, the jury is selected in less than an hour. According to the rules of procedure, nine jurors are selected. At the conclusion of the trial, if all nine jurors are still available, one will be designated the alternate and excused. In Arizona a verdict in a civil case is reached upon agreement of six jurors. Unanimity is not required. If six jurors cannot agree on a verdict, the case must be retried. If you were counsel, would the fact that a less-than-unanimous jury can return a verdict weigh in your approach to the trial? In what way?

O. ORDER OF PRESENTATION OF THE TRIAL

We now proceed to the trial of the case. Normally the order of trial is as follows:

1. The plaintiff's opening statement to the jury.

2. The defendants' opening statements. The defendants may choose instead to make opening statements after stage 4. What factors might be relevant to the decision whether to open at this point in the litigation?

3.   The presentation of plaintiff's case. This process entails calling witnesses for direct examination and the opportunity for cross-examination by opposing counsel, redirect examination by plaintiff, recross, etc. The plaintiff may also introduce exhibits, either through witnesses or pursuant to stipulation, and may read into the record portions of depositions as well as answers to interrogatories and admissions.

4.   The plaintiff rests. At this juncture, the defendants may move for directed verdicts based on insufficiency of the proof. For example, suppose the plaintiff failed to introduce any evidence that Curt drove through a red light. Assume that all the evidence showed that he was proceeding through the intersection with the green light and with care. Curt's lawyer may move for a directed verdict claiming that no rational jury could find negligence on the part of his client. Should the court rule in Curt's favor, that would end the case as to him, barring, of course, a reversal by an appellate court. If directed verdict motions do not abort the trial, then any defendant who did not open at stage two may now make an opening statement.

5.   The presentation of the defendants' cases, if any. The defendants do not have to present any evidence at all. Perhaps the evidence each wants to present has already been introduced during the plaintiff's case. Moreover, since the plaintiff bears the burden of proof, a defendant may prevail by not introducing any evidence whatsoever. Indeed, there is always a danger in presenting evidence that the defendant will unwittingly supply evidence favorable to the plaintiff or will supply an omitted but necessary item of evidence. Can you appreciate now why a defendant may want to reserve an opening statement until the plaintiff has rested?

If the defendants choose to call and examine witnesses, the plaintiff has the opportunity to cross-examine them. Redirect and recross may follow. Defendants may introduce exhibits and admissions obtained in the discovery process. At the conclusion of this stage, the defendants will rest.

6.   The parties present rebuttal evidence, if any.

7.   The parties make appropriate motions. Because the plaintiff has the burden of proof, the likelihood of obtaining a directed verdict in her favor on the issue of negligence is remote. Why? However, the defendants should not overlook the opportunity for a directed verdict in their favor. Jessica does not move for a directed verdict, believing it would be futile. The defendants' motions are denied.

8.   The parties now may address the jury in summation. The plaintiff usually has the right to make the first closing argument. The defendants' arguments are then presented, and the plaintiff has the final opportunity to address the jury.

9.   The court instructs the jury on the law.

10.   The jury retires to deliberate. If the requisite number of jurors concur, the jury renders a verdict. Between the verdict and judgment, or within a short time after judgment, as specified in the rules of procedure,

the parties may make various motions. For example, the losing litigant may request a new trial on the grounds that various errors were committed that materially prejudiced his case.

11. The losing party may exercise the right to seek appellate review. Appeals are typically perfected by filing a notice of appeal with the court.

12. If a judgment is rendered in favor of the plaintiff, she may encounter collection problems. Defendants often pay judgments without further court proceedings; other times they attempt to obtain a favorable settlement of the matter by paying less than the court judgment. On still other occasions, the plaintiff must resort to further court proceedings to satisfy the judgment including proceedings to determine the extent of the defendant's assets. Can you think of reasons why a defendant may prefer one alternative to another?

P. THE TRIAL

1. OPENING STATEMENTS

In those jurisdictions where counsel does not actively participate in *voir dire*, the opening statement is counsel's first formal opportunity to make an organized presentation of the case to the jury. Counsel should take full advantage of the opportunity. Empirical studies have established that in a large percentage of cases, impressions formed by jurors during opening statements persist throughout the trial.

In the opening, plaintiff's counsel should attempt to portray as vividly as possible the scene of the occurrence and the manner in which the collision occurred. She should avoid puffing or exaggerating, for if the evidence does not support the opening, opposing counsel may appropriately comment on the discrepancy. Such puffing has proved to have unfortunate consequences.

The dramatic effect of an opening statement is heightened if the witnesses rather than counsel portray what has happened. For example, suppose the evidence indicates that the defendant said, "Sorry, it was my fault. I ran the red light." If counsel refers to that statement in the opening, the impact may not be as great as if first revealed by the witness. Counsel should alert the jurors in the opening so that they pay careful attention when the admission comes. The following is one way to sensitize the jury:

> What really happened at the intersection? I cannot testify nor can my adversary. We were not there. But the plaintiff was there and so were the defendants. They know. And Harry Smith, a witness to the collision, was also there. And he spoke to one of the defendants right after the accident. The defendant told him how it happened. It was fresh in his mind. And Harry will be here today to tell you exactly what the defendant said. Please listen carefully to what Harry tells you.

An overview of the damages is also essential for the plaintiff's case. If the plaintiff wins but the award is meager, the defendants may well claim victory. It is not enough to establish liability unless the plaintiff can obtain sufficient compensation for her injuries. Counsel may wish to detail every item of damages that will be presented to the jury. But, although it is very important to inform the jury on all elements of damages, counsel must not bore the jury. This is a cardinal sin! A jury that sleeps through the presentation will not deliver a substantial verdict. Nor should counsel lecture the jury. Jurors are neither students nor parishioners.

Kim's lawyer describes to the jurors the function of an opening in the following way:

> Trial of a lawsuit is a very exciting thing, and because we are dealing with human beings, sometimes exciting things happen. Sometimes, though, the telling of the tale is interrupted and doesn't flow smoothly, either because the witness who is here doesn't know everything in a chronological order or knows only a piece of the story, and we get all he does know while he is here, or because, to accommodate a witness' schedule, we take him when he is available, even though what he knows doesn't fall right where we are in the telling of the tale.

> In order to make the evidence more understandable, we start the trial of each lawsuit with an opening statement. It is a time when each lawyer has the opportunity to tell you what the evidence will be. The time to evaluate the evidence, to draw conclusions, and to persuade you all comes later, after you have heard the evidence.

> I don't know how many of you like to work jigsaw puzzles, but if you do, you will know there is a time when you have dumped out all the pieces, turned them right side up, and then it becomes your task to put them all together. Sometimes, if you look at the picture on the front of the box, you will know what it is supposed to look like when you are finished, and it is easier to fit the pieces together and put them in proper places.

> The opening statement of a lawsuit is the picture on the front of the puzzle box. It tells you what this thing is going to look like once you put all the pieces together. And, it will help you to better realize the importance of the testimony as you hear it, and how it relates to this case and other portions of the testimony.

The segments of a trial have been compared to a classroom lecture. The opening should summarize what the listeners will hear, the bulk of the proceedings should elaborate on the theme, and the final portion should recapitulate what has already been said. Repetition is important to the learning process.

The opening should present a theme, and the theme should be reiterated at appropriate times during the trial. If the jigsaw puzzle analogy seemed to go over well in the opening, the lawyer should refer to it again in the summation. For example, Jessica may argue at the close of the case:

> You recall that, in the opening statement, I compared the trial with a jigsaw puzzle. I said that if you look at the picture on the front of the box it is easier to fit the pieces of the puzzle into their proper places. Well, during the remainder of this trial we have been putting pieces together. Now you are to determine whether we have put enough pieces in place for you to form the picture. Ladies and gentlemen, this is not a criminal case. We do not have to put every piece in place. Our burden is not to convince you beyond a reasonable doubt. Our burden is only what the judge will charge—a preponderance—the greater weight of the evidence. If from looking at the pieces in place you believe that the picture on the box is what I told you it was—that is, if you can see from the pieces of puzzle that we've managed to put in place that John turned in front of Curt's car—then the verdict must be for the plaintiff. That is the law.

2. THE EVIDENCE

Each of the parties opened to the jury. The plaintiff presented her case. Selected excerpts of the testimony relating to the liability issue are reprinted below.

Cross-Examination[v] of John Roscoe

Q. As you drove south on Flamingo Drive, there is a hill as it approaches Las Vegas Avenue, is there not?

A. Yes.

Q. It descends as you go south toward the intersection of Flamingo Drive and Las Vegas Avenue?

A. Yes.

Q. You were coming down this hill?

A. Yes.

Q. And, you were traveling at what speed, sir, would you estimate for us?

A. Yes. If I remember right, I didn't catch that stop light above the hill, so I—approximately, it would be, say, 40 miles an hour.

Q. You were coming down that hill at about 40 miles an hour?

A. Yes.

Q. That hill descends right to the intersection, doesn't it?

v. The term "cross-examination" at this stage of the case may be confusing. During a party's case-in-chief, witness examination is usually "direct." Leading questions, ones that suggest to the witness the answer desired by the examiner, are typically disallowed during "direct examination." When, however, counsel examines the adverse party or a witness whose interests are identified with the adverse party he or she may interrogate by the use of leading questions. Thus the examination is termed "cross."

A.   Almost to the intersection.

Q.   Does it level off just before the intersection?

A.   Yeah, about, say 500 feet from the intersection.

Q.   Up to then, it is a downhill ride for you?

A.   Right.

Q.   Now, as you were approximately, oh, let's say 200 feet away from the intersection, were you in the middle lane?

A.   Yes, I was.

Q.   And, did you remain in the middle lane as you approached the intersection?

A.   No. I proceeded into the center lane and then I got over into the left-hand turn lane.

Q.   When you were approximately 200 feet above the intersection, the light had turned from red to green, had it not?

A.   Yes. It proceeded to turn.

Q.   You saw it turn from red to green?

A.   Yes.

Q.   When you were some 200 feet above it?

A.   Yes.

Q.   And you then came out into the intersection, didn't you?

A.   No.

Q.   You didn't?

A.   I stopped. I entered—I pulled up to the line and stopped, because I had to shift down, because the traffic was—I had to wait on traffic to clear before I could turn, so I put my truck in low gears so I eased out into the center.

Q.   Are you telling us then that you came to a complete stop before you entered the intersection?

A.   Yes, I did.

Q.   Even though the light was green?

A.   Yes.

Q.   All right. You then entered the intersection, did you not, sir?

A.   Yes.

Q.   And, when you entered the light was still green?

A.   Yes.

Q.   And, then you came to a second complete stop?

A.   Yes, I had to wait.

Q.   Now, as you were stopped there at the intersection, let's put that on the diagram, if we may, or on the board as a diagram.

If you would draw for us, please, the intersection of Flamingo Drive and Las Vegas Avenue.

A. Oops, I'm not a very good drawer.

Q. Show us, please, where you were in the intersection when you came to that second complete stop.

A. I was approximately right here.

Q. Would you put it in the diagram with—the vehicle with a nose, or a point?

A. Let's see, I was pointed—I was pointing south.

Q. Directly south?

A. Yes.

Q. You were not angled off to your left?

A. No, I couldn't.

Q. You didn't do that?

A. No.

Q. Okay. Now, as you were stopped there in the intersection, the light facing you was green?

A. Right.

Q. Where was that light that you were looking at?

A. See, there were two lights; there was one above me, right about here.

Q. Were you able to see that one?

A. No.

Q. Where was the light that you were able to see?

A. It was off to my right, and I had a clear view of this one.

Q. All right. Now, as you were stopped in the intersection here, where you showed us with the arrow, was there traffic to your immediate right passing through the intersection going south?

A. Yes.

Q. You observed it as you sat there?

A. Yes.

Q. And those cars were passing through on a green light?

A. Yes.

Q. As you looked to your south, you observed a white Chevy pickup truck entering the left-turn lane, did you not?

A. That was—yes, I did. It was just as the light turned yellow.

Q. You were watching a Chevy truck?

A. Yes, it was right here, it was pointing north and getting ready to make his left-hand turn.

Q. And, it was slowing down as you observed it while you were stopped in the intersection?

A. Yes.

Q. You made that observation. And as that pickup truck began to slow down, did you see Curt's vehicle approximately two or three car lengths off to its right in the curb lane?

A. I observed it after some cars went by.

Q. That's not my question.

A. Yes, okay. Okay, I saw the—I observed, I saw the car.

Q. So, you saw Curt's car two or three car lengths back. Would you put that on the diagram for us, please?

A. Let's see, when I first saw it, it was approximately, say, right here.

Q. Now, in regard to the white pickup truck—that is, the Chevy pickup truck—you have indicated to us that it was slowing down in the left-hand turn lane going north and you observed Curt's vehicle off to its side approximately two or three car lengths to its rear in the curb lane?[w]

A. Yes.

Q. When you made that observation of Curt's vehicle, at that point, had the white Chevy pickup truck come to a complete stop or was it still in motion?

A. Complete stop.

Q. How long had it been stopped at that point when you observed Curt's vehicle two or three car lengths back?

A. Oh, it was stopped, I would—what do you want, in minutes or—it was stopped for a while.

Q. Okay. Now, as that white Chevy pickup truck was stopped there, you started to make your left-hand turn, didn't you?

A. After the traffic had cleared.

Q. All right. Now, as you make, or start to make your left-hand turn, had the light facing you turned red?

A. Yes, it turned red just as I made my turn.

Q. You had not started your turn before the light turned red?

A. No.

Q. You are sure of that?

A. Yes.

Q. Now, isn't it a fact that you first saw Curt's car just as you began your left turn?

A. Yes.

w. Consider this testimony in light of witness Henry's statement *supra* p. 71.

Q. And, he was two or three car lengths from the intersection?

A. Yes.

Q. Or closer at that point, isn't that so?

A. Yes. It was approximately three car lengths from the intersection when I saw him.

Q. Now, at what speed was he traveling when you observed him two or three car lengths south of the intersection?

A. I have no idea. All I know—all I know, he was moving at a decent speed.

Q. All right, approximately 40 miles an hour, perhaps?

A. Approximately.

Q. Here is a vehicle two or three car lengths south of the intersection, coming at 40 miles an hour as you started to make a left-hand turn, isn't that what you are telling us?

A. When I started making my left-hand turn?

Q. The answer to that question, sir?

ROSCOE'S LAWYER: Wait just a minute, let him answer.

A. BY THE WITNESS: When I started making my left-hand turn, the light in the corner of my eye had turned red and he was approximately three car lengths from the intersection when that light—when I had seen it turn red out of the corner of my eye.

Q. My question, again, is this: when you observed Curt's vehicle two or three car lengths south of the intersection traveling at approximately 40 miles an hour, you started to make a left-hand turn, didn't you, regardless of the color of the light?

A. When I—

Q. Yes or no.

A. Yes.

Q. Okay. Can automobiles stop at 40 miles an hour, in a distance of three car lengths?

A. It depends on the weight of the car. I have given it a try a couple of times, and I have succeeded.

Q. Dangerously?

A. No.

Q. You could skid to a stop in three car lengths?

A. Yes.

Q. What is the length of the car that you are speaking about?

A. Let's see, oh, say 12 feet, 14 feet, something like that.

Q. 14 feet, three car lengths, 42 feet, and you are telling us that a car can stop in 42 feet at 40 miles an hour?

A.   I have no idea what speed he was traveling at. I am not an expert at it, but—

Q.   I understand that.

A.   But, I have done it at—coming up to a—an intersection, a car all of a sudden darts out in front of me, I have made a good try at it and I had no accident.

Q.   And, you had to slam on your brakes and do it?

A.   Right.

Q.   Okay. That is what I am getting to.

So, if Curt was to be not hit by you when you first observed him traveling at 40 miles an hour, he would have had to slam on his brakes?

ROSCOE'S ATTORNEY: May it please the Court, the question assumes that he was traveling 40 miles an hour. He just testified he had no idea what speed he was going.

JOHNSON'S ATTORNEY: I will withdraw the last question.

THE COURT: Thank you.

Q.   Now, between that observation that you made of Curt's vehicle, two or three car lengths off the intersection, as you commenced your left-hand turn, you observed him a second time, didn't you?

A.   A split second before we collided.

Q.   Just before he hit you?

A.   Yes, a split second.

Q.   And in that interval, you did not keep him in view, did you?

A.   No, because I was—

Q.   All right. Your answer is no?

A.   No, I didn't.

Q.   Now, in that split second that you next saw him, you applied your brakes?

A.   Yes.

Q.   And you skidded?

A.   Yes.

Q.   Does your truck ordinarily skid at five miles an hour?

A.   Yeah.

Q.   Did you speak with Curt or Kim at the accident scene?

A.   Yes, I did.

Q.   All right. You offered some help?

A.   Yes.

Q.   Did you tell Curt that you were sorry?

A. I do not recall that, but I did try to help them. If I said it, I said it. If I didn't, I didn't.

Q. Fair enough.

A. I have no idea.

Direct Examination by Roscoe's Attorney

Q. So, when you came to this stop here, before going into the intersection, did you put it into a low gear so you could start off through the intersection?

A. Yes.

Q. Is that it? Then, after you stopped there, was the light green?

A. Yes.

Q. Did you enter the intersection on that green light?

A. Yes.

Q. You came to a second stop?

A. Yes.

Q. And, you waited for the north-bound traffic to clear the intersection, is that it?

A. Yes.

Q. Then did you observe a white pickup truck pull into the left-turn lane and come to a stop?

A. Yes.

Q. When did you see Curt's vehicle coming north in the curb lane?

A. Just about right then.

Q. And, then, you see the light turn red?

A. Yes.

Q. And that is when you commenced your turn?

A. Yes, but could I say something right here?

Q. Sure, go ahead.

A. Okay. When this white pickup came up to a stop, the light just turned yellow. There were five cars—approximately three cars in the left lane, two cars in the curb lane going through that intersection when the light was already—when it was yellow. I had to wait on them before I proceeded. That's when I noticed the car. See? When I—when those cars got by, I noticed out of the corner of my eye the light turned red, so I proceeded. I could have sworn that Curt's was going to stop.

Q. In other words, this is a point that was missed before in your examination, Curt's vehicle appeared to be slowing down to stop, is that what you are saying?

A. I could have sworn to it, but I was mistaken.

Q.   All right. In any event, they entered the intersection then on a red light?

A.   Yes, I swear to that.

Q.   And, you had the collision.

Now, Curt, in his testimony, said that the impact was someplace here on the north side of the intersection. Does that compare with your recollection?

A.   No. It was right there on the corner.

Q.   In the south half of the intersection?

A.   Yes.

Recross of Roscoe by Johnson's Attorney

Q.   You have told us that you had come to a complete stop within the intersection and you were in second gear.

A.   Yes.

Q.   And the most speed you can get out of that vehicle in that gear range is five miles an hour?

A.   Approximately five.

Q.   And that is putting your foot right down to the floor?

A.   Yes, that's putting it—the torque to it.

Q.   You didn't do that, did you, as you said?

A.   No.

Q.   Bad for the engine, isn't it?

A.   Right.

Q.   So, when you started off in the second gear, in that gear range, you eased on the gas pedal, didn't you?

A.   Yes.

Q.   And, you started slowly?

A.   Yeah.

Q.   The distance that you had to travel from the point at which you were at rest within the intersection to where the impact occurred was how much?

A.   Say 14, 15 feet. It seemed like to me, because it was—

Q.   A short distance?

A.   Right, it was very short. I got out of one lane and got stopped in another lane.

Q.   So, you were traveling at one mile or less per hour at that point?

A.   No.

Q.   At what speed, sir?

A. Approximately five miles an hour.

Q. In other words, in 14 feet distance you were able to get that truck from zero to five miles an hour?

A. Yeah, it doesn't take long.

Q. All right. Now, you have told us that you started to make your left-hand turn after, now, I will repeat the word "after," the light facing you had turned red?

A. Yes. I proceeded.

Q. After it had turned red?

A. Yes.

Q. All right. I'm going to read to you from your deposition, page 34, at line 10, counsel:

> "Question: Before commencing making your left-hand turn, how long were you sitting there at a dead stop?"

Was that question asked of you, at that deposition?

A. Yes, it was.

Q. And, the answer that you gave:

> "Answer: The light turned yellow."

A. Yes.

Q. Okay:

> "Answer: (Continuing) I was still in there waiting for the cars to clear out of the intersection. The light was fixing to turn red. And I started easing to make my left-hand turn because then after the light turned yellow, approximately five more cars went through the light. I had to wait on them, then I started easing on out."

Is it not a fact, sir, that you started to make that left-hand turn before the light turned red?

A. I was already into the intersection, barely moving, until those five cars got by and the light—yes, I was already slowly proceeding.

Q. You were in motion before the light changed to red?

A. Right. I was just starting to move.

JOHNSON'S ATTORNEY: Thank you very much.

Redirect Examination by Roscoe's Attorney

Q. Go ahead and finish what you started to say.

A. As I was starting, I was moving slowly, okay, because I was—there was traffic left and right that afternoon, because it was—in that intersection, it's thick. Anybody can go through there between 4:30 and 6:30 in the afternoon and catch that traffic bad at times. And, that—I was right out in the middle of the intersection, the east to west traffic was heavy, and if you don't get out of the way, you will cause an accident. And, I could have sworn that there—see, I thought that their car was slowing down, but out of the corner of my eye, the light turned red and I proceeded on that.

———

At this juncture of the case, would you as a member of the jury have found John liable to Kim? Would you first want to know the propositions of law controlling the question of negligence? These propositions of law, called jury instructions, are given to the jury at the conclusion of the case. See *infra* p. 145. Do you believe John acted reasonably under the circumstances? What else should plaintiff's counsel have elicited? Should she have elicited evidence regarding John's consumption of alcohol preceding the accident? What about the police officer's citation? Is that admissible evidence? You will learn in the course on Evidence that charges and citations are not usually admissible to prove the facts contained in them. But if John had pled guilty to the charge that plea would be admissible in evidence. How could John effectively counter that evidence? If John were convicted after trial, many jurisdictions would also allow the introduction of that judgment of conviction. Yet, an acquittal could not be used against Kim. Why? Can you understand why criminal proceedings may have important ramifications for the civil trial?

At the trial, John's conviction for driving while intoxicated is submitted to the jury. Jessica also calls Curt to the stand. Relevant portions of this testimony are set forth below:

Cross-Examination of Curt Baker

Q. When you first saw John's truck did you slow down?

A. There was no reason. I had the green light. I mean, I just went on.

Q. Where then was the point of impact?

A. Just a little way beyond the center of the intersection. If this is the center here, it was just about the middle.

Q. Would you please make an "X"?

So within a brief period of time, your car, traveling 40 miles an hour, went from this point to the point where the impact occurred, just a little beyond the center of the intersection, right?

A. Right.

Q. And the truck traveled from a greater distance to the point of impact in that same time span?

A. Yes.

Q. And, do I understand that the path of the truck then was in the center lane?

A. Right.

Q. Would you mind just drawing a dotted line from the first position of the truck, as you believe the truck moved, up to the point of impact?

A. He had to make a wider turn, because of his truck, it was a huge truck.

Q. All right. Curt, when you first saw the truck, did you have any estimate at all as to its speed?

A. Not really. I couldn't tell about the speed.

Q. All right. At any time, from the time you first saw the truck up to the point of impact, at any time were you able to estimate the speed of the truck?

A. I assumed he was going—

Q. No, excuse me.

A. I can't assume?

Q. Excuse me Curt, I realize this is difficult, but we can't ask for guesses from witnesses, so what I am really trying to determine is whether you are actually able to help the jury by giving some kind of an honest estimate. If you can't, well, then, you can't, but—

A. No, I can't. I don't know how fast.

Q. All right. The front of your vehicle came in contact with the side of John's truck, right?

A. Right.

Q. After the accident, did John get out of his truck and speak to you?

A. Yes.

Q. And he was concerned about whether you were hurt and offered his help, right?

A. Yes, yes.

Q. All right. Curt do you have any idea how wide Flamingo Drive is?

A. No, I have no idea how wide it is.

Q. Do you have any idea how wide Las Vegas Avenue is?

A. No.

JOHNSON'S ATTORNEY: Your Honor, may I confer with counsel?

THE COURT: Surely.

(Counsel confer off the record.)

Q. BY JOHNSON'S ATTORNEY: Do you recall what the weather conditions were that afternoon?

A. BY THE WITNESS: It had been raining quite heavily.

Q. Was the road wet?

A. Yes, fairly.

Q. There were no accidents, other accidents in the intersection as you were going through it?

A. No.

Q. Do you recall what the traffic conditions were?

A. Well, seems like I was the only car in the road.

Q. The only car on the road?

A. Seemed like it.

Q. Had you ever gone through that intersection before?

A. No.

Q. Was it a very busy intersection?

A. It wasn't very busy.

Q. Not busy. Were there any other southbound vehicles other than this truck that you saw that afternoon?

A. I didn't notice.

Q. How often did you go by that intersection, Curt?

A. Never before.

Q. Now before the accident occurred were you at the Oceanside bar?

A. Yes.

Q. Did you have any drinks there?

A. Yes, I had a drink or two.

Q. Could it have been three or four?

A. No. It could not have been. I cannot handle that many.

Q. So you admit that three or four drinks would have had an effect on your driving?

      BAKER'S ATTORNEY: Objection.

      COURT: Overruled.

A. Perhaps.

Q. But one or two would not?

A. That's correct.

Q. How many minutes elapsed between your last drink and the accident?

A. Just a few minutes.

Direct Examination by Baker's Attorney

Q. So, you were on your way to the hotel when this accident occurred?

A. Yes.

Q. And would you tell the jury the route of travel that you took?

A. I went north on Flamingo and then I would make a left-hand turn on Main going to the hotel.

Q. So that was—

A. I mean a right-hand turn on Main.

Q. Now, to get to your destination you had to go through the intersection at Las Vegas Boulevard.

A. Right.

Q. How close is the Oceanside Bar to the intersection of Las Vegas and Flamingo, Curt?

A. How close?

Q. Yes, how far away is the bar in relation to that intersection?

A. It is about two blocks, I would say, from the intersection.

Q. On what side of the street is it?

A. It is on—well, the way I am facing, it is the left-hand side.

Q. On the left side of the street?

A. Yes, on the left side of the street.

Q. Okay. Would you tell us what lane of traffic you were proceeding in as you drove from the bar toward the intersection of Flamingo Drive and Las Vegas Avenue?

A. I was on the right-hand side, in the curb lane.

Q. And, as you approached the intersection, Curt, how fast were you driving?

A. I imagine I was going about 40 miles an hour.

Q. And do you recall what the posted speed limit was at that time?

A. 45.

Q. So you were within the speed limit when you were approaching the intersection?

A. Right.

Q. Now, as you were approaching the intersection, would you tell the jury the color of the light that was facing you?

A. Facing me was green.

Q. How far south of the light were you when you first observed it in the condition that you saw it—that is, green?

A. I would say about two car lengths.

Q. It was green at that time?

A. Yes, it was.

Q. And, you proceeded into the intersection, is that correct?

A. Right.

Q. Now, before actually entering the intersection, did you see any vehicles to your left, that is to say in the through lane that was immediately to your left, or in the left-turn lane?

A. No, I hadn't seen any cars that afternoon.

Q. You didn't?

A. No, I hadn't.

Q. Now, when was the first time you observed John's truck?

A. As I was entering the intersection.

Q. Where was he?

A. He was, I would say, about two cars back, or maybe a car length back.

Q. From which direction was he coming?

A. He was coming from the north side.

Q. Do you recall what lane of traffic he was in as he was approaching the intersection?

A. He was not in a turn lane, he was in the other, third lane, the second lane.

Q. We have three lanes of travel here, going south—well, going north, as well, on Flamingo, two of which lanes are left-turn lanes. Now, John's attorney told us in his opening statement that John turned left in the intersection from the left-turn lane.

  Would you step to the board, please? I want you to show us, using the same type of diagram that John's counsel used, that is, put a little block with an arrow where the truck was.

A. When I first saw him?

Q. Yes.

A. Right about here.

Q. Would you put a point on it, like he did it? I think that's good enough. He was not then in the left-turn lane?

A. No, he was not.

Q. Okay. You can resume your seat.

  And, as he came toward you and as he neared the intersection, did he ever change lanes, or did he remain in that lane?

A. I believe he remained in that lane.

Q. Did you observe him actually make his left-hand turn?

A. No. You mean observing turning?

Q. Turning into Las Vegas Avenue.

A. Yes, I saw him turning in.

Q. All right. Where was your vehicle at the time your vehicles collided?

A. It was about a little past the halfway point of Las Vegas, going north.

Q. Would you show us, please, on the diagram? I'm sorry to get you up again.

A. That's all right.

Q. Just put an "X."

A. Center lane here, so it was past this line here, past the center.

Q. Okay. Okay, thank you.

What portion of your vehicle came in contact with John's truck?

A. My front end.

Q. And, what part of his vehicle was damaged?

A. The right side.

Some Remarks on Cross–Examination

Probably no area of trial practice appeals to so many and is mastered by so few as cross-examination. Perhaps too many attorneys see themselves as Perry Mason, breaking down hostile witnesses until they, or someone in the spectator section, admit to the perpetration of the crime. Thanks to television, this image is so much a part of our heritage that some trial lawyers caution the jury at the outset not to expect such feats.

With respect to cross-examination, consider the following items:

1. Ineffective cross-examination may reinforce direct testimony or elicit new, damaging testimony. Extreme caution must be exercised. Some attorneys should even consider foregoing cross-examination.

2. Discrediting a witness is not the same as discrediting his testimony. The latter is a less abrasive and equally effective way of handling many situations and may not alienate jury sympathy to your cause.

3. Obtaining favorable information from a witness is a foremost objective of cross-examination. It is foolish to attack the witness before he has an opportunity to support or reject your account.

4. Simple language is the key. If the jury does not understand the testimony, the examination may be ineffective and perhaps even counterproductive. It has been reported that a juror once became so exasperated over the continued examination of a witness that he said "amen" when the judge refused to allow further questions. The "wear the witness down" approach may work in some cases. Usually, however, it is the jury that becomes worn out.

5. The attorney's demeanor is always important. Indeed, the jury may focus on counsel's behavior. Do not wince or frown when a telling blow has been struck.

6. Do not ordinarily ask questions when unsure of the answers. If counsel must fish in uncharted waters, it should be done in the middle of

the examination, in case the answers prove unfavorable. Cross-examination is but a microcosm of the entire trial process. First and last impressions are usually the strongest. Most good advocates try not to end examinations on a low note.

————

Jessica calls Kim as a witness and reads in portions of the depositions of two of the three occurrence witnesses. She also offers in evidence the hospital report and Kim's employment record. Finally, she examines a physician who testifies that cosmetic surgery would mask the three-inch scar. He states that the surgery would cost approximately $5,000.

The defendants now have the opportunity to present their cases. Since the testimony of the occurrence witnesses has already been received during the plaintiff's case, there is no need to repeat the process. The defendants had been prepared to call a medical expert to testify that Kim's scar is not permanent, but in view of the plaintiff's doctor's admission, they decide not to burden the record with cumulative testimony. Defendants read in portions of Kim's answers to interrogatories and parts of her deposition relating to damages.

After the defendants present their cases, the plaintiff has an opportunity to call rebuttal witnesses. Rebuttal should be limited to matters raised by the adversary, and should not merely repeat what the jury has already heard. What factors would you consider in deciding whether to offer rebuttal? Is the dramatic effect of the evidence offered at this stage heightened? Is there a tactical advantage in holding evidence in abeyance in one's direct case in anticipation of using it later in rebuttal? Can that decision backfire? Note that the trial judge has wide discretion whether to permit rebuttal.

Jessica decides to offer no additional evidence. The jury is excused and the court hears various motions outside its presence.

3. MOTIONS FOR DIRECTED VERDICT AND OTHER RELIEF

Counsel now have the opportunity to address the court on a number of issues before the case is finally submitted to the jury. John's attorney moves for a mistrial. During recross examination of John, Jessica asked the following question:

Q. Now you are the defendant named in this case, the one interested in the outcome of the suit?

A. Well, I don't know what you are driving at—I do have insurance.

ROSCOE'S ATTORNEY: May we approach the bench?

COURT. Yes.

ROSCOE'S ATTORNEY: (outside presence of jury) Judge, we ask for a mistrial. Defendant has been seriously damaged by reference to the insurance. The law in this jurisdiction is that such reference is prejudicial error.

COURT. What do you have to say counsel?

JOHNSON'S ATTORNEY. Well, I think the defendant himself caused the error, if any. My question did not mention insurance. I only meant to reinforce the fact that he was the defendant—not any corporation or anything like that. You will recall that in direct testimony he testified that he owned Roscoe's Rodeo Supply Company. Well, the company has nothing to do with the case. That's all I wanted to show.

COURT. I will overrule the motion and admonish the jury not to consider the question of insurance coverage.

Consider the psychological impact of admonishing the jury not to consider certain evidence. Could it have the opposite effect? John's attorney now presents for the second time his motion for a mistrial based on the reference to insurance coverage. Can you think of situations where he would prefer losing the motion for a mistrial and actually proceeding with the trial? If there are such situations, why make the motion in the first place?

The dilemma confronting trial attorneys may be outlined as follows: Certain procedures, like motions for mistrials, must be made at the trial level in order to preserve the issue for appeal in the event the moving party loses the trial. Often, the moving party believes he will win the trial on the merits. A successful motion for mistrial aborts that possibility. On the other hand, if the moving party does not win on the merits, the issue will not be preserved for appeal unless the motion was made to the trial judge. Either course, making or foregoing the motion, entails some risks. The greater the belief in a jury victory, the more likely it becomes that counsel will risk waiving the motion and allow the trial to continue.

The trial judge denies John's motion for a mistrial.

The defendants proceed to present motions for directed verdicts. These motions address the legal sufficiency of the evidence. The defendants argue that under the applicable legal standards, there is not sufficient evidence to warrant submitting the case to the jury. Courts have developed standards over the centuries to ensure the right to a jury trial on genuine issues of fact. The jury cannot be allowed to act arbitrarily—to award a verdict unsubstantiated by evidence. So the motion tests the court's belief regarding the sufficiency of the evidence on the question of liability. The irony of this procedure is that the weakest case from the judge's standpoint may be the strongest from the standpoint of the jury. If the judge denies the motion, counsel must reassess the jury appeal of the evidence.

The defendants' motions for directed verdicts are denied.

4. INSTRUCTIONS AND CLOSING ARGUMENTS

Finally, the attorneys meet with the judge to discuss jury instructions—that is, the legal standards that will be given to the jury to guide its deliberations. Many of the instructions are standardized "pattern" instructions. Others are tailored to the specific case. The attorneys submit their proposed instructions in writing to the judge during the trial. The court informs counsel of its decisions regarding their requests before the attorneys' closing arguments to the jury. Why should counsel be informed prior to argument? Why shouldn't counsel be informed even before the presentation of the evidence? Would there be any significant problems in advising counsel as early as the opening statement?

The parties deliver closing arguments. After this the court charges the jury on the applicable legal principles. Certain jury instructions relating to liability are printed below:

> Plaintiff claims that each defendant was negligent.

> Negligence is the failure to use reasonable care. Negligence may consist of action or *in*action. A person is negligent if he fails to act as an ordinarily careful person would act under the circumstances.

> Before you can find a defendant liable, you must find that the defendant's negligence caused the plaintiff's injury. Negligence causes an injury if it helps produce the injury, and if the injury would not have happened without the negligence.

> On the defendants' claim that plaintiff was at fault, you must decide whether defendants have proved that plaintiff was at fault and, under all the circumstances of this case, whether any such fault should reduce plaintiff's full damages. These decisions are left to your sole discretion.

> If you decide that plaintiff's fault should reduce her damages, you must then determine the relative degrees of fault of each person whom you find to be at fault.

> The relative degrees of fault are to be entered on the verdict form as percentages of the total fault for plaintiff's injury.

> The fault of one person may be greater or lesser than that of another, but the relative degrees of all fault must add up to 100%. This will be clear from the verdict form.

> If you decide that plaintiff's fault should reduce plaintiff's full damages, the Court will later reduce those damages by the percentage of fault you have assigned to plaintiff.

Are the instructions comprehensible?

5. THE CASE GOES TO THE JURY

The jury deliberates for five hours. It returns a verdict, 6 of 8, finding Curt not liable and finding against John in the sum of $25,000. The court enters judgment accordingly. Various post-trial motions to upset the jury verdict are submitted by John's attorney and denied by the court.

6. POST–TRIAL MOTIONS AND APPELLATE REVIEW

With respect to the verdict against John, who, as a practical matter, is the prevailing party? Does the answer depend on John's potential economic exposure? Suppose Jessica was contemplating a $60,000 recovery and John's attorneys had been willing to settle for $35,000?

After the judgment is rendered, losing parties have the opportunity to file post-trial motions, such as a motion for a new trial. Or the losing party may seek appellate review. John may now appeal from adverse rulings, such as the denial of his motion to dismiss for lack of personal jurisdiction.[x] Recall that he was served with process while attending a rodeo in Arizona and that this was the only contact he had with the forum state. John may also appeal from the denial of the motion for a mistrial made in connection with the divulgence of insurance coverage. Many appeals today are based upon evidence rulings of the trial court. The court must administer the rules under which certain evidence is excluded and other evidence admitted. Sometimes the lines between admissibility and inadmissibility become blurred. If the appellate court finds prejudicial error in the ruling, it will reverse and remand for a new trial.

It appears that the jury verdict in Curt's favor is unassailable unless the court erred in its instructions of law or made improper evidentiary rulings. As to the instructions, suppose the court instructed the jury that if it finds that Kim was Curt's guest, then Curt cannot be liable for injuries unless he was grossly negligent. If an appellate court holds the guest statute not applicable to the case, it would be compelled to reverse and remand for a new trial. Why a new trial? Because the appellate court cannot know what the jury would have found had it been instructed correctly.

Among other issues, John appeals the personal jurisdiction issue. After considering the materials in Chapter III, *infra*, can you predict how the appellate court will rule? If you were Kim, would you settle the case? If you were John would you settle? For how much? There are juridical risks regarding the issue of personal jurisdiction. The economic costs of perfecting an appeal must also be taken into account. Consider, too, that Jessica may cross appeal requesting the appellate court to award a new trial on the issue of damages, claiming that the award is inadequate.

The intermediate appellate court's ruling on personal jurisdiction may not end the matter. The case may be appealed to the state's highest court and may ultimately be reviewed by the United States Supreme Court. Litigation can be a slow and expensive process.

Q. EPILOGUE

In the United States, virtually all lawyers representing plaintiffs in civil actions for personal injuries charge contingent fees. Many diverse

---

x. *See supra* p. 109.

voices have been raised against these fees specifying various perceived ethical improprieties. *See Grady, supra* p. 87. In Kim's case, Jessica will receive one-third of the jury award, assuming the judgment is eventually satisfied. If the retainer agreement so provides, Kim will receive the remainder, less any expenses not taxed to the losing party. The nontaxable expenses advanced by Jessica could easily exceed $1,000. Kim also has to pay hospital bills and other expenses incurred before trial.

Hypothesize for a moment the hours spent by Jessica in the preparation of this case, from the initial interview to the entry of judgment. The hypothesis does not include anticipated time in connection with further proceedings. Before the actual trial, Jessica could have spent thirty hours researching various legal issues, investigating and digesting the facts, preparing for and attending the depositions and answering interrogatories. The trial itself could have taken another two days. If Jessica devoted forty hours to the case, she earned approximately $200 per hour, hardly an exorbitant fee considering its contingent nature. Yet, she would have worked the same hours even had the jury awarded $100,000, and an hourly rate of approximately $800 in this case seems rather high. May Jessica charge a high fee to one client in order to make up for losses in other cases? Are there ethical problems with this payment scheme? Are there problems with respect to charging contingent fees in jurisdictions that have adopted the comparative negligence rule? How can the overall problem of contingent fees be handled in fairness to both the lawyer and the client?

Reconsider footnote 1, p. 95. Was Kim wise to have proceeded to trial?

Chapter III

ANALYSIS AND SYNTHESIS OF JUDICIAL DECISIONS

A. INTRODUCTION

MATERIALS FOR LEGAL METHOD[a]

N. Dowling, E. Patterson, & R. Powell

By derivation the word "synthesis," denotes a "putting together," that is, a determination of the net consequence of two or more contributing factors. Thus the synthesis of decisions requires relational thinking, that is, the determination of what each case contributes to the whole picture in which each decision, is one element. This process of synthesis constitutes the most important single ingredient in legal thinking. Cases are matched, or compared for any one of many purposes. Sometimes the objective is to gain exactness in the formulation of a rule of law. Each added case reveals some new application or some new restriction of the rule under consideration. Sometimes the objective is the very simple one of revealing the existence of inconsistent rules, one accepted in some states, the opposite one in others.[9] Sometimes, and most commonly in the work of a law student, the objective is to show how a rule has evolved, changing in statement as new and varying circumstances raise new facets of the problem for decision,[10] or changing *in substance* as a response to changing social and economic factors.

* * *

a. Second ed. by Harry W. Jones, 163–64 (1952).

9. * * * *See also* Llewellyn, Bramble Bush (1930), 45: "In all of this I have been proceeding upon the assumption—and this is the second further point about case method that I had in mind—that all the cases everywhere can stand together. It is unquestionably the assumption you must also make, at first. If they can be brought together you must bring them. At the same time you must not overlook that our law is built up statewise. It is not built up in one piece.

"Hence, in your matching of cases you may, as a last resort when unable to make the case fit together, fall back upon the answer; here is a conflict: these cases represent two different points of view."

10. This process is described with respect to the required simultaneous existence of "offer" and "acceptance" in the law of contracts by Llewellyn, Bramble Bush (1930), 44 as follows: "The first case

In your law school case books, it is rare to find a single case which is unrelated to its predecessors and successors. Your task, as a seeker after legal skill and knowledge, is to discover the relations between these cases and to do it *before* the instructor has a chance to tell you the relation. What you do for yourself in such relational thinking, exercises, trains and develops your mind. What you soak up from the instructor's synthesis may distend and bloat you temporarily and may even help you to pass an examination (if it comes soon enough), but it adds little, if anything to your development as a legal thinker.[12]

The remainder of this Chapter is designed to show you the techniques of synthesis. By careful study you will begin to develop the skill of

involves a man who makes an offer and gets in his revocation before his offer is accepted. The court decides that he cannot be sued upon his promise, and says that no contract can be made unless the minds of both parties are at one at once. The second case involves a man who has made a similar offer and has mailed a revocation, but to whom a letter of acceptance has been sent before his revocation was received. The court holds that he can be sued upon his promise, and says that his offer was being repeated every moment from the time that it arrived until the letter of acceptance was duly mailed. Here are two rules which are a little difficult to put together, and to square with sense, and which are, too, a little hard to square with the two holdings in the cases. We set to work to seek a way out which will do justice to the holdings. We arrive perhaps at this, that it is not necessary for the two minds to be at one at once, if the person who has received an offer thinks, and thinks reasonably, as he takes the last step of acceptance, that the offeror is standing by the offer. And to test the rule laid down in either case, as also to test our tentative formulation which we have built to cover both, we do two things. First and easiest, is to play variations on the facts, making the case gradually more and more extreme until we find the place beyond which it does not seem sense to go. Suppose, for example, our man does think the offeror still stands to his offer, and thinks it reasonably, on all his information; but yet a revocation has arrived, which his own clerk has failed to bring to his attention? We may find the stopping-place much sooner than we had expected, and thus be forced to recast and narrow the generalization we have made, or to recast it even on wholly different lines. The second and more difficult way of testing is to go to the books and find further cases in which variations on

the facts occur, and in which the importance of such variations has been put to the proof. The first way is the intuitional correction of hypothesis; the second way is the experimental test of whether an hypothesis is sound. Both are needed. The first, to save time. The second, to make sure. For you will remember that in your casebook you have only a sampling, a foundation for discussion, enough cases to set the problem and start you thinking. Before you can trust your results, either those which you achieve yourselves, or those which you take with you out of class, you must go to the writers who have read more cases and see what they have to say."

12. Compare Llewellyn, Bramble Bush (1930) 47: "Precisely for that reason it is necessary, it is vital, it is the very basic element of case law study, for you to have done your matching of the cases before you meet with his [the instructor's]. For it is not by watching him juggle the balls that you will learn. It is by matching his results against your own, by criticizing the process you have gone through in the light of the process he is going through. Indeed if you have not tried the game yourself, *you will not follow him.* The man who sees line-play in the football game is the man who once tried playing on the line himself. A Harlem audience responds to niceties in tap-dancing you do not even know are hard to do. Let me repeat: you will get little out of your instruction unless daily, repeatedly, consistently, you try the game out to the end the weary night before. At the same time, with growing skill you will bring criticism to bear on the man behind the desk as well. You will, if he is human, find inconsistencies between his work today and what he did or said five weeks ago. That will be useful for him. It will be infinitely more for you."

reading cases relationally to ascertain how the rules or principles announced in them contribute to the solution of the legal problem and to
the development of the law.

B.   FIRST EXERCISE IN SYNTHESIS: CASES INVOLVING CONSTITUTIONAL LIMITATIONS ON JURISDICTION OVER NONRESIDENT DEFENDANTS

The cases in this section are landmark United States Supreme Court
decisions imposing constitutional restraints on the assertion of personal
jurisdiction over nonresident defendants.

This area of the law was selected for study for a variety of pedagogical reasons:

First, from its embodiment in *Pennoyer v. Neff,* 95 U.S. (5 Otto) 714
(1877), to the present, the law of personal jurisdiction has responded to
changes in the socio-economic conditions of our society. The influence of
these changes on the development of the legal principles announced by
the Court has been expressly recognized in this area.

Second, constitutional doctrine evolves almost entirely from case
law. Study can therefore appropriately focus on the cases without need
to explore statutory law.

Third, in expounding constitutional principles the Court has wide
latitude to refine or even reject judicial principles. Although precedent
does provide a mooring for establishing judicial doctrine, movement and
change of direction is not stifled. As you read the cases, note how the
Court explains, distinguishes, overlooks, and rejects precedent.

A final reason for selecting the cases in this section is that most
students are unfamiliar with concepts of personal jurisdiction. Everyone,
or most everyone, will therefore begin the study from the same starting
point.

PENNOYER v. NEFF

Supreme Court of the United States, 1877.
95 U.S. (5 Otto) 714, 24 L.Ed. 565.

ERROR to the Circuit Court of the United States for the District of
Oregon.

JUSTICE FIELD delivered the opinion of the Court.

This is an action to recover the possession of a tract of land, of the
alleged value of $15,000, situated in the State of Oregon. The plaintiff
asserts title to the premises by a patent of the United States issued to
him in [March] 1866, under the act of Congress of Sept. 27, 1850, usually
known as the Donation Law of Oregon. The defendant claims to have
acquired the premises under a sheriff's deed, made upon a sale of the
property on execution issued upon a judgment recovered against the

plaintiff in one of the circuit courts of the State. The case turns upon the validity of this judgment.

It appears from the record that the judgment was rendered in February, 1866, in favor of J.H. Mitchell, for less than $300, including costs, in an action brought by him upon a demand for services as an attorney; that, at the time the action was commenced and the judgment rendered, the defendant therein, the plaintiff here, was a non-resident of the State; that he was not personally served with process, and did not appear therein; and that the judgment was entered upon his default in not answering the complaint, upon a constructive service of summons by publication.

The Code of Oregon provides for such service when an action is brought against a non-resident and absent defendant, who has property within the State. It also provides, where the action is for the recovery of money or damages, for the attachment of the property of the non-resident. And it also declares that no natural person is subject to the jurisdiction of a court of the State, "unless he appear in the court, or be found within the State, or be a resident thereof, or have property therein; and, in the last case, only to the extent of such property at the time the jurisdiction attached." Construing this latter provision to mean, that, in an action for money or damages where a defendant does not appear in the court, and is not found within the State, and is not a resident thereof, but has property therein, the jurisdiction of the court extends only over such property, the declaration expresses a principle of general, if not universal, law. The authority of every tribunal is necessarily restricted by the territorial limits of the State in which it is established. Any attempt to exercise authority beyond those limits would be deemed in every other forum, as has been said by this court, an illegitimate assumption of power, and be resisted as mere abuse. In the case against the plaintiff, the property here in controversy sold under the judgment rendered was not attached, nor in any way brought under the jurisdiction of the court. Its first connection with the case was caused by a levy of the execution. It was not, therefore, disposed of pursuant to any adjudication, but only in enforcement of a personal judgment, having no relation to the property, rendered against a non-resident without service of process upon him in the action, or his appearance therein. The court below did not consider that an attachment of the property was essential to its jurisdiction or to the validity of the sale, but held that the judgment was invalid from defects in the affidavit upon which the order of publication was obtained, and in the affidavit by which the publication was proved.

There is some difference of opinion among the members of this court as to the rulings upon these alleged defects. The majority are of opinion that inasmuch as the statute requires, for an order of publication, that certain facts shall appear by affidavit *to the satisfaction of the court or judge,* defects in such affidavit can only be taken advantage of on appeal, or by some other direct proceeding, and cannot be urged to impeach the judgment collaterally. The majority of the court are also of opinion that the provision of the statute requiring proof of the publication in a newspaper to be made by the "affidavit of the printer, or his foreman, or his principal clerk," is satisfied when the affidavit is made by the editor of the paper. The term "printer," in their judgment, is there used not to indicate the person who sets up the type,—he does not usually have a foreman or clerks,—it is rather used as synonymous with publisher. The Supreme Court of New York so held in one case; observing that, for the purpose of making the required proof, publishers were "within the spirit of the statute." And, following this ruling, the Supreme Court of California held that an affidavit made by a "publisher and proprietor" was sufficient. The term "editor," as used when the statute of New York was passed, from which the Oregon law is borrowed, usually included not only the person who wrote or selected the articles for publication, but the person who published the paper and put it into circulation. Webster, in an early edition of his Dictionary, gives as one of the definitions of an editor, a person "who superintends the publication of a newspaper." It is principally since that time that the business of an editor has been separated from that of a publisher and printer, and has become an independent profession.

If, therefore, we were confined to the rulings of the court below upon the defects in the affidavits mentioned, we should be unable to uphold its decision. But it was also contended in that court, and is insisted upon here, that the judgment in the State court against the plaintiff was void for want of personal service of process on him, or of his appearance in the action in which it was rendered, and that the premises in controversy could not be subjected to the payment of the demand of a resident creditor except by a proceeding *in rem;* that is, by a direct proceeding against the property for that purpose. If these positions are sound, the ruling of the Circuit Court as to the invalidity of that judgment must be sustained, notwithstanding our dissent from the reasons upon which it was made. And that they are sound would seem to follow from two well-established principles of public law respecting the jurisdiction of an independent State over persons and property. The several States of the Union are not, it is true, in every respect independent, many of the rights and powers which originally belonged to them being now vested in the government created by the Constitution. But, except as restrained and limited by that instrument, they possess and exercise the authority of independent States, and the principles of public law to which we have referred are applicable to them. One of these principles is, that every State possesses exclusive jurisdiction and sovereignty over persons and property within its territory. As a consequence, every State has the power to determine for itself the civil *status* and capacities of its inhabitants; to prescribe the subjects upon which they may contract, the forms and solemnities with which their contracts shall be executed, the rights and obligations arising from them, and the mode in which their validity shall be determined and their obligations enforced; and also to regulate the manner and conditions upon which property situated within such territory, both personal and real, may be acquired, enjoyed, and transferred. The other principle of public law referred to follows from the one mentioned; that is, that no State can exercise direct jurisdiction and authority over persons or property without its territory. The several States are of equal dignity and authority, and the independence of one implies the exclusion of power from all others. And so it is laid down by jurists, as an elementary principle, that the laws of one State have no operation outside of its territory, except so far as is allowed by comity; and that no tribunal established by it can extend its process beyond that territory so as to subject either persons or property to its decisions. "Any exertion of authority of this sort beyond this limit," says Story, "is a mere nullity, and incapable of binding such persons or property in any other tribunals." Story, Confl.Laws, sect. 539.

But as contracts made in one State may be enforceable only in another State, and property may be held by non-residents, the exercise of the jurisdiction which every State is admitted to possess over persons and property within its own territory will often affect persons and property without it. To any influence exerted in this way by a State affecting persons resident or property situated elsewhere, no objection can be justly taken; whilst any direct exertion of authority upon them, in an attempt to give ex-territorial operation to its laws, or to enforce an ex-territorial jurisdiction by its tribunals, would be deemed an encroachment upon the independence of the State in which the persons are domiciled or the property is situated, and be resisted as usurpation.

Thus the State, through its tribunals, may compel persons domiciled within its limits to execute, in pursuance of their contracts respecting property elsewhere situated, instruments in such form and with such solemnities as to transfer the title, so far as such formalities can be complied with; and the exercise of this jurisdiction in no manner interferes with the supreme control over the property by the State within which it is situated. [Citations omitted.]

So the State, through its tribunals, may subject property situated within its limits owned by non-residents to the payment of the demand of its own citizens against them; and the exercise of this jurisdiction in no respect infringes upon the sovereignty of the State where the owners are domiciled. Every State owes protection to its own citizens; and, when non-residents deal with them, it is a legitimate and just exercise of authority to hold and appropriate any property owned by such non-residents to satisfy the claims of its citizens. It is in virtue of the State's jurisdiction over the property of the non-resident situated within its limits that its tribunals can inquire into that non-resident's obligations to its own citizens, and the inquiry can then be carried only to the extent necessary to control the disposition of the property. If the non-resident have no property in the State, there is nothing upon which the tribunals can adjudicate.

These views are not new. They have been frequently expressed, with more or less distinctness, in opinions of eminent judges, and have been carried into adjudications in numerous cases. Thus, in *Picquet v. Swan,* 5 Mass. 35, Mr. Justice Story said:

> Where a party is within a territory, he may justly be subjected to its process, and bound personally by the judgment pronounced on such process against him. Where he is not within such territory, and is not personally subject to its laws, if, on account of his supposed or actual property being within the territory, process by the local laws may, by attachment, go to compel his appearance, and for his default to appear judgment may be pronounced against him, such a judgment must, upon general principles, be deemed only to bind him to the extent of such property, and cannot have the effect of a conclusive judgment *in personam,* for the plain reason, that, except so far as the property is concerned, it is a judgment *coram non judice.*

And in *Boswell's Lessee v. Otis,* 9 How. 336, where the title of the plaintiff in ejectment was acquired on a sheriff's sale, under a money decree rendered upon publication of notice against non-residents, in a suit brought to enforce a contract relating to land, Mr. Justice McLean said:

> Jurisdiction is acquired in one of two modes: first, as against the person of the defendant by the service of process; or, secondly, by a procedure against the property of the defendant within the jurisdiction of the court. In the latter case, the defendant is not personally bound by the judgment beyond the property in question. And it is immaterial whether the proceeding against the property be by an attachment or bill in chancery. It must be substantially a proceeding *in rem.*

These citations are not made as authoritative expositions of the law; for the language was perhaps not essential to the decision of the cases in which it was used, but as expressions of the opinion of eminent jurists. But in *Cooper v. Reynolds,* reported in the 10th of Wallace, it was essential to the disposition of the case to declare the effect of a personal action against an absent party, without the jurisdiction of the court, not served with process or voluntarily submitting to the tribunal, when it was sought to subject his property to the payment of a demand of a resident complainant; and in the opinion there delivered we have a clear statement of the law as to the efficacy of such actions, and the jurisdiction of the court over them. In that case, the action was for damages for alleged false imprisonment of the plaintiff; and, upon his affidavit that the defendants had fled from the State, or had absconded or concealed themselves so that the ordinary process of law could not reach them, a writ of attachment was sued out against their property. Publication was ordered by the court, giving notice to them to appear and plead, answer or demur, or that the action would be taken as confessed and proceeded in *ex parte* as to them. Publication was had; but they made default, and judgment was entered against them, and the attached property was sold under it. The purchaser having been put into possession of the property, the original owner brought ejectment for its recovery. In considering the character of the proceeding, the court, speaking through Mr. Justice Miller, said:

> Its essential purpose or nature is to establish, by the judgment of the court, a demand or claim against the defendant, and subject his property lying within the territorial jurisdiction of the court to the payment of that demand. But the plaintiff is met at the commencement of his proceedings by the fact that the defendant is not within the territorial jurisdiction, and cannot be served with any process by which he can be brought personally within the power of the court. For this difficulty the statute has provided a remedy. It says that, upon affidavit being made of that fact, a writ of attachment may be issued and levied on any of the defendant's property, and a publication may be made warning him to appear; and that thereafter the court may proceed in the case, whether he appears or not. If the defendant appears, the cause becomes mainly a suit *in personam,* with the added incident, that the property attached remains liable, under the control of the court, to answer to any demand which may be established against the defendant by the final judgment of the court. But if there is no appearance of the defendant, and no service of process on him, the case becomes in its essential nature a proceeding *in rem,* the only effect of which is to subject the property attached to the payment of the demand which the court may find to be due to the plaintiff. That such is the nature of this proceeding in this latter class of cases is clearly evinced by two well-established propositions: first, the judgment of the court, though in form a personal judgment against the defendant, has no effect beyond the property attached in that suit. No general execution can be issued for any balance unpaid after the attached property is exhausted. No suit can be maintained on such a judgment in the same court, or in any other; nor can it be used as evidence in any other proceeding not affecting the attached property; nor could the costs in that proceeding be collected of defendant out of any other property than that attached in the suit. Second, the court, in such a suit, cannot proceed, unless the officer finds some property of defendant on which to levy the writ of attachment. A return that none can be found is the end of the case, and deprives the court of further jurisdiction, though the publication may have been duly made and proven in court.

The fact that the defendants in that case had fled from the State, or had concealed themselves, so as not to be reached by the ordinary process of the court, and were not non-residents, was not made a point in the decision. The opinion treated them as being without the territorial jurisdiction of the court; and the grounds and extent of its authority over persons and property thus situated were considered, when they were not brought within its jurisdiction by personal service or voluntary appearance.

The writer of the present opinion considered that some of the objections to the preliminary proceedings in the attachment suit were well taken, and therefore dissented from the judgment of the court; but to the doctrine declared in the above citation he agreed, and he may add, that it received the approval of all the judges. It is the only doctrine consistent with proper protection to citizens of other States. If, without personal service, judgments *in personam,* obtained *ex parte* against non-residents and absent parties, upon mere publication of process, which, in the great majority of cases, would never be seen by the parties interested, could be upheld and enforced, they would be the constant instruments of fraud and oppression. Judgments for all sorts of claims upon contracts and for torts, real or pretended, would be thus obtained, under which property would be seized, when the evidence of the transactions upon which they were founded, if they ever had any existence, had perished.

Substituted service by publication, or in any other authorized form, may be sufficient to inform parties of the object of proceedings taken where property is once brought under the control of the court by seizure or some equivalent act. The law assumes that property is always in the possession of its owner, in person or by agent; and it proceeds upon the theory that its seizure will inform him, not only that it is taken into the custody of the court, but that he must look to any proceedings authorized by law upon such seizure for its condemnation and sale. Such service may also be sufficient in cases where the object of the action is to reach and dispose of property in the State, or of some interest therein, by enforcing a contract or a lien respecting the same, or to partition it among different owners, or, when the public is a party, to condemn and appropriate it for a public purpose. In other words, such service may answer in all actions which are substantially proceedings *in rem.* But where the entire object of the action is to determine the personal rights and obligations of the defendants, that is, where the suit is merely *in personam,* constructive service in this form upon a non-resident is ineffectual for any purpose. Process from the tribunals of one State cannot run into another State, and summon parties there domiciled to leave its territory and respond to proceedings against them. Publication of process or notice within the State where the tribunal sits cannot create any greater obligation upon the non-resident to appear. Process sent to him out of the State, and process published within it, are equally unavailing in proceedings to establish his personal liability.

The want of authority of the tribunals of a State to adjudicate upon the obligations of non-residents, where they have no property within its limits, is not denied by the court below: but the position is assumed, that, where they have property within the State, it is immaterial whether the property is in the first instance brought under the control of the court by attachment or some other equivalent act, and afterwards applied by its judgment to the satisfaction of demands against its owner; or such demands be first established in a personal action, and the property of the non-resident be afterwards seized and sold on execution. But the answer to this position has already been given in the statement, that the jurisdiction of the court to inquire into and determine his obligations at all is only incidental to its jurisdiction over the property. Its jurisdiction in that respect cannot be made to depend upon facts to be ascertained after it has tried the cause and rendered the judgment. If the judgment be previously void, it will not become valid by the subsequent discovery of property of the defendant, or by his subsequent acquisition of it. The judgment, if void when rendered, will always remain void: it cannot occupy the doubtful position of being valid if property be found, and void if there be none. Even if the position assumed were confined to cases where the non-resident defendant possessed property in the State at the commencement of the action, it would still make the validity of the proceedings and judgment depend upon the question whether, before the levy of the execution, the defendant had or had not disposed of the property. If before the levy the property should be sold, then, according to this position, the judgment would not be binding. This doctrine would introduce a new element of uncertainty in judicial proceedings. The contrary is the law: the validity of every judgment depends upon the jurisdiction of the court before it is rendered, not upon what may occur subsequently.

* * *

The force and effect of judgments rendered against non-residents without personal service of process upon them, or their voluntary appearance, have been the subject of frequent consideration in the courts of the United States and of the several States, as attempts have been made to enforce such judgments in States other than those in which they were rendered, under the provision of the Constitution requiring that "full faith and credit shall be given in each State to the public acts, records, and judicial proceedings of every other State;" and the act of Congress providing for the mode of authenticating such acts, records, and proceedings, and declaring that, when thus authenticated, "they shall have such faith and credit given to them in every court within the United States as they have by law or usage in the courts of the State from which they are or shall be taken." In the earlier cases, it was supposed that the act gave to all judgments the same effect in other States which they had by law in the State where rendered. But this view was afterwards qualified so as to make the act applicable only when the court rendering the judgment had jurisdiction of the parties and of the subject-matter, and not to preclude an inquiry into the jurisdiction of the court in which the judgment was rendered, or the right of the State itself to exercise authority over the person or the subject-matter.

This whole subject has been very fully and learnedly considered in the recent case of *Thompson v. Whitman,* 18 Wall. 457, where all the authorities are carefully reviewed and distinguished, and the conclusion above stated is not only reaffirmed, but the doctrine is asserted, that the record of a judgment rendered in another State may be contradicted as to the facts necessary to give the court jurisdiction against its recital of their existence. In all the cases brought in the State and Federal courts, where attempts have been made under the act of Congress to give effect in one State to personal judgments rendered in another State against non-residents, without service upon them, or upon substituted service by publication, or in some other form, it has been held, without an exception, so far as we are aware, that such judgments were without any binding force, except as to property, or interests in property, within the State, to reach and affect which was the object of the action in which the judgment was rendered, and which property was brought under control of the court in connection with the process against the person. The proceeding in such cases, though in the form of a personal action, has been uniformly treated, where service was not obtained, and the party did not voluntarily appear, as effectual and binding merely as a proceeding *in rem,* and as having no operation beyond the disposition of the property, or some interest therein. And the reason assigned for this conclusion has been that which we have already stated, that the tribunals of one State have no jurisdiction over persons beyond its limits, and can inquire only into their obligations to its citizens when exercising its conceded jurisdiction over their property within its limits. In *Bissell v. Briggs,* decided by the Supreme Court of Massachusetts as early as 1813, the law is stated substantially in conformity with these views. In that case, the court considered at length the effect of the constitutional provision, and the act of Congress mentioned, and after stating that, in order to entitle the judgment rendered in any court of the United States to the full faith and credit mentioned in the Constitution, the court must have had jurisdiction not only of the cause, but of the parties, it proceeded to illustrate its position by observing, that, where a debtor living in one State has goods, effects, and credits in another, his creditor living in the other State may have the property attached pursuant to its laws, and, on recovering judgment, have the property applied to its satisfaction; and that the party in whose hands the property was would be protected by the judgment in the State of the debtor against a suit for it, because the court rendering the judgment had jurisdiction to that extent; but that if the property attached were insufficient to satisfy the judgment, and the creditor should sue on that judgment in the State of the debtor, he would fail, because the defendant was not amenable to the court rendering the judgment. In other words, it was held that over the property within the State the court had jurisdiction by the attachment, but had none over his person; and that any determination of his liability, except so far as was necessary for the disposition of the property, was invalid.

In *Kilburn v. Woodworth,* 5 Johns. (N.Y.) 37, an action of debt was brought in New York upon a personal judgment recovered in Massachusetts. The defendant in that judgment was not served with process; and the suit was commenced by the attachment of a bedstead belonging to the defendant, accompanied with a summons to appear, served on his wife after she had left her place in Massachusetts. The court held that the attachment bound only the property attached as a proceeding *in rem,* and that it could not bind the defendant, observing, that to bind a defendant personally, when he was never personally summoned or had notice of the proceeding, would be contrary to the first principles of justice, repeating the language in that respect of Chief Justice DeGrey, used in the case of *Fisher v. Lane*, 3 Wils. 297, in 1772. To the same purport decisions are found in all the State courts. In several of the cases, the decision has been accompanied with the observation that a personal judgment thus recovered has no binding force without the State in which it is rendered, implying that in such State it may be valid and binding. But if the court has no jurisdiction over the person of the defendant by reason of his non-residence, and, consequently, no authority to pass upon his personal rights and obligations; if the whole proceeding, without service upon him or his appearance, is *coram non judice* and void; if to hold a defendant bound by such a judgment is contrary to the first principles of justice,—it is difficult to see how the judgment can legitimately have any force within the State. The language used can be justified only on the ground that there was no mode of directly reviewing such judgment or impeaching its validity within the State where rendered; and that, therefore, it could be called in question only when its enforcement was elsewhere attempted. In later cases, this language is repeated with less frequency than formerly, it beginning to be considered, as it always ought to have been, that a judgment which can be treated in any State of this Union as contrary to the first principles of justice, and as an absolute nullity, because rendered without any jurisdiction of the tribunal over the party, is not entitled to any respect in the State where rendered.

Be that as it may, the courts of the United States are not required to give effect to judgments of this character when any right is claimed under them. Whilst they are not foreign tribunals in their relations to the State courts, they are tribunals of a different sovereignty, exercising a distinct and independent jurisdiction, and are bound to give to the judgments of the State courts only the same faith and credit which the courts of another State are bound to give to them.

Since the adoption of the Fourteenth Amendment to the Federal Constitution, the validity of such judgments may be directly questioned, and their enforcement in the State resisted, on the ground that proceedings in a court of justice to determine the personal rights and obligations of parties over whom that court has no jurisdiction do not constitute due process of law. Whatever difficulty may be experienced in giving to those terms a definition which will embrace every permissible exertion of power affecting private rights, and exclude such as is forbidden, there can be no doubt of their meaning when applied to judicial proceedings. They then mean a course of legal proceedings according to those rules and principles which have been established in our systems of jurisprudence for the protection and enforcement of private rights. To give such proceedings any validity, there must be a tribunal competent by its constitution—that is, by the law of its creation—to pass upon the subject-matter of the suit; and, if that involves merely a determination of the personal liability of the defendant, he must be brought within its jurisdiction by service of process within the State, or his voluntary appearance.

Except in cases affecting the personal *status* of the plaintiff, and cases in which that mode of service may be considered to have been assented to in advance, as hereinafter mentioned, the substituted service of process by publication, allowed by the law of Oregon and by similar laws in other States, where actions are brought against non-residents, is effectual only where, in connection with process against the person for commencing the action, property in the State is brought under the control of the court, and subjected to its disposition by process adapted to that purpose, or where the judgment is sought as a means of reaching such property or affecting some interest therein; in other words, where the action is in the nature of a proceeding *in rem*.

It is true that, in a strict sense, a proceeding *in rem* is one taken directly against property, and has for its object the disposition of the property, without reference to the title of individual claimants; but, in a larger and more general sense, the terms are applied to actions between parties, where the direct object is to reach and dispose of property owned by them, or of some interest therein. Such are cases commenced by attachment against the property of debtors, or instituted to partition real estate, foreclose a mortgage, or enforce a lien. So far as they affect property in the State, they are substantially proceedings *in rem* in the broader sense which we have mentioned.

It follows from the views expressed that the personal judgment recovered in the State court of Oregon against the plaintiff herein, then a non-resident of the State, was without any validity, and did not authorize a sale of the property in controversy.

To prevent any misapplication of the views expressed in this opinion, it is proper to observe that we do not mean to assert, by any thing we have said, that a State may not authorize proceedings to determine the *status* of one of its citizens towards a non-resident, which would be binding within the State, though made without service of process or personal notice to the non-resident. The jurisdiction which every State possesses to determine the civil *status* and capacities of all its inhabitants involves authority to prescribe the conditions on which proceedings affecting them may be commenced and carried on within its territory. The State, for example, has absolute right to prescribe the conditions upon which the marriage relation between its own citizens shall be created, and the causes for which it may be dissolved. One of the parties guilty of acts for which, by the law of the State, a dissolution may be granted, may have removed to a State where no dissolution is permitted. The complaining party would, therefore, fail if a divorce were sought in the State of the defendant; and if application could not be made to the tribunals of the complainant's domicile in such case, and proceedings be there instituted without personal service of process or personal notice to the offending party, the injured citizen would be without redress.

Neither do we mean to assert that a State may not require a non-resident entering into a partnership or association within its limits, or making contracts enforceable there, to appoint an agent or representative in the State to receive service of process and notice in legal proceedings instituted with respect to such partnership, association, or contracts, or to designate a place where such service may be made and notice given, and provide, upon their failure, to make such appointment or to designate such place that service may be made upon a public officer designated for that purpose, or in some other prescribed way, and that judgments rendered upon such service may not be binding upon the non-residents both within and without the State. Nor do we doubt that a State, on creating corporations or other institutions for pecuniary or charitable purposes, may provide a mode in which their conduct may be investigated, their obligations enforced, or their charters revoked, which shall require other than personal service upon their officers or members. Parties becoming members of such corporations or institutions would hold their interest subject to the conditions prescribed by law.

In the present case, there is no feature of this kind, and, consequently, no consideration of what would be the effect of such legislation in enforcing the contract of a non-resident can arise. The question here respects only the validity of a money judgment rendered in one State, in an action upon a simple contract against the resident of another, without service of process upon him, or his appearance therein.

Judgment affirmed.

JUSTICE HUNT dissenting.

I am compelled to dissent from the opinion and judgment of the court, and, deeming the question involved to be important, I take leave to record my views upon it.

* * *

In my opinion, this decision is at variance with the long-established practice under the statutes of the States of this Union, is unsound in principle, and, I fear, may be disastrous in its effects. It tends to produce confusion in titles which have been obtained under similar statutes in existence for nearly a century; it invites litigation and strife, and overthrows a well-settled rule of property.

To say that a sovereign State has the power to ordain that the property of non-residents within its territory may be subjected to the payment of debts due to its citizens, if the property is levied upon at the commencement of a suit, but that it has not such power if the property is levied upon at the end of the suit, is a refinement and a depreciation of a great general principle that, in my judgment, cannot be sustained.

A reference to the statutes of the different States, and to the statutes of the United States, and to the decided cases, and a consideration of the principles on which they stand, will more clearly exhibit my view of the question.

[Discussion of New York and Oregon statutes omitted.]

Provisions similar in their effect, in authorizing the commencement of suits by attachment against absent debtors, in which all of the property of the absent debtor, real and personal, not merely that seized upon the attachment, is placed under the control of trustees, who sell it for the benefit of all the creditors, and make just distribution thereof, conveying absolute title to the property sold, have been upon the statute-book of New York for more than sixty years.

[Discussion of several state statutes omitted.]

Without going into a wearisome detail of the statutes of the various States, it is safe to say that nearly every State in the Union provides a process by which the lands and other property of a non-resident debtor may be subjected to the payment of his debts, through a judgment or decree against the owner, obtained upon a substituted service of the summons or writ commencing the action.

The principle of substituted service is also a rule of property under the statutes of the United States.

* * *

All these statutes are now adjudged to be unconstitutional and void. The titles obtained under them are not of the value of the paper on which they are recorded, except where a preliminary attachment was issued.

The question whether, in a suit commenced like the present one, a judgment can be obtained, which, if sued upon in another State, will be conclusive against the debtor, is not before us; nor does the question arise as to the faith and credit to be given in one State to a judgment recovered in another. The learning on that subject is not applicable. The point is simply whether land lying in the same State may be subjected to process at the end of a suit thus commenced. I have found no case in which it is adjudged that a statute must require a preliminary seizure of such property as necessary to the validity of the proceeding against it, or that there must have been a previous specific lien upon it; that is, I have found no case where such has been the judgment of the court upon facts making necessary the decision of the point. On the contrary, in the case of the attachment laws of New York and of New Jersey, which distribute all of the non-resident's property, not merely that levied on by the attachment, and in several of the reported cases already referred to, where the judgment was sustained, neither of these preliminary facts existed.

* * *

The case of *Cooper v. Reynolds,* 10 Wall. 308, is cited [in hostility to the views I have expressed]. There the judgment of the court below, refusing to give effect to a judgment obtained upon an order of publication against a non-resident, was reversed in this court. The suit was commenced, or immediately accompanied (it is not clear which) by an attachment which was levied upon the real estate sold, and for the recovery of which this action was brought. This court sustained the title founded upon the suit commenced against the non-resident by attachment. In the opinion delivered in that case there may be remarks, by way of argument or illustration, tending to show that a judgment obtained in a suit not commenced by the levy of an attachment will not give title to land purchased under it. They are, however, extrajudicial, the decision itself sustaining the judgment obtained under the State statute by publication.

* * *

In *Cooper v. Smith*, it is said, that where no process is served on the defendant, nor property attached, nor garnishee charged, nor appearance entered, a judgment based on a publication of the pendency of the suit will be void, and may be impeached, collaterally or otherwise, and forms no bar to a recovery in opposition to it, nor any foundation for a title claimed under it. The language is very general, and goes much beyond the requirement of the case, which was an appeal from a personal judgment obtained by publication against the defendant, and where, as the court say, the petition was not properly verified. All that the court decided was that this judgment should be reversed. This is quite a different question from the one before us. Titles obtained by purchase at a sale upon an erroneous judgment are generally good, although the judgment itself be afterwards reversed.

* * *

It is said that the case where a preliminary seizure has been made, and jurisdiction thereby conferred, differs from that where the property is seized at the end of the action, in this: in the first case, the property is supposed to be so near to its owner, that, if seizure is made of it, he will be aware of the fact, and have his opportunity to defend, and jurisdiction of the person is thus obtained. This, however, is matter of discretion and of judgment only. Such seizure is not in itself notice to the defendant, and it is not certain that he will by that means receive notice. Adopted as a means of communicating it, and although a very good means, it is not the only one, nor necessarily better than a publication of the pendency of the suit, made with an honest intention to reach the debtor.

I am not willing to declare that a sovereign State cannot subject the land within its limits to the payment of debts due to its citizens, or that the power to do so depends upon the fact whether its statute shall authorize the property to be levied upon at the commencement of the suit or at its termination. This is a matter of detail, and I am of opinion, that if reasonable notice be given, with an opportunity to defend when appearance is made, the question of power will be fully satisfied.

Notes and Questions

1. *Pennoyer* is the landmark case impressing territorial sovereignty as a constitutional limitation on the power of states to exercise jurisdiction over

persons and things. Although some of the legal propositions contained in the case are no longer valid, it still presents unique opportunities to hone analytical skills. First year civil procedure courses devote considerable attention to *Pennoyer*. Even after class discussion, however, many students find it difficult to recover from the confusion caused by the case.

J.H. Mitchell sued Marcus Neff in the state court to recover an attorney's fee. Upon what basis did Mitchell believe the state court could assert jurisdiction? Defendant Neff was a nonresident who, at the time the suit was commenced, apparently did not even own property within the state. Was it merely coincidental that Neff thereafter obtained title to property?

Mitchell is designated the plaintiff in the state court proceeding; Neff, the defendant. The plaintiff's name usually appears first in the title of the case, so the state action would have been designated *Mitchell v. Neff*. The case ended in a default judgment in favor of Mitchell since Neff failed to defend. To satisfy the judgment, Mitchell had the sheriff sell Neff's land to Sylvester Pennoyer. Mitchell took the money; Pennoyer, possession of the property. Neff received nothing except the elimination of any obligation to pay the attorney's fee that was the subject of the state suit.

Neff then sued Pennoyer in a federal court. The case, styled *Neff v. Pennoyer,* sought to recover possession of the land. The court found that the default judgment in *Mitchell v. Neff* was invalid and therefore entered a judgment in favor of *Neff.* Pennoyer, the losing party, appealed to the United States Supreme Court. The action in the Supreme Court then became *Pennoyer v. Neff,* rather than *Neff v. Pennoyer,* because of the custom of first naming the party seeking relief in the particular court. Pennoyer sought to reverse the lower court judgment and to establish the validity of the state court judgment upon which his title depended.

Pennoyer, the party appealing from the judgment in the lower court, may be designated as the petitioner, the plaintiff in error, or the appellant. Correspondingly, Neff, the prevailing party in the lower court, is designated as the respondent, the defendant in error, or the appellee. The proper designation depends upon local rules and practice.

By now you have observed that the defendant in the state action became the plaintiff in the original federal action and the defendant in error in the Supreme Court. Still confused? Now reread the case carefully. Had you read it too quickly before? You will soon learn to read more carefully, to look up unfamiliar terms, and to reread difficult passages.

2. The lower federal court rested its decision on defects in the affidavits upon which the order of publication was made and proved. It did not consider attachment of the land at the commencement of the suit essential to the state court's jurisdiction. The Supreme Court stated that alleged defects in the affidavit could not be considered as grounds for upsetting the state court judgment. Why?

The Court distinguished between "direct review" and "collateral impeachment." The former means review by an appellate court of a lower court decision—in other words, had Neff raised the jurisdictional point in the state court action, he could have appealed the adverse judgment to a higher court within the system. The alleged defects contained in the affidavits could properly have been raised by Neff and considered by the appellate court. In American jurisprudence, the usual and customary method of seeking relief from lower court judgments is by appeal to a higher court. Each system has designated a specific time within which to perfect an appeal. In many systems, the period for appeal as of right in civil cases is 30 days. Why didn't Neff appeal? Assuming Neff could have appealed within the time period allowed by state law, would he have been able to obtain complete relief?

Collateral impeachment, on the other hand, involves attacking a judgment in a separate case in a court of original jurisdiction. For example, a *habeas corpus* action is a collateral attack on a judgment of conviction in a criminal case. In varying contexts, collateral impeachment is permissible in civil cases. *Pennoyer* illustrates one such situation. The most common use of this procedure, however, is to attack a judgment of a rendering state in a proceeding instituted by the judgment creditor in another jurisdiction to enforce the judgment.

The Supreme Court in *Pennoyer* asserted that certain irregularities may be relied upon in a direct attack, but may not be the basis for upsetting the judgment in collateral proceedings. Why? What are the criteria for determining the classification into which an irregularity falls?

3. The state court action was never contested; Neff never asserted any defense, and judgment was accordingly entered against him by default. Can you think of reasons why a defendant would allow a default judgment to be entered?

4. The Supreme Court relied on cases decided under the Full Faith and Credit Clause of the Constitution. These precedents held that full faith and credit did not require a state court to enforce another state court's judgments when the rendering court lacked jurisdiction. Prior to the enactment of the Fourteenth Amendment, however, state court judgments could be assailed within the rendering state only on limited federal constitutional grounds. Can you think of any?

Should the principles regarding enforcement of sister states' judicial obligations that underlie the Full Faith and Credit Clause apply when a *federal* court is asked to enforce a state court judgment? Should similar limitations on this enforcement obligation also apply? Although the constitutional provision refers by its terms to the obligations of states, Congress has imposed the obligation of full faith and credit on every court within the United States, state and federal. What is the source of this congressional power?

5. Did the *Pennoyer* opinion adequately articulate the preexisting principles or rules on which the Court based its opinion? What were those principles and rules?

6. Law professors use hypotheticals to focus attention on the reasoning of the court and to demonstrate the art of distinguishing. Hypotheticals are also useful in ferreting out *dicta*. Be clear, however, that even though *dicta* are not controlling, lower courts might wish to consider even passing statements contained in an appellate decision. Of course, the extent to which the lower court will defer to *dicta* will depend upon a number of factors. Can you think of any?

Assume state law allows jurisdiction under the circumstances set forth in the following hypotheticals. Consider whether *Pennoyer* permits the assertion of jurisdiction.

a.   A New York resident sues another New York resident in a New York state court. Assume: (i) process[b] is served in New York; (ii) process is served in Connecticut.

b.   A California resident sues a New York resident in a New York state court. Assume: (i) process is served in New York; (ii) process is served in Connecticut.

c.   A New York resident sues a California resident in a New York state court. Assume: (i) process is served in New York by publication; (ii) process is served in California; (iii) process is served upon the defendant in New York while he is visiting a friend. Recall the facts of *Johnson v. Roscoe & Baker, supra* Chapter II.

d.   A New York resident sues a California resident in a New York state court. At the commencement of the suit the defendant's land in New York is attached. Assume instead that the defendant's car is attached. What if the defendant's bank account is attached? Does your answer depend upon the nature of the cause of action or of the property seized? Does *Pennoyer* consider these factors? *See infra* note 7. Is the place where the cause of action arose significant to your analysis?

e.   May a New York court grant a divorce to a resident petitioner if the respondent (defendant) is not found in New York? Are statements in *Pennoyer* relating to this question *dicta* or necessary steps in the chain of the Court's reasoning?

7.   All the justices agreed that a state may require nonresident property owners to satisfy the demands of its citizens. Moreover, all the justices concurred in the proposition that a judgment entered against a nonappearing nonresident not owning property within the state is constitutionally infirm. The major point of disagreement related to the timing of the seizure of the nonresident's property. Must seizure be effected at the inception of the lawsuit, or may it occur later, for example at the execution stage to satisfy the judgment?

Justice Field, writing for the majority, relied extensively on the decision in *Cooper v. Reynolds. See supra* p. 154. Are the statements in *Cooper* relating to the seizure of property at the outset of the proceedings "essential to the disposition of the case" or, in the words of Justice Hunt, "extra judicial"? Note Justice Hunt's challenge to the Court:

> I have found no case in which it is adjudged that a statute must require a preliminary seizure of nonresident property as necessary to the validity of the proceeding against it * * * that is, I have found no case where such has been the judgment of the court upon facts making necessary the decision of the point.

Did the Court meet that challenge? By citing any cases on point? By any other methods? Consider whether cases involving the right of states to

---

b. Process refers to the summons and complaint.

refuse enforcement of sister-state judgments under the full faith and credit clause are relevant to the precise issue in *Pennoyer*.

Justice Hunt cited statutes permitting seizure of property after the commencement of the action. Of what relevance to the constitutional issue are these enactments?

8. A court may base its decision on more than one ground. If each ground supports the result, each may be an alternative holding. For example, if the Court in *Pennoyer* had also relied upon defects in the affidavit to vitiate the state court judgment, the decision would have rested on two grounds, each of which is entitled to precedential respect under the doctrine of *stare decisis*. *See supra* Chapter I, Sections D and E. In cases, however, where a court articulates alternative bases for a decision, it (and lower courts) may in the future more easily avoid one basis by refocusing on the "true" basis for the decision.

9. Authorities aside, what policy reasons articulated in the majority opinion justify the constitutional mandate requiring seizure at the outset of the proceedings?

One factor supporting seizure at the outset of the proceedings is the greater likelihood that the nonresident owner will receive notice of the pendency of the suit. But are there not better ways to bring the suit to the attention of the nonresident? For example, the Oregon law in question provided as follows:

> In cases of publication, the court or judge shall also direct a copy of the summons and complaint to be forthwith deposited in the post office, directed to the defendant, at his place of residence, unless it shall appear that such residence is neither known to the party making the application, nor can, with reasonable diligence, be ascertained by him.

Can you determine from reading the case whether Neff received actual notice of the suit before judgment? Consider whether the following provision of the Oregon Code bears upon Mitchell's right to institute proceedings:

> When service of the summons cannot be made as prescribed in the last preceding section, and the defendant after due diligence, cannot be found within the State, and when that fact appears, by affidavit, to the satisfaction of the court or judge thereof, * * * and it also appears that a cause of action exists against the defendant, or that he is a proper party to an action relating to real property in this State, such court or judge * * * may grant an order that the service be made by publication of summons in * * * the following cases: * * *
>
> When the defendant is not a resident of the State, but has property therein, and the court has jurisdiction of the subject of the action.

If Neff's non-ownership of property at the outset of the litigation renders the statute inapplicable, could the defect have been raised by collateral attack?

10. Examine just what the Court in *Pennoyer* did and did not consider relevant to its jurisdictional inquiry. It made only passing reference to the nature of the cause of action, and then only to describe the background of the dispute. It did not find convenience of the parties an important factor. It

made passing reference to the concept of fairness—but limited discussion to the fairness of giving the defendant notice of the proceedings commenced against him. The opinion focused on the concept of territorial power. Jurisdiction over the defendant was equivalent to the exercise of power (restraint) directly over the defendant or over his property.

The Court equated jurisdiction over the defendant with notions of territorial sovereignty. Can you recall any of the Court's examples? Later cases elaborate on the traditional notion of territorial sovereignty as it relates to particular bases of personal jurisdiction. Eventually, territorial sovereignty will be rejected as the sole touchstone of jurisdiction. Consequently, certain traditional bases of jurisdiction premised on sovereignty will also be rejected. Concepts born in one era mature in another, and wither in still another. Certain concepts may then be reborn.

11. *Pennoyer* acknowledged that the fortuity of land ownership by a defendant within a state gives the court the power to adjudicate a controversy not related to the land. Would the ownership of movables or intangibles located in the state provide a similar basis for jurisdiction? Should distinctions be made with respect to the nature of the property?

What about the presence of a defendant within the state? In the *Pennoyer* era, would a state have had personal jurisdiction over a nonresident in connection with a controversy simply because the defendant was served with process in the forum? In *Smith v. Gibson,* 83 Ala. 284, 285, 3 So. 321, 321 (1887), the Alabama Supreme Court, citing *Pennoyer,* answered in the affirmative:

> The general rule is that every country has jurisdiction over all persons found within its territorial limits, for the purposes of actions in their nature transitory. It is not a debatable question that such actions may be maintained in any jurisdiction in which the defendant may be found, and is legally served with process. However transiently the defendant may have been in the State, the summons having been legally served upon him, the jurisdiction of his person was complete in the absence of a fraudulent inducement to come.

Cases resolve some issues and spawn others. For example, in *Smith,* the court limited jurisdiction based on mere presence of the defendant to transitory actions. Why? Was *Pennoyer* a transitory action? *Smith* required the development of a set of criteria distinguishing between "transitory" and "local" or fixed causes of action. What criteria should courts use? If the same categories have been employed in different contexts, is the matter of classification made simpler or more difficult?

12. Decide the following case in light of *Pennoyer:* Milliken brings an action in a state court of Wyoming against Meyer. At the time of the suit Meyer is a domiciliary (permanent resident) of Wyoming but is temporarily sojourning in Colorado. Process is served upon Meyer personally within the State of Colorado. He defaults and a judgment is entered for Milliken. Years later Meyer attempts to resist enforcement of the judgment in Colorado claiming that Wyoming did not have jurisdiction over him. *See Milliken v. Meyer,* 311 U.S. 457 (1940). Was Meyer's attack direct or collateral? *See supra* note 2, p. 164.

13. Reconsider the holding/*dictum* dichotomy. *See* Chapter I, p. 42. *Pennoyer,* citing the opinions of *Picquet v. Swan* and *Boswell's Lessee v. Otis,* stated as follows:

> These citations are not made as authoritative expositions of the law; for the language was perhaps not essential to the decision of the cases in which it was used, but as expressions of the opinion of eminent jurists. * * *

The Court then contrasted these cases with *Cooper v. Reynolds,* in which

> [i]t was essential to the disposition of the case to declare the effect of a personal action against an absent defendant, without the jurisdiction of the court, not served with process or voluntarily submitting to the tribunal, when it was sought to subject his property to the payment of a demand of a resident complainant.

Cooper affirmed the judgment of the state court of Tennessee. In view of the affirmance of Tennessee's assertion of jurisdiction, is it correct to refer to statements concerning the *impermissible* reach of state court jurisdiction as holding? Doesn't *Cooper* stand for the more narrow proposition that attachment of property is a permissible basis of state court jurisdiction against a defendant who cannot be found in the state?

Indeed, if *Cooper* were actually dispositive of the outer limits of state court jurisdiction, should not *Pennoyer* merely have affirmed the lower court, citing *Cooper?*

HESS v. PAWLOSKI

Supreme Court of the United States, 1927.
274 U.S. 352, 47 S.Ct. 632, 71 L.Ed. 1091.

JUSTICE BUTLER delivered the opinion of the Court.

This action was brought by defendant in error to recover damages for personal injuries. The declaration alleged that plaintiff in error negligently and wantonly drove a motor vehicle on a public highway in Massachusetts, and that by reason thereof the vehicle struck and injured defendant in error. Plaintiff in error is a resident of Pennsylvania. No personal service was made on him, and no property belonging to him was attached. The service of process was made in compliance with chapter 90, General Laws of Massachusetts, as amended by Stat.1923, c. 431, § 2, the material parts of which follow:

> The acceptance by a nonresident of the rights and privileges conferred by section three or four, as evidenced by his operating a motor vehicle thereunder, or the operation by a nonresident of a motor vehicle on a public way in the commonwealth other than under said sections, shall be deemed equivalent to an appointment by such nonresident of the registrar or his successor in office, to be his true and lawful attorney upon whom may be served all lawful processes in any action or proceeding against him, growing out of any accident or collision in which said nonresident may be involved while operating a motor vehicle on such a way, and said acceptance

or operation shall be a signification of his agreement that any such process against him which is so served shall be of the same legal force and validity as if served on him personally. Service of such process shall be made by leaving a copy of the process with a fee of two dollars in the hands of the registrar, or in his office, and such service shall be sufficient service upon the said nonresident: Provided, that notice of such service and a copy of the process are forthwith sent by registered mail by the plaintiff to the defendant, and the defendant's return receipt and the plaintiff's affidavit of compliance herewith are appended to the writ and entered with the declaration. The court in which the action is pending may order such continuances as may be necessary to afford the defendant reasonable opportunity to defend the action.

Plaintiff in error appeared specially for the purpose of contesting jurisdiction, and filed an answer in abatement and moved to dismiss on the ground that the service of process, if sustained, would deprive him of his property without due process of law, in violation of the Fourteenth Amendment. The court overruled the answer in abatement and denied the motion. The Supreme Judicial Court held the statute to be a valid exercise of the police power, and affirmed the order. At the trial the contention was renewed and again denied. Plaintiff in error excepted. The jury returned a verdict for defendant in error. The exceptions were overruled by the Supreme Judicial Court. Thereupon the superior court entered judgment. The writ of error was allowed by the Chief Justice of that court.

The question is whether the Massachusetts enactment contravenes the due process clause of the Fourteenth Amendment.

The process of a court of one state cannot run into another and summon a party there domiciled to respond to proceedings against him. Notice sent outside the state to a nonresident is unavailing to give jurisdiction in an action against him personally for money recovery. *Pennoyer v. Neff,* 95 U.S. 714, 24 L.Ed. 565. There must be actual service within the state of notice upon him or upon some one authorized to accept service for him. *Goldey v. Morning News,* 156 U.S. 518, 15 S.Ct. 559, 39 L.Ed. 517. A personal judgment rendered against a nonresident, who has neither been served with process nor appeared in the suit, is without validity. *McDonald v. Mabee,* 243 U.S. 90, 37 S.Ct. 343, 61 L.Ed. 608. The mere transaction of business in a state by nonresident natural persons does not imply consent to be bound by the process of its courts. *Flexner v. Farson,* 248 U.S. 289, 39 S.Ct. 97, 63 L.Ed. 250. The power of a state to exclude foreign corporations, although not absolute, but qualified, is the ground on which such an implication is supported as to them. *Pennsylvania Fire Insurance Co. v. Gold Issue Mining Co.,* 243 U.S. 93, 96, 37 S.Ct. 344, 61 L.Ed. 610. But a state may not withhold from nonresident individuals the right of doing business therein. The privileges and immunities clause of the Constitution (section 2, art. 4), safeguards to the citizens of one state the right "to pass through, or to reside in any other state for purposes of trade, agriculture, professional pursuits, or otherwise." And it prohibits state legislation discriminating against citizens of other states.

Motor vehicles are dangerous machines, and, even when skillfully and carefully operated, their use is attended by serious dangers to persons and property. In the public interest the state may make and enforce regulations reasonably calculated to promote care on the part of all, residents and nonresidents alike, who use its highways. The measure in question operates to require a nonresident to answer for his conduct in the state where arise causes of action alleged against him, as well as to provide for a claimant a convenient method by which he may sue to enforce his rights. Under the statute the implied consent is limited to proceedings growing out of accidents or collisions on a highway in which the nonresident may be involved. It is required that he shall actually receive and receipt for notice of the service and a copy of the process. And it contemplates such continuances as may be found necessary to give reasonable time and opportunity for defense. It makes no hostile discrimination against nonresidents, but tends to put them on the same footing as residents. Literal and precise equality in respect of this matter is not attainable; it is not required. The state's power to regulate the use of its highways extends to their use by nonresidents as well as by residents. And, in advance of the operation of a motor vehicle on its highway by a nonresident, the state may require him to appoint one of its officials as his agent on whom process may be served in proceedings growing out of such use. *Kane v. New Jersey,* 242 U.S. 160, 167, 37 S.Ct. 30, 61 L.Ed. 222. That case recognizes power of the state to exclude a nonresident until the formal appointment is made. And, having the power so to exclude, the state may declare that the use of the highway by the nonresident is the equivalent of the appointment of the registrar as agent on whom process may be served. The difference between the formal and implied appointment is not substantial, so far as concerns the application of the due process clause of the Fourteenth Amendment.

Judgment affirmed.

Notes and Questions

1. By now you should have no difficulty identifying the parties to the lawsuit. The original action was brought by Pawloski. Hess, the losing party in the state court system, appealed to the United States Supreme Court and was thereby designated the plaintiff in error. Pawloski, the plaintiff, thus became the defendant in error.

2. An assertion of personal jurisdiction must be authorized by the law of the forum, usually a statute or rule of court. Assuming a state permits the assertion of jurisdiction, a matter solely of construction of state law, a question may then arise whether the state law satisfies the minimum standards of applicable state and federal constitutional provisions.

3. In what ways does *Hess* differ from *Pennoyer* with respect to the nature of the cause of action and its relation to the forum state? Are these differences material?

4. If you had been retained by Pawloski to argue before the United States Supreme Court, upon what judicial authority would you have principally relied? What case(s) would you have attempted to distinguish? Would you have been able to forecast the result with any degree of certainty?

Should *Flexner* have been more thoroughly discussed in the opinion? Expressly overruled? Is *Flexner* still viable after *Hess*?

5. Note the reliance upon *Pennoyer*: "The process of a court of one state cannot run into another and summon a party there domiciled to respond to proceedings against him."

Didn't the Massachusetts summons in effect run into Pennsylvania? Does the appointment of the registrar as an agent on whom process may be served make any sense? What is left of *Pennoyer* should the fiction of implied consent expand to other kinds of transactions? Does *Flexner* impose limitations on that expansion?

6. Recall the question in note 4 regarding the principal judicial authority upon which you would rely as Pawloski's counsel. *Kane v. New Jersey* seems an obvious answer.

Hess makes the leap from *actual* to *implied* consent. But before taking the leap, should the Court have more fully analyzed the fiction of implied consent?

In *Olberding v. Illinois Central Railroad Co.*, 346 U.S. 338 (1953), the Court fully explored the fiction of implied consent in connection with the federal venue statute requiring that a diversity action be brought "only in the judicial district where all plaintiffs or all defendants reside." The plaintiff, in bringing the case in a Kentucky district court, contended on the basis of *Hess* that Olberding had impliedly consented to waive his rights under the federal venue statute by driving into Kentucky. This contention was rejected:

> It is true that * * * there has been some fictive talk to the effect that the reason why a non-resident can be subjected to a state's jurisdiction is that the non-resident has "impliedly" consented to be sued there. In point of fact, however, jurisdiction in these cases does not rest on consent at all. * * * The potentialities of damage by a motorist, in a population as mobile as ours, are such that those whom he injures must have opportunities of redress against him provided only that he is afforded an opportunity to defend himself. We have held that this is a fair rule of law * * * and that the requirements of due process are therefore met. *Hess v. Pawloski* * * *. But to conclude from this holding that the motorist, who never consented to anything and whose consent is altogether immaterial, has actually agreed to be sued and has thus waived his federal venue rights is surely to move in the world of Alice in Wonderland.

Id. at 340–41.

7. The advent of the automobile significantly altered jurisprudential thinking in the early 20th Century, just as the internet is presently affecting various aspects of the law. The automobile shaped the law in the area of personal jurisdiction, just as it had done in products liability. *MacPherson v. Buick Motor Co.*, 217 N.Y. 382, 111 N.E. 1050 (1916). Should *Hess* be limited

to cases involving automobiles? To cases involving dangerous instruments? To in-state torts? Is there supportive language in the opinion for any or all of these positions?

8. Courts and commentators often assert that when the reason for a rule no longer exists, the rule should be discarded. This statement may be somewhat misleading. If the reason articulated in an opinion no longer exists, but another equally valid one does, the rule should be retained. Of course, the original reasoning may be appropriately qualified or rejected.

Hess permitted jurisdiction over nonresident motorists for accidents arising out of the operation of vehicles within the state. If the fiction of implied consent is later rejected by the Court, is jurisdiction still permissible by resort to a more acceptable rationale? Could a court find that *Hess* and its progeny extended jurisdiction for in-state vehicular accidents without regard to consent, either actual or implied? See *International Shoe*, below.

The common law system allows precedent to extend to differing factual situations even if, on occasion, the extension contravenes specific limiting language in an earlier opinion. Suppose *Hess* had explicitly limited its ruling to the operation of automobiles. Such restrictive language could later be rejected by a court seeking to apply *Hess* to other in-state activities by nonresidents. Perhaps then the Court might expressly overrule *Flexner*. Common law doctrine develops incrementally.

INTERNATIONAL SHOE CO. v. STATE OF WASH-INGTON, OFFICE OF UNEMPLOYMENT COM-PENSATION AND PLACEMENT

Supreme Court of the United States, 1945.
326 U.S. 310, 66 S.Ct. 154, 90 L.Ed. 95.

CHIEF JUSTICE STONE delivered the opinion of the Court.

The questions for decision are (1) whether, within the limitations of the due process clause of the Fourteenth Amendment, appellant, a Delaware corporation, has by its activities in the State of Washington rendered itself amenable to proceedings in the courts of that state to recover unpaid contributions to the state unemployment compensation fund exacted by state statutes, Washington Unemployment Compensation Act, Washington Revised Statutes, § 9998–103a through § 9998–123a, 1941 Supp., and (2) whether the state can exact those contributions consistently with the due process clause of the Fourteenth Amendment.

The statutes in question set up a comprehensive scheme of unemployment compensation, the costs of which are defrayed by contributions required to be made by employers to a state unemployment compensation fund. The contributions are a specified percentage of the wages payable annually by each employer for his employees' services in the state. The assessment and collection of the contributions and the fund are administered by respondents. Section 14(c) of the Act, Wash.Rev. Stat.1941 Supp., § 9998–114c, authorizes respondent Commissioner to issue an order and notice of assessment of delinquent contributions upon prescribed personal service of the notice upon the employer if found within the state, or, if not so found, by mailing the notice to the employer by registered mail at his last known address. That section also authorizes the Commissioner to collect the assessment by distraint if it is not paid within ten days after service of the notice.

In this case notice of assessment for the years in question was personally served upon a sales solicitor employed by appellant in the State of Washington, and a copy of the notice was mailed by registered mail to appellant at its address in St. Louis, Missouri. Appellant appeared specially before the office of unemployment and moved to set aside the order and notice of assessment on the ground that the service upon appellant's salesman was not proper service upon appellant; that appellant was not a corporation of the State of Washington and was not doing business within the state; that it had no agent within the state upon whom service could be made; and that appellant is not an employer and does not furnish employment within the meaning of the statute.

The motion was heard on evidence and a stipulation of facts by the appeal tribunal which denied the motion and ruled that respondent Commissioner was entitled to recover the unpaid contributions. That action was affirmed by the Commissioner; both the Superior Court and the Supreme Court affirmed. Appellant in each of these courts assailed the statute as applied, as a violation of the due process clause of the Fourteenth Amendment, and as imposing a constitutionally prohibited burden on interstate commerce.

The facts as found by the appeal tribunal and accepted by the state Superior Court and Supreme Court, are not in dispute. Appellant is a Delaware corporation, having its principal place of business in St. Louis, Missouri, and is engaged in the manufacture and sale of shoes and other footwear. It maintains places of business in several states, other than Washington, at which its manufacturing is carried on and from which its merchandise is distributed interstate through several sales units or branches located outside the State of Washington.

Appellant has no office in Washington and makes no contracts either for sale or purchase of merchandise there. It maintains no stock of merchandise in that state and makes there no deliveries of goods in intrastate commerce. During the years from 1937 to 1940, now in question, appellant employed eleven to thirteen salesmen under direct supervision and control of sales managers located in St. Louis. These salesmen resided in Washington; their principal activities were confined to that state; and they were compensated by commissions based upon the amount of their sales. The commissions for each year totaled more than $31,000. Appellant supplies its salesmen with a line of samples, each consisting of one shoe of a pair, which they display to prospective purchasers. On occasion they rent permanent sample rooms, for exhibiting samples, in business buildings, or rent rooms in hotels or business buildings temporarily for that purpose. The cost of such rentals is reimbursed by appellant.

The authority of the salesmen is limited to exhibiting their samples and soliciting orders from prospective buyers, at prices and on terms fixed by appellant. The salesmen transmit the orders to appellant's office in St. Louis for acceptance or rejection, and when accepted the merchandise for filling the orders is shipped f.o.b. from points outside Washington to the purchasers within the state. All the merchandise shipped into Washington is invoiced at the place of shipment from which collections are made. No salesman has authority to enter into contracts or to make collections.

The Supreme Court of Washington was of opinion that the regular and systematic solicitation of orders in the state by appellant's salesmen, resulting in a continuous flow of appellant's product into the state, was sufficient to constitute doing business in the state so as to make appellant amenable to suit in its courts. But it was also of opinion that there were sufficient additional activities shown to bring the case within the rule frequently stated, that solicitation within a state by the agents of a foreign corporation plus some additional activities there are sufficient to render the corporation amenable to suit brought in the courts of the state to enforce an obligation arising out of its activities there. The court found such additional activities in the salesmen's display of samples sometimes in permanent display rooms, and the salesmen's residence within the state, continued over a period of years, all resulting in a substantial volume of merchandise regularly shipped by appellant to purchasers within the state. The court also held that the statute as applied did not invade the constitutional power of Congress to regulate interstate commerce and did not impose a prohibited burden on such commerce.

Appellant's argument, renewed here, that the statute imposes an unconstitutional burden on interstate commerce need not detain us.

* * *

Appellant also insists that its activities within the state were not sufficient to manifest its "presence" there and that in its absence the state courts were without jurisdiction, that consequently it was a denial of due process for the state to subject appellant to suit. It refers to those cases in which it was said that the mere solicitation of orders for the purchase of goods within a state, to be accepted without the state and filled by shipment of the purchased goods interstate, does not render the corporation seller amenable to suit within the state. And appellant further argues that since it was not present within the state, it is a denial of due process to subject it to taxation or other money exaction. It thus denies the power of the state to lay the tax or to subject appellant to a suit for its collection.

Historically the jurisdiction of courts to render judgment in personam is grounded on their de facto power over the defendant's person. Hence his presence within the territorial jurisdiction of a court was prerequisite to its rendition of a judgment personally binding him. *Pennoyer v. Neff,* 95 U.S. 714, 733, 24 L.Ed. 565. But now that the capias ad respondendum has given way to personal service of summons or other form of notice, due process requires only that in order to subject a defendant to a judgment in personam, if he be not present within the territory of the forum, he have certain minimum contacts with it such that the maintenance of the suit does not offend "traditional notions of fair play and substantial justice." *Milliken v. Meyer,* 311 U.S. 457, 463, 61 S.Ct. 339, 343, 85 L.Ed. 278. See Holmes, J., in *McDonald v. Mabee,* 243 U.S. 90, 91, 37 S.Ct. 343, 61 L.Ed. 608.

Since the corporate personality is a fiction, although a fiction intended to be acted upon as though it were a fact, it is clear that unlike an individual its "presence" without, as well as within, the state of its origin can be manifested only by activities carried on in its behalf by those who are authorized to act for it. To say that the corporation is so far "present" there as to satisfy due process requirements, for purposes of taxation or the maintenance of suits against it in the courts of the state, is to beg the question to be decided. For the terms "present" or "presence" are used merely to symbolize those activities of the corporation's agent within the state which courts will deem to be sufficient to satisfy the demands of due process. L. Hand, J., in *Hutchinson v. Chase & Gilbert,* 2 Cir., 45 F.2d 139, 141. Those demands may be met by such contacts of the corporation with the state of the forum as make it reasonable, in the context of our federal system of government, to require the corporation to defend the particular suit which is brought there. An "estimate of the inconveniences" which would result to the corporation from a trial away from its "home" or principal place of business is relevant in this connection.

"Presence" in the state in this sense has never been doubted when the activities of the corporation there have not only been continuous and systematic, but also give rise to the liabilities sued on, even though no consent to be sued or authorization to an agent to accept service of process has been given. Conversely it has been generally recognized that the casual presence of the corporate agent or even his conduct of single or isolated items of activities in a state in the corporation's behalf are not enough to subject it to suit on causes of action unconnected with the activities there. To require the corporation in such circumstances to defend the suit away from its home or other jurisdiction where it carries on more substantial activities has been thought to lay too great and unreasonable a burden on the corporation to comport with due process.

While it has been held in cases on which appellant relies that continuous activity of some sorts within a state is not enough to support the demand that the corporation be amenable to suits unrelated to that activity, there have been instances in which the continuous corporate operations within a state were thought so substantial and of such a nature as to justify suit against it on causes of action arising from dealings entirely distinct from those activities.

Finally, although the commission of some single or occasional acts of the corporate agent in a state sufficient to impose an obligation or liability on the corporation has not been thought to confer upon the state authority to enforce it, *Rosenberg Bros. & Co. v. Curtis Brown Co.*, 260 U.S. 516, 43 S.Ct. 170, 67 L.Ed. 372, other such acts, because of their nature and quality and the circumstances of their commission, may be deemed sufficient to render the corporation liable to suit. *Cf. Kane v. New Jersey*, 242 U.S. 160, 37 S.Ct. 30, 61 L.Ed. 222; *Hess v. Pawloski, supra; Young v. Masci, supra.* True, some of the decisions holding the corporation amenable to suit have been supported by resort to the legal fiction that it has given its consent to service and suit, consent being implied from its presence in the state through the acts of its authorized agents. *Lafayette Insurance Co. v. French,* 18 How. 404, 407, 15 L.Ed. 451; *St. Clair v. Cox*, 106 U.S. 356, 1 S.Ct. 359, 27 L.Ed. 222; *Commercial Mutual Accident Co. v. Davis*, 213 U.S. 254, 29 S.Ct. 447, 53 L.Ed. 782; *State of Washington v. Superior Court,* 289 U.S. 361, 364, 365, 53 S.Ct. 624, 626, 627, 77 L.Ed. 1256, 89 A.L.R. 653. But more realistically it may be said that those authorized acts were of such a nature as to justify the fiction. *Smolik v. Philadelphia & R. C. & I. Co.,* D.C., 222 F. 148, 151. Henderson, The Position of Foreign Corporations in American Constitutional Law, 94, 95.

It is evident that the criteria by which we mark the boundary line between those activities which justify the subjection of a corporation to suit, and those which do not, cannot be simply mechanical or quantitative. The test is not merely, as has sometimes been suggested, whether the activity, which the corporation has seen fit to procure through its agents in another state, is a little more or a little less. Whether due process is satisfied must depend rather upon the quality and nature of the activity in relation to the fair and orderly administration of the laws which it was the purpose of the due process clause to insure. That clause does not contemplate that a state may make binding a judgment in personam against an individual or corporate defendant with which the state has no contacts, ties, or relations. *Cf. Pennoyer v. Neff, supra.*

But to the extent that a corporation exercises the privilege of conducting activities within a state, it enjoys the benefits and protection of the laws of that state. The exercise of that privilege may give rise to obligations; and, so far as those obligations arise out of or are connected with the activities within the state, a procedure which requires the corporation to respond to a suit brought to enforce them can, in most instances, hardly be said to be undue.

Applying these standards, the activities carried on in behalf of appellant in the State of Washington were neither irregular nor casual. They were systematic and continuous throughout the years in question. They resulted in a large volume of interstate business, in the course of which appellant received the benefits and protection of the laws of the state, including the right to resort to the courts for the enforcement of its rights. The obligation which is here sued upon arose out of those very activities. It is evident that these operations establish sufficient contacts or ties with the state of the forum to make it reasonable and just according to our traditional conception of fair play and substantial justice to permit the state to enforce the obligations which appellant has incurred there. Hence we cannot say that the maintenance of the present suit in the State of Washington involves an unreasonable or undue procedure.

We are likewise unable to conclude that the service of the process within the state upon an agent whose activities establish appellant's "presence" there was not sufficient notice of the suit, or that the suit was so unrelated to those activities as to make the agent an inappropriate vehicle for communicating the notice. It is enough that appellant has established such contacts with the state that the particular form of substituted service adopted there gives reasonable assurance that the notice will be actual. *Milliken v. Meyer, supra.* Nor can we say that the mailing of the notice of suit to appellant by registered mail at its home office was not reasonably calculated to apprise appellant of the suit.

Appellant having rendered itself amenable to suit upon obligations arising out of the activities of its salesmen in Washington, the state may maintain the present suit in personam to collect the tax laid upon the exercise of the privilege of employing appellant's salesmen within the state. For Washington has made one of those activities, which taken together establish appellant's "presence" there for purposes of suit, the taxable event by which the state brings appellant within the reach of its taxing power. The state thus has constitutional power to lay the tax and to subject appellant to a suit to recover it. The activities which establish its "presence" subject it alike to taxation by the state and to suit to recover the tax.

Affirmed.

JUSTICE JACKSON took no part in the consideration or decision of this case.

JUSTICE BLACK delivered the following opinion.

* * *

Certainly appellant cannot in the light of our past decisions meritoriously claim that notice by registered mail and by personal service on its sales solicitors in Washington did not meet the requirements of procedural due process. And the due process clause is not brought in issue any more by appellant's further conceptualistic contention that Washington could not levy a tax or bring suit against the corporation because it did not honor that State with its mystical "presence." For it is unthinkable that the vague due process clause was ever intended to prohibit a State from regulating or taxing a business carried on within its boundaries simply because this is done by agents of a corporation organized and having its headquarters elsewhere. To read this into the due process clause would in fact result in depriving a State's citizens of due process by taking from the State the power to protect them in their business dealings within its boundaries with representatives of a foreign corporation. Nothing could be more irrational or more designed to defeat the function of our federative system of government. Certainly a State, at the very least, has power to tax and sue those dealing with its citizens within its boundaries, as we have held before. Were the Court to follow this principle, it would provide a workable standard for cases where, as here, no other questions are involved. The Court has not chosen to do so, but instead has engaged in an unnecessary discussion in the course of which it has announced vague Constitutional criteria applied for the first time to the issue before us. It has thus introduced uncertain elements confusing the simple pattern and tending to curtail the exercise of State powers to an extent not justified by the Constitution.

The criteria adopted insofar as they can be identified read as follows: Due process does permit State courts to "enforce the obligations which appellant has incurred" if it be found "reasonable and just according to our traditional conception of fair play and substantial justice." And this in turn means that we will "permit" the State to act if upon "an 'estimate of the inconveniences' which would result to the corporation from a trial away from its 'home' or principal place of business," we conclude that it is "reasonable" to subject it to suit in a State where it is doing business.

It is true that this Court did use the terms "fair play" and "substantial justice" in explaining the philosophy underlying the holding that it could not be "due process of law" to render a personal judgment against a defendant without notice to and an opportunity to be heard by him. *Milliken v. Meyer,* 311 U.S. 457, 61 S.Ct. 339, 85 L.Ed. 278, 132 A.L.R. 1357. In *McDonald v. Mabee,* 243 U.S. 90, 91, 37 S.Ct. 343, 61 L.Ed. 608, cited in the *Milliken* case, Mr. Justice Holmes speaking for the Court warned against judicial curtailment of this opportunity to be heard and referred to such a curtailment as a denial of "fair play," which even the common law would have deemed "contrary to natural justice." And previous cases had indicated that the ancient rule against judgments without notice had stemmed from "natural justice" concepts. These cases, while giving additional reasons why notice under particular circumstances is inadequate, did not mean thereby that all legislative enactments which this Court might deem to be contrary to natural justice ought to be held invalid under the due process clause. None of the cases purport to support or could support a holding that a State can tax and sue corporations only if its action comports with this Court's notions of "natural justice." I should have thought the Tenth Amendment settled that.

I believe that the Federal Constitution leaves to each State, without any "ifs" or "buts," a power to tax and to open the doors of its courts for its citizens to sue corporations whose agents do business in those States. Believing that the Constitution gave the States that power, I think it a judicial deprivation to condition its exercise upon this Court's notion of "fair play," however appealing that term may be. Nor can I stretch the meaning of due process so far as to authorize this Court to deprive a State of the right to afford judicial protection to its citizens on the ground that it would be more "convenient" for the corporation to be sued somewhere else.

There is a strong emotional appeal in the words "fair play," "justice," and "reasonableness." But they were not chosen by those who wrote the original Constitution or the Fourteenth Amendment as a measuring rod for this Court to use in invalidating State or Federal laws passed by elected legislative representatives. No one, not even those who most feared a democratic government, ever formally proposed that courts should be given power to invalidate legislation under any such elastic standards. Express prohibitions against certain types of legislation are found in the Constitution, and under the long settled practice, courts invalidate laws found to conflict with them. This requires interpretation, and interpretation, it is true, may result in extension of the Constitution's purpose. But that is no reason for reading the due process clause so as to restrict a State's power to tax and sue those whose activities affect persons and businesses within the State, provided proper service can be had. Superimposing the natural justice concept on the Constitution's specific prohibitions could operate as a drastic abridgment of democratic safeguards they embody, such as freedom of speech, press and religion, and the right to counsel. This has already happened. For application of this natural law concept, whether under the terms "reasonableness," "justice," or "fair play," makes judges the supreme arbiters of the country's laws and practices. This result, I believe, alters the form of government our Constitution provides. I cannot agree.

True, the State's power is here upheld. But the rule announced means that tomorrow's judgment may strike down a State or Federal enactment on the ground that it does not conform to this Court's idea of natural justice. I therefore find myself moved by the same fears that caused Mr. Justice Holmes to say in 1930:

> I have not yet adequately expressed the more than anxiety that I feel at the ever increasing scope given to the Fourteenth Amendment in cutting down what I believe to be the constitutional rights of the States. As the decisions now stand, I see hardly any limit but the sky to the invalidating of those rights if they happen to strike a majority of this Court as for any reason undesirable. *Baldwin v. Missouri*, 281 U.S. 586, 595, 50 S.Ct. 436, 439, 74 L.Ed. 1056, 72 A.L.R. 1303.

Notes and Questions

1. The Court has come a long way since the days of *Pennoyer*.

Consider the passages in the *International Shoe* opinion that refer to *Pennoyer*. Is *Pennoyer* still good law after *International Shoe*? If so, for what propositions? What happened to *Flexner*?

2. The opening paragraph of the Supreme Court opinion in *International Shoe* specified two issues: one dealt with the subject matter of this section, namely, whether a state may render a nonresident amenable to the jurisdiction of its courts by virtue of its in-state activities; the other, outside the scope of the present analysis, concerned the right of the state to exact

contributions to its state unemployment fund based upon these same activities.

The former issue relates to judicial jurisdiction; the latter, to legislative jurisdiction. Do you see any differences? What consequences would have resulted had the Court abrogated judicial jurisdiction, yet permitted the exaction of contributions? How could the state have judicially enforced its right? Would it be compelled to bring suit in sister-state courts having jurisdiction over the defendant? Can you envisage problems with maintaining these suits? If insurmountable burdens stand in the way of enforcing rights in sister-state jurisdictions, may *International Shoe* then be classified as a "jurisdiction by necessity" case?

The issue relating to judicial jurisdiction was narrowly drawn by the Court as follows:

> The questions for decision are (1) whether, within the limitations of the due process clause of the Fourteenth Amendment, appellant, a Delaware corporation, has by its activities in the State of Washington rendered itself amenable to proceedings in the courts of that state to recover unpaid contributions to the state unemployment compensation fund exacted by state statutes * * *

This precise phrasing of the question presented assists the student in ascertaining the holding of the case. Would you have phrased the issue differently?

3.   Put on your procedural spectacles. What method did the defendant employ to resist judicial jurisdiction? Recall the discussion in note 2 following *Pennoyer, supra* p. 164, regarding the distinction between collateral attack and direct review. Was the defendant wise to enter the jurisdiction for the purposes of raising the jurisdictional issue? Are there risks involved in allowing a default to be entered and later contesting the jurisdictional issue in a collateral proceeding? Before choosing between direct and collateral attack, would you want to know more about the benefits and risks inherent in each alternative?

4.   *International Shoe* paid only fleeting attention to *Pennoyer*. The foundational blocks were *Milliken, Kane,* and *Hess.* This building process illustrates the art of judicial synthesis. Note how the Court revamped the rationale of certain precedents to accommodate its new "reasonableness" test. For example, in citing cases ostensibly relying upon implied consent of foreign corporations to in-state suit, the Court disregarded the legal fiction and instead focused on the underlying in-state activities of the corporation:

> True, some of the decisions holding the corporation amenable to suit have been supported by resort to the legal fiction that it has given its consent to service and suit, consent being implied from its presence in the state through the acts of its authorized agents. * * * But more realistically it may be said that those authorized acts were of such a nature as to justify the fiction. * * *

326 U.S. at 318, 66 S. Ct. at 159.

5.   The United States Supreme Court found that the state court had based its decision on two grounds:

The Supreme Court of Washington was of the opinion that the regular and systematic solicitation of orders in the state by appellant's salesmen, resulting in a continuous flow of appellant's product into the state, was sufficient to constitute doing business in the state so as to make appellant amenable to suit in its courts. But it was also of the opinion that there were sufficient additional activities shown to bring the case within the rule frequently stated, that solicitation within a state by the agents of a foreign corporation plus some additional activities there are sufficient to render the corporation amenable to suit brought in the courts of the state to enforce an obligation arising out of its activities there. * * * The court found such additional activities in the salesmen's display of samples sometimes in permanent display rooms, and the salesmen's residence within the state, continued over a period of years, all resulting in a substantial volume of merchandise regularly shipped by appellant to purchasers within the state. * * *

326 U.S. at 314–15, 66 S. Ct. at 157.

Would the International Shoe Corporation be subject to the jurisdiction of the Washington courts on the basis of activities unrelated to the forum state? The Washington Supreme Court would uphold the assertion of jurisdiction. Does it appear clearly from the opinion what the United States Supreme Court would do? Is there room for argument?

Reread the Court's statement of the question presented. Does it not focus on the second and alternative basis for the state court's decision—that is, that the suit arose out of the very activities relied upon as a basis for jurisdiction?

6. In *Shaffer v. Heitner, infra* p. 188, the Court stated: "[A]ll assertions of state court jurisdiction must be evaluated according to the standards set forth in *International Shoe* and its progeny." What are these standards?

7. The parameters of the *International Shoe* doctrine were further delineated in *McGee v. International Life Insurance Co.,* 355 U.S. 220 (1957). In *McGee,* a California resident, in accordance with an offer of insurance mailed to him, purchased an insurance policy from a nonresident company. The insurance contract in question was delivered in California, the premiums were mailed from that state, and the insured died a resident of California. The defendant never maintained any offices or agents in California, nor did it solicit any business there, apart from the policy sued upon.

In rejecting the argument that California lacked jurisdiction over the nonresident insurer, the Court canvassed the law from *Pennoyer* to *International Shoe* and made the following observations:

Since *Pennoyer v. Neff,* 95 U.S. 714, 24 L.Ed. 565, this Court has held that the Due Process Clause of the Fourteenth Amendment places some limit on the power of state courts to enter binding judgments against persons not served with process within their boundaries. But just where this line of limitation falls has been the subject of prolific controversy, particularly with respect to foreign corporations. In a continuing process of evolution this Court accepted and then abandoned "consent," "doing business," and "presence" as the standard for measuring the extent of state judicial power over such corporations. *See*

Henderson, The Position of Foreign Corporations in American Constitutional Law, ch. V. More recently in *International Shoe Co. v. State of Washington,* 326 U.S. 310, 66 S.Ct. 154, 90 L.Ed. 95, the Court decided that "due process requires only that in order to subject a defendant to a judgment *in personam,* if he be not present within the territory of the forum, he have certain minimum contacts with it such that the maintenance of the suit does not offend 'traditional notions of fair play and substantial justice.'" *Id.,* 326 U.S. at page 316, 66 S.Ct. at page 158.

Looking back over this long history of litigation a trend is clearly discernible toward expanding the permissible scope of state jurisdiction over foreign corporations and other nonresidents. In part this is attributable to the fundamental transformation of our national economy over the years. Today many commercial transactions touch two or more States and may involve parties separated by the full continent. With this increasing nationalization of commerce has come a great increase in the amount of business conducted by mail across state lines. At the same time modern transportation and communication have made it much less burdensome for a party sued to defend himself in a State where he engages in economic activity.

Turning to this case we think it apparent that the Due Process Clause did not preclude the California court from entering a judgment binding on respondent. It is sufficient for purposes of due process that the suit was based on a contract which had substantial connection with that State. *Cf. Hess v. Pawloski,* 274 U.S. 352, 47 S.Ct. 632, 71 L.Ed. 1091; *Henry L. Doherty & Co. v. Goodman,* 294 U.S. 623, 55 S.Ct. 553, 79 L.Ed. 1097; *Pennoyer v. Neff,* 95 U.S. 714, 735, 24 L.Ed. 565. The contract was delivered in California, the premiums were mailed from there and the insured was a resident of that State when he died. It cannot be denied that California has a manifest interest in providing effective means of redress for its residents when their insurers refuse to pay claims. These residents would be at a severe disadvantage if they were forced to follow the insurance company to a distant State in order to hold it legally accountable. When claims were small or moderate individual claimants frequently could not afford the cost of bringing an action in a foreign forum—thus in effect making the company judgment proof. Often the crucial witnesses—as here on the company's defense of suicide—will be found in the insured's locality. Of course there may be inconvenience to the insurer if it is held amenable to suit in California where it had this contract but certainly nothing which amounts to a denial of due process. *Cf. Travelers Health Ass'n v. Commonwealth of Virginia ex rel. State Corporation Comm.,* 339 U.S. 643, 70 S.Ct. 927, 94 L.Ed. 1154. There is no contention that respondent did not have adequate notice of the suit or sufficient time to prepare its defenses and appear.

Did *McGee* broaden the *International Shoe* doctrine? Was it a necessary outgrowth? Recall the following passage from *International Shoe:*

Finally, although the commission of some single or occasional acts of the corporate agent in a state sufficient to impose an obligation or liability on the corporation has not been thought to confer upon the state authority to enforce it, * * * other such acts, because of their nature and quality and the circumstances of their commission, may be deemed sufficient to render the corporation liable to suit. *Cf. Kane v. New Jersey; Hess v. Pawloski* * * *

Note the use of *Kane* and *Hess* as the foundational building blocks.

What relevant contacts occurred in the State of California? Were all those contacts essential to the exercise of jurisdiction? If not, which ones were essential?

Was "insurance" to *McGee* as the automobile was to *Hess*? Should the subject of the contact with the forum be relevant in deciding whether to extend jurisdiction? Does not the *International Shoe* test of reasonableness invite the inquiry?

8.   Assume a nonresident defendant manufacturer causes its product to be shipped to State X. The product explodes, causing injury. The plaintiff institutes suit in State X against the nonresident manufacturer. As the defendant's attorney, would you have a reasonable chance of distinguishing *McGee* and *Hess* on the grounds that *McGee* is merely an insurance case and *Hess*, an automobile case? Assuming there is some merit to these distinctions, which jurisdiction do you believe would be more receptive to the argument—the forum state or the manufacturer's home base? If the latter, the manufacturer may wish to default and set up the defense of lack of jurisdiction in a subsequent collateral attack in its home state. What risks are involved in that litigation strategy?

Regardless which forum is chosen for the assertion of the jurisdictional issue, the Supreme Court of the United States has potential appellate jurisdiction to review the constitutional issues.

9.   In *Johnson v. Roscoe & Baker,* the plaintiff asserted jurisdiction on the basis of John's presence in Arizona. Under *Pennoyer,* such an assertion would have been constitutionally permissible. What would be the result after *International Shoe*? Can you present arguments in support of the exercise of jurisdiction? Against it? Which ones are more persuasive?

10.   *International Shoe* and *McGee* represent high-water marks in the constitutional expansion of the right of states to extend jurisdiction over nonresidents based upon activities within the forum state. Just one year after it decided *McGee*, the Court attempted to stem the tide of state court jurisdiction. In *Hanson v. Denckla,* 357 U.S. 235 (1958), a Florida court exerted jurisdiction over a Delaware trust company on the basis of the latter's contacts with the state. These contacts were limited to the company's maintaining business relations and communicating with its settlor who had moved to Florida after entering into a trust relationship with the Delaware trustee. In a 5–4 opinion, the Supreme Court reversed, stating:

> Principal reliance is placed upon *McGee v. International Life Ins. Co.,* 355 U.S. 220, 78 S.Ct. 199, 2 L.Ed.2d 223. In *McGee* the Court noted the trend of expanding personal jurisdiction over nonresidents. As technological progress has increased the flow of commerce between States, the need for jurisdiction over nonresidents has undergone a similar increase. At the same time, progress in communications and transportation has made the defense of a suit in a foreign tribunal less burdensome. In

response to these changes, the requirements for personal jurisdiction over nonresidents have evolved from the rigid rule of *Pennoyer v. Neff,* 95 U.S. 714, 24 L.Ed. 565, to the flexible standard of *International Shoe Co. v. State of Washington,* 326 U.S. 310, 66 S.Ct. 154, 90 L.Ed. 95. But it is a mistake to assume that this trend heralds the eventual demise of all restrictions on the personal jurisdiction of state courts. *See Vanderbilt v. Vanderbilt,* 354 U.S. 416, 418, 77 S.Ct. 1360, 1362, 1 L.Ed.2d 1456. Those restrictions are more than a guarantee of immunity from inconvenient or distant litigation. They are a consequence of territorial limitations on the power of the respective States. However minimal the burden of defending in a foreign tribunal, a defendant may not be called upon to do so unless he has had the "minimal contacts" with that State that are a prerequisite to its exercise of power over him. *See International Shoe Co. v. State of Washington,* 326 U.S. 310, 319, 66 S.Ct. 154, 159, 90 L.Ed. 95.

We fail to find such contacts in the circumstances of this case. The defendant trust company has no office in Florida, and transacts no business there. None of the trust assets has ever been held or administered in Florida, and the record discloses no solicitation of business in that State either in person or by mail. *Cf. International Shoe Co. v. State of Washington,* 326 U.S. 310, 66 S.Ct. 154, 90 L.Ed. 95; *McGee v. International Life Ins. Co.,* 355 U.S. 220, 78 S.Ct. 199, 2 L.Ed.2d 223; *Travelers Health Ass'n v. Com. of Virginia ex rel. State Corporation Comm.,* 339 U.S. 643, 70 S.Ct. 927, 94 L.Ed. 1154.

The cause of action in this case is not one that arises out of an act done or transaction consummated in the forum State. In that respect, it differs from *McGee v. International Life Ins. Co.,* 355 U.S. 220, 78 S.Ct. 199, 201, 2 L.Ed.2d 223, and the cases there cited. In *McGee,* the nonresident defendant solicited a reinsurance agreement with a resident of California. The offer was accepted in that State, and the insurance premiums were mailed from there until the insured's death. Noting the interest California has in providing effective redress for its residents when nonresident insurers refuse to pay claims on insurance they have solicited in that State, the Court upheld jurisdiction because the suit "was based on a contract which had substantial connection with that State." In contrast, this action involves the validity of an agreement that was entered without any connection with the forum State. The agreement was executed in Delaware by a trust company incorporated in that State and a settlor domiciled in Pennsylvania. The first relationship Florida had to the agreement was years later when the settlor became domiciled there, and the trustee remitted the trust income to her in that State. From Florida Mrs. Donner carried on several bits of trust administration that may be compared to the mailing of premiums in *McGee.* But the record discloses no instance in which the *trustee* performed any acts in Florida that bear the same relationship to the agreement as the solicitation in *McGee.* Consequently, this suit cannot be said to be one to enforce an obligation that arose from a privilege the defendant exercised in Florida. *Cf. International Shoe Co. v. State of Washington,* 326 U.S. 310, 319, 66 S.Ct. 154, 159, 90 L.Ed. 95. This case is also different from *McGee* in that there the State had enacted special legislation (Unauthorized Insurers Process Act, West's Ann.Cal.Insurance Code, § 1610 *et seq.*) to exercise what *McGee* called its "manifest interest" in providing effective redress for citizens who had been injured by nonresidents engaged in an activity that the State treats as exceptional and subjects to special regulation.

* * * The unilateral activity of those who claim some relationship with a nonresident defendant cannot satisfy the requirement of contact with the forum State. The application of that rule will vary with the quality and nature of the defendant's activity, but it is essential in each case that there be some act by which the defendant purposefully avails itself of the privilege of conducting activities within the forum State, thus invoking the benefits and protections of its laws. *International Shoe Co. v. State of Washington*, 326 U.S. 310, 319, 66 S.Ct. 154, 159, 90 L.Ed. 95. The settlor's execution in Florida of her power of appointment cannot remedy the absence of such an act in this case.

* * *

Introductory Notes to Shaffer v. Heitner

1. Ever since *International Shoe, Pennoyer* had been ripe for reconsideration. But a doctrine so securely rooted in history and founded on principles heralded by great jurists did not die easily.

International Shoe fashioned the minimum contacts test for determining the power of a state to exercise in personam jurisdiction over a nonresident. A remaining question was whether that standard was the exclusive test for assertions of jurisdiction. The decision in *International Shoe* added to the confusion, for the Court stated:

> [D]ue process requires only that in order to subject a defendant to a judgment in personam, *if he be not present within the territory of the forum,* he have certain minimum contacts with it such that the maintenance of the suit does not offend "traditional notions of fair play and substantial justice."

(Emphasis added.)

Mere presence of the defendant within the territory still conferred personal jurisdiction. What about the presence of the defendant's property? In other words, was *Pennoyer* still good law?

2. As *Pennoyer* recognized, courts could properly adjudicate a controversy involving a nonresident defendant in limited situations. For example, a court in the jurisdiction in which the defendant's property was located could attach her interest in the property for the purpose of adjudicating a controversy between the plaintiff and the nonresident owner. This type of jurisdiction was later termed "quasi in rem." Why *quasi* in rem?

An action in personam is one that seeks to impose personal liability upon the defendant, either in the form of a money judgment or an obligation to do or refrain from doing an act. An action in rem is one that seeks to affect the interests of persons in a specific thing or *res*. Some such actions purport to affect the interests of the entire world, others just the interests of particular persons. Examples of in rem proceedings affecting property include actions to partition property among several owners and suits to foreclose mortgages or other liens on property.[c] Actions in rem also include actions affecting status, such as divorce and custody suits. Quasi in rem proceedings, on the other hand, include actions based upon a claim for money damages commenced by a seizure of the defendant's property where the court lacks jurisdiction over the person of the defendant, but has jurisdiction over her property. In this type of proceeding, the plaintiff admits or asserts the defendant's ownership in the property and requests the court to convey all or part of that ownership in satisfaction of a claim for money damages.

A quasi in rem proceeding may properly adjudicate only the interests of the defendant in the seized property. It may not foreclose nonparties from later claiming that the defendant did not own the property in question. Thus, a quasi in rem proceeding cannot extinguish the interests of strangers to the litigation.

Where a court had in personam jurisdiction, any money judgment rendered is enforceable against assets of the judgment debtor in the rendering state and in other states. This latter accommodation is obligatory upon other states by virtue of the full faith and credit clause of the United States Constitution. A judgment based upon quasi in rem jurisdiction, on the other hand, typically is enforceable only against the property seized. If the value of property seized exceeds the debt sued upon (for example in *Pennoyer* the indebtedness was $300, the value of the property, $15,000), the judgment creditor will be fully satisfied. In cases, however, where the debt exceeds the value of the property (*see Shaffer, infra* p. 188), the scope of the litigation traditionally had been determined by and limited to the value of the property itself. Thus, a victory for either party would not necessarily foreclose additional litigation. There would be no *res judicata* consequences of the first litigation; in fairness, however, any property awarded the successful plaintiff would be credited against the obligation in future actions. The inefficiency of multiple litigation with its concomitant possibility of inconsistent results led to laws conditioning a defense on the merits upon a general appearance, thus subjecting the defendant to in personam jurisdiction. This legislative response compelling personal appearances as the price of defending on the merits evoked vigorous criticism from commentators.

3. Historically, quasi in rem jurisdiction ameliorated the harshness to resident plaintiffs of the *Pennoyer* rule requiring in-state service of process for in personam jurisdiction. The *Pennoyer* rule favored nonresidents who could not be reached by in-state service and forced plaintiffs seeking redress against nonresidents to institute proceedings in distant and at times inaccessible fora. The benefits derived by nonresidents from the *Pennoyer* rule, however, were largely reduced by the plaintiff's ability to seize property within the forum state. Two famous cases, *Harris v. Balk* and *Seider v. Roth*, illustrate the extremes to which courts expanded quasi in rem jurisdiction to aid hapless residents in obtaining a convenient forum.

Shaffer v. Heitner, 433 U.S. 186 (1977), contains the following pithy recapitulation of *Harris v. Balk:*

c. *But cf.* Shaffer v. Heitner, 433 U.S. 186 n. 17 (1977).

[I]n the well-known case of *Harris v. Balk,* 198 U.S. 215, 25 S.Ct. 625, 49 L.Ed. 1023 (1905), Epstein, a resident of Maryland, had a claim against Balk, a resident of North Carolina. Harris, another North Carolina resident, owed money to Balk. When Harris happened to visit Maryland, Epstein garnished his debt to Balk. Harris did not contest the debt to Balk and paid it to Epstein's North Carolina attorney. When Balk later sued Harris in North Carolina, this Court held that the Full Faith and Credit Clause, U.S. Const, Art. IV, § 1, required that Harris' payment to Epstein be treated as a discharge of his debt to Balk. This Court reasoned that the debt Harris owed Balk was an intangible form of property belonging to Balk, and that the location of that property traveled with the debtor. By obtaining personal jurisdiction over Harris, Epstein had "arrested" his debt to Balk, 198 U.S. at 223, 25 S.Ct. 625, 49 L.Ed. 1023, and brought it into the Maryland court. Under the structure established by Pennoyer, Epstein was then entitled to proceed against that debt to vindicate his claim against Balk, even though Balk himself was not subject to the jurisdiction * * * of a Maryland tribunal.

433 U.S. at 197.

In *Seider v. Roth,* 17 N.Y.2d 111, 269 N.Y.S.2d 99, 216 N.E.2d 312 (1966), the New York courts went even a step farther. The plaintiffs, New York residents, were injured in an automobile accident in Vermont. They alleged that it was caused by the negligence of a Canadian national who fortuitously was insured by the Hartford Insurance Company, a company headquartered in Connecticut, but doing business in New York. Claiming that Hartford's obligation of indemnification to the nonresident was a debt within the reach of the New York courts, the plaintiff attached the obligation. The New York courts permitted the seizure.

Against this historical background, the constitutionality of quasi in rem jurisdiction reached the Court in *Shaffer v. Heitner,* excerpted below:

SHAFFER v. HEITNER
Supreme Court of the United States, 1977.
433 U.S. 186, 97 S.Ct. 2569, 53 L.Ed.2d 683.

JUSTICE MARSHALL delivered the opinion of the Court.

The controversy in this case concerns the constitutionality of a Delaware statute that allows a court of that State to take jurisdiction of a lawsuit by sequestering any property of the defendant that happens to be located in Delaware. Appellants contend that the sequestration statute as applied in this case violates the Due Process Clause of the Fourteenth Amendment both because it permits the state courts to exercise jurisdiction despite the absence of sufficient contacts among the defendants, the litigation, and the State of Delaware and because it authorizes the deprivation of defendants' property without providing adequate procedural safeguards. We find it necessary to consider only the first of these contentions.

I

Appellee Heitner, a nonresident of Delaware, is the owner of one share of stock in the Greyhound Corp., a business incorporated under the laws of Delaware with its principal place of business in Phoenix, Ariz. On May 22, 1974, he filed a shareholder's derivative suit in the Court of Chancery for New Castle County, Del., in which he named as defendants Greyhound, its wholly owned subsidiary Greyhound Lines, Inc., and 28 present or former officers or directors of one or both of the corporations. In essence, Heitner alleged that the individual defendants had violated their duties to Greyhound by causing it and its subsidiary to engage in actions that resulted in the corporations being held liable for substantial damages in a private antitrust suit and a large fine in a criminal contempt action. The activities which led to these penalties took place in Oregon.

Simultaneously with his complaint, Heitner filed a motion for an order of sequestration of the Delaware property of the individual defendants pursuant to Del.Code Ann., Tit. 10, § 366 (1975). This motion was accompanied by a supporting affidavit of counsel which stated that the individual defendants were nonresidents of Delaware. The affidavit identified the property to be sequestered as [shares and stock options of] Greyhound Corporation. The requested sequestration order was signed the day the motion was filed. Pursuant to that order, the sequestrator "seized" approximately 82,000 shares of Greyhound common stock belonging to 19 of the defendants, and options belonging to another 2 defendants. These seizures were accomplished by placing "stop transfer" orders or their equivalents on the books of the Greyhound Corp. So far as the record shows, none of the certificates representing the seized property was physically present in Delaware. The stock was considered to be in Delaware, and so subject to seizure, by virtue of Del.Code Ann., Tit. 8, § 169 (1975), which makes Delaware the situs of ownership of all stock in Delaware corporations.

All 28 defendants were notified of the initiation of the suit by certified mail directed to their last known addresses and by publication in a New Castle County newspaper. The 21 defendants whose property was seized (hereafter referred to as appellants) responded by entering a special appearance for the purpose of moving to quash service of process and to vacate the sequestration order. They contended that the *ex parte* sequestration procedure did not accord them due process of law and that the property seized was not capable of attachment in Delaware. In addition, appellants asserted that under the rule of *International Shoe Co. v. Washington,* 326 U.S. 310, 66 S.Ct. 154, 90 L.Ed. 95 (1945), they did not have sufficient contacts with Delaware to sustain the jurisdiction of that State's courts.

The Court of Chancery rejected these arguments.

On appeal, the Delaware Supreme Court affirmed the judgment of the Court of Chancery. *Greyhound Corp. v. Heitner,* 361 A.2d 225 (1976). Most of the Supreme Court's opinion was devoted to rejecting appellants' contention that the sequestration procedure is inconsistent with the due process analysis developed in the *Sniadach* line of cases.[d] The court

d. *See infra* Chapter III, Exercise 2.

based its rejection of that argument in part on its agreement with the Court of Chancery that the purpose of the sequestration procedure is to compel the appearance of the defendant, a purpose not involved in the *Sniadach* cases. The court also relied on what it considered the ancient origins of the sequestration procedure and approval of that procedure in the opinions of this Court,[10] Delaware's interest in asserting jurisdiction to adjudicate claims of mismanagement of a Delaware corporation, and the safeguards for defendants that it found in the Delaware statute.

Appellants' claim that the Delaware courts did not have jurisdiction to adjudicate this action received much more cursory treatment. The court's analysis of the jurisdictional issue is contained in two paragraphs:

There are significant constitutional questions at issue here but we say at once that we do not deem the rule of *International Shoe* to be one of them. * * * The reason of course, is that jurisdiction under § 366 remains * * * *quasi in rem* founded on the presence of capital stock here, not on prior contact by defendants with this forum. Under 8 Del.C. § 169 the "situs of the ownership of the capital stock of all corporations existing under the laws of this State * * * [is] in this State," and that provides the initial basis for jurisdiction. Delaware may constitutionally establish situs of such shares here, * * * it has done so and the presence thereof provides the foundation for § 366 in this case ... On this issue we agree with the analysis made and the conclusion reached by Judge Stapleton in *U.S. Industries, Inc. v. Gregg*, D.Del., 348 F.Supp. 1004 (1972).[11]

We hold that seizure of the Greyhound shares is not invalid because plaintiff has failed to meet the prior contacts tests of *International Shoe*. *Id.* at 229.

We noted probable jurisdiction. 429 U.S. 813, 97 S.Ct. 52, 50 L.Ed.2d 72.[12] We reverse.

10. The court relied, 361 A.2d, at 228, 230–231, on our decision in *Ownbey v. Morgan*, 256 U.S. 94, 41 S.Ct. 433, 65 L.Ed. 837 (1921), and references to that decision in *North Georgia Finishing, Inc. v. Di-Chem, Inc.*, 419 U.S. 601, 610, 95 S.Ct. 719, 724, 42 L.Ed.2d 751 (1975) (Powell, J., concurring in judgment); *Calero-Toledo v. Pearson Yacht Leasing Co.*, 416 U.S. 663, 679 n. 14, 94 S.Ct. 2080, 2090, 40 L.Ed.2d 452 (1974); *Mitchell v. W.T. Grant Co.*, 416 U.S. 600, 613, 94 S.Ct. 1895, 1903, 40 L.Ed.2d 406 (1974); *Fuentes v. Shevin*, 407 U.S. 67, 91 n. 23, 92 S.Ct. 1983, 32 L.Ed.2d 556 (1972); *Sniadach v. Family Finance Corp., supra*, 395 U.S. at 339, 89 S.Ct. at 1821. The only question before the Court in *Ownbey* was the constitutionality of a requirement that a defendant whose property has been attached file a bond before entering an appearance. We do not read the recent references to *Ownbey* as necessarily suggesting that *Ownbey* is consistent with more recent decisions interpreting the Due Process Clause.

Sequestration is the equity counterpart of the process of foreign attachment in suits at law considered in *Ownbey*.

11. The District Court judgment in *U.S. Industries* was reversed by the Court of Appeals for the Third Circuit. 540 F.2d 142 (1976), cert. pending, No. 76–359. The Court of Appeals characterized the passage from the Delaware Supreme Court's opinion quoted in text as "cryptic conclusions." *Id.* at 149.

12. Under Delaware law, defendants whose property has been sequestered must enter a general appearance, thus subjecting themselves to *in personam* liability, before they can defend on the merits. *See Greyhound Corp. v. Heitner*, 361 A.2d 225, at 235–236 (1976).

II

The Delaware courts rejected appellants' jurisdictional challenge by noting that this suit was brought as a *quasi in rem* proceeding. Since *quasi in rem* jurisdiction is traditionally based on attachment or seizure of property present in the jurisdiction, not on contacts between the defendant and the State, the courts considered appellants' claimed lack of contacts with Delaware to be unimportant. This categorical analysis assumes the continued soundness of the conceptual structure founded on the century-old case of *Pennoyer v. Neff*, 95 U.S. 714, 24 L.Ed. 565 (1878).

Pennoyer was an ejectment action brought in federal court under the diversity jurisdiction. Pennoyer, the defendant in that action, held the land under a deed purchased in a sheriff's sale conducted to realize on a judgment for attorney's fees obtained against Neff in a previous action by one Mitchell. At the time of Mitchell's suit in an Oregon State court, Neff was a nonresident of Oregon. An Oregon statute allowed service by publication on nonresidents who had property in the State,[13] and Mitchell had used that procedure to bring Neff before the court. The United States Circuit Court for the District of Oregon, in which Neff brought his ejectment action, refused to recognize the validity of the judgment against Neff in Mitchell's suit, and accordingly awarded the land to Neff.[14] This Court affirmed.

Mr. Justice Field's opinion for the Court focused on the territorial limits of the States' judicial powers. Although recognizing that the States are not truly independent sovereigns, Mr. Justice Field found that their jurisdiction was defined by the "principles of public law" that regulate the relationships among independent nations. The first of those principles was "that every State possesses exclusive jurisdiction and sovereignty over persons and property within its territory." The second was "that no State can exercise direct jurisdiction and authority over persons or property without its territory." *Id.* at 722. Thus, "in virtue of the State's jurisdiction over the property of the non-resident situated within its limits," the state courts "can inquire into that non-resident's obligations to its own citizens * * * to the extent necessary to control the disposition of the property." *Id.* at 723. The Court recognized that if the conclusions of that inquiry were adverse to the non-resident property owner, his interest in the property would be affected. *Ibid.* Similarly, if the defendant consented to the jurisdiction of the state courts or was personally served within the State, a judgment could affect his interest

---

13. The statute also required that a copy of the summons and complaint be mailed to the defendant if his place of residence was known to the plaintiff or could be determined with reasonable diligence. 95 U.S. at 718. Mitchell had averred that he did not know and could not determine Neff's address, so that the publication was the only "notice" given. *Id.* at 717.

14. The Federal Circuit Court based its ruling on defects in Mitchell's affidavit in support of the order for service by publication and in the affidavit by which publication was proved. *Id.* at 720. Mr. Justice Field indicated that if this Court had confined itself to considering those rulings, the judgment would have been reversed. *Id.* at 721.

in property outside the State. But any attempt "directly" to assert extraterritorial jurisdiction over persons or property would offend sister States and exceed the inherent limits of the State's power. A judgment resulting from such an attempt, Mr. Justice Field concluded, was not only unenforceable in other States,[15] but was also void in the rendering State because it had been obtained in violation of the Due Process Clause of the Fourteenth Amendment.

This analysis led to the conclusion that Mitchell's judgment against Neff could not be validly based on the State's power over persons within its borders, because Neff had not been personally served in Oregon, nor had he consensually appeared before the Oregon court. The Court reasoned that even if Neff had received personal notice of the action, service of process outside the State would have been ineffectual since the State's power was limited by its territorial boundaries. Moreover, the Court held, the action could not be sustained on the basis of the State's power over property within its borders because that property had not been brought before the court by attachment or any other procedure prior to judgment.[16] Since the judgment which authorized the sheriff's sale was therefore invalid, the sale transferred no title. Neff regained his land.

From our perspective, the importance of *Pennoyer* is not its result, but the fact that its principles and corollaries derived from them became the basic elements of the constitutional doctrine governing state-court jurisdiction. As we have noted, under *Pennoyer* state authority to adjudicate was based on the jurisdiction's power over either persons or property. This fundamental concept is embodied in the very vocabulary which we use to describe judgments. If a court's jurisdiction is based on its authority over the defendant's person, the action and judgment are denominated *"in personam"* and can impose a personal obligation on the defendant in favor of the plaintiff. If jurisdiction is based on the court's power over property within its territory, the action is called *"in rem"* or *"quasi in rem."* The effect of a judgment in such a case is limited to the property that supports jurisdiction and does not impose a personal liability on the property owner, since he is not before the court.[17] In

15. The doctrine that one State does not have to recognize the judgment of another State's courts if the latter did not have jurisdiction was firmly established at the time of *Pennoyer*.

16. Attachment was considered essential to the state court's jurisdiction for two reasons. First, attachment combined with substituted service would provide greater assurance that the defendant would actually receive notice of the action than would publication alone. Second, since the court's jurisdiction depended on the defendant's ownership of property in the State and could be defeated if the defendant disposed of that property, attachment was necessary to assure that the court had jurisdiction

when the proceedings began and continued to have jurisdiction when it entered judgment. 95 U.S. at 727–728.

17. "A judgment *in rem* affects the interests of all persons in designated property. A judgment *quasi in rem* affects the interests of particular persons in designated property. The latter is of two types. In one the plaintiff is seeking to secure a preexisting claim in the subject property and to extinguish or establish the nonexistence of similar interests of particular persons. In the other the plaintiff seeks to apply what he concedes to be the property of the defendant to the satisfaction of a claim against him. Restatement, Judgments, 5–9." *Han-*

Pennoyer's terms, the owner is affected only "indirectly" by an *in rem* judgment adverse to his interest in the property subject to the court's disposition.

By concluding that "[t]he authority of every tribunal is necessarily restricted by the territorial limits of the State in which it is established," 95 U.S. at 720, *Pennoyer* sharply limited the availability of *in personam* jurisdiction over defendants not resident in the forum State. If a nonresident defendant could not be found in a State, he could not be sued there. On the other hand, since the State in which property was located was considered to have exclusive sovereignty over that property, *in rem* actions could proceed regardless of the owner's location. Indeed, since a State's process could not reach beyond its borders, this Court held after *Pennoyer* that due process did not require any effort to give a property owner personal notice that his property was involved in an *in rem* proceeding.

The *Pennoyer* rules generally favored nonresident defendants by making them harder to sue. This advantage was reduced, however, by the ability of a resident plaintiff to satisfy a claim against a nonresident defendant by bringing into court any property of the defendant located in the plaintiff's State. For example, in the well-known case of *Harris v. Balk*, 198 U.S. 215, 25 S.Ct. 625, 49 L.Ed. 1023 (1905), Epstein, a resident of Maryland, had a claim against Balk, a resident of North Carolina. Harris, another North Carolina resident, owed money to Balk. When Harris happened to visit Maryland, Epstein garnished his debt to Balk. Harris did not contest the debt to Balk and paid it to Epstein's North Carolina attorney. When Balk later sued Harris in North Carolina, this Court held that the Full Faith and Credit Clause, U.S. Const., Art. IV, § 1, required that Harris' payment to Epstein be treated as a discharge of his debt to Balk. This Court reasoned that the debt Harris owed Balk was an intangible form of property belonging to Balk, and that the location of that property traveled with the debtor. By obtaining personal jurisdiction over Harris, Epstein had "arrested" his debt to Balk, and brought it into the Maryland court. Under the structure established by *Pennoyer*, Epstein was then entitled to proceed against that debt to vindicate his claim against Balk, even though Balk himself was not subject to the jurisdiction of a Maryland tribunal.

Pennoyer itself recognized that its rigid categories, even as blurred by the kind of action typified by *Harris,* could not accommodate some necessary litigation. Accordingly, Mr. Justice Field's opinion carefully noted that cases involving the personal status of the plaintiff, such as divorce actions, could be adjudicated in the plaintiff's home State even though the defendant could not be served within that State. Similarly, the opinion approved the practice of considering a foreign corporation doing business in a State to have consented to being sued in that State.

son v. Denckla, 357 U.S. 235, 246 n. 12, 78 S.Ct. 1228, 1235, 2 L.Ed.2d 1283 (1958).

As did the Court in *Hanson*, we will for convenience generally use the term *"in rem"* in place of *"in rem and quasi in rem."*

This basis for *in personam* jurisdiction over foreign corporations was later supplemented by the doctrine that a corporation doing business in a State could be deemed "present" in the State, and so subject to service of process under the rule of *Pennoyer.*

The advent of automobiles, with the concomitant increase in the incidence of individuals causing injury in States where they were not subject to *in personam* actions under *Pennoyer,* required further moderation of the territorial limits on jurisdictional power. This modification, like the accommodation to the realities of interstate corporate activities, was accomplished by use of a legal fiction that left the conceptual structure established in *Pennoyer* theoretically unaltered. The fiction used was that the out-of-state motorist, who it was assumed could be excluded altogether from the State's highways, had by using those highways appointed a designated state official as his agent to accept process. *See Hess v. Pawloski,* 274 U.S. 352, 47 S.Ct. 632, 71 L.Ed. 1091 (1927). Since the motorist's "agent" could be personally served within the State, the state courts could obtain *in personam* jurisdiction over the nonresident driver.

The motorists' consent theory was easy to administer since it required only a finding that the out-of-state driver had used the State's roads. By contrast, both the fictions of implied consent to service on the part of a foreign corporation and of corporate presence required a finding that the corporation was "doing business" in the forum State. Defining the criteria for making that finding and deciding whether they were met absorbed much judicial energy. *See, e.g., International Shoe Co. v. Washington,* 326 U.S. at 317–319, 66 S.Ct. at 158–160. While the essentially quantitative tests which emerged from these cases purported simply to identify circumstances under which presence or consent could be attributed to the corporation, it became clear that they were in fact attempting to ascertain "what dealings make it just to subject a foreign corporation to local suit". *Hutchinson v. Chase & Gilbert,* 45 F.2d 139, 141 (C.A.2 1930) (L. Hand, J.). In *International Shoe,* we acknowledged that fact.

The question in *International Shoe* was whether the corporation was subject to the judicial and taxing jurisdiction of Washington. Mr. Chief Justice Stone's opinion for the Court began its analysis of that question by noting that the historical basis of *in personam* jurisdiction was a court's power over the defendant's person. That power, however, was no longer the central concern:

> But now that the *capias ad respondendum* has given way to personal service of summons or other form of notice, due process requires only that in order to subject a defendant to a judgment *in personam,* if he be not present within the territory of the forum, he have certain minimum contacts with it such that the maintenance of the suit does not offend "traditional notions of fair play and substantial justice."

Milliken v. Meyer, 311 U.S. 457, 463, 61 S.Ct. 339, 343, 85 L.Ed. 278. 326 U.S. at 316, 66 S.Ct. at 158.

Thus, the inquiry into the State's jurisdiction over a foreign corporation appropriately focused not on whether the corporation was "present" but on whether there have been

> such contacts of the corporation with the state of the forum as make it reasonable, in the context of our federal system of government, to require the corporation to defend the particular suit which is brought there.

* * *

Id. at 317, 66 S.Ct. at 158. Mechanical or quantitative evaluations of the defendant's activities in the forum could not resolve the question of reasonableness:

> Whether due process is satisfied must depend rather upon the quality and nature of the activity in relation to the fair and orderly administration of the laws which it was the purpose of the due process clause to insure. That clause does not contemplate that a state may make binding a judgment *in personam* against an individual or corporate defendant with which the state has no contacts, ties, or relations. *Id.* at 319, 66 S.Ct. at 160. Thus, the relationship among the defendant, the forum, and the litigation, rather than the mutually exclusive sovereignty of the States on which the rules of *Pennoyer* rest, became the central concern of the inquiry into personal jurisdiction. The immediate effect of this departure from *Pennoyer's* conceptual apparatus was to increase the ability of the state courts to obtain personal jurisdiction over nonresident defendants.

No equally dramatic change has occurred in the law governing jurisdiction *in rem.* There have, however, been intimations that the collapse of the *in personam* wing of *Pennoyer* has not left that decision unweakened as a foundation for *in rem* jurisdiction. Well-reasoned lower court opinions have questioned the proposition that the presence of property in a State gives that State jurisdiction to adjudicate rights to the property regardless of the relationship of the underlying dispute and the property owner to the forum. The overwhelming majority of commentators have also rejected *Pennoyer's* premise that a proceeding "against" property is not a proceeding against the owners of that property. Accordingly, they urge that the "traditional notions of fair play and substantial justice" that govern a State's power to adjudicate *in personam* should also govern its power to adjudicate personal rights to property located in the State.

Although this Court has not addressed this argument directly, we have held that property cannot be subjected to a court's judgment unless reasonable and appropriate efforts have been made to give the property owners actual notice of the action. This conclusion recognizes, contrary to *Pennoyer,* that an adverse judgment *in rem* directly affects the property owner by divesting him of his rights in the property before the court. Moreover, in *Mullane* we held that Fourteenth Amendment rights cannot depend on the classification of an action as *in rem* or *in personam*.

It is clear, therefore, that the law of state-court jurisdiction no longer stands securely on the foundation established in *Pennoyer*. We think that the time is ripe to consider whether the standard of fairness and substantial justice set forth in *International Shoe* should be held to govern actions *in rem* as well as *in personam*.

III

The case for applying to jurisdiction *in rem* the same test of "fair play and substantial justice" as governs assertions of jurisdiction *in personam* is simple and straightforward. It is premised on recognition that "[t]he phrase, 'judicial jurisdiction over a thing,' is a customary elliptical way of referring to jurisdiction over the interests of persons in a thing." Restatement (Second) of Conflict of Laws § 56, Introductory Note (1971) (hereafter Restatement). This recognition leads to the conclusion that in order to justify an exercise of jurisdiction *in rem*, the basis for jurisdiction must be sufficient to justify exercising "jurisdiction over the interests of persons in a thing." The standard for determining whether an exercise of jurisdiction over the interests of persons is consistent with the Due Process Clause is the minimum-contacts standard elucidated in *International Shoe*.

This argument, of course, does not ignore the fact that the presence of property in a State may bear on the existence of jurisdiction by providing contacts among the forum State, the defendant, and the litigation. For example, when claims to the property itself are the source of the underlying controversy between the plaintiff and the defendant, it would be unusual for the State where the property is located not to have jurisdiction. In such cases, the defendant's claim to property located in the State would normally indicate that he expected to benefit from the State's protection of his interest. The State's strong interests in assuring the marketability of property within its borders and in providing a procedure for peaceful resolution of disputes about the possession of that property would also support jurisdiction, as would the likelihood that important records and witnesses will be found in the State. The presence of property may also favor jurisdiction in cases such as suits for injury suffered on the land of an absentee owner, where the defendant's ownership of the property is conceded but the cause of action is otherwise related to rights and duties growing out of that ownership.

It appears, therefore, that jurisdiction over many types of actions which now are or might be brought *in rem* would not be affected by a holding that any assertion of state-court jurisdiction must satisfy the *International Shoe* standard. For the type of *quasi in rem* action typified by *Harris v. Balk* and the present case, however, accepting the proposed analysis would result in significant change. These are cases where the property which now serves as the basis for state-court jurisdiction is completely unrelated to the plaintiff's cause of action. Thus, although the presence of the defendant's property in a State might suggest the existence of other ties among the defendant, the State, and the litigation, the presence of the property alone would not support the State's jurisdiction. If those other ties did not exist, cases over which the State is now thought to have jurisdiction could not be brought in that forum.

Since acceptance of the *International Shoe* test would most affect this class of cases, we examine the arguments against adopting that standard as they relate to this category of litigation. Before doing so, however, we note that this type of case also presents the clearest illustration of the argument in favor of assessing assertions of jurisdiction by a single standard. For in cases such as *Harris* and this one, the only role played by the property is to provide the basis for bringing the defendant into court. Indeed, the express purpose of the Delaware sequestration procedure is to compel the defendant to enter a personal appearance. In such cases, if a direct assertion of personal jurisdiction over the defendant would violate the Constitution, it would seem that an indirect assertion of that jurisdiction should be equally impermissible.

The primary rationale for treating the presence of property as a sufficient basis for jurisdiction to adjudicate claims over which the State would not have jurisdiction if *International Shoe* applied is that a wrongdoer

> should not be able to avoid payment of his obligations by the expedient of removing his assets to a place where he is not subject to an in personam suit. Restatement § 66, Comment a.

This justification, however, does not explain why jurisdiction should be recognized without regard to whether the property is present in the State because of an effort to avoid the owner's obligations. Nor does it support jurisdiction to adjudicate the underlying claim. At most, it suggests that a State in which property is located should have jurisdiction to attach that property, by use of proper procedures, as security for a judgment being sought in a forum where the litigation can be maintained consistently with *International Shoe*. Moreover, we know of nothing to justify the assumption that a debtor can avoid paying his obligations by removing his property to a State in which his creditor cannot obtain personal jurisdiction over him. The Full Faith and Credit Clause, after all, makes the valid *in personam* judgment of one State enforceable in all other States.

It might also be suggested that allowing *in rem* jurisdiction avoids the uncertainty inherent in the *International Shoe* standard and assures a plaintiff of a forum.[37] *See* Folk & Moyer, *supra*, n. 10, at 749, 767. We believe, however, that the fairness standard of *International Shoe* can be easily applied in the vast majority of cases. Moreover, when the existence

---

37. This case does not raise, and we therefore do not consider, the question whether the presence of a defendant's property in a State is a sufficient basis for jurisdiction when no other forum is available to the plaintiff.

of jurisdiction in a particular forum under *International Shoe* is unclear, the cost of simplifying the litigation by avoiding the jurisdictional question may be the sacrifice of "fair play and substantial justice." That cost is too high.

We are left, then, to consider the significance of the long history of jurisdiction based solely on the presence of property in a State. Although the theory that territorial power is both essential to and sufficient for jurisdiction has been undermined, we have never held that the presence of property in a State does not automatically confer jurisdiction over the owner's interest in that property. This history must be considered as supporting the proposition that jurisdiction based solely on the presence of property satisfies the demands of due process, cf. *Ownbey v. Morgan*, 256 U.S. 94, 111, 41 S.Ct. 433, 438, 65 L.Ed. 837 (1921), but it is not decisive. "[T]raditional notions of fair play and substantial justice" can be as readily offended by the perpetuation of ancient forms that are no longer justified as by the adoption of new procedures that are inconsistent with the basic values of our constitutional heritage. The fiction that an assertion of jurisdiction over property is anything but an assertion of jurisdiction over the owner of the property supports an ancient form without substantial modern justification. Its continued acceptance would serve only to allow state-court jurisdiction that is fundamentally unfair to the defendant.

We therefore conclude that all assertions of state-court jurisdiction must be evaluated according to the standards set forth in *International Shoe* and its progeny.[39]

IV

The Delaware courts based their assertion of jurisdiction in this case solely on the statutory presence of appellants' property in Delaware. Yet that property is not the subject matter of this litigation, nor is the underlying cause of action related to the property. Appellants' holdings in Greyhound do not, therefore, provide contacts with Delaware sufficient to support the jurisdiction of that State's courts over appellants. If it exists, that jurisdiction must have some other foundation.[40]

---

39. It would not be fruitful for us to reexamine the facts of cases decided on the rationales of *Pennoyer* and *Harris* to determine whether jurisdiction might have been sustained under the standard we adopt today. To the extent that prior decisions are inconsistent with this standard, they are overruled.

40. Appellants argue that our determination that the minimum-contacts standard of *International Shoe* governs jurisdiction here makes unnecessary any consideration of the existence of such contacts. They point out that they were never personally served with a summons, that Delaware has no long-arm statute which would authorize

such service, and that the Delaware Supreme Court has authoritatively held that the existence of contacts is irrelevant to jurisdiction under Del.Code Ann., Tit. 10, § 366 (1975). As part of its sequestration order, however, the Court of Chancery directed its clerk to send each appellant a copy of the summons and complaint by certified mail. The record indicates that those mailings were made and contains return receipts from at least 19 of the appellants. None of the appellants has suggested that he did not actually receive the summons which was directed to him in compliance with a Delaware statute designed to provide jurisdiction over nonresidents. In these circumstances, we will assume that

Appellee Heitner did not allege and does not now claim that appellants have ever set foot in Delaware. Nor does he identify any act related to his cause of action as having taken place in Delaware. Nevertheless, he contends that appellants' positions as directors and officers of a corporation chartered in Delaware provide sufficient "contacts, ties, or relations," *International Shoe Co. v. Washington,* with that State to give its courts jurisdiction over appellants in this stockholder's derivative action. This argument is based primarily on what Heitner asserts to be the strong interest of Delaware in supervising the management of a Delaware corporation. That interest is said to derive from the role of Delaware law in establishing the corporation and defining the obligations owed to it by its officers and directors. In order to protect this interest, appellee concludes, Delaware's courts must have jurisdiction over corporate fiduciaries such as appellants.

This argument is undercut by the failure of the Delaware Legislature to assert the state interest appellee finds so compelling. Delaware law bases jurisdiction, not on appellants' status as corporate fiduciaries, but rather on the presence of their property in the State. Although the sequestration procedure used here may be most frequently used in derivative suits against officers and directors, the authorizing statute evinces no specific concern with such actions. Sequestration can be used in any suit against a nonresident, and reaches corporate fiduciaries only if they happen to own interests in a Delaware corporation, or other property in the State. But as Heitner's failure to secure jurisdiction over seven of the defendants named in his complaint demonstrates, there is no necessary relationship between holding a position as a corporate fiduciary and owning stock or other interests in the corporation. If Delaware perceived its interest in securing jurisdiction over corporate fiduciaries to be as great as Heitner suggests, we would expect it to have enacted a statute more clearly designed to protect that interest.

Moreover, even if Heitner's assessment of the importance of Delaware's interest is accepted, his argument fails to demonstrate that Delaware is a fair forum for this litigation. The interest appellee has identified may support the application of Delaware law to resolve any controversy over appellants' actions in their capacities as officers and directors. But we have rejected the argument that if a State's law can properly be applied to a dispute, its courts necessarily have jurisdiction over the parties to that dispute.

Appellee suggests that by accepting positions as officers or directors of a Delaware corporation, appellants performed the acts required by *Hanson v. Denckla.* He notes that Delaware law provides substantial benefits to corporate officers and directors, and that these benefits were at least in part the incentive for appellants to assume their positions. It is, he says, "only fair and just" to require appellants, in return for these

the procedures followed would be sufficient to bring appellants before the Delaware courts, if minimum contacts existed.

benefits, to respond in the State of Delaware when they are accused of misusing their power.

But like Heitner's first argument, this line of reasoning establishes only that it is appropriate for Delaware law to govern the obligations of appellants to Greyhound and its stockholders. It does not demonstrate that appellants have "purposefully avail[ed themselves] of the privilege of conducting activities within the forum State," *Hanson v. Denckla, supra,* at 253, 78 S.Ct. at 1240, in a way that would justify bringing them before a Delaware tribunal. Appellants have simply had nothing to do with the State of Delaware. Moreover, appellants had no reason to expect to be haled before a Delaware court. Delaware, unlike some States, has not enacted a statute that treats acceptance of a directorship as consent to jurisdiction in the State. And "[i]t strains reason * * * to suggest that anyone buying securities in a corporation formed in Delaware 'impliedly consents' to subject himself to Delaware's * * * jurisdiction on any cause of action." Folk & Moyer, [73 Colum.L.Rev.] at 785. Appellants, who were not required to acquire interests in Greyhound in order to hold their positions, did not by acquiring those interests surrender their right to be brought to judgment only in States with which they had had "minimum contacts." Delaware's assertion of jurisdiction over appellants in this case is inconsistent with that constitutional limitation on state power. The judgment of the Delaware Supreme Court must, therefore, be reversed.

It is so ordered.

JUSTICE REHNQUIST took no part in the consideration or decision of this case.

JUSTICE POWELL, concurring.

I agree that the principles of *International Shoe Co. v. Washington,* 326 U.S. 310, 66 S.Ct. 154, 90 L.Ed. 95 (1945), should be extended to govern assertions of *in rem* as well as *in personam* jurisdiction in a state court. I also agree that neither the statutory presence of appellants' stock in Delaware nor their positions as directors and officers of a Delaware corporation can provide sufficient contacts to support the Delaware courts' assertion of jurisdiction in this case.

I would explicitly reserve judgment, however, on whether the ownership of some forms of property whose situs is indisputably and permanently located within a State may, without more, provide the contacts necessary to subject a defendant to jurisdiction within the State to the extent of the value of the property. In the case of real property, in particular, preservation of the common-law concept of *quasi in rem* jurisdiction arguably would avoid the uncertainty of the general *International Shoe* standard without significant cost to " 'traditional notions of fair play and substantial justice.' "

Subject to the foregoing reservation, I join the opinion of the Court.

JUSTICE STEVENS, concurring in the judgment.

One who purchases shares of stock on the open market can hardly be expected to know that he has thereby become subject to suit in a forum remote from his residence and unrelated to the transaction. As a practical matter, the Delaware sequestration statute creates an unacceptable risk of judgment without notice. Unlike the 49 other States, Delaware treats the place of incorporation as the situs of the stock, even though both the owner and the custodian of the shares are elsewhere. Moreover, Delaware denies the defendant the opportunity to defend the merits of the suit unless he subjects himself to the unlimited jurisdiction of the court. Thus, it coerces a defendant either to submit to personal jurisdiction in a forum which could not otherwise obtain such jurisdiction or to lose the securities which have been attached. If its procedure were upheld, Delaware would, in effect, impose a duty of inquiry on every purchaser of securities in the national market. For unless the purchaser ascertains both the State of incorporation of the company whose shares he is buying, and also the idiosyncrasies of its law, he may be assuming an unknown risk of litigation. I therefore agree with the Court that on the record before us no adequate basis for jurisdiction exists and that the Delaware statute is unconstitutional on its face.

How the Court's opinion may be applied in other contexts is not entirely clear to me. I agree with Mr. Justice Powell that it should not be read to invalidate *quasi in rem* jurisdiction where real estate is involved. I would also not read it as invalidating other long-accepted methods of acquiring jurisdiction over persons with adequate notice of both the particular controversy and the fact that their local activities might subject them to suit. My uncertainty as to the reach of the opinion, and my fear that it purports to decide a great deal more than is necessary to dispose of this case, persuade me merely to concur in the judgment.

JUSTICE BRENNAN, concurring in part and dissenting in part.

I join Parts I–III of the Court's opinion. I fully agree that the minimum-contacts analysis developed in *International Shoe Co. v. Washington,* 326 U.S. 310, 66 S.Ct. 154, 90 L.Ed. 95 (1945), represents a far more sensible construct for the exercise of state-court jurisdiction than the patchwork of legal and factual fictions that has been generated from the decision in *Pennoyer v. Neff,* 95 U.S. 714, 24 L.Ed. 565 (1878). It is precisely because the inquiry into minimum contacts is now of such overriding importance, however, that I must respectfully dissent from Part IV of the Court's opinion.

I

The primary teaching of Parts I–III of today's decision is that a State, in seeking to assert jurisdiction over a person located outside its borders, may only do so on the basis of minimum contacts among the parties, the contested transaction, and the forum State. The Delaware Supreme Court could not have made plainer, however, that its sequestration statute, Del.Code Ann., Tit. 10, § 366 (1975), does not operate on this basis, but instead is strictly an embodiment of *quasi in rem* jurisdiction, a jurisdictional predicate no longer constitutionally viable. * * * This state-court ruling obviously comports with the understanding of the parties, for the issue of the existence of minimum contacts was never pleaded by appellee, made the subject of discovery, or ruled upon by the Delaware courts. These facts notwithstanding, the Court in Part IV reaches the minimum-contacts question and finds such contacts lacking as applied to appellants. Succinctly stated, once having properly and persuasively decided that the *quasi in rem* statute that Delaware admits to having enacted is invalid, the Court then proceeds to find that a minimum-contacts law that Delaware expressly *denies* having enacted also could not be constitutionally applied in this case.

In my view, a purer example of an advisory opinion is not to be found. True, appellants do not deny having received actual notice of the action in question. However, notice is but one ingredient of a proper assertion of state-court jurisdiction. The other is a statute authorizing the exercise of the State's judicial power along constitutionally permissible grounds—which henceforth means minimum contacts. As of today, § 366 is not such a law. Recognizing that today's decision fundamentally alters the relevant jurisdictional ground rules, I certainly would not want to rule out the possibility that Delaware's courts might decide that the legislature's overriding purpose of securing the personal appearance in state courts of defendants would best be served by reinterpreting its statute to permit state jurisdiction on the basis of constitutionally permissible contacts rather than stock ownership. Were the state courts to take this step, it would then become necessary to address the question of whether minimum contacts exist here. But in the present posture of this case, the Court's decision of this important issue is purely an abstract ruling.

My concern with the inappropriateness of the Court's action is highlighted by two other considerations. First, an inquiry into minimum contacts inevitably is highly dependent on creating a proper factual foundation detailing the contacts between the forum State and the controversy in question. Because neither the plaintiff-appellee nor the state courts viewed such an inquiry as germane in this instance, the Court today is unable to draw upon a proper factual record in reaching its conclusion; moreover, its disposition denies appellee the normal opportunity to seek discovery on the contacts issue. Second, it must be remembered that the Court's ruling is a constitutional one and necessarily will affect the reach of the jurisdictional laws of all 50 States. Ordinarily this would counsel restraint in constitutional pronouncements. Certainly it should have cautioned the Court against reaching out to decide a question that, as here, has yet to emerge from the state courts ripened for review on the federal issue.

II

Nonetheless, because the Court rules on the minimum-contacts question, I feel impelled to express my view. While evidence derived through discovery might satisfy me that minimum contacts are lacking in a given case, I am convinced that as a general rule a state forum has jurisdiction to adjudicate a shareholder derivative action centering on the conduct and policies of the directors and officers of a corporation chartered by that State. Unlike the Court, I therefore would not foreclose Delaware from asserting jurisdiction over appellants were it persuaded to do so on the basis of minimum contacts.

It is well settled that a derivative lawsuit as presented here does not inure primarily to the benefit of the named plaintiff. Rather, the primary beneficiaries are the corporation and its owners, the shareholders.

Viewed in this light, the chartering State has an unusually powerful interest in insuring the availability of a convenient forum for litigating claims involving a possible multiplicity of defendant fiduciaries and for vindicating the State's substantive policies regarding the management of its domestic corporations. I believe that our cases fairly establish that the State's valid substantive interests are important considerations in assessing whether it constitutionally may claim jurisdiction over a given cause of action.

In this instance, Delaware can point to at least three interrelated public policies that are furthered by its assertion of jurisdiction. First, the State has a substantial interest in providing restitution for its local corporations that allegedly have been victimized by fiduciary misconduct, even if the managerial decisions occurred outside the State. The importance of this general state interest in assuring restitution for its own residents previously found expression in cases that went outside the then-prevailing due process framework to authorize state-court jurisdiction over nonresident motorists who injure others within the State. *Hess v. Pawloski*, 274 U.S. 352, 47 S.Ct. 632, 71 L.Ed. 1091 (1927). More recently, it has led States to seek and to acquire jurisdiction over nonresident tortfeasors whose purely out-of-state activities produce domestic consequences. Second, state courts have legitimately read their jurisdiction expansively when a cause of action centers in an area in which the forum State possesses a manifest regulatory interest. *E.g., McGee v. International Life Ins. Co.*, 355 U.S. 220, 78 S.Ct. 199, 2 L.Ed.2d 223 (1957) (insurance regulation). Only this Term we reiterated that the conduct of corporate fiduciaries is just such a matter in which the policies and interests of the domestic forum are ordinarily presumed to be paramount. Finally, a State like Delaware has a recognized interest in affording a convenient forum for supervising and overseeing the affairs of an entity that is purely the creation of that State's law. For example, even following our decision in *International Shoe,* New York courts were permitted to exercise complete judicial authority over nonresident beneficiaries of a trust created under state law, even though, unlike appellants here, the beneficiaries personally entered into no association whatsoever with New York. *Mullane v. Central Hanover Bank & Trust Co.*, 339 U.S. 306, 313, 70 S.Ct. 652, 656, 94 L.Ed. 865 (1950). I, of course, am not suggesting that Delaware's varied interests would justify its acceptance of jurisdiction over any transaction touching upon the affairs of its domestic corporations. But a derivative action which raises allegations of abuses of the basic management of an institution whose existence is created by the State and whose powers and duties are defined by state law fundamentally implicates the public policies of that forum.

To be sure, the Court is not blind to these considerations. It notes that the State's interests "may support the application of Delaware law to resolve any controversy over appellants' actions in their capacities as officers and directors." But this, the Court argues, pertains to choice of law, not jurisdiction. I recognize that the jurisdictional and choice-of-law inquiries are not identical. But I would not compartmentalize thinking in this area quite so rigidly as it seems to me the Court does today, for both inquiries "are often closely related and to a substantial degree depend upon similar considerations." In either case an important linchpin is the extent of contacts between the controversy, the parties, and the forum State. While constitutional limitations on the choice of law are by no means settled, important considerations certainly include the expectancies of the parties and the fairness of governing the defendants' acts and behavior by rules of conduct created by a given jurisdiction. These same factors bear upon the propriety of a State's exercising jurisdiction over a legal dispute. At the minimum, the decision that it is fair to bind a defendant by a State's laws and rules should prove to be highly relevant to the fairness of permitting that same State to accept jurisdiction for adjudicating the controversy.

Furthermore, I believe that practical considerations argue in favor of seeking to bridge the distance between the choice-of-law and jurisdictional inquiries. Even when a court would apply the law of a different forum, as a general rule it will feel less knowledgeable and comfortable in interpretation, and less interested in fostering the policies of that foreign jurisdiction, than would the courts established by the State that provides the applicable law. Obviously, such choice-of-law problems cannot entirely be avoided in a diverse legal system such as our own. Nonetheless, when a suitor seeks to lodge a suit in a State with a substantial interest in seeing its own law applied to the transaction in question, we could wisely act to minimize conflicts, confusion, and uncertainty by adopting a liberal view of jurisdiction, unless considerations of fairness or efficiency strongly point in the opposite direction.

This case is not one where, in my judgment, this preference for jurisdiction is adequately answered. Certainly nothing said by the Court persuades me that it would be unfair to subject appellants to suit in Delaware. The fact that the record does not reveal whether they "set foot" or committed "act[s] related to [the] cause of action" in Delaware, is not decisive, for jurisdiction can be based strictly on out-of-state acts having foreseeable effects in the forum State. I have little difficulty in applying this principle to nonresident fiduciaries whose alleged breaches of trust are said to have substantial damaging effect on the financial posture of a resident corporation. Further, I cannot understand how the existence of minimum contacts in a constitutional sense is at all affected by Delaware's failure statutorily to express an interest in controlling corporate fiduciaries. To me this simply demonstrates that Delaware did not elect to assert jurisdiction to the extent the Constitution would allow. Nor would I view as controlling or even especially meaningful Delaware's failure to exact from appellants their consent to be sued. Once we have rejected the jurisdictional framework created in *Pennoyer v. Neff,* I see no reason to rest jurisdiction on a fictional outgrowth of that system such as the existence of a consent statute, expressed or implied.[6]

I, therefore, would approach the minimum-contacts analysis differently than does the Court. Crucial to me is the fact that appellants voluntarily associated themselves with the State of Delaware, "invoking the benefits and protections of its laws," by entering into a long-term and fragile relationship with one of its domestic corporations. They thereby elected to assume powers and to undertake responsibilities wholly derived from that State's rules and regulations, and to become eligible for those benefits that Delaware law makes available to its corporations' officials. *E.g.,* Del.Code Ann., Tit. 8, § 143 (1975) (interest-free loans); § 145 (1975 ed. and Supp. 1976) (indemnification). While it is possible that countervailing issues of judicial efficiency and the like might clearly favor a different forum, they do not appear on the meager record before us; and, of course, we are concerned solely with "minimum" contacts, not the "best" contacts. I thus do not believe that it is unfair to insist that appellants make themselves available to suit in a competent forum that Delaware might create for vindication of its important public policies directly pertaining to appellants' fiduciary associations with the State.

Notes and Questions

1. In its opening paragraph, the Court noted two issues: First, the jurisdiction of the state court over a controversy based simply on the presence of property within the state; second, the constitutionality of the sequestration procedure. The Court never reached the second issue, having disposed of the case on the constitutionality of quasi in rem jurisdiction. For analysis and synthesis of significant Supreme Court opinions relating to the second issue, *see infra* Section C, Exercise II.

2. The Delaware legislation in question required a general appearance before nonresidents were permitted to defend a lawsuit on the merits, thus

---

6. Admittedly, when one consents to suit in a forum, his expectation is enhanced that he may be haled into that State's courts. To this extent, I agree that consent may have bearing on the fairness of accepting jurisdiction. But whatever is the degree of personal expectation that is necessary to warrant jurisdiction should not depend on the formality of establishing a consent law. Indeed, if one's expectations are to carry such weight, then appellants here might be fairly charged with the understanding that Delaware would decide to protect its sub-stantial interests through its own courts, for they certainly realized that in the past the sequestration law has been employed primarily as a means of securing the appearance of corporate officials in the State's courts. Even in the absence of such a statute, however, the close and special association between a state corporation and its managers should apprise the latter that the State may seek to offer a convenient forum for addressing claims of fiduciary breach of trust.

transforming the limited quasi in rem jurisdiction into full in personam jurisdiction. Why did the Delaware legislature take this approach? Did this transformation influence the Court's thinking regarding the fairness of the Delaware procedure and perhaps set the stage for reexamination of quasi in rem jurisdiction generally? Could the Court have left undisturbed quasi in rem jurisdiction in general, yet have held unconstitutional the legislative bar on "limited appearances"? Would your answer depend on prior Court pronouncements in analogous areas? *See York v. Texas,* 137 U.S. 15 (1890) (upholding the Texas practice barring special appearances).

3. Clearly Justice Marshall was correct in discarding the fiction that a proceeding against property is not a proceeding against the person. And once that hoary fiction was abandoned, did any justification or sound policy reason remain for retaining quasi in rem jurisdiction?

4. The Court fully analyzed *Pennoyer* and *Harris v. Balk.* Why did the Court neither discuss nor cite *Seider,* excerpted at p. 188? Can you convincingly argue that *Seider* was not affected by the decision? *See Rush v. Savchuk,* 444 U.S. 320 (1980) (rejecting *Seider*). Perhaps apprehensive that litigants and courts would attempt to resuscitate *Pennoyer* and *Harris,* the Court asserted in footnote 39:

> It would not be fruitful for us to reexamine the facts of cases decided on the rationales of *Pennoyer* and *Harris* to determine whether jurisdiction might have been sustained under the standard we adopt today. To the extent that prior decisions are inconsistent with this standard, they are overruled.

5. Assume a state legislature desired to extend its judicial jurisdiction over nonresident directors and officers of domestic corporations who cause injury to the corporation. After *Shaffer,* could a state render these nonresident corporate officials amenable to its jurisdiction? Note carefully the following passage of the opinion:

> [The nonresident directors and officers] have simply had nothing to do with the State of Delaware. Moreover [they] had no reason to expect to be haled before a Delaware Court. Delaware, unlike some States, has not enacted a statute that treats acceptance of a directorship as consent to jurisdiction in the State.

433 U.S. at 216. Within a few weeks of the *Shaffer* decision Delaware enacted the following statute:

> Every nonresident of this State who after September 1, 1977, accepts election or appointment as a director, trustee or member of the governing body of a corporation organized under the laws of this State or who after June 30, 1978, serves in such capacity and every resident of this State who so accepts election or appointment or serves in such capacity and thereafter removes his residence from this State shall, by such acceptance or by such service, be deemed thereby to have consented to the appointment of the registered agent of such corporation (or, if there is none, the Secretary of State) as his agent upon whom service of process may be made in all civil actions or proceedings brought in this State, by or on behalf of, or against such corporation, in which such director, trustee or member is a necessary or proper party, or in any

action or proceeding against such director, trustee or member for violation of his duty in such capacity, whether or not he continues to serve as such director, trustee or member at the time suit is commenced. Such acceptance or service as such director, trustee or member shall be a signification of the consent of such director, trustee or member that any process when so served shall be of the same legal force and validity as if served upon such director, trustee or member within this State and such appointment of the registered agent (or, if there is none, the Secretary of State) shall be irrevocable. 10 Del. C. § 3114.

Is *Shaffer* much ado about nothing? Is the statute constitutional?

6. In *Shaffer* the Court stated:

> We therefore conclude that *all* assertions of state-court jurisdiction must be evaluated according to the standards set forth in *International Shoe* and its progeny.

433 U.S. at 212 (emphasis added).

May Arizona now assume personal jurisdiction over a nonresident causing an injury in Nevada simply because the summons is served on the nonresident while he is physically present in Arizona? Recall the following passage in *International Shoe:* "[D]ue process requires that in order to subject a defendant to a judgment in personam, *if he be not present within the territory of the forum*, he have certain minimum contacts with it such that the maintenance of the suit does not offend 'traditional notions of fair play and substantial justice.' " 326 U.S. at 316 (emphasis added).

Suppose the nonresident's property in Arizona is seized for jurisdictional purposes? Do you entertain doubts after *Shaffer?* Reexamine *Johnson v. Roscoe & Baker, supra* Chapter II. Was jurisdiction over John's person and property constitutional? Let's revisit the issue after you read *Burnham*, the following case.

7. Assume an American citizen is injured by an alien in an incident occurring in a foreign country. The citizen locates a New York bank account belonging to the nonresident. May the bank account be seized for purposes of asserting quasi in rem jurisdiction? The Court in *Shaffer* expressly left the issue open in "jurisdiction by necessity" cases:

> This case does not raise, and we therefore do not consider, the question whether the presence of a defendant's property in a State is a sufficient basis for jurisdiction when no other forum is available to the plaintiff.

433 U.S. at 211 n. 37. Assume, instead, that the alien is served with process while on a one-day visit to New York. What result? If the American court exercises jurisdiction in the latter situation, what problems might the plaintiff face in attempting to satisfy the judgment?

8. *Shaffer* may affect other areas. For example, suppose the owner of the property seized by attachment does not appear to contest the jurisdiction of the court. May he later upset the title passed through the default judgment? In addressing this problem, Professor Casad states:

> While presence of property in the state may be insufficient to force a defendant to adjudicate a claim unrelated to that property, it may

provide a sufficient basis for forcing a defendant to present any objection he may have on *International Shoe* grounds in that forum.

Casad, Shaffer v. Heitner: *An End to Ambivalence in Jurisdiction Theory?,* 26 Kan. L. Rev. 61, 80 (1977). Do you agree?

9.   The Internet, and more specifically the use of Internet domain names, has caused a rethinking of jurisdictional principles. Because of the ubiquitous nature of the Internet, problems of obtaining jurisdiction over poachers and infringers are likely to occur. In 1999, Congress addressed several of these problems in 15 U.S.C. § 1125d (2000), entitled Cyberpiracy Prevention. Where the owner of a mark alleges that a domain name violates its rights under the laws protecting trademarks, the statute allows the plaintiff to institute *in rem* proceedings where the name has been registered in the following circumstances:

(2)(A) The owner of a mark may file an in rem civil action against a domain name in the judicial district in which the domain name registrar, domain name registry, or other domain name authority that registered or assigned the domain name is located if

* * *

(ii) the court finds that the owner—

(I) is not able to obtain in personam jurisdiction over a person who would have been a defendant in a civil action under paragraph (1); or

(II) through due diligence was not able to find a person who would have been a defendant in a civil action under paragraph (1) by—

(aa) sending a notice of the alleged violation and intent to proceed under this paragraph to the registrant of the domain name at the postal and e-mail address provided by the registrant to the registrar; and

(bb) publishing notice of the action as the court may direct promptly after filing the action.

(B) The actions under subparagraph (A)(ii) shall constitute service of process.

(C) In an in rem action under this paragraph, a domain name shall be deemed to have its situs in the judicial district in which

(i) the domain name registrar, registry, or other domain name authority that registered or assigned the domain name is located; or

(ii) documents sufficient to establish control and authority regarding the disposition of the registration and use of the domain name are deposited with the court.

(D)(i) The remedies in an in rem action under this paragraph shall be limited to a court order for the forfeiture or cancellation of the domain name or the transfer of the domain name to the owner of the mark.

* * *

(3) The civil action established under paragraph (1) [not included herein] and the in rem action established under paragraph (2), and any remedy available under either such action, shall be in addition to any other civil action or remedy otherwise applicable.

(4) The in rem jurisdiction established under paragraph (2) shall be in addition to any other jurisdiction that otherwise exists, whether in rem or in personam.

————

Under the principles of *Shaffer*, are these provisions constitutional? Remember that the provisions are limited to *in rem* forfeiture proceedings. Could the statute provide for personal jurisdiction in the judicial district in which the registrar is located? Is injury through piracy like injury caused by an accident on land to a nonresident plaintiff? Does the injury have to occur in the situs state? What about a nuisance created in one state and causing injury in another? If these examples seem problematic, would you favor an amendment to provide that the assertion of any substantive defense by the user of the domain name in the *in rem* proceeding constitutes a general appearance for purposes of personal jurisdiction? How often do you suppose that the court will be able to make the finding required by section 2Aii? Does the inability to obtain in personam jurisdiction refer to the court in which the domain name registrant is located, any court in the United States, any court in the world?

Finally, suppose a rogue nation allows the registration of domain names and refuses to recognize causes of action for trademark piracy. What can the United States do to protect its owners of trademarks?

BURNHAM v. SUPERIOR COURT

Supreme Court of the United States, 1990.
495 U.S. 604, 110 S.Ct. 2105, 109 L.Ed.2d 631.

Justice Scalia announced the judgment of the Court and delivered an opinion in which The Chief Justice and Justice Kennedy join, and in which Justice White joins with respect to Parts I, II–A, II–B, and II–C.

The question presented is whether the Due Process Clause of the Fourteenth Amendment denies California courts jurisdiction over a nonresident, who was personally served with process while temporarily in that State, in a suit unrelated to his activities in the State.

I

* * *

In late January, petitioner visited southern California on business, after which he went north to visit his children in the San Francisco Bay area, where his wife resided. He took the older child to San Francisco for the weekend. Upon returning the child to Mrs. Burnham's home on January 24, 1988, petitioner was served with a California court summons and a copy of Mrs. Burnham's divorce petition. He then returned to New Jersey.

Later that year, petitioner made a special appearance in the California Superior Court, moving to quash the service of process on the ground that the court lacked personal jurisdiction over him because his only contacts with California were a few short visits to the State for the purposes of conducting business and visiting his children. The Superior Court denied the motion, and the California Court of Appeal denied mandamus relief, rejecting petitioner's contention that the Due Process Clause prohibited California courts from asserting jurisdiction over him because he lacked "minimum contacts" with the State. The court held it to be "a valid jurisdictional predicate for *in personam* jurisdiction" that the "defendant [was] present in the forum state and personally served with process." App. to Pet. for Cert. 5. We granted certiorari. 493 U.S. 807, 110 S.Ct. 47, 107 L.Ed.2d 16 (1989).

II

A

* * * In what has become the classic expression of the criterion, we said in *International Shoe Co. v. Washington,* 326 U.S. 310 (1945), that a State court's assertion of personal jurisdiction satisfies the Due Process Clause if it does not violate " 'traditional notions of fair play and substantial justice.' " *Id.* at 316 (quoting *Milliken v. Meyer,* 311 U.S. 457, 463 (1940)). * * * Since *International Shoe,* we have only been called upon to decide whether these "traditional notions" permit States to exercise jurisdiction over absent defendants in a manner that deviates from the rules of jurisdiction applied in the 19th century. We have held such deviations permissible, but only with respect to suits arising out of the absent defendant's contacts with the State. *See, e.g., Helicopteros Nacionales de Colombia v. Hall,* 466 U.S. 408, 414, 104 S.Ct. 1868, 1872, 80 L.Ed.2d 404 (1984). The question we must decide today is whether due process requires a similar connection between the litigation and the defendant's contacts with the State in cases where the defendant is physically present in the State at the time process is served upon him.

B

Among the most firmly established principles of personal jurisdiction in American tradition is that the courts of a State have jurisdiction over nonresidents who are physically present in the State. The view developed early that each State had the power to hale before its courts any individual who could be found within its borders, and that once having acquired jurisdiction over such a person by properly serving him with process, the State could retain jurisdiction to enter judgment against him, no matter how fleeting his visit. * * *

Decisions in the courts of many States in the 19th and early 20th centuries held that personal service upon a physically present defendant sufficed to confer jurisdiction, without regard to whether the defendant was only briefly in the State or whether the cause of action was related to his activities there. * * * Particularly striking is the fact that, as far as we have been able to determine, *not one* American case from the period (or, for that matter, not one American case until 1978) held, or even suggested, that in-state personal service on an individual was insufficient to confer personal jurisdiction. * * * We do not know of a single State or federal statute, or a single judicial decision resting upon State law, that has abandoned in-State service as a basis of jurisdiction. Many recent cases reaffirm it. * * *

C

Despite this formidable body of precedent, petitioner contends, in reliance on our decisions applying the *International Shoe* standard, that in the absence of "continuous and systematic" contacts with the forum, * * * a non-resident defendant can be subjected to judgment only as to matters that arise out of or relate to his contacts with the forum. This argument rests on a thorough misunderstanding of our cases.

The view of most courts in the 19th century was that a court simply could not exercise *in personam* jurisdiction over a nonresident who had not been personally served with process in the forum. * * * In the late 19th and early 20th centuries, changes in the technology of transportation and communication, and the tremendous growth of interstate business activity, led to an "inevitable relaxation of the strict limits on state jurisdiction" over nonresident individuals and corporations. *Hanson v. Denckla,* 357 U.S. 235, 260 (1958) (Black, J., dissenting). * * * Subsequent cases have derived from the *International Shoe* standard the general rule that a State may dispense with in-forum personal service on nonresident defendants in suits arising out of their activities in the State. *See generally Helicopteros Nacionales de Colombia v. Hall,* 466 U.S. at 414–415. As *International Shoe* suggests, the defendant's litigation-related "minimum contacts" may take the place of physical presence as the basis for jurisdiction * * *.

Nothing in *International Shoe* or the cases that have followed it, however, offers support for the very different proposition petitioner seeks to establish today: that a defendant's presence in the forum is not only unnecessary to validate novel, nontraditional assertions of jurisdiction, but is itself no longer sufficient to establish jurisdiction. That proposition is unfaithful to both elementary logic and the foundations of our due process jurisprudence. The distinction between what is needed to support novel procedures and what is needed to sustain traditional ones is fundamental, as we observed over a century ago:

> "[A] process of law, which is not otherwise forbidden, must be taken to be due process of law, if it can show the sanction of settled usage both in England and in this country; but it by no means follows that nothing else can be due process of law * * *. [That which], in substance, has been immemorially the actual law of the land * * * therefor[e] is due process of law. But to hold that such a characteristic is essential to due process of law, would be to deny every quality of the law but its age, and to render it incapable of progress or improvement. It would be to stamp upon our jurispru-

dence the unchangeableness attributed to the laws of the Medes and Persians." *Hurtado v. California,* 110 U.S. 516, 528–529, 4 S.Ct. 111, 117–118, 28 L.Ed. 232 (1884).

The short of the matter is that jurisdiction based on physical presence alone constitutes due process because it is one of the continuing traditions of our legal system that define the due process standard of "traditional notions of fair play and substantial justice." That standard was developed by *analogy* to "physical presence," and it would be perverse to say it could now be turned against that touchstone of jurisdiction.

D

Petitioner's strongest argument, though we ultimately reject it, relies upon our decision in *Shaffer v. Heitner,* 433 U.S. 186 (1977). In that case, a Delaware court hearing a shareholder's derivative suit against a corporation's directors secured jurisdiction *quasi in rem* by sequestering the out-of-State defendants' stock in the company, the situs of which was Delaware under Delaware law. Reasoning that Delaware's sequestration procedure was simply a mechanism to compel the absent defendants to appear in a suit to determine their personal rights and obligations, we concluded that the normal rules we had developed under *International Shoe* for jurisdiction over suits against absent defendants should apply—*viz.,* Delaware could not hear the suit because the defendants' sole contact with the State (ownership of property there) was unrelated to the lawsuit. 433 U.S. at 213–215.

It goes too far to say, as petitioner contends, that *Shaffer* compels the conclusion that a State lacks jurisdiction over an individual unless the litigation arises out of his activities in the State. *Shaffer,* like *International Shoe,* involved jurisdiction over an *absent defendant,* and it stands for nothing more than the proposition that when the "minimum contact" that is a substitute for physical presence consists of property ownership it must, like other minimum contacts, be related to the litigation. Petitioner wrenches out of its context our statement in *Shaffer* that "all assertions of state-court jurisdiction must be evaluated according to the standards set forth in *International Shoe* and its progeny," 433 U.S. at 212. When read together with the two sentences that preceded it, the meaning of this statement becomes clear:

> The fiction that an assertion of jurisdiction over property is anything but an assertion of jurisdiction over the owner of the property supports an ancient form without substantial modern justification. Its continued acceptance would serve only to allow state-court jurisdiction that is fundamentally unfair to the defendant.
>
> We *therefore conclude* that all assertions of state-court jurisdiction must be evaluated according to the standards set forth in *International Shoe* and its progeny. *Ibid.* (emphasis added).

Shaffer was saying, in other words, not that all bases for the assertion of *in personam* jurisdiction (including, presumably, in-state service) must be treated alike and subjected to the "minimum contacts" analysis of *International Shoe;* but rather that *quasi in rem* jurisdiction, that fictional "ancient form," and *in personam* jurisdiction, are really one and the same and must be treated alike—leading to the conclusion that *quasi in rem* jurisdiction, *i.e.,* that form of *in personam* jurisdiction based upon a "property ownership" contact and by definition unaccompanied by personal, in-state service, must satisfy the litigation-relatedness requirement of *International Shoe.* * * *

It is fair to say, however, that while our holding today does not contradict *Shaffer,* our basic approach to the due process question is different. We have conducted no independent inquiry into the desirability or fairness of the prevailing in-state service rule, leaving that judgment to the legislatures that are free to amend it; for our purposes, its validation is its pedigree, as the phrase *"traditional notions* of fair play and substantial justice" makes clear. *Shaffer* did conduct such an independent inquiry, asserting that " 'traditional notions of fair play and substantial justice' can be as readily offended by the perpetuation of ancient forms that are no longer justified as by the adoption of new procedures that are inconsistent with the basic values of our constitutional heritage." 433 U.S. at 212. Perhaps that assertion can be sustained when the "perpetuation of ancient forms" is engaged in by only a very small minority of the States. Where, however, as in the present case, a jurisdictional principle is both firmly approved by tradition and still favored, it is impossible to imagine what standard we could appeal to for the judgment that it is "no longer justified." While in no way receding from or casting doubt upon the holding of *Shaffer* or any other case, we reaffirm today our time-honored approach * * *. For new procedures, hitherto unknown, the Due Process clause requires analysis to determine whether "traditional notions of fair play and substantial justice" have been offended. *International Shoe,* 326 U.S. at 316. But a doctrine of personal jurisdiction that dates back to the adoption of the Fourteenth Amendment and is still generally observed unquestionably meets that standard.

III

A few words in response to Justice Brennan's concurrence: It insists that we apply "contemporary notions of due process" to determine the constitutionality of California's assertion of jurisdiction. * * *

But the concurrence's proposed standard of "contemporary notions of due process" requires more: it measures state-court jurisdiction not only against traditional doctrines in this country, including current state-court practice, but against each Justice's subjective assessment of what is fair and just. Authority for that seductive standard is not to be found in any of our personal jurisdiction cases. It is, indeed, an out-right break with the test of "traditional notions of fair play and substantial justice," which would have to be reformulated *"our* notions of fair play and substantial justice."

The subjectivity, and hence inadequacy, of this approach becomes apparent when the concurrence tries to explain *why* the assertion of jurisdiction in the present case meets its standard of continuing-American-tradition-*plus*-innate-fairness. Justice Brennan lists the "benefits" Mr. Burnham derived from the State of California—the fact that, during the few days he was there, "his health and safety [were] guaranteed by the State's police, fire, and emergency medical services; he [was] free to travel on the State's roads and waterways; he likely enjoy[ed] the fruits of the State's economy." * * * Three days' worth of these benefits strike us as powerfully inadequate to establish, as an abstract matter, that it is "fair" for California to decree the ownership of all Mr. Burnham's worldly goods acquired during the ten years of his marriage, and the custody over his children. * * * It would create "an asymmetry," we are told, if Burnham were *permitted* (as he is) to appear in California courts as a plaintiff, but were not *compelled* to appear in California courts as defendant; and travel being as easy as it is nowadays, and modern procedural devices being so convenient, it is no great hardship to appear in California courts. * * * The problem with these assertions is that they justify the exercise of jurisdiction over *everyone, whether or not* he ever comes to California. * * *

Because the Due Process Clause does not prohibit the California courts from exercising jurisdiction over petitioner based on the fact of in-state service of process, the judgment is

Affirmed.

JUSTICE WHITE, concurring in part and concurring in the judgment.

I join Part I and Parts II–A, II–B, and II–C of Justice Scalia's opinion and concur in the judgment of affirmance. The rule allowing jurisdiction to be obtained over a non-resident by personal service in the forum state, without more, has been and is so widely accepted throughout this country that I could not possibly strike it down, either on its face or as applied in this case, on the ground that it denies due process of law guaranteed by the Fourteenth Amendment. * * *

JUSTICE BRENNAN, with whom JUSTICE MARSHALL, JUSTICE BLACKMUN, and JUSTICE O'CONNOR join, concurring in the judgment.

* * *

I

I believe that the approach adopted by Justice Scalia's opinion today—reliance solely on historical pedigree—is foreclosed by our decisions in *International Shoe Co. v. Washington,* 326 U.S. 310 (1945), and *Shaffer v. Heitner,* 433 U.S. 186 (1977). * * *

While our *holding* in *Shaffer* may have been limited to *quasi in rem* jurisdiction, our mode of analysis was not. Indeed, that we were willing in *Shaffer* to examine anew the appropriateness of the *quasi in rem* rule—until that time dutifully accepted by American courts for at least a century—demonstrates that we did not believe that the "pedigree" of a jurisdictional practice was dispositive in deciding whether it was consistent with due process. * * *

II

Tradition, though alone not dispositive, is of course *relevant* to the question whether the rule of transient jurisdiction is consistent with due process. Tradition is salient not in the sense that practices of the past are automatically reasonable today; indeed, under such a standard, the legitimacy of transient jurisdiction would be called into question because the rule's historical "pedigree" is a matter of intense debate. * * * For much of the 19th century, American courts did not uniformly recognize the concept of transient jurisdiction, and it appears that the transient rule did not receive wide currency until well after our decision in *Pennoyer v. Neff,* 95 U.S. 714, 24 L.Ed. 565 (1878). * * * The transient rule is consistent with reasonable expectations and is entitled to a strong presumption that it comports with due process. * * *

By visiting the forum State, a transient defendant actually "avail[s]" himself * * * of significant benefits provided by the State. His health and safety are guaranteed by the State's police, fire, and emergency medical services; he is free to travel on the State's roads and waterways; he likely enjoys the fruits of the State's economy as well. * * *

The potential burdens on a transient defendant are slight. " '[M]odern transportation and communications have made it much less burdensome for a party sued to defend himself' " in a State outside his place of residence. *Burger King,* 471 U.S. at 474, quoting *McGee v. International Life Insurance Co.,* 355 U.S. 220, 223, 78 S.Ct. 199, 201 (1957). That the defendant has already journeyed at least once before to the forum—as evidenced by the fact that he was served with process there—is an indication that suit in the forum likely would not be prohibitively inconvenient. Finally, any burdens that do arise can be ameliorated by a variety of procedural devices. For these reasons, as a rule the exercise of personal jurisdiction over a defendant based on his voluntary presence in the forum will satisfy the requirements of due process. * * *

In this case, it is undisputed that petitioner was served with process while voluntarily and knowingly in the State of California. I therefore concur in the judgment.

JUSTICE STEVENS, concurring in the judgment.

As I explained in my separate writing, I did not join the Court's opinion in *Shaffer v. Heitner,* 433 U.S. 186, 97 S.Ct. 2569, 53 L.Ed.2d 683 (1977), because I was concerned by its unnecessarily broad reach. *Id.* at 217–219 (opinion concurring in judgment). The same concern prevents me from joining either Justice Scalia's or Justice Brennan's opinion in this case. For me, it is sufficient to note that the historical evidence and consensus identified by Justice Scalia, the considerations of fairness identified by Justice Brennan, and the common sense displayed by Justice White, all combine to demonstrate that this is, indeed, a very easy case. Accordingly, I agree that the judgment should be affirmed.

Notes and Questions

1. Note the plurality's framing of the issue. Do you agree that the suit was "unrelated to [defendant's] activities in the State"? Certainly the cause of action did not arise out of defendant's activities in the state, but was the cause of action *unrelated* to his activities there? Could you construct an argument that his agreement that Mrs. Burnham go to California where she would file for divorce and his later visit in California with his children is related to the support suit? Might this relationship be sufficient? *See Helicopteros Nacionales de Colombia, S.A. v. Hall,* 466 U.S. 408 (1984).

2. Recall *Johnson v. Roscoe & Baker, supra* Chapter II. Would Arizona have personal jurisdiction over John if he were served in Arizona while attending the rodeo? Under Justice Scalia's approach? Under Justice Brennan's approach? Under Justice Stevens' approach?

3. Under any analysis, California would have jurisdiction over the *Burnham* divorce action. *See Pennoyer.* Is it fair to limit *Burnham* to a situation in which the court acquires ancillary personal jurisdiction over a support action because it may adjudicate the divorce action? Although the Court has not expressly adopted this position, may not later decisions explain *Burnham* on this ground? May lower courts distinguish *Burnham* in this manner? Should they await explication by the Supreme Court?

4. Notice how Justice Scalia explains *International Shoe.* He states that it creates a new basis for asserting personal jurisdiction—that is, minimum contacts with the forum. It does not reject the traditional grounds of presence. Why else *Shoe*'s language: "if he be not present"?

5. The plurality opinion suggests that the Court should not invalidate traditional notions of fair play except perhaps where "perpetuation of ancient forms" has been rejected by the vast majority of states. Do you agree? We will return to this debate on the role of the Court in the adjudication of constitutional rights under the due process clause. *See infra* pp. 218–61. What are your views?

6. Assume *Shaffer* had not been decided in 1978 but came to the Supreme Court for review after *Burnham.* What result? Do you now more fully appreciate Lon Fuller's analysis that the timing of a case affects its disposition? *See supra* pp. 39–40.

7. The Court has said that the minimum contacts test performs "two related, but distinguishable functions." It protects the defendant against the burden of litigating in an inconvenient forum, and it ensures that states do not reach out beyond permissible limits. *See World–Wide Volkswagen Corp. v. Woodson,* 444 U.S. 286 (1980). Does due process embody the latter federalism function? If not, what does? If there is concern that states should not reach beyond their borders, a concern that admittedly transcends mere convenience to the defendant, then why countenance and even encourage doctrines permitting waiver of the jurisdictional defect?

8. Was Justice Brennan correct in his dissent in *Volkswagen* in stating that the principles of *International Shoe,* which focus almost exclusively on the rights of defendants, may be outdated? Can you foresee Brennan's dissent becoming tomorrow's law? Before responding too quickly, recall the fate of *Pennoyer.* Also consider two Supreme Court cases, *Keeton* and *Calder,* excerpted below.

Although the Court has primarily focused on the defendant's contacts with the forum, it has indicated that it will give some weight to the plaintiff's residence. In *Keeton v. Hustler Magazine, Inc.,* 465 U.S. 770 (1984), the Court, in upholding jurisdiction over a nonresident's claim for defamation against a nationwide magazine, commented on the plaintiff's residence, as follows:

> The plaintiff's residence is not, of course, completely irrelevant to the jurisdictional inquiry. As noted, that inquiry focuses on the relations among the defendant, the forum and the litigation. Plaintiff's residence may well play an important role in determining the propriety of entertaining a suit against the defendant in the forum. That is, plaintiff's residence in the forum may, because of defendant's relationship with the plaintiff, enhance defendant's contacts with the forum. Plaintiff's residence may be the focus of the activities of the defendant out of which the suit arises. *See Calder v. Jones,* 465 U.S. 783, 104 S.Ct. 1482, 1486–87, 79 L.Ed.2d 804; *McGee v. International Life Ins. Co.,* 355 U.S. 220, 78 S.Ct. 199, 2 L.Ed.2d 223 (1957). But plaintiff's residence in the forum State is not a separate requirement, and lack of residence will not defeat jurisdiction established on the basis of defendant's contacts.

In *Calder v. Jones,* 465 U.S. 783 (1984), the Court upheld jurisdiction of a libel action brought by a resident of the forum state against two nonresidents, the reporter and editor of the magazine that circulated in the forum state. The Court again noted the importance of the plaintiff's contacts with the forum state in the following passage:

> The Due Process Clause of the Fourteenth Amendment to the United States Constitution permits personal jurisdiction over a defendant in any State with which the defendant has "certain minimum contacts * * * such that the maintenance of the suit does not offend 'traditional notions of fair play and substantial justice.' *Milliken v. Meyer,* 311 U.S. 457, 463 [61 S.Ct. 339, 342, 85 L.Ed. 278 (1940)]." *International Shoe Co. v. Washington,* 326 U.S. 310, 316, 66 S.Ct. 154, 158, 90 L.Ed. 95 (1945). In judging minimum contacts, a court properly focuses on "the relationship among the defendant, the forum, and the litigation." *Shaffer v. Heitner,* 433 U.S. 186, 204, 97 S.Ct. 2569, 2579, 53 L.Ed.2d 683 (1977). *See also Rush v. Savchuk,* 444 U.S. 320, 332, 100 S.Ct. 571, 579, 62 L.Ed.2d 516 (1980). The plaintiff's lack of "contacts" will not defeat otherwise proper jurisdiction, *see Keeton v. Hustler Magazine, Inc.,* 465 U.S. 770, 104 S.Ct. 1473, 1480–1482, 79 L.Ed.2d 790 (1984), but they may be so manifold as to permit jurisdiction when it would not exist in their absence. Here, the plaintiff is the focus of the activities of the defendants out of which the suit arises. *See McGee v. International Life Ins. Co.,* 355 U.S. 220, 78 S.Ct. 199, 2 L.Ed.2d 223 (1957).

9. Just as the advent of the automobile posed challenges to the property-based doctrine of *Pennoyer (see Hess v. Pawloski)*, the world-wide accessibility of the Internet now significantly challenges and strains the contacts-based tests of personal jurisdiction based on *International Shoe* and its progeny. Under these tests, a defendant must perform some act by which it "purposefully avails itself of the privilege of conducting activities within the forum state." *See Hanson v. Denkla, supra* note 10 following *International Shoe.*

Suppose that the owner of a website advertises around the world via the Internet in the expectation of receiving orders. Suppose further that a potential customer responds to the solicitation, receives the goods, and becomes embroiled in a legal dispute with the website owner. Should the buyer's home state have personal jurisdiction over the owner of the website? Should the answer depend on whether the website is "active" or "passive"?

Let's take another example, this time from the field of torts. In a ground-breaking case, a California-based website offered to auction hundreds of Nazi objects, such as flags and medals. The website was accessible throughout the world, including France, whose penal laws prohibited the display or sale of these items. In a civil case brought in France seeking to filter the messages from the view of French visitors to the site, the defendant website owner sought dismissal on the grounds of lack of jurisdiction. The French court denied the motion, reasoning that the American company had committed a wrong in the territory of France. How would an American court rule? An American court eventually upset the French judgment because of concerns that enforcement in America would abridge constitutional guarantees of freedom of speech. *See Yahoo!, Inc. v. La Ligue Contre Le Racisme et L'Antisemitisme,* 169 F. Supp. 2d 1181 (N.D. Cal. 2001).

C. SECOND EXERCISE IN SYNTHESIS: CASES INVOLVING THE RIGHT TO A HEARING IN CONNECTION WITH SEIZURES OF PROPERTY

We have already considered seizure of property as a basis of acquiring quasi in rem jurisdiction. Seizures of defendants' property before the adjudication of the merits of the controversy may also serve other purposes. For example, seizures preserve the status quo and assure the plaintiff of the existence of assets from which to satisfy a judgment. Seizures, of course, may have grave economic and social consequences to a defendant who, in certain circumstances, may be willing to forego valid defenses rather than suffer the deprivation of the property during the proceedings. Do you perceive any ethical considerations in invoking prejudgment seizure in these situations?

In permitting plaintiffs to seize property at the commencement of a lawsuit for purposes of acquiring jurisdiction, *Pennoyer* did not address the process due the defendant as a result of the taking. Indeed, early Supreme Court cases did not address the issues of notice or opportunity to be heard in connection with the seizure. We now turn to more recent judicial pronouncements attempting to accommodate the respective interests of creditors and debtors in connection with prejudgment seizures of property.

SNIADACH v. FAMILY FINANCE CORP.

Supreme Court of the United States, 1969.
395 U.S. 337, 89 S.Ct. 1820, 23 L.Ed.2d 349.

JUSTICE DOUGLAS delivered the opinion of the Court.

Respondents instituted a garnishment action against petitioner as defendant and Miller Harris Instrument Co., her employer, as garnishee. The complaint alleged a claim of $420 on a promissory note. The garnishee filed its answer stating it had wages of $63.18 under its control earned by petitioner and unpaid, and that it would pay one-half to petitioner as a subsistence allowance and hold the other half subject to the order of the court.

Petitioner moved that the garnishment proceedings be dismissed for failure to satisfy the due process requirements of the Fourteenth Amendment. The Wisconsin Supreme Court sustained the lower state court in approving the procedure. The case is here on a petition for a writ of certiorari.

The Wisconsin statute gives a plaintiff 10 days in which to serve the summons and complaint on the defendant after service on the garnishee. In this case petitioner was served the same day as the garnishee. She nonetheless claims that the Wisconsin garnishment procedure violates that due process required by the Fourteenth Amendment, in that notice and an opportunity to be heard are not given before the *in rem* seizure of the wages. What happens in Wisconsin is that the clerk of the court issues the summons at the request of the creditor's lawyer; and it is the latter who by serving the garnishee sets in motion the machinery whereby the wages are frozen. They may, it is true, be unfrozen if the trial of the main suit is ever had and the wage earner wins on the merits. But in the interim the wage earner is deprived of his enjoyment of earned wages without any opportunity to be heard and to tender any defense he may have, whether it be fraud or otherwise.

Such summary procedure may well meet the requirements of due process in extraordinary situations. *Cf. Fahey v. Mallonee,* 332 U.S. 245, 253–254, 67 S.Ct. 1552, 1554–1556, 91 L.Ed. 2030; *Ewing v. Mytinger & Casselberry, Inc.,* 339 U.S. 594, 598–600, 70 S.Ct. 870, 872–873, 94 L.Ed. 1088; *Ownbey v. Morgan,* 256 U.S. 94, 110–112, 41 S.Ct. 433, 437–438, 65 L.Ed. 837; *Coffin Bros. & Co. v. Bennett,* 277 U.S. 29, 31, 48 S.Ct. 422, 423, 72 L.Ed. 768. But in the present case no situation requiring special protection to a state or creditor interest is presented by the facts; nor is the Wisconsin statute narrowly drawn to meet any such unusual condition. Petitioner was a resident of this Wisconsin community and *in personam* jurisdiction was readily obtainable.

The question is not whether the Wisconsin law is a wise law or unwise law. Our concern is not what philosophy Wisconsin should or should not embrace. We do not sit as a super-legislative body. In this case the sole question is whether there has been a taking of property without that procedural due process that is required by the Fourteenth Amendment. We have dealt over and over again with the question of what constitutes "the right to be heard" (*Schroeder v. New York*, 371 U.S. 208, 212, 83 S.Ct. 279, 282, 9 L.Ed.2d 255) within the meaning of procedural due process. *See Mullane v. Central Hanover Trust Co.*, 339 U.S. 306, 314, 70 S.Ct. 652, 657, 94 L.Ed. 865. In the latter case we said that the right to be heard "has little reality or worth unless one is informed that the matter is pending and can choose for himself whether to appear or default, acquiesce or contest." In the context of this case the question is whether the interim freezing of the wages without a chance to be heard violates procedural due process.

A procedural rule that may satisfy due process for attachments in general, *see McKay v. McInnes*, 279 U.S. 820, 49 S.Ct. 344, 73 L.Ed. 975, does not necessarily satisfy procedural due process in every case. The fact that a procedure would pass muster under a feudal regime does not mean it gives necessary protection to all property in its modern forms. We deal here with wages—a specialized type of property presenting distinct problems in our economic system. We turn then to the nature of that property and problems of procedural due process.

A prejudgment garnishment of the Wisconsin type is a taking which may impose tremendous hardship on wage earners with families to support. Until a recent Act of Congress, § 304 of which forbids discharge of employees on the ground that their wages have been garnished, garnishment often meant the loss of a job. Over and beyond that was the great drain on family income.

Recent investigations of the problem have disclosed the grave injustices made possible by prejudgment garnishment whereby the sole opportunity to be heard comes after the taking. Congressman Sullivan, Chairman of the House Subcommittee on Consumer Affairs who held extensive hearings on this and related problems stated:

> What we know from our study of this problem is that in a vast number of cases the debt is a fraudulent one, saddled on a poor ignorant person who is trapped in an easy credit nightmare, in which he is charged double for something he could not pay for even if the proper price was called for, and then hounded into giving up his pound of flesh, and being fired besides. 114 Cong.Rec. 1832.

The leverage of the creditor on the wage earner is enormous. The creditor tenders not only the original debt but the "collection fees" incurred by his attorneys in the garnishment proceedings:

> The debtor whose wages are tied up by a writ of garnishment, and who is usually in need of money, is in no position to resist demands for collection fees. If the debt is small, the debtor will be under considerable pressure to pay the debt and collection charges in order to get his wages back. If the debt is large, he will often sign

a new contract of [sic] "payment schedule" which incorporates these additional charges.

Apart from those collateral consequences, it appears that in Wisconsin the statutory exemption granted the wage earner is "generally insufficient to support the debtor for any one week."

The result is that a prejudgment garnishment of the Wisconsin type may as a practical matter drive a wage-earning family to the wall.[9] Where the taking of one's property is so obvious, it needs no extended argument to conclude that absent notice and a prior hearing (*cf. Coe v. Armour Fertilizer Works*, 237 U.S. 413, 423, 35 S.Ct. 625, 628, 59 L.Ed. 1027) this prejudgment garnishment procedure violates the fundamental principles of due process.

Reversed.

JUSTICE HARLAN, concurring.

Particularly in light of my Brother Black's dissent, I think it not amiss for me to make explicit the precise basis on which I join the Court's opinion. The "property" of which petitioner has been deprived is the *use* of the garnished portion of her wages during the interim period between the garnishment and the culmination of the main suit. Since this deprivation cannot be characterized as *de minimis,* she must be accorded the usual requisites of procedural due process: notice and a prior hearing.

The rejoinder which this statement of position has drawn from my Brother Black prompts an additional word. His and my divergence in this case rests, I think, upon a basic difference over whether the Due Process Clause of the Fourteenth Amendment limits state action by norms of "fundamental fairness" whose content in any given instance is to be judicially derived not alone as my colleague believes it should be, from the specifics of the Constitution, but also, as I believe, from concepts which are part of the Anglo–American legal heritage—not, as my Brother Black continues to insist, from the mere predilections of individual judges.

From my standpoint, I do not consider that the requirements of "notice" and "hearing" are satisfied by the fact that the petitioner was advised of the garnishment simultaneously with the garnishee, or by the fact that she will not permanently lose the garnished property until after a plenary adverse adjudication of the underlying claim against her, or by the fact that relief from the garnishment may have been available in the interim under less than clear circumstances. Compare the majority and dissenting opinions in the Wisconsin Supreme Court, 37 Wis.2d 163, 178,

9. "For a poor man—and whoever heard of the wage of the affluent being attached?—to lose part of his salary often means his family will go without the essentials. No man sits by while his family goes hungry or without heat. He either files for consumer bankruptcy and tries to begin again, or just quits his job and goes on relief. Where is the equity, the common sense, in such a process?" Congressman Gonzales, 114 Cong.Rec. 1833. For the impact of garnishment on personal bankruptcies *see* H.R.Rep. No. 1040, 90th Cong., 1st Sess., 20–21.

154 N.W.2d 259, 267 (1967). Apart from special situations, some of which are referred to in this Court's opinion, I think that due process is afforded only by the kinds of "notice" and "hearing" which are aimed at establishing the validity, or at least the probable validity, of the underlying claim against the alleged debtor *before* he can be deprived of his property or its unrestricted use. I think this is the thrust of the past cases in this Court. *See, e.g., Mullane v. Central Hanover Bank & Trust Co.,* 339 U.S. 306, 313, 70 S.Ct. 652, 657, 94 L.Ed. 865 (1950); *Opp Cotton Mills v. Administrator,* 312 U.S. 126, 152–153, 61 S.Ct. 524, 535–536, 85 L.Ed. 624 (1941); *United States v. Illinois Cent. R. Co.,* 291 U.S. 457, 463, 54 S.Ct. 471, 473, 78 L.Ed. 909 (1934); *Londoner v. City & County of Denver,* 210 U.S. 373, 385–386, 28 S.Ct. 708, 713–714, 52 L.Ed. 1103 (1908).[10] And I am quite unwilling to take the unexplicated *per curiam* in *McKay v. McInnes,* 279 U.S. 820, 49 S.Ct. 344, 73 L.Ed. 975 (1929), as vitiating or diluting these essential elements of due process.

JUSTICE BLACK, dissenting.

* * *

The state court * * * pointed out that the garnishment proceedings did not involve "any final determination of the title to a defendant's property, but merely preserve[d] the status quo thereof pending determination of the principal action." 37 Wis.2d, at 169, 154 N.W.2d, at 262. The court then relied on *McInnes v. McKay,* 127 Me. 110, 141 A. 699. That suit related to a Maine attachment law which, of course, is governed by the same rule as garnishment law. *See* "garnishment," Bouvier's Law Dictionary; *see also Pennoyer v. Neff,* 95 U.S. 714, 24 L.Ed. 565. The Maine law was subjected to practically the same challenges that Brother Harlan and the Court raise against this Wisconsin law. About that law the Supreme Court of Maine said:

> But, although an attachment may, within the broad meaning of the preceding definition, deprive one of property, yet conditional and temporary as it is, and part of the legal remedy and procedure by which the property of a debtor may be taken in satisfaction of the debt, if judgment be recovered, we do not think it is the deprivation of property contemplated by the Constitution. And if it be, it is not a deprivation without "due process of law" for it is a part of a process, which during its proceeding gives notice and opportunity for hearing and judgment of some judicial or other authorized tribunal. The requirements of "due process of law" and "law of the land" are satisfied. 127 Me. 110, 116, 141 A. 699, 702–703.

10. There are other decisions to the effect that one may be deprived of property by summary administrative action taken before hearing when such action is essential to protect a vital governmental interest. *See, e.g., Ewing v. Mytinger & Casselberry, Inc.,* 339 U.S. 594, 70 S.Ct. 870, 94 L.Ed. 1088 (1950); *Fahey v. Mallonee,* 332 U.S. 245, 67 S.Ct. 1552, 91 L.Ed. 2030 (1947); *Bowles v. Willingham,* 321 U.S. 503, 64 S.Ct. 641, 88 L.Ed. 892 (1944); *North Amer. Cold Storage Co. v. City of Chicago,* 211 U.S. 306, 29 S.Ct. 101, 53 L.Ed. 195 (1908). However, no such justification has been advanced in behalf of Wisconsin's garnishment law.

This Court did not even consider the challenge to the Maine law worthy of a Court opinion but affirmed it in a *per curiam* opinion, 279 U.S. 820, 49 S.Ct. 344, 73 L.Ed. 975 on the authority of two prior decisions of this Court.

The Supreme Court of Wisconsin, in upholding the constitutionality of its law also cited the following statement of our Court made in *Rothschild v. Knight,* 184 U.S. 334, 341, 22 S.Ct. 391, 393, 46 L.Ed. 573:

> To what actions the remedy of attachment may be given is for the legislature of a State to determine and its courts to decide * * *.

The Supreme Court of Wisconsin properly pointed out:

> The ability to place a lien upon a man's property, such as to temporarily deprive him of its beneficial use, without any judicial determination of probable cause dates back not only to medieval England but also to Roman times. 37 Wis.2d at 171, 154 N.W.2d at 264.

The State Supreme Court then went on to point out a statement made by Mr. Justice Holmes in *Jackman v. Rosenbaum Co.,* 260 U.S. 22, 31, 43 S.Ct. 9, 10, 67 L.Ed. 107:

> The Fourteenth Amendment, itself a historical product, did not destroy history for the States and substitute mechanical compartments of law all exactly alike. If a thing has been practiced for two hundred years by common consent, it will need a strong case for the Fourteenth Amendment to affect it, as is well illustrated by *Ownbey v. Morgan,* 256 U.S. 94, 104, 112, 41 S.Ct. 433, 65 L.Ed. 837.

The *Ownbey* case, which was one of the two cited by this Court in its *per curiam* affirmance of *McInnes v. McKay, supra,* sustained the constitutionality of a Delaware attachment law. And see *Byrd v. Rector,* 112 W.Va. 192, 163 S.E. 845.

I can only conclude that the Court is today overruling a number of its own decisions and abandoning the legal customs and practices in this country with reference to attachments and garnishments wholly on the ground that the garnishment laws of this kind are based on unwise policies of government which might some time in the future do injury to some individuals. In the first sentence of the argument in her brief, petitioner urges that this Wisconsin law "is contrary to public policy"; the Court apparently finds that a sufficient basis for holding it unconstitutional. This holding savors too much of the "Natural Law," "Due Process," "Shock-the-conscience" test of what is constitutional for me to agree to the decision. See my dissent in *Adamson v. California,* 332 U.S. 46, 68, 67 S.Ct. 1672, 1683, 91 L.Ed. 1903.

Notes and Questions

1. Garnishment is a procedure by which a debt owing to the defendant by a third person (the garnishee) is seized by judicial process initiated by the plaintiff and held pending further orders of the court. All forms of property,

tangible and intangible, may be subject to garnishment: Simple debts, as in *Harris, supra* p. 188; wages, as in *Sniadach;* bank accounts as in *Di Chem, infra* p. 251. Note the employment of other seizure devices: Attachment, as in *Pennoyer, supra* p. 150; replevin, as in *Fuentes, infra* p. 225; sequestration, as in *Mitchell, infra* p. 240. All these devices, by whatever designation, seize and hold property pending further court proceedings. The due process implications are therefore similar, regardless of the form of the seizure.

2. Today, few cases involving constitutional law are written on a totally clean slate. Where relevant authority exists, as it usually does, the Court should cite and consider it. Indeed, one significant value of concurring and dissenting opinions is the effect that they have on the majority, forcing it to focus on precedents.

What were the pre-*Sniadach* precedents? Did the majority opinion adequately distinguish them? Was Justice Black correct in dissent in concluding that the Court was in effect overruling many of its decisions? Should the majority have discussed the *McKay* decision more fully? Are you satisfied with the treatment it received in Justice Harlan's concurring opinion: "And I am quite unwilling to take the unexplicated *per curiam* in McKay * * * as vitiating or diluting these essential elements of due process"? In contrast to Justice Harlan, Justice Black noted that *McKay* did not even consider the challenge to the Maine law "worthy of a Court opinion but affirmed it in a *per curiam* decision." What is the precedential effect of an unexplicated *per curiam* opinion?

3. *Sniadach* cited four cases presenting "extraordinary situations" justifying summary seizure:

(a) *Fahey* permitted the Federal Home Loan Bank Commissioner to take summary possession of a failing saving and loan association upon allegations that it was being operated in an unlawful manner;

(b) *Ewing* justified summary seizure of mislabeled articles upon an *ex parte* finding of probable cause that the article was dangerous to the health of consumers;

(c) *Ownbey* involved the attachment of property essential to secure jurisdiction in a state court;

(d) *Coffin* involved the immediate and irreparable harm of an imminent bank failure.

Were all these cases extraordinary? Note that three of the cases involved the intercession of public officials to prevent irreparable harm to the public. *Ownbey*, on the other hand, concerned a private party seeking access to a particular court. Can this truly be deemed extraordinary?

Was *McKay* an extraordinary situation? In a later case, *Fuentes v. Shevin, see infra* p. 225, the Court, referring to *McKay* asserted: "As far as essential procedural due process doctrine goes, *McKay* cannot stand for any more than was established in the *Coffin Bros.* and *Ownbey* cases on which it relied completely." Why?

4. Reconsider *Shaffer, supra* p. 188. One issue, briefed and argued by the parties but never reached by the Court, concerned the continuing vitality of the *Ownbey* doctrine. The appellant argued that summary seizure for

purposes of acquiring quasi in rem jurisdiction could not constitutionally be effected without prior notice and an opportunity to be heard. Do you agree? In any event, the existence of an extraordinary situation merely permits the initial summary procedure. It does not sustain the right to keep the property indefinitely.

5. Did *Sniadach* constitutionally require notice and a *prior* hearing before prejudgment garnishment of wages? Did the opinions reveal when under the Wisconsin statute the debtor would be accorded a hearing? The majority asserted that the wage garnishment "may * * * be unfrozen if the trial of the main suit is ever had and the wage earner wins on the merits." The concurring opinion questioned whether relief from the garnishment could have been available during the interim. Does any of this make any difference? Was the timing of the hearing an important factor in analyzing the precise holding of the case? Assume a resourceful researcher now discovers that the Wisconsin statute did not permit any interim relief to the debtor before the trial on the merits. Would that discovery render a prior hearing mandatory even if the legislature has provided an opportunity for a hearing immediately after seizure? We shall return to these questions shortly.

FUENTES v. SHEVIN

Supreme Court of the United States, 1972.
407 U.S. 67, 92 S.Ct. 1983, 32 L.Ed.2d 556.

JUSTICE STEWART delivered the opinion of the Court.

We here review the decisions of two three-judge federal District Courts that upheld the constitutionality of Florida and Pennsylvania laws authorizing the summary seizure of goods or chattels in a person's possession under a writ of replevin. Both statutes provide for the issuance of writs ordering state agents to seize a person's possessions, simply upon the *ex parte* application of any other person who claims a right to them and posts a security bond. Neither statute provides for notice to be given to the possessor of the property, and neither statute gives the possessor an opportunity to challenge the seizure at any kind of prior hearing. The question is whether these statutory procedures violate the Fourteenth Amendment's guarantee that no State shall deprive any person of property without due process of law.

I

The appellant in No. 5039, Margarita Fuentes, is a resident of Florida. She purchased a gas stove and service policy from the Firestone Tire and Rubber Co. (Firestone) under a conditional sales contract calling for monthly payments over a period of time. A few months later, she purchased a stereophonic phonograph from the same company under the same sort of contract. The total cost of the stove and stereo was about $500, plus an additional financing charge of over $100. Under the contracts, Firestone retained title to the merchandise, but Mrs. Fuentes was entitled to possession unless and until she should default on her installment payments.

For more than a year, Mrs. Fuentes made her installment payments. But then, with only about $200 remaining to be paid, a dispute developed between her and Firestone over the servicing of the stove. Firestone instituted an action in a small-claims court for repossession of both the stove and the stereo claiming that Mrs. Fuentes had refused to make her remaining payments. Simultaneously with the filing of that action and before Mrs. Fuentes had even received a summons to answer its complaint, Firestone obtained a writ of replevin ordering a sheriff to seize the disputed goods at once.

In conformance with Florida procedure, Firestone had only to fill in the blanks on the appropriate form documents and submit them to the clerk of the small-claims court. The clerk signed and stamped the documents and issued a writ of replevin. Later the same day, a local deputy sheriff and an agent of Firestone went to Mrs. Fuentes' home and seized the stove and stereo.

Shortly thereafter, Mrs. Fuentes instituted the present action in a federal district court, challenging the constitutionality of the Florida prejudgment replevin procedures under the Due Process Clause of the Fourteenth Amendment.[2] She sought declaratory and injunctive relief against continued enforcement of the procedural provisions of the state statutes that authorize prejudgment replevin.

The appellants in No. 5138 filed a very similar action in a federal district court in Pennsylvania, challenging the constitutionality of that State's prejudgment replevin process. Like Mrs. Fuentes, they had had possessions seized under writs of replevin. Three of the appellants had purchased personal property—a bed, a table, and other household goods—under installment sales contracts like the one signed by Mrs. Fuentes; and the sellers of the property had obtained and executed summary writs of replevin, claiming that the appellants had fallen behind in their installment payments. The experience of the fourth appellant, Rosa Washington, had been more bizarre. She had been divorced from a local deputy sheriff and was engaged in a dispute with him over the custody of their son. Her former husband, being familiar with the routine forms used in the replevin process, had obtained a writ that ordered the seizure of the boy's clothes, furniture, and toys.

In both No. 5039 and No. 5138, three-judge District Courts were convened to consider the appellants' challenges to the constitutional validity of the Florida and Pennsylvania statutes. The courts in both cases upheld the constitutionality of the statutes. * * *[5]

---

2. Both Mrs. Fuentes and the appellants in No. 5138 also challenged the prejudgment replevin procedures under the Fourth Amendment, made applicable to the States by the Fourteenth. We do not, however, reach that issue. *See* n.32, *infra.*

5. Since the announcement of this Court's decision in *Sniadach v. Family Finance Corp.*, summary prejudgment remedies have come under constitutional challenge throughout the country. The summary deprivation of property under statutes very similar to the Florida and Pennsylvania statutes at issue here has been held unconstitutional by at least two courts. Applying *Sniadach* to other closely related forms of summary prejudgment remedies, some courts have construed that

II

Under the Florida statute challenged here, "[a]ny person whose goods or chattels are wrongfully detained by any other person * * * may have a writ of replevin to recover them * * *." Fla.Stat.Ann. § 78.01 (Supp.1972–1973). There is no requirement that the applicant make a convincing showing before the seizure that the goods are, in fact, "wrongfully detained." Rather, Florida law automatically relies on the bare assertion of the party seeking the writ that he is entitled to one and allows a court clerk to issue the writ summarily. It requires only that the applicant file a complaint, initiating a court action for repossession and reciting in conclusory fashion that he is "lawfully entitled to the possession" of the property, and that he file a security bond. On the sole basis of the complaint and bond, a writ is issued "command[ing] the officer to whom it may be directed to replevy the goods and chattels in possession of defendant * * * and to summon the defendant to answer the complaint." Fla.Stat.Ann. § 78.08 (Supp.1972–1973). If the goods are "in any dwelling house or other building or enclosure," the officer is required to demand their delivery; but if they are not delivered, "he shall cause such house, building or enclosure to be broken open and shall make replevin according to the writ * * *." Fla.Stat.Ann. § 78.10 (Supp. 1972–1973).

Thus, at the same moment that the defendant receives the complaint seeking repossession of property through court action, the property is seized from him. He is provided no prior notice and allowed no opportunity whatever to challenge the issuance of the writ. *After* the property has been seized, he will eventually have an opportunity for a hearing, as the defendant in the trial of the court action for repossession, which the plaintiff is required to pursue. And he is also not wholly without recourse in the meantime. For under the Florida statute, the officer who seizes the property must keep it for three days, and during that period the defendant may reclaim possession of the property by posting his own security bond in double its value. But if he does not post such a bond, the property is transferred to the party who sought the writ, pending a final judgment in the underlying action for repossession. Fla.Stat.Ann. § 78.13 (Supp.1972–1973).

The Pennsylvania law differs, though not in its essential nature, from that of Florida. As in Florida, a private party may obtain a prejudgment writ of replevin through a summary process of *ex parte* application to a prothonotary. As in Florida, the party seeking the writ may simply post with his application a bond in double the value of the property to be seized. Pa.Rule Civ.Proc. 1073(a). There is no opportunity for a prior hearing and no prior notice to the other party. On this basis, a sheriff is required to execute the writ by seizing the specified property. Unlike the Florida statute, however, the Pennsylvania law does not require that there *ever* be opportunity for a hearing on the merits of the

decision as setting forth general principles of procedural due process and have struck down such remedies. Other courts, however, have construed *Sniadach* as closely confined to its own facts and have upheld such summary prejudgment remedies.

conflicting claims to possession of the replevied property. The party seeking the writ is not obliged to initiate a court action for repossession. Indeed, he need not even formally allege that he is lawfully entitled to the property. The most that is required is that he file an "affidavit of the value of the property to be replevied." Pa.Rule Civ.Proc. 1073(a). If the party who loses property through replevin seizure is to get even a post-seizure hearing, he must initiate a lawsuit himself. He may also, as under Florida law, post his own counterbond within three days after the seizure to regain possession. Pa.Rule Civ.Proc. 1076.

III

Although these prejudgment replevin statutes are descended from the common law replevin action of six centuries ago, they bear very little resemblance to it. Replevin at common law was an action for the return of specific goods wrongfully taken or "distrained." Typically, it was used after a landlord (the "distrainor") had seized possessions from a tenant (the "distrainee") to satisfy a debt allegedly owed. If the tenant then instituted a replevin action and posted security, the landlord could be ordered to return the property at once, pending a final judgment in the underlying action. However, this prejudgment replevin of goods at common law did *not* follow from an entirely *ex parte* process of pleading by the distrainee. For "[t]he distrainor could always stop the action of replevin by claiming to be the owner of the goods; and as this claim was often made merely to delay the proceedings, the writ *de proprietate probanda* was devised early in the fourteenth century, which enabled the sheriff to determine summarily the question of ownership. If the question of ownership was determined against the distrainor the goods were delivered back to the distrainee [pending final judgment]."

Prejudgment replevin statutes like those of Florida and Pennsylvania are derived from this ancient possessory action in that they authorize the seizure of property before a final judgment. But the similarity ends there. As in the present cases, such statutes are most commonly used by creditors to seize goods allegedly wrongfully detained—not wrongfully taken—by debtors. At common law, if a creditor wished to invoke state power to recover goods wrongfully detained, he had to proceed through the action of debt or detinue. These actions, however, did not provide for a return of property before final judgment.[12] And, more importantly, on the occasions when the common law did allow prejudgment seizure by state power, it provided some kind of notice and opportunity to be heard to the party then in possession of the property, and a state official made at least a summary determination of the relative rights of the disputing parties before stepping into the dispute and taking goods from one of them.

IV

For more than a century the central meaning of procedural due process has been clear: "Parties whose rights are to be affected are

---

12. The creditor could, of course, proceed without the use of state power, through self-help, by "distraining" the property before a judgment.

entitled to be heard; and in order that they may enjoy that right they must first be notified." *Baldwin v. Hale,* 1 Wall. 223, 233, 17 L.Ed. 531. It is equally fundamental that the right to notice and an opportunity to be heard "must be granted at a meaningful time and in a meaningful manner." *Armstrong v. Manzo,* 380 U.S. 545, 552, 85 S.Ct. 1187, 1191, 14 L.Ed.2d 62.

The primary question in the present cases is whether these state statutes are constitutionally defective in failing to provide for hearings "at a meaningful time." The Florida replevin process guarantees an opportunity for a hearing after the seizure of goods, and the Pennsylvania process allows a post-seizure hearing if the aggrieved party shoulders the burden of initiating one. But neither the Florida nor the Pennsylvania statute provides for notice or an opportunity to be heard *before* the seizure. The issue is whether procedural due process in the context of these cases requires an opportunity for a hearing *before* the State authorizes its agents to seize property in the possession of a person upon the application of another.

The constitutional right to be heard is a basic aspect of the duty of government to follow a fair process of decisionmaking when it acts to deprive a person of his possessions. The purpose of this requirement is not only to ensure abstract fair play to the individual. Its purpose, more particularly, is to protect his use and possession of property from arbitrary encroachment—to minimize substantively unfair or mistaken deprivations of property, a danger that is especially great when the State seizes goods simply upon the application of and for the benefit of a private party. So viewed, the prohibition against the deprivation of property without due process of law reflects the high value, embedded in our constitutional and political history, that we place on a person's right to enjoy what is his, free of governmental interference.

The requirement of notice and an opportunity to be heard raises no impenetrable barrier to the taking of a person's possessions. But the fair process of decision making that it guarantees works, by itself, to protect against arbitrary deprivation of property. For when a person has an opportunity to speak up in his own defense, and when the State must listen to what he has to say, substantively unfair and simply mistaken deprivations of property interests can be prevented. It has long been recognized that "fairness can rarely be obtained by secret, one-sided determination of facts decisive of rights. * * * [And n]o better instrument has been devised for arriving at truth than to give a person in jeopardy of serious loss notice of the case against him and opportunity to meet it."

If the right to notice and a hearing is to serve its full purpose, then, it is clear that it must be granted at a time when the deprivation can still be prevented. At a later hearing, an individual's possessions can be returned to him if they were unfairly or mistakenly taken in the first place. Damages may even be awarded to him for the wrongful deprivation. But no later hearing and no damage award can undo the fact that the arbitrary taking that was subject to the right of procedural due process has already occurred. "This Court has not * * * embraced the general proposition that a wrong may be done if it can be undone." *Stanley v. Illinois,* 405 U.S. 645, 647, 92 S.Ct. 1208, 1210, 31 L.Ed.2d 551.

This is no new principle of constitutional law. The right to a prior hearing has long been recognized by this Court under the Fourteenth and Fifth Amendments. Although the Court has held that due process tolerates variances in the *form* of a hearing "appropriate to the nature of the case," *Mullane v. Central Hanover Tr. Co.,* and "depending upon the importance of the interests involved and the nature of the subsequent proceedings [if any]," *Boddie v. Connecticut,* 401 U.S. 371, 378, 91 S.Ct. 780, 786, 28 L.Ed.2d 113, the Court has traditionally insisted that, whatever its form, opportunity for that hearing must be provided before the deprivation at issue takes effect. "That the hearing required by due process is subject to waiver, and is not fixed in form does not affect its root requirement that an individual be given an opportunity for a hearing *before* he is deprived of any significant property interest, except for extraordinary situations where some valid governmental interest is at stake that justifies postponing the hearing until after the event." *Boddie v. Connecticut, supra,* 401 U.S. at 378–379, 91 S.Ct. at 786 (emphasis in original).

The Florida and Pennsylvania prejudgment replevin statutes fly in the face of this principle. To be sure, the requirements that a party seeking a writ must first post a bond, allege conclusorily that he is entitled to specific goods, and open himself to possible liability in damages if he is wrong, serve to deter wholly unfounded applications for a writ. But those requirements are hardly a substitute for a prior hearing, for they test no more than the strength of the applicant's own belief in his rights.[13] Since his private gain is at stake, the danger is all too great that his confidence in his cause will be misplaced. Lawyers and judges are familiar with the phenomenon of a party mistakenly but firmly convinced that his view of the facts and law will prevail, and therefore quite willing to risk the costs of litigation. Because of the understandable, self-interested fallibility of litigants, a court does not decide a dispute until it has had an opportunity to hear both sides—and does not generally take even tentative action until it has itself examined the support for the plaintiff's position. The Florida and Pennsylvania statutes do not even require the official issuing a writ of replevin to do that much.

The minimal deterrent effect of a bond requirement is, in a practical sense, no substitute for an informed evaluation by a neutral official. More specifically, as a matter of constitutional principle, it is no replace-

13. They may not even test that much. For if an applicant for the writ knows that he is dealing with an uneducated, uninformed consumer with little access to legal help and little familiarity with legal procedures, there may be a substantial possibility that a summary seizure of property—however unwarranted—may go unchallenged, and the applicant may feel that he can act with impunity.

ment for the right to a prior hearing that is the only truly effective safeguard against arbitrary deprivation of property. While the existence of these other, less effective, safeguards may be among the considerations that affect the form of hearing demanded by due process, they are far from enough by themselves to obviate the right to a prior hearing of some kind.

V

The right to a prior hearing, of course, attaches only to the deprivation of an interest encompassed within the Fourteenth Amendment's protection. In the present cases, the Florida and Pennsylvania statutes were applied to replevy chattels in the appellants' possession. The replevin was not cast as a final judgment; most, if not all, of the appellants lacked full title to the chattels; and their claim even to continued possession was a matter in dispute. Moreover, the chattels at stake were nothing more than an assortment of household goods. Nonetheless, it is clear that the appellants were deprived of possessory interests in those chattels that were within the protection of the Fourteenth Amendment.

A

A deprivation of a person's possessions under a prejudgment writ of replevin, at least in theory, may be only temporary. The Florida and Pennsylvania statutes do not require a person to wait until a post-seizure hearing and final judgment to recover what has been replevied. Within three days after the seizure, the statutes allowing him to recover the goods if he, in return, surrenders other property—a payment necessary to secure a bond in double the value of the goods seized from him. But it is now well settled that a temporary, nonfinal deprivation of property is nonetheless a "deprivation" in the terms of the Fourteenth Amendment. *Sniadach v. Family Finance Corp.,* 395 U.S. 337, 89 S.Ct. 1820, 23 L.Ed.2d 349; *Bell v. Burson,* 402 U.S. 535, 91 S.Ct. 1586, 29 L.Ed.2d 90. Both *Sniadach* and *Bell* involved takings of property pending a final judgment in an underlying dispute. In both cases, the challenged statutes included recovery provisions, allowing the defendants to post security to quickly regain the property taken from them.[15] Yet the Court firmly held that these were deprivations of property that had to be preceded by a fair hearing.

* * * The Fourteenth Amendment draws no bright lines around three-day, 10–day or 50–day deprivations of property. Any significant taking of property by the State is within the purview of the Due Process Clause. While the length and consequent severity of a deprivation may be another factor to weigh in determining the appropriate form of

15. *Bell v. Burson,* 402 U.S. 535, 536, 91 S.Ct. 1586, 1587, 29 L.Ed.2d 90. Although not mentioned in the *Sniadach* opinion, there clearly was a quick recovery provision in the Wisconsin prejudgment garnishment statute at issue. Wis.Stat.Ann. § 267.21(1) (Supp.1970–1971). *Family Finance Corp. v. Sniadach,* 37 Wis.2d 163, 173–174, 154 N.W.2d 259, 265. Mr. Justice Harlan adverted to the recovery provision in his concurring opinion.

hearing, it is not decisive of the basic right to a prior hearing of some kind.

B

The appellants who signed conditional sales contracts lacked full legal title to the replevied goods. The Fourteenth Amendment's protection of "property," however, has never been interpreted to safeguard only the rights of undisputed ownership. Rather, it has been read broadly to extend protection to "any significant property interest."

The appellants were deprived of such an interest in the replevied goods—the interest in continued possession and use of the goods. *See Sniadach v. Family Finance Corp.*, 395 U.S. at 342, 89 S.Ct. at 1823 (Harlan, J., concurring). They had acquired this interest under the conditional sales contracts that entitled them to possession and use of the chattels before transfer of title. In exchange for immediate possession, the appellants had agreed to pay a major financing charge beyond the basic price of the merchandise. Moreover, by the time the goods were summarily repossessed, they had made substantial installment payments. Clearly, their possessory interest in the goods, dearly bought and protected by contract,[16] was sufficient to invoke the protection of the Due Process Clause.

Their ultimate right to continued possession was, of course, in dispute. If it were shown at a hearing that the appellants had defaulted on their contractual obligations, it might well be that the sellers of the goods would be entitled to repossession. But even assuming that the appellants had fallen behind in their installment payments, and that they had no other valid defenses,[17] that is immaterial here. The right to be heard does not depend upon an advance showing that one will surely prevail at the hearing.

C

Nevertheless, the District Courts rejected the appellants' constitutional claim on the ground that the goods seized from them—a stove, a stereo, a table, a bed, and so forth—were not deserving of due process protection, since they were not absolute necessities of life. The courts based this holding on a very narrow reading of *Sniadach v. Family Finance Corp., supra,* and *Goldberg v. Kelly,* [397 U.S. 254, 90 S.Ct. 1011, 25 L.Ed.2d 287 (1970)] in which this Court held that the Constitu-

---

16. The possessory interest of Rosa Washington, an appellant in No. 5138, in her son's clothes, furniture, and toys was no less sufficient to invoke due process safeguards. Her interest was not protected by contract. Rather, it was protected by ordinary property law, there being a dispute between her and her estranged husband over which of them had a legal right not only to custody of the child but also to possession of the chattels.

17. Mrs. Fuentes argues that Florida law allows her to defend on the ground that Firestone breached its obligations under the sales contract by failing to repair serious defects in the stove it sold her. We need not consider this issue here. It is enough that the right to continued possession of the goods was open to *some* dispute at a hearing since the sellers of the goods had to show, at the least, that the appellants had defaulted in their payments.

tion requires a hearing before prejudgment wage garnishment and before the termination of certain welfare benefits. They reasoned that *Sniadach* and *Goldberg,* as a matter of constitutional principle, established no more than that a prior hearing is required with respect to the deprivation of such basically "necessary" items as wages and welfare benefits.

This reading of *Sniadach* and *Goldberg* reflects the premise that those cases marked a radical departure from established principles of procedural due process. They did not. Both decisions were in the mainstream of past cases, having little or nothing to do with the absolute "necessities" of life but establishing that due process requires an opportunity for a hearing before a deprivation of property takes effect.[19] [Citations of eight cases omitted.] In none of those cases did the Court hold that this most basic due process requirement is limited to the protection of only a few types of property interests. While *Sniadach* and *Goldberg* emphasized the special importance of wages and welfare benefits, they did not convert that emphasis into a new and more limited constitutional doctrine.

Nor did they carve out a rule of "necessity" for the sort of nonfinal deprivations of property that they involved. That was made clear in *Bell v. Burson,* holding that there must be an opportunity for a fair hearing before mere suspension of a driver's license. A driver's license clearly does not rise to the level of "necessity" exemplified by wages and welfare benefits. Rather, as the Court accurately stated, it is an "important interest," entitled to the protection of procedural due process of law.

The household goods, for which the appellants contracted and paid substantial sums, are deserving of similar protection.

VI

There are "extraordinary situations" that justify postponing notice and opportunity for a hearing. These situations, however, must be truly unusual. Only in a few limited situations has this Court allowed outright seizure[23] without opportunity for a prior hearing. First, in each case, the

19. The Supreme Court of California recently put the matter accurately: "*Sniadach* does not mark a radical departure in constitutional adjudication. It is not a rivulet of wage garnishment but part of the mainstream of the past procedural due process decisions of the United States Supreme Court." *Randone v. Appellate Dept.,* 5 Cal.3d 536, 550, 96 Cal.Rptr. 709, 718, 488 P.2d 13, 22.

23. Of course, outright seizure of property is not the only kind of deprivation that must be preceded by a prior hearing. *See, e.g., Sniadach v. Family Finance Corp., supra.* In three cases, the Court has allowed the attachment of property without a prior hearing. In one, the attachment was neces-

sary to protect the public against the same sort of immediate harm involved in the seizure cases—a bank failure. *Coffin Bros. & Co. v. Bennett,* 277 U.S. 29, 48 S.Ct. 422, 72 L.Ed. 768. Another case involved attachment necessary to secure jurisdiction in state court—clearly a most basic and important public interest. *Ownbey v. Morgan,* 256 U.S. 94, 41 S.Ct. 433, 65 L.Ed. 837. It is much less clear what interests were involved in the third case, decided with an unexplicated *per curiam* opinion simply citing *Coffin Bros.* and *Ownbey. McKay v. McInnes,* 279 U.S. 820, 49 S.Ct. 344, 73 L.Ed. 975. As far as essential procedural due process doctrine goes, *McKay* cannot stand for any more than was established in the *Coffin Bros.* and *Ownbey* cases on which

seizure has been directly necessary to secure an important governmental or general public interest. Second, there has been a special need for very prompt action. Third, the State has kept strict control over its monopoly of legitimate force: the person initiating the seizure has been a government official responsible for determining, under the standards of a narrowly drawn statute, that it was necessary and justified in the particular instance. Thus, the Court has allowed summary seizure of property to collect the internal revenue of the United States, to meet the needs of a national war effort, to protect against the economic disaster of a bank failure, and to protect the public from misbranded drugs and contaminated food.

The Florida and Pennsylvania prejudgment replevin statutes serve no such important governmental or general public interest. They allow summary seizure of a person's possessions when no more than private gain is directly at stake.[29] The replevin of chattels, as in the present cases, may satisfy a debt or settle a score. But state intervention in a private dispute hardly compares to state action furthering a war effort or protecting the public health.

Nor do the broadly drawn Florida and Pennsylvania statutes limit the summary seizure of goods to special situations demanding prompt action. There may be cases in which a creditor could make a showing of immediate danger that a debtor will destroy or conceal disputed goods. But the statutes before us are not "narrowly drawn to meet any such unusual condition." *Sniadach v. Family Finance Corp., supra.* And no such unusual situation is presented by the facts of these cases.

The statutes, moreover, abdicate effective state control over state power. Private parties, serving their own private advantage, may unilat-

---

it relied completely. *See Sniadach v. Family Finance Corp., supra,* 395 U.S. at 340, 89 S.Ct. at 1822; *id.* at 344, 89 S.Ct. 1823 (Harlan, J., concurring).

In cases involving deprivation of other interests, such as government employment, the Court similarly has required an unusually important governmental need to outweigh the right to a prior hearing. *See, e.g., Cafeteria and Restaurant Workers v. McElroy,* 367 U.S. 886, 895–896, 81 S.Ct. 1743, 1748–1749, 6 L.Ed.2d 1230.

Seizure under a search warrant is quite a different matter, *see* n.30, *infra.*

29. By allowing repossession without an opportunity for a prior hearing, the Florida and Pennsylvania statutes may be intended specifically to reduce the costs for the private party seeking to seize goods in another party's possession. Even if the private gain at stake in repossession actions were equal to the great public interests recognized in this Court's past decisions, the Court has made clear that the avoidance of the ordi-

nary costs imposed by the opportunity for a hearing is not sufficient to override the constitutional right. The appellees argue that the cost of holding hearings may be especially onerous in the context of the creditor-debtor relationship. But the Court's holding in *Sniadach v. Family Finance Corp., supra,* indisputably demonstrates that ordinary hearing costs are no more able to override due process rights in the creditor-debtor context than in other contexts.

In any event, the aggregate cost of an opportunity to be heard before repossession should not be exaggerated. For we deal here only with the right to an *opportunity* to be heard. Since the issues and facts decisive of rights in repossession suits may very often be quite simple, there is a likelihood that many defendants would forgo their opportunity, sensing the futility of the exercise in the particular case. And, of course, no hearing need be held unless the defendant, having received notice of his opportunity, takes advantage of it.

erally invoke state power to replevy goods from another. No state official participates in the decision to seek a writ; no state official reviews the basis for the claim to repossession; and no state official evaluates the need for immediate seizure. There is not even a requirement that the plaintiff provide any information to the court on these matters. The State acts largely in the dark.[30]

* * *

VIII

We hold that the Florida and Pennsylvania prejudgment replevin provisions work a deprivation of property without due process of law insofar as they deny the right to a prior opportunity to be heard before chattels are taken from their possessor.[32] Our holding, however, is a narrow one. We do not question the power of a State to seize goods before a final judgment in order to protect the security interests of creditors so long as those creditors have tested their claim to the goods through the process of a fair prior hearing. The nature and form of such prior hearings, moreover, are legitimately open to many potential variations and are a subject, at this point, for legislation—not adjudication.[33]

For the foregoing reasons, the judgments of the District Courts are vacated and these cases are remanded for further proceedings consistent with this opinion.

It is so ordered.

Vacated and remanded.

JUSTICE POWELL and JUSTICE REHNQUIST did not participate in the consideration or decision of these cases.

JUSTICE WHITE, with whom THE CHIEF JUSTICE and JUSTICE BLACKMUN join, dissenting.

30. The seizure of possessions under a writ of replevin is entirely different from the seizure of possessions under a search warrant. First, a search warrant is generally issued to serve a highly important governmental need—e.g., the apprehension and conviction of criminals—rather than the mere private advantage of a private party in an economic transaction. Second, a search warrant is generally issued in situations demanding prompt action. The danger is all too obvious that a criminal will destroy or hide evidence or fruits of his crime if given any prior notice. Third, the Fourth Amendment guarantees that the State will not issue search warrants merely upon the conclusory application of a private party. It guarantees that the State will not abdicate control over the issuance of warrants and that no warrant will be issued without a prior showing of probable cause. Thus, our decision today in no way implies that there must be opportunity for an adversary hearing before a search warrant is issued.

32. We do not reach the appellants' argument that the Florida and Pennsylvania statutory procedures violate the Fourth Amendment, made applicable to the States by the Fourteenth. See n.2, supra. For once a prior hearing is required, at which the applicant for a writ must establish the probable validity of his claim for repossession, the Fourth Amendment problem may well be obviated. There is no need for us to decide that question at this point.

33. Leeway remains to develop a form of hearing that will minimize unnecessary cost and delay while preserving the fairness and effectiveness of the hearing in preventing seizures of goods where the party seeking the writ has little probability of succeeding on the merits of the dispute.

Because the Court's opinion and judgment improvidently, in my view, call into question important aspects of the statutes of almost all the States governing secured transactions and the procedure for repossessing personal property, I must dissent for the reasons that follow.

* * *

The narrow issue, as the Court notes, is whether it comports with due process to permit the seller, pending final judgment, to take possession of the property through a writ of replevin served by the sheriff without affording the buyer opportunity to insist that the seller establish at a hearing that there is reasonable basis for his claim of default. The interests of the buyer and seller are obviously antagonistic during this interim period: the buyer wants the use of the property pending final judgment; the seller's interest is to prevent further use and deterioration of his security. By the Florida and Pennsylvania laws the property is to all intents and purposes placed in custody and immobilized during this time. The buyer loses use of the property temporarily but is protected against loss; the seller is protected against deterioration of the property but must undertake by bond to make the buyer whole in the event the latter prevails.

In considering whether this resolution of conflicting interests is unconstitutional, much depends on one's perceptions of the practical considerations involved. The Court holds it constitutionally essential to afford opportunity for a probable-cause hearing prior to repossession. Its stated purpose is "to prevent unfair and mistaken deprivations of property." But in these typical situations, the buyer-debtor has either defaulted or he has not. If there is a default, it would seem not only "fair," but essential, that the creditor be allowed to repossess; and I cannot say that the likelihood of a mistaken claim of default is sufficiently real or recurring to justify a broad constitutional requirement that a creditor do more than the typical state law requires and permits him to do. Sellers are normally in the business of selling and collecting the price for their merchandise. I could be quite wrong, but it would not seem in the creditor's interest for a default occasioning repossession to occur; as a practical matter it would much better serve his interests if the transaction goes forward and is completed as planned. Dollar-and-cents considerations weigh heavily against false claims of default as well as against precipitate action that would allow no opportunity for mistakes to surface and be corrected. Nor does it seem to me that creditors would lightly undertake the expense of instituting replevin actions and putting up bonds.

The Court relies on prior cases, particularly *Goldberg v. Kelly,* 397 U.S. 254, 90 S.Ct. 1011, 25 L.Ed.2d 287 (1970); *Bell v. Burson,* 402 U.S. 535, 91 S.Ct. 1586, 29 L.Ed.2d 90 (1971); and *Stanley v. Illinois,* 405 U.S. 645, 92 S.Ct. 1208, 31 L.Ed.2d 551 (1972). But these cases provide no automatic test for determining whether and when due process of law requires adversary proceedings. Indeed, "[t]he very nature of due process negates any concept of inflexible procedures universally applicable to every imaginable situation. * * *." "[W]hat procedures due process may require under any given set of circumstances must begin with a determination of the precise nature of the government function involved as well as of the private interest that has been affected by governmental action." *Cafeteria and Restaurant Workers v. McElroy*, 367 U.S. 886, 895, 81 S.Ct. 1743, 1748, 6 L.Ed.2d 1230 (1961). *See also Stanley v. Illinois*, *supra*, 405 U.S. at 650, 92 S.Ct. at 1212; *Goldberg v. Kelly*, *supra*, 397 U.S. at 263, 90 S.Ct. at 1018. Viewing the issue before us in this light, I would not construe the Due Process Clause to require the creditors to do more than they have done in these cases to secure possession pending final hearing. Certainly, I would not ignore, as the Court does, the creditor's interest in preventing further use and deterioration of the property in which he has substantial interest. Surely under the Court's own definition, the creditor has a "property" interest as deserving of protection as that of the debtor. At least the debtor, who is very likely uninterested in a speedy resolution that could terminate his use of the property, should be required to make those payments, into court or otherwise, upon which his right to possession is conditioned.

* * *

The Court's rhetoric is seductive, but in end analysis, the result it reaches will have little impact and represents no more than ideological tinkering with state law. It would appear that creditors could withstand attack under today's opinion simply by making clear in the controlling credit instruments that they may retake possession without a hearing, or, for that matter, without resort to judicial process at all. Alternatively, they need only give a few days' notice of a hearing, take possession if hearing is waived or if there is default; and if hearing is necessary merely establish probable cause for asserting that default has occurred. It is very doubtful in my mind that such a hearing would in fact result in protections for the debtor substantially different from those the present laws provide. On the contrary, the availability of credit may well be diminished or, in any event, the expense of securing it increased.

None of this seems worth the candle to me. The procedure that the Court strikes down is not some barbaric hangover from bygone days. The respective rights of the parties in secured transactions have undergone the most intensive analysis in recent years. * * * I am content to rest on the judgment of those who have wrestled with these problems so long and often and upon the judgment of the legislatures that have considered and so recently adopted provisions that contemplate precisely what has happened in these cases.

Notes and Questions

1. The Court in *Fuentes* was squarely faced with the scope of its earlier decisions in *Sniadach* (requiring a hearing before taking of wages) and *Goldberg v. Kelly* (requiring a hearing before termination of welfare benefits). The lower courts believed that *Sniadach* and *Goldberg* dealt with deprivations of absolute necessities of life, wages and welfare benefits, and

"marked a radical departure from established principles of procedural due process." Reread *Sniadach, supra* p. 219. Were the lower courts in error in treating *Sniadach* as they did? Did *Sniadach* lend itself to such treatment?

The *Fuentes* opinion noted that *Sniadach* was in the mainstream of cases having "little or nothing to do with the absolute 'necessities' of life but establishing that due process requires an opportunity for a hearing before a deprivation of property takes effect," citing numerous cases in support. Are you convinced that *Sniadach* was in the mainstream? In the mainstream requiring a hearing *prior* to seizure? Note how the mainstream turned into a rivulet just a few years later. *See Mitchell, infra* p. 240.

2. Recall the discussion of quasi in rem jurisdiction. Assuming the continued constitutionality of that basis of jurisdiction, would the creditor have to give notice before seizing property to secure jurisdiction? Would the nature of the property affect the result? If notice were first given, might the debtor not flee with movable property, thereby avoiding jurisdiction? *See Ownbey.* Did *Fuentes* address that situation? Recall the following passage:

> Nor do the broadly drawn Florida and Pennsylvania statutes limit the summary seizure of goods to special situations demanding prompt action. There may be cases in which a creditor could make a showing of immediate danger that a debtor will destroy or conceal disputed goods. But the statutes before us are not "narrowly drawn to meet any such unusual condition." [Citation omitted.] And no such unusual situation is presented by the facts of these cases.

407 U.S. at 93.

3. Did *Fuentes* require that the debtor be given an opportunity for a hearing *before* prejudgment seizure in all non-extraordinary situations? Consider the Court's framing of the issue:

> The issue is whether procedural due process in the context of these cases requires an opportunity for a hearing *before* the State authorizes its agents to seize property in the possession of a person upon the application of another.

407 U.S. at 80. Do any of the opinions indicate that due process could be satisfied by a hearing held *after* the seizure?

4. Note that the Court's holding is restricted to the right to prior notice and opportunity to be heard. The Court refrains from commenting on the nature and form of the hearing and reserves the subject for legislation rather than adjudication. Was this approach fostered by a desire to conserve judicial resources? To avoid premature judicial decision? To give each state an opportunity to develop laws that could later be tested in light of experience?

5. *Fuentes* contained the seeds of several ironies. Neither Justice Powell nor Justice Rehnquist participated in the consideration or decision of the case. The opinion was rendered by four justices, with three justices dissenting. As you may imagine, many creditor-oriented states welcomed neither the decision nor its impact on state law. Many avoidance techniques were utilized. The Supreme Court of Arizona adopted a rather novel one in *Roofing Wholesale, Inc. v. Palmer,* 108 Ariz. 508, 502 P.2d 1327 (1972).

When, however, we have doubts that once the full Court hears the case that the opinion will stand, we are reluctant to declare unconstitutional Arizona statutes based upon a decision by less than a clear majority.

108 Ariz. at 510–11, 502 P.2d at 1329.

6. Another irony lay in the Court's reliance upon the state judicial process as the "state action" necessary to implement Fourteenth Amendment scrutiny. *Fuentes* left open the questions whether "self-help" by the creditor pursuant to a consensual agreement or authorized by legislative enactments would be constitutional. Whether such self-help constitutes "state action" for purposes of Fourteenth Amendment scrutiny was subsequently decided by the Court. *See Flagg Brothers, Inc. v. Brooks,* 436 U.S. 149 (1978) (no state action). Note that the decision was handed down after *Mitchell, infra* p. 240, and *Di–Chem, infra* p. 251.

7. Does *Fuentes* apply to post-judgment seizures to satisfy judgments? For example, suppose a judgment debtor wishes to contest a seizure on the ground that the property in question is exempt from levy. Should the debtor be allowed an opportunity to demonstrate the exempt status before seizure? *See infra* note 11, p. 260.

8. The Court asserted that seizure pursuant to a lawful search warrant is a different matter from ordinary seizures. Similarly, a temporary restraining order under Rule 65 of the Federal Rules of Civil Procedure may also differ. Rule 65(b) provides in pertinent part as follows:

> A temporary restraining order may be granted without written or oral notice to the adverse party or that party's attorney only if (1) it clearly appears from specific facts shown by affidavit or by the verified complaint that immediate and irreparable injury, loss, or damage will result to the applicant before the adverse party or that party's attorney can be heard in opposition, and (2) the applicant's attorney certifies to the court in writing the efforts, if any, which have been made to give the notice and the reasons supporting the claim that notice should not be required. Every temporary restraining order granted without notice shall * * * expire by its terms within such time after entry, not to exceed 10 days, as the court fixes, unless within the time so fixed the order, for good cause shown, is extended for a like period or unless the party against whom the order is directed consents that it may be extended for a longer period. * * * In case a temporary restraining order is granted without notice, the motion for a preliminary injunction shall be set down for hearing at the earliest possible time and takes precedence of all matters except older matters of the same character; * * *. On 2 days' notice to the party who obtained the temporary restraining order without notice or on such shorter notice to that party as the court may prescribe, the adverse party may appear and move its dissolution or modification and in that event the court shall proceed to hear and determine such motion as expeditiously as the ends of justice require.

What differences do you see? Is Rule 65 constitutional?

9. The Fourth Amendment to the United States Constitution is made applicable to the states through incorporation into the Fourteenth Amend-

ment. The Court expressly refrained from deciding whether the Fourth Amendment proscription against unreasonable governmental seizures applies to the summary seizures described in this section. The Court stated that a prior hearing would satisfy any Fourth Amendment problem. Perhaps the judicial restraint in refusing to decide an issue not necessary to the decision was commendable. But if later cases overrule or distinguish the rationale of *Fuentes,* should they not then address the Fourth Amendment issue?

10.   Reread the paragraph on p. 229, starting with the words, "[t]he primary question in the present cases * * *." Would an opportunity for an immediate post-seizure hearing satisfy the "meaningful time" reference?

11.   The Court in *dictum* approved attachment of property without a prior hearing where necessary to secure jurisdiction. After *Shaffer,* however, all assertions of jurisdiction in civil proceedings must be based on the principles of *International Shoe, supra* p. 173—that is, if the defendant be not present, she must have such minimum contacts with the forum that the maintenance of the suit does not offend traditional notions of fair play and substantial justice. In any situation there presumably either are or are not sufficient minimum contacts for the assertion of personal jurisdiction. If there are not, *Shaffer* forbids attachment for purposes of acquiring jurisdiction; if there are, a state should be able to obtain in personam jurisdiction over a nonresident. Is there any longer a need for attachment to secure jurisdiction?

MITCHELL v. W.T. GRANT CO.

Supreme Court of the United States, 1974.
416 U.S. 600, 94 S.Ct. 1895, 40 L.Ed.2d 406.

JUSTICE WHITE delivered the opinion of the Court.

In this case, a state trial judge in Louisiana ordered the sequestration of personal property on the application of a creditor who had made an installment sale of the goods to petitioner and whose affidavit asserted delinquency and prayed for sequestration to enforce a vendor's lien under state law. The issue is whether the sequestration violated the Due Process Clause of the Fourteenth Amendment because it was ordered *ex parte,* without prior notice or opportunity for a hearing.

I

On February 2, 1972, respondent W.T. Grant Co. filed suit in the First City Court of the City of New Orleans, Louisiana, against petitioner, Lawrence Mitchell. The petition alleged the sale by Grant to Mitchell of a refrigerator, range, stereo, and washing machine, and an overdue and unpaid balance of the purchase price for said items in the amount of $574.17. Judgment for that sum was demanded. It was further alleged that Grant had a vendor's lien on the goods and that a writ of sequestration should issue to sequester the merchandise pending the outcome of the suit. The accompanying affidavit of Grant's credit manager swore to the truth of the facts alleged in the complaint. It also asserted that Grant had reason to believe petitioner would "encumber, alienate or otherwise dispose of the merchandise described in the foregoing petition during the pendency of these proceedings, and that a writ of sequestration is necessary in the premises." Based on the foregoing petition and affidavit, and without prior notice to Mitchell or affording him opportunity for hearing, the judge of the First City Court, Arthur J. O'Keefe, then signed an order that "a writ of sequestration issue herein" and that "the Constable of this court sequester and take into his possession the articles of merchandise described in the foregoing petition, upon plaintiff furnishing bond in the amount of $1,125." Bond in that amount having been filed by the respondent, the writ of sequestration issued, along with citation to petitioner Mitchell, citing him to file a pleading or make appearance in the First City Court of the city of New Orleans within five days. The citation recited the filing of the writ of sequestration and the accompanying affidavit, order, and bond. On March 3 Mitchell filed a motion to dissolve the writ of sequestration issued on February 2. The motion asserted that the personal property at issue had been seized under the writ of February 7, 1972, and claimed, first, that the goods were exempt from seizure under state law and, second, that the seizure violated the Due Process Clauses of the State and Federal Constitutions in that it had occurred without prior notice and opportunity to defend petitioner's right to possession of the property. The motion came on for hearing on March 14. It was then stipulated that a vendor's lien existed on the items, arguments of counsel were heard, and on March 16 the motion to dissolve was denied. The goods were held not exempt from seizure under state law. The trial court also ruled that "the provisional seizure enforced through sequestration" was not a denial of due process of law. "To the contrary," the trial judge said, "plaintiff insured defendant's right to due process by proceeding in accordance with Louisiana Law as opposed to any type of self-help seizure which would have denied defendant possession of his property without due process." The appellate courts of Louisiana refused to disturb the rulings of the trial court, the Supreme Court of Louisiana expressly rejecting petitioner's due process claims pressed under the Federal Constitution. 263 La. 627, 269 So.2d 186 (1972). We granted certiorari, and now affirm the judgment of the Louisiana Supreme Court.

II

* * * Petitioner no doubt "owned" the goods he had purchased under an installment sales contract, but his title was heavily encumbered. The seller W.T. Grant Co., also had an interest in the property, for state law provided it with a vendor's lien to secure the unpaid balance of the purchase price. Because of the lien, Mitchell's right to possession and his title were subject to defeasance in the event of default in paying the installments due from him. His interest in the property, until the purchase price was paid in full, was no greater than the surplus remaining, if any, after foreclosure and sale of the property in the event of his default and satisfaction of outstanding claims. *See* La.Code Civ. Proc.Ann., Art. 2373 (1961). The interest of Grant, as seller of the

property and holder of a vendor's lien, was measured by the unpaid balance of the purchase price. The monetary value of that interest in the property diminished as payments were made, but the value of the property as security also steadily diminished over time as it was put to its intended use by the purchaser.

Plainly enough, this is not a case where the property sequestered by the court is exclusively the property of the defendant debtor. The question is not whether a debtor's property may be seized by his creditors, *pendente lite,* where they hold no present interest in the property sought to be seized. The reality is that both seller and buyer had current, real interests in the property, and the definition of property rights is a matter of state law. Resolution of the due process question must take account not only of the interests of the buyer of the property but those of the seller as well.

Louisiana statutes provide for sequestration where "one claims the ownership or right to possession of property, or a mortgage, lien, or privilege thereon * * * if it is within the power of the defendant to conceal, dispose of, or waste the property or the revenues therefrom, or remove the property from the parish, during the pendency of the action." Art. 3571. The writ, however, will not issue on the conclusory allegation of ownership or possessory rights. Article 3501 provides that the writ of sequestration shall issue "only when the nature of the claim and the amount thereof, if any, and the grounds relied upon for the issuance of the writ clearly appear from specific facts" shown by a verified petition or affidavit. In the parish where this case arose, the clear showing required must be made to a judge,[5] and the writ will issue only upon his authorization and only after the creditor seeking the writ has filed a sufficient bond to protect the vendee against all damages in the event the sequestration is shown to have been improvident. Arts. 3501 and 3574.

The writ is obtainable on the creditor's *ex parte* application, without notice to the debtor or opportunity for a hearing, but the statute entitles the debtor immediately to seek dissolution of the writ, which must be ordered unless the creditor "proves the grounds upon which the writ was issued," Art. 3506, the existence of the debt, lien, and delinquency, failing which the court may order return of the property and assess damages in favor of the debtor, including attorney's fees.

The debtor, with or without moving to dissolve the sequestration, may also regain possession by filing his own bond to protect the creditor against interim damage to him should he ultimately win his case and have judgment against the debtor for the unpaid balance of the purchase price which was the object of the suit and of the sequestration. Arts. 3507 and 3508.

---

5. Articles 282 and 283 of the Code provide, generally, that the court clerk may issue writs of sequestration. But Art. 281 confines the authority to the judge in Orleans Parish. There is no dispute in this case that judicial authority for the writ was required and that it was obtained as the statute requires. The validity of procedures obtaining in areas outside Orleans Parish is not at issue.

In our view, this statutory procedure effects a constitutional accommodation of the conflicting interests of the parties. We cannot accept petitioner's broad assertion that the Due Process Clause of the Fourteenth Amendment guaranteed to him the use and possession of the goods until all issues in the case were judicially resolved after full adversary proceedings had been completed.

* * *

Second, there is the real risk that the buyer, with possession and power over the goods, will conceal or transfer the merchandise to the damage of the seller. This is one of the considerations weighed in the balance by the Louisiana law in permitting initial sequestration of the property. An important factor in this connection is that under Louisiana law, the vendor's lien expires if the buyer transfers possession.

Third, there is scant support in our cases for the proposition that there must be final judicial determination of the seller's entitlement before the buyer may be even temporarily deprived of possession of the purchased goods. On the contrary, it seems apparent that the seller with his own interest in the disputed merchandise would need to establish in any event only the probability that his case will succeed to warrant the bonded sequestration of the property pending outcome of the suit. The issue at this stage of the proceeding concerns possession pending trial and turns on the existence of the debt, the lien, and the delinquency. These are ordinarily uncomplicated matters that lend themselves to documentary proof; and we think it comports with due process to permit the initial seizure on sworn *ex parte* documents, followed by the early opportunity to put the creditor to his proof. The nature of the issues at stake minimizes the risk that the writ will be wrongfully issued by a judge. The potential damages award available, if there is a successful motion to dissolve the writ, as well as the creditor's own interest in avoiding interrupting the transaction, also contributes to minimizing this risk.

Fourth, we remain unconvinced that the impact on the debtor of deprivation of the household goods here in question overrides his inability to make the creditor whole for wrongful possession, the risk of destruction or alienation if notice and a prior hearing are supplied, and the low risk of a wrongful determination of possession through the procedures now employed.

Finally, the debtor may immediately have a full hearing on the matter of possession following the execution of the writ, thus cutting to a bare minimum the time of creditor- or court-supervised possession. The debtor in this case, who did not avail himself of this opportunity, can hardly expect that his argument on the severity of deprivation will carry much weight, and even assuming that there is real impact on the debtor from loss of these goods, pending the hearing on possession, his basic source of income is unimpaired.

* * *

III

Petitioner asserts that his right to a hearing before his possession is in any way disturbed is nonetheless mandated by a long line of cases in this Court, culminating in *Sniadach v. Family Finance Corp.*, 395 U.S. 337, 89 S.Ct. 1820, 23 L.Ed.2d 349 (1969), and *Fuentes v. Shevin*, 407 U.S. 67, 92 S.Ct. 1983, 32 L.Ed.2d 556 (1972). The pre-*Sniadach* cases are said by petitioner to hold that "the opportunity to be heard must precede any actual deprivation of private property." Their import, however, is not so clear as petitioner would have it: they merely stand for the proposition that a hearing must be had before one is finally deprived of his property and do not deal at all with the need for a pretermination hearing where a full and immediate post-termination hearing is provided.

More precisely in point, the Court had unanimously approved pre-judgment attachment liens effected by creditors, without notice, hearing, or judicial order, saying that "nothing is more common than to allow parties alleging themselves to be creditors to establish in advance by attachment a lien dependent for its effect upon the result of the suit." "The fact that the execution is issued in the first instance by an agent of the State but not from a court, followed as it is by personal notice and a right to take the case into court, is a familiar method in Georgia and is open to no objection." *Coffin Bros. v. Bennett*, 277 U.S. 29, 31, 48 S.Ct. 422, 423, 72 L.Ed. 768 (1929). To the same effect was the earlier case of *Ownbey v. Morgan*, 256 U.S. 94, 41 S.Ct. 433, 65 L.Ed. 837 (1921). Furthermore, based on *Ownbey* and *Coffin,* the Court later sustained the constitutionality of the Maine attachment statute. *McKay v. McInnes*, 279 U.S. 820, 49 S.Ct. 344, 73 L.Ed. 975 (1928). In that case, a nonresident of Maine sued in the Maine courts to collect a debt from a resident of the State. As permitted by statute, and as an integral part of instituting the suit, the creditor attached the properties of the defendant, without notice and without judicial process of any kind. In sustaining the procedure, the Maine Supreme Court, 127 Me. 110, 141 A. 699 (1928), described the attachment as designed to create a lien for the creditor at the outset of the litigation. "Its purpose is simply to secure to the creditor the property which the debtor has at the time it is made so that it may be seized and levied upon in satisfaction of the debt after judgment and execution may be obtained." *Id.* at 115, 141 A. at 702. The attachment was deemed "part of the remedy provided for the collection of the debt," *ibid.*, and represented a practice that "had become fully established in Massachusetts, part of which Maine was, at the time of the adoption of the Federal Constitution." *Id.* at 114, 115, 141 A. at 702. The judgment of the Maine court was affirmed without opinion, citing *Ownbey* and *Coffin.*

In *Sniadach v. Family Finance Corp., supra,* it was said that *McKay* and like cases dealt with "[a] procedural rule that may satisfy due process for attachments in general" but one that would not "necessarily satisfy procedural due process in every case," nor one that "gives necessary protection to all property in its modern forms." 395 U.S. at

340, 89 S.Ct. at 1822. *Sniadach* involved the prejudgment garnishment of wages—"a specialized type of property presenting distinct problems in our economic system." *Ibid.* Because "[t]he leverage of the creditor on the wage earner is enormous" and because "prejudgment garnishment of the Wisconsin type may as a practical matter drive a wage-earning family to the wall," it was held that the Due Process Clause forbade such garnishment absent notice and prior hearing. In *Sniadach,* the Court also observed that garnishment was subject to abuse by creditors without valid claims, a risk minimized by the nature of the security interest here at stake and the protections to the debtor offered by Louisiana procedure. Nor was it apparent in *Sniadach* with what speed the debtor could challenge the validity of the garnishment, and obviously the creditor's claim could not rest on the danger of destruction of wages, the property seized, since their availability to satisfy the debt remained within the power of the debtor who could simply leave his job. The suing creditor in *Sniadach* had no prior interest in the property attached, and the opinion did not purport to govern the typical case of the installment seller who brings a suit to collect an unpaid balance and who does not seek to attach wages pending the outcome of the suit but to repossess the sold property on which he had retained a lien to secure the purchase price. This very case soon came before the Court in *Fuentes v. Shevin,* where the constitutionality of the Florida and Pennsylvania replevin statutes was at issue. Those statutes permitted the secured installment seller to repossess the goods sold, without notice or hearing and without judicial order or supervision, but with the help of the sheriff operating under a writ issued by the court clerk at the behest of the seller. Because carried out without notice or opportunity for hearing and without judicial participation, this kind of seizure was held violative of the Due Process Clause. This holding is the mainstay of petitioner's submission here. But we are convinced that *Fuentes* was decided against a factual and legal background sufficiently different from that now before us and that it does not require the invalidation of the Louisiana sequestration statute, either on its face or as applied in this case.

* * *

The Louisiana law provides for judicial control of the process from beginning to end.[12]

* * *

12. The approval of a writ of sequestration is not, as petitioner contends, a mere ministerial act. "Since a writ of sequestration issues without a hearing, specific facts as to the grounds relied upon for issuance must be contained in the verified petition in order that the issuing judge can properly evaluate the grounds." *Wright v. Hughes,* 254 So.2d 293, 296–297 (La.Ct.App.1971) (on rehearing). To the same effect is *Hancock Bank v. Alexander,* 256 La. 643, 237 So.2d 669 (1970), where the court held that a simple allegation of indebtedness for money due on an automobile, where no deed of trust was referred to or produced, did not satisfy the "specific facts" test. The court stated:

"Strict application of the rules established for the issuance of conservatory writs has been uniformly required by the Courts in the past. It is implicit in those remedies that they should not be availed of unless the conditions which permit them exist;

Of course, as in *Fuentes*, consideration of the impact on the debtor remains. Under Louisiana procedure, however, the debtor, Mitchell, was not left in limbo to await a hearing that might or might not "eventually" occur, as the debtors were under the statutory schemes before the Court in *Fuentes*. Louisiana law expressly provides for an immediate hearing and dissolution of the writ "unless the plaintiff proves the grounds upon which the writ was issued." Art. 3506.

To summarize, the Louisiana system seeks to minimize the risk of error of a wrongful interim possession by the creditor. The system protects the debtor's interest in every conceivable way, except allowing him to have the property to start with, and this is done in pursuit of what we deem an acceptable arrangement *pendente lite* to put the property in the possession of the party who furnishes protection against loss or damage to the other pending trial on the merits. Here, the initial hardship to the debtor is limited, the seller has a strong interest, the process proceeds under judicial supervision and management, and the prevailing party is protected against all loss. Our conclusion is that the Louisiana standards regulating the use of the writ of sequestration are constitutional. Mitchell was not deprived of procedural due process in this case. The judgment of the Supreme Court of Louisiana is affirmed.

So ordered.

JUSTICE POWELL, concurring.

In sweeping language, *Fuentes v. Shevin,* 407 U.S. 67, 92 S.Ct. 1983, 32 L.Ed.2d 556 (1972), enunciated the principle that the constitutional guarantee of procedural due process requires an adversary hearing before an individual may be temporarily deprived of any possessory interest in tangible personal property, however brief the dispossession and however slight his monetary interest in the property. The Court's decision today withdraws significantly from the full reach of that principle, and to this extent I think it fair to say that the *Fuentes* opinion is overruled.

I could have agreed that the Florida and Pennsylvania statutes in *Fuentes* were violative of due process because of their arbitrary and unreasonable provisions. It seems to me, however, that it was unnecessary for the *Fuentes* opinion to have adopted so broad and inflexible a rule, especially one that considerably altered settled law with respect to commercial transactions and basic creditor-debtor understandings. Narrower grounds existed for invalidating the replevin statutes in that case.

* * *

that is to say, it is a prerequisite to their issuance that proper grounds be alleged and sworn to." *Id.* at 653–654, 237 So.2d at 672. (Emphasis added.) *Zion Mercantile Co. v. Pierce,* 163 La. 477, 112 So. 371 (1927), upon which petitioner relies, is not to the contrary. The Louisiana court merely held there that it is not necessary to "file" papers requesting the writ with the clerk, or pay court costs, before the judge is empowered to issue the writ.

II

Justice Stewart reproves the Court for not adhering strictly to the doctrine of *stare decisis*. To be sure, *stare decisis* promotes the important considerations of consistency and predictability in judicial decisions and represents a wise and appropriate policy in most instances. But that doctrine has never been thought to stand as an absolute bar to reconsideration of a prior decision, especially with respect to matters of constitutional interpretation.[2] Where the Court errs in its construction of a statute, correction may always be accomplished by legislative action. Revision of a constitutional interpretation, on the other hand, is often impossible as a practical matter, for it requires the cumbersome route of constitutional amendment. It is thus not only our prerogative but also our duty to re-examine a precedent where its reasoning or understanding of the Constitution is fairly called into question. And if the precedent or its rationale is of doubtful validity, then it should not stand. As Mr. Chief Justice Taney commented more than a century ago, a constitutional decision of this Court should be "always open to discussion when it is supposed to have been founded in error, [so] that [our] judicial authority should hereafter depend altogether on the force of the reasoning by which it is supported." *Passenger Cases*, 48 U.S. (7 How.) 283, 470, 12 L.Ed. 702 (1849).

Moreover, reconsideration is particularly appropriate in the present case. To the extent that the *Fuentes* opinion established a Procrustean rule of a prior adversary hearing, it marked a significant departure from past teachings as to the meaning of due process.[3] As the Court stated in *Cafeteria & Restaurant Workers Union v. McElroy*, 367 U.S. at 895, 81 S.Ct. at 1748, "[t]he very nature of due process negates any concept of inflexible procedures universally applicable to every imaginable situation." The *Fuentes* opinion not only eviscerated that principle but also sounded a potential death knell for a panoply of statutes in the commercial field. This fact alone justifies a re-examination of its premises. The

2. See *St. Joseph Stock Yards Co. v. United States*, 298 U.S. 38, 93, 56 S.Ct. 720, 744, 80 L.Ed. 1033 (1936) (Stone and Cardozo, JJ., concurring in result); *Burnet v. Coronado Oil & Gas Co.*, 285 U.S. 393, 405, 406–408, 52 S.Ct. 443, 446, 447–448, 76 L.Ed. 815 (1932) (Brandeis, J., dissenting). For the view that *stare decisis* need not always apply even to questions of statutory interpretation, see *Boys Markets, Inc. v. Retail Clerks Union*, 398 U.S. 235, 255, 90 S.Ct. 1583, 1594, 26 L.Ed.2d 199 (1970) (Stewart, J., concurring).

3. The *Fuentes* opinion relied primarily on *Sniadach v. Family Finance Corp.*, 395 U.S. 337, 89 S.Ct. 1820, 23 L.Ed.2d 349 (1969). That case involved a prejudgment garnishment of wages in which the creditor had no pre-existing property interest. It is readily distinguishable from the instant case where the creditor does have a pre[-]existing property interest as a result of the vendor's lien which attached upon execution of the installment sales contract. Indeed, depending on the number of installments which have been paid, the creditor's interest may often be greater than the debtor's. Thus, we deal here with mutual property interests, both of which are entitled to be safeguarded. *Fuentes* overlooked this vital point.

In addition, the Court recognized in *Sniadach* that prejudgment garnishment of wages could as a practical matter "impose tremendous hardship" and "drive a wage-earning family to the wall." By contrast, there is no basis for assuming that sequestration of a debtor's goods would necessarily place him in such a "brutal need" situation.

Court today reviews these at length, and I join its opinion because I think it represents a reaffirmation of the traditional meaning of procedural due process.

JUSTICE STEWART, with whom JUSTICE DOUGLAS and JUSTICE MARSHALL concur, dissenting.

The Louisiana sequestration procedure now before us is remarkably similar to the statutory provisions at issue in *Fuentes v. Shevin,* 407 U.S. 67, 92 S.Ct. 1983, 32 L.Ed.2d 556 (1972). In both cases the purchaser-in-possession of the property is not afforded any prior notice of the seizure or any opportunity to rebut the allegations of the vendor before the property is summarily taken from him by agents of the State. In both cases all that is required to support the issuance of the writ and seizure of the goods is the filing of a complaint and an affidavit containing *pro forma* allegations in support of the seller's purported entitlement to the goods in question. Since the procedure in both cases is completely *ex parte,* the state official charged with issuing the writ can do little more than determine the formal sufficiency of the plaintiff's allegations before ordering the state agents to take the goods from the defendant's possession.

The question before the Court in *Fuentes* was what procedures are required by the Due Process Clause of the Fourteenth Amendment when a State, at the behest of a private claimant, seizes goods in the possession of another, pending judicial resolution of the claimant's assertion of superior right to possess the property. The Court's analysis of this question began with the proposition that, except in exceptional circumstances, the deprivation of a property interest encompassed within the Fourteenth Amendment's protection must be preceded by notice to the affected party and an opportunity to be heard. The Court then went on to hold that a debtor-vendee's interest in the continued possession of purchased goods was "property" within the Fourteenth Amendment's protection and that the "temporary, nonfinal deprivation of [this] property [is] * * * a 'deprivation' in the terms of the Fourteenth Amendment." 407 U.S. at 85, 92 S.Ct. at 1996. Accordingly, *Fuentes* held that such a deprivation of property must be preceded by notice to the possessor and by an opportunity for a hearing appropriate under the circumstances. Matters such as requirements for the posting of bond and the filing of sworn factual allegations, the length and severity of the deprivation, the relative simplicity of the issues underlying the creditor's claim to possession, and the comparative "importance" or "necessity" of the goods involved were held to be relevant to determining the form of notice and hearing to be provided, but not to the constitutional need for notice and an opportunity for a hearing of some kind.

The deprivation of property in this case is identical to that at issue in *Fuentes,* and the Court does not say otherwise. Thus, under *Fuentes,* due process of law permits Louisiana to effect this deprivation only after notice to the possessor and opportunity for a hearing. Because I would adhere to the holding of *Fuentes,* I dissent from the Court's opinion and judgment upholding Louisiana's *ex parte* sequestration procedure, which provides that the possessor of the property shall never have advance notice or a hearing of any kind.

As already noted, the deprivation of property in this case is identical to that in *Fuentes*. But the Court says that this is a different case for three reasons: (1) the plaintiff who seeks the seizure of the property must file an affidavit stating "specific facts" that justify the sequestration; (2) the state official who issues the writ of sequestration is a judge instead of a clerk of the court; and (3) the issues that govern the plaintiff's right to sequestration are limited to "the existence of a vendor's lien and the issue of default," and "[t]here is thus far less danger here that the seizure will be mistaken and a corresponding decrease in the utility of an adversary hearing." The Court's opinion in *Fuentes,* however, explicitly rejected each of these factors as a ground for a difference in decision.

The first two purported distinctions relate solely to the procedure by which the creditor-vendor secures the State's aid in summarily taking goods from the purchaser's possession. But so long as the Louisiana law routinely permits an *ex parte* seizure without notice to the purchaser, these procedural distinctions make no constitutional difference.

The Louisiana affidavit requirement can be met by any plaintiff who fills in the blanks on the appropriate form documents and presents the completed forms to the court. Although the standardized form in this case called for somewhat more information than that required by the Florida and Pennsylvania statutes challenged in *Fuentes,* such *ex parte* allegations "are hardly a substitute for a prior hearing, for they test no more than the strength of the applicant's own belief in his rights. Since his private gain is at stake, the danger is all too great that his confidence in his cause will be misplaced. Lawyers and judges are familiar with the phenomenon of a party mistakenly but firmly convinced that his view of the facts and law will prevail, and therefore quite willing to risk the costs of litigation." 407 U.S. at 83, 92 S.Ct. at 1995.

Similarly, the fact that the official who signs the writ after the *ex parte* application is a judge instead of a court clerk is of no constitutional significance. Outside Orleans Parish, this same function is performed by the court clerk. There is nothing to suggest that the nature of this duty was at all changed when the law was amended to vest it in a judge rather than a clerk in this one parish. Indeed, the official comments declare that this statutory revision was intended to "mak[e] no change in the law." Whether the issuing functionary be a judge or a court clerk, he can in any event do no more than ascertain the formal sufficiency of the plaintiff's allegations, after which the issuance of the summary writ becomes a simple ministerial act.[4]

4. The Louisiana authorities cited by the Court are not to the contrary. *Wright v. Hughes,* 254 So.2d 293 (La.Ct.App.1971), and *Hancock Bank v. Alexander,* 256 La. 643, 237 So.2d 669 (1970), stand only for the proposition that a writ should not issue unless the sworn allegations are formally sufficient, which may mean nothing more

The third distinction the Court finds between this case and *Fuentes* is equally insubstantial. The Court says the issues in this case are "particularly suited" to *ex parte* determination, in contrast to the issues in *Fuentes,* which were "inherently subject to factual determination and adversarial input." There is, however, absolutely no support for this purported distinction. In this case the Court states the factual issues as "the existence of a vendor's lien and the issue of default." The issues upon which replevin depended in *Fuentes* were no different; the creditor-vendor needed only to establish his security interest and the debtor-vendee's default. As Mr. Justice White acknowledged in his *Fuentes* dissent, the essential issue at any hearing would be whether "there is reasonable basis for his [the creditor-vendor's] claim of default." 407 U.S. at 99–100, 92 S.Ct. at 2004. Thus, the Court produces this final attempted distinction out of whole cloth.

Moreover, *Fuentes* held that the relative complexity of the issues in dispute is not relevant to determining whether a prior hearing is required by due process. "The issues decisive of the ultimate right to continued possession, of course, may be quite simple. The simplicity of the issues might be relevant to the formality or scheduling of a prior hearing. But it certainly cannot undercut the right to a prior hearing of some kind." *Id.* at 87 n. 18, 92 S.Ct. at 1998 (citation omitted). Similarly, the probability of success on the factual issue does not affect the right to prior notice and an opportunity to be heard.

In short, this case is constitutionally indistinguishable from *Fuentes v. Shevin,* and the Court today has simply rejected the reasoning of that case and adopted instead the analysis of the *Fuentes* dissent. In light of all that has been written in *Fuentes* and in this case, it seems pointless to prolong the debate. Suffice it to say that I would reverse the judgment before us because the Louisiana sequestration procedure fails to comport with the requirements of due process of law.

I would add, however, a word of concern. It seems to me that unless we respect the constitutional decisions of this Court, we can hardly expect that others will do so. *Cf. Roofing Wholesale Co. v. Palmer,* 108 Ariz. 508, 502 P.2d 1327 (1972). A substantial departure from precedent can only be justified, I had thought, in the light of experience with the application of the rule to be abandoned or in the light of an altered historic environment. Yet the Court today has unmistakably overruled a considered decision of this Court that is barely two years old, without pointing to any change in either societal perceptions or basic constitutional understandings that might justify this total disregard of *stare decisis.*

The *Fuentes* decision was in a direct line of recent cases in this Court that have applied the procedural due process commands of the Fourteenth Amendment to prohibit governmental action that deprives a person of a statutory or contractual property interest with no advance

than that the proper standardized form be completely filled in.

notice or opportunity to be heard.[5] In the short time that has elapsed since the *Fuentes* case was decided, many state and federal courts have followed it in assessing the constitutional validity of state replevin statutes and other comparable state laws. No data have been brought to our attention to indicate that these decisions, granting to otherwise defenseless consumers the simple rudiments of due process of law, have worked any untoward change in the consumer credit market or in other commercial relationships. The only perceivable change that has occurred since *Fuentes* is in the makeup of this Court.[8]

A basic change in the law upon a ground no firmer than a change in our membership invites the popular misconception that this institution is little different from the two political branches of the Government. No misconception could do more lasting injury to this Court and to the system of law which it is our abiding mission to serve.

JUSTICE BRENNAN is in agreement that *Fuentes v. Shevin*, 407 U.S. 67, 92 S.Ct. 1983, 32 L.Ed.2d 556 (1972), requires reversal of the judgment of the Supreme Court of Louisiana.

NORTH GEORGIA FINISHING, INC. v. DI-CHEM, INC.

Supreme Court of the United States, 1975.
419 U.S. 601, 95 S.Ct. 719, 42 L.Ed.2d 751.

JUSTICE WHITE delivered the opinion of the Court.

Under the statutes of the State of Georgia, plaintiffs in pending suits are "entitled to the process of garnishment." Ga.Code Ann. § 46–101. To employ the process, plaintiff or his attorney must make an affidavit before "some officer authorized to issue an attachment, or the clerk of any court of record in which the said garnishment is being filed or in which the main case is filed, stating the amount claimed to be due in such action * * * and that he has reason to apprehend the loss of the same or some part thereof unless process of garnishment shall issue." § 146–102. To protect defendant against loss or damage in the event plaintiff fails to recover, that section also requires plaintiff to file a bond in a sum double the amount sworn to be due. Section 46–401 permits the defendant to dissolve the garnishment by filing a bond "conditioned for the payment of any judgment that shall be rendered on said garnishment." Whether these provisions satisfy the Due Process Clause of the Fourteenth Amendment is the issue before us in this case.

On August 20, 1971, respondent filed suit against petitioner in the Superior Court of Whitfield County, Ga., alleging an indebtedness due

---

5. *See, e.g., Goldberg v. Kelly*, 397 U.S. 254, 90 S.Ct. 1011, 25 L.Ed.2d 287 (1970); *Sniadach v. Family Finance Corp.*, 395 U.S. 337, 89 S.Ct. 1820, 23 L.Ed.2d 349 (1969); and *Bell v. Burson*, 402 U.S. 535, 91 S.Ct. 1586, 29 L.Ed.2d 90 (1971).

8. Although Mr. Justice Powell and Mr. Justice Rehnquist were Members of the Court at the time that *Fuentes v. Shevin* was announced, they were not Members of the Court when that case was argued, and they did not participate in its "consideration or decision." 407 U.S. at 97, 92 S.Ct. at 2002.

and owing from petitioner for goods sold and delivered in the amount of $51,279.17. Simultaneously with the filing of the complaint and prior to its service on petitioner, respondent filed affidavit and bond for process of garnishment, naming the First National Bank of Dalton as garnishee. The affidavit asserted the debt and "reason to apprehend the loss of said sum or some part thereof unless process of Garnishment issues."[2] The clerk of the Superior Court forthwith issued summons of garnishment to the bank, which was served that day. On August 23, petitioner filed a bond in the Superior Court conditioned to pay any final judgment in the main action up to the amount claimed, and the judge of that court thereupon discharged the bank as garnishee. On September 15, petitioner filed a motion to dismiss the writ of garnishment and to discharge its bond, asserting, among other things, that the statutory garnishment procedure was unconstitutional in that it violated "defendant's due process and equal protection rights guaranteed him by the Constitution of the United States and the Constitution of the State of Georgia." App. 11. The motion was heard and overruled on November 29. The Georgia Supreme Court,[3] finding that the issue of the constitutionality of the statutory garnishment procedure was properly before it, sustained the statute and rejected petitioner's claims that the statute was invalid for failure to provide notice and hearing in connection with the issuance of the writ of garnishment. 231 Ga. 260, 201 S.E.2d 321 (1973).[4] We granted certiorari. We reverse.

The Georgia court recognized that *Sniadach v. Family Finance Corp.,* 395 U.S. 337, 89 S.Ct. 1820, 23 L.Ed.2d 349 (1969) had invalidated a statute permitting the garnishment of wages without notice and opportunity for hearing, but considered that case to have done nothing more than to carve out an exception, in favor of wage earners, "to the general rule of legality of garnishment statutes." The garnishment of other assets or properties pending the outcome of the main action, although the effect was to " 'impound [them] in the hands of the

2. The affidavit in its entirety was as follows:

"SUPERIOR COURT OF *Whitfield* COUNTY GEORGIA, *Whitfield* COUNTY.

"Personally appeared *R. L. Foster, President of Di–Chem, Inc.,* who on oath says that he is *President of DiChem, Inc.,* plaintiff herein and that *North Georgia Finishing, Inc.,* defendant, is indebted to said plaintiff in the sum of $51,279.17 DOLLARS, principal, $_____, interest, $_____, attorney's fees, and $_____ cost and that said plaintiff has—a suit pending—*returnable to the* Superior Court of *Whitfield* County, and that affiant has reason to apprehend the loss of said sum or some part thereof unless process of Garnishment issues.

"Sworn to and subscribed before me, this *August* 20, 1971.

"/s/*Dual Broadrick,* Clerk

"/s/ *R. L. Foster,* Affiant.

"Superior Court of *Whitfield* County." App. 3–4.

3. Appeal was taken in the first instance to the Georgia Supreme Court. That court, without opinion, transferred the case to the Georgia Court of Appeals. The latter court issued an opinion, 127 Ga.App. 593, 194 S.E.2d 508 (1972). The Georgia Supreme Court then issued certiorari, 230 Ga. 623, 198 S.E.2d 284 (1973).

4. Subsequent to the Georgia Supreme Court's decision in this case, a three-judge federal court, sitting in the Northern District of Georgia declared these same statutory provisions unconstitutional. *Morrow Electric Co. v. Cruse,* 370 F.Supp. 639 (N.D.Ga.1974).

garnishee,' " was apparently thought not to implicate the Due Process Clause.

This approach failed to take account of *Fuentes v. Shevin,* 407 U.S. 67, 92 S.Ct. 1983, 32 L.Ed.2d 556 (1972), a case decided by this Court more than a year prior to the Georgia court's decision. There the Court held invalid the Florida and Pennsylvania replevin statutes which permitted a secured installment seller to repossess the goods sold, without notice or hearing and without judicial order or supervision, but with the help of the sheriff operating under a writ issued by the clerk of the court at the behest of the seller. That the debtor was deprived of only the use and possession of the property, and perhaps only temporarily, did not put the seizure beyond scrutiny under the Due Process Clause. "The Fourteenth Amendment draws no bright lines around three-day, 10–day, or 50–day deprivations of property. Any significant taking of property by the State is within the purview of the Due Process Clause." *Id.* at 86, 92 S.Ct. at 1997. Although the length or severity of a deprivation of use or possession would be another factor to weigh in determining the appropriate form of hearing, it was not deemed to be determinative of the right to a hearing of some sort. Because the official seizures had been carried out without notice and without opportunity for a hearing or other safeguard against mistaken repossession they were held to be in violation of the Fourteenth Amendment.

The Georgia statute is vulnerable for the same reasons. Here, a bank account, surely a form of property, was impounded and, absent a bond, put totally beyond use during the pendency of the litigation on the alleged debt, all by a writ of garnishment issued by a court clerk without notice or opportunity for an early hearing and without participation by a judicial officer.

Nor is the statute saved by the more recent decision in *Mitchell v. W. T. Grant Co.,* 416 U.S. 600, 94 S.Ct. 1895, 40 L.Ed.2d 406 (1974).

The Georgia garnishment statute has none of the saving characteristics of the Louisiana statute. The writ of garnishment is issuable on the affidavit of the creditor or his attorney, and the latter need not have personal knowledge of the facts. § 46–103. The affidavit, like the one filed in this case, need contain only conclusory allegations. The writ is issuable, as this one was, by the court clerk, without participation by a judge. Upon service of the writ, the debtor is deprived of the use of the property in the hands of the garnishee. Here a sizable bank account was frozen, and the only method discernible on the face of the statute to dissolve the garnishment was to file a bond to protect the plaintiff creditor. There is no provision for an early hearing at which the creditor would be required to demonstrate at least probable cause for the garnishment. Indeed, it would appear that without the filing of a bond the defendant debtor's challenge to the garnishment will not be entertained, whatever the grounds may be.

Respondent also argues that neither *Fuentes* nor *Mitchell* is apposite here because each of those cases dealt with the application of due process protections to consumers who are victims of contracts of adhesion and who might be irreparably damaged by temporary deprivation of household necessities, whereas this case deals with its application in the commercial setting to a case involving parties of equal bargaining power. *See also Sniadach v. Family Finance Corp.*, 395 U.S. 337, 89 S.Ct. 1820, 23 L.Ed.2d 349 (1969). It is asserted in addition that the double bond posted here gives assurance to petitioner that it will be made whole in the event the garnishment turns out to be unjustified. It may be that consumers deprived of household appliances will more likely suffer irreparably than corporations deprived of bank accounts, but the probability of irreparable injury in the latter case is sufficiently great so that some procedures are necessary to guard against the risk of initial error. We are no more inclined now than we have been in the past to distinguish among different kinds of property in applying the Due Process Clause. *Fuentes v. Shevin*, 407 U.S. at 89–90, 92 S.Ct. at 1998–1999.

Enough has been said, we think, to require the reversal of the judgment of the Georgia Supreme Court. The case is remanded to that court for further proceedings not inconsistent with this opinion.

So ordered.

Judgment reversed and case remanded.

JUSTICE STEWART, concurring.

It is gratifying to note that my report of the demise of *Fuentes v. Shevin*, 407 U.S. 67, 92 S.Ct. 1983, 32 L.Ed.2d 556, see *Mitchell v. W.T. Grant Co.*, 416 U.S. 600, 629–36, 94 S.Ct. 1895, 1910–14, 40 L.Ed.2d 406 (dissenting opinion), seems to have been greatly exaggerated. *Cf.* S. Clemens, Cable from Europe to the Associated Press, quoted in 2 A. Paine, Mark Twain: A Biography 1039 (1912).

JUSTICE POWELL, concurring in the judgment.

I join in the Court's judgment, but I cannot concur in the opinion as I think it sweeps more broadly than is necessary and appears to resuscitate *Fuentes v. Shevin*. * * * Only last term in *Mitchell v. W. T. Grant Co.*, 416 U.S. 600, 629–30, 94 S.Ct. 1895, 40 L.Ed.2d 406, the Court significantly narrowed the precedential scope of *Fuentes*. In my concurrence in *Mitchell,* I noted:

> The Court's decision today withdraws significantly from the full reach of [*Fuentes'*] principle, and to this extent I think it fair to say that the *Fuentes* opinion is overruled. 416 U.S. at 623, 94 S.Ct. at 1908 (Powell, J., concurring).

Three dissenting Justices, including the author of *Fuentes*, went further in their description of the impact of *Mitchell:*

> [T]he Court today has unmistakably overruled a considered decision of this Court that is barely two years old, without pointing to any change * * * that might justify this total disregard of *stare decisis*.

416 U.S. at 635, 94 S.Ct. at 1913 (Stewart, J., joined by Douglas and Marshall, JJ., dissenting).

The Court's opinion in this case, relying substantially on *Fuentes,* suggests that that decision will again be read as calling into question much of the previously settled law governing commercial transactions. I continue to doubt whether *Fuentes* strikes a proper balance, especially in cases where the creditor's interest in the property may be as significant or even greater than that of the debtor. Nor do I find it necessary to relegate *Mitchell* to its narrow factual setting in order to determine that the Georgia garnishment statutes fail to satisfy the requirements of procedural due process.

* * *

Pregarnishment notice and a prior hearing have not been constitutionally mandated in the past. Despite the ambiguity engendered by the Court's reliance on *Fuentes,* I do not interpret its opinion today as imposing these requirements for the future.[2] Such restrictions, antithetical to the very purpose of the remedy, would leave little efficacy to the garnishment and attachment laws of the 50 States.

* * *

The most compelling deficiency in the Georgia procedure is its failure to provide a prompt and adequate postgarnishment hearing. Under Georgia law, garnishment is a separate proceeding between the garnishor and the garnishee. The debtor is not a party and can intervene only by filing a dissolution bond and substituting himself for the garnishee. [Citations omitted.]

I consider the combination of these deficiencies to be fatal to the Georgia statute. Quite simply, the Georgia provisions fail to afford fundamental fairness in their accommodation of the respective interests of creditor and debtor. For these reasons, I join in the judgment of the Court.

JUSTICE BLACKMUN, with whom JUSTICE REHNQUIST joins, dissenting.

The Court once again—for the third time in less than three years—struggles with what it regards as the due process aspects of a State's old and long-unattacked commercial statutes designed to afford a way for relief to a creditor against a delinquent debtor. On this third occasion, the Court, it seems to me, does little more than make very general and very sparse comparisons of the present case with *Fuentes v. Shevin,* 407 U.S. 67, 92 S.Ct. 1983, 32 L.Ed.2d 556 (1972), on the one hand, and with

---

2. The Court also cites *Sniadach v. Family Finance Corp.,* 395 U.S. 337, 89 S.Ct. 1820, 23 L.Ed.2d 349 (1969), which established an exception for garnishment of an individual's wages. In such cases, the Due Process Clause requires notice and a hearing *prior* to application of the garnishment remedy. As the opinion itself indicates, however, the *Sniadach* rule is limited to wages, "a specialized type of property presenting distinct problems in our economic system." The Court did not purport to impose requirements of pregarnishment notice and hearing in other instances. I therefore do not consider *Sniadach* to be more than peripherally relevant to the present case.

Mitchell v. W. T. Grant Co., 416 U.S. 600, 94 S.Ct. 1895, 40 L.Ed.2d 406 (1974), on the other; concludes that this case resembles *Fuentes* more than it does *Mitchell;* and then strikes down the Georgia statutory structure as offensive to due process. One gains the impression, particularly from the final paragraph of its opinion, that the Court is endeavoring to say as little as possible in explaining just why the Supreme Court of Georgia is being reversed. And, as a result, the corresponding commercial statutes of all other States, similar to but not exactly like those of Florida or Pennsylvania or Louisiana or Georgia, are left in questionable constitutional status, with little or no applicable standard by which to measure and determine their validity under the Fourteenth Amendment. This, it seems to me, is an undesirable state of affairs, and I dissent. I do so for a number of reasons:

1. *Sniadach v. Family Finance Corp.*, 395 U.S. 337, 89 S.Ct. 1820, 23 L.Ed.2d 349 (1969), mentioned in passing by the Court in its present opinion, was correctly regarded by the Georgia Supreme Court as a case relating to the garnishment of *wages*. The opinion in *Sniadach* makes this emphasis:

> We deal here with wages—a specialized type of property presenting distinct problems in our economic system. We turn then to the nature of that property and problems of procedural due process.

> 395 U.S. at 340, 89 S.Ct. at 1822.

It goes on to speak of possible "tremendous hardship on wage earners with families to support," *ibid.*, and the "enormous" leverage of the creditor "on the wage earner." *Sniadach* should be allowed to remain in its natural environment—wages—and not be expanded to arm's-length relationships between business enterprises of such financial consequence as North Georgia Finishing and Di–Chem.

* * *

3. I would have thought that, whatever *Fuentes* may have stood for in this area of debtor-creditor commercial relationships, with its 4–3 vote by a bobtailed Court, it was substantially cut back by *Mitchell*. Certainly, Mr. Justice Stewart, the author of *Fuentes* and the writer of the dissenting opinion in *Mitchell*, thought so:

> The deprivation of property in this case is identical to that at issue in *Fuentes,* and the Court does not say otherwise. 416 U.S. at 631, 94 S.Ct. at 1911.

> In short, this case is constitutionally indistinguishable from *Fuentes v. Shevin*, and the Court today has simply rejected the reasoning of that case and adopted instead the analysis of the *Fuentes* dissent. *Id.* at 634, 94 S.Ct. at 1913.

> Yet the Court today has unmistakably overruled a considered decision of this Court that is barely two years old * * *. The only perceivable change that has occurred since the *Fuentes* case is in the makeup of this Court. *Id.* at 635, 94 S.Ct. at 1913.

Surely, Mr. Justice Brennan thought so when he asserted in dissent that he was "in agreement that *Fuentes* * * * requires reversal" of the Louisiana judgment. And surely, Mr. Justice Powell thought so, substantially, when, in his concurrence, he observed:

> The Court's decision today withdraws significantly from the full reach of [the *Fuentes*] principle, and to this extent I think it fair to say that the *Fuentes* opinion is overruled. *Id.* at 623, 94 S.Ct. at 1908.

I accept the views of these dissenting and concurring Justices in *Mitchell* that *Fuentes* at least was severely limited by *Mitchell,* and I cannot regard *Fuentes* as of much influence or precedent for the present case.

4. *Fuentes,* a constitutional decision, obviously should not have been brought down and decided by a 4–3 vote when there were two vacancies on the Court at the time of argument. It particularly should not have been decided by a 4–3 vote when Justices filling the vacant seats had qualified and were on hand and available to participate on reargument. Announcing the constitutional decision, with a four-Justice majority of a seven-Justice shorthanded Court, did violence to Mr. Chief Justice Marshall's wise assurance, in *Briscoe v. Commonwealth's Bank of Kentucky,* 8 Pet. 118, 122, 9 L.Ed. 709 (1834), that the practice of the Court "except in cases of absolute necessity" is not to decide a constitutional question unless there is a majority "of the whole court."

The Court encountered the same situation a century ago with respect to the *Legal Tender Cases;* mishandled the decisional process similarly; and came to regret the error. Originally, in *Hepburn v. Griswold,* 8 Wall. 603, 19 L.Ed. 513 (1870), the Court, assertedly by a 5–3 vote, with one vacancy, held the Legal Tender Act of 1862, 12 Stat. 345, to be unconstitutional with respect to prior debts. Mr. Justice Grier, who was in failing health, was noted as concurring. 8 Wall. at 626. It was stated that the case "was decided in conference" on November 27, 1869, and the opinion "directed to be read" on January 29, 1870. *Ibid.* Mr. Justice Grier, however, had submitted his resignation to the President in December 1869, effective February 1, 1870, and it had been accepted on December 15. The Justice last sat on January 31. 8 Wall. at vii–viii. The opinion and judgment in *Hepburn* actually were rendered on February 7, when Mr. Justice Grier was no longer on the bench.

A year later, with the two vacancies filled, the Court, by a 5–4 vote, overruled *Hepburn* and held the Legal Tender Act constitutional with respect to all debts. *Legal Tender Cases,* 12 Wall. 457, 20 L.Ed. 287 (1871). The Court said:

> That case [*Hepburn v. Griswold*] was decided by a divided court, and by a court having a less number of judges than the law then in existence provided this court shall have. * * * We have been in the habit of treating cases involving a consideration of constitutional power differently from those which concern merely private right [citing *Briscoe v. Commonwealth's Bank of Kentucky*]. We are not

accustomed to hear them in the absence of a full court, if it can be avoided. *Id.* at 553–554.

The failure in *Hepburn* to recall or adhere to the practice announced by the Marshall Court resulted in confusion, prompt reversal of position, embarrassment, and recrimination. *See* the opinion of Mr. Chief Justice Chase in dissent. 12 Wall. at 572.

* * *

The admonition of the Great Chief Justice, in my view, should override any natural, and perhaps understandable, eagerness to decide. Had we bowed to that wisdom when *Fuentes* was before us, and waited a brief time for reargument before a full Court, whatever its decision might have been, I venture to suggest that we would not be immersed in confusion, with *Fuentes* one way, *Mitchell* another, and now this case decided in a manner that leaves counsel and the commercial communities in other States uncertain as to whether their own established and long-accepted statutes pass constitutional muster with a wavering tribunal off in Washington, D.C. This Court surely fails in its intended purpose when confusing results of this kind are forthcoming and are imposed upon those who owe and those who lend.

5. Neither do I conclude that, because this is a garnishment case, rather than a lien or vendor-vendee case, it is automatically controlled by *Sniadach. Sniadach,* as has been noted, concerned and reeks of wages. North Georgia Finishing is no wage earner. It is a corporation engaged in business. It was protected (a) by the fact that the garnishment procedure may be instituted in Georgia only after the primary suit has been filed or judgment obtained by the creditor, thus placing on the creditor the obligation to initiate the proceedings and the burden of proof, and assuring a full hearing to the debtor; (b) by the respondent's statutorily required and deposited double bond; and (c) by the requirement of the respondent's affidavit of apprehension of loss. It was in a position to dissolve the garnishment by the filing of a single bond. These are transactions of a day-to-day type in the commercial world. They are not situations involving contracts of adhesion or basic unfairness, imbalance, or inequality.

* * *

6. Despite its apparent disclaimer, the Court now has embarked on a case-by-case analysis (weighted heavily in favor of *Fuentes* and with little hope under *Mitchell*) of the respective state statutes in this area. That road is a long and unrewarding one, and provides no satisfactory answers to issues of constitutional magnitude.

I would affirm the judgment of the Supreme Court of Georgia.

CHIEF JUSTICE BURGER dissents for the reasons stated in numbered paragraph 5 of the opinion of JUSTICE BLACKMUN.

Notes and Questions

1.   Justice White, joined by the Chief Justice and Justice Blackmun (the dissenters in *Fuentes*), and Justices Rehnquist and Powell (the non-participating Justices in *Fuentes*), wrote the majority opinion in *Mitchell*. What effect did the change in the Court's membership after *Fuentes* have on the law respecting a debtor's right to a pre-garnishment hearing? Justice Blackmun, dissenting in *Di-Chem*, faulted the *Fuentes* Court for deciding an important constitutional case when there were two vacancies on the Court at the time of argument and particularly where the two Justices (Rehnquist and Powell) were available to participate prior to the decision. Does this background help you understand the *Mitchell* Court's handling of *Fuentes*? Was the Arizona Supreme Court correct in not following *Fuentes*? *See* note 5, *supra* pp. 238–39.

2.   Are *Fuentes* and *Mitchell* distinguishable on their facts? Or are the distinctions specified in the *Mitchell* majority opinion contrived? Consider the following factors relied upon in *Mitchell:*

a.   the affidavit in support of the writ of sequestration must contain specific facts clearly establishing "the nature of the claim, and the amount thereof, if any, and the grounds relied upon." How does this differ from *Fuentes?*

b.   the order of sequestration is signed by a judge rather than a clerk.

c.   the debtor is expressly provided the opportunity for an immediate post-sequestration hearing to dissolve the writ.

3.   *Sniadach* is distinguishable from *Fuentes* and *Mitchell* in at least one significant respect. The *Sniadach* creditor did not possess any co-existing interest in the debtor's wages. Should *Fuentes* have analyzed this distinction more comprehensively? Should the *Fuentes* Court have expressly attempted to balance the interests of creditors and debtors having co-existing interests in the property?

4.   Consider the following language from the dissent of Justice Stewart (who, incidentally, authored *Fuentes*):

[*Mitchell*] * * * has unmistakenly overruled a considered decision of this Court that is barely two years old, without pointing to any change in either societal perceptions or basic constitutional understandings that might justify this total disregard of *stare decisis.*

416 U.S. at 635. Yet in *Di-Chem* Justice Stewart admitted that this report of the demise of *Fuentes* was exaggerated. Would you characterize the *Fuentes, Mitchell,* and *Di-Chem* trilogy as a comedy of errors?

5.   What should the Court do when it is convinced that a doctrine of constitutional law is no longer viable? Resort to the constitutional amendatory process has been extremely rare. What accounts for this sparing use of the amendatory process?

While a judicial precedent on a constitutional issue stands, it is a barrier against mere legislative overrule.

Justice Powell, concurring in *Mitchell*, expressed his belief that *Mitchell* overruled *Fuentes*. Carefully analyze his justification for departing from *stare decisis* in constitutional adjudication. For further discussion of the doctrine of *stare decisis*, see *supra* Chapter I, Section E.

6. *Mitchell* characterized the pre-*Sniadach* cases as follows: "They merely stand for the proposition that a hearing must be had before one is finally deprived of his property and do not deal at all with the need for a predetermination hearing where a full and immediate post-termination hearing is provided." Reconsider *Sniadach* and *Fuentes*. Was the Court's characterization fair? Are the repeated references in these cases to the right to a prior hearing now relegated to mere *dicta*?

7. The majority in *Mitchell* asserted that *Fuentes* was decided "against a factual and legal background sufficiently different" from the one before the Court. Certainly the statement did not refer to the nonparticipation of Justices Powell and Rehnquist? To what then did it refer?

8. *Di-Chem* was decided just one year after *Mitchell*. The Court recast (or if you prefer Justice Powell's term, "resuscitated") *Fuentes* as constitutionally requiring an opportunity for a "hearing *or other safeguard* against mistaken repossession." What happened to the pre-seizure hearing? And what was meant by the phrase "or other safeguard"? The participation of a judicial officer? A detailed factual affidavit? An opportunity for an immediate post-seizure hearing? All of the foregoing?

9. Did *Di-Chem* reject *Sniadach* as controlling authority? Should a pre-seizure hearing be constitutionally mandated when dealing with wages?

10. You are requested by a state legislative committee to draft a statute that would allow creditors, in connection with prejudgment civil proceedings, to constitutionally seize a debtor's property without notice and without an opportunity for a pre-seizure hearing. Do the Supreme Court cases give sufficient guidance for such a statute? Must the statute require the posting of a bond? *See Connecticut v. Doehr,* 501 U.S. 1, 111 S. Ct. 2105 (1991) (striking down a state statute authorizing prejudgment attachment without prior notice or hearing and without requiring that the creditor post a bond).

11. Do the principles of *Sniadach, Fuentes, Mitchell,* and *Di-Chem* radiate beyond the realm of prejudgment seizures? Consider the plight of Beatrice Finberg, a widow solely dependent upon social security retirement benefits for her income. Sterling Consumer Discount Company sued her in the Pennsylvania courts to enforce a debt. It obtained a default judgment and immediately moved to execute on the judgment by garnishing Mrs. Finberg's checking and savings accounts in a Philadelphia bank. The garnishment process enjoined the bank from paying out any of the monies on deposit in Mrs. Finberg's accounts. Under the Social Security Act, the money in these accounts was entirely exempt from attachment and execution. Mrs. Finberg received no notice of the proceedings before the garnishment and had no opportunity to litigate her exemption claims. The Pennsylvania law gave the creditor fifteen days within which to respond to any motion filed by Mrs. Finberg to set aside the garnishment proceedings. Is the Pennsylvania procedure constitutional? *See Finberg v. Sullivan,* 634 F.2d 50 (3d Cir. 1980) (*en banc.*) *See supra* note 7, p. 239.

12. For further developments in this area, see *Trainor v. Hernandez*, Chapter VI, Section D.

D. THIRD EXERCISE IN SYNTHESIS: CASES INVOLVING CHOICE OF LAW IN SUITS BROUGHT BY GUESTS AGAINST HOSTS

In tort cases, the traditional choice of law rule mandated that the law of the place of the wrong be applied to resolve substantive legal issues. The place of the wrong usually referred to the place where the injury occurred. This rule, known as *lex loci delictus,* caused few problems since the wrongful act and the resulting injury normally occurred in the same state. But what if the state where the injury occurred had no other contact with the case? For example, suppose a commercial plane carrying passengers from New York to San Francisco fortuitously crashes in the four corners area (the point where Arizona, Utah, New Mexico, and Colorado meet). If the substantive tort laws of these states differ, should the result of a case depend upon the exact location of the crash? Or to take another case, why should the liability of a host to her guest be governed by the law of the state of the injury if that state has no other meaningful contacts with the case? We now examine four New York cases involving choice of law issues in suits by guests against their hosts.

BABCOCK v. JACKSON
Court of Appeals of New York, 1963.
12 N.Y.2d 473, 191 N.E.2d 279, 240 N.Y.S.2d 743.

FULD, JUDGE. On Friday, September 16, 1960, Miss Georgia Babcock and her friends, Mr. and Mrs. William Jackson, all residents of Rochester, left that city in Mr. Jackson's automobile, Miss Babcock as guest, for a week-end trip to Canada. Some hours later, as Mr. Jackson was driving in the Province of Ontario, he apparently lost control of the car; it went off the highway into an adjacent stone wall, and Miss Babcock was seriously injured. Upon her return to this State, she brought the present action against William Jackson, alleging negligence on his part in operating his automobile.

At the time of the accident, there was in force in Ontario a statute providing that "the owner or driver of a motor vehicle, other than a vehicle operated in the business of carrying passengers for compensation, is not liable for any loss or damage resulting from bodily injury to, or the death of any person being carried in * * * the motor vehicle" (Highway Traffic Act of Province of Ontario [Ontario Rev.Stat. (1960), ch. 172], § 105, subd. [2]). Even though no such bar is recognized under this State's substantive law of torts * * * the defendant moved to dismiss the complaint on the ground that the law of the place where the accident occurred governs and that Ontario's guest statute bars recovery. The court at Special Term, agreeing with the defendant, granted the motion and the Appellate Division * * * affirmed the judgment of dismissal without opinion.

The question presented is simply drawn. Shall the law of the place of the tort[2] *invariably* govern the availability of relief for the tort or shall the applicable choice of law rule also reflect a consideration of other factors which are relevant to the purposes served by the enforcement or denial of the remedy?

The traditional choice of law rule, embodied in the original Restatement of Conflict of Laws (§ 384), and until recently unquestioningly followed in this court * * * has been that the substantive rights and liabilities arising out of a tortious occurrence are determinable by the law of the place of the tort. * * * It had its conceptual foundation in the vested rights doctrine, namely, that a right to recover for a foreign tort owes its creation to the law of the jurisdiction where the injury occurred and depends for its existence and extent solely on such law. * * * [T]he vested rights doctrine has long since been discredited * * *. More particularly, as applied to torts, the theory ignores the interest which jurisdictions other than that where the tort occurred may have in the resolution of particular issues. It is for this very reason that, despite the advantages of certainty, ease of application and predictability which it affords * * * there has in recent years been increasing criticism of the traditional rule by commentators and a judicial trend towards its abandonment or modification.

* * *

In *Auten v. Auten,* 308 N.Y. 155, 124 N.E.2d 99, * * * this court * * * applied what has been termed the "center of gravity" or "grouping of contacts" theory of the conflict of laws. "Under this theory," we declared in the Auten case, "the courts, instead of regarding as conclusive the parties' intention or the place of making or performance, lay emphasis rather upon the law of the place 'which has the most significant contacts with the matter in dispute' " (308 N.Y. at 160, 124 N.E.2d at 101–102). * * *

The "center of gravity" or "grouping of contacts" doctrine adopted by this court in conflicts cases involving contracts impresses us as likewise affording the appropriate approach for accommodating the competing interests in tort cases with multi-State contacts. Justice, fairness and "the best practical result" (*Swift & Co. v. Bankers Trust Co.,* 280 N.Y. 135, 141, 19 N.E.2d 992, 995) * * * may best be achieved by giving controlling effect to the law of the jurisdiction which, because of its relationship or contact with the occurrence or the parties, has the greatest concern with the specific issue raised in the litigation. * * *

2. In this case, as in nearly all such cases, the conduct causing injury and the injury itself occurred in the same jurisdiction. The phrase "place of the tort," as distinguished from "place of wrong" and "place of injury," is used herein to designate the place where both the wrong and the injury took place.

Comparison of the relative "contacts" and "interests" of New York and Ontario in this litigation, vis-a-vis the issue here presented, makes it clear that the concern of New York is unquestionably the greater and more direct and that the interest of Ontario is at best minimal. The present action involves injuries sustained by a New York guest as the result of the negligence of a New York host in the operation of an automobile, garaged, licensed and undoubtedly insured in New York, in the course of a week-end journey which began and was to end there. In sharp contrast, Ontario's sole relationship with the occurrence is the purely adventitious circumstance that the accident occurred there.

New York's policy of requiring a tort-feasor to compensate his guest for injuries caused by his negligence cannot be doubted—as attested by the fact that the Legislature of this State has repeatedly refused to enact a statute denying or limiting recovery in such cases (*see, e.g.,* 1930 Sen.Int.No. 339, Pr.No. 349; 1935 Sen.Int.No. 168, Pr. No. 170; 1960 Sen.Int.No. 3662, Pr.No. 3967)—and our courts have neither reason nor warrant for departing from that policy simply because the accident, solely affecting New York residents and arising out of the operation of a New York based automobile, happened beyond its borders. Per contra, Ontario has no conceivable interest in denying a remedy to a New York guest against his New York host for injuries suffered in Ontario by reason of conduct which was tortious under Ontario law. The object of Ontario's guest statute, it has been said, is "to prevent the fraudulent assertion of claims by passengers, in collusion with the drivers, against insurance companies" (Survey of Canadian Legislation, 1 U. Toronto L.J. 358, 366) and, quite obviously, the fraudulent claims intended to be prevented by the statute are those asserted against Ontario defendants and their insurance carriers, not New York defendants and their insurance carriers. Whether New York defendants are imposed upon or their insurers defrauded by a New York plaintiff is scarcely a valid legislative concern of Ontario simply because the accident occurred there, any more so than if the accident had happened in some other jurisdiction.

It is hardly necessary to say that Ontario's interest is quite different from what it would have been had the issue related to the manner in which the defendant had been driving his car at the time of the accident. Where the defendant's exercise of due care in the operation of his automobile is in issue, the jurisdiction in which the allegedly wrongful conduct occurred will usually have a predominant, if not exclusive, concern. In such a case, it is appropriate to look to the law of the place of the tort so as to give effect to that jurisdiction's interest in regulating conduct within its borders, and it would be almost unthinkable to seek the applicable rule in the law of some other place.

The issue here, however, is not whether the defendant offended against a rule of the road prescribed by Ontario for motorists generally or whether he violated some standard of conduct imposed by that jurisdiction, but rather whether the plaintiff, because she was a guest in the defendant's automobile, is barred from recovering damages for a wrong concededly committed. As to that issue, it is New York, the place where the parties resided, where their guest-host relationship arose and where the trip began and was to end, rather than Ontario, the place of the fortuitous occurrence of the accident, which has the dominant contacts and the superior claim for application of its law. Although the rightness or wrongness of defendant's conduct may depend upon the law of the particular jurisdiction through which the automobile passes, the rights and liabilities of the parties which stem from their guest-host relationship should remain constant and not vary and shift as the automobile proceeds from place to place. Indeed, such a result, we note, accords with "the interests of the host in procuring liability insurance adequate under the applicable law, and the interests of his insurer in reasonable calculability of the premium." (Ehrenzweig, *Guest Statutes in the Conflict of Laws,* 69 Yale L.J. 595, 603.)

Although the traditional rule has in the past been applied by this court in giving controlling effect to the guest statute of the foreign jurisdiction in which the accident occurred * * * it is not amiss to point out that the question here posed was neither raised nor considered in those cases and that the question has never been presented in so stark a manner as in the case before us with a statute so unique as Ontario's. Be that as it may, however, reconsideration of the inflexible traditional rule persuades us, as already indicated, that, in failing to take into account essential policy considerations and objectives, its application may lead to unjust and anomalous results. This being so, the rule, formulated as it was by the courts, should be discarded. * * *

In conclusion, then, there is no reason why all issues arising out of a tort claim must be resolved by reference to the law of the same jurisdiction. Where the issue involves standards of conduct, it is more than likely that it is the law of the place of the tort which will be controlling but the disposition of other issues must turn, as does the issue of the standard of conduct itself, on the law of the jurisdiction which has the strongest interest in the resolution of the particular issue presented.

The judgment appealed from should be reversed, with costs, and the motion to dismiss the complaint denied.

VAN VOORHIS, JUDGE (dissenting). The decision about to be made of this appeal changes the established law of this State * * *. * * * The decision in *Auten v. Auten* rationalized and rendered more workable the existing law of contracts. * * * The difference between the present case and *Auten v. Auten* is that Auten did not materially change the law, but sought to formulate what had previously been decided. The present case makes substantial changes in the law of torts. * * *

In my view there is no overriding consideration of public policy which justifies or directs this change in the established rule or renders necessary or advisable the confusion which such a change will introduce. * * *

Notes and Questions

1. Recall the Anatomy from Chapter II. Assume Arizona would follow *Babcock*. What laws would apply to determine Curt's liability to Kim? Nevada's? Arizona's? Can you predict without knowing the content of the laws? For example, would *Babcock* have been decided the same way if Ontario permitted guest suits based on mere negligence but New York did not? You may wish to return to this inquiry after you read *Neumeier, infra* page 275.

2. Suppose Kim had brought suit in Nevada. Assume that Nevada requires that a guest show gross negligence before imposing liability on a host, but that Arizona applies a traditional negligence standard. Would Nevada subordinate its laws to Arizona's laws? Should it?

3. If Kim brought suit in California, a neutral forum, what law would apply to establish Curt's liability?

4. As you can see, selection of forum may be the most critical decision in the lawsuit. It should not be made without considering many factors, not the least of which includes conflict of laws issues.

DYM v. GORDON

Court of Appeals of New York, 1965.
16 N.Y.2d 120, 209 N.E.2d 792, 262 N.Y.S.2d 463.

[Plaintiff and Defendant, New York residents, attended summer school at the University of Colorado in Boulder, Colorado. Defendant offered Plaintiff a ride to a nearby town in Colorado and en route collided with another car, injuring Plaintiff and, possibly, others. The Appellate Division ruled that ordinary negligence was not a sufficient basis for recovery, since the Colorado guest statute applied, requiring "willful and wanton disregard" of the passenger's safety.]

BURKE, J. * * * Following our approach in *Babcock*, it is necessary first to isolate the issue, next to identify the policies embraced in the laws in conflict, and finally to examine the contacts of the respective jurisdictions to ascertain which has a superior connection with the occurrence and thus would have a superior interest in having its policy or law applied. The issue here is simply whether in an automobile host-guest relationship a negligent driver should be liable to his injured passenger. The New York law finds nothing in the host-guest relationship which warrants a digression from the usual negligence rule of ordinary care. In Colorado, however, this relationship is treated specially and, while ordinary negligence is usually enough for recovery in that state, injuries arising out of this relationship are compensable only if they result from "willful and wanton" conduct. Contrary to the narrow view advanced by plaintiff, the policy underlying Colorado's law is threefold: the protection of Colorado drivers and their insurance carriers against fraudulent claims, the prevention of suits by "ungrateful guests", and the priority of injured parties in other cars in the assets of the negligent defendant. Examining Colorado's interest in light of its public policy we find that over and above the usual interest which Colorado may bring to bear on all conduct occurring within its boundaries, Colorado has an interest in seeing that the negligent defendant's assets are not dissipated in order that the persons in the car of the blameless driver will not have their right to recovery diminished by the present suit.

Finally we come to the question of which state has the more significant contacts with the case such that its interest should be upheld. In this regard, the factual distinctions between this case and *Babcock* do have considerable influence. *Babcock* did not involve a collision between two cars; thus only New Yorkers were involved and it was unnecessary for us to consider the interest of Ontario in the rights of those in a car of a nonnegligent driver. In *Babcock* we pointed out that the host-guest relationship was seated in New York and that the place of the accident was "entirely fortuitous." In this case the parties were dwelling in Colorado when the relationship was formed and the accident arose out of Colorado based activity; therefore, the fact that the accident occurred in Colorado could in no sense be termed fortuitous. Thus it is that in this case where Colorado has such significant contacts with the *relationship itself* and the *basis of its formation* the application of its law and underlying policy are clearly warranted.

Of compelling importance in this case is the fact that here the parties had come to rest in the State of Colorado and had thus chosen to live their daily lives under the protective arm of Colorado law. Having accepted the benefits of that law for such a prolonged period, it is spurious to maintain that Colorado has no interest in a relationship which was formed there. In *Babcock* the New Yorkers at all times were *in transitu* and we were impressed with the fundamental unfairness of subjecting them to a law which they in no sense had adopted.

To say that this relationship was formed in Colorado implies that the parties had acquired so sufficient a nexus with that jurisdiction that relationships formed there were in the real sense Colorado relationships. In other words, it is neither the physical situs where the relationship was created nor the time of its creation which is controlling but rather these factors in conjunction with the general intent of the parties as inferred from their actions. * * *

The alleged contacts referred to by plaintiff may be classified under the heading of domicile. Certainly it is merely a long-handed method of reciting that the parties were domiciled in New York to state that the car was registered here and that the insurance was written here. These and many other factors may usually be presumed from the fact of domicile; they have no independent significance as regards the host-guest relationship apart from their inclusion as natural incidents of domicile.

Judicial hostility to "guest" statutes and a preoccupation with New York social welfare problems and the relative liability of insurers should not be treated as "contacts" which are found then to outweigh the factual contacts. * * *

Here, necessarily, the only valid competing consideration bearing on the host-guest relationship is that of domicile. However appealing it might seem to give effect to our own public policy on this issue, merely because the negligent driver of the car in the collision, and his guest, are domiciled here, to do so would be to totally neglect the interests of the jurisdiction where the accident occurred, where the relationship arose and where the parties were dwelling * * *. To give domicile or an alleged public policy such a preferred status is to substitute a conflicts rule every bit as inflexible and arbitrary as its *lex loci* predecessor. Such was not our intention in *Babcock*. It is suggested that New York has a dominant governmental interest in seeing that the plaintiff receives compensation because it is this State that she will look to for welfare payments should she become a public charge as a result of her injuries. Such an argument is hardly a legal one. Were we to give our attention to such considerations we might just as well speculate about the possibility that the New York defendant could become a public charge if the plaintiff were to be given recovery. There is no guarantee that the recovery will not far exceed the insurance coverage in this or in any other case. A reflection on the import of this argument gives one the feeling that a preference for whatever law will compensate the New York tort plaintiff lurks in the background. The suggestion that our courts should apply this State's policy of compensation for innocent tort victims to all cases of returning domiciliaries is tantamount to saying that different rules or interests of other jurisdictions should be denied application in a New York forum on the ground of their not suiting our public policy. The principles justifying our refusal to apply foreign law on the ground of public policy are well defined, and a mere difference between the foreign rule and our own will not warrant such refusal.

Public policy, *per se,* plays no part in a *choice* of law problem. * * *

The present decision represents no departure from the rule announced in *Babcock;* merely an example of its application. * * *

Accordingly, the order of the Appellate Division should be affirmed, without costs.

FULD, JUDGE (dissenting).

* * *

The [*Babcock*] rule is not, and does not profess to be, a talisman of legal certainty, nor does it of itself provide a formulary means for resolving conflicts problems. What it does provide is a method, a conceptual framework, for the disposition of tort cases having contacts with more than one jurisdiction. Although the majority in this case reaffirms *Babcock*'s abandonment of the prior inflexible rule of *lex loci delicti*, its decision, nevertheless, in essence, reflects the adoption of an equally mechanical and arbitrary rule that, in litigation involving a special relationship, controlling effect must be given to the law of the jurisdiction in which the relationship originated, notwithstanding that that jurisdiction may not have the slightest concern with the specific issue raised or that some other state's relationship or contact with the occurrence or the parties may be such as to give it the predominant interest in the resolution of that issue.

There is, indeed, no material distinction between the factual situation here presented and that in the *Babcock* case. * * *

* * * Under the circumstances of the present case, then, Colorado, to paraphrase what we wrote in *Babcock*, "has no conceivable interest in denying a remedy to a New York guest against his New York host for injuries suffered in [Colorado] by reason of conduct which was tortious under [Colorado] law" (12 N.Y.2d at 482, 240 N.Y.S.2d at 750, 191 N.E.2d at 284).

Nor is the majority's position advanced by its further suggestion * * * that the Colorado statute also reflects (1) an antipathy on the part of Colorado to suits by "ungrateful" guests (*see Dobbs v. Sugioka*, 117 Colo. 218, 220, 185 P.2d 784,) and (2) a policy to assure "the priority of injured parties in other cars in the assets of the negligent defendant." Indeed, as regards the latter asserted policy, there does not appear to be any Colorado pronouncement even to intimate that the Colorado Legislature was motivated by any such objective. In any event, though, Colorado would be legitimately concerned with the application of these alleged policies only in relation to matters within its legislative competence, such as the burdens of the Colorado courts, the regulation of the affairs and relationships of Colorado citizens or the protection of Colorado claimants or insurers. * * *

CHIEF JUDGE DESMOND (dissenting). * * * What we did in the [*Babcock* and *Kilberg*] decisions was to announce for New York a modern public policy which abandoned the old sweeping rule that the law to be applied in every tort case was the law of the place of the wrong. *Babcock* and *Kilberg* together should be the law of this present case.

* * *

No guides satisfactory to me are found in the concepts currently favored by teachers and writers on conflict of laws, such as "significant contacts", "center of gravity", and "interests of the respective states" * * *. Counting up "contacts" or locating the "center of gravity" or weighing the respective "interests" of two states can never be a satisfactory way of deciding actual lawsuits. * * *

Notes and Questions

1. *Dym* retreats from *Babcock*. Are you persuaded by the distinction that *Babcock* did not involve a collision between two cars?

2. Do you agree with the three policies underlying the Colorado guest statute? From what source did the court divine these policies? From the legislative history? Logic? Which policy supported the court's preference for Colorado law?

3. Are you satisfied that the place where the relationship is formed justifies application of its guest/host laws if the accident occurs there? What if the accident occurs in another state?

4. Should the legislature (rather than courts) resolve these intractable problems?

5. *Macey v. Rozbicki,* 18 N.Y.2d 289, 221 N.E.2d 380, 274 N.Y.S.2d 591 (1966), involved two sisters who lived in Buffalo, New York. The guest sister visited her host sister who was vacationing in Ontario. An accident occurred on a round trip within Ontario to church. The New York Court of Appeals applied the New York law and allowed recovery. Should it have? Which of the three policies supports the decision? Judge Keating argued for the overrule of *Dym.* Consider your answer in light of the following case.

TOOKER v. LOPEZ

Court of Appeals of New York, 1969.
24 N.Y.2d 569, 249 N.E.2d 394, 301 N.Y.S.2d 519.

KEATING, JUDGE. On October 16, 1964, Catharina Tooker, a 20–year–old coed at Michigan State University, was killed when the Japanese sports car in which she was a passenger overturned after the driver had lost control of the vehicle while attempting to pass another car. The accident also took the life of the driver of the vehicle, Marcia Lopez, and seriously injured another passenger, Susan Silk. The two girls were classmates of Catharina Tooker at Michigan State University and lived in the same dormitory. They were en route from the University to Detroit, Michigan, to spend the weekend.

Catharina Tooker and Marcia Lopez were both New York domiciliaries. The automobile which Miss Lopez was driving belonged to her father who resided in New York, where the sports car he had given his daughter was registered and insured.

This action for wrongful death was commenced by Oliver P. Tooker, Jr., the father of Catharina Tooker, as the administrator of her estate. The defendant asserted as an affirmative defense the Michigan "guest statute" (C.L.S. § 257.401 [Stat.Ann.1960, § 9.2101]) which permits recovery by guests only by showing willful misconduct or gross negligence of the driver. The plaintiff moved to dismiss the affirmative defense on the ground that under the governing choice-of-law rules it was New York law rather than Michigan law which applied. The motion was granted by the Special Term Justice who concluded that: "New York State 'has the greatest concern with the specific issue raised in the litigation' and New York law should apply." The Appellate Division (Third Department) agreed with "the cogent argument advanced by Special Term" but felt "constrained" by the holding in *Dym v. Gordon,* 16 N.Y.2d 120, 209 N.E.2d 792, 262 N.Y.S.2d 463 [1965] to apply the Michigan guest statute.

We are presented here with a choice-of-law problem which we have had occasion to consider in several cases since our decision in *Babcock v. Jackson,* 12 N.Y.2d 473, 191 N.E.2d 279, 240 N.Y.S.2d 743 [1963] rejected the traditional rule which looked invariably to the law of the place of the wrong. Unfortunately, as we recently had occasion to observe, our decisions subsequent to rejection of the *lex loci delictus* rule "have lacked a precise consistency" (*Miller v. Miller,* 22 N.Y.2d 12, 15, 237 N.E.2d 877, 878, 290 N.Y.S.2d 734, 736 [1968]; *see also* D. Currie, Comments on Reich v. Purcell, 15 U.C.L.A. L. Rev. 595–598). This case gives us the opportunity to resolve those inconsistencies in a class of cases which have been particularly troublesome.

* * *

The decision in *Dym v. Gordon,* upon which the Appellate Division relied in the instant case, is clearly distinguishable from the facts here. There is here no third-party "non-guest" who was injured and there is no question of denying such a party priority in the assets of the negligent defendant. We cannot, however, in candor rest our decision on this basis in light of a subsequent decision which refused to apply the Ontario guest statute in a case indistinguishable from *Dym v. Gordon* (*supra*). (*See Macey v. Rozbicki,* 18 N.Y.2d 289, 221 N.E.2d 380, 274 N.Y.S.2d 591 [1966].)

* * *

The teleological argument advanced by some (*see* Cavers, Choice-of-Law Process, p. 298) that the guest statute was intended to assure the priority of injured nonguests in the assets of a negligent host, in addition to the prevention of fraudulent claims, overlooks not only the statutory history but the fact that the statute permits recovery by guests who can establish that the accident was due to the gross negligence of the driver. If the purpose of the statute is to protect the rights of the injured "nonguest," as opposed to the owner or his insurance carrier, we fail to perceive any rational basis for predicating that protection on the degree of negligence which the guest is able to establish. The only justification for discrimination between injured guests which can withstand logical as well as constitutional scrutiny * * * is that the legitimate purpose of the statute—prevention of fraudulent claims against local insurers or the protection of local automobile owners—is furthered by increasing the guest's burden of proof. This purpose can never be vindicated when the insurer is a New York carrier and the defendant is sued in the courts of this State. Under such circumstances, the jurisdiction enacting such a guest statute has absolutely no interest in the application of its law.

* * *

* * * [T]he instant case is one of the simplest in the choice-of-law area. If the facts are examined in light of the policy considerations which underlie the ostensibly conflicting laws it is clear that New York has the only real interest in whether recovery should be granted and that the application of Michigan law "would defeat a legitimate interest of the forum State without serving a legitimate interest of any other State" (*Intercontinental Planning v. Daystrom, Inc.,* [24 N.Y.2d 372, 248 N.E.2d 576, 300 N.Y.S.2d 817 (1969)]).

The policy of this State with respect to all those injured in automobile accidents is reflected in the legislative declaration which prefaces New York's compulsory insurance law: "The legislature is concerned over the rising toll of motor vehicle accidents and the suffering and loss thereby inflicted. The legislature determines that it is a matter of grave concern that motorists shall be financially able to respond in damages for their negligent acts, so that innocent victims of motor vehicle accidents may be recompensed for the injury and financial loss inflicted upon them." (Vehicle and Traffic Law, Consol.Laws, c. 71, § 310.)

Neither this declaration of policy nor the standard required provisions for an auto liability insurance policy make any distinction between guests, pedestrians or other insured parties.

New York's "grave concern" in affording recovery for the injuries suffered by Catharina Tooker, a New York domiciliary, and the loss suffered by her family as a result of her wrongful death, is evident merely in stating the policy which our law reflects. On the other hand, Michigan has no interest in whether a New York plaintiff is denied recovery against a New York defendant where the car is insured here.[1] The fact that the deceased guest and driver were in Michigan for an extended period of time is plainly irrelevant. Indeed, the Legislature, in requiring that insurance policies cover liability for injuries regardless of where the accident takes place (Vehicle & Traffic Law, § 311, subd. 4) has evinced commendable concern not only for residents of this State, but residents of other States who may be injured as a result of the activities of New York residents. Under these circumstances we cannot be concerned with whether Miss Tooker or Miss Lopez were in Michigan for a summer session or for a full college education (*see* Baade, Counter–Revolution or Alliance for Progress? Reflections on Reading Cavers, The Choice-of-Law Process, 46 Tex.L.Rev. 141, 168–170).

The argument that the choice of law in tort cases should be governed by the fictional expectation of the parties has been rejected unequivocally by this court. * * *

Moreover, when the Legislature has chosen to compel an owner of an automobile to provide a fund for recovery for those who will be injured, and thus taken the element of choice and expectation out of the question, it seems unreasonable to look to that factor as a basis for a choice of law. And, even if we were to engage in such fictions as the expectations of the parties, it seems only fair to infer that the owner of the vehicle by purchasing a New York insurance policy which provided for the specific liability "intended to protect [the] passenger against negligent injury, as well as to secure indemnity for liability, in whatever

---

1. The Michigan courts have suggested that the purpose of their guest statute is to protect the owner of the vehicle (*Castle v. McKeown*, 327 Mich. 518, 42 N.W.2d 733 [1950]; *Hunter v. Baldwin*, 268 Mich. 106, 255 N.W. 431 [1934]). It is no longer clear that a Michigan court would apply Michigan law here (*see Abendschein v. Farrell*, 11 Mich.App. 662, 162 N.W.2d 165 [1968]; *House v. Gibbs*, 4 Mich.App. 519, 145 N.W.2d 248 [1966]).

state an accident might occur" (*Kopp v. Rechtzigel*, 273 Minn. 441, 443, 141 N.W.2d 526, 528 [1966]).

* * *

The dissent is, of course, correct that it was "adventitious" that Miss Tooker was a guest in an automobile registered and insured in New York. For all we know, her decision to go to Michigan State University as opposed to New York University may have been "adventitious." Indeed, her decision to go to Detroit on the weekend in question instead of staying on campus and studying may equally have been "adventitious." The fact is, however, that Miss Tooker went to Michigan State University; that she decided to go to Detroit on October 16, 1964; that she was a passenger in a vehicle registered and insured in New York; and that as a result of all these "adventitious" occurrences, she is dead and we have a case to decide. Why we should be concerned with what might have been is unclear.

* * *

We rejected the *lex loci delictus* rule because it placed controlling reliance upon one factor totally unrelated to the policies reflected by the ostensibly conflicting laws. The only fact less relevant to those policies in guest statute cases is whether the presence of the guest in the particular automobile was "adventitious."[2]

* * * Applying the choice-of-law rule which we have adopted, it is not an "implicit consequence" that the Michigan passenger injured along with Miss Lopez should be denied recovery. Under the reasoning adopted here, it is not at all clear that Michigan law would govern (*Gaither v. Myers,* 404 F.2d 216, 224 [D.C.Cir.1968]). We do not, however, find it necessary or desirable to conclusively resolve a question which is not now before us. It suffices to note that any anomaly resulting from the application of Michigan law to bar an action brought by Miss Silk is "the implicit consequence" of a Federal system which, at a time when we have truly become one nation, permits a citizen of one State to recover for injuries sustained in an automobile accident and denies a citizen of another State the right to recover for injuries sustained in a similar accident. The anomaly does not arise from any choice-of-law rule.

* * *

The order of the Appellate Division should be reversed, with costs, and the order of Special Term reinstated.

Fuld, Chief Judge (concurring).

2. Similar reasons compel the rejection of the rule suggested by the Restatement, 2d, Conflict of Laws, P.O.D., pt. II, § 159, upon which the dissent relies. Where the guest-host relationship "arose" or is "centered" is wholly irrelevant to policies reflected by the laws in conflict. Any language in our earlier opinions lending support to a contrary view has, as Judge Burke notes in his concurring opinion * * *, been overruled. We would note that there is some question as to whether the portion of the Restatement, relied upon by the dissent, is applicable to the precise facts present here.

The time has come * * * to endeavor to minimize what some have characterized as an *ad hoc* case-by-case approach by laying down guidelines as well as we can for the solution of guest-host conflicts problems. [Chief Judge Fuld then advanced three principles, which, in *Neumeier v. Kuehner, see infra* page 275, were accepted by a majority of the judges of the Court of Appeals.]

Guidelines of the sort suggested will not always be easy of application, nor will they furnish guidance to litigants and lower courts in all cases. They are proffered as a beginning, not as an end, to the problems of sound and fair adjudication in the troubled world of the automobile guest statute.

Burke, Judge (concurring).

* * *

From all that has been written, it is apparent that our decision in *Dym* is overruled. * * * It is evident that the philosophy of the court has changed since *Dym* and, as a result of this transformation, we have firmly embarked upon an interest analysis approach to a conflicts problem. * * * [T]his approach * * * does not, I feel, remove all future problems from the [guest-passenger] area. Reference to the status of Miss Silk illustrates this point.

It is not at all clear whether the majority would conclude that she too, although not a New York resident, could recover should she bring an action against this defendant. Logically, the majority might declare, as they have in this case * * *, that "the Legislature, in requiring that insurance policies cover liability for injuries regardless of where the accident takes place * * * has evinced commendable concern not only for residents of this State, but residents of other States who may be injured as a result of the activities of New York residents." The dissenters, however, intimate that since Miss Silk could not recover in Michigan, she would presumably be barred from a recovery in this court.

I am not now prepared to decide that question nor am I ready to suggest what this State's interest would be in the present situation if the car were not insured in New York. I merely refer to these situations to illustrate the difficulty which we shall encounter in future guest statute cases even under the standard adopted by the majority today. * * * For this reason, and because of the nature of automotive traffic today, I view the entire matter as one of national concern which cannot be settled by any rule this court might proffer. As the matter is of Federal dimension, only Federal legislation will ultimately succeed in resolving these continuing controversies in a rational and equitable manner. * * *

Breitel, Judge (dissenting).

* * *

Except for the facts that plaintiff and the deceased were New York residents, that defendant's deceased daughter had a New York operator's license, that the registered owner of the car was a New York resident, and that the car was registered and insured in New York, every other facet of the accident was based in Michigan and was as localized as it could be in that State. The students were in residence at the university, were not in sojourn for short courses or interim sessions, or on tour. The trip was intrinsically and exclusively a Michigan trip, concerned only with Michigan places, roads, and conditions.

The registration and ownership of the car and the residence of its driver, as well as that of plaintiff's deceased daughter, were adventitious so far as this trip was concerned. The same trip with the same purposes with some automobile would have or could have taken place among a similar group of students from other States or Michigan, or by the same students, even if the States of residence and automobile ownership and insurance were changed. Indeed, defendant might have chosen to have the automobile registered and insured in either Michigan or New York, and in his daughter's name, since the car, as a matter of family arrangements, was really hers rather than his.

In this highly mobile and automotive Nation the slight admixture of multi-state contacts as occurred here is now very frequent, and is becoming increasingly so. Unless conflicts rules move over to substitute a completely personal law for the territorial system that infuses Anglo–American jurisprudence and underlies the understanding and expectations of Americans, it is still true that the law of a territory governs the conduct and qualifiedly the status of persons, resident and nonresident, within it, except in the extraordinary situation where the localization of persons and conduct is adventitious. At least this has been true until quite recently. * * *

The incidental registration and ownership of the car, and the domicile of these Michigan students, did not influence their conduct or the establishment or nature of the relationship among them. Regardless of these facts they would undoubtedly have entered into the same relationship, made the same trip, and behaved the same way. These facts were, therefore, extrinsic or adventitious.

On this view, *Dym v. Gordon*, 16 N.Y.2d 120, 209 N.E.2d 792, 262 N.Y.S.2d 463, was soundly decided, and this case, which is even stronger on its intrinsic facts because of the young women's being students in residence, as that term is used in the academic world, should be decided the same way (Cavers, Choice-of-Law Process, pp. 300–304). * * *

Intra-mural speculation on the policies of other States has obvious limitations because of restricted information and wisdom. It is difficult enough to interpret the statutes and decisional rules of one's own State. To be sure, there is no total escape from considering the policies of other States. But this necessity should not be extended to produce anomalies of results out of the same accident, with unpredictability, and lack of consistency in determinations. Thus, it is hard to accept the implicit consequence that Miss Silk, the Michigan resident injured in the accident, should not be able to recover in Michigan (and presumably in New

York) but a recovery can be had for her deceased fellow-passenger in the very same accident.

If the trend continues uninterruptedly, the shift to a personal law approach in conflicts law, especially in the torts field, will continue apace (*see* Cavers, Choice-of-Law Process, *supra*, pp. 150–156). * * *

Notes and Questions

1.   Note the contradictory views of the lower courts. The Court of Appeals finds that *Dym* is clearly distinguishable from *Tooker*. Do you agree?

2.   Has *Dym* been effectively overruled?

3.   Would a New York court permit Ms. Silk to recover?

NEUMEIER v. KUEHNER

Court of Appeals of New York, 1972.
31 N.Y.2d 121, 286 N.E.2d 454, 335 N.Y.S.2d 64.

FULD, CHIEF JUDGE. A domiciliary of Ontario, Canada, was killed when the automobile in which he was riding, owned and driven by a New York resident, collided with a train in Ontario. That jurisdiction has a guest statute, and the primary question posed by this appeal is whether in this action brought by the Ontario passenger's estate, Ontario law should be applied and the New York defendant permitted to rely on its guest statute as a defense.

The facts are quickly told. On May 7, 1969, Arthur Kuehner, the defendant's intestate, a resident of Buffalo, drove his automobile from that city to Fort Erie in the Province of Ontario, Canada, where he picked up Amie Neumeier, who lived in that town with his wife and their children. Their trip was to take them to Long Beach, also in Ontario, and back again to Neumeier's home in Fort Erie. However, at a railroad crossing in the Town of Sherkston—on the way to Long Beach—the auto was struck by a train of the defendant Canadian National Railway Company. Both Kuehner and his guest-passenger were instantly killed.

Neumeier's wife and administratrix, a citizen of Canada and a domiciliary of Ontario, thereupon commenced this wrongful death action in New York against both Keuhner's estate and the Canadian National Railway Company. The defendant estate pleaded, as an affirmative defense, the Ontario guest statute and the defendant railway also interposed defenses in reliance upon it. In substance, the statute provides that the owner or driver of a motor vehicle is not liable for damages resulting from injury to, or the death of, a guest-passenger unless he was guilty of gross negligence (Highway Traffic Act of Province of Ontario [Ont.Rev.Stat. (1960), ch. 172], § 105, subd. [2], as amd. by Stat. of 1966, ch. 64, § 20, subd. [2]). It is worth noting, at this point, that, although our court originally considered that the sole purpose of the Ontario statute was to protect Ontario defendants and their insurers against collusive claims (*see Babcock v. Jackson,* 12 N.Y.2d 473, 482–483,

240 N.Y.S.2d 743, 749–750, 191 N.E.2d 279, 283–284). "Further research * * * has revealed the distinct possibility that one purpose, and perhaps the only purpose, of the statute was to protect owners and drivers against ungrateful guests." (Reese, Chief Judge Fuld and Choice of Law, 71 Col.L.Rev. 548, 558; see Trautman, Two Views on Kell v. Henderson: A Comment, 67 Col.L.Rev. 465, 469.)

The plaintiff, asserting that the Ontario statute "is not available * * * in the present action", moved, pursuant to CPLR 3211 (subd. [b]), to dismiss the affirmative defenses pleaded. The court at Special Term holding the guest statute applicable, denied the motions (63 Misc.2d 766, 313 N.Y.S.2d 468) but, on appeal, a closely divided Appellate Division reversed and directed dismissal of the defenses (37 A.D.2d 70, 322 N.Y.S.2d 867). It was the court's belief that such a result was dictated by *Tooker v. Lopez*, 24 N.Y.2d 569, 301 N.Y.S.2d 519, 249 N.E.2d 394.

In reaching that conclusion, the Appellate Division misread our decision in the *Tooker* case—a not unnatural result in light of the variant views expressed in the three separate opinions written on behalf of the majority. It is important to bear in mind that in *Tooker*, the guest-passenger and the host-driver were both domiciled in New York, and our decision—that New York law was controlling—was based upon, and limited to, that fact situation. Indeed [both] * * * Judge Keating (24 N.Y.2d at 580, 301 N.Y.S.2d at 528, 249 N.E.2d at 400) and Judge Burke (at p. 591, 301 N.Y.S.2d at p. 537, 249 N.E.2d at 407) expressly noted that the determination then being made left open the question whether New York law would be applicable if the plaintiff passenger happened to be a domiciliary of the very jurisdiction which had a guest statute.[1] Thus, *Tooker v. Lopez* did no more than hold that, when the passenger and driver are residents of the same jurisdiction and the car is there registered and insured, its law, and not the law of the place of accident, controls and determines the standard of care which the host owes to his guest.

What significantly and effectively differentiates the present case is the fact that, although the host was a domiciliary of New York, the guest, for whose death recovery is sought, was domiciled in Ontario, the place of accident and the very jurisdiction which had enacted the statute designed to protect the host from liability for ordinary negligence. It is clear that although New York has a deep interest in protecting its own residents, injured in a foreign state, against unfair or anachronistic statutes of that state, it has no legitimate interest in ignoring the public policy of a foreign jurisdiction—such as Ontario—and in protecting the plaintiff guest domiciled and injured there from legislation obviously addressed, at the very least, to a resident riding in a vehicle traveling within its borders.

---

1. In the other concurring opinion (24 N.Y.2d at 585, 249 N.E.2d at 404, 301 N.Y.S.2d at 533), I wrote that in such a case—where the passenger is a resident of the state having a guest statute—"the applicable rule of decision will [normally] be that of the state where the accident occurred."

To distinguish *Tooker* on such a basis is not improperly discriminatory. It is quite true that, in applying the Ontario guest statute to the Ontario-domiciled passenger, we, in a sense, extend a right less generous than New York extends to a New York passenger in a New York vehicle with New York insurance. That, though, is not a consequence of invidious discrimination; it is, rather, the result of the existence of disparate rules of law in jurisdictions that have diverse and important connections with the litigants and the litigated issue.

The fact that insurance policies issued in this State on New York-based vehicles cover liability, regardless of the place of the accident (Vehicle and Traffic Law, Consol.Laws, c. 71 § 311, subd. 4), certainly does not call for the application of internal New York law in this case. The compulsory insurance requirement is designed to cover a car-owner's liability, not create it; in other words, the applicable statute was not intended to impose liability where none would otherwise exist. This being so, we may not properly look to the New York insurance requirement to dictate a choice-of-law rule which would invariably impose liability. * * *

When, in *Babcock v. Jackson* (12 N.Y.2d 473, 240 N.Y.S.2d 743, 191 N.E.2d 279), we rejected the inexorable choice-of-law rule in personal injury cases because it failed to take account of underlying policy considerations, we were willing to sacrifice the certainty provided by the old rule for the more just, fair and practical result that may best be achieved by giving controlling effect to the law of the jurisdiction which has the greatest concern with, or interest in, the specific issue raised in the litigation. * * * In consequence of the change effected—and this was to be anticipated—our decisions in multi-state highway accident cases, particularly in those involving guest-host controversies, have, it must be acknowledged, lacked consistency. This stemmed, in part, from the circumstance that it is frequently difficult to discover the purposes or policies underlying the relevant local law rules of the respective jurisdictions involved. It is even more difficult, assuming that these purposes or policies are found to conflict, to determine on some principled basis which should be given effect at the expense of the others.

The single all-encompassing rule which called, invariably, for selection of the law of the place of injury was discarded, and wisely, because it was too broad to prove satisfactory in application. There, is, however, no reason why choice-of-law rules, more narrow than those previously devised, should not be successfully developed, in order to assure a greater degree of predictability and uniformity, on the basis of our present knowledge and experience. * * * "The time has come," I wrote in *Tooker* (24 N.Y.2d at 584, 301 N.Y.S.2d at 532, 249 N.E.2d at 403), "to endeavor to minimize what some have characterized as an *ad hoc* case-by-case approach by laying down guidelines, as well as we can, for the solution of guest-host conflicts problems." *Babcock* and its progeny enable us to formulate a set of basic principles that may be profitably utilized, for they have helped us uncover the underlying values and policies which are operative in this area of the law. * * * "Now that these values and policies have been revealed, we may proceed to the next stage in the evolution of the law—the formulation of a few rules of general applicability, promising a fair level of predictability." Although it was recognized that no rule may be formulated to guarantee a satisfactory result in every case, the following principles were proposed as sound for situations involving guest statutes in conflicts settings (24 N.Y.2d at 585, 301 N.Y.S.2d at 532, 249 N.E.2d at 404):

1. When the guest-passenger and the host-driver are domiciled in the same state, and the car is there registered, the law of that state should control and determine the standard of care which the host owes to his guest.

2. When the driver's conduct occurred in the state of his domicile and that state does not cast him in liability for that conduct, he should not be held liable by reason of the fact that liability would be imposed upon him under the tort law of the state of the victim's domicile. Conversely, when the guest was injured in the state of his own domicile and its law permits recovery, the driver who has come into that state should not—in the absence of special circumstances—be permitted to interpose the law of his state as a defense.

3. In other situations, when the passenger and the driver are domiciled in different states, the rule is necessarily less categorical. Normally, the applicable rule of decision will be that of the state where the accident occurred but not if it can be shown that displacing that normally applicable rule will advance the relevant substantive law purposes without impairing the smooth working of the multi-state system or producing great uncertainty for litigants. (Cf. Restatement, 2d, Conflict of Laws, P.O.D., pt. II, §§ 146, 159 [later adopted and promulgated May 23, 1969].)

The variant views expressed not only in *Tooker* but by Special Term and the divided Appellate Division in this litigation underscore and confirm the need for these rules. Since the passenger was domiciled in Ontario and the driver in New York, the present case is covered by the third stated principle. The law to be applied is that of the jurisdiction where the accident happened unless it appears that "displacing [that] normally applicable rule will advance the relevant substantive law purposes" of the jurisdictions involved. Certainly, ignoring Ontario's policy requiring proof of gross negligence in a case which involves an Ontario-domiciled guest at the expense of a New Yorker does not further the substantive law purposes of New York. In point of fact, application of New York law would result in the exposure of this State's domiciliaries to a greater liability than that imposed upon resident users of Ontario's highways. Conversely, the failure to apply Ontario's law would "impair"—to cull from the rule set out above—"the smooth working of the multi-state system [and] produce great uncertainty for litigants" by sanctioning forum shopping and thereby allowing a party to select a forum which could give him a larger recovery than the court of his own domicile. In short, the plaintiff has failed to show that this State's connection with the controversy was sufficient to justify displacing the rule of *lex loci delictus.* * * *

In each action, the Appellate Division's order should be reversed, that of Special Term reinstated, without costs, and the questions certified answered in the negative.

BREITEL, JUDGE (concurring).

I agree that there should be a reversal, but would place the reversal on quite narrow grounds. It is undesirable to lay down prematurely major premises based on shifting ideologies in the choice of law. True, Chief Judge Fuld in his concurring opinion in the *Tooker* case * * * took the view that there had already occurred sufficient experience to lay down some rules of law which would reduce the instability and uncertainty created by the recent departures from traditional *lex loci delictus.* This case, arising so soon after, shows that the permutations in accident cases, especially automobile accident cases, is disproof that the time has come.

Problems engendered by the new departures have not gone unnoticed and they are not confined to the courts of this State (Juenger, *Choice of Law in Interstate Torts,* 118 U.Pa.L.Rev. 202, 214–220). They arise not merely because any new departure of necessity creates problems, but much more because the departures have been accompanied by an unprecedented competition of ideologies, largely of academic origin, to explain and reconstruct a whole field of law, each purporting or aspiring to achieve a single universal principle.

Babcock v. Jackson, 12 N.Y.2d 473, 240 N.Y.S.2d 743, 191 N.E.2d 279, an eminently correctly and justly decided case, applied the then current new doctrine of grouping of contacts. Troubles arose only when the universality of a single doctrine was assumed * * *. By the time of *Miller v. Miller,* 22 N.Y.2d 12, 290 N.Y.S.2d 734, 237 N.E.2d 877 and the *Tooker* case, *supra,* the new doctrine had been displaced by a still newer one, that of governmental interests developed most extensively by the late Brainerd Currie, and the court was deeply engaged in probing the psychological motivation of legislatures of other States in enacting statutes restricting recoveries in tort cases. Now, evidently, it is suggested that this State and other States may have less parochial concerns in enacting legislation restricting tort recoveries than had been believed only a short time ago. The trouble this case has given the courts below and now this court stems, it is suggested, more from a concern in sorting out ideologies than in applying narrow rules of law in the traditional common-law process (Juenger, *op. cit., supra,* at 233).

What the *Babcock* case * * * taught and what modern day commentators largely agree is that *lex loci delictus* is unsoundly applied if it is done indiscriminately and without exception. It is still true, however, that the *lex loci delictus* is the normal rule, as indeed Chief Judge Fuld noted in the *Tooker* case, * * * to be rejected only when it is evident that the situs of the accident is the least of the several factors or influences to which the accident may be attributed. * * * Certain it is that States are not concerned only with their own citizens or residents. They are concerned with events that occur within their territory, and are also concerned with the "stranger within the gates" (Juenger, *op. cit., supra,* at 209–210).

In this case, none would have ever assumed that New York law should be applied just because one of the two defendants was a New York resident and his automobile was New York insured, except for the overbroad statements of Currie doctrine in the *Tooker* case. * * *

Consequently, I agree that there should be a reversal and the defenses allowed to stand. The conclusion, however, rests simply on the proposition that plaintiff has failed by her allegations to establish that the relationship to this State was sufficient to displace the normal rule that the *lex loci delictus* should be applied, the accident being associated with Ontario, from inception to tragic termination, except for adventitious facts and where the lawsuit was brought.

BERGAN, JUDGE (dissenting). * * *

There is a difference of fundamental character between justifying a departure from *lex loci delictus* because the court will not, as a matter of policy, permit a New York owner of a car licensed and insured in New York to escape a liability that would be imposed on him here; and a departure based on the fact a New York resident makes the claim for injury. The first ground of departure is justifiable as sound policy; the second is justifiable only if one is willing to treat the rights of a stranger permitted to sue in New York differently from the way a resident is treated. Neither because of "interest" nor "contact" nor any other defensible ground is it proper to say in a court of law that the rights of one man whose suit is accepted shall be adjudged differently on the merits on the basis of where he happens to live. * * *

* * * What the court is deciding today is that although it will prevent a New York car owner from asserting the defense of a protective foreign statute when a New York resident in whose rights it has an "interest" sues; it has no such "interest" when it accepts the suit in New York of a nonresident. This is an inadmissible distinction.

Notes and Questions

1. Should courts engage in formulating rules? Are not the rules that go beyond the facts of the case *dicta?* Even so, may not *dicta* provide guidance to lower courts?

2. The result of the case seems evident. Why should the New York court be more solicitous of an Ontario citizen than Ontario would be of its own citizen?

3. Review Judge Fuld's three principles. Now examine the facts of each case in this synthesis in light of those principles. How would each be decided? Specifically, how would *Dym* be decided under these rules?

E.   FOURTH EXERCISE IN SYNTHESIS: CASES INVOLVING INJURY RESULTING FROM NEGLIGENTLY INFLICTED MENTAL DISTRESS

The following line of cases examines the development of the common law bases of compensation for injury resulting from negligently inflicted mental distress. Analyze the law of New York from its wholesale rejection of such compensation in *Mitchell v. Rochester Railway Co.*, to the refinement of the rule denying compensation, to the later abandonment of *Mitchell* and the acceptance of the tort of bodily injury resulting from negligently inflicted mental distress. Note that the change in the law was accomplished without legislative reform.

Consider the following hypothetical in light of each principal case. Assume that in *Johnson v. Roscoe & Baker, supra* Chapter II, two bystanders, A and B, barely escaped being hit by the skidding vehicles after the collision. A and B suffered identical fright, accompanied by emotional and mental distress. A, however, was struck by flying glass that caused a minor physical injury. B was not physically injured in any way.

MITCHELL v. ROCHESTER RAILWAY CO.

Court of Appeals of New York, 1896.
151 N.Y. 107, 45 N.E. 354.

MARTIN, J. The facts in this case are few, and may be briefly stated. On the 1st day of April, 1891, the plaintiff was standing upon a crosswalk on Main street, in the city of Rochester, awaiting an opportunity to board one of the defendant's cars which had stopped upon the street at that place. While standing there, and just as she was about to step upon the car, a horse car of the defendant came down the street. As the team attached to the car drew near, it turned to the right, and came close to the plaintiff, so that she stood between the horses' heads when they were stopped. She testified that from fright and excitement caused by the approach and proximity of the team she became unconscious, and also that the result was a miscarriage, and consequent illness. Medical testimony was given to the effect that the mental shock which she then received was sufficient to produce that result. Assuming that the evidence tended to show that the defendant's servant was negligent in the management of the car and horses, and that the plaintiff was free from contributory negligence, the single question presented is whether the plaintiff is entitled to recover for the defendant's negligence which occasioned her fright and alarm, and resulted in the injuries already mentioned. While the authorities are not harmonious upon this question, we think the most reliable and better-considered cases, as well as public policy, fully justify us in holding that the plaintiff cannot recover for injuries occasioned by fright, as there was no immediate personal injury.

[Citations omitted.] The learned counsel for the respondent in his brief very properly stated that "the consensus of opinion would seem to be that no recovery can be had for mere fright," as will be readily seen by an examination of the following additional authorities: [Citations omitted.] If it be admitted that no recovery can be had for fright occasioned by the negligence of another, it is somewhat difficult to understand how a defendant would be liable for its consequences. Assuming that fright cannot form the basis of an action, it is obvious that no recovery can be had for injuries resulting therefrom. That the result may be nervous disease, blindness, insanity, or even a miscarriage, in no way changes the principle. These results merely show the degree of fright, or the extent of the damages. The right of action must still depend upon the question whether a recovery may be had for fright. If it can, then an action may be maintained, however slight the injury. If not, then there can be no recovery, no matter how grave or serious the consequences. Therefore the logical result of the respondent's concession would seem to be, not only that no recovery can be had for mere fright, but also that none can be had for injuries which are the direct consequences of it. If the right of recovery in this class of cases should be once established, it would naturally result in a flood of litigation in cases where the injury complained of may be easily feigned without detection, and where the damages must rest upon mere conjecture or speculation. The difficulty which often exists in cases of alleged physical injury, in determining whether they exist, and, if so, whether they were caused by the negligent act of the defendant, would not only be greatly increased, but a wide field would be opened for fictitious or speculative claims. To establish such a doctrine would be contrary to principles of public policy. Moreover, it cannot be properly said that the plaintiff's miscarriage was the proximate result of the defendant's negligence. Proximate damages are such as are the ordinary and natural results of the negligence charged, and those that are usual, and may, therefore, be expected. It is quite obvious that the plaintiff's injuries do not fall within the rule as to proximate damages. The injuries to the plaintiff were plainly the result of an accidental or unusual combination of circumstances, which could not have been reasonably anticipated, and over which the defendant had no control, and hence her damages were too remote to justify a recovery in this action. These considerations lead to the conclusion that no recovery can be had for injuries sustained by fright occasioned by the negligence of another, where there is no immediate personal injury. The orders of the general and special terms should be reversed, and the order of the trial term granting a nonsuit affirmed, with costs. All concur, except Haight, J., not sitting, and Vann, J., not voting. Ordered accordingly.

Notes and Questions

1. Consider the testimony that the plaintiff stood between the horses' heads when they were stopped. Of course, had she been struck ever so slightly, the issue before the court would have been different. What might

have accounted for the damaging testimony? Ethics? Would it have been proper for the plaintiff's counsel to advise her of the damaging effect of such testimony? Suppose the plaintiff then changed her story? What obligation does plaintiff's counsel have in these situations? *See supra* pp. 78–84.

2. The court held that the plaintiff could not recover for injuries occasioned by mere fright if she did not suffer immediate personal injury. It relied on the "most reliable and better-considered cases, as well as public policy." What public policy? The court apparently would have permitted recovery for emotional and mental distress as long as the plaintiff suffered some immediate personal injury. Why?

3. Suppose the plaintiff hit her head on the ground when she fainted. Would this have satisfied the "immediate personal injury" requirement, thereby permitting her to recover for the subsequent emotional and mental distress?

4. Did the plaintiff concede that no recovery could be had for mere fright? Was this concession wise? Did the court take unfair advantage of it? If you were the plaintiff and had an opportunity to rebut the court's reasoning, how would you have responded?

COMSTOCK v. WILSON

Court of Appeals of New York, 1931.
257 N.Y. 231, 177 N.E. 431.

LEHMAN, J. Plaintiff's automobile, in which the plaintiff's testratrix was a passenger, came into collision with an automobile operated by the defendant. The collision caused some noise or "grating sound." The left fender of plaintiff's car was loosened from the running board. The plaintiff's testatrix stepped from the automobile and started to write down the defendant's name and license number. While doing so, she fainted and fell to the sidewalk, fracturing her skull. All this occurred within a few minutes after the accident. She lived about twenty minutes after the fall. The plaintiff, claiming that the death of his testatrix was the result of defendant's negligence, has recovered judgment for $5,000 against her.

The trial judge submitted to the jury, as a question of fact, whether the alleged negligence of the defendant was the proximate cause of the death of plaintiff's testatrix. He refused the defendant's request to charge that, "if the Jury find that the deceased at the time of the collision sustained only shock or fright, without physical injury, they must find for the defendant." The defendant appealed to the Appellate Division from an order denying her motion for a new trial, and the Appellate Division in granting leave to appeal from its order of affirmance has certified the question whether it was error for the trial court to refuse the defendant's request to charge. No other question may be reviewed upon this appeal.

In the case of *Mitchell v. Rochester Ry. Co.*, this court stated: "No recovery can be had for injuries sustained by fright occasioned by the negligence of another, where there is no immediate personal injury."

There, while the plaintiff was standing upon a crosswalk, awaiting an opportunity to board one of the defendant's cars which had stopped there, a team attached to another horse car of the defendant, coming down the street, turned to the right and came so close to the plaintiff that she stood between the horses' heads when they were stopped. From fright and excitement, caused by the approach and proximity of the team, she became unconscious, and the result was a miscarriage and consequent illness. Recovery was denied to her on the ground that, "assuming that fright cannot form the basis of an action, it is obvious that no recovery can be had for injuries resulting therefrom." The appellant maintains upon this appeal that it was error, under the authority of that case, to refuse her request to charge.

That case has been much discussed and frequently criticized by legal scholars. Judicial authority supports its conclusions in some jurisdictions. Elsewhere the courts have reached other conclusions. Its conclusions cannot be tested by pure logic. The court recognized that its views of public policy to some extent dictated its decision. In fixing the limits of legal liability, such considerations may be given due weight. Only for consequences which follow from an infraction of a duty, to the injured party, from an invasion of his legal rights, is legal liability imposed. Even then legal liability does not extend beyond "proximate" consequences. Practical considerations must at times determine the bounds of correlative rights and duties as well as the point beyond which the courts will decline to trace causal connection.

"The question of liability is always anterior to the question of the measure of the consequences that go with liability. If there is no tort to be redressed, there is no occasion to consider what damage might be recovered if there were a finding of a tort." *Palsgraf v. Long Island R.R. Co.,* 248 N.Y. 339, 346, 162 N.E. 99, 101, 59 A.L.R. 1253, per Cardozo, C.J. In deciding that no action lies for fright and, therefore, no action for the consequences of fright, the court was dealing with the question of liability rather than the measure of consequences that go with liability. "In actions of negligence damage is of the very gist and essence of the plaintiff's cause." 1 Street, Foundations of Legal Liability, 444. Mental suffering or disturbance, even without consequences of physical injury, may in fact constitute actual damage; nevertheless the courts generally do not regard it as such damage as gives rise to a cause of action, though it be the direct result of the careless act. Whether the true explanation of that conclusion lies in an historical conception of injury or in supposed considerations of public policy may for the present be put aside. In either event the reason fails where fright or nervous shock causes visible physical injury. Then the careless act carries consequences of physical injury which, if caused directly, would undoubtedly be recognized as legal damages sufficient to support a cause of action for negligence. Refusal to sustain such a cause of action can be based only on one of two grounds: Either that the careless act invaded no right of the injured party and is not a tort, or that the physical injury consequent upon the mental disturbance or shock is not a proximate result of the tort.

Either alternative presents both theoretical and practical difficulties. The development of the law on this subject in Massachusetts strikingly illustrates these difficulties. In *Canning v. Inhabitants of Williamstown*, 1 Cush. (Mass.) 451, recovery was denied for fright and mental suffering without physical injury. In *Warren v. Boston & Maine R.R. Co.*, 163 Mass. 484, 40 N.E. 895, the driver of a vehicle thrown to the ground by a collision with a railroad train was permitted to recover for physical injuries caused mainly by the nervous shock. There the court did not refuse to trace the chain of causation from nervous shock to physical injury; at least where there was a physical impact: In *Spade v. Lynn & Boston R.R. Co.*, 168 Mass. 285, 288, 47 N.E. 88, it denied recovery for similar injuries where the evidence did not show such physical impact.

In that case the plaintiff claimed damages for physical injuries caused by fright and excitement due to the eviction of a disorderly passenger. The court, speaking per Allen, J., recognized that "exemption from liability for mere fright, terror, alarm, or anxiety, does not rest on the assumption that these do not constitute an actual injury," and that "a physical injury may be directly traceable to fright, and so may be caused by it. We cannot say, therefore, that such consequences may not flow proximately from unintentional negligence." The court, conscious that such consequences are unusual, placed its decision on the ground that the defendant was under a duty "to anticipate and guard against the probable consequences to ordinary people, but to carry the rule of damages further imposes an undue measure of responsibility upon those who are guilty only of unintentional negligence."

Upon an appeal from a judgment in favor of the plaintiff after a second trial in the same action, the record showed that in evicting the disorderly passenger the conductor "jostled another drunken man, who was standing in front of the plaintiff, and threw him upon her." The fall upon her seems to have been a trifling matter, taken by itself, but the fright caused by that and the antecedent disorder produced bodily ills. It was held that "the plaintiff could recover only for the pain and fright caused by the contact with her person, and not for such mental disturbance and injury as was caused by other acts of the conductor, and the general disturbance in the car." "The wrong to the plaintiff, if any, began with the battery; and it is for the consequences of the battery only that the defendant is liable, not for all the consequences of the drunken man's presence in the car, or of the defendant's attempt to remove him." *Spade v. Lynn & Boston R.R. Co.*, 172 Mass. 488, 52 N.E. 747.

To some extent the law on this subject has developed in this jurisdiction along similar lines. True, no case has since been presented to this court where the plaintiff claimed damages for physical injuries which resulted from mental distress caused by a careless act. In the intermediate appellate courts, such recovery has been generally allowed where there has been a physical impact. Without attempting detailed analyses of such cases, we may assume that they evince the view that, where there has been a physical impact, even though slight, accompanied by shock, there may be a recovery for damages to health caused by the shock, even though that shock was the result produced by the impact and fright concurrently. Recovery was not limited to or made dependent upon immediate visible or physical injuries.

The courts in such case attempt no differentiation between the direct physical injury caused by the impact and the damage caused by the fright, even where the fright preceded the impact. The result may seem at times anomalous, for the direct physical injury may be insignificant in relation to the damages consequent upon the fright. That anomaly did not escape the keen mind of Mr. Justice Holmes. "As has been explained repeatedly, it is an arbitrary exception, based upon a notion of what is practicable, that prevents a recovery for visible illness resulting from nervous shock alone. But when there has been a battery and the nervous shock results from the same wrongful management as the battery, it is at least equally impracticable to go further and to inquire whether the shock comes through the battery or along with it. Even were it otherwise, recognizing as we must the logic in favor of the plaintiff when a remedy is denied because the only immediate wrong was a shock to the nerves, we think that when the reality of the cause is guarantied by proof of a substantial battery of the person there is no occasion to press further the exception to general rules." *Homans v. Boston Elevated Ry. Co.*, 180 Mass., 456, 457, 62 N.E. 737.

We think that these considerations must sustain the trial judge's refusal to charge. Whether there can be a recovery for the consequences of fright caused by unintentional want of care depends in the first place upon the question whether a legal right of the plaintiff has been invaded by the defendant's negligence. In the cases of *Mitchell v. Rochester Ry. Co., supra,* and *Spade v. Lynn & Boston R.R. Co., supra,* the courts decided that for practical reasons there is ordinarily no duty to exercise care to avoid causing mental disturbance, and no legal right to mental security. Serious consequences from mere mental disturbance unaccompanied by physical shock cannot be anticipated, and no person is bound to be alert to avert a danger that foresight does not disclose. The conclusion is fortified by the practical consideration that, where there has been no physical contact, there is danger that fictitious claims may be fabricated. Therefore, where no wrong was claimed other than a mental disturbance, the courts refused to sanction a recovery for the consequences of that disturbance. Here there was more. The defendant should have foreseen that a collision with the car in which plaintiff's testatrix was a passenger would cause injury to the passengers. She did collide with the car through lack of care, and she did cause injury to the plaintiff's testatrix. That injury was not confined to fright. The fright was only a link in the chain of causation between collision and fractured skull. The collision itself, the consequent jar to the passengers in the car, was a battery and an invasion of their legal right. Their cause of action is complete when they suffered consequent damages.

Doubtless the question still remains whether the fractured skull was the proximate result of the collision. That question was presented to the jury as a question of fact. Assuming that upon this appeal we may determine whether it was a question of fact or of law, we are clear that it was a question of fact. We do not say that in all cases the courts will hold a defendant liable for remote physical injuries resulting from nervous shock. Here the physical injuries are not remote, either in time or space. They were almost immediate, and the evident result of the defendant's lack of care. No slight physical injuries in addition to those resulting from the shock would fortify the plaintiff's claim.

The order should be affirmed, with costs, and the question certified answered in the negative.

CARDOZO, C.J., and POUND, CRANE, KELLOGG, O'BRIEN, and HUBBS, JJ., concur.

Judgment affirmed.

Notes and Questions

1. Put on your procedural spectacles for a moment. Note how the issue in *Comstock* arose. The defendant requested a charge to the jury that would have compelled a defendant's verdict if at the time of the collision the plaintiff sustained only shock and fright, but no physical injury. The lower court refused to charge the jury in that manner, and the court of appeals affirmed. In the court's view, "where there has been a physical impact, even though slight, accompanied by shock, there may be a recovery for damages to health caused by the shock, even though that shock was the result produced by the impact and fright concurrently." Is the court no longer concerned about fictitious fright cases?

Does the physical impact rule at least assure the defendant some notice of an eventual claim or lawsuit? Suppose a defendant negligently swerves her vehicle to avoid an apparent obstruction, causing the driver in the adjacent lane to experience fright and emotional distress. How may a defendant protect herself against these types of lawsuits? Should this dilemma tip the scales toward rejection of the underlying cause of action in every nonimpact case?

2. What was left of the *Mitchell* rule after *Comstock*, at least in cases where there was (or arguably could have been) physical contact? Does *Comstock* encourage false claims of physical impact? What are the limitations on compensation for consequences caused by fright accompanied by some physical impact? Note the court's admonition: "We do not say that in all cases the courts will hold a defendant liable for remote physical injuries resulting from nervous shock. Here the physical injuries are not remote, either in time or space." The court forged two limitations: First, the injuries must be physical, not emotional or mental; second, the physical injuries must not be remote. By "remote," did the court only mean that the physical injuries must occur almost immediately? Or does the limitation serve another function?

3. What is the meaning of "physical injury" as used in the foregoing statement? Consider the statement of Judge McEntee in *Petition of United States*, 418 F.2d 264 (1st Cir. 1969): "The term 'physical' is not used in its ordinary sense for purposes of applying the 'physical consequences' rule.

Rather, the word is used to indicate that the condition or illness for which recovery is sought must be one susceptible of objective determination. Hence, a definite nervous disorder is a 'physical injury' sufficient to support an action for damages for negligence." *See also Wallace v. Coca–Cola Bottling Plants, Inc.,* 269 A.2d 117, 121 (Me. 1970), *overruled, Culbert v. Sampson's Supermarkets Inc.,* 444 A.2d 433 (Me. 1982) ("The mental and emotional suffering, to be compensable, must be substantial and manifested by objective symptomatology.").

4. The impact rule has produced some amusing cases. In *Christy Brothers Circus v. Turnage,* 38 Ga. App. 581, 144 S.E. 680 (1928), the plaintiff sat in the front row at the defendant's circus; one of the horses backed up and evacuated its bowels into her lap. The court permitted recovery for humiliation and illness resulting from the "impact."

BATTALLA v. NEW YORK

Court of Appeals of New York, 1961.
10 N.Y.2d 237, 219 N.Y.S.2d 34, 176 N.E.2d 729.

BURKE, JUDGE. The question presented is whether the claim states a cause of action when it alleges that claimant was negligently caused to suffer "severe emotional and neurological disturbances with residual physical manifestations."

The appellant avers that in September of 1956, at Bellayre Mountain Ski Center, the infant plaintiff was placed in a chair lift by an employee of the State who failed to secure and properly lock the belt intended to protect the occupant. As a result of this alleged negligent act, the infant plaintiff became frightened and hysterical upon the descent, with consequential injuries.

The Court of Claims, on a motion to dismiss the complaint, held that a cause of action does lie. The Appellate Division found itself constrained to follow *Mitchell v. Rochester Ry. Co.,* 151 N.Y. 107, 45 N.E. 354, and, therefore, reversed and dismissed the claim. The *Mitchell* case decided that there could be no recovery for injuries, physical or mental, incurred by fright negligently induced.

It is our opinion that *Mitchell* should be overruled. It is undisputed that a rigorous application of its rule would be unjust, as well as opposed to experience and logic. On the other hand, resort to the somewhat inconsistent exceptions would merely add further confusion to a legal situation which presently lacks that coherence which precedent should possess. "We act in the finest common-law tradition when we adapt and alter decisional law to produce common-sense justice. * * * Legislative action there could, of course, be, but we abdicate our own function, in a field peculiarly nonstatutory, when we refuse to reconsider an old and unsatisfactory court-made rule." *Woods v. Lancet,* 303 N.Y. 349, 355, 102 N.E.2d 691, 694.

Before passing to a résumé of the evolution of the doctrine in this State, it is well to note that it has been thoroughly repudiated by the English courts which initiated it, rejected by a majority of American jurisdictions, abandoned by many which originally adopted it, and diluted, through numerous exceptions, in the minority which retained it. Moreover, it is the opinion of scholars that *the right* to bring an action should be enforced.

It is fundamental to our common-law system that one may seek redress for every substantial wrong. "The best statement of the rule is that a wrong-doer is responsible for the natural and proximate consequences of his misconduct; and what are such consequences must generally be left for the determination of the jury." *Ehrgott v. Mayor of City of New York,* 96 N.Y. 264, 281. A departure from this axiom was introduced by *Mitchell,* wherein recovery was denied to plaintiff, a pregnant woman, who, although not physically touched, was negligently caused to abort her child. Defendant's horses were driven in such a reckless manner that, when finally restrained, plaintiff was trapped between their heads. The court indicated essentially three reasons for dismissing the complaint. It stated first that, since plaintiff could not recover for mere fright, there could be no recovery for injuries resulting therefrom. It was assumed, in addition, that the miscarriage was not the proximate result of defendant's negligence, but rather was due to an accidental or unusual combination of circumstances. Finally, the court reasoned that a recovery would be contrary to public policy because that type of injury could be feigned without detection and it would result in a flood of litigation where damages must rest on speculation.

With the possible exception of the last, it seems "[a]ll these objections have been demolished many times, and it is threshing old straw to deal with them." (Prosser, Torts [2d ed.], § 37, pp. 176–177.) Moreover, we have stated that the conclusions of the *Mitchell* case "cannot be tested by pure logic." *Comstock v. Wilson,* 1931, 257 N.Y. 231, 234, 177 N.E. 431, 432. Although finding impact and granting recovery, the unanimous court in *Comstock* rejected all but the public policy arguments of the *Mitchell* decision.

We presently feel that even the public policy argument is subject to challenge. Although fraud, extra litigation and a measure of speculation are, of course, possibilities, it is no reason for a court to eschew a measure of its jurisdiction. "The argument from mere expediency cannot commend itself to a Court of justice, resulting in the denial of a logical legal right and remedy in *all* cases because in *some* a fictitious injury may be urged as a real one." *Green v. T.A. Shoemaker & Co.,* 111 Md. 69, 81, 73 A. 688, 692.

In any event, it seems that fraudulent accidents and injuries are just as easily feigned in the slight-impact cases and other exceptions wherein New York permits a recovery, as in the no-impact cases which it has heretofore shunned. As noted by the Law Revision Commission: "The exceptions to the rule cannot be said to insure recovery to any substantial number of meritorious claimants and there is good ground for believing that they breed dishonest attempts to mold the facts so as to fit them within the grooves leading to recovery." (1936 Report of N.Y.Law

Rev.Comm., p. 450.) The ultimate result is that the honest claimant is penalized for his reluctance to fashion the facts within the framework of the exceptions.

Not only, therefore, are claimants in this situation encouraged by the *Mitchell* disqualification to perjure themselves, but the constant attempts to either come within an old exception, or establish a new one, lead to excess appellate litigation. In any event, even if a flood of litigation were realized by abolition of the exception, it is the duty of the courts to willingly accept the opportunity to settle these disputes.

The only substantial policy argument of *Mitchell* is that the damages or injuries are somewhat speculative and difficult to prove. However, the question of proof in individual situations should not be the arbitrary basis upon which to bar all actions, and "it is beside the point * * * in determining sufficiency of a pleading." *Woods v. Lancet*, 303 N.Y. 349, 356, 102 N.E.2d 691, 695. In many instances, just as in impact cases, there will be no doubt as to the presence and extent of the damage and the fact that it was proximately caused by defendant's negligence. In the difficult cases, we must look to the quality and genuineness of proof and rely to an extent on the contemporary sophistication of the medical profession and the ability of the court and jury to weed out the dishonest claims. Claimant should, therefore, be given an opportunity to prove that her injuries were proximately caused by defendant's negligence.

Accordingly, the judgment should be reversed and the claim reinstated, with costs.

VAN VOORHIS, JUDGE (dissenting).

In following the Massachusetts rule, which corresponded to that enunciated in this State by *Mitchell v. Rochester Ry. Co.*, 151 N.Y. 107, 45 N.E. 354, Mr. Justice Holmes described it as "an arbitrary exception, based upon a notion of what is practicable, that prevents a recovery for visible illness resulting from nervous shock alone." *Spade v. Lynn & Boston Railroad*, 168 Mass. 285, 288, 47 N.E. 88, 38 L.R.A. 512, 60 Am.St.Rep. 393. Illogical as the legal theoreticians acknowledge this rule to be, it was Justice Holmes who said that the life of the law has not been logic but experience. Experience has produced this rule to prevent the ingenuity of special pleaders and paid expert witnesses from getting recoveries in negligence for nervous shock without physical injury, which was stated as well as possible in *Mitchell v. Rochester Ry. Co.*

The opinion likewise points out the speculative nature of the usual evidence of causation where it is contended that mere fright has resulted in "nervous disease, blindness, insanity, or even a miscarriage."

These statements in the *Mitchell* opinion are not archaic or antiquated, but are even more pertinent today than when they were first stated. At a time like the present, with constantly enlarging recoveries both in scope and amount in all fields of negligence law, and when an influential portion of the Bar is organized as never before to promote ever-increasing recoveries for the most intangible and elusive injuries, little imagination is required to envision mental illness and psychosomatic medicine as encompassed by the enlargement of the coverage of negligence claims to include this fertile field. In *Comstock v. Wilson*, 257 N.Y. 231, 177 N.E. 431, *Mitchell v. Rochester Ry. Co.* is not overruled, but the opinion by Judge Lehman cites it as well as the Massachusetts rule of *Spade v. Lynn & Boston R.R. Co.*, 168 Mass. 285, 47 N.E. 88, as holding that "for practical reasons there is ordinarily no duty to exercise care to avert causing mental disturbance, and no legal right to mental security." Judge Lehman's opinion continues: "Serious consequences from mere mental disturbance unaccompanied by physical shock cannot be anticipated, and no person is bound to be alert to avert a danger that foresight does not disclose. The conclusion is fortified by the practical consideration that where there has been no physical contact there is danger that fictitious claims may be fabricated. Therefore, where no wrong was claimed other than a mental disturbance, the courts refuse to sanction a recovery for the consequence of that disturbance." (257 N.Y. at 238–239, 177 N.E. at 433).

The problem involved in enlarging the scope of recovery in negligence, even in instances where, as here, an enlargement might be justified on purely theoretical grounds, is that, when once the door has been opened, the new and broader rule is in practice pressed to its extreme conclusion. Courts and juries become prone to accept as established fact that fright has been the cause of mental or physical consequences which informed medical men of balanced judgment find too complicated to trace. Once a medical expert has been found who, for a consideration, expresses an opinion that the relationship of cause and effect exists, courts and juries tend to lay aside critical judgment and accept the fact as stated.

This is the practical reason mentioned by Judges Holmes and Lehman. The Pennsylvania Supreme Court has recently decided that to hold otherwise "would open a Pandora's box." *Bosley v. Andrews*, 393 Pa. 161, 168, 142 A.2d 263, 266.

In my view the judgment dismissing the claim should be affirmed.

FULD, FROESSEL and FOSTER, JJ., concur with BURKE, J.

VAN VOORHIS, J., dissents in an opinion in which DESMOND, C.J., and DYE, J., concur.

Judgment reversed and order of the Court of Claims reinstated, with costs in this court and in the Appellate Division.

Notes and Questions

1. Why did the majority overrule *Mitchell v. Rochester Railway Co.*? Are there sound policy reasons for adhering to common law precedent even if the court is convinced that the precedent is unsound? Explain. Are you concerned that prospective plaintiffs or defendants may have relied upon *Mitchell* in conducting their affairs? Why? *See Rush, supra* p. 42. Should the court have considered whether liability insurance would cover losses unaccompanied by impact?

2.   Does *Battalla* answer the question posed at the beginning of this section whether B, the bystander in *Johnson v. Roscoe & Baker*, may recover for emotional and mental distress? How is B's situation distinguishable from that of the plaintiff in *Battalla?*

3.   Before 1968, case authority generally rejected recovery by bystanders suffering emotional harm after observing an accident negligently caused to another. Then in *Dillon v. Legg,* 68 Cal. 2d 728, 441 P.2d 912, 69 Cal. Rptr. 72 (1968), the California court permitted a bystander to recover. In *Dillon,* the plaintiff was the injured victim's relative who was present at the scene of the accident. Suppose the bystander is not a relative, or the suing relative did not observe the accident. What then? Should courts additionally require "a sudden and brief event causing the child's injury"? *See Jansen v. Children's Hospital Medical Center,* 31 Cal. App. 3d 22, 106 Cal. Rptr. 883 (1973). Should courts defer to legislative judgment in drawing the lines, or should they define the parameters of liability on a case by case basis? Which method is preferable? Why? *Thing v. La Chusa,* 48 Cal. 3d 644, 771 P.2d 814, 257 Cal. Rptr. 865 (1989), resolves some of these issues.

JOHNSON v. NEW YORK

Court of Appeals of New York, 1975.
37 N.Y.2d 378, 372 N.Y.S.2d 638, 334 N.E.2d 590.

BREITEL, CHIEF JUDGE. On claimant Fleeter Thorpe's appeal, the issue is whether the daughter of a patient in a State hospital, falsely advised that the patient, her mother, had died, may recover from the State for emotional harm. She sustained the harm as a direct result of the negligent misinformation provided by the hospital in the course of it advising relatives of the death of a patient. The mother was in fact alive and well.

Claimant and her aunt, Nellie Johnson, since deceased, had filed a claim against the State for funeral expenses incurred, emotional harm and punitive damages. The Court of Claims awarded claimant $7,500 for funeral expenses undertaken on the false information, and for emotional harm. It denied her punitive damages, and dismissed the aunt's claim for insufficiency. The State appealed to the Appellate Division and claimants cross-appealed. The Appellate Division modified, limiting the daughter's award to her pecuniary losses of $1,658.47, and otherwise affirmed as to both claimants. The aunt's estate, unlike the daughter, took no further appeal to this court.

There should be a reversal. The daughter of a hospital patient may recover for emotional harm sustained by her as a result of negligent misinformation given by the hospital that her mother had died. Key to liability, of course, is the hospital's duty, borne or assumed, to advise the proper next of kin of the death of a patient.

Claimant's mother, Emma Johnson, had been a patient in the Hudson River State Hospital since 1960. On August 6, 1970, another patient, also named Emma Johnson, died. Later that day, the hospital sent a telegram addressed to Nellie Johnson of Albany, claimant's aunt and the sister of the living Emma Johnson. The telegram read:

REGRET TO INFORM YOU OF DEATH OF EMMA JOHNSON PLEASE NOTIFY RELATIVES MAKE BURIAL ARRANGEMENTS HAVE UNDERTAKER CONTACT HOSPITAL BEFORE COMING FOR BODY HOSPITAL WISHES TO STUDY ALL DEATHS FOR SCIENTIFIC REASONS PLEASE WIRE POST MORTEM CONSENT

HUDSON RIVER STATE HOSPITAL

In accordance with the instructions in the telegram, claimant was notified of her mother's death by her aunt. An undertaker was engaged; the body of the deceased Emma Johnson was released by the hospital and taken to Albany that night. A wake was set for August 11, with burial the next day. In the interim claimant incurred expenses in preparing the body for the funeral, and in notifying other relatives of her mother's death.

On the afternoon of the wake, claimant and her aunt went to the funeral home to view the body. After examining the body, both claimant and her aunt remarked that the mother's appearance had changed. Nellie Johnson also expressed doubt that the corpse was that of her sister Emma. Thereafter the doubts built up, and upon returning that evening for the wake, claimant, in a state of extreme distress, examined the corpse more closely and verified that it was not that of her mother. At this point, claimant became "very, very hysterical," and had to be helped from the funeral chapel.

The hospital was called, and the mistake confirmed. Claimant's mother was alive and well in another wing of the hospital. Later that evening at the hospital, the deputy director, with the authorization of the director, admitted the mistake to claimant and her aunt. Upon the trial it appeared that the hospital had violated its own procedures and with gross carelessness had "pulled" the wrong patient record.

After this incident, claimant did not work in her employment for more than 11 days. She complained of "[r]ecurrent nightmares, terrifying dreams of death, seeing the coffin * * * difficulty in concentrating, irritability, inability to function at work properly, general tenseness and anxiety." Her psychiatrist testified that "She appeared to be somewhat depressed, tremulous. She seemed to be under a considerable amount of pressure. She cried easily when relating events that occurred. I thought that she spoke rather rapidly and she was obviously perspiring." Both her psychiatrist and that of the State agreed that, as a result of the incident, claimant suffered "excessive anxiety," that is, anxiety neurosis. Her expert, as indicated, testified that she showed objective manifestations of that condition.

One to whom a duty of care is owed, it has been held, may recover for harm sustained solely as a result of an initial, negligently-caused psychological trauma, but with ensuing psychic harm with residual physical manifestations. *Battalla v. State of New York*, 10 N.Y.2d 237, 238–239, 219 N.Y.S.2d 34, 35, 176 N.E.2d 729; *Ferrara v. Galluchio*, 5 N.Y.2d 16, 21–22, 176 N.Y.S.2d 996, 999–1000, 152 N.E.2d 249, 252. In the absence of contemporaneous or consequential physical injury, courts have been reluctant to permit recovery for negligently caused psychological trauma, with ensuing emotional harm alone. The reasons for the more restrictive rule were best summarized by Prosser: "The temporary emotion of fright, so far from serious that it does no physical harm, is so evanescent a thing, so easily counterfeited, and usually so trivial, that the courts have been quite unwilling to protect the plaintiff against mere negligence, where the elements of extreme outrage and moral blame which have had such weight in the case of the intentional tort are lacking." Contemporaneous or consequential physical harm, coupled with the initial psychological trauma, was, however, thought to provide an index of reliability otherwise absent in a claim for psychological trauma with only psychological consequences.

There have developed, however, two exceptions. The first is the minority rule permitting recovery for emotional harm resulting from negligent transmission by a telegraph company of a message announcing death.

The second exception permits recovery for emotional harm to a close relative resulting from negligent mishandling of a corpse. Recovery in these cases has ostensibly been grounded on a violation of the relative's quasi-property right in the body. It has been noted, however, that in this context such a "property right" is little more than a fiction; in reality the personal feelings of the survivors are being protected.

In both the telegraph cases and the corpse mishandling cases, there exists "an especial likelihood of genuine and serious mental distress, arising from the special circumstances, which serves as a guarantee that the claim is not spurious." Prosser notes that "[t]here may perhaps be other such cases." The instant claim provides an example of such a case.

As the Appellate Division correctly found and the State in truth concedes, the hospital was negligent in failing to ascertain the proper next of kin when it mistakenly transmitted the death notice to claimant's aunt and through her, at its behest, to claimant. While for one to be held liable in negligence he need not foresee novel or extraordinary consequences, it is enough that he be aware of the risk of danger. The consequential funeral expenditures and the serious psychological impact on claimant of a false message informing her of the death of her mother, were all within the "orbit of the danger" and therefore within the "orbit of the duty" for the breach of which a wrongdoer may be held liable. Thus, the hospital owed claimant a duty to refrain from such conduct, a duty breached when it negligently sent the false message. The false message and the events flowing from its receipt were the proximate cause of claimant's emotional harm. Hence, claimant is entitled to recover for that harm, especially if supported by objective manifestations of that harm.

Tobin v. Grossman, 24 N.Y.2d 609, 301 N.Y.S.2d 554, 249 N.E.2d 419, is not relevant. In the *Tobin* case, the court held that no cause of action lies for unintended harm sustained by one, solely as a result of injuries inflicted directly upon another, regardless of the relationship and whether the one was an eyewitness to the incident which resulted in the direct injuries. In this case, however, the injury was inflicted by the hospital directly on claimant by its negligent sending of a false message announcing her mother's death. Claimant was not indirectly harmed by injury caused to another; she was not a mere eyewitness of or bystander to injury caused to another. Instead, she was the one to whom a duty was directly owed by the hospital, and the one who was directly injured by the hospital's breach of that duty. Thus, the rationale underlying the *Tobin* case, namely, the real dangers of extending recovery for harm to others than those directly involved, is inapplicable to the instant case.

Moreover, not only justice but logic compels the further conclusion that if claimant was entitled to recover her pecuniary losses she was also entitled to recover for the emotional harm caused by the same tortious act. The recovery of the funeral expenses stands only because a duty to claimant was breached. Such a duty existing and such a breach of that duty occurring, she is entitled to recover the proven harmful consequences proximately caused by the breach. In the light of the *Battalla* and *Ferrara* cases, and the reasoning upon which they were based, recovery for emotional harm to one subjected directly to the tortious act may not be disallowed so long as the evidence is sufficient to show causation and substantiality of the harm suffered, together with a "guarantee of genuineness" to which the court referred in the *Ferrara* case 5 N.Y.2d 16, 21, 176 N.Y.S.2d 996, 999, 152 N.E.2d 249, 252; *see also Battalla v. State of New York*, 10 N.Y.2d 237, 242, 219 N.Y.S.2d 34, 38, 176 N.E.2d 729, 731.

Order reversed, with costs, and case remitted to Appellate Division, Third Department, for further proceedings in accordance with the opinion herein.

Notes and Questions

1. After *Battalla*, may a plaintiff sue for negligent infliction of emotional harm? Although the impact rule was rejected in *Battalla*, physical harm is still essential. *See Johnson*. But what does "physical harm" mean? *See supra* note 3, p. 287.

2. *Johnson* recognized two existing exceptions to the physical harm rule. Did this case represent a logical extension of these exceptions? Or did the court merely embrace one of them? Where should the courts draw the line in extending liability for negligent infliction of emotional harm?

3. In *Molien v. Kaiser Foundation Hospitals*, 27 Cal. 3d 916, 616 P.2d 813, 167 Cal. Rptr. 831 (1980), the defendant negligently diagnosed a wife's condition as syphilis, instructed her to advise her husband of the diagnosis and have him submit to a blood test. His test proved negative. Recriminations followed, and the marriage ultimately broke up. The husband sued

for infliction of mental distress and for loss of consortium. In holding that there might be recovery, the court declared that "the attempted distinction between physical and psychological injury merely clouds the issue. The essential question is one of proof." *Id.* at 930, 616 P.2d at 821, 167 Cal. Rptr. at 839. "[A] cause of action may be stated for the negligent infliction of serious emotional distress." *Id.* at 931, 616 P.2d at 821, 167 Cal. Rptr. at 839. In light of this observation, refer to hypothetical bystanders A and B in *Johnson v. Roscoe & Baker.* See hypothetical posed at page 281. Can B recover for mental or emotional distress?

Chapter IV

THE CRIMINAL JUSTICE SYSTEM

A. AN OVERVIEW OF THE CRIMINAL PROCESS

The vast majority of criminal proceedings are instituted by the states and their various subdivisions. In the fifty-one jurisdictions—the federal government and the fifty states—there are many variations in structure and in practice. Moreover, at almost every stage of the criminal process the police officers, prosecutors, and judges exercise considerable discretion in determining how or whether to proceed. Many potential prosecutions will be screened out in the process of deciding whether to go forward. Charging decisions may be modified. Prospective punishments may be altered by plea bargaining.

Despite the variations and the discretion in administration, basic similarities permit us to describe, in summary fashion, the typical stages in the operation of the criminal justice system. All of the states have been strongly influenced by the English common law. The rights of English citizens as against the Crown, as those rights had been shaped by the English courts by the late Eighteenth Century, are reflected in large measure in the United States Constitution and the constitutions of the several states. Moreover, as we shall see, vital procedural protections written into the United States Constitution are binding upon the states. By virtue of Supreme Court decisions interpreting the relevant constitutional provisions, criminal procedure has become in large measure constitutionalized. That is not a contradiction of our earlier observation that there are many variations from state to state. It does mean, however, that in very important respects the United States Constitution imposes nationwide a set of minimum standards.

B. PROGRESSION OF THE CRIMINAL CASE

Typically, serious criminal cases progress through predictable stages. Crimes are ordinarily classified as felonies (crimes for which punishment of more than one year of imprisonment is authorized), misdemeanors (crimes for which a penalty of one year or less is prescribed), and petty offenses (those for which a violator can be confined for no more than six months). Because the procedures required in felony cases are more demanding than those imposed in lesser offenses, we will focus on a felony prosecution in a typical state jurisdiction.

1. INVESTIGATION

Most offenses come to the attention of law enforcement authorities through direct observation by police officers or through reports from witnesses or victims. Many crimes, of course, are unreported and obviously not all that are reported are investigated with the same diligence.

Let us suppose, however, that a household burglary has been reported to the local police department; that police officers have been dispatched to the scene and have obtained descriptions of the offender from the owner of the premises and from a neighbor who saw a suspicious-looking stranger leaving the scene and noted the license number of the car in which he departed; and that the police, having checked the registration of the vehicle and briefly investigated the identity and the criminal record of the owner (one John Roscoe), believe that he is the culprit. In the law's terminology, they now have "probable cause"—a reasonable belief, founded on common sense and specific, articulable facts, that he has committed the crime. As the words imply, probable cause is more than mere suspicion, but may fall considerably short of certainty.

2. ARREST, SEARCH, AND STATIONHOUSE PROCESSING

Because they have probable cause, the police could arrest Roscoe immediately—that is, take him into custody and charge him with the crime without pausing to procure an arrest warrant. If they wish to arrest Roscoe in his home, as distinguished from a public place, the Fourth Amendment to the United States Constitution would obligate the officers to secure an arrest warrant from a magistrate or judge. In this instance, the police have practical reasons for wanting to go to Roscoe's home. If they were to find some of the items stolen during the burglary there, it would strengthen the case against him. Accordingly, they decide to apply to a magistrate for both an arrest warrant and a warrant to search Roscoe's residence.

To secure the warrants, the police officers prepare an affidavit setting forth the information supporting their belief that Roscoe has committed the crime in question and setting forth what they hope to find and where they hope to find it, and why they believe it is there. Once satisfied that the affidavit shows probable cause, the magistrate will issue a warrant for Roscoe's arrest and a search warrant designating with particularity the place to be searched and the items subject to seizure.

Next, the officers execute the warrants—that is, they go to Roscoe's home, announce their presence, and serve the warrants. When they arrest John, they may search him. For the arresting officer's protection, a search of the person may be conducted any time a suspect is arrested, whether or not a search warrant has been obtained. The police then search the premises. In the attic, they find silverware that they believe is a fruit of the burglary. This they seize as evidence of the crime. Had the officers failed to get a search warrant, the seizure of the silverware would have been illegal and its introduction in evidence subject to suppression.

Roscoe is then escorted to the stationhouse and "booked." This is simply an administrative procedure, a notation for the records of the police department of the suspect's name, the offense for which he has been arrested, the time of his arrest, and related details. Roscoe will be fingerprinted and probably will be questioned. As all television viewers know, the police are required to give the *Miranda* warnings[a] before seeking to elicit information from a person in their custody. The warnings include advice that the suspect has the right to remain silent, that anything he says can be used against him in a court of law, that he has the right to the presence of an attorney, and that, if he cannot afford an attorney, one will be appointed for him prior to any questioning if he so desires.

Police station processing may take several hours. The police, however, must take the arrestee before a judicial officer without unnecessary delay.[b] Before taking John before a judge, a police officer or one of the local prosecutors writes a "complaint" setting forth the charges against him. It will be presented to the judge at the initial appearance.

3. INITIAL APPEARANCE

The first, or initial, appearance before a magistrate or judge is usually a brief administrative, rather than evidentiary, proceeding. The magistrate will wish to make sure that Roscoe is the person named in the complaint. She will then inform him of the charge set forth in the complaint and the various rights that he will have in the course of the proceedings. This will include the advice that Roscoe has the right to be represented by counsel and that counsel will be appointed for him if he is indigent and wishes to have representation. If he does request an attorney, the magistrate will initiate the necessary arrangements. The magistrate will also set a date for the preliminary hearing, the next stage of the process. Finally, the magistrate will set the conditions upon which the defendant may obtain his release from custody pending final disposition of the case. This may involve posting bail or satisfying other conditions of release.

4. PRELIMINARY HEARING

At this stage, the prosecutor must satisfy the magistrate that sufficient evidence justifies further proceedings—in traditional language,

a.   The warnings stem from *Miranda v. Arizona*, 384 U.S. 436 (1966).

b.   The Supreme Court has held that the initial appearance must occur as soon as reasonably feasible. *County of Riverside v. McLaughlin*, 500 U.S. 44 (1991) (upholding 48–hour delay).

the prosecution must show reason to "bind the case over" for trial. This hearing is an evidentiary one, although less formal than a trial. Ordinarily, the prosecutor will present one or more of his key witnesses, but will not develop his full case. He need only convince the magistrate that there is probable cause to believe that the defendant committed the crime; the matter of proof of guilt beyond a reasonable doubt is reserved for the trial. The defendant has a right to be represented by counsel at the hearing. Ordinarily, defense counsel will merely cross-examine the prosecution's witnesses and will otherwise refrain from exposing the defendant's strategy. If the magistrate finds probable cause, the case moves on. If she finds that the charge is not supported by substantial evidence, she will dismiss it. May the State refile a charge that has been dismissed?

In Roscoe's case, the evidence satisfies the judge that there is probable cause to believe that Roscoe committed the crime charged. The magistrate therefore directs that the case be bound over for trial. At this stage, the prosecutor will prepare an "information" and file it with the trial court. An "information" is simply a formal written accusation signed by the prosecuting official, a substitute for the less formal "complaint."

Alternatively, in a few states and in federal prosecutions, the written accusation charging a felony must be made by a grand jury. In that instance, the charging instrument is known as an indictment. In "information" states, the prosecutor has the option to present the matter to a grand jury, but does so only infrequently, usually when he believes that it will be advantageous to make use of the grand jury's power to call witnesses and subpoena documents. Grand jury proceedings are customarily conducted in secret and in the absence of defense counsel.

5. ARRAIGNMENT

At the arraignment, the defendant makes his first official appearance before the court designated to try him. He is informed of the charge set forth in the information or indictment and the pleas available to him. If he elects to plead guilty, as many defendants do, he waives the right to trial and all of the other rights associated with the conduct of a fair trial such as the right to confront witnesses, the right to a jury, and the right to require the state to prove guilt beyond a reasonable doubt. Before accepting that plea, the judge must assure that the defendant understands the nature of the charge and the applicable penalties, and that his decision to waive his rights is not coerced. If the defendant pleads not guilty, the matter is set for trial.

In our criminal justice system, many guilty pleas are entered pursuant to plea bargains—that is, agreements between the prosecution and the defense. In return for the plea and the consequent saving of prosecutorial and judicial resources, the prosecution offers concessions. These may take various forms. The prosecutor may drop one or more of the charges; reduce a charge to a lower level offense, for example, from burglary to theft; propose, subject to court approval, an agreed-upon sentence; or simply agree to recommend a particular penalty to the sentencing judge.

Plea bargaining is a controversial subject. Critics argue that it may make the outcome of the case turn on inappropriate considerations, such as the prosecutor's caseload or the degree of court congestion, rather than on the societal interest in a just punishment. Plea bargaining may also encourage prosecutors to over-charge in order to increase the leverage that they can exert. Some defendants may believe that judges impose heavier penalties on those defendants who go to trial and lose than on similarly situated offenders who waive their right to a trial, thus putting a price on the exercise of the constitutionally guaranteed right to a jury trial.

Plea bargaining also has its defenders and has received widespread judicial approval. Most jurisdictions have also adopted rules to regulate the practice. In *Santobello v. New York,* 404 U.S. 257 (1971), Chief Justice Burger, speaking for the Supreme Court, approved plea bargaining in the following terms:

> The disposition of criminal charges by agreement between the prosecutor and the accused, sometimes loosely called "plea bargaining," is an essential component of the administration of justice. Properly administered, it is to be encouraged. If every criminal charge were subjected to a full-scale trial, the States and the Federal Government would need to multiply by many times the number of judges and court facilities.

> Disposition of charges after plea discussions is not only an essential part of the process but a highly desirable part for many reasons. It leads to prompt and largely final disposition of most criminal cases; it avoids much of the corrosive impact of enforced idleness during pretrial confinement for those who are denied release pending trial; it protects the public from those accused persons who are prone to continue criminal conduct even while on pretrial release; and, by shortening the time between charge and disposition, it enhances whatever may be the rehabilitative prospects of the guilty when they are ultimately imprisoned.

A final note on guilty pleas: For every felony case that goes to trial in an American court, many more are terminated by guilty plea. Does this suggest that many defendants who plead may be bowing to pressure?

6. PRETRIAL MOTIONS

In most jurisdictions, several kinds of motions[c] must be presented before trial. Among these are motions that challenge the prosecution, for example, attacks upon the preliminary hearing or the composition of the grand jury, motions asserting defects in the indictment or information,

---

c. Requests for a ruling by the judge.

or claims that the charge was not brought within applicable time limitations. Motions to suppress on the ground that evidence was obtained in violation of the defendant's rights, such as motions challenging the validity of a confession or claiming that physical evidence was illegally seized, must also be promptly filed. The same is true of motions requesting discovery of evidence within the control of the prosecution, such as a request that the government produce for examination by the defense the results of laboratory tests.[d] Other examples of pretrial motions are motions for a change of judge, motions for a change of venue, and motions for continuance of the trial.

7. TRIAL

In a felony case or a misdemeanor case punishable by more than six months' imprisonment, the defendant has a constitutional right to trial by jury. In most jurisdictions, the jury consists of twelve persons and unanimity is required for a verdict, although juries of six or more have also been held to be constitutionally permissible, as have guilty verdicts supported by ten of twelve jurors. The right to a jury trial may be waived and many defendants elect a "bench" trial, in which event the judge determines the ultimate question of guilt or innocence.

The most important difference between a criminal and a civil trial is the standard of proof: In a criminal trial, guilt must be established beyond a reasonable doubt; civil verdicts require only proof by a preponderance of the evidence.[e] There are several other notable differences: The defendant in a criminal court enjoys many rights, including a presumption of innocence, a right to counsel at the government's expense if he cannot afford to pay counsel, and a right not to take the witness stand. A criminal defendant is also entitled to exclude evidence obtained through unconstitutional police procedures.

In most other respects, the criminal trial and the civil trial are similar. *See supra* Chapter II, Section O. The prosecution, like the civil plaintiff, presents its case first. The defense follows. Each side, of course, has the opportunity to cross-examine opposing witnesses. If the trial is by jury, each side submits proposed jury instructions and the judge

---

d. In most jurisdictions, discovery in criminal cases is very limited. Physical evidence is subject to pretrial examination, but compulsory pretrial examination of witnesses by depositions or interrogatories is not available in the federal system or in most state systems. Compare discovery procedures in the civil context, *supra* pp. 110–19. In all jurisdictions, the defendant is protected from the compulsion to testify, both in criminal trial and pretrial proceedings, by the Fifth Amendment privilege against self-incrimination. Both sides, of course, may interview prospective witnesses who consent to talk. Also, as observed above, the state has available to it the investigatory power of the grand jury.

Quite apart from rules relating to discovery, a prosecutor is required to disclose to defense counsel evidence favorable to the accused which, were it suppressed, would deprive the defendant of a fair trial. This is a constitutional requirement resting on the Due Process Clauses of the Fifth and Fourteenth Amendments. *See Brady v. Maryland,* 373 U.S. 83 (1963) (requiring disclosure of exculpatory evidence); *United States v. Agurs,* 427 U.S. 97 (1976).

e. A few limited categories of civil cases require "clear and convincing" proof. In general, however, civil liability is imposed if the jury believes that the plaintiff's version of the facts is more likely than not.

decides which instructions to give to the jury. If the jury cannot agree on a verdict of guilty or acquittal, a relatively infrequent occurrence, the matter is subject to retrial.

8.   POST–TRIAL MOTIONS

The defendant who has been found guilty by the jury may ask the court to intervene. He may move for a new trial on the ground that the prosecutor engaged in misconduct or that the trial was infected by error, for example, evidence that was improperly admitted. He may also move for judgment on the ground that no jury could reasonably have found, on the basis of the evidence adduced, that the defendant was guilty beyond a reasonable doubt. Such measures failing, the case reaches the sentencing phase.

9.   SENTENCING

Before sentencing the unfortunate Roscoe, the trial judge will request a presentence report. In some states, this is a mandatory procedure. The report, usually prepared by a probation officer, provides background information and personal data that may assist the judge in exercising her discretion to impose an appropriate sentence. How much discretion the judge has depends on the governing sentencing statute. In some instances, the judge may have broad discretion, extending from "no time" in jail or prison to a substantial term of years. In others, the judge's discretion may be narrowly confined by a legislative prescription of a mandatory minimum term.

10.   POST–CONVICTION REMEDIES

The convicted defendant may appeal the judgment against him by asserting error on the part of the trial court. In the federal system and most state systems there are three tiers of courts—the trial courts, intermediate appellate courts, and the highest court of the jurisdiction.[f] The first appeal is a matter of right. Allowance of a further appeal is ordinarily subject to the discretion of the high court. A state court defendant who has gone through the state appellate system thereafter may seek discretionary review in the United States Supreme Court if his claim rests on a violation of the United States Constitution or of federal laws.

A defendant may pursue yet another set of remedies, one that may be described as extraordinary. A prisoner may file petition for *habeas corpus* ("you should have the body"), alleging that he is illegally confined by his jailer. Some jurisdictions call these "petitions for post-conviction relief." These indirect or collateral attacks upon a conviction are available only when the opportunities for review by way of direct appeal have been exhausted. They are available, moreover, only to cure fundamental defects in the prior proceedings. In addition, if the petitioner failed to claim a defect in the earlier proceedings, he will be required

---

f.   *See* Chapter I, *supra* p. 52.

to show an excusable cause for that failure. Relief by way of *habeas corpus* is a possibility, albeit a very limited one, in both the state and federal systems. Again, a state prisoner seeking relief in federal court must show that the defect is one arising under the United States Constitution or federal law.

C. THE ROOTS OF CONSTITUTIONAL CRIMINAL PROCEDURE

1. THE ENGLISH BACKGROUND

Justice William O. Douglas once asserted that the knowledge of one's rights against the government and the restraints on the police should be known to all. He concluded, however, that they were understood by relatively few. Another late justice of our Supreme Court, Felix Frankfurter, observed that the history of liberty is in large part the story of the continuing struggle for fair procedure.

The roots of our constitutional criminal procedure run deep. The ancestor of the modern grand jury took shape in England in the 1100's. The idea that no one, not even the King, is above the law of the land was expressed in Magna Carta in 1215. The institution of trial by jury was established by the 14th Century. The term "due process of law" appears during the same era. In 1645, in the famed case of Puritan dissenter John Lilburne, the House of Lords upheld a privilege against self-incrimination, vindicating Lilburne's adamant refusal to submit to inquisitorial interrogation by the Star Chamber. The English Bill of Rights of 1689 condemned the requirement of "excessive bail" and the infliction of "cruel and unusual punishments." The English common law courts inveighed against unreasonable searches and seizures well before James Otis, on this side of the Atlantic, denounced the random searches made by British officers seeking evidence of smuggling by the colonists.

The historic rights of English citizens, however, stood on shaky ground. What was declared by a staunch Parliament one day might be undone by one subservient to the Crown on the next. Sir Edward Coke, in his *Second Institutes* (1628), noted that the Magna Carta had been enacted thirty-two times—which means that thirty-one times it had fallen out of the unwritten British Constitution.

The point was not lost on the leaders of the New World. Shortly after their delegates signed the Declaration of Independence, Virginia and Pennsylvania incorporated bills of rights in their written constitutions so that their constitutions would be less vulnerable to political windstorms. Other states followed suit. When the framers of the United States Constitution failed to include similar provisions restraining the federal government, participants in the state ratifying conventions demanded that this be promptly remedied. The First Congress responded in 1789, proposing twelve amendments to the newly adopted Constitution. Ten of these, since known as the Bill of Rights, were ratified two years later.

2. THE BILL OF RIGHTS

What, then, are the critical provisions of the Bill of Rights that bear on criminal procedure?

The Fourth Amendment of the United States Constitution affirms the right to be free from unreasonable governmental searches and seizures. It requires that governmental searches and arrests be based on probable cause, rather than mere suspicion, and that any intrusion upon privacy be confined to the necessities of the situation.

Amendment IV

The right of the people to be secure in their persons, houses, papers, and effects, against unreasonable searches and seizures, shall not be violated, and no Warrants shall issue, but upon probable cause, supported by Oath or affirmation, and particularly describing the place to be searched, and the persons or things to be seized.

The Fifth Amendment protects against double jeopardy and prohibits the government from charging a person with a serious crime without securing approval of a grand jury. It also guarantees that no one will be deprived of life, liberty, or property without due process of law or be compelled to be a witness against himself.

Amendment V

No person shall be held to answer for a capital, or otherwise infamous crime, unless on a presentment or indictment of a Grand Jury, except in cases arising in the land or naval forces, or in the Militia, when in actual service in time of War or public danger; nor shall any person be subject for the same offence to be twice put in jeopardy of life or limb; nor shall be compelled in any criminal case to be a witness against himself, nor be deprived of life, liberty, or property, without due process of law; nor shall private property be taken for public use, without just compensation.

The Sixth Amendment states that an accused shall enjoy the rights to a speedy, public trial before an impartial jury, to be informed of the nature and cause of the charges against him, to confront witnesses, to have the power to subpoena witnesses, and to have counsel assist him with his defense.

Amendment VI

In all criminal prosecutions, the accused shall enjoy the right to a speedy and public trial, by an impartial jury of the State and district wherein the crime shall have been committed, which district shall have been previously ascertained by law, and to be informed of the nature and cause of the accusation; to be confronted with the witnesses against him; to have compulsory process for obtaining witnesses in his favor, and to have the Assistance of Counsel for his defense.

The Eighth Amendment prohibits excessive fines or bail and cruel and unusual punishments.

Amendment VIII

Excessive bail shall not be required, nor excessive fines imposed, nor cruel and unusual punishments inflicted.

The words of the constitutional provisions are relatively few, but their potential reach extends far. After all, a constitution, unlike a statute or rule, is written for the ages. A declaration of rights must be sufficiently general in its terms to apply to countless differing factual situations, many of them beyond anticipation by its framers. Not surprisingly, the terms in the Bill of Rights are largely undefined. The standards it adopts are neither precise nor self-executing. What is probable cause? Where is the line to be drawn between a reasonable and an unreasonable search? At what point does police questioning encroach upon the Fifth Amendment privilege? What are the essential features of a trial by jury? In what circumstances will the imposition of punishment be deemed cruel and unusual? Did the defendant have a "fair trial," one satisfying the standard of "due process"? These and many other constitutional questions can be answered concretely only by a process of case-by-case adjudication.

That, of course, is the task of the judiciary. Ultimately, the Supreme Court, proceeding within the constitutional framework, must mark the reach of the constitutional guarantees and the boundaries that confine the exercise of governmental authority.

D. THE BILL OF RIGHTS AND THE STATES

The first ten amendments to the Constitution were adopted at the insistence of the states to restrain the newly created federal government. The foundation for applying those amendments to the states came in 1868 with the adoption of the Fourteenth Amendment, one clause of which provides that no state shall "deprive any person of life, liberty, or property, without due process of law." Reasoning that due process broadly embraces the notion of fundamental fairness, the Supreme Court has ruled over the last half of the Twentieth Century that the states are required to adhere to virtually all of the express guarantees of the Bill of Rights.[g] This process is known as incorporation. Due process encompasses as well elements of fair procedure not explicitly identified in the Constitution, for example, the presumption of innocence and the requirement that guilt be established beyond a reasonable doubt.

In combination, the actions taken by the First Congress, following the American Revolution, and by the Thirty-ninth, following the Civil

g. A principal exception is the requirement, imposed upon the United States, that the prosecution of serious crimes be initiated by the indictment of a grand jury. As noted in Section B, *supra*, in most states the prosecutor may bring a charge by filing an information.

War, established the framework for what has evolved into a national code of constitutional criminal procedure, one that permits variation but sets minimum standards to which both state and nation must adhere.

In the remaining portions of this chapter, we shall consider the concept of due process and how it has served as the engine by which criminal procedure has developed and become heavily constitutionalized. Our primary examples will be drawn from three important areas: the right to trial by jury, the right to the assistance of counsel, and the right to be free from unreasonable searches and seizures.

E. THE CONCEPT OF DUE PROCESS

ROCHIN v. CALIFORNIA

Supreme Court of the United States, 1952.
342 U.S. 165, 72 S.Ct. 205, 96 L.Ed. 183.

JUSTICE FRANKFURTER delivered the opinion of the Court.

Having "some information that [the petitioner here] was selling narcotics," three deputy sheriffs of the County of Los Angeles, on the morning of July 1, 1949, made for the two-story dwelling house in which Rochin lived with his mother, common-law wife, brothers and sisters. Finding the outside door open, they entered and then forced open the door to Rochin's room on the second floor. Inside they found petitioner sitting partly dressed on the side of the bed, upon which his wife was lying. On a "night stand" beside the bed the deputies spied two capsules. When asked "Whose stuff is this?" Rochin seized the capsules and put them in his mouth. A struggle ensued, in the course of which the three officers "jumped upon him" and attempted to extract the capsules. The force they applied proved unavailing against Rochin's resistance. He was handcuffed and taken to a hospital. At the direction of one of the officers a doctor forced an emetic solution through a tube into Rochin's stomach against his will. This "stomach pumping" produced vomiting. In the vomited matter were found two capsules which proved to contain morphine.

Rochin was brought to trial before a California Superior Court, sitting without a jury, on the charge of possessing "a preparation of morphine" in violation of the California Health and Safety Code, 1947, § 11,500. Rochin was convicted and sentenced to sixty days' imprisonment. The chief evidence against him was the two capsules. They were admitted over petitioner's objection, although the means of obtaining them was frankly set forth in the testimony by one of the deputies, substantially as here narrated.

On appeal, the District Court of Appeal affirmed the conviction, despite the finding that the officers "were guilty of unlawfully breaking into and entering defendant's room and were guilty of unlawfully assaulting and battering defendant while in the room," and "were guilty of unlawfully assaulting, battering, torturing and falsely imprisoning the defendant at the alleged hospital." 101 Cal.App.2d 140, 143, 225 P.2d 1,

3. One of the three judges, while finding that "the record in this case reveals a shocking series of violations of constitutional rights," concurred only because he felt bound by decisions of his Supreme Court. These, he asserted, "have been looked upon by law enforcement officers as an encouragement, if not an invitation, to the commission of such lawless acts." *Id.* The Supreme Court of California denied without opinion Rochin's petition for a hearing. Two justices dissented from this denial, and in doing so expressed themselves thus: " * * * a conviction which rests upon evidence of incriminating objects obtained from the body of the accused by physical abuse is as invalid as a conviction which rests upon a verbal confession extracted from him by such abuse. * * * Had the evidence forced from the defendant's lips consisted of an oral confession that he illegally possessed a drug * * * he would have the protection of the rule of law which excludes coerced confessions from evidence. But because the evidence forced from his lips consisted of real objects the People of this state are permitted to base a conviction upon it. [We] find no valid ground of distinction between a verbal confession extracted by physical abuse and a confession wrested from defendant's body by physical abuse." 101 Cal.App.2d 143, 149–150, 225 P.2d 913, 917–918.

This Court granted certiorari, 341 U.S. 939, 71 S.Ct. 997, 95 L.Ed. 1366, because a serious question is raised as to the limitations which the Due Process Clause of the Fourteenth Amendment imposes on the conduct of criminal proceedings by the States.

In our federal system the administration of criminal justice is predominantly committed to the care of the States. * * *

However, this Court too has its responsibility. Regard for the requirements of the Due Process Clause "inescapably imposes upon this Court an exercise of judgment upon the whole course of the proceedings [resulting in a conviction] in order to ascertain whether they offend those canons of decency and fairness which express the notions of justice of English-speaking peoples even toward those charged with the most heinous offenses." *Malinski v. New York, supra,* 324 U.S. at pages 416–417, 65 S.Ct. at page 789. These standards of justice are not authoritatively formulated anywhere as though they were specifics. Due process of law is a summarized constitutional guarantee of respect for those personal immunities which, as Mr. Justice Cardozo twice wrote for the Court, are "so rooted in the traditions and conscience of our people as to be ranked as fundamental," *Snyder v. Massachusetts,* 291 U.S. 97, 105, 54 S.Ct. 330, 332, 78 L.Ed. 674, or are "implicit in the concept of ordered liberty." *Palko v. Connecticut,* 302 U.S. 319, 325, 58 S.Ct. 149, 152, 82 L.Ed. 288.

The Court's function in the observance of this settled conception of the Due Process Clause does not leave us without adequate guides in subjecting State criminal procedures to constitutional judgment. In dealing not with the machinery of government but with human rights, the absence of formal exactitude, or want of fixity of meaning, is not an unusual or even regrettable attribute of constitutional provisions. Words being symbols do not speak without a gloss. On the one hand the gloss may be the deposit of history, whereby a term gains technical content. Thus the requirements of the Sixth and Seventh Amendments for trial by jury in the federal courts have a rigid meaning. No changes or chances can alter the content of the verbal symbol of "jury"—a body of twelve men who must reach a unanimous conclusion if the verdict is to go against the defendant. On the other hand, the gloss of some of the verbal symbols of the Constitution does not give them a fixed technical content. It exacts a continuing process of application.

When the gloss has thus not been fixed but is a function of the process of judgment, the judgment is bound to fall differently at different times and differently at the same time through different judges. Even more specific provisions, such as the guaranty of freedom of speech and the detailed protection against unreasonable searches and seizures, have inevitably evoked as sharp divisions in this Court as the least specific and most comprehensive protection of liberties, the Due Process Clause.

The vague contours of the Due Process Clause do not leave judges at large. We may not draw on our merely personal and private notions and disregard the limits that bind judges in their judicial function. Even though the concept of due process of law is not final and fixed, these limits are derived from considerations that are fused in the whole nature of our judicial process. See Cardozo, The Nature of the Judicial Process; The Growth of the Law; The Paradoxes of Legal Science. These are considerations deeply rooted in reason and in the compelling traditions of the legal profession. The Due Process Clause places upon this Court the duty of exercising a judgment, within the narrow confines of judicial power in reviewing State convictions, upon interests of society pushing in opposite directions.

Due process of law thus conceived is not to be derided as resort to a revival of "natural law." To believe that this judicial exercise of judgment could be avoided by freezing "due process of law" at some fixed stage of time or thought is to suggest that the most important aspect of constitutional adjudication is a function for inanimate machines and not for judges, for whom the independence safeguarded by Article III of the Constitution was designed and who are presumably guided by established standards of judicial behavior. Even cybernetics has not yet made that haughty claim. To practice the requisite detachment and to achieve sufficient objectivity no doubt demands of judges the habit of self-discipline and self-criticism, incertitude that one's own views are incontestable and alert tolerance toward views not shared. But these are precisely the presuppositions of our judicial process. They are precisely the qualities society has a right to expect from those entrusted with ultimate judicial power.

Restraints on our jurisdiction are self-imposed only in the sense that there is from our decisions no immediate appeal short of impeachment or constitutional amendment. But that does not make due process of law a matter of judicial caprice. The faculties of the Due Process Clause may be indefinite and vague, but the mode of their ascertainment is not self-willed. In each case "due process of law" requires an evaluation based on a disinterested inquiry pursued in the spirit of science, on a balanced order of facts exactly and fairly stated, on the detached consideration of conflicting claims, *see Hudson County Water Co. v. McCarter,* 209 U.S. 349, 355, 28 S.Ct. 529, 531, 52 L.Ed. 828, on a judgment not *ad hoc* and episodic but duly mindful of reconciling the needs both of continuity and of change in a progressive society.

Applying these general considerations to the circumstances of the present case, we are compelled to conclude that the proceedings by which this conviction was obtained do more than offend some fastidious squeamishness or private sentimentalism about combatting crime too energetically. This is conduct that shocks the conscience. Illegally breaking into the privacy of the petitioner, the struggle to open his mouth and remove what was there, the forcible extraction of his stomach's contents—this course of proceeding by agents of government to obtain evidence is bound to offend even hardened sensibilities. They are methods too close to the rack and the screw to permit of constitutional differentiation.

It has long since ceased to be true that due process of law is heedless of the means by which otherwise relevant and credible evidence is obtained. This was not true even before the series of recent cases enforced the constitutional principle that the States may not base convictions upon confessions, however much verified, obtained by coercion. These decisions are not arbitrary exceptions to the comprehensive right of States to fashion their own rules of evidence for criminal trials. They are not sports in our constitutional law but applications of a general principle. They are only instances of the general requirement that States in their prosecutions respect certain decencies of civilized conduct. Due process of law, as a historic and generative principle, precludes defining, and thereby confining, these standards of conduct more precisely than to say that convictions cannot be brought about by methods that offend "a sense of justice." *See* Mr. Chief Justice Hughes, speaking for a unanimous Court in *Brown v. Mississippi,* 297 U.S. 278, 285–286, 56 S.Ct. 461, 464–465, 80 L.Ed. 682. It would be a stultification of the responsibility which the course of constitutional history has cast upon this Court to hold that in order to convict a man the police cannot extract by force what is in his mind but can extract what is in his stomach.

To attempt in this case to distinguish what lawyers call "real evidence" from verbal evidence is to ignore the reasons for excluding coerced confessions. Use of involuntary verbal confessions in State criminal trials is constitutionally obnoxious not only because of their unreliability. They are inadmissible under the Due Process Clause even though statements contained in them may be independently established as true. Coerced confessions offend the community's sense of fair play and decency. So here, to sanction the brutal conduct which naturally enough was condemned by the court whose judgment is before us, would be to afford brutality the cloak of law. Nothing would be more calculated to discredit law and thereby to brutalize the temper of a society.

In deciding this case we do not heedlessly bring into question decisions in many States dealing with essentially different, even if related, problems. We therefore put to one side cases which have arisen in the State courts through use of modern methods and devices for discovering wrongdoers and bringing them to book. It does not fairly represent these decisions to suggest that they legalize force so brutal and so offensive to human dignity in securing evidence from a suspect as is revealed by this record. Indeed the California Supreme Court has not sanctioned this mode of securing a conviction. It merely exercised its discretion to decline a review of the conviction. All the California judges who have expressed themselves in this case have condemned the conduct in the strongest language.

We are not unmindful that hypothetical situations can be conjured up, shading imperceptibly from the circumstances of this case and by gradations producing practical differences despite seemingly logical extensions. But the Constitution is "intended to preserve practical and substantial rights, not to maintain theories." *Davis v. Mills,* 194 U.S. 451, 457, 24 S.Ct. 692, 695, 48 L.Ed. 1067.

On the facts of this case the conviction of the petitioner has been obtained by methods that offend the Due Process Clause. The judgment below must be

Reversed.

JUSTICE BLACK, concurring.

Adamson v. California, 332 U.S. 46, 68–123, 67 S.Ct. 1672, 1683, 1684–1711, 91 L.Ed. 1903, sets out reasons for my belief that state as well as federal courts and law enforcement officers must obey the Fifth Amendment's command that "No person * * * shall be compelled in any criminal case to be a witness against himself." I think a person is compelled to be a witness against himself not only when he is compelled to testify, but also when as here, incriminating evidence is forcibly taken from him by a contrivance of modern science. * * * California convicted this petitioner by using against him evidence obtained in this manner, and I agree with Mr. Justice Douglas that the case should be reversed on this ground.

In the view of a majority of the Court, however, the Fifth Amendment imposes no restraint of any kind on the states. They nevertheless hold that California's use of this evidence violated the Due Process Clause of the Fourteenth Amendment. Since they hold as I do in this case, I regret my inability to accept their interpretation without protest. But I believe that faithful adherence to the specific guarantees in the Bill of Rights insures a more permanent protection of individual liberty than that which can be afforded by the nebulous standards stated by the majority.

What the majority hold is that the Due Process Clause empowers this Court to nullify any state law if its application "shocks the conscience," offends "a sense of justice" or runs counter to the "decencies of civilized conduct." The majority emphasize that these statements do not refer to their own consciences or to their senses of justice and decency. For we are told that "we may not draw on our merely personal and private notions"; our judgment must be grounded on "considerations deeply rooted in reason and in the compelling traditions of the legal profession." We are further admonished to measure the validity of state practices, not by our reason, or by the traditions of the legal profession, but by "the community's sense of fair play and decency"; by the "traditions and conscience of our people"; or by "those canons of decency and fairness which express the notions of justice of English-speaking peoples." These canons are made necessary, it is said, because of "interests of society pushing in opposite directions."

If the Due Process Clause does vest this Court with such unlimited power to invalidate laws, I am still in doubt as to why we should consider only the notions of English-speaking peoples to determine what are immutable and fundamental principles of justice. Moreover, one may well ask what avenues of investigation are open to discover "canons" of conduct so universally favored that this Court should write them into the Constitution? All we are told is that the discovery must be made by an "evaluation based on a disinterested inquiry pursued in the spirit of science, on a balanced order of facts."

Some constitutional provisions are stated in absolute and unqualified language such, for illustration, as the First Amendment stating that no law shall be passed prohibiting the free exercise of religion or abridging the freedom of speech or press. Other constitutional provisions do require courts to choose between competing policies, such as the Fourth Amendment which, by its terms, necessitates a judicial decision as to what is an "unreasonable" search or seizure. There is, however, no express constitutional language granting judicial power to invalidate *every* state law of *every* kind deemed "unreasonable" or contrary to the Court's notion of civilized decencies; yet the constitutional philosophy used by the majority has, in the past, been used to deny a state the right to fix the price of gasoline, *Williams v. Standard Oil Co.,* 278 U.S. 235, 49 S.Ct. 115, 73 L.Ed. 287; and even the right to prevent bakers from palming off smaller for larger loaves of bread, *Jay Burns Baking Co. v. Bryan,* 264 U.S. 504, 44 S.Ct. 412, 68 L.Ed. 813. These cases, and others, show the extent to which the evanescent standards of the majority's philosophy have been used to nullify state legislative programs passed to suppress evil economic practices. What paralyzing role this same philosophy will play in the future economic affairs of this country is impossible to predict. Of even graver concern, however, is the use of the philosophy to nullify the Bill of Rights. I long ago concluded that the accordion-like qualities of this philosophy must inevitably imperil all the individual liberty safeguards specifically enumerated in the Bill of Rights. Reflection and recent decisions of this Court sanctioning abridgement of the freedom of speech and press have strengthened this conclusion.

JUSTICE DOUGLAS, concurring.

The evidence obtained from this accused's stomach would be admissible in the majority of states where the question has been raised. So far as the reported cases reveal, the only states which would probably exclude the evidence would be Arkansas, Iowa, Michigan, and Missouri. Yet the Court now says that the rule which the majority of the states have fashioned violates the "decencies of civilized conduct." To that I cannot agree. It is a rule formulated by responsible courts with judges as sensitive as we are to the proper standards for law administration.

As an original matter it might be debatable whether the provision in the Fifth Amendment that no person "shall be compelled in any criminal case to be a witness against himself" serves the ends of justice. Not all civilized legal procedures recognize it. But the choice was made by the Framers, a choice which sets a standard for legal trials in this country. The Framers made it a standard of due process for prosecutions by the Federal Government. If it is a requirement of due process for a trial in the federal courthouse, it is impossible for me to say it is not a requirement of due process for a trial in the state courthouse. That was the issue recently surveyed in *Adamson v. California,* 332 U.S. 46, 67 S.Ct. 1672, 91 L.Ed. 1903. The Court rejected the view that compelled testimony should be excluded and held in substance that the accused in a state trial can be forced to testify against himself. I disagree. Of course an accused can be compelled to be present at the trial, to stand, to sit, to turn this way or that, and to try on a cap or a coat. *See Holt v. United States,* 218 U.S. 245, 252–253, 31 S.Ct. 2, 6, 54 L.Ed. 1021. But I think that words taken from his lips, capsules taken from his stomach, blood taken from his veins are all inadmissible provided they are taken from him without his consent. They are inadmissible because of the command of the Fifth Amendment.

That is an unequivocal, definite and workable rule of evidence for state and federal courts. But we cannot in fairness free the state courts from that command and yet excoriate them for flouting the "decencies of civilized conduct" when they admit the evidence. That is to make the rule turn not on the Constitution but on the idiosyncrasies of the judges who sit here.

The damage of the view sponsored by the Court in this case may not be conspicuous here. But it is part of the same philosophy that produced *Betts v. Brady,* 316 U.S. 455, 62 S.Ct. 1252, 86 L.Ed. 1595, denying counsel to an accused in a state trial against the command of the Sixth Amendment, and *Wolf v. Colorado,* 338 U.S. 25, 69 S.Ct. 1359, 93 L.Ed. 1782, allowing evidence obtained as a result of a search and seizure that is illegal under the Fourth Amendment to be introduced in a state trial. It is part of the process of erosion of civil rights of the citizen in recent years.

Notes and Questions

1. You will note that Justice Frankfurter's opinion makes scant reference to the Fourth Amendment's prohibition of unreasonable searches and seizures or the Fifth Amendment's prohibition of compelled self-incrimination as possible bases for the decision. Rather, he relies on what might be termed the self-generative power of due process, as he interprets that term. Due process, he tells us, provides the "most comprehensive protection of liberties." It embraces those "canons of decency and fairness" implicit in our notions of justice. The decision condemns the state's use of evidence obtained by conduct that "shocks the conscience."

Justice Black's opinion begins by adverting to his dissenting opinion in the *Adamson* case, in which Justice Douglas joined. In that dissent, Justice Black argued that the history of the Fourteenth Amendment reflected a purpose to incorporate all of the federal Bill of Rights. In that same case, Justice Frankfurter had stated, in his concurring opinion, that the Fourteenth Amendment has "independent potency" and that it "neither comprehends the specific provisions by which the founders deemed it appropriate to restrict the federal government nor is confined to them." The Black–Douglas view of total incorporation has never commanded a majority of the Supreme Court. Rather, the Court has proceeded by selective incorporation, considering with respect to individual provisions of the Bill of Rights whether they are "fundamental" in our system of jurisprudence. If the Black–Douglas position lost several battles, it may nonetheless be said to have won the war. Over the course of decades the continuing process of selective incorporation has resulted in something very close to total incorporation. Further consideration of the subject of incorporation is provided by the opinions in *Duncan v. Louisiana* that follow.

2. Recall the discussion of stare decisis, *supra* Chapter I, Section E.

One of the judges of the California District Court of Appeal concurred "only because he felt bound by decisions of his Supreme Court." You have now witnessed the potency of the doctrine of *stare decisis.* Lower court judges are bound to follow even those decisions that they consider improperly decided. The recurring question is, of course, whether the precedent truly controls. Reconsider Llewellen's position in The Bramble Bush, *supra* p. 57.

3. What were the Supreme Court precedents that guided Justice Frankfurter? He refers to the "series of recent cases [that] enforced the constitutional principle that the States may not base convictions upon confessions, however much verified, obtained by coercion." Now let us revisit the California District Court. Assume for purposes of discussion that these precedents were decided after the decisions of the Supreme Court of California that had been alluded to as binding by one of the judges. What analytic approach should the trial judge now adopt? May a judge disregard the California decisions as not controlling—in effect, as having been overruled by the supervening federal decisions? Or, since reasonable minds could differ as to the reach of those federal precedents, should the judge adhere to the California precedents and let the matter be resolved by higher authority?

Suppose, on the other hand, that the confession precedents antedated the California Supreme Court decisions. What should the District Judge now do? Clearly if the California Supreme Court held that these decisions were not binding in "real evidence" cases, that would end the matter. The judge would be bound to follow that rule. But what if the Supreme Court of California never mentioned these cases? In all probability the California judge would still follow the California precedent. Consider one further extension. Assume the California Supreme Court expressly refused to consider the applicability of the Supreme Court precedents because these precedents had not been adequately briefed by the parties. Is the District Judge freed of the constraints of *stare decisis?*

4. Justice Black's concurring opinion in *Rochin* maintains that the majority's approach grants the Justices too much discretion and that they should be confined to the safeguards "specifically enumerated in the Bill of Rights." But, one may ask, how specific is the specific language? History reveals that the Justices have very often disagreed as to its reach. This, too, we shall have occasion to illustrate.

Justices Black and Douglas were of the opinion that the stomach-pumping in *Rochin* violated the Fifth Amendment's command that no person "shall be compelled in any criminal case to be a witness against himself." Subsequently, however, a majority of the Court concluded, in a case decided after the Fifth Amendment privilege had been held applicable to the states, that the privilege applied only to testimonial or communicative evidence, as distinguished from "real evidence." *See Schmerber v. California,* 384 U.S. 757 (1966).

The *Schmerber* Court also ruled that the search of the body and the seizure of the blood were not unreasonable within the meaning of the Fourth Amendment, which also had been held, after *Rochin,* to be binding on the states. *See Mapp v. Ohio, infra.* The Court reasoned that the taking of a blood sample, performed in accordance with accepted medical procedures, was not a serious intrusion; that the state had probable cause to believe that the defendant had been driving while intoxicated; and that the failure to seek a warrant was excusable because the delay incident to its procurement would have impaired or defeated the purpose of the test. *Rochin* was distinguished on the ground that it involved a far more intrusive and offensive procedure. Is the distinction persuasive? Is the taking of a DNA sample permissible under *Schmerber?*

F. DUE PROCESS AND THE RIGHT TO TRIAL BY JURY

DUNCAN v. LOUISIANA

Supreme Court of the United States, 1968.
391 U.S. 145, 88 S.Ct. 1444, 20 L.Ed.2d 491.

Justice White delivered the opinion of the Court.

Appellant, Gary Duncan, was convicted of simple battery in the Twenty-fifth Judicial District Court of Louisiana. Under Louisiana law simple battery is a misdemeanor, punishable by a maximum of two

years' imprisonment and a $300 fine. Appellant sought trial by jury, but because the Louisiana Constitution grants jury trials only in cases in which capital punishment or imprisonment at hard labor may be imposed, the trial judge denied the request. Appellant was convicted and sentenced to serve 60 days in the parish prison and pay a fine of $150. Appellant sought review in the Supreme Court of Louisiana, asserting that the denial of jury trial violated rights guaranteed to him by the United States Constitution. The Supreme Court, finding "[n]o error of law in the ruling complained of," denied appellant a writ of certiorari. Pursuant to 28 U.S.C. § 1257(2) appellant sought review in this Court, alleging that the Sixth and Fourteenth Amendments to the United States Constitution secure the right to jury trial in state criminal prosecutions where a sentence as long as two years may be imposed.
* * *

Appellant was 19 years of age when tried. While driving on Highway 23 in Plaquemines Parish on October 18, 1966, he saw two younger cousins engaged in a conversation by the side of the road with four white boys. Knowing his cousins, Negroes who had recently transferred to a formerly all-white high school, had reported the occurrence of racial incidents at the school, Duncan stopped the car, got out, and approached the six boys. At trial the white boys and a white onlooker testified, as did appellant and his cousins. The testimony was in dispute on many points, but the witnesses agreed that appellant and the white boys spoke to each other, that appellant encouraged his cousins to break off the encounter and enter his car, and that appellant was about to enter the car himself for the purpose of driving away with his cousins. The whites testified that just before getting in the car appellant slapped Herman Landry, one of the white boys, on the elbow. The Negroes testified that appellant had not slapped Landry, but had merely touched him. The trial judge concluded that the State had proved beyond a reasonable doubt that Duncan had committed simple battery, and found him guilty.

I.

The Fourteenth Amendment denies the States the power to "deprive any person of life, liberty, or property, without due process of law." In resolving conflicting claims concerning the meaning of this spacious language, the Court has looked increasingly to the Bill of Rights for guidance; many of the rights guaranteed by the first eight Amendments to the Constitution have been held to be protected against state action by the Due Process Clause of the Fourteenth Amendment. That clause now protects the right to compensation for property taken by the State; the rights of speech, press, and religion covered by the First Amendment; the Fourth Amendment rights to be free from unreasonable searches and seizures and to have excluded from criminal trials any evidence illegally seized; the right guaranteed by the Fifth Amendment to be free of compelled self-incrimination; and the Sixth Amendment rights to counsel, to a speedy and public trial, to confrontation of opposing witnesses, and to compulsory process for obtaining witnesses.

The test for determining whether a right extended by the Fifth and Sixth Amendments with respect to federal criminal proceedings is also protected against state action by the Fourteenth Amendment has been phrased in a variety of ways in the opinions of this Court. The question has been asked whether a right is among those " 'fundamental principles of liberty and justice which lie at the base of all our civil and political institutions,' " *Powell v. Alabama,* 287 U.S. 45, 67, 53 S.Ct. 55, 63, 77 L.Ed. 158 (1932); whether it is "basic in our system of jurisprudence," *In re Oliver,* 333 U.S. 257, 273, 68 S.Ct. 499, 507, 92 L.Ed. 682 (1948); and whether it is "a fundamental right, essential to a fair trial," *Gideon v. Wainwright,* 372 U.S. 335, 343–344, 83 S.Ct. 792, 796, 9 L.Ed.2d 799 (1963); *Malloy v. Hogan,* 378 U.S. 1, 6, 84 S.Ct. 1489, 1492, 12 L.Ed.2d 653 (1964); *Pointer v. Texas,* 380 U.S. 400, 403, 85 S.Ct. 1065, 1067, 13 L.Ed.2d 923 (1965). The claim before us is that the right to trial by jury guaranteed by the Sixth Amendment meets these tests. The position of Louisiana, on the other hand, is that the Constitution imposes upon the States no duty to give a jury trial in any criminal case, regardless of the seriousness of the crime or the size of the punishment which may be imposed. Because we believe that trial by jury in criminal cases is fundamental to the American scheme of justice, we hold that the Fourteenth Amendment guarantees a right of jury trial in all criminal cases which—were they to be tried in a federal court—would come within the Sixth Amendment's guarantee.[14] Since we consider the appeal

14. In one sense recent cases applying provisions of the first eight Amendments to the States represent a new approach to the "incorporation" debate. Earlier the Court can be seen as having asked, when inquiring into whether some particular procedural safeguard was required of a State, if a civilized system could be imagined that would not accord the particular protection. For example, *Palko v. Connecticut,* 302 U.S. 319, 325, 58 S.Ct. 149, 152, 82 L.Ed. 288 (1937), stated: "The right to trial by jury and the immunity from prosecution except as the result of an indictment may have value and importance. Even so, they are not of the very essence of a scheme of ordered liberty. * * * Few would be so narrow or provincial as to maintain that a fair and enlightened system of justice would be impossible without them." The recent cases, on the other hand, have proceeded upon the valid assumption that state criminal processes are not imaginary and theoretical schemes but actual systems bearing virtually every characteristic of the common-law system that has been developing contemporaneously in England and in this country. The question thus is whether given this kind of system a particular procedure is fundamental—whether, that is, a procedure is necessary to an Anglo–American regime of ordered liberty. It is this sort of inquiry that can justify the conclusions that state courts must exclude evidence seized in violation of the Fourth Amendment, *Mapp v. Ohio,* 367 U.S. 643, 81 S.Ct. 1684, 6 L.Ed.2d 1081 (1961); that state prosecutors may not comment on a defendant's failure to testify, *Griffin v. California,* 380 U.S. 609, 85 S.Ct. 1229, 14 L.Ed.2d 106 (1965); and that criminal punishment may not be imposed for the status of narcotics addiction, *Robinson v. California,* 370 U.S. 660, 82 S.Ct. 1417, 8 L.Ed.2d 758 (1962). Of immediate relevance for this case are the Court's holdings that the States must comply with certain provisions of the Sixth Amendment, specifically that the States may not refuse a speedy trial, confrontation of witnesses, and the assistance, at state expense if necessary, of counsel. * * * Of each of these determinations that a constitutional provision originally written to bind the Federal Government should bind the States as well it might be said that the limitation in question is not necessarily fundamental to fairness in every criminal system that might be imagined but is fundamental in the context of the criminal processes maintained by the American States.

When the inquiry is approached in this way the question whether the States can impose criminal punishment without granting a jury trial appears quite different from

before us to be such a case, we hold that the Constitution was violated when appellant's demand for jury trial was refused.

The history of trial by jury in criminal cases has been frequently told. It is sufficient for present purposes to say that by the time our Constitution was written, jury trial in criminal cases had been in existence in England for several centuries and carried impressive credentials traced by many to Magna Carta. Its preservation and proper operation as a protection against arbitrary rule were among the major objectives of the revolutionary settlement which was expressed in the Declaration and Bill of Rights of 1689. In the 18th century Blackstone could write:

> Our law has therefore wisely placed this strong and two-fold barrier, of a presentment and a trial by jury, between the liberties of the people and the prerogative of the crown. It was necessary, for preserving the admirable balance of our constitution, to vest the executive power of the laws in the prince: and yet this power might be dangerous and destructive to that very constitution, if exerted without check or control, by justices of *oyer* and *terminer* occasionally named by the crown; who might then, as in France or Turkey, imprison, dispatch, or exile any man that was obnoxious to the government, by an instant declaration that such is their will and pleasure. But the founders of the English law have, with excellent forecast, contrived that * * * the truth of every accusation, whether preferred in the shape of indictment, information, or appeal, should afterwards be confirmed by the unanimous suffrage of twelve of his equals and neighbours, indifferently chosen and superior to all suspicion.

Jury trial came to America with English colonists, and received strong support from them. Royal interference with the jury trial was deeply resented. Among the resolutions adopted by the First Congress of the American Colonies (the Stamp Act Congress) on October 19, 1765—resolutions deemed by their authors to state "the most essential rights and liberties of the colonists"—was the declaration:

> That trial by jury is the inherent and invaluable right of every British subject in these colonies.

The First Continental Congress, in the resolve of October 14, 1774, objected to trials before judges dependent upon the Crown alone for their

the way it appeared in the older cases opining that States might abolish jury trial. *See, e.g., Maxwell v. Dow,* 176 U.S. 581, 20 S.Ct. 448, 44 L.Ed. 597 (1900). A criminal process which was fair and equitable but used no juries is easy to imagine. It would make use of alternative guarantees and protections which would serve the purposes that the jury serves in the English and American systems. Yet no American State has undertaken to construct such a system. Instead, every American State, including Louisiana, uses the jury extensively, and imposes very serious punishments only after a trial at which the defendant has a right to a jury's verdict. In every State, including Louisiana, the structure and style of the criminal process—the supporting framework and the subsidiary procedures—are of the sort that naturally complement jury trial, and have developed in connection with and in reliance upon jury trial.

salaries and to trials in England for alleged crimes committed in the colonies; the Congress therefore declared:

> That the respective colonies are entitled to the common law of England, and more especially to the great and inestimable privilege of being tried by their peers of the vicinage, according to the course of that law.

The Declaration of Independence stated solemn objections to the King's making "Judges dependent on his Will alone, for the tenure of their offices, and the amount and payment of their salaries," to his "depriving us in many cases, of the benefits of Trial by Jury," and to his "transporting us beyond Seas to be tried for pretended offenses." The Constitution itself, in Art. III, § 2, commanded:

> The Trial of all Crimes, except in Cases of Impeachment, shall be by Jury; and such Trial shall be held in the State where the said Crimes shall have been committed.

Objections to the Constitution because of the absence of a bill of rights were met by the immediate submission and adoption of the Bill of Rights. Included was the Sixth Amendment which, among other things, provided:

> In all criminal prosecutions, the accused shall enjoy the right to a speedy and public trial, by an impartial jury of the State and district wherein the crime shall have been committed.

The constitutions adopted by the original States guaranteed jury trial. Also, the constitution of every State entering the Union thereafter in one form or another protected the right to jury trial in criminal cases.

Even such skeletal history is impressive support for considering the right to jury trial in criminal cases to be fundamental to our system of justice, an importance frequently recognized in the opinions of this Court. * * *

Jury trial continues to receive strong support. The laws of every State guarantee a right to jury trial in serious criminal cases; no State has dispensed with it; nor are there significant movements underway to do so. Indeed, the three most recent state constitutional revisions, in Maryland, Michigan, and New York, carefully preserved the right of the accused to have the judgment of a jury when tried for a serious crime.

We are aware of prior cases in this Court in which the prevailing opinion contains statements contrary to our holding today that the right to jury trial in serious criminal cases is a fundamental right and hence must be recognized by the States as part of their obligation to extend due process of law to all persons within their jurisdiction. Louisiana relies especially on *Maxwell v. Dow,* 176 U.S. 581, 20 S.Ct. 448, 44 L.Ed. 597 (1900); *Palko v. Connecticut,* 302 U.S. 319, 58 S.Ct. 149, 82 L.Ed. 288 (1937); and *Snyder v. Massachusetts,* 291 U.S. 97, 54 S.Ct. 330, 78 L.Ed. 674 (1934). None of these cases, however, dealt with a State which had purported to dispense entirely with a jury trial in serious criminal cases. *Maxwell* held that no provision of the Bill of Rights applied to the

States—a position long since repudiated—and that the Due Process Clause of the Fourteenth Amendment did not prevent a State from trying a defendant for a noncapital offense with fewer than 12 men on the jury. It did not deal with a case in which no jury at all had been provided. In neither *Palko* nor *Snyder* was jury trial actually at issue, although both cases contain important *dicta* asserting that the right to jury trial is not essential to ordered liberty and may be dispensed with by the States regardless of the Sixth and Fourteenth Amendments. These observations, though weighty and respectable, are nevertheless *dicta,* unsupported by holdings in this Court that a State may refuse a defendant's demand for a jury trial when he is charged with a serious crime. Perhaps because the right to jury trial was not directly at stake, the Court's remarks about the jury in *Palko* and *Snyder* took no note of past or current developments regarding jury trials, did not consider its purposes and functions, attempted no inquiry into how well it was performing its job, and did not discuss possible distinctions between civil and criminal cases. In *Malloy v. Hogan, supra,* the Court rejected *Palko's* discussion of the self-incrimination clause. Respectfully, we reject the prior *dicta* regarding jury trial in criminal cases.

The guarantees of jury trial in the Federal and State Constitutions reflect a profound judgment about the way in which law should be enforced and justice administered. A right to jury trial is granted to criminal defendants in order to prevent oppression by the Government. Those who wrote our constitutions knew from history and experience that it was necessary to protect against unfounded criminal charges brought to eliminate enemies and against judges too responsive to the voice of higher authority. * * * We would not assert, however, that every criminal trial—or any particular trial—held before a judge alone is unfair or that a defendant may never be as fairly treated by a judge as he would be by a jury. Thus we hold no constitutional doubts about the practices, common in both federal and state courts, of accepting waivers of jury trial and prosecuting petty crimes without extending a right to jury trial. However, the fact is that in most places more trials for serious crimes are to juries than to a court alone; a great many defendants prefer the judgment of a jury to that of a court. Even where defendants are satisfied with bench trials, the right to a jury trial very likely serves its intended purpose of making judicial or prosecutorial unfairness less likely.[30]

30. Louisiana also asserts that if due process is deemed to include the right to jury trial, States will be obligated to comply with all past interpretations of the Sixth Amendment, an amendment which in its inception was designed to control only the federal courts and which throughout its history has operated in this limited environment where uniformity is a more obvious and immediate consideration. In particular, Louisiana objects to application of the decisions of this Court interpreting the Sixth Amendment as guaranteeing a 12–man jury in serious criminal cases, *Thompson v. Utah,* 170 U.S. 343, 18 S.Ct. 620, 42 L.Ed. 1061 (1898); as requiring a unanimous verdict before guilt can be found, *Maxwell v. Dow,* 176 U.S. 581, 586, 20 S.Ct. 448, 450, 44 L.Ed. 597 (1900); and as barring procedures by which crimes subject to the Sixth Amendment jury trial provision are tried in the first instance without a jury but at the first appellate stage by *de novo* trial with a jury, *Callan v. Wilson,* 127 U.S. 540, 557, 8

II.

Louisiana's final contention is that even if it must grant jury trials in serious criminal cases, the conviction before us is valid and constitutional because here the petitioner was tried for simple battery and was sentenced to only 60 days in the parish prison. We are not persuaded. It is doubtless true that there is a category of petty crimes or offenses which is not subject to the Sixth Amendment jury trial provision and should not be subject to the Fourteenth Amendment jury trial requirement here applied to the States. Crimes carrying possible penalties up to six months do not require a jury trial if they otherwise qualify as petty offenses, *Cheff v. Schnackenberg,* 384 U.S. 373, 86 S.Ct. 1523, 16 L.Ed.2d 629 (1966). But the penalty authorized for a particular crime is of major relevance in determining whether it is serious or not and may in itself, if severe enough, subject the trial to the mandates of the Sixth Amendment. *District of Columbia v. Clawans,* 300 U.S. 617, 57 S.Ct. 660, 81 L.Ed. 843 (1937). The penalty authorized by the law of the locality may be taken "as a gauge of its social and ethical judgments," 300 U.S. at 628, 57 S.Ct. at 663, of the crime in question. In *Clawans* the defendant was jailed for 60 days, but it was the 90-day authorized punishment on which the Court focused in determining that the offense was not one for which the Constitution assured trial by jury. In the case before us the Legislature of Louisiana has made simple battery a criminal offense punishable by imprisonment for up to two years and a fine. The question, then, is whether a crime carrying such a penalty is an offense which Louisiana may insist on trying without a jury.

We think not. So-called petty offenses were tried without juries both in England and in the Colonies and have always been held to be exempt from the otherwise comprehensive language of the Sixth Amendment's jury trial provisions. There is no substantial evidence that the Framers intended to depart from this established common-law practice, and the possible consequences to defendants from convictions for petty offenses have been thought insufficient to outweigh the benefits to efficient law enforcement and simplified judicial administration resulting from the availability of speedy and inexpensive nonjury adjudications. These same considerations compel the same result under the Fourteenth Amendment. Of course the boundaries of the petty offense category have always been ill-defined, if not ambulatory. In the absence of an explicit constitu-

S.Ct. 1301, 1307, 32 L.Ed. 223 (1888). It seems very unlikely to us that our decision today will require widespread changes in state criminal processes. First, our decisions interpreting the Sixth Amendment are always subject to reconsideration, a fact amply demonstrated by the instant decision. In addition, most of the States have provisions for jury trials equal in breadth to the Sixth Amendment, if that amendment is construed, as it has been, to permit the trial of petty crimes and offenses without a jury. Indeed, there appear to be only four States in which juries of fewer than 12 can be used without the defendant's consent for offenses carrying a maximum penalty of greater than one year. Only in Oregon and Louisiana can a less-than-unanimous jury convict for an offense with a maximum penalty greater than one year. However 10 States authorize first-stage trials without juries for crimes carrying lengthy penalties; these States give a convicted defendant the right to a *de novo* trial before a jury in a different court. The statutory provisions are listed in the briefs filed in this case.

tional provision, the definitional task necessarily falls on the courts, which must either pass upon the validity of legislative attempts to identify those petty offenses which are exempt from jury trial or, where the legislature has not addressed itself to the problem, themselves face the question in the first instance. In either case it is necessary to draw a line in the spectrum of crime, separating petty from serious infractions. This process, although essential, cannot be wholly satisfactory, for it requires attaching different consequences to events which, when they lie near the line, actually differ very little.

In determining whether the length of the authorized prison term or the seriousness of other punishment is enough in itself to require a jury trial, we are counseled by *District of Columbia v. Clawans, supra,* to refer to objective criteria, chiefly the existing laws and practices in the Nation. In the federal system, petty offenses are defined as those punishable by no more than six months in prison and a $500 fine. In 49 of the 50 States crimes subject to trial without a jury, which occasionally include simple battery, are punishable by no more than one year in jail. Moreover, in the late 18th century in America crimes triable without a jury were for the most part punishable by no more than a six-month prison term, although there appear to have been exceptions to this rule. We need not, however, settle in this case the exact location of the line between petty offenses and serious crimes. It is sufficient for our purposes to hold that a crime punishable by two years in prison is, based on past and contemporary standards in this country, a serious crime and not a petty offense. Consequently, appellant was entitled to a jury trial and it was error to deny it.

The judgment below is reversed and the case is remanded for proceedings not inconsistent with this opinion.

JUSTICE BLACK, with whom JUSTICE DOUGLAS joins, concurring.

The Court today holds that the right to trial by jury guaranteed defendants in criminal cases in federal courts by Art. III of the United States Constitution and by the Sixth Amendment is also guaranteed by the Fourteenth Amendment to defendants tried in state courts. With this holding I agree for reasons given by the Court. I also agree because of reasons given in my dissent in *Adamson v. California,* 332 U.S. 46, 68, 67 S.Ct. 1672, 1683, 91 L.Ed. 1903.

* * *

While I do not wish at this time to discuss at length my disagreement with Brother Harlan's forthright and frank restatement of the now discredited *Twining* doctrine, I do want to point out what appears to me to be the basic difference between us. His view, as was indeed the view of *Twining,* is that "due process is an evolving concept" and therefore that it entails a "gradual process of judicial inclusion and exclusion" to ascertain those "immutable principles * * * of free government which no member of the Union may disregard." Thus the Due Process Clause is treated as prescribing no specific and clearly ascertainable constitutional command that judges must obey in interpreting the Constitution, but rather as leaving judges free to decide at any particular time whether a particular rule or judicial formulation embodies an "immutable principl[e] of free government" or is "implicit in the concept of ordered liberty," or whether certain conduct "shocks the judge's conscience" or runs counter to some other similar, undefined and undefinable standard. Thus due process, according to my Brother Harlan, is to be a phrase with no permanent meaning, but one which is found to shift from time to time in accordance with judges' predilections and understandings of what is best for the country. If due process means this, the Fourteenth Amendment, in my opinion, might as well have been written that "no person shall be deprived of life, liberty or property except by laws that the judges of the United States Supreme Court shall find to be consistent with the immutable principles of free government." It is impossible for me to believe that such unconfined power is given to judges in our Constitution that is a written one in order to limit governmental power.

Another tenet of the *Twining* doctrine as restated by my Brother Harlan is that "due process of law requires only fundamental fairness." But the "fundamental fairness" test is one on a par with that of shocking the conscience of the Court. Each of such tests depends entirely on the particular judge's idea of ethics and morals instead of requiring him to depend on the boundaries fixed by the written words of the Constitution. Nothing in the history of the phrase "due process of law" suggests that constitutional controls are to depend on any particular judge's sense of values. * * * [T]he Due Process Clause gives all Americans, whoever they are and wherever they happen to be, the right to be tried by independent and unprejudiced courts using established procedures and applying valid pre-existing laws. There is not one word of legal history that justifies making the term "due process of law" mean a guarantee of a trial free from laws and conduct which the courts deem at the time to be "arbitrary," "unreasonable," "unfair," or "contrary to civilized standards." The due process of law standard for a trial is one in accordance with the Bill of Rights and laws passed pursuant to constitutional power, guaranteeing to all alike a trial under the general law of the land.

Finally I want to add that I am not bothered by the argument that applying the Bill of Rights to the States, "according to the same standards that protect those personal rights against federal encroachment," interferes with our concept of federalism in that it may prevent States from trying novel social and economic experiments. I have never believed that under the guise of federalism the States should be able to experiment with the protections afforded our citizens through the Bill of Rights. As Justice Goldberg said so wisely in his concurring opinion in *Pointer v. Texas,* 380 U.S. 400, 85 S.Ct. 1065, 13 L.Ed.2d 923:

> to deny to the States the power to impair a fundamental constitutional right is not to increase federal power, but, rather, to limit the power of both federal and state governments in favor of safeguard-

ing the fundamental rights and liberties of the individual. In my view this promotes rather than undermines the basic policy of avoiding excess concentration of power in government, federal or state, which underlies our concepts of federalism.

380 U.S. at 414, 85 S.Ct. at 1073.

It seems to me totally inconsistent to advocate, on the one hand, the power of this Court to strike down any state law or practice which it finds "unreasonable" or "unfair" and, on the other hand, urge that the States be given maximum power to develop their own laws and procedures. Yet the due process approach of my Brothers Harlan and Fortas does just that since in effect it restricts the States to practices which a majority of this Court is willing to approve on a case-by-case basis. No one is more concerned than I that the States be allowed to use the full scope of their powers as their citizens see fit. And that is why I have continually fought against the expansion of this Court's authority over the States through the use of a broad, general interpretation of due process that permits judges to strike down state laws they do not like.

In closing I want to emphasize that I believe as strongly as ever that the Fourteenth Amendment was intended to make the Bill of Rights applicable to the States. I have been willing to support the selective incorporation doctrine, however, as an alternative, although perhaps less historically supportable than complete incorporation. The selective incorporation process, if used properly, does limit the Supreme Court in the Fourteenth Amendment field to specific Bill of Rights' protections only and keeps judges from roaming at will in their own notions of what policies outside the Bill of Rights are desirable and what are not. And, most importantly for me, the selective incorporation process has the virtue of having already worked to make most of the Bill of Rights' protections applicable to the States.

JUSTICE FORTAS, concurring.

I join the judgments and opinions of the Court because I agree that the Due Process Clause of the Fourteenth Amendment requires that the States accord the right to jury trial in prosecutions for offenses that are not petty.

* * *

But although I agree with the decision of the Court, I cannot agree with the implication that the tail must go with the hide: that when we hold, influenced by the Sixth Amendment, that "due process" requires that the States accord the right of jury trial for all but petty offenses, we automatically import all of the ancillary rules which have been or may hereafter be developed incidental to the right to jury trial in the federal courts. I see no reason whatever, for example, to assume that our decision today should require us to impose federal requirements such as unanimous verdicts or a jury of 12 upon the States. We may well conclude that these and other features of federal jury practice are by no means fundamental—that they are not essential to due process of law—and that they are not obligatory on the States.

I would make these points clear today. Neither logic nor history nor the intent of the draftsmen of the Fourteenth Amendment can possibly be said to require that the Sixth Amendment or its jury trial provision be applied to the States together with the total gloss that this Court's decisions have supplied. The draftsmen of the Fourteenth Amendment intended what they said, not more or less: that no State shall deprive any person of life, liberty, or property without due process of law. It is ultimately the duty of this Court to interpret, to ascribe specific meaning to this phrase. There is no reason whatever for us to conclude that, in so doing, we are bound slavishly to follow not only the Sixth Amendment but all of its bag and baggage, however securely or insecurely affixed they may be by law and precedent to federal proceedings.

* * *

This Court has heretofore held that various provisions of the Bill of Rights such as the freedom of speech and religion guarantees of the First Amendment, the prohibition of unreasonable searches and seizures in the Fourth Amendment, the privilege against self-incrimination of the Fifth Amendment, and the right to counsel and to confrontation under the Sixth Amendment "are all to be enforced against the States under the Fourteenth Amendment according to the same standards that protect those personal rights against federal encroachment." *Malloy v. Hogan,* 378 U.S. 1, 10, 84 S.Ct. 1489, 1495, 12 L.Ed.2d 653 (1964); *Pointer v. Texas,* 380 U.S. 400, 406, 85 S.Ct. 1065, 1069, 13 L.Ed.2d 923 (1965); *Miranda v. Arizona,* 384 U.S. 436, 464, 86 S.Ct. 1602, 1622, 16 L.Ed.2d 694 (1966). I need not quarrel with the specific conclusion in those specific instances. But unless one adheres slavishly to the incorporation theory, body and substance, the same conclusion need not be superimposed upon the jury trial right. I respectfully but urgently suggest that it should not be. Jury trial is more than a principle of justice applicable to individual cases. It is a system of administration of the business of the State. While we may believe (and I do believe) that the right of jury trial is fundamental, it does not follow that the particulars of according that right must be uniform. We should be ready to welcome state variations which do not impair—indeed, which may advance—the theory and purpose of trial by jury.

Justice Harlan, whom Justice Stewart joins, dissenting.

Every American jurisdiction provides for trial by jury in criminal cases. The question before us is not whether jury trial is an ancient institution, which it is; nor whether it plays a significant role in the administration of criminal justice, which it does; nor whether it will endure, which it shall. The question in this case is whether the State of Louisiana, which provides trial by jury for all felonies, is prohibited by the Constitution from trying charges of simple battery to the court alone. In my view, the answer to that question, mandated alike by our constitutional history and by the longer history of trial by jury, is clearly "no."

The States have always borne primary responsibility for operating the machinery of criminal justice within their borders, and adapting it to their particular circumstances. In exercising this responsibility, each State is compelled to conform its procedures to the requirements of the Federal Constitution. The Due Process Clause of the Fourteenth Amendment requires that those procedures be fundamentally fair in all respects. It does not, in my view, impose or encourage nationwide uniformity for its own sake; it does not command adherence to forms that happen to be old; and it does not impose on the States the rules that may be in force in the federal courts except where such rules are also found to be essential to basic fairness.

The Court's approach to this case is an uneasy and illogical compromise among the views of various Justices on how the Due Process Clause should be interpreted. The Court does not say that those who framed the Fourteenth Amendment intended to make the Sixth Amendment applicable to the States. And the Court concedes that it finds nothing unfair about the procedure by which the present appellant was tried. Nevertheless, the Court reverses his conviction: it holds, for some reason not apparent to me, that the Due Process Clause incorporates the particular clause of the Sixth Amendment that requires trial by jury in federal criminal cases—including, as I read its opinion, the sometimes trivial accompanying baggage of judicial interpretation in federal contexts. I have raised my voice many times before against the Court's continuing undiscriminating insistence upon fastening on the States federal notions of criminal justice, and I must do so again in this instance. With all respect, the Court's approach and its reading of history are altogether topsy-turvy.

I.

I believe I am correct in saying that every member of the Court for at least the last 135 years has agreed that our Founders did not consider the requirements of the Bill of Rights so fundamental that they should operate directly against the States. They were wont to believe rather that the security of liberty in America rested primarily upon the dispersion of governmental power across a federal system. The Bill of Rights was considered unnecessary by some but insisted upon by others in order to curb the possibility of abuse of power by the strong central government they were creating.

The Civil War Amendments dramatically altered the relation of the Federal Government to the States. The first section of the Fourteenth Amendment imposes highly significant restrictions on state action. But the restrictions are couched in very broad and general terms: citizenship; privileges and immunities; due process of law; equal protection of the laws. Consequently, for 100 years this Court has been engaged in the difficult process Professor Jaffe has well called "the search for intermediate premises." The question has been, Where does the Court properly look to find the specific rules that define and give content to such terms as "life, liberty, or property" and "due process of law"?

A few members of the Court have taken the position that the intention of those who drafted the first section of the Fourteenth Amendment was simply, and exclusively, to make the provisions of the first eight Amendments applicable to state action. This view has never been accepted by this Court. In my view, often expressed elsewhere, the first section of the Fourteenth Amendment was meant neither to incorporate, nor to be limited to, the specific guarantees of the first eight Amendments. The overwhelming historical evidence marshalled by Professor Fairman demonstrates, to me conclusively, that the Congressmen and state legislators who wrote, debated, and ratified the Fourteenth Amendment did not think they were "incorporating" the Bill of Rights and the very breadth and generality of the Amendment's provisions suggest that its authors did not suppose that the Nation would always be limited to mid–19th century conceptions of "liberty" and "due process of law" but that the increasing experience and evolving conscience of the American people would add new "intermediate premises." In short, neither history, nor sense, supports using the Fourteenth Amendment to put the States in a constitutional straitjacket with respect to their own development in the administration of criminal or civil law.

Although I therefore fundamentally disagree with the total incorporation view of the Fourteenth Amendment, it seems to me that such a position does at least have the virtue, lacking in the Court's selective incorporation approach, of internal consistency: we look to the Bill of Rights, word for word, clause for clause, precedent for precedent because, it is said, the men who wrote the Amendment wanted it that way. For those who do not accept this "history," a different source of "intermediate premises" must be found. The Bill of Rights is not necessarily irrelevant to the search for guidance in interpreting the Fourteenth Amendment, but the reason for and the nature of its relevance must be articulated.

Apart from the approach taken by the absolute incorporationists, I can see only one method of analysis that has any internal logic. That is to start with the words "liberty" and "due process of law" and attempt to define them in a way that accords with American traditions and our system of government. This approach, involving a much more discriminating process of adjudication than does "incorporation," is, albeit difficult, the one that was followed throughout the 19th and most of the present century. It entails a "gradual process of judicial inclusion and exclusion," seeking, with due recognition of constitutional tolerance for state experimentation and disparity, to ascertain those "immutable principles * * * of free government which no member of the Union may disregard." Due process was not restricted to rules fixed in the past, for that "would be to deny every quality of the law but its age, and to render it incapable of progress or improvement." Nor did it impose nationwide uniformity in details, for

[t]he Fourteenth Amendment does not profess to secure to all persons in the United States the benefit of the same laws and the same remedies. Great diversities in these respects may exist in two States separated only by an imaginary line. On one side of this line there may be a right of trial by jury, and on the other side no such right. Each State prescribes its own modes of judicial proceeding. [Citation omitted.]

Through this gradual process, this Court sought to define "liberty" by isolating freedoms that Americans of the past and of the present considered more important than any suggested countervailing public objective. The Court also, by interpretation of the phrase "due process of law," enforced the Constitution's guarantee that no State may imprison an individual except by fair and impartial procedures.

The relationship of the Bill of Rights to this "gradual process" seems to me to be twofold. In the first place it has long been clear that the Due Process Clause imposes some restrictions on state action that parallel Bill of Rights restrictions on federal action. Second, and more important than this accidental overlap, is the fact that the Bill of Rights is evidence, at various points, of the content Americans find in the term "liberty" and of American standards of fundamental fairness.

An example, both of the phenomenon of parallelism and the use of the first eight Amendments as evidence of a historic commitment, is found in the partial definition of "liberty" offered by Mr. Justice Holmes, dissenting in *Gitlow v. New York,* 268 U.S. 652, 45 S.Ct. 625, 69 L.Ed. 1138.

The general principle of free speech * * * must be taken to be included in the Fourteenth Amendment, in view of the scope that has been given to the word "liberty" as there used, although perhaps it may be accepted with a somewhat larger latitude of interpretation than is allowed to Congress by the sweeping language that governs or ought to govern the laws of the United States.

Id. at 672.

* * *

Today's Court still remains unwilling to accept the total incorporationists' view of the history of the Fourteenth Amendment. This, if accepted, would afford a cogent reason for applying the Sixth Amendment to the States. The Court is also, apparently, unwilling to face the task of determining whether denial of trial by jury in the situation before us, or in other situations, is fundamentally unfair. Consequently, the Court has compromised on the ease of the incorporationist position, without its internal logic. It has simply assumed that the question before us is whether the Jury Trial Clause of the Sixth Amendment should be incorporated into the Fourteenth, jot-for-jot and case-for-case, or ignored. Then the Court merely declares that the clause in question is "in" rather than "out."

The Court has justified neither its starting place nor its conclusion. If the problem is to discover and articulate the rules of fundamental fairness in criminal proceedings, there is no reason to assume that the whole body of rules developed in this Court constituting Sixth Amendment jury trial must be regarded as a unit. The requirement of trial by jury in federal criminal cases has given rise to numerous subsidiary questions respecting the exact scope and content of the right. * * *

Examples abound. I should suppose it obviously fundamental to fairness that a "jury" means an "impartial jury." I should think it equally obvious that the rule, imposed long ago in the federal courts, that "jury" means "jury of exactly twelve," is not fundamental to anything: there is no significance except to mystics in the number 12. Again, trial by jury has been held to require a unanimous verdict of jurors in the federal courts, although unanimity has not been found essential to liberty in Britain, where the requirement has been abandoned.

* * *

Even if I could agree that the question before us is whether Sixth Amendment jury trial is totally "in" or totally "out," I can find in the Court's opinion no real reasons for concluding that it should be "in." The basis for differentiating among clauses in the Bill of Rights cannot be that only some clauses are in the Bill of Rights or that only some are old and much praised, or that only some have played an important role in the development of federal law. These things are true of all. The Court says that some clauses are more "fundamental" than others, but it turns out to be using this word in a sense that would have astonished Mr. Justice Cardozo and which, in addition, is of no help. The word does not mean "analytically critical to procedural fairness" for no real analysis of the role of the jury in making procedures fair is even attempted. Instead, the word turns out to mean "old," "much praised," and "found in the Bill of Rights." The definition of "fundamental" thus turns out to be circular.

II.

Since, as I see it, the Court has not even come to grips with the issues in this case, it is necessary to start from the beginning. When a criminal defendant contends that his state conviction lacked "due process of law," the question before this Court, in my view, is whether he was denied any element of fundamental procedural fairness. Believing, as I do, that due process is an evolving concept and that old principles are subject to re-evaluation in light of later experience, I think it appropriate to deal on its merits with the question whether Louisiana denied appellant due process of law when it tried him for simple assault without a jury.

The obvious starting place is the fact that this Court has, in the past, *held* that trial by jury is not a requisite of criminal due process.

* * *

Although it is of course open to this Court to re-examine these decisions, I can see no reason why they should now be overturned. It can hardly be said that time has altered the question, or brought significant new evidence to bear upon it. The virtues and defects of the jury system have been hotly debated for a long time, and are hotly debated today, without significant change in the lines of argument.

The argument that jury trial is not a requisite of due process is quite simple. The central proposition of *Palko, supra,* a proposition to which I would adhere, is that "due process of law" requires only that criminal trials be fundamentally fair. As stated above, apart from the theory that it was historically intended as a mere shorthand for the Bill of Rights, I do not see what else "due process of law" can intelligibly be thought to mean. If due process of law requires only fundamental fairness, then the inquiry in each case must be whether a state trial process was a fair one. The Court has held, properly I think, that in an adversary process it is a requisite of fairness, for which there is no adequate substitute, that a criminal defendant be afforded a right to counsel and to cross-examine opposing witnesses. But it simply has not been demonstrated, nor, I think, can it be demonstrated, that trial by jury is the only fair means of resolving issues of fact.

The jury is of course not without virtues. It affords ordinary citizens a valuable opportunity to participate in a process of government, an experience fostering, one hopes, a respect for law. It eases the burden on judges by enabling them to share a part of their sometimes awesome responsibility. A jury may, at times, afford a higher justice by refusing to enforce harsh laws (although it necessarily does so haphazardly, raising the questions whether arbitrary enforcement of harsh laws is better than total enforcement, and whether the jury system is to be defended on the ground that jurors sometimes disobey their oaths). And the jury may, or may not, contribute desirably to the willingness of the general public to accept criminal judgments as just.

It can hardly be gainsaid, however, that the principal original virtue of the jury trial—the limitations a jury imposes on a tyrannous judiciary—has largely disappeared. We no longer live in a medieval or colonial society. Judges enforce laws enacted by democratic decision, not by regal fiat. They are elected by the people or appointed by the people's elected officials, and are responsible not to a distant monarch alone but to reviewing courts, including this one.

The jury system can also be said to have some inherent defects, which are multiplied by the emergence of the criminal law from the relative simplicity that existed when the jury system was devised. It is a cumbersome process, not only imposing great cost in time and money on both the State and the jurors themselves, but also contributing to delay in the machinery of justice. Untrained jurors are presumably less adept at reaching accurate conclusions of fact than judges, particularly if the issues are many or complex. And it is argued by some that trial by jury, far from increasing public respect for law, impairs it: the average man, it is said, reacts favorably neither to the notion that matters he knows to be complex are being decided by other average men, nor to the way the jury system distorts the process of adjudication.

That trial by jury is not the only fair way of adjudicating criminal guilt is well attested by the fact that it is not the prevailing way, either in England or in this country. * * *

In the United States, where it has not been as generally assumed that jury waiver is permissible, the statistics are * * * revealing. Two experts have estimated that, of all prosecutions for crimes triable to a jury, 75% are settled by guilty plea and 40% of the remainder are tried to the court. In one State, Maryland, which has always provided for waiver, the rate of court trial appears in some years to have reached 90%. The Court recognizes the force of these statistics in stating,

> We would not assert, however, that every criminal trial—or any particular trial—held before a judge alone is unfair or that a defendant may never be as fairly treated by a judge as he would be by a jury.

I agree. I therefore see no reason why this Court should reverse the conviction of appellant, absent any suggestion that his particular trial was in fact unfair, or compel the State of Louisiana to afford jury trial in an as yet unbounded category of cases that can, without unfairness, be tried to a court.

Indeed, even if I were persuaded that trial by jury is a fundamental right in some criminal cases, I could see nothing fundamental in the rule, not yet formulated by the Court, that places the prosecution of appellant for simple battery within the category of "jury crimes" rather than "petty crimes." Trial by jury is ancient, it is true. Almost equally ancient, however, is the discovery that, because of it,

> the King's most loving Subjects are much travailed and otherwise encumbered in coming and keeping of the said six Weeks Sessions, to their Costs, Charges, Unquietness. [Citation omitted.]

As a result, through the long course of British and American history, summary procedures have been used in a varying category of lesser crimes as a flexible response to the burden jury trial would otherwise impose.

* * *

In sum, there is a wide range of views on the desirability of trial by jury, and on the ways to make it most effective when it is used; there is also considerable variation from State to State in local conditions such as the size of the criminal caseload, the ease or difficulty of summoning jurors, and other trial conditions bearing on fairness. We have before us, therefore, an almost perfect example of a situation in which the celebrated dictum of Mr. Justice Brandeis should be invoked. It is, he said, one of the happy incidents of the federal system that a single courageous State may, if its citizens choose, serve as a laboratory * * *.

New State Ice Co. v. Liebmann, 285 U.S. 262, 280, 311, 52 S.Ct. 371, 386, 76 L.Ed. 747 (dissenting opinion).

This Court, other courts, and the political process are available to correct any experiments in criminal procedure that prove fundamentally unfair to defendants. That is not what is being done today: instead, and quite without reason, the Court has chosen to impose upon every State one means of trying criminal cases; it is a good means, but it is not the only fair means, and it is not demonstrably better than the alternatives States might devise.

I would affirm the judgment of the Supreme Court of Louisiana.

Notes and Questions

1. Noted scholar Lon Fuller believed that the order in which cases are decided affects the decision process. *See supra* Chapter I, Section D. Let's test this legal method thesis. Review footnote 14 of the Court's opinion discussing *Palko*, which, in 1937, held that the states are not bound by the indictment provision of the Fifth Amendment. Assume that *Palko* came to the Supreme Court for the first time in 1969, one year after *Duncan*. Would the case have been decided differently? If so, do you perceive how important a factor history might be in the determination of cases? Recall Cardozo's discussion, *supra* Chapter I, Section G.

Let's examine another thesis. If you believe the grand jury indictments are not as critical to ordered liberty as jury trials, is it possible that *Palko* nurtured or even created this belief? Because state prosecutions are not required to proceed by grand jury indictment, states, in effect, act as laboratories for experimenting with whether the grand jury provision is necessary for a fair process. Based upon the experiment, we have accepted the commencement of proceedings without the protections of the grand jury indictment.

2. Note the way the Supreme Court discards prior cases that one might have thought stood in the way of the decision. For the most part, the Court characterizes the statements in the cases as *dicta,* unsupported by any holdings of the Court. And even if the statements were not *dicta,* one case was discarded as embracing a position since repudiated by the Court.

3. One of the recurring and intractable problems confronting the criminal justice system is the effect of new Supreme Court pronouncements on pending or adjudicated cases. For example, if the Supreme Court decides that a jury trial is a fundamental right in state court, may a prisoner attack his confinement under an earlier conviction entered by a judge who denied his request for a jury trial? Under what circumstances?

4. Justice White's opinion for the Court fully expounds the doctrine of selective incorporation—the idea that those provisions of the United States Constitution that are "fundamental to the American scheme of justice" are embraced by the concept of due process and hence are binding upon the

states by operation of the Fourteenth Amendment. Justices Black and Douglas, concurring in the judgment, adhere to their view, earlier expressed in *Rochin,* that the Fourteenth Amendment's due process clause requires total incorporation of the guarantees of the Bill of Rights. On the other hand, Justices Harlan and Stewart, dissenting, maintain the view held by the Court in an earlier day and illustrated by Justice Frankfurter's opinion in *Rochin*: that provisions of the Bill of Rights are not to be applied *as such* to the states, and that the question to be decided in each case is whether the procedure adopted by the state satisfies the idea of fundamental fairness implicated by the words "due process of law." In their view, there was no unfairness or injustice in Louisiana's practice of having a judge, rather than a jury, determine the guilt of a misdemeanant.

5. Does the Court's holding that Duncan was entitled to a jury trial mean that Louisiana is bound to accord jury trials in criminal cases in the same way that they are accorded in federal courts? The prevailing view of the Court is that the provisions of the Bill of Rights that apply to the states are to be enforced against the states according to the same constitutional standards that protect those personal rights against federal encroachment. In this connection, see the concluding paragraph of Justice Fortas' concurring opinion (*supra* p. 324) and note 30 to Justice White's opinion for the Court (*supra* p. 320).

That formulation, however, raises a further question: What aspects of jury trials as conducted in federal criminal cases are compelled by the Constitution rather than by statute, rule, or custom? This question was central to a series of cases that followed on the heels of *Duncan.*

6. In *Duncan,* the Court said that some petty offenses are not subject to the Sixth Amendment jury trial provisions. This exception for petty offenses cannot be derived from the text of the amendment, which refers to "all criminal prosecutions." Rather, it was based upon history. In both England and the colonies, minor derelictions had been tried without a jury. The First Congress had defined petty offenses as those for which no more than six months' imprisonment was authorized. In turn, the Supreme Court had adopted the six-month line as its basis for deciding when a jury must be impanelled in federal criminal cases.

Was that same dividing line conclusive on the states after *Duncan? Duncan* had decided only that a charge carrying a potential two year term of imprisonment was too serious to admit of trial without jury. The question presented by *Baldwin v. New York,* 399 U.S. 66 (1970), was whether New York could constitutionally draw the line at one year, providing jury trial only when the authorized penalty was in excess of that figure. "No" was the response of a divided Supreme Court: The six-month line is a constitutional rule, not merely a rule of federal practice.

7. What, then, of the rule of unanimity—that a guilty verdict requires the assent of all jurors—a fixture of the common law and of federal practice since the founding of the Republic? Here, the closely divided Court ruled, a state could depart from the federal practice. The federal requirement of unanimity, it stated, was not constitutionally mandated. Accordingly, Oregon could convict a defendant of a serious crime under a statute providing that a

guilty verdict could be returned by agreement of ten or more of twelve jurors. *Apodaca v. Oregon,* 406 U.S. 404 (1972).

8. A jury of twelve persons was a federal practice rooted in history. Was it a constitutional requirement binding on the States after *Duncan?* The Court's majority held that it was not; the rule of twelve was a historical accident. Florida's practice of convening six-person juries was consistent with the purpose of a jury system, and therefore constitutionally permissible. *Williams v. Florida,* 399 U.S. 78 (1970).

Would a smaller jury pass constitutional muster? Georgia, it developed, permitted five-person juries. This, the Supreme Court struck down. There comes a point, it said, at which a progressively smaller jury becomes unacceptable, because it is less likely to foster effective group deliberation and less likely to draw from an adequate cross section of the community. *Ballew v. Georgia,* 435 U.S. 223 (1978).

9. Consider again the question, "How specific are the 'specific guarantees' of the Bill of Rights?" Should the standards be the same for the states and the United States? Would you allow the states some latitude in filling in the gaps?

G. THE RIGHT TO COUNSEL

BETTS v. BRADY

Supreme Court of the United States, 1942.
316 U.S. 455, 62 S.Ct. 1252, 86 L.Ed. 1595.

JUSTICE ROBERTS delivered the opinion of the Court.

The petitioner was indicted for robbery in the Circuit Court of Carroll County, Maryland. Due to lack of funds, he was unable to employ counsel, and so informed the judge at his arraignment. He requested that counsel be appointed for him. The judge advised him that this would not be done, as it was not the practice in Carroll County to appoint counsel for indigent defendants, save in prosecutions for murder and rape.

Without waiving his asserted right to counsel, the petitioner pleaded not guilty and elected to be tried without a jury. At his request witnesses were summoned in his behalf. He cross-examined the State's witnesses and examined his own. The latter gave testimony tending to establish an alibi. Although afforded the opportunity, he did not take the witness stand. The judge found him guilty and imposed a sentence of eight years.

While serving his sentence, the petitioner filed with a judge of the Circuit Court for Washington County, Maryland, a petition for a writ of *habeas corpus* alleging that he had been deprived of the right to assistance of counsel guaranteed by the Fourteenth Amendment of the Federal Constitution. The writ issued, the cause was heard, his contention was rejected, and he was remanded to the custody of the prison warden.

Some months later, a petition for a writ of *habeas corpus* was presented to Hon. Carroll T. Bond, Chief Judge of the Court of Appeals of Maryland, setting up the same grounds for the prisoner's release as the former petition. The respondent answered, a hearing was afforded, at which an agreed statement of facts was offered by counsel for the parties, the evidence taken at the petitioner's trial was incorporated in the record, and the cause was argued. Judge Bond granted the writ but, for reasons set forth in an opinion, denied the relief prayed and remanded the petitioner to the respondent's custody.

* * *

The question we are now to decide is whether due process of law demands that in every criminal case, whatever the circumstances, a State must furnish counsel to an indigent defendant. Is the furnishing of counsel in all cases whatever dictated by natural, inherent, and fundamental principles of fairness? The answer to the question may be found in the common understanding of those who have lived under the Anglo–American system of law. By the Sixth Amendment the people ordained that, in all criminal prosecutions, the accused should "enjoy the right * * * to have the assistance of counsel for his defence." We have construed the provision to require appointment of counsel in all cases where a defendant is unable to procure the services of an attorney, and where the right has not been intentionally and competently waived. Though, as we have noted, the Amendment lays down no rule for the conduct of the States, the question recurs whether the constraint laid by the Amendment upon the national courts expresses a rule so fundamental and essential to a fair trial, and so, to due process of law, that it is made obligatory upon the States by the Fourteenth Amendment. Relevant data on the subject are afforded by constitutional and statutory provisions subsisting in the colonies and the States prior to the inclusion of the Bill of Rights in the national Constitution, and in the constitutional, legislative, and judicial history of the States to the present date. These constitute the most authoritative sources for ascertaining the considered judgment of the citizens of the States upon the question.

* * *

This material demonstrates that, in the great majority of the States, it has been the considered judgment of the people, their representatives and their courts that appointment of counsel is not a fundamental right, essential to a fair trial. On the contrary, the matter has generally been deemed one of legislative policy. In the light of this evidence, we are unable to say that the concept of due process incorporated in the Fourteenth Amendment obligates the States, whatever may be their own views, to furnish counsel in every such case. Every court has power, if it deems proper, to appoint counsel where that course seems to be required in the interest of fairness.

The practice of the courts of Maryland gives point to the principle that the States should not be straight-jacketed in this respect, by a construction of the Fourteenth Amendment. Judge Bond's opinion states, and counsel at the bar confirmed the fact, that in Maryland the usual practice is for the defendant to waive a trial by jury. This the petitioner did in the present case. Such trials, as Judge Bond remarks, are much more informal than jury trials and it is obvious that the judge can much better control the course of the trial and is in a better position to see impartial justice done than when the formalities of a jury trial are involved.

In this case there was no question of the commission of a robbery. The State's case consisted of evidence identifying the petitioner as the perpetrator. The defense was an alibi. Petitioner called and examined witnesses to prove that he was at another place at the time of the commission of the offense. The simple issue was the veracity of the testimony for the State and that for the defendant. As Judge Bond says, the accused was not helpless, but was a man forty-three years old, of ordinary intelligence, and ability to take care of his own interests on the trial of that narrow issue. He had once before been in a criminal court, pleaded guilty to larceny and served a sentence and was not wholly unfamiliar with criminal procedure. It is quite clear that in Maryland, if the situation had been otherwise and it had appeared that the petitioner was, for any reason, at a serious disadvantage by reason of the lack of counsel, a refusal to appoint would have resulted in the reversal of a judgment of conviction. Only recently the Court of Appeals has reversed a conviction because it was convinced on the whole record that an accused, tried without counsel, had been handicapped by the lack of representation.

To deduce from the due process clause a rule binding upon the States in this matter would be to impose upon them, as Judge Bond points out, a requirement without distinction between criminal charges of different magnitude or in respect of courts of varying jurisdiction. As he says: "Charges of small crimes tried before justices of the peace and capital charges tried in the higher courts would equally require the appointment of counsel. Presumably it would be argued that trials in the Traffic Court would require it." And, indeed, it was said by petitioner's counsel both below and in this court, that as the Fourteenth Amendment extends the protection of due process to property as well as to life and liberty, if we hold with the petitioner, logic would require the furnishing of counsel in civil cases involving property.

As we have said, the Fourteenth Amendment prohibits the conviction and incarceration of one whose trial is offensive to the common and fundamental ideas of fairness and right, and while want of counsel in a particular case may result in a conviction lacking in such fundamental fairness, we cannot say that the Amendment embodies an inexorable command that no trial for any offense, or in any court, can be fairly conducted and justice accorded a defendant who is not represented by counsel.

The judgment is affirmed.

[JUSTICES BLACK, DOUGLAS and MURPHY dissented.]

Notes and Questions

1. *Betts* was decided during the pre-incorporation era. The Court rejects the idea that the Sixth Amendment's guarantee of counsel binds the states and confines itself to deciding whether the failure to provide a lawyer for Betts was "offensive to the common and fundamental ideas of fairness and right" and hence violative of due process. As *Duncan* shows, by 1968 selective incorporation had gone a very considerable distance. Most of this development took place in the era of the Warren Court. (Chief Justice Warren was appointed by President Eisenhower in 1953 and served until 1969.) *Betts* itself, as you will observe from the next selection, led a troubled life until it was overruled in 1963.

2. During the pre-incorporation era, the justices took differing positions on the relevance of the states' experience in determining the breadth of the Due Process Clause. In *Betts,* the Court refused to extend due process to require appointed counsel in light of the view of the "great majority of the States that appointment of counsel is not a fundamental right, essential to a fair trial." Yet in *Rochin,* Justice Douglas decried the Court's extension of due process guarantees to exclude evidence when the reported cases of only four states would have excluded the evidence. *See supra* p. 313. Why the differing treatment of the states' experiences?

3. Some believe that counsel may have an impact upon the decisional process as well as the end result. Note the concession by defendant's counsel that his argument, if accepted, would inexorably lead to appointed counsel in civil cases. Was the concession wise? Necessary? Can you devise a principled argument that would avoid the concession?

GIDEON v. WAINWRIGHT

Supreme Court of the United States, 1963.
372 U.S. 335, 83 S.Ct. 792, 9 L.Ed.2d 799.

JUSTICE BLACK delivered the opinion of the Court.

Petitioner was charged in a Florida state court with having broken and entered a poolroom with intent to commit a misdemeanor. This offense is a felony under Florida law. Appearing in court without funds and without a lawyer, petitioner asked the court to appoint counsel for him, whereupon the following colloquy took place:

> The COURT: Mr. Gideon, I am sorry, but I cannot appoint Counsel to represent you in this case. Under the laws of the State of Florida, the only time the Court can appoint Counsel to represent a Defendant is when that person is charged with a capital offense. I am sorry, but I will have to deny your request to appoint Counsel to defend you in this case.

> The DEFENDANT: The United States Supreme Court says I am entitled to be represented by Counsel.

Put to trial before a jury, Gideon conducted his defense about as well as could be expected from a layman. He made an opening statement to the jury, cross-examined the State's witnesses, presented witnesses in his own defense, declined to testify himself, and made a short argument "emphasizing his innocence to the charge contained in the Information filed in this case." The jury returned a verdict of guilty, and petitioner was sentenced to serve five years in the state prison. Later, petitioner filed in the Florida Supreme Court this *habeas corpus* petition attacking his conviction and sentence on the ground that the trial court's refusal to appoint counsel for him denied him rights "guaranteed by the Constitution and the Bill of Rights by the United States Government." Treating the petition for *habeas corpus* as properly before it, the State Supreme Court, "upon consideration thereof" but without an opinion, denied all relief. Since 1942, when *Betts v. Brady,* 316 U.S. 455, 62 S.Ct. 1252, 86 L.Ed. 1595, was decided by a divided Court, the problem of a defendant's federal constitutional right to counsel in a state court has been a continuing source of controversy and litigation in both state and federal courts. To give this problem another review here, we granted certiorari. 370 U.S. 908, 82 S.Ct. 1259, 8 L.Ed.2d 403. Since Gideon was proceeding *in forma pauperis,* we appointed counsel to represent him and requested both sides to discuss in their briefs and oral arguments the following: "Should this Court's holding in *Betts v. Brady,* 316 U.S. 455, 62 S.Ct. 1252, 86 L.Ed. 1595, be reconsidered?"

I

The facts upon which Betts claimed that he had been unconstitutionally denied the right to have counsel appointed to assist him are strikingly like the facts upon which Gideon here bases his federal constitutional claim. Betts was indicted for robbery in a Maryland state court. On arraignment, he told the trial judge of his lack of funds to hire a lawyer and asked the court to appoint one for him. Betts was advised that it was not the practice in that county to appoint counsel for indigent defendants except in murder and rape cases. He then pleaded not guilty, had witnesses summoned, cross-examined the State's witnesses, examined his own, and chose not to testify himself. He was found guilty by the judge, sitting without a jury, and sentenced to eight years in prison. Like Gideon, Betts sought release by *habeas corpus,* alleging that he had been denied the right to assistance of counsel in violation of the Fourteenth Amendment. Betts was denied any relief, and on review this Court affirmed. It was held that a refusal to appoint counsel for an indigent defendant charged with a felony did not necessarily violate the Due Process Clause of the Fourteenth Amendment, which for reasons given the Court deemed to be the only applicable federal constitutional provision. The Court said:

> Asserted denial [of due process] is to be tested by an appraisal of the totality of facts in a given case. That which may, in one setting, constitute a denial of fundamental fairness, shocking to the universal sense of justice, may, in other circumstances, and in the light of other considerations, fall short of such denial.

316 U.S. at 462, 62 S.Ct., at 1256, 86 L.Ed. 1595.

Treating due process as "a concept less rigid and more fluid than those envisaged in other specific and particular provisions of the Bill of Rights," the Court held that refusal to appoint counsel under the particular facts and circumstances in the *Betts* case was not so "offensive to the common and fundamental ideas of fairness" as to amount to a denial of due process. Since the facts and circumstances of the two cases are so nearly indistinguishable, we think the Betts v. Brady holding if left standing would require us to reject Gideon's claim that the Constitution guarantees him the assistance of counsel. Upon full reconsideration we conclude that *Betts v. Brady* should be overruled.

II

The Sixth Amendment provides, "In all criminal prosecutions, the accused shall enjoy the right * * * to have the Assistance of Counsel for his defence." We have construed this to mean that in federal courts counsel must be provided for defendants unable to employ counsel unless the right is competently and intelligently waived. Betts argued that this right is extended to indigent defendants in state courts by the Fourteenth Amendment. In response the Court stated that, while the Sixth Amendment laid down "no rule for the conduct of the States, the question recurs whether the constraint laid by the Amendment upon the national courts expresses a rule so fundamental and essential to a fair trial, and so, to due process of law, that it is made obligatory upon the States by the Fourteenth Amendment." 316 U.S. at 465, 62 S.Ct. at 1257, 86 L.Ed. 1595. In order to decide whether the Sixth Amendment's guarantee of counsel is of this fundamental nature, the Court in *Betts* set out and considered "[r]elevant data on the subject * * * afforded by constitutional and statutory provisions subsisting in the colonies and the States prior to the inclusion of the Bill of Rights in the national Constitution, and in the constitutional, legislative, and judicial history of the States to the present date." 316 U.S. at 465, 62 S.Ct. at 1257. On the basis of this historical data the Court concluded that "appointment of counsel is not a fundamental right, essential to a fair trial." 316 U.S. at 471, 62 S.Ct. at 1261. It was for this reason the *Betts* Court refused to accept the contention that the Sixth Amendment's guarantee of counsel for indigent federal defendants was extended to or, in the words of that Court, "made obligatory upon the States by the Fourteenth Amendment." Plainly, had the Court concluded that appointment of counsel for an indigent criminal defendant was "a fundamental right, essential to a fair trial," it would have held that the Fourteenth Amendment requires appointment of counsel in a state court, just as the Sixth Amendment requires in a federal court.

* * *

We accept *Betts v. Brady*'s assumption, based as it was on our prior cases, that a provision of the Bill of Rights which is "fundamental and essential to a fair trial" is made obligatory upon the States by the Fourteenth Amendment. We think the Court in *Betts* was wrong, however, in concluding that the Sixth Amendment's guarantee of counsel is not one of these fundamental rights. Ten years before *Betts v. Brady,* this Court, after full consideration of all the historical data examined in *Betts,* had unequivocally declared that "the right to the aid of counsel is of this fundamental character." *Powell v. Alabama,* 287 U.S. 45, 68, 53 S.Ct. 55, 63, 77 L.Ed. 158 (1932). While the Court at the close of its *Powell* opinion did by its language, as this Court frequently does, limit its holding to the particular facts and circumstances of that case, its conclusions about the fundamental nature of the right to counsel are unmistakable. Several years later, in 1936, the Court reemphasized what it had said about the fundamental nature of the right to counsel in this language:

> We concluded that certain fundamental rights, safeguarded by the first eight amendments against federal action, were also safeguarded against state action by the due process of law clause of the Fourteenth Amendment, and among them the fundamental right of the accused to the aid of counsel in a criminal prosecution.

Grosjean v. American Press Co., 297 U.S. 233, 243–44, 56 S.Ct. 444, 446, 80 L.Ed. 660 (1936).

And again in 1938 this Court said:

> [The assistance of counsel] is one of the safeguards of the Sixth Amendment deemed necessary to insure fundamental human rights of life and liberty. * * * The Sixth Amendment stands as a constant admonition that if the constitutional safeguards it provides be lost, justice will not "still be done." *Johnson v. Zerbst,* 304 U.S. 458, 462, 58 S.Ct. 1019, 1022, 82 L.Ed. 1461 (1938). To the same effect, see *Avery v. Alabama,* 308 U.S. 444, 60 S.Ct. 321 (1940), and *Smith v. O'Grady,* 312 U.S. 329, 61 S.Ct. 572, 85 L.Ed. 859 (1941).

In light of these and many other prior decisions of this Court, it is not surprising that the *Betts* Court, when faced with the contention that "one charged with crime, who is unable to obtain counsel, must be furnished counsel by the State," conceded that "[e]xpressions in the opinions of this court lend color to the argument * * *." 316 U.S. at 462–63. The fact is that in deciding as it did—that "appointment of counsel is not a fundamental right, essential to a fair trial"—the Court in *Betts v. Brady* made an abrupt break with its own well-considered precedents. In returning to these old precedents, sounder we believe than the new, we but restore constitutional principles established to achieve a fair system of justice. Not only these precedents but also reason and reflection require us to recognize that in our adversary system of criminal justice, any person haled into court, who is too poor to hire a lawyer, cannot be assured a fair trial unless counsel is provided for him. This seems to us to be an obvious truth. Governments, both state and federal, quite properly spend vast sums of money to establish machinery to try defendants accused of crime. Lawyers to prosecute are everywhere deemed essential to protect the public's interest in an orderly society. Similarly, there are few defendants charged with crime, few indeed, who fail to hire the best lawyers they can get to prepare and present their defenses. That government hires lawyers to prosecute and defendants who have the money hire lawyers to defend are the strongest indications of the widespread belief that lawyers in criminal courts are necessities, not luxuries. The right of one charged with crime to counsel may not be deemed fundamental and essential to fair trials in some countries, but it is in ours. From the very beginning, our state and national constitutions and laws have laid great emphasis on procedural and substantive safeguards designed to assure fair trials before impartial tribunals in which every defendant stands equal before the law. This noble ideal cannot be realized if the poor man charged with crime has to face his accusers without a lawyer to assist him.

* * *

The Court in *Betts v. Brady* departed from the sound wisdom upon which the Court's holding in *Powell v. Alabama* rested. Florida, supported by two other States, has asked that *Betts v. Brady* be left intact. Twenty-two States, as friends of the Court, argue that *Betts* was "an anachronism when handed down" and that it should now be overruled. We agree.

The judgment is reversed and the cause is remanded to the Supreme Court of Florida for further action not inconsistent with this opinion.

JUSTICE HARLAN, concurring.

I agree that *Betts v. Brady* should be overruled, but consider it entitled to a more respectful burial than has been accorded, at least on the part of those of us who were not on the Court when that case was decided.

I cannot subscribe to the view that *Betts v. Brady* represented "an abrupt break with its own well-considered precedents." In 1932, in *Powell v. Alabama,* 287 U.S. 45, 53 S.Ct. 55, 77 L.Ed. 158, a capital case, this Court declared that under the particular facts there presented— "the ignorance and illiteracy of the defendants, their youth, the circumstances of public hostility * * * and above all that they stood in deadly peril of their lives" (287 U.S., at 71, 53 S.Ct., at 65)—the state court had a duty to assign counsel for the trial as a necessary requisite of due process of law. It is evident that these limiting facts were not added to the opinion as an afterthought; they were repeatedly emphasized, see 287 U.S. at 52, 57–58, 71, 53 S.Ct., at 58, 59–60, 65, and were clearly regarded as important to the result.

Thus when this Court, a decade later, decided *Betts v. Brady,* it did no more than to admit of the possible existence of special circumstances in noncapital as well as capital trials, while at the same time insisting that such circumstances be shown in order to establish a denial of due process. The right to appointed counsel had been recognized as being considerably broader in federal prosecutions, *see Johnson v. Zerbst,* 304 U.S. 458, 58 S.Ct. 1019, 82 L.Ed. 1461, but to have imposed these requirements on the States would indeed have been "an abrupt break" with the almost immediate past. The declaration that the right to appointed counsel in state prosecutions, as established in *Powell v. Alabama,* was not limited to capital cases was in truth not a departure from, but an extension of, existing precedent.

The principles declared in *Powell* and in *Betts,* however, have had a troubled journey throughout the years that have followed first the one case and then the other. Even by the time of the *Betts* decision, dictum in at least one of the Court's opinions had indicated that there was an absolute right to the services of counsel in the trial of state capital cases. Such dicta continued to appear in subsequent decisions, and any lingering doubts were finally eliminated by the holding of *Hamilton v. Alabama,* 368 U.S. 52, 82 S.Ct. 157, 7 L.Ed.2d 114.

In noncapital cases, the "special circumstances" rule has continued to exist in form while its substance has been substantially and steadily eroded. In the first decade after *Betts,* there were cases in which the Court found special circumstances to be lacking, but usually by a sharply divided vote. However, no such decision has been cited to us, and I have found none, after *Quicksall v. Michigan,* 339 U.S. 660, 70 S.Ct. 910, 94 L.Ed. 1188, decided in 1950. At the same time, there have been not a few cases in which special circumstances were found in little or nothing more than the "complexity" of the legal questions presented, although those questions were often of only routine difficulty. The Court has come to recognize, in other words, that the mere existence of a serious criminal charge constituted in itself special circumstances requiring the services of counsel at trial. In truth the *Betts v. Brady* rule is no longer a reality.

This evolution, however, appears not to have been fully recognized by many state courts, in this instance charged with the front-line responsibility for the enforcement of constitutional rights. To continue a rule which is honored by this Court only with lip service is not a healthy thing and in the long run will do disservice to the federal system.

The special circumstances rule has been formally abandoned in capital cases, and the time has now come when it should be similarly abandoned in noncapital cases, at least as to offenses which, as the one involved here, carry the possibility of a substantial prison sentence. (Whether the rule should extend to *all* criminal cases need not now be decided.) This indeed does no more than to make explicit something that has long since been foreshadowed in our decisions.

In agreeing with the Court that the right to counsel in a case such as this should now be expressly recognized as a fundamental right embraced in the Fourteenth Amendment, I wish to make a further observation. When we hold a right or immunity, valid against the Federal Government, to be "implicit in the concept of ordered liberty" and thus valid against the States, I do not read our past decisions to suggest that by so holding, we automatically carry over an entire body of federal law and apply it in full sweep to the States. Any such concept would disregard the frequently wide disparity between the legitimate interests of the States and of the Federal Government, the divergent problems that they face, and the significantly different consequences of their actions. Cf. *Roth v. United States,* 354 U.S. 476, 496–508, 77 S.Ct. 1304, 1315–1321, 1 L.Ed.2d 1498 (separate opinion of this writer). In what is done today I do not understand the Court to depart from the principles laid down in *Palko v. Connecticut,* 302 U.S. 319, 58 S.Ct. 149, 82 L.Ed. 288, or to embrace the concept that the Fourteenth Amendment "incorporates" the Sixth Amendment as such.

On these premises I join in the judgment of the Court.

Notes and Questions

1.　Both *Betts* and *Gideon* involved felony charges. Cases that followed *Gideon* raised the question whether indigents charged with minor offenses were entitled to counsel. The answer ultimately provided by the Supreme Court in *Scott v. Illinois,* 440 U.S. 367 (1979), was that counsel must be provided if the sentence imposed involves imprisonment rather than a fine.

2.　Was it necessary for the Court to overrule *Betts?* Could it have distinguished *Betts* based on the severity of the crimes? The sentences imposed? The complexity of the proceedings? The presence of the jury? The education level of the defendant? Would you have been satisfied with any of these attempted distinctions? With any combination of these distinctions?

H.　UNREASONABLE SEARCHES AND SEIZURES

The Fourth Amendment has been a prolific source of litigation. Obviously, concepts of probability ("probable cause") and reasonableness ("unreasonable searches and seizures") can be given concrete meaning in the legal system only through the adjudication of actual cases. Another thorny question that arises is what remedy should lie for a violation of the amendment. Suppose that a police officer has uncovered a cache of illicit drugs in "X's" possession by means of an illegally conducted search of his wine cellar. Is "X" entitled to prevent the use of that highly probative evidence in an ensuing prosecution, or should he be remitted to some other remedy, such as damages for the trespass? The language of the amendment does not provide an explicit answer. Compare the language of the Fourth Amendment to the specific language of the self-incrimination clause of the Fifth Amendment. Does the Fourth Amendment have a built-in exclusionary principle?

In the two cases that follow, *Wolf* and *Mapp,* the Supreme Court considers whether the exclusionary rule, which it had already adopted in the federal arena, should be made binding upon the states. The Supreme Court, of course, has broad supervisory power over the lower federal courts. To impose the exclusionary rule upon the states, however, required a determination that it was constitutionally necessary.

WOLF v. COLORADO

Supreme Court of the United States, 1949.
338 U.S. 25, 69 S.Ct. 1359, 93 L.Ed. 1782.

JUSTICE FRANKFURTER delivered the opinion of the Court.

The precise question for consideration is this: Does a conviction by a State court for a State offense deny the "due process of law" required by the Fourteenth Amendment, solely because evidence that was admitted at the trial was obtained under circumstances which would have rendered it inadmissible in a prosecution for violation of a federal law in a court of the United States because there deemed to be an infraction of the Fourth Amendment as applied in *Weeks v. United States,* 232 U.S. 383, 34 S.Ct. 341, 58 L.Ed. 652, L.R.A.1915B, 834, Ann.Cas.1915C, 1177? The Supreme Court of Colorado has sustained convictions in which such evidence was admitted, 117 Col. 279, 187 P.2d 926; 117 Col. 321, 187 P.2d 928, and we brought the cases here. 333 U.S. 879, 68 S.Ct. 910, 92 L.Ed. 1155.

Unlike the specific requirements and restrictions placed by the Bill of Rights (Amendments I to VIII) upon the administration of criminal justice by federal authority, the Fourteenth Amendment did not subject criminal justice in the States to specific limitations. The notion that the "due process of law" guaranteed by the Fourteenth Amendment is shorthand for the first eight amendments of the Constitution and thereby incorporates them has been rejected by this Court again and again, after impressive consideration. *See, e.g., Hurtado v. California,* 110 U.S. 516, 4 S.Ct. 111, 292, 28 L.Ed. 232; *Twining v. New Jersey,* 211 U.S. 78, 29 S.Ct. 14, 53 L.Ed. 97; *Brown v. Mississippi,* 297 U.S. 278, 56 S.Ct. 461, 80 L.Ed. 682; *Palko v. Connecticut,* 302 U.S. 319, 58 S.Ct. 149, 82 L.Ed. 288. Only the other day the Court reaffirmed this rejection after thorough reexamination of the scope and function of the Due Process Clause of the Fourteenth Amendment. *Adamson v. California,* 332 U.S. 46, 67 S.Ct. 1672, 91 L.Ed. 1903, 171 A.L.R. 1223. The issue is closed.

For purposes of ascertaining the restrictions which the Due Process Clause imposed upon the States in the enforcement of their criminal law, we adhere to the views expressed in *Palko v. Connecticut, supra,* 302 U.S. 319. That decision speaks to us with the great weight of the authority, particularly in matters of civil liberty, of a court that included Mr. Chief Justice Hughes, Mr. Justice Brandeis, Mr. Justice Stone and Mr. Justice Cardozo, to name only the dead. In rejecting the suggestion that the Due Process Clause incorporated the original Bill of Rights, Mr. Justice Cardozo reaffirmed on behalf of that Court a different but deeper and more pervasive conception of the Due Process Clause. This Clause exacts from the States for the lowliest and the most outcast all that is "implicit in the concept of ordered liberty." 302 U.S. at page 325, 58 S.Ct. at page 152.

Due process of law thus conveys neither formal nor fixed nor narrow requirements. It is the compendious expression for all those rights which the courts must enforce because they are basic to our free society. But basic rights do not become petrified as of any one time, even though, as a matter of human experience, some may not too rhetorically be called eternal verities. It is of the very nature of a free society to advance in its standards of what is deemed reasonable and right. Representing as it does a living principle, due process is not confined within a permanent catalogue of what may at a given time be deemed the limits or the essentials of fundamental rights.

To rely on a tidy formula for the easy determination of what is a fundamental right for purposes of legal enforcement may satisfy a longing for certainty but ignores the movements of a free society. It belittles the scale of the conception of due process. The real clue to the problem confronting the judiciary in the application of the Due Process Clause is not to ask where the line is once and for all to be drawn but to recognize that it is for the Court to draw it by the gradual and empiric process of "inclusion and exclusion." *Davidson v. New Orleans*, 96 U.S. 97, 104, 24 L.Ed. 616. This was the Court's insight when first called upon to consider the problem; to this insight the Court has on the whole been faithful as case after case has come before it since *Davidson v. New Orleans* was decided.

The security of one's privacy against arbitrary intrusion by the police—which is at the core of the Fourth Amendment—is basic to a free society. It is therefore implicit in "the concept of ordered liberty" and as such enforceable against the States through the Due Process Clause. The knock at the door, whether by day or by night, as a prelude to a search, without authority of law but solely on the authority of the police, did not need the commentary of recent history to be condemned as inconsistent with the conception of human rights enshrined in the history and the basic constitutional documents of English-speaking peoples.

Accordingly, we have no hesitation in saying that were a State affirmatively to sanction such police incursion into privacy it would run counter to the guaranty of the Fourteenth Amendment. But the ways of enforcing such a basic right raise questions of a different order. How such arbitrary conduct should be checked, what remedies against it should be afforded, the means by which the right should be made effective, are all questions that are not to be so dogmatically answered as to preclude the varying solutions which spring from an allowable range of judgment on issues not susceptible of quantitative solution.

In *Weeks v. United States, supra,* this Court held that in a federal prosecution the Fourth Amendment barred the use of evidence secured through an illegal search and seizure. This ruling was made for the first time in 1914. It was not derived from the explicit requirements of the Fourth Amendment; it was not based on legislation expressing Congressional policy in the enforcement of the Constitution. The decision was a matter of judicial implication. Since then it has been frequently applied and we stoutly adhere to it. But the immediate question is whether the basic right to protection against arbitrary intrusion by the police demands the exclusion of logically relevant evidence obtained by an unreasonable search and seizure because, in a federal prosecution for a federal crime, it would be excluded. As a matter of inherent reason, one would suppose this to be an issue as to which men with complete devotion to the protection of the right of privacy might give different answers. When we find that in fact most of the English-speaking world does not regard as vital to such protection the exclusion of evidence thus obtained, we must hesitate to treat this remedy as an essential ingredient of the right. The contrariety of views of the States is particularly impressive in view of the careful reconsideration which they have given the problem in the light of the *Weeks* decision.

I.   Before the *Weeks* decision 27 States had passed on the admissibility of evidence obtained by unlawful search and seizure.

     (a)   Of these, 26 States opposed the *Weeks* doctrine.

     (b)   Of these, 1 State anticipated the *Weeks* doctrine.

II.   Since the *Weeks* decision 47 States all told have passed on the *Weeks* doctrine.

     (a)   Of these, 20 passed on it for the first time.

         (1)   Of the foregoing States, 6 followed the *Weeks* doctrine.

         (2)   Of the foregoing States, 14 rejected the *Weeks* doctrine.

     (b)   Of these, 26 States reviewed prior decisions contrary to the *Weeks* doctrine.

         (1)   Of these, 10 States have followed *Weeks,* overruling or distinguishing their prior decisions.

         (2)   Of these, 16 States adhered to their prior decisions against *Weeks*.

     (c)   Of these, 1 State repudiated its prior formulation of the *Weeks* doctrine.

III.   As of today 31 States reject the *Weeks* doctrine, 16 States are in agreement with it.

IV.   Of 10 jurisdictions within the United Kingdom and the British Commonwealth of Nations which have passed on the question, none has held evidence obtained by illegal search and seizure inadmissible.

The jurisdictions which have rejected the *Weeks* doctrine have not left the right to privacy without other means of protection. Indeed, the exclusion of evidence is a remedy which directly serves only to protect those upon whose person or premises something incriminating has been found. We cannot, therefore, regard it as a departure from basic standards to remand such persons, together with those who emerge scatheless from a search, to the remedies of private action and such protection as the internal discipline of the police, under the eyes of an alert public opinion, may afford. Granting that in practice the exclusion of evidence may be an effective way of deterring unreasonable searches, it is not for this Court to condemn as falling below the minimal standards assured by the Due Process Clause a State's reliance upon other methods which, if consistently enforced, would be equally effective. Weighty testimony against such an insistence on our own view is furnished by the opinion of Mr. Justice (then Judge) Cardozo in *People v. Defore*, 242 N.Y. 13, 150 N.E. 585. We cannot brush aside the experience of States which deem the incidence of such conduct by the police too slight to call for a deterrent remedy not by way of disciplinary measures but by overriding the relevant rules of evidence. There are, moreover, reasons for excluding evidence unreasonably obtained by the federal police which are less compelling in the case of police under State or local authority. The public opinion of a community can far more effectively be exerted against oppressive conduct on the part of police directly responsible to the community itself than can local opinion, sporadically aroused, be brought to bear upon remote authority pervasively exerted throughout the country.

We hold, therefore, that in a prosecution in a State court for a State crime the Fourteenth Amendment does not forbid the admission of evidence obtained by an unreasonable search and seizure. And though we have interpreted the Fourth Amendment to forbid the admission of such evidence, a different question would be presented if Congress under its legislative powers were to pass a statute purporting to negate the *Weeks* doctrine. We would then be faced with the problem of the respect to be accorded the legislative judgment on an issue as to which, in default of that judgment, we have been forced to depend upon our own. Problems of a converse character, also not before us, would be presented should Congress under § 5 of the Fourteenth Amendment undertake to enforce the rights there guaranteed by attempting to make the *Weeks* doctrine binding upon the States.

Affirmed.

JUSTICE MURPHY, with whom JUSTICE RUTLEDGE joins, dissenting.

It is disheartening to find so much that is right in an opinion which seems to me so fundamentally wrong. Of course I agree with the Court that the Fourteenth Amendment prohibits activities which are proscribed by the search and seizure clause of the Fourth Amendment. See my dissenting views, and those of Mr. Justice Black, in *Adamson v. California*, 332 U.S. 46, 68, 123, 67 S.Ct. 1672, 1684, 1711, 91 L.Ed.1903, 171 A.L.R. 1223. Quite apart from the blanket application of the Bill of Rights to the States, a devotee of democracy would ill suit his name were he to suggest that his home's protection against unlicensed governmental invasion was not "of the very essence of a scheme of ordered liberty." *Palko v. Connecticut*, 302 U.S. 319, 325, 58 S.Ct. 149, 152, 82 L.Ed. 288. It is difficult for me to understand how the Court can go this far and yet be unwilling to make the step which can give some meaning to the pronouncements it utters.

Imagination and zeal may invent a dozen methods to give content to the commands of the Fourth Amendment. But this Court is limited to the remedies currently available. It cannot legislate the ideal system. If we would attempt the enforcement of the search and seizure clause in the ordinary case today, we are limited to three devices: judicial exclusion of the illegally obtained evidence; criminal prosecution of violators; and civil action against violators in the action of trespass.

Alternatives are deceptive. Their very statement conveys the impression that one possibility is as effective as the next. In this case their statement is blinding. For there is but one alternative to the rule of exclusion. That is no sanction at all.

This has been perfectly clear since 1914, when a unanimous Court decided *Weeks v. United States,* 232 U.S. 383, 393, 34 S.Ct. 341, 344, 58 L.Ed. 652, L.R.A.1915B, 834, Ann.Cas.1915C, 1177. "If letters and private documents can thus be seized and held and used in evidence against a citizen accused of an offense," we said, "the protection of the Fourth Amendment declaring his right to be secure against such searches and seizures is of no value, and, so far as those thus placed are concerned, might as well be stricken from the Constitution." "It reduces the Fourth Amendment to a form of words." Holmes, J., for the Court, in *Silverthorne Lumber Co. v. United States,* 251 U.S. 385, 392, 40 S.Ct. 182, 183, 64 L.Ed. 319, 24 A.L.R. 1426.

Today the Court wipes those statements from the books with its bland citation of "other remedies." Little need be said concerning the possibilities of criminal prosecution. Self-scrutiny is a lofty ideal, but its exaltation reaches new heights if we expect a District Attorney to prosecute himself or his associates for well-meaning violations of the search and seizure clause during a raid the District Attorney or his associates have ordered. But there is an appealing ring in another alternative. A trespass action for damages is a venerable means of securing reparation for unauthorized invasion of the home. Why not put the old writ to a new use? When the Court cites cases permitting the action, the remedy seems complete.

But what an illusory remedy this is, if by "remedy" we mean a positive deterrent to police and prosecutors tempted to violate the Fourth Amendment. The appealing ring softens when we recall that in a trespass action the measure of damages is simply the extent of the injury to physical property. If the officer searches with care, he can avoid all but nominal damages—a penny, or a dollar. Are punitive damages possible? Perhaps. But a few states permit none, whatever the circumstances. In those that do, the plaintiff must show the real ill will or malice of the defendant and surely it is not unreasonable to assume that one in honest pursuit of crime bears no malice toward the search victim. If that burden is carried, recovery may yet be defeated by the rule that there must be physical damages before punitive damages may be awarded. In addition, some states limit punitive damages to the actual expenses of litigation. *See* 61 Harv.L.Rev. 113, 119–120. Others demand some arbitrary ratio between actual and punitive damages before a verdict may stand. *See* Morris, Punitive Damages in Tort Cases, 44 Harv.L.Rev. 1173, 1180–81. Even assuming the ill will of the officer, his reasonable grounds for belief that the home he searched harbored evidence of crime is admissible in mitigation of punitive damages. *Gamble v. Keyes,* 35 S.D. 644, 153 N.W. 888; *Simpson v. McCaffrey,* 13 Ohio 508. The bad reputation of the plaintiff is likewise admissible. *Banfill v. Byrd,* 122 Miss. 288, 84 So. 227. If the evidence seized was actually used at a trial, that fact has been held a complete justification of the search, and a defense against the trespass action. *Elias v. Pasmore* [1934] 2 K.B. 164. And even if the plaintiff hurdles all these obstacles, and gains a substantial verdict, the individual officer's finances may well make the judgment useless—for the municipality, of course, is not liable without its consent. Is it surprising that there is so little in the books concerning trespass actions for violation of the search and seizure clause?

The conclusion is inescapable that but one remedy exists to deter violations of the search and seizure clause. That is the rule which excludes illegally obtained evidence. Only by exclusion can we impress upon the zealous prosecutor that violation of the Constitution will do him no good. And only when that point is driven home can the prosecutor be expected to emphasize the importance of observing constitutional demands in his instructions to the police.

* * *

I cannot believe that we should decide due process questions by simply taking a poll of the rules in various jurisdictions, even if we follow the *Palko* "test." Today's decision will do inestimable harm to the cause of fair police methods in our cities and states. Even more important, perhaps, it must have tragic effect upon public respect for our judiciary. For the Court now allows what is indeed shabby business: lawlessness by officers of the law.

Since the evidence admitted was secured in violation of the Fourth Amendment, the judgment should be reversed.

MAPP v. OHIO

Supreme Court of the United States, 1961.
367 U.S. 643, 81 S.Ct. 1684, 6 L.Ed.2d 1081.

JUSTICE CLARK delivered the opinion of the Court.

Appellant stands convicted of knowingly having had in her possession and under her control certain lewd and lascivious books, pictures, and photographs in violation of § 2905.34 of Ohio's Revised Code. As officially stated in the syllabus to its opinion, the Supreme Court of Ohio found that her conviction was valid though "based primarily upon the introduction in evidence of lewd and lascivious books and pictures

unlawfully seized during an unlawful search of defendant's home * * *."
170 Ohio St. 427–28, 166 N.E.2d 387, 388.

On May 23, 1957, three Cleveland police officers arrived at appellant's residence in that city pursuant to information that "a person [was] hiding out in the home, who was wanted for questioning in connection with a recent bombing, and that there was a large amount of policy paraphernalia being hidden in the home." Miss Mapp and her daughter by a former marriage lived on the top floor of the two-family dwelling. Upon their arrival at that house, the officers knocked on the door and demanded entrance but appellant, after telephoning her attorney, refused to admit them without a search warrant. They advised their headquarters of the situation and undertook a surveillance of the house.

The officers again sought entrance some three hours later when four or more additional officers arrived on the scene. When Miss Mapp did not come to the door immediately, at least one of the several doors to the house was forcibly opened[2] and the policemen gained admittance. Meanwhile Miss Mapp's attorney arrived, but the officers, having secured their own entry, and continuing in their defiance of the law, would permit him neither to see Miss Mapp nor to enter the house. It appears that Miss Mapp was halfway down the stairs from the upper floor to the front door when the officers, in this highhanded manner, broke into the hall. She demanded to see the search warrant. A paper, claimed to be a warrant, was held up by one of the officers. She grabbed the "warrant" and placed it in her bosom. A struggle ensued in which the officers recovered the piece of paper and as a result of which they handcuffed appellant because she had been "belligerent" in resisting their official rescue of the "warrant" from her person. Running roughshod over appellant, a policeman "grabbed" her, "twisted [her] hand," and she "yelled [and] pleaded with him" because "it was hurting." Appellant, in handcuffs, was then forcibly taken upstairs to her bedroom where the officers searched a dresser, a chest of drawers, a closet and some suitcases. They also looked into a photo album and through personal papers belonging to the appellant. The search spread to the rest of the second floor including the child's bedroom, the living room, the kitchen and a dinette. The basement of the building and a trunk found therein were also searched. The obscene materials for possession of which she was ultimately convicted were discovered in the course of that widespread search.

At the trial no search warrant was produced by the prosecution, nor was the failure to produce one explained or accounted for. At best, "There is, in the record, considerable doubt as to whether there ever was any warrant for the search of defendant's home." 170 Ohio St. at 430, 166 N.E.2d at 389. The Ohio Supreme Court believed a "reasonable argument" could be made that the conviction should be reversed "be-

---

2. A police officer testified that "we did pry the screen door to gain entrance"; the attorney on the scene testified that a policeman "tried * * * to kick in the door" and then "broke the glass in the door and somebody reached in and opened the door and let them in"; the appellant testified that "The back door was broken."

cause the 'methods' employed to obtain the [evidence] * * * were such as to 'offend "a sense of justice,"'" but the court found determinative the fact that the evidence had not been taken "from defendant's person by the use of brutal or offensive physical force against defendant." 170 Ohio St. at 431, 166 N.E.2d at 389–390.

The State says that even if the search were made without authority, or otherwise unreasonably, it is not prevented from using the unconstitutionally seized evidence at trial, citing *Wolf v. People of the State of Colorado,* 1949, 338 U.S. 25, 69 S.Ct. 1359, 1364, 93 L.Ed. 1782, in which this Court did indeed hold "that in a prosecution in a State court for a State crime the Fourteenth Amendment does not forbid the admission of evidence obtained by an unreasonable search and seizure." At p. 33. On this appeal, of which we have noted probable jurisdiction, 364 U.S. 868, 81 S.Ct. 111, 5 L.Ed.2d 90, it is urged once again that we review that holding.

I

Seventy-five years ago, in *Boyd v. United States,* 1886, 116 U.S. 616, 630, 6 S.Ct. 524, 532, 29 L.Ed. 746, considering the Fourth and Fifth Amendments as running "almost into each other" on the facts before it, this Court held that the doctrines of those Amendments

> apply to all invasions on the part of the government and its employés of the sanctity of a man's home and the privacies of life. It is not the breaking of his doors, and the rummaging of his drawers, that constitutes the essence of the offence; but it is the invasion of his indefeasible right of personal security, personal liberty and private property. * * * Breaking into a house and opening boxes and drawers are circumstances of aggravation; but any forcible and compulsory extortion of a man's own testimony or of his private papers to be used as evidence to convict him of crime or to forfeit his goods, is within the condemnation * * * [of those Amendments].

The Court noted that

> constitutional provisions for the security of person and property should be liberally construed. * * * It is the duty of courts to be watchful for the constitutional rights of the citizen, and against any stealthy encroachments thereon.

In this jealous regard for maintaining the integrity of individual rights, the Court gave life to Madison's prediction that "independent tribunals of justice * * * will be naturally led to resist every encroachment upon rights expressly stipulated for in the Constitution by the declaration of rights." I Annals of Cong. 439 (1789). Concluding, the Court specifically referred to the use of the evidence there seized as "unconstitutional."

Less than 30 years after *Boyd,* this Court, in *Weeks v. United States,* 1914, 232 U.S. 383, 391–392, 34 S.Ct. 341, 344, 58 L.Ed. 652, stated that

> the Fourth Amendment * * * put the courts of the United States and Federal officials, in the exercise of their power and authority,

under limitations and restraints [and] * * * forever secure[d] the people, their persons, houses, papers and effects against all unreasonable searches and seizures under the guise of law * * * and the duty of giving to it force and effect is obligatory upon all entrusted under our Federal system with the enforcement of the laws.

Specifically dealing with the use of the evidence unconstitutionally seized, the Court concluded:

If letters and private documents can thus be seized and held and used in evidence against a citizen accused of an offense, the protection of the Fourth Amendment declaring his right to be secure against such searches and seizures is of no value, and, so far as those thus placed are concerned, might as well be stricken from the Constitution. The efforts of the courts and their officials to bring the guilty to punishment, praiseworthy as they are, are not to be aided by the sacrifice of those great principles established by years of endeavor and suffering which have resulted in their embodiment in the fundamental law of the land.

Finally, the Court in that case clearly stated that use of the seized evidence involved "a denial of the constitutional rights of the accused." Thus, in the year 1914, in the *Weeks* case, this Court "for the first time" held that "in a federal prosecution the Fourth Amendment barred the use of evidence secured through an illegal search and seizure." *Wolf v. Colorado, supra,* 338 U.S. at 28, 69 S.Ct. at 1361. This Court has ever since required of federal law officers a strict adherence to that command which this Court has held to be a clear, specific, and constitutionally required—even if judicially implied—deterrent safeguard without insistence upon which the Fourth Amendment would have been reduced to "a form of words." Holmes, J., *Silverthorne Lumber Co. v. United States,* 1920, 251 U.S. 385, 392, 40 S.Ct. 182, 183, 64 L.Ed. 319. It meant, quite simply, that "conviction by means of unlawful seizures and enforced confessions * * * should find no sanction in the judgments of the courts * * *," *Weeks v. United States, supra,* 232 U.S. at 392, 34 S.Ct. at 344, and that such evidence "shall not be used at all." *Silverthorne Lumber Co. v. United States, supra,* 251 U.S. at 392, 40 S.Ct. at 183. * * *

II

In 1949, 35 years after *Weeks* was announced, this Court, in *Wolf v. Colorado, supra,* again for the first time, discussed the effect of the Fourth Amendment upon the States through the operation of the Due Process Clause of the Fourteenth Amendment. It said:

[W]e have no hesitation in saying that were a State affirmatively to sanction such police incursion into privacy it would run counter to the guaranty of the Fourteenth Amendment.

Nevertheless, after declaring that the "security of one's privacy against arbitrary intrusion by the police" is "implicit in 'the concept of ordered liberty' and as such enforceable against the States through the Due Process Clause," cf. *Palko v. Connecticut,* 302 U.S. 319, 58 S.Ct. 149, 82

L.Ed. 288 (1937), and announcing that it "stoutly adhere[d]" to the *Weeks* decision, the Court decided that the *Weeks* exclusionary rule would not then be imposed upon the States as "an essential ingredient of the right." 338 U.S. at 27–29, 69 S.Ct. at 1362. The Court's reasons for not considering essential to the right to privacy, as a curb imposed upon the States by the Due Process Clause, that which decades before had been posited as part and parcel of the Fourth Amendment's limitation upon federal encroachment of individual privacy, were bottomed on factual considerations.

While they are not basically relevant to a decision that the exclusionary rule is an essential ingredient of the Fourth Amendment as the right it embodies is vouchsafed against the States by the Due Process Clause, we will consider the current validity of the factual grounds upon which *Wolf* was based.

The Court in *Wolf* first stated that "[t]he contrariety of views of the States" on the adoption of the exclusionary rule of *Weeks* was "particularly impressive"; and, in this connection, that it could not "brush aside the experience of States which deem the incidence of such conduct by the police too slight to call for a deterrent remedy * * * by overriding the [States'] relevant rules of evidence." While in 1949, prior to the *Wolf* case, almost two-thirds of the States were opposed to the use of the exclusionary rule, now, despite the *Wolf* case, more than half of those since passing upon it, by their own legislative or judicial decision, have wholly or partly adopted or adhered to the *Weeks* rule. *See Elkins v. United States,* 1960, 364 U.S. 206, Appendix, at 224–32, 80 S.Ct. 1437, at 1448–53, 4 L.Ed.2d 1669. Significantly, among those now following the rule is California, which, according to its highest court, was "compelled to reach that conclusion because other remedies have completely failed to secure compliance with the constitutional provisions * * *." *People v. Cahan,* 1955, 44 Cal.2d 434, 445, 282 P.2d 905, 911, 50 A.L.R.2d 513. In connection with this California case, we note that the second basis elaborated in *Wolf* in support of its failure to enforce the exclusionary doctrine against the States was that "other means of protection" have been afforded "the right to privacy." 338 U.S. 30, 69 S.Ct. 1362. The experience of California that such other remedies have been worthless and futile is buttressed by the experience of other States. The obvious futility of relegating the Fourth Amendment to the protection of other remedies has, moreover, been recognized by this Court since *Wolf. See Irvine v. California,* 1954, 347 U.S. 128, 137, 74 S.Ct. 381, 385, 98 L.Ed. 561.

Likewise, time has set its face against what *Wolf* called the "weighty testimony" of *People v. Defore,* 1926, 242 N.Y. 13, 150 N.E. 585. There Justice (then Judge) Cardozo, rejecting adoption of the *Weeks* exclusionary rule in New York, had said that "[t]he Federal rule as it stands is either too strict or too lax." 242 N.Y. at 22, 150 N.E. at 588. However, the force of that reasoning has been largely vitiated by later decisions of this Court. These include the recent discarding of the "silver platter" doctrine which allowed federal judicial use of evidence seized in violation of the Constitution by state agents, *Elkins v. United States, supra;* the relaxation of the formerly strict requirements as to standing to challenge the use of evidence thus seized, so that now the procedure of exclusion, "ultimately referable to constitutional safeguards," is available to anyone even "legitimately on [the] premises" unlawfully searched, *Jones v. United States,* 1960, 362 U.S. 257, 266–267, 80 S.Ct. 725, 734, 4 L.Ed.2d 697; and, finally, the formulation of a method to prevent state use of evidence unconstitutionally seized by federal agents, *Rea v. United States,* 1956, 350 U.S. 214, 76 S.Ct. 292, 100 L.Ed. 233. Because there can be no fixed formula, we are admittedly met with "recurring questions of the reasonableness of searches," but less is not to be expected when dealing with a Constitution, and, at any rate, "[r]easonableness is in the first instance for the [trial court] * * * to determine." *United States v. Rabinowitz,* 1950, 339 U.S. 56, 63, 70 S.Ct. 430, 434, 94 L.Ed. 653.

It, therefore, plainly appears that the factual considerations supporting the failure of the *Wolf* Court to include the *Weeks* exclusionary rule when it recognized the enforceability of the right to privacy against the States in 1949, while not basically relevant to the constitutional consideration, could not, in any analysis, now be deemed controlling.

III

Some five years after *Wolf,* in answer to a plea made here Term after Term that we overturn its doctrine on applicability of the *Weeks* exclusionary rule, this Court indicated that such should not be done until the States had "adequate opportunity to adopt or reject the [*Weeks*] rule." *Irvine v. California, supra,* 347 U.S. at 134, 74 S.Ct. at 384. There again it was said:

> Never until June of 1949 did this Court hold the basic search-and-seizure prohibition in any way applicable to the states under the Fourteenth Amendment.

And only last Term, after again carefully re-examining the *Wolf* doctrine in *Elkins v. United States, supra,* the Court pointed out that "the controlling principles" as to search and seizure and the problem of admissibility "seemed clear" until the announcement in *Wolf* "that the Due Process Clause of the Fourteenth Amendment does not itself require state courts to adopt the exclusionary rule" of the *Weeks* case. At the same time, the Court pointed out, "the underlying constitutional doctrine which *Wolf* established * * * that the Federal Constitution * * * prohibits unreasonable searches and seizures by state officers" had undermined the "foundation upon which the admissibility of state-seized evidence in a federal trial originally rested * * *." The Court concluded that it was therefore obliged to hold, although it chose the narrower ground on which to do so, that all evidence obtained by an unconstitutional search and seizure was inadmissible in a federal court regardless of its source. Today we once again examine *Wolf's* constitutional documentation of the right of privacy free from unreasonable state intrusion, and, after its dozen years on our books, are led by it to close the only courtroom door remaining open to evidence secured by official lawlessness in flagrant abuse of that basic right, reserved to all persons as a specific guarantee against that very same unlawful conduct. We hold that all evidence obtained by searches and seizures in violation of the Constitution is, by that same authority, inadmissible in a state court.

IV

Since the Fourth Amendment's right of privacy has been declared enforceable against the States through the Due Process Clause of the Fourteenth, it is enforceable against them by the same sanction of exclusion as is used against the Federal Government. Were it otherwise, then just as without the *Weeks* rule the assurance against unreasonable federal searches and seizures would be "a form of words," valueless and undeserving of mention in a perpetual charter of inestimable human liberties, so too, without that rule the freedom from state invasions of privacy would be so ephemeral and so neatly severed from its conceptual nexus with the freedom from all brutish means of coercing evidence as not to merit this Court's high regard as a freedom "implicit in the concept of ordered liberty." * * * Therefore, in extending the substantive protections of due process to all constitutionally unreasonable searches—state or federal—it was logically and constitutionally necessary that the exclusion doctrine—an essential part of the right to privacy—be also insisted upon as an essential ingredient of the right newly recognized by the *Wolf* case. In short, the admission of the new constitutional right by *Wolf* could not consistently tolerate denial of its most important constitutional privilege, namely, the exclusion of the evidence which an accused had been forced to give by reason of the unlawful seizure. To hold otherwise is to grant the right but in reality to withhold its privilege and enjoyment. Only last year the Court itself recognized that the purpose of the exclusionary rule "is to deter—to compel respect for the constitutional guaranty in the only effectively available way—by removing the incentive to disregard it." *Elkins v. United States, supra*, 364 U.S. at 217, 80 S.Ct. at 1444.

* * *

V

Moreover, our holding that the exclusionary rule is an essential part of both the Fourth and Fourteenth Amendments is not only the logical dictate of prior cases, but it also makes very good sense. There is no war between the Constitution and common sense. Presently, a federal prosecutor may make no use of evidence illegally seized, but a State's attorney across the street may, although he supposedly is operating under the enforceable prohibitions of the same Amendment. Thus the State, by admitting evidence unlawfully seized, serves to encourage disobedience to the Federal Constitution which it is bound to uphold. * * * In non-exclusionary States, federal officers, being human, were by it invited to and did, as our cases indicate, step across the street to the State's attorney with their unconstitutionally seized evidence. Prosecution on the basis of that evidence was then had in a state court in utter disregard of the enforceable Fourth Amendment. If the fruits of an unconstitutional search had been inadmissible in both state and federal courts, this inducement to evasion would have been sooner eliminated.

Federal-state cooperation in the solution of crime under constitutional standards will be promoted, if only by recognition of their now mutual obligation to respect the same fundamental criteria in their approaches. "However much in a particular case insistence upon such rules may appear as a technicality that inures to the benefit of a guilty person, the history of the criminal law proves that tolerance of shortcut methods in law enforcement impairs its enduring effectiveness." *Miller v. United States,* 1958, 357 U.S. 301, 313, 78 S.Ct. 1190, 1197, 2 L.Ed.2d 1332. Denying shortcuts to only one of two cooperating law enforcement agencies tends naturally to breed legitimate suspicion of "working arrangements" whose results are equally tainted. *Byars v. United States,* 1927, 273 U.S. 28, 47 S.Ct. 248, 71 L.Ed. 520; *Lustig v. United States,* 1949, 338 U.S. 74, 69 S.Ct. 1372, 93 L.Ed. 1819.

There are those who say, as did Justice (then Judge) Cardozo, that under our constitutional exclusionary doctrine "[t]he criminal is to go free because the constable has blundered." *People v. Defore,* 242 N.Y. at 21, 150 N.E. at 587. In some cases this will undoubtedly be the result. But, as was said in *Elkins,* "there is another consideration—the imperative of judicial integrity." 364 U.S. at 222, 80 S.Ct. at 1447. The criminal goes free, if he must, but it is the law that sets him free. Nothing can destroy a government more quickly than its failure to observe its own laws, or worse, its disregard of the charter of its own existence. As Mr. Justice Brandeis, dissenting, said in *Olmstead v. United States,* 1928, 277 U.S. 438, 485, 48 S.Ct. 564, 575, 72 L.Ed. 944: "Our Government is the potent, the omnipresent teacher. For good or for ill, it teaches the whole people by its example. * * * If the Government becomes a lawbreaker, it breeds contempt for law; it invites every man to become a law unto himself; it invites anarchy." Nor can it lightly be assumed that, as a practical matter, adoption of the exclusionary rule fetters law enforcement. Only last year this Court expressly considered that contention and found that "pragmatic evidence of a sort" to the contrary was not wanting. *Elkins v. United States, supra,* 364 U.S. at 218, 80 S.Ct. at 1444. The Court noted that

> The federal courts themselves have operated under the exclusionary rule of *Weeks* for almost half a century; yet it has not been suggested either that the Federal Bureau of Investigation has thereby been rendered ineffective, or that the administration of criminal justice in the federal courts has thereby been disrupted. Moreover, the experience of the states is impressive. * * * The movement towards the rule of exclusion has been halting but seemingly inexorable.

The ignoble shortcut to conviction left open to the State tends to destroy the entire system of constitutional restraints on which the liberties of the people rest. Having once recognized that the right to privacy embodied in the Fourth Amendment is enforceable against the States, and that the right to be secure against rude invasions of privacy by state officers is, therefore, constitutional in origin, we can no longer permit that right to remain an empty promise. Because it is enforceable in the same manner and to like effect as other basic rights secured by the Due Process Clause, we can no longer permit it to be revocable at the whim of any police officer who, in the name of law enforcement itself, chooses to suspend its enjoyment. Our decision, founded on reason and truth, gives to the individual no more than that which the Constitution guarantees him, to the police officer no less than that to which honest law enforcement is entitled, and, to the courts, that judicial integrity so necessary in the true administration of justice.

The judgment of the Supreme Court of Ohio is reversed and the cause remanded for further proceedings not inconsistent with this opinion.

Reversed and remanded.

JUSTICE BLACK, concurring.

JUSTICE DOUGLAS, concurring.

* * *

I am still not persuaded that the Fourth Amendment, standing alone, would be enough to bar the introduction into evidence against an accused of papers and effects seized from him in violation of its commands. For the Fourth Amendment does not itself contain any provision expressly precluding the use of such evidence, and I am extremely doubtful that such a provision could properly be inferred from nothing more than the basic command against unreasonable searches and seizures. Reflection on the problem, however, in the light of cases coming before the Court since *Wolf,* has led me to conclude that when the Fourth Amendment's ban against unreasonable searches and seizures is considered together with the Fifth Amendment's ban against compelled self-incrimination, a constitutional basis emerges which not only justifies but actually requires the exclusionary rule.

* * *

JUSTICE HARLAN, whom JUSTICE FRANKFURTER and JUSTICE WHITTAKER join, dissenting.

* * *

Essential to the majority's argument against *Wolf* is the proposition that the rule of *Weeks v. United States,* 232 U.S. 383, 34 S.Ct. 341, 58 L.Ed. 652, excluding in federal criminal trials the use of evidence obtained in violation of the Fourth Amendment, derives not from the "supervisory power" of this Court over the federal judicial system, but from Constitutional requirement. This is so because no one, I suppose, would suggest that this Court possesses any general supervisory power over the state courts. Although I entertain considerable doubt as to the soundness of this foundational proposition of the majority, *cf. Wolf v. Colorado,* 338 U.S. at 39–40, 69 S.Ct. at 1367–1368 (concurring opinion), I shall assume, for present purposes, that the *Weeks* rule "is of constitutional origin."

At the heart of the majority's opinion in this case is the following syllogism: (1) the rule excluding in federal criminal trials evidence which is the product of an illegal search and seizure is "part and parcel" of the Fourth Amendment; (2) *Wolf* held that the "privacy" assured against federal action by the Fourth Amendment is also protected against state action by the Fourteenth Amendment; and (3) it is therefore "logically and constitutionally necessary" that the *Weeks* exclusionary rule should also be enforced against the States.

This reasoning ultimately rests on the unsound premise that because *Wolf* carried into the States, as part of "the concept of ordered liberty" embodied in the Fourteenth Amendment, the principle of "privacy" underlying the Fourth Amendment (338 U.S. at 27, 69 S.Ct. at 1361), it must follow that whatever configurations of the Fourth Amendment have been developed in the particularizing federal precedents are likewise to be deemed a part of "ordered liberty," and as such are enforceable against the States. For me, this does not follow at all.

It cannot be too much emphasized that what was recognized in *Wolf* was not that the Fourth Amendment *as such* is enforceable against the States as a facet of due process, a view of the Fourteenth Amendment which, as *Wolf* itself pointed out (338 U.S. at 26, 69 S.Ct. at 1360), has long since been discredited, but the principle of privacy "which is at the core of the Fourth Amendment." (*Id.*, 338 U.S. at 27, 69 S.Ct. at 1361.) It would not be proper to expect or impose any precise equivalence, either as regards the scope of the right or the means of its implementation, between the requirements of the Fourth and Fourteenth Amendments. For the Fourth, unlike what was said in *Wolf* of the Fourteenth, does not state a general principle only; it is a particular command, having its setting in a pre-existing legal context on which both interpreting decisions and enabling statutes must at least build.

Thus, even in a case which presented simply the question of whether a particular search and seizure was constitutionally "unreasonable"—say in a tort action against state officers—we would not be true to the Fourteenth Amendment were we merely to stretch the general principle of individual privacy on a Procrustean bed of federal precedents under the Fourth Amendment. But in this instance more than that is involved, for here we are reviewing not a determination that what the state police did was Constitutionally permissible (since the state court quite evidently assumed that it was not), but a determination that appellant was properly found guilty of conduct which, for present purposes, it is to be assumed the State could Constitutionally punish. Since there is not the slightest suggestion that Ohio's policy is "affirmatively to sanction * * * police incursion into privacy" (338 U.S. at 28), *compare Marcus v.*

Search Warrants, what the Court is now doing is to impose upon the States not only federal substantive standards of "search and seizure" but also the basic federal remedy for violation of those standards. For I think it entirely clear that the *Weeks* exclusionary rule is but a remedy which, by penalizing past official misconduct, is aimed at deterring such conduct in the future.

I would not impose upon the States this federal exclusionary remedy. The reasons given by the majority for now suddenly turning its back on *Wolf* seem to me notably unconvincing.

First, it is said that "the factual grounds upon which *Wolf* was based" have since changed, in that more States now follow the *Weeks* exclusionary rule than was so at the time *Wolf* was decided. While that is true, a recent survey indicates that at present one-half of the States still adhere to the common-law non-exclusionary rule, and one, Maryland, retains the rule as to felonies. Berman and Oberst, Admissibility of Evidence Obtained by an Unconstitutional Search and Seizure, 55 N.W.L.Rev. 525, 532–33. But in any case surely all this is beside the point, as the majority itself indeed seems to recognize. Our concern here, as it was in *Wolf,* is not with the desirability of that rule but only with the question whether the States are Constitutionally free to follow it or not as they may themselves determine, and the relevance of the disparity of views among the States on this point lies simply in the fact that the judgment involved is a debatable one. Moreover, the very fact on which the majority relies, instead of lending support to what is now being done, points away from the need of replacing voluntary state action with federal compulsion.

The preservation of a proper balance between state and federal responsibility in the administration of criminal justice demands patience on the part of those who might like to see things move faster among the States in this respect. Problems of criminal law enforcement vary widely from State to State. * * * For us the question remains, as it has always been, one of state power, not one of passing judgment on the wisdom of one state course or another. In my view this Court should continue to forbear from fettering the States with an adamant rule which may embarrass them in coping with their own peculiar problems in criminal law enforcement.

Further, we are told that imposition of the *Weeks* rule on the States makes "very good sense," in that it will promote recognition by state and federal officials of their "mutual obligation to respect the same fundamental criteria" in their approach to law enforcement, and will avoid " 'needless conflict between state and federal courts.' " Indeed the majority now finds an incongruity in *Wolf's* discriminating perception between the demands of "ordered liberty" as respects the basic right of "privacy" and the means of securing it among the States. That perception, resting both on a sensitive regard for our federal system and a sound recognition of this Court's remoteness from particular state problems, is for me the strength of that decision.

An approach which regards the issue as one of achieving procedural symmetry or of serving administrative convenience surely disfigures the boundaries of this Court's functions in relation to the state and federal courts. Our role in promulgating the *Weeks* rule and its extensions in such cases as *Rea, Elkins,* and *Rios* was quite a different one than it is here. There, in implementing the Fourth Amendment, we occupied the position of a tribunal having the ultimate responsibility for developing the standards and procedures of judicial administration within the judicial system over which it presides. Here we review state procedures whose measure is to be taken not against the specific substantive commands of the Fourth Amendment but under the flexible contours of the Due Process Clause. I do not believe that the Fourteenth Amendment empowers this Court to mould state remedies effectuating the right to freedom from "arbitrary intrusion by the police" to suit its own notions of how things should be done, as, for instance, the California Supreme Court did in *People v. Cahan,* 44 Cal.2d 434, 282 P.2d 905, with reference to procedures in the California courts or as this Court did in *Weeks* for the lower federal courts.

A state conviction comes to us as the complete product of a sovereign judicial system. Typically a case will have been tried in a trial court, tested in some final appellate court, and will go no further. In the comparatively rare instance when a conviction is reviewed by us on due process grounds we deal then with a finished product in the creation of which we are allowed no hand, and our task, far from being one of overall supervision, is, speaking generally, restricted to a determination of whether the prosecution was Constitutionally fair. The specifics of trial procedure, which in every mature legal system will vary greatly in detail, are within the sole competence of the States. I do not see how it can be said that a trial becomes unfair simply because a State determines that evidence may be considered by the trier of fact, regardless of how it was obtained, if it is relevant to the one issue with which the trial is concerned, the guilt or innocence of the accused. Of course, a court may use its procedures as an incidental means of pursuing other ends than the correct resolution of the controversies before it. Such indeed is the *Weeks* rule, but if a State does not choose to use its courts in this way, I do not believe that this Court is empowered to impose this much-debated procedure on local courts, however efficacious we may consider the *Weeks* rule to be as a means of securing Constitutional rights.

Finally, it is said that the overruling of *Wolf* is supported by the established doctrine that the admission in evidence of an involuntary confession renders a state conviction Constitutionally invalid. Since such a confession may often be entirely reliable, and therefore of the greatest relevance to the issue of the trial, the argument continues, this doctrine is ample warrant in precedent that the way evidence was obtained, and not just its relevance, is Constitutionally significant to the fairness of a trial. I believe this analogy is not a true one. The "coerced confession" rule is certainly not a rule that any illegally obtained statements may not be used in evidence. I would suppose that a statement which is procured during a period of illegal detention, *McNabb v. United States,* 318 U.S. 332, 63 S.Ct. 608, 87 L.Ed. 819, is, as much as unlawfully seized evidence, illegally obtained, but this Court has consistently refused to reverse state convictions resting on the use of such statements. Indeed it would seem the Court laid at rest the very argument now made by the majority when in *Lisenba v. California,* 314 U.S. 219, at 235, 62 S.Ct. 280, at 289, 86 L.Ed. 166, a state-coerced confession case, it said (at 235):

> It may be assumed [that the] treatment of the petitioner [by the police] * * * deprived him of his liberty without due process and that the petitioner would have been afforded preventive relief if he could have gained access to a court to seek it.
>
> But illegal acts, as such, committed in the course of obtaining a confession * * * do not furnish an answer to the constitutional question we must decide. * * * The gravamen of his complaint is the unfairness of the *use* of his confessions, and what occurred in their procurement is relevant only as it bears on that issue. (Emphasis supplied.)

The point, then, must be that in requiring exclusion of an involuntary statement of an accused, we are concerned not with an appropriate remedy for what the police have done, but with something which is regarded as going to the heart of our concepts of fairness in judicial procedure. * * * The pressures brought to bear against an accused leading to a confession, unlike an unconstitutional violation of privacy, do not, apart from the use of the confession at trial, necessarily involve independent Constitutional violations. What is crucial is that the trial defense to which an accused is entitled should not be rendered an empty formality by reason of statements wrung from him, for then "a prisoner * * * [has been] made the deluded instrument of his own conviction." 2 Hawkins, Pleas of the Crown (8th ed., 1824), c. 46, § 34. That this is a *procedural right,* and that its violation occurs at the time his improperly obtained statement is admitted at trial, is manifest. For without this right all the careful safeguards erected around the giving of testimony, whether by an accused or any other witness, would become empty formalities in a procedure where the most compelling possible evidence of guilt, a confession, would have already been obtained at the unsupervised pleasure of the police.

This, and not the disciplining of the police, as with illegally seized evidence, is surely the true basis for excluding a statement of the accused which was unconstitutionally obtained. In sum, I think the coerced confession analogy works strongly *against* what the Court does today.

* * *

I regret that I find so unwise in principle and so inexpedient in policy a decision motivated by the high purpose of increasing respect for Constitutional rights. But in the last analysis I think this Court can increase respect for the Constitution only if it rigidly respects the limitations which the Constitution places upon it, and respects as well the principles inherent in its own processes. In the present case I think we exceed both, and that our voice becomes only a voice of power, not of reason.

Notes and Questions

1. *In Wolf v. Colorado,* Justice Frankfurter declared that the incorporation doctrine "has been rejected by this Court again and again, after impressive consideration. * * * The issue is closed." But as we have already seen, reports of an issue's demise may have been premature. *See supra* p. 254.

2. Justice Frankfurter limits the scope of inquiry regarding "the concept of ordered liberty" to the "basic constitutional documents of English-speaking peoples." In a nation that contains a large population of non English-speaking heritage, are such limitations wise? Necessary? Historically mandated?

3. Once again the Justices cite the experiences of the states in determining whether to regard the "exclusionary rule" as an essential ingredient of the Fourth Amendment right. In declining to embrace the exclusionary rule, Justice Frankfurter notes the preponderance of jurisdictions that have not applied the doctrine. Ironically, however, in *Rochin* the same Justice embraces as constitutionally mandated a doctrine that, according to Justice Douglas, had been adopted in only a handful of states. Can you reconcile these positions?

4. How did *Mapp* handle *Wolf?* According to the Court, *Mapp* was "bottomed on factual considerations" "that could not * * * now be deemed controlling." Recall the Court's "reasoning" in *Mitchell* distinguishing *Fuentes. See* Chapter III, *supra* pp. 245–46.

5. States are free to impose statutory, common law, and constitutional limitations on state executive authority. California, for example, adopted the exclusionary rule for its courts after "reach[ing] the conclusion [that] other remedies have completely failed to secure compliance with the constitutional provisions." Indeed as the Court has retreated from an expansive interpretation of the Bill of Rights, some states, looking to their own constitutional provisions, have afforded the criminal defendant broader protection than that mandated by the United States Constitution. Should the Court have left the exclusionary rule decision to the states?

6. Suppression of the fruits of unconstitutional searches and seizures has remained a feature of our constitutional order since *Mapp,* although the exclusionary rule has been criticized in many quarters on the ground that its cost (loss of critical evidence) exceeds the benefit (discouragement of official misconduct). In 1984, however, the Supreme Court, by a 6–3 margin, adopted a limited exception to the exclusionary principle. In companion cases, it ruled that when an officer proceeds in good faith on the basis of a search warrant issued by a magistrate, the evidence obtained will be admitted, even though it is subsequently determined that there was a defect in the warrant or in the underlying showing of probable cause. *United States v. Leon,* 468 U.S. 897 (1984); *Massachusetts v. Sheppard,* 468 U.S. 981 (1984).

There is continuing speculation whether the Court will expand, or accept a Congressional expansion of, the so-called "good-faith exception" to other situations.

I.   MORE ON THE FOURTH AMENDMENT: THE ISSUE OF POLICE SURVEILLANCE

First, it is well to take another close look at the text of the amendment:

> The right of the people to be secure in their persons, houses, papers, and effects, against unreasonable searches and seizures, shall not be violated, and no Warrants shall issue, but upon probable cause, supported by Oath or affirmation, and particularly describing the place to be searched, and the persons or things to be seized.

Although the amendment was prompted more by fear of arbitrary intrusions on the part of law officers than by the prospect of their spying and eavesdropping, its terms long proved adequate to inhibit both. Since the amendment addressed unreasonable incursions upon private property, the owner or occupant of premises could ordinarily protect his secrets from the prying eyes and uninvited ears of police agents by simple precautions–drawing the shades or avoiding loud disclosures at open windows.

That, of course, was before the electronic age. *Olmstead v. United States*, 277 U.S. 438, 48 S. Ct. 564 (1928), is a mark of the transition. Olmstead, a bootlegger, was charged with violating of the National Prohibition Act. Treasury agents had gathered the evidence against him by tapping telephone wires located outside his premises. Relying on the language of the Fourth Amendment (*"persons, houses, papers,* and *effects"*) Chief Justice Taft, speaking for a majority of five, concluded that there had been no violation of Olmstead's constitutional rights. There had been no physical seizure of the person, he observed, no physical invasion of the premises, and no taking of any effects.

Justice Brandeis, in a memorable dissent, considered it immaterial that officers had not trespassed or seized tangible objects. The essence of the amendment, he stated, was to guard against "every unjustifiable intrusion by the Government upon the privacy of the individual, whatever the means employed." The "right to be let alone is the most comprehensive of rights and the right most valued by civilized men." Prophetically, he added that ways "may some day be developed by which the government ... will be enabled to expose to a jury the most intimate occurrences of the home." Can it be, he asked, that "the Constitution affords no protection against such invasions of individual security?"

Almost forty years later, in *Katz v. United States*, 389 U.S. 347, 88 S. Ct. 507 (1967), the Court for the first time unqualifiedly endorsed the precept that the amendment "protects people—and not simply 'areas' " and that its reach "cannot turn upon the presence or absence of a physical intrusion into any given enclosure." In *Katz*, FBI agents attached a listening and recording device to the outside of a public telephone booth, which they correctly surmised was used by the defendant to transmit wagering information. The Government's activities, Justice Stewart stated for the Court, violated the privacy upon which Katz "justifiably relied" and "thus constituted a 'search and seizure' within the meaning of the Fourth Amendment," even though Katz had no proprietary interest in the premises and the "seizure" was confined to sound waves.

On its face, *Katz* struck a blow against surreptitious monitoring of private conversations by law enforcement officers. But *Katz* proved to be a decision with a backlash, contributing ultimately to a heavy increase in official eavesdropping and electronic surveillance.

Justice Stewart's opinion noted that the FBI agents who monitored Katz's calls exercised restraint. They did not initiate the surveillance until they had observed his habits and established probable cause to believe that he was using the booth to transmit gambling information. The surveillance was limited to six occasions and the agents took care not to monitor when other persons were inside the booth. On this basis, the Justice concluded that if the agents had obtained advance approval from a duly authorized magistrate, their "limited search and seizure" would have been constitutionally permissible.

The idea that police might lawfully tap a citizen's phone conversations or "bug" his living room by securing the leave of the magistrate was a novel one. To be sure, the Supreme Court had approved the prosecutorial use of recorded conversations between a defendant and a wired government agent or informer. In *Lopez v. United States*, 373 U.S. 427, 83 S. Ct. 1381 (1963), an Internal Revenue Agent had concealed a recorder on his person in order to obtain evidence confirming a taxpayer's prior attempt to bribe him. It is a risk inherent in society, the Court reasoned, that a person to whom one speaks may choose to disclose the contents even though the words are spoken in confidence. Hence, it concluded, there was no valid objection to the use of evidence which reproduced the conversation more reliably than the agent's memory. Three dissenting Justices (Justice Brennan, joined by Justices Douglas and Goldberg) held the view that the prospect of having the other party to a conversation record the event is itself a serious inhibition upon communication. In any case, there is a marked difference between the situation in which one's face-to-face communicant is the instrument of disclosure and the situation in which an outside intruder monitors the exchange. Justice Stewart's opinion for the Court suggested that even the latter might be permissible if grounded upon an appropriate showing to a judicial officer.

Congress promptly responded, enacting in 1968 legislation that undertook, subject to certain limitations, to legitimate the official conduct of electronic surveillance by federal and state law enforcement officers. Wire and Electronics Interception and Interception of Oral Communications, 18 U.S.C. § 2510 *et seq.*

Under the statute, wire interception and interception of oral communications (bugging) may be authorized, subject to specified limitations, in order to investigate a wide variety of offenses. Among the federal offenses are murder, kidnapping, robbery, extortion, embezzlement, theft, interstate transportation of stolen property, bribery, transmission of wagering information, obstruction of justice or of criminal investigations, racketeering and labor offenses, bankruptcy fraud, and violations of the narcotics laws, as well as any conspiracy to commit any of the named offenses. Additionally, the enabling legislation extends to a wide variety of specifically listed state offenses and to other state crimes "dangerous to life, limb, or property, and punishable by imprisonment for more than one year." Conspiracies to commit any of the designated crimes are also included.

The authorization procedure is initiated in much the same way as an application for an ordinary search warrant. It begins by an ex parte proceeding in which the prosecutor presents supporting statements or affidavits to a "judge of competent jurisdiction." In substance, the prosecutor must offer evidence constituting probable cause to believe that an offense to which the statute applies "has been, is being, or is about to be committed." He is further required to set forth the place of the proposed interception, the type of communications sought to be intercepted, and the identity, if known, of the suspected offender. He must also state what other means of investigation have been attempted and why other means are not feasible. If the judge finds the showing sufficient, she may authorize interception for a period not to exceed thirty days. Extensions for a like period may be granted on further application.

There are two notable exceptions to the requirement that judicial authorization be sought. An interception made with consent of one of the parties is deemed lawful. Hence there is no need to seek permission from a magistrate. See *Lopez*, discussed above.

A second exception provided that nothing contained in the Act should be deemed to limit the power of the President to take such measures as deemed necessary to safeguard national security.

Evidence obtained by an authorized interception may be used in any criminal proceeding, federal or state. Even if the evidence goes to an offense far removed from that which provided the basis of the order to intercept, it may be utilized upon a finding that the interception was conducted in conformity with the Act. Information or evidence obtained in the course of an authorized interception may be circulated to other investigative or law enforcement officers to the extent that the disclosure is "appropriate to the proper performance of the official duties of the officer making or receiving the disclosure."

Notes and Questions

1. The opinions of Chief Justice Taft and Justice Brandeis in *Olmstead* reflect a marked difference in approach. The Chief Justice relies heavily on

the wording of the Fourth Amendment. It speaks to the security of "things." Moreover, spoken words, in his view, are hardly subject to search or seizure. Is he being too literal? Or is Justice Brandeis more imaginative than is appropriate for a judge in looking to unexpressed purposes of the framers? The Constitution says nothing of the right to be let alone. It never uses the word "privacy."

Is it significant that the Court is dealing not with a statute, but with a constitutional provision designed for the governance of future generations?

2. *Katz* did not say that the Fourth Amendment creates "a general constitutional 'right of privacy'." It only "protects individual privacy against certain kinds of governmental intrusion." In this connection, the Court observed that the public telephone had come to play "a vital role" in private communication. Is there anything wrong with the idea that constitutional terms or standards may take on new meaning with changes in technology? Is there any expectation of privacy in a cell-phone user's publicly conducted conversation? Since cell-phone conversations are easily intercepted, should cell-phone users have any reasonable expectation of privacy in the calls they make?

Justice Black, dissenting in *Katz*, countered the majority's suggestion that interpretation of the Constitution may change with the times by responding that eavesdropping was "an ancient practice" condemned at common law as a nuisance, and that, had the framers wished to outlaw the use of evidence so obtained, they would have found appropriate language to do so.

3. *Katz* assumed that since the clause of the Fourth Amendment setting forth minimal requirements for procurement of a search warrant contemplates that "things" may be seized upon a proper antecedent showing to a magistrate, it would also be permissible to seek evidence by surveillance of oral communications under a statutory scheme calling for judicial authorization pursuant to appropriate standards and limitations. That, of course, is the premise upon which the 1968 legislation rests.

Is that an obvious conclusion? So far as we know, no common law judge had ever considered it within his province to issue the constable a warrant to lurk under a householder's eaves or to hide in his attic or broom closet to listen for incriminating conversation. Has it somehow become more congenial—and more constitutionally tolerable—in our society to admit an electronic intruder that can pick up every whisper in living room, bedroom or bath?

Before proceeding to the next paragraph, ask yourself this: What are the significant differences between a conventional search warrant—say, a search for a murder weapon or loot from a robbery—and the planting of a "bug" for evidence of what is thought to be a criminal scheme?

4. Would you say that the following factors, when considered in the aggregate, should make a constitutional difference?

Notice. In carrying out a conventional search of a home or office, the police officer is called upon to produce the authorizing warrant. The occupant is in a position to limit the invasion of privacy by producing or facilitating the production of the designated item or items. The law provides a civil remedy if the officer's search exceeds the authority set forth in the warrant. In the case of wire tapping or bugging, advance notice would, of course, be self-defeating.

Duration. The conventional search will ordinarily be served and executed within a few hours or less. The search is for a thing in being. If not found on the person or premises, the search ends. Electronic searches involve lying in wait for evidence to develop. The authorization usually is for thirty days of listening and in practice it usually continues for the full term.

Generality of the Search. The warrant clause of the Fourth Amendment uses the words "particularly describing the place to be searched and the persons or things to be seized." This was no accident. The framers were keenly aware that during the colonial era officers of the crown, armed with so-called writs of assistance, had made unconfined searches of houses for contraband, such as goods obtained in violation of customs laws, that might be uncovered. They wanted to condemn the "general search." The tap on the telephone and the bug in the living room do not discriminate; they are omnivorous in their appetites. For however long the device operates, the lives and thoughts of many people—not merely the immediate target but all who chance to wander into the web—are exposed. Such a search has no channel and is bound to be far more pervasive and intrusive than a properly conducted search for a specific, tangible object at a defined location.

In light of the above considerations, is the conduct of electronic searches inherently "unreasonable" within the meaning of the Fourth Amendment, and hence not redeemable by the stamp of a magistrate? Stated in terms of the *Katz* decision, does the practice unjustifiably or unreasonably override the individual's expectation of privacy?

5. The 5–4 ruling in *Berger v. New York*, 388 U.S. 41, 87 S. Ct. 1873 (1967), decided shortly before *Katz* and in the year preceding the sweeping federal statute legitimating electronic surveillance pursuant to warrant, strongly suggested that the answer to the above questions might be "yes."

In *Berger*, five Justices concluded that a New York eavesdrop statute was unconstitutional on its face. The statute permitted a judge to issue a warrant authorizing electronic surveillance upon the oath of the attorney general, a district attorney, or a police officer above the rank of sergeant "that there is a reasonable ground to believe that evidence of crime may be thus obtained, and particularly describing the person or persons whose communications, conversations or discussions are to be overheard or recorded and the purpose thereof." The authorization could be for periods up to sixty days and might be renewed on application. Observing that the law did not require mention of the particular crime under investigation, the place to be searched, or the "things" to be seized, Justice Clark's opinion concludes that the statute cannot be squared with the Fourth Amendment. The inherent obtrusiveness of eavesdropping, he states, makes the need for particularity "especially great." He concluded:

> It is said that neither a warrant nor a statute authorizing eavesdropping can be drawn so as to meet the Fourth Amendment's requirements. If that be true then the "fruits" of eavesdropping devices are barred under the Amendment.

Justice Douglas' concurring opinion clearly states his constitutional doubts:

> If a statute were to authorize placing a policeman in every home or office where it was shown that there was probable cause to believe that evidence would be obtained, there is little doubt that it would be struck down as a bald invasion of privacy, far worse than the general warrants prohibited by the Fourth Amendment. I can see no difference between such a statute and one authorizing electronic surveillance, which, in effect, places an invisible policeman in the home. If anything, the latter is more offensive because the homeowner is completely unaware of the invasion of privacy.

6. *Berger* notwithstanding, several federal circuits rejected challenges to the 1968 federal statute, relying on the fact that, though it was far reaching in its potential effect on privacy, it was not as loosely drafted as New York's eavesdrop law. Somewhat surprisingly, the Supreme Court declined to review those decisions and has never explicitly considered the facial validity of the federal Act. A possible explanation is that during the several years that the issue was percolating in the lower federal courts, President Nixon made four appointments to the Court and it had taken on a more conservative hue.

7. The Court, however, has interpreted and given broad effect to various provisions of the statute and clearly indicated its approval of the basic statutory scheme. *See Dalia v. United States*, 441 U.S. 238, 99 S. Ct. 1682 (1979), is an example. Finding probable cause to believe that Petitioner Dalia was conspiring to commit an offense involving interstate commerce and that his business office was being used for that purpose, a federal district court authorized interception of all oral communications at that location. Although the order did not authorize entry into petitioner's office, the FBI broke in at night and installed a bug in the ceiling. Some six weeks later, they secretly re-entered and removed the device. Partly on the basis of the intercepted conversations, Dalia was convicted of receiving stolen goods. Upholding the conviction, the Court's majority stated that the "Fourth Amendment does not prohibit *per se* a covert entry for the purpose of installing legal electronic bugging equipment," and that those considering the surveillance legislation must have understood that "by authorizing electronic interception of oral communications in addition to wire communications, they were necessarily authorizing surreptitious entries."

8. *Kyllo v. United States*, 533 U.S. 27, 121 S. Ct. 2038 (2001), involved police use of a thermal imaging device to detect activity in Kyllo's house. The device measures the intensity of heat emanating from the walls of the building being scanned. A relatively high degree of heat is consistent with the use of high intensity lamps typically used to grow marijuana indoors. Relying on the indications of high heat given off by one of the walls in Kyllo's residence, the police obtained a warrant to search the premises. Invalidating the ensuing search, which yielded proof of marijuana possession, a majority of five concluded that "obtaining by sense-enhancing technology any information regarding the interior of the home that could not otherwise have been obtained without physical intrusion into a constitution-

ally protected area constitutes a search—at least where (as here) the technology in question is not in general use."

The dissenters reasoned that a thermal imaging device only measures heat after it has escaped from the home and has become exposed to the general public. Hence, they concluded, there has been no intrusion upon a constitutionally protected area.

Who is right?

9. Should the atrocities at the World Trade Center and the Pentagon on September 11, 2001, cause the Court to rethink the permissible scope of governmental searches and seizures?

CONCLUSION

One generalization to be drawn from our limited survey of constitutional criminal procedure is that several vital provisions of the Constitution are drafted in sweeping general terms that set forth broad standards. "Due process," "probable cause," and "unreasonable searches and seizures" are terms freighted with history, but they are also concepts that leave wide latitude for the exercise of judgment. It is not surprising, then, that the course of constitutional adjudication in such areas is far from straight and smooth, and that it takes its character in no small measure from changes society and in the composition of the Supreme Court.

This book's focus upon significant areas of criminal procedure that have been shaped by constitutional precepts should not obscure the fact that significant areas are governed by procedural rules adopted by legislatures and courts at both the federal and state level.

In speaking of standards, we had in mind criteria that *require* the exercise of judgment—judgment that may require consideration of a variety of factors. Rules may be distinguished from standards in that they seek to anticipate the variant situations that may arise and to prescribe the result or consequence that is to follow. But one should not press the distinction too far. Some rules are fairly general; others, very specific. Moreover, even a rule that seems explicit may sometimes require interpretation, especially when applying it in an unusual context.

Chapter V

THE INTERPRETATION
OF STATUTES

A. READING STATUTES

1. INTRODUCTION

The study of the legislative process is too important to relegate to a mere chapter in an introductory book on legal method. Nevertheless, before becoming "case hardened," students must learn to deal with and appreciate the role of statutes. Law school teaching has always emphasized judge-made law, rather than law enacted by legislative bodies.[a] This remains true today even though legislation is the primary instrument of social change. Interpretation and application of statutes and administrative rules and regulations form the great bulk of material in most judicial decisions. Furthermore, most problems with which lawyers deal are likely to require the ability to understand provisions of a statute, ordinance, rule, or regulation. The lawyer must be able to read a statute and to make a logical prediction as to its meaning and the applicability of its provisions to a given situation.

The lawyer who acts as counselor—that is, one who guides the future actions of clients—reads a statutory provision in quite a different light from the advocate who is called upon to champion a given reading and interpretation of the statute after a dispute has surfaced. The counselor may view her role as protecting the client from litigation. She may very well adopt the view least likely to cause dispute and litigation. Yet in attempting to avoid potential disputes, the counselor may tip the scales against interpretations more favorable to the client. Ideally, the counselor should advise the client of the alternative courses of action with regard to potential statutory interpretations and evaluate the risks and benefits attendant upon each course of action. Only then will the client have an informed basis for making a decision.

---

a. The subject of Chapter V—the legal method employed in the interpretation of statutes—also embraces constitutional provisions, ordinances, rules, and regulations promulgated by legislative and administrative bodies, as contrasted with cases and opinions, the product of the judicial process.

The lawyer performs quite a different role when acting as an advocate. Once a controversy over the meaning of the statute has arisen, the advocate must convince the tribunal called upon to resolve the dispute of the correctness of her views regarding the meaning and scope of the statutory language. The advocate's skill entails effective argumentation of the impact of a statute upon events that have already taken place, not counseling a client regarding future action.

The roles of advocate and counselor do not necessarily encompass two separate spheres. As a practical matter, a lawyer often acts as both counselor and advocate for the same client in a given situation. For example, even in the litigation context, decisions may be made with a view toward reducing the client's potential exposure. The lawyer who guides the client's course of conduct in these situations combines the attributes of advocate and counselor.

Lawyers are also called upon to draft legislation. Although the materials in this chapter are not designed to teach the art of drafting statutes, the student should gain a healthy respect for the techniques involved in transforming thoughts into clear statutory language. The following is an excerpt from the minutes of an English Borough Council Meeting:[b]

> Councillor Trafford took exception to the proposed notice at the entrance of South Park: "No dogs must be brought to this Park except on a lead." He pointed out that this order would not prevent an owner from releasing his pets, or pet, from a lead when once safely inside the Park.
>
> *The Chairman* (Colonel Vine): What alternative wording would you propose, Councillor?
>
> *Councillor Trafford:* "Dogs are not allowed in this Park without leads."
>
> *Councillor Hogg:* Mr. Chairman, I object. The order should be addressed to the owners, not to the dogs.
>
> *Councillor Trafford:* That is a nice point. Very well then: "Owners of dogs are not allowed in this Park unless they keep them on leads."
>
> *Councillor Hogg:* Mr. Chairman, I object. Strictly speaking, this would prevent me as a dog-owner from leaving my dog in the back-garden at home and walking with Mrs. Hogg across the Park.
>
> *Councillor Trafford:* Mr. Chairman, I suggest that our legalistic friend be asked to redraft the notice himself.
>
> *Councillor Hogg:* Mr. Chairman, since Councillor Trafford finds it so difficult to improve on my original wording, I accept. "Nobody without his dog on a lead is allowed in this Park."

Councillor Trafford: Mr. Chairman, I object. Strictly speaking, this notice would prevent me, as a citizen who owns no dog, from walking in the Park without first acquiring one.

Councillor Hogg (with some warmth): Very simply, then: "Dogs must be led in this Park."

Councillor Trafford: Mr. Chairman, I object: this reads as if it were a general injunction to the Borough to lead their dogs into the Park.

Councillor Hogg interposed a remark for which he was called to order; upon his withdrawing it, it was directed to be expunged from the Minutes.

The Chairman: Councillor Trafford, Councillor Hogg has had three tries; you have had only two * * *.

Councillor Trafford: "All dogs must be kept on leads in this Park."

The Chairman: I see Councillor Hogg rising quite rightly to raise another objection. May I anticipate him with another amendment: "All dogs in this Park must be kept on the lead."

This draft was put to the vote and carried unanimously, with two abstentions.

————

The legal method employed in interpreting and construing statutes must be premised upon respect for statutory language. This is an essential change (and often an unwelcome one) from the legal method employed in extrapolating a rule of law from a case or line of cases. In Chapters III and IV, we analyzed and synthesized judicial decisions for the purpose of drawing rules of law from them. Liberties were often taken with the language of the court. At times the language of the court was deliberately disregarded in order to reach the true *ratio decidendi* of the case—the narrow rule of law derived after analysis of the facts of the case and the precise legal issue presented. Not so with a statute! The statutory rule is cast exclusively in the wording of the provision—no more, no less. All legal methods employed by courts to interpret statutes start with the text.[c]

Students may initially be somewhat uncomfortable with this method, preferring to take the liberties with statutes to which they have become accustomed with judicial decisions. The only sure guide to the interpretation of a statute, however, is to state the issue facing the court using the exact language of the statute—approximations and paraphrasing are not sufficient. Use the exact language!

The legal method employed in statutory analysis is forcefully set forth by Erwin N. Griswold, formerly Dean of the Harvard Law School

c. For a different view see pp. 437–47, *infra.*

and Solicitor General of the United States, in an address to the Association of the Bar of the City of New York.[d] In commenting on effective argument to a court on the meaning of statutes, he stated:

> [L]et the court see—and I mean "see"—the exact language with which they have to deal. Tell them, right at the beginning: "The statutory language involved appears at page 4 of my brief. Though the clause is a somewhat long one, the issue turns, I believe, on the proper construction or effect of words in two lines near the top of the page." Give the court time to find the two lines, and then read the words to them. At this point, the eye can be as important as the ear in oral argument, and the court will follow all of the rest of your argument much better if you have taken pains to tell them exactly what it is about, and where to find the words if they want to look at them again.

> In the years when I was a law teacher, I suppose that my most famous classroom remark was "Look at the statute"—or "What does the statute say?" Over the years, I have had literally hundreds of my former students write me and say that this was the most important thing they learned in law school. There is something about the student, and some oral advocates, too, which leads them to think great thoughts without ever taking the time and care to see just exactly what they are thinking about. Now I would not suggest that the court would make such a mistake. But courts are accustomed to think in terms of concrete, rather specific cases. The oral advocate takes a great step in advancing his cause, I think, if, right at the beginning of his argument, after the procedural setting has been established, he tells the court exactly what the case is about, including specific reference to any statutory language which must be construed or evaluated in bringing the case to a decision. With orientation, the court finds moorings. It is no longer cast adrift on the great sea of all the law. If you can get the court moored to the question as you see it, and so that they see it clearly and distinctly, you may be off to a good start towards leading them to decide the case your way.

2. STATING ISSUES IN STATUTORY TERMS

a. *Introduction*

Statutory analysis is traditionally taught by having students read cases. Such reliance on judicial authority puts the cart before the horse. Before reading cases setting forth guidelines on statutory construction, students must develop the habit of first reading the statute in light of the given problem. Only in this way will they master the art of culling the relevant statutory language. Students who first peek at the cases or secondary sources for clues to the meaning of a statute without wading through the process of isolating the text of the statute under consider-

---

d. 26 The Record of the Association of the Bar of the City of New York 342 (1971).

ation, may be unequipped to handle later problems in the practice of law, for not every statute has been judicially interpreted. Indeed, a large percentage of the work of contemporary lawyers involves interpreting statutes of first impression—that is, statutes that have not previously been subject to judicial review. This statement becomes especially significant if interpretation of contract provisions is also included. After all, a contract is, in a sense, merely private legislation.

We shall soon examine statutory language in light of hypotheticals. Analyze the hypotheticals strictly in terms of the statutory language. Frame the legal issues confronting the court. Later you will analyze some of the cases on which the hypotheticals were based. If you proceed through these exercises in the suggested manner, you will appreciate that the careful reading of the precise statutory language is an indispensable key to its interpretation.

Keep in mind, however, two factors that render these exercises quite different from the task of the lawyer. First, the given facts are assumed to govern the resolution of the controversy. The adversary process involves the resolution of disputed facts. Counseling involves forecasting or shaping future facts. Second, the problems set forth the statutory language to be construed. In practice, lawyers may spend many hours researching applicable statutes. Often several statutes or regulations seem to affect the same transaction or dispute. At other times, no relevant statutes or regulations seem to govern the situation.

b. Problems

Problem 1

McBoyle was convicted of transporting from Ottawa, Illinois, to Guymon, Oklahoma, an airplane that he knew had been stolen. It is alleged that he violated the National Motor Vehicle Theft Act, which provides, in pertinent part, as follows:

> 2. That when used in this Act: (a) The term "motor vehicle" shall include an automobile, automobile truck, automobile wagon, motor cycle, or any other self-propelled vehicle not designed for running on rails. * * *

> 3. That whoever shall transport or cause to be transported in interstate or foreign commerce a motor vehicle, knowing the same to have been stolen, shall be punished by a fine of not more than $5,000, or by imprisonment of not more than five years, or both.

State the issue or issues of statutory construction raised by the problem, using the precise language of the statute.

Problem 2

The defendants, members of the White House staff, were charged with soliciting political contributions from three individuals. In return, the defendants promised to support and use influence on behalf of the contributors to secure for them appointments as Chairs of the County

Rations Boards of Pike, Amite, and Lawrence Counties. No such offices existed at the time of the solicitation or at any time thereafter up to the return of the indictment. Authority to create such offices, however, had been granted to the President well before the alleged violations occurred.

The statute upon which the indictment was based provided as follows:

> Whoever solicits or receives, either as a political contribution, or for personal emolument, any money or thing of value, in consideration of the promise of support or use of influence in obtaining for any person any appointive office or place under the United States, shall be fined not more than $1,000 or imprisoned not more than one year, or both.

State the issue or issues of statutory construction raised by the problem, using the precise language of the statute.

Problem 3

John D. Temple acquired lot number 169 in Petersburg and erected a residence on it. The residence faces St. Andrews Street and is bounded on one side by Talliaferro Street.

At the time that John Temple erected his residence, Peoples Memorial Cemetery was already established on a tract of eight acres, a portion of which extended to within 80 feet of his residence. Between the residence and the cemetery lies Talliaferro street, which is 30 feet wide, and a vacant strip of land belonging to the City of Petersburg, 50 feet in width. On this vacant strip of land are a number of graves, the nearest of which is 74 feet east of the residence.

The cemetery tract on one side abutted Crater road. It became necessary for the city to widen and improve Crater road. To do so, a strip of the cemetery property was required to be taken by the exercise of eminent domain. Many bodies had been interred upon this strip, and it was necessary to exhume them to complete the improvement of the road. The city, desiring to provide a proper place to re-inter these bodies, acquired the tract of 1.01 acres of land on the south side of St. Andrews street adjoining the cemetery tract. The 1.01–acre tract lies directly across St. Andrews street in front of the appellants' residence, and 70 feet distant therefrom at the nearest point. The City of Petersburg plans to re-inter the bodies in this proposed addition to the cemetery. Afterward, it plans to make the tract an integral part of the cemetery.[e]

Temple sued the City of Petersburg to enjoin it from using the 1.01 acres of land acquired by it for cemetery purposes. He relied upon the following statute, which was in effect at all relevant times:

> No cemetery shall be hereafter established within the corporate limits of any city or town; nor shall any cemetery be established within two hundred and fifty yards of any residence without the

e. Facts taken from *Temple v. Petersburg*, 182 Va. 418, 29 S.E.2d 357 (1944).

consent of the owner of the legal and equitable title of such residence * * *.

State the issue or issues of statutory construction raised by the problem, using the precise language of the statute.

Notes and Questions

1. The underlying question is whether the city would violate the statute by using the 1.01 acre parcel for cemetery purposes. Specifically, the issue may be framed as whether the use of the 1.01 tract of land falls within the statutory prohibition against any cemetery being "established" in a city or town or within two hundred and fifty yards of any residence. The meaning of the term "established" is the critical focal point. Is the enlargement of an existing cemetery an establishment within the meaning of the statute? Phrased differently, does establishment mean origination and creation, or may it also embrace enlargements of or additions to existing cemeteries?

2. Assume Temple did not sue to enjoin the use of the land. Instead, with knowledge of the use of the tract for cemetery purposes, he waited two years and then brought a suit for damages against the city. What additional statutory language might become relevant to the resolution of the problem?

Problem 4

Johnson was acting as head brakeman on a freight train of the Southern Pacific Company, which was making its regular trip between San Francisco, California, and Ogden, Utah. On reaching Promontory, Utah, Johnson was directed to uncouple the engine from the train and couple it to a dining car, which belonged to the company, and which was standing on a side track, for the purpose of turning the car around so that it could be picked up and put on the next westbound passenger train. The engine and the dining car were equipped, respectively, with the Janney coupler and the Miller hook, which would not couple together automatically by impact but would couple automatically with a connector made by the same company, and it was therefore necessary for Johnson, and he was ordered, to go between the engine and the dining car to accomplish the coupling. In so doing, Johnson's hand was caught between the engine bumper and the dining car bumper and crushed, which necessitated amputation of the hand above the wrist. The accident occurred on August 5, 1900.[f]

Johnson sued the railroad seeking to recover damages for his injuries resulting from the coupling operation. The defendant contended that it was not liable for the injuries on the ground that the plaintiff, under the rules of the common law, had "assumed the risk" involved in coupling the dining car and the locomotive. The plaintiff contended, on the other hand, that the defendant was violating a federal statute and

---

f. Facts taken from *W.O. Johnson v. Southern Pacific Co.*, 196 U.S. 1, 25 S. Ct. 158 (1904).

that by virtue of this violation the plaintiff was not deemed to have assumed the risk. The federal statute provided:

Chap. 196.—An act to promote the safety of employees and travelers upon railroads by compelling common carriers engaged in interstate commerce to equip their cars with automatic couplers and continuous brakes and their locomotives with driving-wheel brakes, and for other purposes.

Be it enacted by the Senate and House of Representatives of the United States of America in Congress assembled

* * *

Sec. 2. That on and after the first day of January, eighteen hundred and ninety-eight, it shall be unlawful for any common carrier [engaged in interstate commerce] to haul or permit to be hauled or used on its line any car used in moving interstate traffic not equipped with couplers coupling automatically by impact, and which can be uncoupled without the necessity of men going between the ends of the cars.

* * *

Sec. 6. That any such common carrier using any locomotive engine, running any train, or hauling or permitting to be hauled or used on its line any car in violation of any of the provisions of this act, shall be liable to a penalty of one hundred dollars for each and every such violation, to be recovered in a suit or suits to be brought by the United States district attorney in the district court of the United States having jurisdiction in the locality where such violation shall have been committed, and it shall be the duty of such district attorney to bring such suits upon duly verified information being lodged with him of such violation having occurred. And it shall also be the duty of the Interstate Commerce Commission to lodge with the proper district attorneys information of any such violations as may come to its knowledge: *Provided,* that nothing in this act contained shall apply to trains composed of four-wheel cars or to locomotives used in hauling such trains.

Sec. 7. That the Interstate Commerce Commission may from time to time upon full hearing and for good cause extend the period within which any common carrier shall comply with the provisions of this act.

Sec. 8. That any employee of any such common carrier who may be injured by any locomotive, car, or train in use contrary to the provision of this act shall not be deemed thereby to have assumed the risk thereby occasioned, although continuing in the employment of such carrier after the unlawful use of such locomotive, car, or train had been brought to his knowledge.

State the issue or issues of statutory construction raised by the problem, using the precise language of the statute.

Notes and Questions

1. The problem turns upon whether the employee assumed the risk in undertaking the coupling operation. Section 8 of the Federal Act abrogated the doctrine in suits by employees injured by "any locomotive, car or train in use contrary to the provision" of the act. What provisions of the act are relevant to this inquiry? Examine closely section 2.

    a. Does the term "car" within the text of section 2 include an engine? If it does not embrace an engine, then section 2 is inapplicable to the facts of the case, and the doctrine of assumption of risk has not been statutorily abrogated. See also section 6 of the statute.

    b. If the term "car" does embrace engines, then consider whether the engine and dining car were "equipped with couplers coupling automatically by impact, and which can be uncoupled without the necessity of men going between the ends of the cars."

    c. Assuming the statute does require the engine and dining car to be equipped with couplers capable of coupling automatically with each other upon impact, were they "used in moving interstate traffic"?

2. After first identifying the statutory language in question, you should proceed to construe each element of the statute.

Problem 5

Holy Trinity Church is a corporation duly organized and incorporated as a religious society under the laws of the State of New York. E. Walpoe Warren was an Englishman residing abroad. Holy Trinity Church entered into a contract with him to become its rector and pastor. Warren moved to New York and entered the service of the church. The United States brought an action to recover a penalty under the terms of the following statute:

    Be it enacted by the senate and house of representatives of the United States of America, in congress assembled, that from and after the passage of this act it shall be unlawful for any person, company, partnership, or corporation, in any manner whatsoever, to prepay the transportation, or in any way assist or encourage the importation or migration, of any alien or aliens, any foreigner or foreigners, into the United States, its territories, or the District of Columbia, under contract or agreement, parol or special, express or implied, made previous to the importation or migration of such alien or aliens, foreigner or foreigners, to perform labor or service of any kind in the United States, its territories, or the District of Columbia.

State the issue or issues of statutory construction raised by the problem, using the precise language of the statute.

Notes and Questions

The statute contained a section withdrawing several classes of persons and contracts from the operation of the act. One proviso stated: "Nor shall the provisions of this act apply to professional actors, artists, lecturers, or singers, nor to persons employed strictly as personal or domestic servants." Does this proviso aid in determining whether a minister performs labor or service of any kind? Assume the proviso excluded "actors, artists, lecturers, and other professionals." Now state the issue raised by the problem.

B.   RESOLVING STATUTORY ISSUES

1.   INTRODUCTION

Reading the literal text of the statute, although indispensable, is just the first step in the process of statutory construction. After isolating the relevant language of the legislative provision, the lawyer must seek its meaning. Only then will she be able to act effectively as counselor or advocate.

The materials that follow examine various methods and rules employed in construing statutes. Before reaching them, however, let us first attempt to understand why there exists uncertainty in interpreting legislation.

SOME CAUSES OF UNCERTAINTY IN STATUTES[g]

Every lawyer who holds himself out as a legislative draftsman dreams of one perfect job. Let the painter aspire to his one flawlessly balanced composition, the composer to his one consummate harmony, and the big league pitcher to that one crowning game at which no opposing batter will reach first base. The draftsman of bills will be ready to pronounce his *nunc dimittis* the day he sees enacted into law a statute of his devising that leaves no contingency unprovided for and that is clear and unambiguous in its direction as to each and every conceivable fact situation which may take place in the world of affairs.

Unhappily, the gap between aspiration and accomplishment stretches as wide in legislative craftsmanship as in any other professional field. The draftsman can narrow the area of statutory uncertainty by painstaking fact-gathering and intensive study of every facet of existing case and statute law bearing on the matter at hand. He can reduce the incidence of statutory ambiguity by conjuring up hundreds of hypothetical fact-situations which may arise in the future for decision under the statute. But, when the job is done and the bill added to the statute books, there will still be cases for which the statute affords no certain guide. It is the purpose of this sketch to suggest a few of the reasons why any statute, however carefully and imaginatively drawn up, must fall short of the goal of perfect certainty.

WORDS ARE IMPERFECT SYMBOLS TO COMMUNICATE INTENT

Certain of the draftsman's difficulties are not unique to legislative work but arise in connection with the preparation of all legal documents. The draftsman must express his understanding and purpose in words,

g. Department of Legislation, 36 A.B.A.J. 321 (1950).

and words are notoriously imperfect symbols for the communication of ideas. Justice Cardozo was speaking for our entire word-bound profession when he began his little classic, The Paradoxes of Legal Science, with the mournful exclamation, "They do things better with logarithms." What makes the legislative draftsman's job more trying than the task of the draftsman of a contract or a will is that the words of the statute must communicate the intention to at least three crucial classes of readers: the legislators who are to examine the bill to decide whether it is in accordance with their specifications, the lawyers who must make use of the statute in counseling and litigation, and the judges who will give the statute its final and authoritative interpretation. One does not have to be an expert in semantics to know that words rarely mean the same thing to all men or at all times. An intent that seems "plainly" expressed to the legislative experts on a standing committee may be ambiguous to affected persons and their lawyers and quite unintelligible to judges with no special knowledge or experience in the field of regulation.

Unforeseen Situations Are Inevitable

Unforeseen cases account for the great majority of the instances of statutory uncertainty. The problem here is that the typical drive for legislative action originates not in a desire for an overall codification of the law but in some felt necessity for a better way of dealing with some specific situation or group of situations. The draftsman must make effective provision for the specific needs that are urged upon him, but he must write the statute in the form of a proposition of general applicability. In our legal system we have a long-standing distrust of legislation so narrowly drawn as to affect only designated persons or a few particularized situations. Inequality in the application of legislation is the evil aimed at in such provisions of the federal Constitution as the Equal Protection and Bill of Attainder Clauses, and the same general idea is reflected in the provision of most state constitutions against local and special legislation. The policy is sound, beyond any question at all, but it leaves to the draftsman of statutes the hard task of formulating a general rule that adequately takes care of the specific situations before the legislature without including in its apparent scope unthought-of cases somewhat similar in fact content but distinguishable on policy grounds.

Case-minded judges and lawyers might be a little less caustic in their comments on the ambiguity of statutes if they were to reflect that the problem of uncertainty in relation to the unthought-of case arises also in the use of case precedents. Every first year law student learns that he must distinguish between the *holding* of a case and the *dicta* which may be set out in the court's opinion. In our common law tradition, we take as binding precedent only the decision of the court on the material facts of the case actually before it. All else we discount as *dicta*—persuasive, perhaps, but not authoritative. This immemorial common law distinction between *holding* and *dictum* is based on a recognition that even the finest judge is at his best only when dealing with the facts of the case at hand, the issues on which he has had the benefit of argument of counsel. The same is true of the statute-law maker and his technical drafting assistants. If the draftsman is respectably skilled and careful, he will make unmistakably clear provision for the specific situations called to his attention at committee hearings and in other ways. If he is at all imaginative, he will anticipate and take care of other situations within the reach of reasonable anticipation. But human foresight is limited and the variety of fact-situations endless. Every generally worded statute, sooner or later, will fail to provide a certain direction as to the handling of those inevitable legislative nuisances, the cases nobody thought of.

UNCERTAINTIES MAY BE ADDED IN COURSE OF ENACTMENT

So far in this sketch, the problems of the legislative draftsman have been considered without reference to the political realities in Congress and the state legislatures. But legislative drafting is not a branch of art for art's sake. After the statute has been drafted it has to be passed, and there are many stages in the process of enactment at which uncertainty may be introduced into the most tightly drafted legislative proposal. The sponsoring legislator or the responsible standing committee is likely to make changes in the bill without having the time to consider the effect of the changes on the articulation of the bill as a whole. An amendment from the floor may add confused or inconsistent provisions which fit awkwardly into the statutory pattern. It sometimes becomes necessary as a matter of political compromise to eliminate some precise key-word in the bill and substitute for it some less exact term, chosen deliberately to leave a controversial issue to the courts for decision. In short, it is wholly unrealistic to read a statute as if it were the product of wholly scientific, detached and uneventful deliberation.

2. EXTRINSIC SOURCES

If a statute is ambiguous or unclear, resort is often had to "extrinsic sources," sources outside the statutory provisions. A common source is the legislative history surrounding the enactment of the provision. This history is compiled from the records and documents produced by the legislative process. Materials used to compile a federal legislative history are the printed bill (both before and after any amendments), the transcript or report of committee hearings, debates (recorded in the Congressional Record), and the public law as signed by the President and published in the Statutes at Large. These documents are printed by Congress and are available in law libraries. Unfortunately this material is often unavailable for most state legislation.

In the following excerpt,[h] Professor Boris Bittker comments upon the importance of extrinsic sources in interpreting ambiguous or unclear terms.

h. 1 Boris Bittker, FEDERAL TAXATION OF INCOME ESTATES AND GIFTS ¶ 4.2.2 (1981).

The courts and commentators once vigorously debated the propriety of resorting to such "extrinsic" aids to statutory construction as legislative debates, committee hearings and reports, prior laws, and administrative interpretations; but the practice is now so common that it is difficult to recapture the intensity of that ancient war of words. Its principal contemporary legacy is an occasional assertion that the statute must be "ambiguous" on its face before resort to extrinsic aids is permissible; and its corollary—that a "plain meaning" must be enforced, however much it may conflict with the legislative history, since the latter may be used only to resolve, and not to create, ambiguity. The opposite view is that judges should not "make a fortress out of the dictionary" by rejecting any source of enlightenment, even if the statutory language is clear. This approach is sometimes caricatured by the maxim, "Look at the Code only if the committee reports are ambiguous"—or, as students of Roman law used to say, *quid non agnoscit glossa, id non agnoscit curia.*[19]

Judicial readiness to go outside the four corners of the statute even when the language is unambiguous is sometimes thought to be a recent innovation, but it has ancient and honorable precedents. As long ago as *Heydon's Case* (1584), it was held that "the office of all the Judges is always to make such * * * construction [of statutes] as shall suppress the mischief [which the statute was intended to remedy] and advance the remedy, and to suppress subtle inventions and evasions for continuance of the mischief * * * and to add force and life to the remedy, according to the true intent of the makers of the Act, *pro bono publico.*" This early groping for something more than the literal meaning of a statute was superseded in England in the early nineteenth century by the more explicit "Golden Rule" of statutory construction:

> The rule by which we are to be guided in construing acts of Parliament is to look at the precise words, and to construe them in their ordinary sense, unless it would lead to any absurdity or manifest injustice; and if it should, so to vary and modify them as to avoid that which it certainly could not have been the intention of the legislature should be done.

The current American rule, as enunciated by the Supreme Court in 1940, sanctions the use of extrinsic aids in an even broader spectrum of cases than was contemplated by the English Golden Rule:

> There is, of course, no more persuasive evidence of the purpose of a statute than the words by which the legislature undertook to give expression to its wishes. Often these words are sufficient in and of themselves to determine the purpose of the legislation. In such cases we have followed their plain meaning. When that meaning has led to absurd or futile results, however, this Court has looked

---

19. Roughly translated: "If it can't be found in the commentaries, judges won't believe it." *See* Babeaux v. CIR, 601 F.2d 730, 732 (4th Cir. 1979) (Judge Dumbauld, dissenting, in his role as Yankee interloper on the Fourth Circuit, Latinist, and legal historian).

beyond the words to the purpose of the act. Frequently, however, even when the plain meaning did not produce absurd results but merely an unreasonable one "plainly at variance with the policy of the legislation as a whole" this Court has followed that purpose, rather than the literal words.

On concluding that the "plain meaning" of the statutory language warranted looking "beyond the words to the purpose of the act," the Court embarked on an extensive examination of the law's legislative history, including prior drafts of the bill as enacted, committee reports and hearings, legislative debate, and other pending legislation.

Given this approach to statutory language with a troublesome "plain meaning," the threshold decision for a court is whether simply to go ahead and enforce the statutory language as written, leaving correction of its deficiencies to Congress, or to resort to extrinsic aids to interpretation and then to decide, with the aid of this "outside" light, whether the plain meaning or something less obvious was intended by Congress. Such an inquiry does not require courts to delude themselves or others into believing that the Congress had an "intent" comparable to the intent of individuals. Judge Learned Hand's comment on this point cannot be improved:

> The issue involves the baffling question which comes up so often in the interpretation of all kinds of writings: how far is it proper to read the words out of their literal meaning in order to realize their overriding purpose? It is idle to add to the acres of paper and streams of ink that have been devoted to the discussion. When we ask what Congress "intended," usually there can be no answer, if what we mean is what any person or group of persons actually had in mind. Flinch as we may, what we do, and must do, is to project ourselves, as best we can, into the position of those who uttered the words, and to impute to them how they would have dealt with the concrete occasion. He who supposes that he can be certain of the result is the least fitted for the attempt.

Turning from the theory of statutory interpretation to actual practice, courts seldom if ever refuse to consider these extrinsic aids, no matter how plain the statutory language. It is easy enough to adhere to the statute's plain meaning if the legislative history proves to be ambiguous; conversely, if the extrinsic evidence is persuasive, the judge may conclude that the meaning of the statutory language is less clear than it initially appeared to be. In the latter case, it is common to quote Mr. Justice Holmes: "A word is not a crystal, transparent and unchanged, it is the skin of a living thought and may vary greatly in color and content according to the circumstances and the time in which it is used." This excursion into semantic theory encourages the view that statutes never have a "plain meaning," as does Judge Learned Hand's famous observation in *Helvering v. Gregory:*

> [T]he meaning of a sentence may be more than that of the separate words, as a melody is more than the notes, and no degree of

particularity [of the statutory language] can ever obviate recourse to the setting in which all appear, and which all collectively create.

Knowing that a statute's "plain meaning," as originally perceived, may be altered by a blinding flash of extrinsic light, tax lawyers routinely refer to committee reports and similar sources in arguments before the IRS and the courts.

Once a court has decided to look beyond the four corners of the Internal Revenue Code, there are no formal restrictions on the material that may be taken into account in interpreting the statutory language. Just as a trial judge, when sitting without a jury, will often let in almost any evidence "for what it is worth" even if it is incompetent or immaterial under the normal rules of evidence, so the basic test for a proffered extrinsic aid to statutory construction is whether it can reasonably be thought to shed light on the issue to be decided. Thus, courts in federal tax cases look not only to such formal sources of legislative history as committee reports and legislative debates but also to less formal sources such as hearings, memoranda by trade groups, and commentators. Prior judicial decisions and administrative interpretations and regulations are also frequently examined because, whether endorsed, qualified, or rejected by legislation, they can illuminate its purpose. The *weight* of any particular bit of evidence is, of course, a different matter from its relevance.

3. DOCTRINES OF STATUTORY CONSTRUCTION

Several rules of statutory interpretation have evolved over the years. The most basic of these strictures is that the "plain meaning" of the statute must be first ascertained and applied. In most situations this rule is not difficult to follow. These cases are rarely litigated. As the passage below demonstrates, the decided cases largely involve special facts that raise debatable issues of meaning or application.

A NOTE ON CERTAINTY IN STATUTES[i]

The cases on statutory interpretation considered in the course on Legal Method deal for the most part with what might be termed the "pathology" of statutes. That is, they deal with serious difficulties and disputes arising out of legislative language.

There is real danger that a reader confronted with such materials will begin to confuse the pathological with the normal. He may conclude that grave interpretive doubts attend every effort to use statutes. But such a conclusion is far from the facts.

Thousands of questions are daily disposed of in lawyers' offices, and in the offices of government, and elsewhere, by recourse to statutory provisions. Only a fraction of the verbiage in our statute books finds its way to the courts for construction. Some of the causes of interpretive problems that do arise have been described earlier. The nature and

i. H. Jones, J. Kernochan and A. Murphy, Legal Method 400–01 (1980).

volume of these problems vary greatly, of course, from statute to statute. But it is essential to an understanding and effective use of legislation to realize that for many, if not most, acts there is normally a substantial body of situations, an "area of no dispute," to which the terms can be applied with assurance and without difficulty.

Consider the bearing of the foregoing upon interpretation in accordance with "plain meaning." In an article entitled An Evaluation of the Rules of Statutory Interpretation, 3 Kan. L. Rev. 1 (1954), Professor Quintin Johnstone states (pp. 12–13):

> "If no statute can be perfectly plain, should the plain meaning rule be abolished? Not necessarily. Although no statute may be absolutely unambiguous, the degree of ambiguity in most statutes is very slight when applied to most situations. The degree of ambiguity is likely to be substantial only in limited peripheral sets of situations. The result is that to a large extent statutes are substantially plain, so plain that except in marginal situations it would be a ridiculous forcing of a statute to put more than one meaning on the statutory language. For purposes of interpretation, a vast area of plain meaning exists. If the term plain in the plain meaning rule is understood as plain beyond reasonable question, then the rule makes sense, although admittedly a problem arises as to what is reasonable doubt or substantial lack of ambiguity.

> "To deny that the plain meaning rule has any force or validity opens the door to violation of a fundamental objective in statutory interpretation. This position leads to a denial of legislative supremacy in the statutory field. Under such a view, statutes never are binding on a court as they never are clear. A court can always make whatever rule it wishes and decide cases in any way it wishes, despite statutory meanings because it cannot be restricted by statutory language."

In short, where the language of a statute is clear, do not twist or torture the wording to arrive at a contrived result. Apply the plain meaning!

There are situations, however, when either the language of a statute is ambiguous, or the statute seems intelligible but the facts do not clearly fall within it. What then?

A traditional doctrine for ascertaining the meaning or applicability of a statute in such a case is to discover and apply the "intent of the legislature." But this concept is elusive. Sometimes it refers to the specific intent of the legislators, at other times, to the purpose of the enactment. The former meaning assumes that Congress or the body enacting the legislation foresaw the issue and meant to decide it in a particular way. The latter, admitting that the precise issue was never contemplated by the legislators, interprets the statute in a manner to achieve its objectives. Which legal method was employed in the following case?

> And after all the Barons openly argued in Court in the same term, and it was unanimously resolved by Sir Roger Manwood, Chief Baron, and the other Barons of the Exchequer, that the said lease made to Heydon of the said parcels, whereof Ware and Ware were seised for life by copy of court-roll, was void; for it was agreed by them, that the said copyhold estate was an estate for life, within the words and meaning of the said Act. And it was resolved by them, that for the sure and true interpretation of all statutes in general (be they penal or beneficial, restrictive or enlarging of the common law) four things are to be discerned and considered:—

> 1st. What was the common law before the making of the Act.

> 2nd. What was the mischief and defect for which the common law did not provide.

> 3rd. What remedy the Parliament hath resolved and appointed to cure the disease of the commonwealth.

> And, 4th. The true reason of the remedy; and then the office of all the Judges is always to make such construction as shall suppress the mischief, and advance the remedy, and to suppress subtle inventions and evasions for continuance of the mischief, and *pro privato commodo,* and to add force and life to the cure and remedy, according to the true intent of the makers of the Act, *pro bono publico.*

Heydon's Case, 3 Coke 7a, 76 Eng. Rep. 637 (Court of Exchequer, 1584).

The two rules just discussed—the plain meaning and the intent of the legislature maxims—are seemingly antithetical. If the meaning is clear, why should one look beyond it to the intent of the framers of the legislation?

There are judicial authorities supporting the plain meaning rule and refusing to resort to the intent of the statute to avoid the plain meaning. Some of the following cases are in this current. Note, however, how some decisions support the plain meaning with reference to legislative intent. Others avoid the plain meaning by resort to extrinsic sources.

CAMINETTI v. UNITED STATES

Supreme Court of the United States, 1917.
242 U.S. 470, 37 S.Ct. 192, 61 L.Ed. 442.

JUSTICE DAY delivered the opinion of the Court.

These three cases were argued together, and may be disposed of in a single opinion. In each of the cases there was a conviction and sentence for violation of the so-called White Slave Traffic Act of June 25, 1910 (36 Stat. at L. 825, chap. 395, Comp. Stat. 1913, § 8813), the judgments were affirmed by the circuit courts of appeals, and writs of certiorari bring the cases here.

In the Caminetti Case, the petitioner was indicted in the United States district court for the northern district of California, upon the 6th day of May, 1913, for alleged violations of the act. The indictment was in four counts, the first of which charged him with transporting and causing to be transported, and aiding and assisting in obtaining transportation for a certain woman from Sacramento, California, to Reno, Nevada, in interstate commerce, for the purpose of debauchery, and for an immoral purpose, to wit, that the aforesaid woman should be and become his mistress and concubine. A verdict of not guilty was returned as to the other three counts of this indictment. As to the first count, defendant was found guilty and sentenced to imprisonment for eighteen months and to pay a fine of $1,500. Upon writ of error to the United States circuit court of appeals for the ninth circuit, that judgment was affirmed. 136 C.C.A. 147, 220 Fed. 545.

It is contended that the act of Congress is intended to reach only "commercialized vice," or the traffic in women for gain, and that the conduct for which the several petitioners were indicted and convicted, however reprehensible in morals, is not within the purview of the statute when properly construed in the light of its history and the purposes intended to be accomplished by its enactment. In none of the cases was it charged or proved that the transportation was for gain or for the purpose of furnishing women for prostitution for hire, and it is insisted that, such being the case, the acts charged and proved, upon which conviction was had, do not come within the statute.

It is elementary that the meaning of a statute must, in the first instance, be sought in the language in which the act is framed, and if that is plain, and if the law is within the constitutional authority of the law-making body which passed it, the sole function of the courts is to enforce it according to its terms.

Where the language is plain and admits of no more than one meaning, the duty of interpretation does not arise, and the rules which are to aid doubtful meanings need no discussion. There is no ambiguity in the terms of this act. It is specifically made an offense to knowingly transport or cause to be transported, etc., in interstate commerce, any woman or girl for the purpose of prostitution or debauchery, or for "any other immoral purpose," or with the intent and purpose to induce any such woman or girl to become a prostitute or to give herself up to debauchery, or to engage in any other immoral practice.

Statutory words are uniformly presumed, unless the contrary appears, to be used in their ordinary and usual sense, and with the meaning commonly attributed to them. To cause a woman or girl to be transported for the purposes of debauchery, and for an immoral purpose, to wit, becoming a concubine or mistress, for which Caminetti and Diggs[j] were convicted; or to transport an unmarried woman, under eighteen years of age, with the intent to induce her to engage in prostitution, debauchery, and other immoral practices, for which Hays was convicted,

---

j. A defendant in another case before the Court.

would seem by the very statement of the facts to embrace transportation for purposes denounced by the act, and therefore fairly within its meaning.

While such immoral purpose would be more culpable in morals and attributed to baser motives if accompanied with the expectation of pecuniary gain, such considerations do not prevent the lesser offense against morals of furnishing transportation in order that a woman may be debauched, or become a mistress or a concubine, from being the execution of purposes within the meaning of this law. To say the contrary would shock the common understanding of what constitutes an immoral purpose when those terms are applied, as here, to sexual relations.

In *United States v. Bitty,* 208 U.S. 393, 52 L.Ed. 543, 28 Sup.Ct.Rep. 396, it was held that the act of Congress against the importation of alien women and girls for the purpose of prostitution "and any other immoral purpose" included the importation of an alien woman to live in concubinage with the person importing her. In that case this court said:

> All will admit that full effect must be given to the intention of Congress as gathered from the words of the statute. There can be no doubt as to what class was aimed at by the clause forbidding the importation of alien women for purposes of "prostitution." It refers to women who, for hire or without hire, offer their bodies to indiscriminate intercourse with men. The lives and example of such persons are in hostility to "the idea of the family, as consisting in and springing from the union for life of one man and one woman in the holy estate of matrimony; the sure foundation of all that is stable and noble in our civilization; the best guaranty of that reverent morality which is the source of all beneficent progress in social and political improvement." *Murphy v. Ramsey,* 114 U.S. 15, 45, 29 L.Ed. 47, 57, 5 Sup.Ct.Rep. 747. * * * Now the addition in the last statute of the words, "or for any other immoral purpose," after the word "prostitution," must have been made for some practical object. Those added words show beyond question that Congress had in view the protection of society against another class of alien women other than those who might be brought here merely for purposes of "prostitution." In forbidding the importation of alien women "for any other immoral purpose," Congress evidently thought that there were purposes in connection with the importations of alien women which, as in the case of importations for prostitution, were to be deemed immoral. It may be admitted that, in accordance with the familiar rule of *ejusdem generis,* the immoral purpose referred to by the words "any other immoral purpose" must be one of the same general class or kind as the particular purpose of "prostitution" specified in the same clause of the statute. 2 Lewis's Sutherland, Stat.Constr. § 423, and authorities cited. But that rule cannot avail the accused in this case; for the immoral purpose charged in the indictment is of the same general class or kind as the one that controls in the importation of an alien woman for the purpose strictly of prostitution. The prostitute may, in the popular

sense, be more degraded in character than the concubine, but the latter none the less must be held to lead an immoral life, if any regard whatever be had to the views that are almost universally held in this country as to the relations which may rightfully, from the standpoint of morality, exist between man and woman in the matter of sexual intercourse.

This definition of an immoral purpose was given prior to the enactment of the act now under consideration, and must be presumed to have been known to Congress when it enacted the law here involved. (See the sections of the act[1] set forth in the margin.)

But it is contended that though the words are so plain that they cannot be misapprehended when given their usual and ordinary inter-

---

1. Sections 2, 3, and 4 of the act are as follows:

"Sec. 2. That any person who shall knowingly transport or cause to be transported, or aid or assist in obtaining transportation for, or in transporting, in interstate or foreign commerce, or in any territory or in the District of Columbia, any woman or girl for the purpose of prostitution or debauchery, or for any other immoral purpose, or with the intent and purpose to induce, entice, or compel such woman or girl to become a prostitute or to give herself up to debauchery, or to engage in any other immoral practice; or who shall knowingly procure or obtain, or cause to be procured or obtained, or aid or assist in procuring or obtaining, any ticket or tickets, or any form of transportation or evidence of the right thereto, to be used by any woman or girl in interstate or foreign commerce, or in any territory or the District of Columbia, in going to any place for the purpose of prostitution or debauchery, or for any other immoral purpose, or with the intent or purpose on the part of such person to induce, entice, or compel her to give herself up to the practice of prostitution, or to give herself up to debauchery, or any other immoral practice, whereby any such woman or girl shall be transported in interstate or foreign commerce, or in any territory or the District of Columbia, shall be deemed guilty of a felony, and upon conviction thereof shall be punished by a fine not exceeding five thousand dollars, or by imprisonment of not more than five years, or by both such fine and imprisonment, in the discretion of the court.

Sec. 3. That any person who shall knowingly persuade, induce, entice, or coerce, or cause to be persuaded, induced, enticed, or coerced, or aid or assist in persuading, inducing, enticing, or coerc-

ing any woman or girl to go from one place to another in interstate or foreign commerce, or in any territory or the District of Columbia, for the purpose of prostitution or debauchery, or for any other immoral purpose, or with the intent and purpose on the part of such person that such woman or girl shall engage in the practice of prostitution or debauchery, or any other immoral practice, whether with or without her consent, and who shall thereby knowingly cause or aid or assist in causing such woman or girl to go and to be carried or transported as a passenger upon the line or route of any common carrier or carriers in interstate or foreign commerce, or any territory or the District of Columbia, shall be deemed guilty of a felony and on conviction thereof shall be punished by a fine of not more than five thousand dollars, or by imprisonment for a term not exceeding five years, or by both such fine and imprisonment, in the discretion of the court.

Sec. 4. That any person who shall knowingly persuade, induce, entice or coerce any woman or girl under the age of eighteen years, from any state or territory or the District of Columbia, to any other state or territory or the District of Columbia, with the purpose and intent to induce or coerce her, or that she shall be induced or coerced to engage in prostitution or debauchery, or any other immoral practice, and shall in furtherance of such purpose knowingly induce or cause her to go and to be carried or transported as a passenger in interstate commerce upon the line or route of any common carrier or carriers, shall be deemed guilty of a felony, and on conviction thereof shall be punished by a fine of not more than ten thousand dollars, or by imprisonment for a term not exceeding ten years, or by both such fine and imprisonment, in the discretion of the court."

pretation, and although the sections in which they appear do not in terms limit the offense defined and punished to acts of "commercialized vice," or the furnishing or procuring of transportation of women for debauchery, prostitution, or immoral practices for hire, such limited purpose is to be attributed to Congress and engrafted upon the act in view of the language of § 8 and the report which accompanied the law upon its introduction into and subsequent passage by the House of Representatives.

In this connection, it may be observed that while the title of an act cannot overcome the meaning of plain and unambiguous words used in its body, the title of this act embraces the regulation of interstate commerce "by prohibiting the transportation therein for immoral purposes of women and girls, and for other purposes." It is true that § 8 of the act provides that it shall be known and referred to as the "White Slave Traffic Act," and the report accompanying the introduction of the same into the House of Representatives set forth the fact that a material portion of the legislation suggested was to meet conditions which had arisen in the past few years, and that the legislation was needed to put a stop to a villainous interstate and international traffic in women and girls. Still, the name given to an act by way of designation or description, or the report which accompanies it, cannot change the plain import of its words. If the words are plain, they give meaning to the act, and it is neither the duty nor the privilege of the courts to enter speculative fields in search of a different meaning.

Reports to Congress accompanying the introduction of proposed laws may aid the courts in reaching the true meaning of the legislature in cases of doubtful interpretation. But, as we have already said, and it has been so often affirmed as to become a recognized rule, when words are free from doubt they must be taken as the final expression of the legislative intent, and are not to be added to or subtracted from by considerations drawn from titles or designating names or reports accompanying their introduction, or from any extraneous source. In other words, the language being plain, and not leading to absurd or wholly impracticable consequences, it is the sole evidence of the ultimate legislative intent.

The fact, if it be so, that the act as it is written opens the door to blackmailing operations upon a large scale, is no reason why the courts should refuse to enforce it according to its terms, if within the constitutional authority of Congress. Such considerations are more appropriately addressed to the legislative branch of the government, which alone had authority to enact and may, if it sees fit, amend the law.

The judgment in each of the cases is affirmed.

JUSTICE McREYNOLDS took no part in the consideration or decision of these cases.

JUSTICE McKENNA, dissenting:

Undoubtedly, in the investigation of the meaning of a statute we resort first to its words, and, when clear, they are decisive. The principle has attractive and seemingly disposing simplicity, but that it is not easy of application, or, at least, encounters other principles, many cases demonstrate. The words of a statute may be uncertain in their signification or in their application. If the words be ambiguous, the problem they present is to be resolved by their definition; the subject matter and the lexicons become our guides. But here, even, we are not exempt from putting ourselves in the place of the legislators. If the words be clear in meaning, but the objects to which they are addressed be uncertain, the problem then is to determine the uncertainty. And for this a realization of conditions that provoked the statute must inform our judgment. Let us apply these observations to the present case.

The transportation which is made unlawful is of a woman or girl "to become a prostitute or to give herself up to debauchery, or to engage in any other immoral practice." Our present concern is with the words "any other immoral practice," which, it is asserted, have a special office. The words are clear enough as general descriptions; they fail in particular designation; they are class words, not specifications. Are they controlled by those which precede them? If not, they are broader in generalization and include those that precede them, making them unnecessary and confusing. To what conclusion would this lead us? "Immoral" is a very comprehensive word. It means a dereliction of morals. In such sense it covers every form of vice, every form of conduct that is contrary to good order. It will hardly be contended that in this sweeping sense it is used in the statute. But, if not used in such sense, to what is it limited and by what limited? If it be admitted that it is limited at all, that ends the imperative effect assigned to it in the opinion of the court. But not insisting quite on that, we ask again, By what is it limited? By its context, necessarily, and the purpose of the statute.

For the context I must refer to the statute; of the purpose of the statute Congress itself has given us illumination. It devotes a section to the declaration that the "act shall be known and referred to as the 'White Slave Traffic Act.' " And its prominence gives it prevalence in the construction of the statute. It cannot be pushed aside or subordinated by indefinite words in other sentences, limited even there by the context. It is a peremptory rule of construction that all parts of a statute must be taken into account in ascertaining its meaning, and it cannot be said that § 8 has no object. Even if it gives only a title to the act, it has especial weight. *United States v. Union P.R. Co.*, 91 U.S. 72, 82, 23 L.Ed. 224, 229. But it gives more than a title; it makes distinctive the purpose of the statute. The designation "white slave traffic" has the sufficiency of an axiom. If apprehended, there is no uncertainty as to the conduct it describes. It is commercialized vice, immoralities having a mercenary purpose, and this is confirmed by other circumstances.

The author of the bill was Mr. Mann, and in reporting it from the House committee on interstate and foreign commerce he declared for the committee that it was not the purpose of the bill to interfere with or usurp in any way the police power of the states, and further, that it was not the intention of the bill to regulate prostitution or the places where prostitution or immorality was practised, which were said to be matters wholly within the power of the states, and over which the Federal government had no jurisdiction. And further explaining the bill, it was said that the sections of the act had been "so drawn that they are limited to the cases in which there is an act of transportation in interstate commerce of women for the purposes of prostitution." And again:

> "The White Slave Trade. A material portion of the legislation suggested and proposed is necessary to meet conditions which have arisen within the past few years. The legislation is needed to put a stop to a villainous interstate and international traffic in women and girls. The legislation is not needed or intended as an aid to the states in the exercise of their police powers in the suppression or regulation of immorality in general. It does not attempt to regulate the practice of voluntary prostitution, but aims solely to prevent panderers and procurers from compelling thousands of women and girls against their will and desire to enter and continue in a life of prostitution." Cong.Rec. vol. 50, pp. 3368, 3370.

In other words, it is vice as a business at which the law is directed, using interstate commerce as a facility to procure or distribute its victims.

In 1912 the sense of the Department of Justice was taken of the act in a case where a woman of twenty-four years went from Illinois, where she lived, to Minnesota, at the solicitation and expense of a man. She was there met by him and engaged with him in immoral practices like those for which petitioners were convicted. The assistant district attorney forwarded her statement to the Attorney General, with the comment that the element of traffic was absent from the transaction and that therefore, in his opinion, it was not "within the spirit and intent of the Mann Act." Replying, the Attorney General expressed his concurrence in the view of his subordinate.

Of course, neither the declarations of the report of the committee on interstate commerce of the House nor the opinion of the Attorney General are conclusive of the meaning of the law, but they are highly persuasive. The opinion was by one skilled in the rules and methods employed in the interpretation or construction of laws, and informed, besides, of the conditions to which the act was addressed. The report was by the committee charged with the duty of investigating the necessity for the act, and to inform the House of the results of that investigation, both of evil and remedy. The report of the committee has, therefore, a higher quality than debates on the floor of the House. The representations of the latter may indeed be ascribed to the exaggerations of advocacy or opposition. The report of a committee is the execution of a duty and has the sanction of duty. There is a presumption, therefore, that the measure it recommends has the purpose it declares and will accomplish it as declared.

This being the purpose, the words of the statute should be construed to execute it, and they may be so construed even if their literal meaning be otherwise. In *Church of the Holy Trinity v. United States,* 143 U.S. 457, 36 L.Ed. 226, 12 Sup.Ct.Rep. 511, there came to this court for construction an act of Congress which made it unlawful for anyone in any of the United States "to prepay the transportation, or in any way assist or encourage the importation or migration of any alien or aliens, any foreigner or foreigners, into the United States * * * under contract or agreement * * * to perform labor or *service of any kind* [italics mine] in the United States, its territories or the District of Columbia." The Trinity Church made a contract with one E.W. Warren, a resident of England, to remove to the city of New York and enter its service as rector and pastor. The church was proceeded against under the act and the circuit court held that it applied, and rendered judgment accordingly. 36 Fed. 303.

It will be observed that the language of the statute is very comprehensive—fully as much so as the language of the act under review—having no limitation whatever from the context; and the circuit court, in submission to what the court considered its imperative quality, rendered judgment against the church. This court reversed the judgment, and, in an elaborate opinion by Mr. Justice Brewer, declared that "it is a familiar rule that a thing may be within the letter of the statute and yet not within the statute, because not within its spirit, nor within the intention of its makers." And the learned justice further said: "This has been often asserted, and the reports are full of cases illustrating its application."

It is hardly necessary to say that the application of the rule does not depend upon the objects of the legislation, to be applied or not applied as it may exclude or include good things or bad things. Its principle is the simple one that the words of a statute will be extended or restricted to execute its purpose.

Another pertinent illustration of the rule is *Reiche v. Smythe,* 13 Wall. 162, 20 L.Ed. 566, in which the court declared that if at times it was its duty to regard the words of a statute, at times it was also its duty to disregard them, limit or extend them, in order to execute the purpose of the statute. And applying the principle, it decided that in a tariff act the provision that a duty should be imposed on horses, etc., and other *live animals* imported from foreign countries should not include canary birds, ignoring the classification of nature. And so again in *Silver v. Ladd,* 7 Wall. 219, 19 L.Ed. 138, where the benefit of the Oregon Donation Act was extended by making the words "single man" used in the statute mean an unmarried woman, disregarding a difference of genders clearly expressed in the law.

The rule that these cases illustrate is a valuable one and in varying degrees has daily practice. It not only rescues legislation from absurdity (so far the opinion of the court admits its application), but it often rescues it from invalidity—a useful result in our dual form of governments and conflicting jurisdictions. It is the dictate of common sense. Language, even when most masterfully used, may miss sufficiency and give room for dispute. Is it a wonder, therefore, that when used in the haste of legislation, in view of conditions perhaps only partly seen or not seen at all, the consequences, it may be, beyond present foresight, it often becomes necessary to apply the rule? And it is a rule of prudence and highest sense. It rescues from crudities, excesses, and deficiencies, making legislation adequate to its special purpose, rendering unnecessary repeated qualifications, and leaving the simple and best exposition of a law the mischief it was intended to redress. Nor is this judicial legislation. It is seeking and enforcing the true sense of a law notwithstanding its imperfection or generality of expression.

There is much in the present case to tempt to a violation of the rule. Any measure that protects the purity of women from assault or enticement to degradation finds an instant advocate in our best emotions; but the judicial function cannot yield to emotion—it must, with poise of mind, consider and decide. It should not shut its eyes to the facts of the world and assume not to know what everybody else knows. And everybody knows that there is a difference between the occasional immoralities of men and women and that systematized and mercenary immorality epitomized in the statute's graphic phrase "white slave traffic." And it was such immorality that was in the legislative mind, and not the other. The other is occasional, not habitual—inconspicuous—does not offensively obtrude upon public notice. Interstate commerce is not its instrument as it is of the other, nor is prostitution its object or its end. It may, indeed, in instances, find a convenience in crossing state lines, but this is its accident, not its aid.

There is danger in extending a statute beyond its purpose, even if justified by a strict adherence to its words. The purpose is studied, all effects measured, not left at random—one evil practice prevented, opportunity given to another. The present case warns against ascribing such improvidence to the statute under review. Blackmailers of both sexes have arisen, using the terrors of the construction now sanctioned by this court as a help—indeed, the means—for their brigandage. The result is grave and should give us pause. It certainly will not be denied that legal authority justifies the rejection of a construction which leads to mischievous consequences, if the statute be susceptible of another construction.

United States v. Bitty, 208 U.S. 393, 52 L.Ed. 543, 28 Sup.Ct.Rep. 396, is not in opposition. The statute passed upon was a prohibition against the importation of alien women or girls—a statute, therefore, of broader purpose than the one under review. Besides, the statute finally passed upon was an amendment to a prior statute, and the words construed were an addition to the prior statute, and necessarily, therefore, had an added effect. The first statute prohibited the importation of any alien woman or girl into the United States *for the purpose of prostitution* [italics mine]. The second statute repeated the words and added *"or for any other immoral purpose."* Necessarily there was an enlargement of purpose, and besides, the act was directed against the importation of foreign corruption, and was construed accordingly. The case, therefore, does not contradict the rule; it is an example of it.

For these reasons I dissent from the opinion and judgment of the court, expressing no opinion of the other propositions in the cases.

I am authorized to say that the CHIEF JUSTICE and MR. JUSTICE CLARKE concur in this dissent.

Notes and Questions

1. The majority embraced the proposition that if the language of the statute is plain, the courts must enforce it according to its terms. The Court should not enter "speculative fields" to discover the intent of the legislature. Yet it embraced the "absurd or wholly impracticable consequences" exception to the plain meaning rule. Did the exception apply?

2. The question in *Caminetti* was the meaning of the phrase "any other immoral practice." Was the phrase limited by the specific words that immediately preceded it—that is, "practices involving pecuniary gain"? Shouldn't the Court also have analyzed the term "debauchery"? The dissent used the canons *ejusdem generis*[k] and *noscitur a sociis*,[l] without identifying them by name, in deriving the import of the language. Should the meaning of a word in a statute be determined from the words and phrases associated with it? If a man takes his wife across state lines in order to beat her or to have her assist in robbing a bank, would these acts fall within the statutory proscription, "any other immoral purpose"?

This case, and a long line of Mann Act cases, became rather famous, or perhaps infamous. How would you decide the following cases under the statute at issue in *Caminetti*:

(A) In the District of Columbia, a lady of the evening is taken for a four block taxi ride to a hotel for the purpose of prostitution. Is this within the Act? *United States v. Beach*, 324 U.S. 193, 65 S. Ct. 602 (1945).

(B) A madam and her husband take several prostitutes working for them on a well deserved vacation. The vacation trip crossed state lines both while going from and returning to the house that was not quite a home. Did this good will gesture violate the Mann Act? *Mortensen v. United States*, 322 U.S. 369, 64 S. Ct. 1037 (1944).

3. Courts have developed several maxims and canons of construction for ascertaining the meaning of statutes. Although there is an enormous array of scholarly literature debunking the use of the canons of construction, the canons continue to appear in judicial decisions. It has been forcefully

k. This phrase embodies the notion that, in interpreting statutes, if general terms follow a list of specifically enumerated items, the general terms are to be construed as referring to items of the same class, kind or nature as those specifically enumerated.

l. This doctrine provides that words or phrases in a statute should be interpreted by reference to and in harmony with the words or phrases that surround those to be interpreted.

demonstrated that every canon has an equal and opposite one. Regrettably, there is no rule for choosing between opposing canons. Yet for all their shortcomings, the canons are useful tools for advocating a particular interpretation. For additional materials relating the canons of constructions, see *infra* p. 436.

TEMPLE v. PETERSBURG

Supreme Court of Appeals of Virginia, 1944.
182 Va. 418, 29 S.E.2d 357.

GREGORY, JUSTICE.

The appellants, who were the complainants in the court below, filed their bill in equity against the city of Petersburg, praying that it be restrained and enjoined from using a tract of 1.01 acres of land acquired by it in 1942 for cemetery purposes. This plot of land adjoined Peoples Memorial Cemetery, which had been established and used as a cemetery for more than one hundred years.

The court below temporarily restrained the city from using the 1.01–acre tract as an addition to the cemetery. Later the city filed its answer to the bill and, by consent, the cause was set for hearing upon the bill, the answer, and a stipulation of counsel. The court dissolved the injunction and refused the prayer for relief.

Code, sec. 56 (Michie 1942), provides in part as follows:

> No cemetery shall be hereafter established within the corporate limits of any city or town; nor shall any cemetery be established within two hundred and fifty yards of any residence without the consent of the owner of the legal and equitable title of such residence; * * *.

We are called upon to ascertain the proper meaning of the statute, and to decide whether or not it has been violated by the city. Specifically the controversy concerns the meaning to be given to the word, "established", used therein. The appellants maintain that under the statute the enlargement of an existing cemetery, such as is sought here, in reality is the establishment of a cemetery, while the appellee contends that to enlarge an existing cemetery is not the establishment of a cemetery and, therefore, constitutes no violation of the statute.

In 1916, John D. Temple, the predecessor in title of the appellants, acquired lot number 169 in the city of Petersburg, and erected a residence thereon. In 1917 he acquired the adjoining lot, number 168. Upon his death, intestate, in 1921, this real estate descended to the appellants, who have maintained a residence thereon since that time. The residence faces St. Andrews street, and is bounded on one side by Talliaferro street.

At the time that John D. Temple erected his residence, Peoples Memorial Cemetery was already established on a tract of eight acres, a portion of which extended to within 80 feet of his residence. Between the residence and the cemetery there is Talliaferro street, which is 30 feet wide, and a vacant strip of land belonging to the city of Petersburg, 50 feet in width. Upon this vacant strip of land there are a number of graves, the nearest of which is 74 feet east of the residence.

The cemetery tract on one side adjoined Crater road. It became necessary for the city to widen and improve Crater road. In order to do so, a strip of the cemetery property was required to be taken by the exercise of eminent domain. Many bodies had been interred upon this strip, and it is necessary to exhume them in order to complete the improvement of the road. The city, desiring to provide a proper place to re-inter these bodies, acquired the tract of 1.01 acres of land on the south side of St. Andrews street adjoining the cemetery tract. The 1.01–acre tract so acquired lies directly across St. Andrews street in front of the appellants' residence, and 70 feet distant therefrom at the nearest point. It is the plan of the city of Petersburg to re-inter the bodies in this proposed addition to the cemetery. Afterwards, the city plans to convey the said tract to trustees to be appointed by the hustings court of the city in order that it may be incorporated in the Peoples Memorial Cemetery and be made an integral part thereof.

The principal and determinative issue to be determined in this cause is whether or not the proposed enlargement of Peoples Memorial Cemetery, by the additional 1.01–acre tract, is prohibited by section 56 of the Code.

The appellants most strongly contend that the word, "established", as used in the statute, means "located", and that the evil intended to be inhibited is the location of a cemetery in a city or town upon ground not previously dedicated for cemetery purposes, or the location of a cemetery within 250 yards of a residence, whether by enlargement or otherwise. They contend that the purpose of the statute is to protect residences and lands from the ill effects growing out of close proximity to a cemetery. They further contend that it is unreasonable to say that residences and lands are to be protected against the "establishment" of cemeteries, but are not to be protected against the encroachment or enlargement of existing cemeteries; that the evil created by one is equally as real as that created by the other.

The position of the appellee is that the word "established", has such a clear and precise meaning that no question of statutory construction arises. That the statute provides that no cemetery shall be "hereafter established" in a city or town, and that this language does not mean that a cemetery already established shall not be hereafter enlarged. To hold otherwise would be not to construe the statute, but in effect, to amend it.

It is elementary that the ultimate aim of rules of interpretation is to ascertain the intention of the legislature in the enactment of a statute, and that intention, when discovered, must prevail. If, however, the intention of the legislature is perfectly clear from the language used, rules of construction are not to be applied. We are not allowed to construe that which has no need of construction.

If the language of a statute is plain and unambiguous, and its meaning perfectly clear and definite, effect must be given to it regardless of what courts think of its wisdom or policy. In such cases courts must find the meaning within the statute itself.

In *Commonwealth v. Sanderson,* 170 Va. 33, 195 S.E. 516, 519, we quoted with approval from *Saville v. Virginia Ry. & Power Co.,* 114 Va. 444, 76 S.E. 954, 957, this statement of the rule:

> " 'It is contended that the construction insisted upon by the plaintiff in error is violative of the spirit or reason of the law. The argument would seem to concede that the contention is within the letter of the law. We hear a great deal about the spirit of the law, but the duty of this court is not to make law, but to construe it; not to wrest its letter from its plain meaning in order to conform to what is conceived to be its spirit, in order to subserve and promote some principle of justice and equality which it is claimed the letter of the law has violated. It is our duty to take the words which the legislature has seen fit to employ and give to them their usual and ordinary signification, and, having thus ascertained the legislative intent, to give effect to it, unless it transcends the legislative power as limited by the Constitution.' "

In *Fairbanks, etc., Co. v. Cape Charles, supra* [144 Va. 56, 131 S.E. 439], the court says: "Under the distribution of powers by the Constitution, it is the function of this court to interpret and not to enact laws. The latter power belongs to the Legislature alone."

The word "established" is defined in Webster's New International Dictionary, 2d Ed., 1936, thus: "To originate and secure the permanent existence of; to found; to institute; to create and regulate;—said of a colony, a State or other institutions."

Just why the Legislature, in its wisdom, saw fit to prohibit the establishment of cemeteries in cities and towns, and did not see fit to prohibit enlargements or additions, is no concern of ours. Certain it is that language could not be plainer than that employed to express the legislative will. From it we can see with certainty that while a cemetery may not be established in a city or town, it may be added to or enlarged without running counter to the inhibition found in section 56. We are not permitted to read into the statute an inhibition which the Legislature, perhaps advisedly, omitted. Our duty is to construe the statute as written.

If construction of the statute were necessary and proper in this case, we would be forced to the same conclusion. Even if it be assumed that there is ambiguity in the language in section 56, the legislative history of its enactment and a consideration of Code, sec. 53, a related statute, would remove all doubt as to what the legislature intended by its language in section 56.

Code, sec. 53, affords a complete answer to the question of legislative intent in the use of the word "established" in section 56, for the former section makes a distinction between "establish" and "enlarge" in these words: "If it be desired at any time to establish a cemetery, for the use of a city, town, county, or magisterial district, or to enlarge any such already established, and the title to land needed cannot be otherwise acquired, land sufficient for the purpose may be condemned. * * *"

The foregoing language, taken from section 53, completely demonstrates that the Legislature did not intend the words "establish" and "enlarge" to be used interchangeably, but that the use of one excluded any idea that it embraced or meant the other. As used, they are mutually exclusive. To enlarge or add to a cemetery is not to establish one within the meaning of section 56.

The language of the statute being so plain and unambiguous, and the intention and meaning of the Legislature so clear, we hold that the city of Petersburg has not violated Code, sec. 56, and the decree accordingly should be affirmed.

Affirmed.

Notes and Questions

1. Do you agree with the court that the "language could not be plainer than that employed to express the legislative will"? Even if the language were plain, should not the court have further inquired whether the result would lead to "absurd or wholly impracticable consequences"? See *Caminetti, supra* p. 386.

2. Assume the city had purchased a parcel of property on the other side of the town and had conveyed the tract and incorporated it into the Peoples Memorial Cemetery. Is the conveyance an establishment or an enlargement of an existing cemetery? Must the parcels be contiguous?

3. Aside from the question whether the term "established" is plain, doesn't the use of the terms "establish" and "enlarge" in a related statute demonstrate the correctness of the court's view? But does it "completely demonstrate" its correctness? Can you think of plausible arguments to the contrary?

4. Is it significant that the existing cemetery already had extended to within eighty feet of Temple's residence? Should the court be guided by factors peculiar to the specific case when interpreting statutes of general applicability? In a subsequent case involving a different resident, could *Temple* be distinguished on its peculiar facts? Is it significant that the court noted this fact in the opinion?

5. How does the court's formulation of the issue compare with your statement thereof in response to problem 3, pp. 375–76, *supra.*

CHUNG FOOK v. WHITE

Supreme Court of the United States, 1924.
264 U.S. 443, 44 S.Ct. 361, 68 L.Ed. 781.

JUSTICE SUTHERLAND delivered the opinion of the Court.

Chung Fook is a native-born citizen of the United States. Lee Shee, his wife, is an alien Chinese woman, ineligible for naturalization. In 1922 she sought admission to the United States, but was refused and detained at the immigration station, on the ground that she was an alien, afflicted with a dangerous contagious disease. No question is raised as to her alienage or the effect and character of her disease; but the contention is that, nevertheless, she is entitled to admission under the proviso found in section 22 of the Immigration Act of February 5, 1917, 39 Stat. 891, c. 29 (Comp.St.1918, Comp.St.Ann.Supp.1919, § 4289¼l). The section is copied in the margin.[1]

A petition for a writ of habeas corpus was denied by the federal District Court for the Northern District of California, and upon appeal to the Circuit Court of Appeals, the judgment was affirmed. 287 Fed. 533.

The pertinent words of the proviso are:

> That if the person sending for wife or minor child is naturalized, a wife to whom married or a minor child born subsequent to such husband or father's naturalization shall be admitted without detention for treatment in hospital. * * *

The measure of the exemption is plainly stated and, in terms, extends to the wife of a naturalized citizen only.

But it is argued that it cannot be supposed that Congress intended to accord to a naturalized citizen a right and preference beyond that enjoyed by a native-born citizen. The court below thought that the exemption from detention was meant to relate only to a wife who by marriage had acquired her husband's citizenship, and not to one who, notwithstanding she was married to a citizen, remained an alien under section 1994, Rev.Stats. (Comp.St. § 3948):

> Any woman who is now or may hereafter be married to a citizen of the United States, and who might herself be lawfully naturalized, shall be deemed a citizen.

To the same effect, *see Ex parte Leong Shee* (D.C.) 275 Fed. 364. We are inclined to agree with this view; but, in any event, the statute plainly relates only to the wife or children of a naturalized citizen and we cannot

---

1. Sec. 22. That whenever an alien shall have been naturalized or shall have taken up his permanent residence in this country, and thereafter shall send for his wife or minor children to join him, and said wife or any of said minor children shall be found to be affected with any contagious disorder, such wife or minor children shall be held, under such regulations as the Secretary of Labor shall prescribe, until it shall be determined whether the disorder will be easily curable or whether they can be permitted to land without danger to other persons; and they shall not be either admitted or deported until such facts have been ascertained; and if it shall be determined that the disorder is easily curable and the husband or father or other responsible person is willing to bear the expense of the treatment, they may be accorded treatment in hospital until cured and then be admitted, or if it shall be determined that they can be permitted to land without danger to other persons, they may, if otherwise admissible, thereupon be admitted: Provided, that if the person sending for wife or minor children is naturalized, a wife to whom married or a minor child born subsequent to such husband or father's naturalization shall be admitted without detention for treatment in hospital, and with respect to a wife to whom married or a minor child born prior to such husband or father's naturalization the provisions of this section shall be observed, even though such person is unable to pay the expense of treatment, in which case the expense shall be paid from the appropriation for the enforcement of this act.

interpolate the words "native-born citizen" without usurping the legislative function. The words of the statute being clear, if it unjustly discriminates against the native-born citizen, or is cruel and inhuman in its results, as forcefully contended, the remedy lies with Congress and not with the courts. Their duty is simply to enforce the law as it is written, unless clearly unconstitutional.

Affirmed.

Notes and Questions

1. The Court enforced the statute as written, notwithstanding potential "cruel and inhuman" results. What happened to the "absurd or wholly impracticable consequences" exception of *Caminetti,* decided only seven years earlier?

2. The Court stated that its "duty is simply to enforce the law as it is written, unless clearly unconstitutional." This proposition has eminent judicial antecedents. *See* Chapter VI, Section C, *infra.* What if the statute is unconstitutional on its face? Should the Court rewrite it to include "native born citizens" within its ambit, in which event Chung Fook would presumably prevail, or will it simply invalidate the provision, in which event Chung Fook would still lose? Or would he?

UNITED STATES v. AMERICAN TRUCKING ASSOCIATIONS

Supreme Court of the United States, 1940.
310 U.S. 534, 60 S.Ct. 1059, 84 L.Ed. 1345.

JUSTICE REED delivered the opinion of the Court.

This appeal requires determination of the power of the Interstate Commerce Commission under the Motor Carrier Act, 1935, to establish reasonable requirements with respect to the qualifications and maximum hours of service of employees of motor carriers, other than employees whose duties affect safety of operation.

After detailed consideration, the Motor Carrier Act, 1935, was passed. It followed generally the suggestion of form made by the Federal Coordinator of Transportation. The difficulty and wide scope of the problems raised by the growth of the motor carrier industry were obvious. Congress sought to set out its purpose and the range of its action in a declaration of policy which covered the preservation and fostering of motor transportation in the public interest, tariffs, the coordination of motor carriage with other forms of transportation and cooperation with the several states in their efforts to systematize the industry.

While efficient and economical movement in interstate commerce is obviously a major objective of the Act, there are numerous provisions which make it clear that Congress intended to exercise its powers in the non-transportation phases of motor carrier activity. Safety of operation was constantly before the committees and Congress in their study of the situation.

The pertinent portions of the section of the Act immediately under discussion read as follows:

Sec. 204 [§ 304] (a). It shall be the duty of the Commission—

(1) To regulate common carriers by motor vehicle as provided in this [chapter], and to that end the Commission may establish reasonable requirements with respect to continuous and adequate service, transportation of baggage and express, uniform systems of accounts, records, and reports, preservation of records, qualifications and maximum hours of service of employees, and safety of operation and equipment.

(2) To regulate contract carriers by motor vehicle as provided in this [chapter], and to that end the Commission may establish reasonable requirements with respect to uniform systems of accounts, records, and reports, preservation of records, qualifications and maximum hours of service of employees, and safety of operation and equipment.

(3) To establish for private carriers of property by motor vehicle, if need therefor is found, reasonable requirements to promote safety of operation, and to that end prescribe qualifications and maximum hours of service of employees, and standards of equipment. * * *

Shortly after the approval of the Act, the Commission on its own motion undertook to and did fix maximum hours of service for "employees whose functions in the operation of motor vehicles make such regulations desirable because of safety considerations." A few months after this determination, the Fair Labor Standards Act was enacted. Section 7 of this act limits the workweek at the normal rate of pay of all employees subject to its terms and Section 18 makes the maximum hours of the Fair Labor Standards Act subject to further reduction by applicable federal or state law or municipal ordinances. There were certain employees excepted, however, from these regulations by Section 13(b). It reads as follows:

Sec. 13 [§ 213]. * * * (b) The provisions of section 7 [207] shall not apply with respect to (1) any employee with respect to whom the Interstate Commerce Commission has power to establish qualifications and maximum hours of service pursuant to the provisions of section 204 [304 of Title 49] of the Motor Carrier Act, 1935 * * *.

This exemption brought sharply into focus the coverage of employees by Motor Carrier Act, Section 204(a). Clerical, storage and other non-transportation workers are under this or the Fair Labor Standards Act, dependent upon the sweep of the word employee in this act. The Commission again examined the question of its jurisdiction and in Ex parte No. MC–28 again reached the conclusion that its power under "section 204(a)(1) and (2) is limited to prescribing qualifications and maximum hours of service for those employees * * * whose activities affect the safety of operation." It added: "The provisions of section 202 evince a clear intent of Congress to limit our jurisdiction to regulating the motor-carrier industry as a part of the transportation system of the nation. To extend that regulation to features which are not characteristic of transportation nor inherent in that industry strikes us as an enlargement of our jurisdiction unwarranted by any express or implied provision in the act, which vests in us all the powers we have." The Wage and Hour Division of the Department of Labor arrived at the same result in an interpretation.

Shortly thereafter appellees, an association of truckmen and various common carriers by motor, filed a petition with the Commission in the present case seeking an exercise of the Commission's jurisdiction under Section 204(a) to fix reasonable requirements "with respect to qualifications and maximum hours of service of all employees of common and contract carriers, except employees whose duties are related to safety of operations; (3) to disregard its report and order in Ex parte MC–28." The Commission reaffirmed its position and denied the petition. The appellees petitioned a three-judge district court to compel the Commission to take jurisdiction and consider the establishment of qualifications and hours of service of all employees of common and contract carriers by motor vehicle. The Administrator of the Wage and Hour Division was permitted to intervene. The district court reversed the Commission, set aside its order and directed it to take jurisdiction of the appellees' petition. A direct appeal to this Court was granted.

In the broad domain of social legislation few problems are enmeshed with the difficulties that surround a determination of what qualifications an employee shall have and how long his hours of work may be. Upon the proper adjustment of these factors within an industry and in relation to competitive activities may well depend the economic success of the enterprises affected as well as the employment and efficiency of the workers. The Motor Carrier Act lays little emphasis upon the clause we are called upon now to construe, "qualifications and maximum hours of service of employees." None of the words are defined by the Section, 203, devoted to the explanation of the meaning of the words used in the Act. They are a part of an elaborate enactment drawn and passed in an attempt to adjust a new and growing transportation service to the needs of the public. To find their content, they must be viewed in their setting.

In the interpretation of statutes, the function of the courts is easily stated. It is to construe the language so as to give effect to the intent of Congress. There is no invariable rule for the discovery of that intention. To take a few words from their context and with them thus isolated to attempt to determine their meaning, certainly would not contribute greatly to the discovery of the purpose of the draftsmen of a statute, particularly in a law drawn to meet many needs of a major occupation.

There is, of course, no more persuasive evidence of the purpose of a statute than the words by which the legislature undertook to give expression to its wishes. Often these words are sufficient in and of themselves to determine the purpose of the legislation. In such cases we have followed their plain meaning. When that meaning has led to absurd or futile results, however, this Court has looked beyond the words to the purpose of the act. Frequently, however, even when the plain meaning did not produce absurd results but merely an unreasonable one "plainly at variance with the policy of the legislation as a whole" this Court has followed that purpose, rather than the literal words. When aid to construction of the meaning of words, as used in the statute, is available, there certainly can be no "rule of law" which forbids its use, however clear the words may appear on "superficial examination." The interpretation of the meaning of statutes, as applied to justiciable controversies, is exclusively a judicial function. This duty requires one body of public servants, the judges, to construe the meaning of what another body, the legislators, has said. Obviously there is danger that the courts' conclusion as to legislative purpose will be unconsciously influenced by the judges' own views or by factors not considered by the enacting body. A lively appreciation of the danger is the best assurance of escape from its threat but hardly justifies an acceptance of a literal interpretation dogma which withholds from the courts available information for reaching a correct conclusion. Emphasis should be laid, too, upon the necessity for appraisal of the purposes as a whole of Congress in analyzing the meaning of clauses or sections of general acts. A few words of general connotation appearing in the text of statutes should not be given a wide meaning, contrary to a settled policy, "excepting as a different purpose is plainly shown."

The language here under consideration, if construed as appellees contend, gives to the Commission a power of regulation as to qualifications and hours of employees quite distinct from the settled practice of Congress. That policy has been consistent in legislating for such regulation of transportation employees in matters of movement and safety only. The Hours of Service Act imposes restrictions on the hours of labor of employees "actually engaged in or connected with the movement of any train." The Seamen's Act limits employee regulations under it to members of ships' crews. The Civil Aeronautics Authority has authority over hours of service of employees "in the interest of safety." It is stated by appellants in their brief with detailed citations, and the statement is uncontradicted, that at the time of the passage of the Motor Vehicle Act "forty states had regulatory measures relating to the hours of service of employees" and every one "applied exclusively to drivers or helpers on the vehicles." In the face of this course of legislation, coupled with the supporting interpretation of the two administrative agencies concerned with its interpretation, the Interstate Commerce Commission and the Wage and Hour Division, it cannot be said that the word "employee" as used in Section 204(a) is so clear as to the workmen it embraces that we would accept its broadest meaning. The word, of course, is not a word of art. It takes color from its surroundings and frequently is carefully defined by the statute where it appears.

We are especially hesitant to conclude that Congress intended to grant the Commission other than the customary power to secure safety in view of the absence in the legislative history of the Act of any discussion of the desirability of giving the Commission broad and unusual powers over all employees. The clause in question was not contained in the bill as introduced. Nor was it in the Coordinator's draft. It was presented on the Senate Floor as a committee amendment following a suggestion of the Chairman of the Legislative Committee of the Commission, Mr. McManamy. The committee reports and the debates contain no indication that a regulation of the qualifications and hours of service of all employees was contemplated; in fact the evidence points the other way. The Senate Committee's report explained the provisions of Section 204(a)(1), (2) as giving the Commission authority over common and contract carriers similar to that given over private carriers by Section 204(a)(3). The Chairman of the Senate Committee expressed the same thought while explaining the provisions on the floor of the Senate. When suggesting the addition of the clause, the Chairman of the Commission's Legislative Committee said: " * * * it relates to safety." In the House the member in charge of the bill characterized the provisions as tending "greatly to promote careful operation for safety on the highways," and spoke with assurance of the Commission's ability to "formulate a set of reasonable rules * * * including therein maximum labor-hours service on the highway." And in the report of the House Committee a member set out separate views criticizing the delegation of discretion to the Commission and proposing an amendment providing for an eight-hour day for "any employee engaged in the operation of such motor vehicle."

The Commission and the Wage and Hour Division, as we have said, have both interpreted Section 204(a) as relating solely to safety of operation. In any case such interpretations are entitled to great weight. This is peculiarly true here where the interpretations involve "contemporaneous construction of a statute by the men charged with the responsibility of setting its machinery in motion; of making the parts work efficiently and smoothly while they are yet untried and new." Furthermore, the Commission's interpretation gains much persuasiveness from the fact that it was the Commission which suggested the provisions' enactment to Congress.

It is important to remember that the Commission has three times concluded that its authority was limited to securing safety of operation.

It is contended by appellees that the difference in language between subsections (1) and (2) and subsection (3) is indicative of a congressional purpose to restrict the regulation of employees of private carriers to "safety of operation" while inserting broader authority in (1) and (2) for employees of common and contract carriers. Appellants answer that the difference in language is explained by the difference in the powers. As (1) and (2) give powers beyond safety for service, goods, accounts and records, language limiting those subsections to safety would be inapt.

Appellees call our attention to certain pending legislation as sustaining their view of the congressional purpose in enacting the Motor Carrier Act. We do not think it can be said that the action of the Senate and House of Representatives on this pending transportation legislation throws much light on the policy of Congress or the meaning attributed by that body to Section 204(a). Aside from the very pertinent fact that the legislation is still unadopted, the legislative history up to now points only to a hesitation to determine a controversy as to the meaning of the present Motor Carrier Act, pending a judicial determination.

Reversed with directions.

[The dissenting opinion of THE CHIEF JUSTICE, JUSTICE MCREYNOLDS, JUSTICE STONE and JUSTICE ROBERTS is omitted.]

Notes and Questions

1.   The Court shifted its approach in *American Trucking.* Although it still looked to the plain meaning of the statute—that is, to the "words by which the legislature undertook to give expression to its wishes"—it did so not as an end but as a means of construing the intention of the legislature. The Court clearly perceived that its function was "to construe the language so as to give effect to the intent of Congress."

2.   Consider how lawyers marshal legislative history in close cases. Perusal of the Court's decisions and literature on the meaning of the Fourteenth Amendment or the Civil Rights Acts should amply demonstrate the inconclusiveness of legislative history. Raoul Berger, Government by Judiciary (1977). Is this phenomenon disturbing? Does it suggest a reason to return to the plain meaning rule?

RECTOR, HOLY TRINITY CHURCH
v. UNITED STATES

Supreme Court of the United States, 1892.
143 U.S. 457, 12 S.Ct. 511, 36 L.Ed. 226.

JUSTICE BREWER delivered the opinion of the Court.

Plaintiff in error is a corporation duly organized and incorporated as a religious society under the laws of the state of New York. E. Walpole Warren was, prior to September, 1887, an alien residing in England. In that month the plaintiff in error made a contract with him, by which he was to remove to the city of New York, and enter into its service as rector and pastor; and, in pursuance of such contract, Warren did so remove and enter upon such service. It is claimed by the United States that this contract on the part of the plaintiff in error was forbidden by chapter 164, 23 St. p. 332; and an action was commenced to recover the penalty prescribed by that act. The circuit court held that the contract was within the prohibition of the statute, and rendered judgment accordingly (36 Fed.Rep. 303), and the single question presented for our determination is whether it erred in that conclusion.

The first section describes the act forbidden, and is in these words:

Be it enacted by the senate and house of representatives of the United States of America, in congress assembled, that from and after the passage of this act it shall be unlawful for any person, company, partnership, or corporation, in any manner whatsoever, to prepay the transportation, or in any way assist or encourage the importation or migration, of any alien or aliens, any foreigner or foreigners, into the United States, its territories, or the District of Columbia, under contract or agreement, parol or special, express or implied, made previous to the inportation or migration of such alien or aliens, foreigner or foreigners, to perform labor or service of any kind in the United States, its territories, or the District of Columbia.

It must be conceded that the act of the corporation is within the letter of this section, for the relation of rector to his church is one of service, and implies labor on the one side with compensation on the other. Not only are the general words "labor" and "service" both used, but also, as it were to guard against any narrow interpretation and emphasize a breadth of meaning, to them is added "of any kind"; and, further, as noticed by the circuit judge in his opinion, the fifth section, which makes specific exceptions, among them professional actors, artists, lecturers, singers, and domestic servants, strengthens the idea that every other kind of labor and service was intended to be reached by the first section. While there is great force to this reasoning, we cannot think congress intended to denounce with penalties a transaction like that in the present case. It is a familiar rule that a thing may be within the letter of the statute and yet not within the statute, because not within its spirit nor within the intention of its makers. This has been often asserted, and the Reports are full of cases illustrating its application. This is not the substitution of the will of the judge for that of the legislator; for frequently words of general meaning are used in a statute, words broad enough to include an act in question, and yet a consideration of the whole legislation, or of the circumstances surrounding its enactment, or of the absurd results which follow from giving such broad meaning to the words, makes it unreasonable to believe that the legislator intended to include the particular act. As said in *Stradling v. Morgan,* Plow. 205: "From which cases it appears that the sages of the law heretofore have construed statutes quite contrary to the letter in some appearance, and those statutes which comprehend all things in the letter they have expounded to extend to but some things, and those which generally prohibit all people from doing such an act they have interpreted to permit some people to do it, and those which include every person in the letter they have adjudged to reach to some persons only, which expositions have always been founded upon the intent of the legislature, which they have collected sometimes by considering the cause and necessity of making the act, sometimes by comparing one part of the act with another, and sometimes by foreign circumstances."

In *Pier Co. v. Hannam,* 3 Barn. & Ald. 266, Abbott, C.J., quotes from Lord Coke as follows: "Acts of parliament are to be so construed as no man that is innocent or free from injury or wrong be, by a literal construction, punished or endangered." In the case of *State v. Clark*, 29 N.J.Law, 96, 99, it appeared that an act had been passed, making it a misdemeanor to willfully break down a fence in the possession of another person. Clark was indicted under that statute. The defense was that the act of breaking down the fence, though willful, was in the exercise of a legal right to go upon his own lands. The trial court rejected the testimony offered to sustain the defense, and the supreme court held that this ruling was error. In its opinion the court used this language: "The act of 1855, in terms, makes the willful opening, breaking down, or injuring of any fences belonging to or in the possession of any other person a misdemeanor. In what sense is the term 'willful' used? In common parlance, 'willful' is used in the sense of 'intentional,' as distinguished from 'accidental' or 'involuntary.' Whatever one does intentionally, he does willfully. Is it used in that sense in this act? Did the legislature intend to make the intentional opening of a fence for the purpose of going upon the land of another indictable, if done by permission or for a lawful purpose? * * * We cannot suppose such to have been the actual intent. To adopt such a construction would put a stop to the ordinary business of life. The language of the act, if construed literally, evidently leads to an absurd result. If a literal construction of the words of a statute be absurd, the act must be so construed as to avoid the absurdity. The court must restrain the words. The object designed to be reached by the act must limit and control the literal import of the terms and phrases employed." In *U.S. v. Kirby*, 7 Wall. 482, 486, the defendants were indicted for the violation of an act of congress providing "that if any person shall knowingly and willfully obstruct or retard the passage of the mail, or of any driver or carrier, or of any horse or carriage carrying the same, he shall, upon conviction, for every such offense, pay a fine not exceeding one hundred dollars." The specific charge was that the defendants knowingly and willfully retarded the passage of one Farris, a carrier of the mail, while engaged in the performance of his duty, and also in like manner retarded the steamboat Gen. Buell, at that time engaged in carrying the mail. To this indictment the defendants pleaded specially that Farris had been indicted for murder by a court of competent authority in Kentucky; that a bench-warrant had been issued and placed in the hands of the defendant Kirby, the sheriff of the county, commanding him to arrest Farris, and bring him before the court to answer to the indictment; and that, in obedience to this warrant, he and the other defendants, as his posse, entered upon the steamboat Gen. Buell and arrested Farris, and used only such force as was necessary to accomplish that arrest. The question as to the sufficiency of this plea was certified to this court, and it was held that the arrest of Farris upon the warrant from the state court was not an obstruction of the mail, or the retarding of the passage of a carrier of the mail, within the meaning of the act. In its opinion the court says: "All laws should receive a sensible construction. General terms should be so limited in their application as not to lead to injustice, oppression, or an absurd consequence. It will always, therefore, be presumed that the legislature intended exceptions to its language which would avoid results of this character. The reason of the law in such cases should prevail over its letter. The common sense of man approves the judgment mentioned by Puffendorf, that the Bolognian law which enacted 'that whoever drew blood in the streets should be punished with the utmost severity,' did not extend to the surgeon who opened the vein of a person that fell down in the street in a fit. The same common sense accepts the ruling, cited by *Plowden,* that the statute of 1 Edw. II., which enacts that a prisoner who breaks prison shall be guilty of felony, does not extend to a prisoner who breaks out when the prison is on fire, 'for he is not to be hanged because he would not stay to be burnt.' And we think that a like common sense will sanction the ruling we make, that the act of congress which punishes the obstruction or retarding of the passage of the mail, or of its carrier, does not apply to a case of temporary detention of the mail caused by the arrest of the carrier upon an indictment for murder."

Among other things which may be considered in determining the intent of the legislature is the title of the act. We do not mean that it may be used to add to or take from the body of the statute, but it may help to interpret its meaning. In the case of *U.S. v. Fisher,* 2 Cranch, 358, 386, Chief Justice Marshall said: "On the influence which the title ought to have in construing the enacting clauses, much has been said, and yet it is not easy to discern the point of difference between the opposing counsel in this respect. Neither party contends that the title of an act can control plain words in the body of the statute; and neither denies that, taken with other parts, it may assist in removing ambiguities. Where the intent is plain, nothing is left to construction. Where the mind labors to discover the design of the legislature, it seizes everything from which aid can be derived; and in such case the title claims a degree of notice, and will have its due share of consideration." And in the case of *U.S. v. Palmer,* 3 Wheat. 610, 631, the same judge applied the doctrine in this way: "The words of the section are in terms of unlimited extent. The words 'any person or persons' are broad enough to comprehend every human being. But general words must not only be limited to cases within the jurisdiction of the state, but also to those objects to which the legislature intended to apply them. Did the legislature intend to apply these words to the subjects of a foreign power, who in a foreign ship may commit murder or robbery on the high seas? The title of an act cannot control its words, but may furnish some aid in showing what was in the mind of the legislature. The title of this act is, 'An act for the punishment of certain crimes against the United States.' It would seem that offenses against the United States, not offenses against the human race, were the crimes which the legislature intended by this law to punish."

It will be seen that words as general as those used in the first section of this act were by that decision limited, and the intent of congress with respect to the act was gathered partially, at least, from its title. Now, the title of this act is, "An act to prohibit the importation and migration of foreigners and aliens under contract or agreement to perform labor in the United States, its territories, and the District of

Columbia." Obviously the thought expressed in this reaches only to the work of the manual laborer, as distinguished from that of the professional man. No one reading such a title would suppose that congress had in its mind any purpose of staying the coming into this country of ministers of the gospel, or, indeed, of any class whose toil is that of the brain. The common understanding of the terms "labor" and "laborers" does not include preaching and preachers, and it is to be assumed that words and phrases are used in their ordinary meaning. So whatever of light is thrown upon the statute by the language of the title indicates an exclusion from its penal provisions of all contracts for the employment of ministers, rectors, and pastors.

Again, another guide to the meaning of a statute is found in the evil which it is designed to remedy; and for this the court properly looks at contemporaneous events, the situation as it existed, and as it was pressed upon the attention of the legislative body. The situation which called for this statute was briefly but fully stated by Mr. Justice Brown when, as district judge, he decided the case of *U.S. v. Craig,* 28 Fed.Rep. 795, 798: "The motives and history of the act are matters of common knowledge. It had become the practice for large capitalists in this country to contract with their agents abroad for the shipment of great numbers of an ignorant and servile class of foreign laborers, under contracts by which the employer agreed, upon the one hand, to prepay their passage, while, upon the other hand, the laborers agreed to work after their arrival for a certain time at a low rate of wages. The effect of this was to break down the labor market, and to reduce other laborers engaged in like occupations to the level of the assisted immigrant. The evil finally became so flagrant that an appeal was made to congress for relief by the passage of the act in question, the design of which was to raise the standard of foreign immigrants, and to discountenance the migration of those who had not sufficient means in their own hands, or those of their friends, to pay their passage."

It appears, also, from the petitions, and in the testimony presented before the committees of congress, that it was this cheap, unskilled labor which was making the trouble, and the influx of which congress sought to prevent. It was never suggested that we had in this country a surplus of brain toilers, and, least of all, that the market for the services of Christian ministers was depressed by foreign competition. Those were matters to which the attention of congress, or of the people, was not directed. So far, then, as the evil which was sought to be remedied interprets the statute, it also guides to an exclusion of this contract from the penalties of the act.

A singular circumstance, throwing light upon the intent of congress, is found in this extract from the report of the senate committee on education and labor, recommending the passage of the bill: "The general facts and considerations which induce the committee to recommend the passage of this bill are set forth in the report of the committee of the house. The committee report the bill back without amendment, although there are certain features thereof which might well be changed or modified, in the hope that the bill may not fail of passage during the present session. Especially would the committee have otherwise recommended amendments, substituting for the expression, 'labor and service,' whenever it occurs in the body of the bill, the words 'manual labor' or 'manual service,' as sufficiently broad to accomplish the purposes of the bill, and that such amendments would remove objections which a sharp and perhaps unfriendly criticism may urge to the proposed legislation. The committee, however, believing that the bill in its present form will be construed as including only those whose labor or service is manual in character, and being very desirous that the bill become a law before the adjournment, have reported the bill without change." Page 6059, Congressional Record, 48th Cong. And, referring back to the report of the committee of the house, there appears this language: "It seeks to restrain and prohibit the immigration or importation of laborers who would have never seen our shores but for the inducements and allurements of men whose only object is to obtain labor at the lowest possible rate, regardless of the social and material well-being of our own citizens, and regardless of the evil consequences which result to American laborers from such immigration. This class of immigrants care nothing about our institutions, and in many instances never even heard of them. They are men whose passage is paid by the importers. They come here under contract to labor for a certain number of years. They are ignorant of our social condition, and, that they may remain so, they are isolated and prevented from coming into contact with Americans. They are generally from the lowest social stratum, and live upon the coarsest food, and in hovels of a character before unknown to American workmen. They, as a rule, do not become citizens, and are certainly not a desirable acquisition to the body politic. The inevitable tendency of their presence among us is to degrade American labor, and to reduce it to the level of the imported pauper labor." Page 5359, Congressional Record, 48th Cong.

We find, therefore, that the title of the act, the evil which was intended to be remedied, the circumstances surrounding the appeal to congress, the reports of the committee of each house, all concur in affirming that the intent of congress was simply to stay the influx of this cheap, unskilled labor.

But, beyond all these matters, no purpose of action against religion can be imputed to any legislation, state or national, because this is a religious people. This is historically true.

If we examine the constitutions of the various states, we find in them a constant recognition of religious obligations.

Even the constitution of the United States, which is supposed to have little touch upon the private life of the individual, contains in the first amendment a declaration common to the constitutions of all the states, as follows: "Congress shall make no law respecting an establishment of religion, or prohibiting the free exercise thereof," etc.—and also provides in article 1, § 7 (a provision common to many constitutions), that the executive shall have 10 days (Sundays excepted) within which to determine whether he will approve or veto a bill.

There is no dissonance in these declarations. There is a universal language pervading them all, having one meaning. They affirm and reaffirm that this is a religious nation. These are not individual sayings, declarations of private persons. They are organic utterances. They speak the voice of the entire people.

Suppose, in the congress that passed this act, some member had offered a bill which in terms declared that, if any Roman Catholic church in this country should contract with Cardinal Manning to come to this country, and enter into its service as pastor and priest, or any Episcopal church should enter into a like contract with Canon Farrar, or any Baptist church should make similar arrangements with Rev. Mr. Spurgeon, or any Jewish synagogue with some eminent rabbi, such contract should be adjudged unlawful and void, and the church making it be subject to prosecution and punishment. Can it be believed that it would have received a minute of approving thought or a single vote? Yet it is contended that such was, in effect, the meaning of this statute. The construction invoked cannot be accepted as correct. It is a case where there was presented a definite evil, in view of which the legislature used general terms with the purpose of reaching all phases of that evil; and thereafter, unexpectedly, it is developed that the general language thus employed is broad enough to reach cases and acts which the whole history and life of the country affirm could not have been intentionally legislated against. It is the duty of the courts, under those circumstances, to say that, however broad the language of the statute may be, the act, although within the letter, is not within the intention of the legislature, and therefore cannot be within the statute.

The judgment will be reversed, and the case remanded for further proceedings in accordance with this opinion.

Notes and Questions

1. Ascertaining the meaning of the statute by reference to its "purpose" has been traced to the classic *Heydon's Case,* 3 Coke 7a, 76 Eng. Rep. 637 (Court of Exchequer, 1584). *See* p. 386, *supra.* It has since been scrutinized by many scholars.

From the time of *Heydon's Case* courts have examined the purpose of the statute and the history of its enactment. Justice Frankfurter once asserted:

> A statute, like other living organisms, derives significance and sustenance from its environment, from which it cannot be severed without being mutilated. Especially is this true where the statute, like the one before us, is part of a legislative process having a history and a purpose. The meaning of such a statute cannot be gained by confining inquiry within its four corners. Only the historic process of which such legislation is an incomplete fragment—that to which it gave rise as well as that which gave rise to it—can yield its true meaning.

United States v. Monia, 317 U.S. 424, 432 (1943).

Learned Hand further explained:

> We can best reach the meaning here, as always, by recourse to the underlying purpose, and, with that as a guide, by trying to project upon the specific occasion how we think persons, actuated by such a purpose, would have dealt with it, if it had been presented to them at the time. To say that it is a hazardous process is indeed a truism, but we cannot escape it, once we abandon literal interpretation—a method far more unreliable.

Borella v. Borden Co., 145 F.2d 63, 64–65 (2d Cir. 1944), *aff'd*, 325 U.S. 679 (1945).

2. Had there existed a surplus of foreign Christian ministers, would the decision have been any different? How did the Court arrive at the "common understanding" of the term "labor"? From what sources did the Supreme Court in *American Trucking*, p. 401 *supra*, and *Holy Trinity* derive the meaning of the statutes? What sources did the Court overlook or disregard? Why would the lower court in *American Trucking* disregard the interpretation of the statute by the administrative body charged with the enforcement of the Act? *See Demarest v. Manspeaker*, 498 U.S. 184 (1991).

3. What should a court do when the relevant sources are themselves contradictory? *See Fishgold v. Sullivan Drydock & Repair Corp.*, 154 F.2d 785 (2d Cir. 1946), *aff'd*, 328 U.S. 275 (1946).

4. In his provocative book, A MATTER OF INTERPRETATION 22–23 (Princeton University Press, 1997), Justice Antonin Scalia, a textualist/originalist, attacks the methodology of the Court in *Holy Trinity*:

> It may well be that the statutory interpretation adopted by the Court in *Church of the Holy Trinity* produced a desirable result; and it may even be (though I doubt it) that it produced the unexpressed result actually intended by Congress, rather than merely the one desired by the Court. Regardless, the decision was wrong because it failed to follow the text. The text is the law, and it is the text that must be observed. I agree with Justice Holmes's remark, quoted approvingly by Justice Frankfurter in his article on the construction of statutes: "Only a day or two ago—when counsel talked of the intention of a legislature, I was indiscreet enough to say I don't care what their intention was. I only want to know what the words mean."[28] And I agree with Homes's other remark, quoted approvingly by Justice Jackson: "We do not inquire what the legislature meant; we ask only what the statute means."[29]

Professor Laurence Tribe opines that had the statute not exempted religious leaders it might have abridged the First Amendment's free speech and free exercise of religion clauses. *Id.* at 92–93. Justice Scalia rejoins that "holding a provision unconstitutional is quite different from holding that it says what it does not." *Id.* at 20 n.22.

28. Felix Frankfurter, *Some Reflections on the Reading of Statutes*, 47 Colum. L. Rev. 527, 538 (1947).

29. Oliver Wendell Holmes, *Collected Legal Papers* 207 (1920), *quoted in* Schwegmann Bros. v. Calvert Distillers Corp., 341 U.S. 384, 397 (1951) (Jackson, J., concurring).

Who has the better argument? Recall that the statute excluded "professional actors, artists, lecturers, or singers, [and] persons employed as personal or domestic servants." See notes and questions following Problem 5, *supra* pp. 378–79. Should a procrustean interpretation of the statute be adopted to avoid constitutional invalidity?

5. One scholarly camp justifies judicial power to rewrite statutes to fit the legal landscape. Ordinarily reserved for obsolete statutes, the power could also be expanded to cover any statute that violates constitutional or other deep-seated societal conventions. For example, Guido Calabresi expressed his views on the role of the courts in the interpretation of obsolete statutes as follows:

> [B]ecause a statute is hard to revise once it is passed, laws are governing us that would not and could not be enacted today, and ... *some* of these laws not only could not be reenacted but also do not fit, are in some sense inconsistent with, our whole legal landscape....
>
> ... There is an alternate way of dealing with [this] problem of legal obsolescence: granting to courts the authority to determine whether a statute is obsolete, whether in one way or another it should be consciously reviewed. At times this doctrine would approach granting to courts the authority to treat statutes as if they were no more and no less than part of the common law.[1]

Professor Eskridge goes a step further in allowing the judge to depart from the meaning of the statutory language in order to consider "what it ought to mean in terms of the needs and goals of our present day society." William N. Eskridge, Jr., Dynamic Statutory Interpretation 50 (1994) (quoting Arthur Phelps, Factors Influencing Judges in Interpreting Statutes, 3 Vand. L. Rev. 456, 469 (1950)).

Should courts have this power to treat statutes the same way they consider common law precedents?

RIGGS v. PALMER

Court of Appeals of New York, 1889.
115 N.Y. 506, 22 N.E. 188.

EARL, J. On the 13th day of August, 1880, Francis B. Palmer made his last will and testament, in which he gave small legacies to his two daughters, Mrs. Riggs and Mrs. Preston, the plaintiffs in this action, and the remainder of his estate to his grandson, the defendant Elmer E. Palmer, subject to the support of Susan Palmer, his mother, with a gift over to the two daughters, subject to the support of Mrs. Palmer in case Elmer should survive him and die under age, unmarried, and without any issue. The testator, at the date of his will, owned a farm, and considerable personal property. He was a widower, and thereafter, in March, 1882, he was married to Mrs. Bresee, with whom, before his marriage, he entered into an antenuptial contract, in which it was

---

1. Guido Calabresi, A COMMON LAW FOR THE AGE OF STATUTES 2 (1982) (emphasis in original).

agreed that in lieu of dower and all other claims upon his estate in case she survived him she should have her support upon his farm during her life, and such support was expressly charged upon the farm. At the date of the will, and subsequently to the death of the testator, Elmer lived with him as a member of his family, and at his death was 16 years old. He knew of the provisions made in his favor in the will, and, that he might prevent his grandfather from revoking such provisions, which he had manifested some intention to do, and to obtain the speedy enjoyment and immediate possession of his property, he willfully murdered him by poisoning him. He now claims the property, and the sole question for our determination is, can he have it?

The defendants say that the testator is dead; that his will was made in due form, and has been admitted to probate; and that therefore it must have effect according to the letter of the law. It is quite true that statutes regulating the making, proof, and effect of wills and the devolution of property, if literally construed, and if their force and effect can in no way and under no circumstances be controlled or modified, give this property to the murderer. The purpose of those statutes was to enable testators to dispose of their estates to the objects of their bounty at death, and to carry into effect their final wishes legally expressed; and in considering and giving effect to them this purpose must be kept in view. It was the intention of the law-makers that the donees in a will should have the property given to them. But it never could have been their intention that a donee who murdered the testator to make the will operative should have any benefit under it. If such a case had been present to their minds, and it had been supposed necessary to make some provision of law to meet it, it cannot be doubted that they would have provided for it. It is a familiar canon of construction that a thing which is within the intention of the makers of a statute is as much within the statute as if it were within the letter; and a thing which is within the letter of the statute is not within the statute unless it be within the intention of the makers. The writers of laws do not always express their intention perfectly, but either exceed it or fall short of it, so that judges are to collect it from probable or rational conjectures only, and this is called "rational interpretation"; and Rutherford, in his Institutes, (page 420) says: "Where we make use of rational interpretation, sometimes we restrain the meaning of the writer so as to take in less, and sometimes we extend or enlarge his meaning so as to take in more, than his words express." Such a construction ought to be put upon a statute as will best answer the intention which the makers had in view, for *qui hyret in litera, hyret in cortice.* In Bac. Abr. "Statutes," 1, 5; Puff. Law Nat. bk. 5, c. 12; Ruth. Inst. 422, 427, and in Smith's Commentaries, 814, many cases are mentioned where it was held that matters embraced in the general words of statutes nevertheless were not within the statutes, because it could not have been the intention of the law-makers that they should be included. They were taken out of the statutes by an equitable construction; and it is said in Bacon: "By an equitable construction a case not within the letter of a statute is sometimes holden to be within the meaning, because it is within the mischief for which a remedy is provided. The reason for such construction is that the law-makers could not set down every case in express terms. In order to form a right judgment whether a case be within the equity of a statute, it is a good way to suppose the law-maker present, and that you have asked him this question: Did you intend to comprehend this case? Then you must give yourself such answer as you imagine he, being an upright and reasonable man, would have given. If this be that he did mean to comprehend it, you may safely hold the case to be within the equity of the statute; for while you do no more than he would have done, you do not act contrary to the statute, but in conformity thereto." 9 Bac. Abr. 248. In some cases the letter of a legislative act is restrained by an equitable construction; in others, it is enlarged; in others, the construction is contrary to the letter. The equitable construction which restrains the letter of a statute is defined by Aristotle as frequently quoted in this manner: *Aequitas est correctio legis generaliter laty qua parte deficit.* If the lawmakers could, as to this case, be consulted, would they say that they intended by their general language that the property of a testator or of an ancestor should pass to one who had taken his life for the express purpose of getting his property? In 1 Bl.Comm. 91, the learned author, speaking of the construction of statutes, says: "If there arise out of them collaterally any absurd consequences manifestly contradictory to common reason, they are with regard to those collateral consequences void. * * * Where some collateral matter arises out of the general words, and happens to be unreasonable, there the judges are in decency to conclude that this consequence was not foreseen by the parliament, and therefore they are at liberty to expound the statute by equity, and only *quoad hoc* disregard it;" and he gives as an illustration, if an act of parliament gives a man power to try all causes that arise within his manor of Dale, yet, if a cause should arise in which he himself is party, the act is construed not to extend to that, because it is unreasonable that any man should determine his own quarrel. There was a statute in Bologna that whoever drew blood in the streets should be severely punished, and yet it was held not to apply to the case of a barber who opened a vein in the street. It is commanded in the decalogue that no work shall be done upon the Sabbath, and yet giving the command a rational interpretation founded upon its design the Infallible Judge held that it did not prohibit works of necessity, charity, or benevolence on that day.

What could be more unreasonable than to suppose that it was the legislative intention in the general laws passed for the orderly, peaceable, and just devolution of property that they should have operation in favor of one who murdered his ancestor that he might speedily come into the possession of his estate? Such an intention is inconceivable. We need not, therefore, be much troubled by the general language contained in the laws. Besides, all laws, as well as all contracts, may be controlled in their operation and effect by general, fundamental maxims of the common law. No one shall be permitted to profit by his own fraud, or to take advantage of his own wrong, or to found any claim upon his own iniquity, or to acquire property by his own crime. These maxims are dictated by public policy, have their foundation in universal law administered in all civilized countries, and have nowhere been superseded by statutes. They were applied in the decision of the case of *Insurance Co. v. Armstrong,* 117 U.S. 599, 6 Sup.Ct.Rep. 877. There it was held that the person who procured a policy upon the life of another, payable at his death, and then murdered the assured to make the policy payable, could not recover thereon. Mr. Justice Field, writing the opinion, said: "Independently of any proof of the motives of Hunter in obtaining the policy, and even assuming that they were just and proper, he forfeited all rights under it when, to secure its immediate payment, he murdered the assured. It would be a reproach to the jurisprudence of the country if one could recover insurance money payable on the death of a party whose life he had feloniously taken. As well might he recover insurance money upon a building that he had willfully fired." These maxims, without any statute giving them force or operation, frequently control the effect and nullify the language of wills. A will procured by fraud and deception, like any other instrument, may be decreed void, and set aside; and so a particular portion of a will may be excluded from probate, or held inoperative, if induced by the fraud or undue influence of the person in whose favor it is. *Allen v. McPherson,* 1 H.L.Cas. 191; *Harrison's Appeal,* 48 Conn. 202. So a will may contain provisions which are immoral, irreligious, or against public policy, and they will be held void.

Here there was no certainty that this murderer would survive the testator, or that the testator would not change his will, and there was no certainty that he would get this property if nature was allowed to take its course. He therefore murdered the testator expressly to vest himself with an estate. Under such circumstances, what law, human or divine, will allow him to take the estate and enjoy the fruits of his crime? The will spoke and became operative at the death of the testator. He caused that death, and thus by his crime made it speak and have operation. Shall it speak and operate in his favor? If he had met the testator, and taken his property by force, he would have had no title to it. Shall he acquire title by murdering him? If he had gone to the testator's house, and by force compelled him, or by fraud or undue influence had induced him, to will him his property, the law would not allow him to hold it. But can he give effect and operation to a will by murder, and yet take the property? To answer these questions in the affirmative it seems to me would be a reproach to the jurisprudence of our state, and an offense against public policy. Under the civil law, evolved from the general principles of natural law and justice by many generations of jurisconsults, philosophers, and statesmen, one cannot take property by inheritance or will from an ancestor or benefactor whom he has murdered. Our revisers and law-makers were familiar with the civil law, and they did not deem it important to incorporate into our statutes its provisions upon this subject. This is not a *casus omissus.* It was evidently supposed that the maxims of the common law were sufficient to regulate such a case, and that a specific enactment for that purpose was not needed. For the same reasons the defendant Palmer cannot take any of this property as heir. Just before the murder he was not an heir, and it was not certain that he ever would be. He might have died before his grandfather, or might have been disinherited by him. He made himself an heir by the murder, and he seeks to take property as the fruit of his crime. What has before been said as to him as legatee applies to him with equal force as an heir. He cannot vest himself with title by crime. My view of this case does not inflict upon Elmer any greater or other punishment for his crime than the law specifies. It takes from him no property, but simply holds that he shall not acquire property by his crime, and thus be rewarded for its commission.

* * *

The facts found entitled the plaintiffs to the relief they seek. The error of the referee was in his conclusion of law. Instead of granting a new trial, therefore, I think the proper judgment upon the facts found should be ordered here. The facts have been passed upon twice with the same result—first upon the trial of Palmer for murder, and then by the referee in this action. We are therefore of opinion that the ends of justice do not require that they should again come in question. The judgment of the general term and that entered upon the report of the referee should therefore be reversed, and judgment should be entered as follows: That Elmer E. Palmer and the administrator be enjoined from using any of the personalty or real estate left by the testator for Elmer's benefit; that the devise and bequest in the will to Elmer be declared ineffective to pass the title to him; that by reason of the crime of murder committed upon the grandfather he is deprived of any interest in the estate left by him; that the plaintiffs are the true owners of the real and personal estate left by the testator, subject to the charge in favor of Elmer's mother and the widow of the testator, under the antenuptial agreement, and that the plaintiffs have costs in all the courts against Elmer.

GRAY, J. (dissenting).

The appellants' argument is not helped by reference to those rules of the civil law, or to those laws of other governments, by which the heir, or legatee, is excluded from benefit under the testament if he has been convicted of killing, or attempting to kill, the testator. In the absence of such legislation here, the courts are not empowered to institute such a system of remedial justice. The deprivation of the heir of his testamentary succession by the Roman law, when guilty of such a crime, plainly was intended to be in the nature of a punishment imposed upon him. The succession, in such a case of guilt, escheated to the exchequer. I concede that rules of law which annul testamentary provisions made for the benefit of those who have become unworthy of them may be based on principles of equity and of natural justice. It is quite reasonable to suppose that a testator would revoke or alter his will, where his mind has been so angered and changed as to make him unwilling to have his will executed as it stood. But these principles only suggest sufficient reasons for the enactment of laws to meet such cases.

The statutes of this state have prescribed various ways in which a will may be altered or revoked; but the very provision defining the modes of alteration and revocation implies a prohibition of alteration or revocation in any other way. The words of the section of the statute are: "No will in writing, except in the cases hereinafter mentioned, nor any part thereof, shall be revoked or altered otherwise," etc. Where, therefore, none of the cases mentioned are met by the facts, and the revocation is not in the way described in the section, the will of the testator is unalterable. I think that a valid will must continue as a will always, unless revoked in the manner provided by the statutes.

I cannot find any support for the argument that the respondent's succession to the property should be avoided because of his criminal act, when the laws are silent. Public policy does not demand it; for the demands of public policy are satisfied by the proper execution of the laws and the punishment of the crime. There has been no convention between the testator and his legatee; nor is there any such contractual element, in such a disposition of property by a testator, as to impose or imply conditions in the legatee. The appellants' argument practically amounts to this: that, as the legatee has been guilty of a crime, by the commission of which he is placed in a position to sooner receive the benefits of the testamentary provision, his rights to the property should be forfeited, and he should be divested of his estate. To allow their argument to prevail would involve the diversion by the court of the testator's estate into the hands of persons whom, possibly enough, for all we know, the testator might not have chosen or desired as its recipients. Practically the court is asked to make another will for the testator. The laws do not warrant this judicial action, and mere presumption would not be strong enough to sustain it. But, more than this, to concede the appellants' views would involve the imposition of an additional punishment or penalty upon the respondent. What power or warrant have the courts to add to the respondent's penalties by depriving him of property? The law has punished him for his crime, and we may not say that it was an insufficient punishment. In the trial and punishment of the respondent the law has vindicated itself for the outrage which he committed, and further judicial utterance upon the subject of punishment or deprivation of rights is barred. We may not, in the language of the court in *People v. Thornton*, 25 Hun. 456, "enhance the pains, penalties, and forfeitures provided by law for the punishment of crime." The judgment should be affirmed, with costs.

DANFORTH, J., concurs.

Notes and Questions

1. The *Riggs* court referred to the technique of "equitable construction." It did not wish to permit a criminal to acquire property by his crime. Courts today do not speak in terms of "equitable construction," perhaps to

avoid the charge that they are legislating rather than interpreting existing laws. Nevertheless, courts are not inclined to allow one to take advantage of wrongdoing. *See Glus v. Brooklyn Eastern District Terminal,* 359 U.S. 231 (1959).

2. The majority in *Riggs* attempted to divine the legislative intent. Was the focus really on intent or rather on purpose? *See* pp. 385–86, *supra.* From what sources did the court discern the intention of the legislators? Did it deal effectively with the specific wording of the statute? In what respects did the focus of the dissent differ from that of the majority? Which approach is preferable?

3. Was *Riggs* an exercise in statutory interpretation? Or rather was it a case where the court fashioned a result out of whole cloth in view of the statute's silence? Should *Riggs* be considered a case where, absent a clear legislative directive, the court simply refused to aid a claimant because of sound judicial and public policy? Is there any danger in this approach? Is the danger any different from that inherent in the "equitable construction" doctrine?

Courts have engrafted judicial exceptions upon seemingly clear legislative commands in various situations without resort to the equitable construction fiction. They simply construe the statutory language in light of public policy. Are cases dealing with questions of jurisdiction and procedure different from cases, such as *Riggs,* involving substantive rights? Why?

Whatever approach is used, note the ability of the legislature to alter the rule, subject only to constitutional limitations.

4. Reexamine Benjamin Cardozo's discussion of *Riggs,* p. 61, *supra.*

5. Professors Hart and Sacks analyze alternative approaches to a wooden application of a rule that general words in a statute must always be read without qualification. In a passage discussing the *Riggs* case, they offer the following insight regarding statutory interpretation:

> A much more tough-minded approach is possible. This would be to say that the law rests upon a body of hard-won and deeply embedded principles and policies—such, precisely, as the principle that one should not be allowed to profit by his own wrong; that this body of thought about the problems of social living is a previous inheritance and possession of the whole society; that the legislature as an institution must necessarily have authority, within broad constitutional limits, to modify or depart from one or more of these traditional principles and policies when after due consideration it deems it wise to do so; but that no body of men and women constituting for the time being merely one session of the legislature has authority to abandon any part of this inheritance unthinkingly or without making clear openly and responsibly its purpose to do so; and that accordingly every statute is to be read as subject to established principles and policies of the general law save only as a decision to modify or depart from them is made unmistakably plain.[m]

m. Hart & Sacks, The Legal Process: Basic Problems in the Making and Application of Law 92–93 (1994).

This insight is not limited to statutory interpretation, but may even be applied to Supreme Court pronouncements. If the Court renders a decision that totally alters 200 years of understanding, may the system properly refuse to follow it in future cases, given "the chance that it may be overruled and never become a precedent for other cases?" *See* Abraham Lincoln's address on the *Dred Scott* decision, *infra* at p. 475.

6. Some scholars believe that the Court in *Riggs* interpreted the statute the way it did in order to avoid a possible clash with the First Amendment to the Constitution. That amendment provides that Congress should pass no law abridging the freedom of religion. But should the Court engage in this interpretive device without clearly noting it? In other circumstances, the Court has been forthright in its use of the doctrine of avoidance of constitutional adjudication by narrowly construing the statute. Indeed in very sensitive areas such as state sovereign immunity, the Court has required Congress to speak with plain and unmistakable language in the text. It leaves no room for guesswork. Should the Court dictate to Congress how to draft statutes?

7. When interpreting statutes, two sources should always be consulted: judicial precedents and administrative interpretations. Reexamine the cases in this chapter. Were these sources effectively analyzed?

Consider the following:

(1) Judicial precedents[n]

As with nearly all legal problems, the lawyer working on statutory interpretation is safest if the highest court of appeal has already answered his question. Not only is he protected by general *stare decisis,* but judges often state that they are especially reluctant to overrule a prior decision that merely construes a statute. There are instances where this rule has been rejected, but the lawyer who seeks its rejection in a specific case travels a rough road indeed.

Usually, controversies involving prior judicial interpretations arise when the applicable precedent came from a court that is not the highest court of appeal.

Difficulties involving the doctrine of precedent also arise when one word as used in different statutes has more than one meaning. *E.g., see U.S. v. Amer. Trucking Ass'ns,* 310 U.S. 534, 545 n. 29 (1940) ("That the word 'employees' is not treated by Congress as a word of art having a definite meaning is apparent from an examination of recent legislation.").

(2) Administrative interpretations

Lawyers troubled by words in a statute should always find out whether administrative officials have interpreted those words. The best way to find out is to consult the relevant loose-leaf service or to communicate directly with the administrators who work with the statute. If a loose-leaf service is not available, or if direct communication is impracticable or unproductive, pertinent interpretations can often be

n. F. Newman & S. Surrey, LEGISLATION, CASES AND MATERIALS 653–56 (1955).

found in the *Code of Federal Regulations* or the *Federal Register,* in state administrative codes, in reports of agency adjudications, and in other publications.°

What must be stressed is that the administrative interpretations are very often final. Within an agency, officials tend to follow an administrative *stare decisis* rule that is just as strong as its judicial counterpart. Within a government, officials of one agency are very reluctant to disregard the interpretations of another agency. Officials in one state government only rarely overrule officials of another state government, or of the federal government; and federal officials reciprocate. Finally, lawyers' successes in persuading courts to invalidate an agency's interpretation are becoming less frequent.

* * *

(3) Judicial deference to administrative interpretations

In the landmark case, *Chevron, U.S.A., Inc. v. Natural Resources Defense Council,* 467 U.S. 837 (1984), the Court held that if a statute is ambiguous and the implementing agency's interpretation is reasonable, great deference should be accorded to the agency interpretation. The Court has recently limited the *Chevron* deference principle to agency action that is embodied in the rulemaking function, as contrasted, for example, to the adjudicative function, *see U.S. v. Mead Corp.,* 533 U.S. 218 (2001). Agency interpretations that are not made in the rulemaking process are only entitled to such respect as may be warranted by the formality of the agency's process, the consistency of the agency's interpretation, and the overall persuasiveness of the agency's interpretation.

———

Reread problem 4, *supra* pp. 376–78, and compare your statement of the issues with the Court's formulation in the following case:

W.O. JOHNSON v. SOUTHERN PACIFIC CO.

Supreme Court of the United States, 1904.
196 U.S. 1, 25 S.Ct. 158, 49 L.Ed. 363.

CHIEF JUSTICE FULLER delivered the opinion of the Court.

The plaintiff claimed that he was relieved of assumption of risk under common-law rules by the act of Congress of March 2, 1893 (27 Stat. at L. 531, chap. 196, U.S.Comp.Stat.1901, p. 3174), entitled "An Act to Promote the Safety of Employees and Travelers upon Railroads by Compelling Common Carriers Engaged in Interstate Commerce to Equip

o. Many of these resources can also be accessed through the Internet, on individual administrative agency home pages, through commercial legal research web sites, or through the web site for the Government Printing Office, which offers on-line versions of both the *Federal Register* and the *Code of Federal Regulations.* In addition, the Administrative Codes and Registers (ACR) section of the National Association of Secretaries of State (NASS) web site provides links to on-line resources for many state agency decisions.

their Cars with Automatic Couplers and Continuous Brakes and their Locomotives with Driving–Wheel Brakes, and for Other Purposes.''

The issues involved questions deemed of such general importance that the government was permitted to file brief and be heard at the bar.

The act of 1893 provided:

> That from and after the first day of January, eighteen hundred and ninety-eight, it shall be unlawful for any common carrier engaged in interstate commerce by railroad to use on its line any locomotive engine in moving interstate traffic not equipped with a power driving-wheel brake and appliances for operating the train-brake system. * * *

> Sec. 2. That on and after the first day of January, eighteen hundred and ninety-eight, it shall be unlawful for any such common carrier to haul or permit to be hauled or used on its line any car used in moving interstate traffic not equipped with couplers coupling automatically by impact, and which can be uncoupled without the necessity of men going between the ends of the cars.

> Sec. 6. That any such common carrier using any locomotive engine, running any train, or hauling or permitting to be hauled or used on its line any car in violation of any of the provisions of this act, shall be liable to a penalty of one hundred dollars for each and every such violation, to be recovered in a suit or suits to be brought by the United States District Attorney in the district court of the United States having jurisdiction in the locality where such violation shall have been committed, and it shall be the duty of such district attorney to bring such suits upon duly verified information being lodged with him of such violation having occurred.

> Sec. 8. That any employee of any such common carrier who may be injured by any locomotive, car, or train in use contrary to the provision of this act shall not be deemed thereby to have assumed the risk thereby occasioned, although continuing in the employment of such carrier after the unlawful use of such locomotive, car, or train had been brought to his knowledge.

The circuit court of appeals held, in substance, Sanborn, J., delivering the opinion and Lochren, J., concurring, that the locomotive and car were both equipped as required by the act, as the one had a power driving-wheel brake and the other a coupler; that § 2 did not apply to locomotives; that at the time of the accident the dining car was not "used in moving interstate traffic" ; and, moreover, that the locomotive, as well as the dining car, was furnished with an automatic coupler, so that each was equipped as the statute required if § 2 applied to both. Thayer, J., concurred in the judgment on the latter ground, but was of opinion that locomotives were included by the words "any car" in the 2d section, and that the dining car was being "used in moving interstate traffic."

We are unable to accept these conclusions, notwithstanding the able opinion of the majority, as they appear to us to be inconsistent with the plain intention of Congress, to defeat the object of the legislation, and to be arrived at by an inadmissible narrowness of construction.

The intention of Congress, declared in the preamble and in §§ 1 and 2 of the act, was "to promote the safety of employees and travelers upon railroads by compelling common carriers engaged in interstate commerce to equip their cars with automatic couplers and continuous brakes and their locomotives with driving-wheel brakes," those brakes to be accompanied with "appliances for operating the train-brake system;" and every car to be "equipped with couplers coupling automatically by impact, and which can be uncoupled without the necessity of men going between the ends of the cars," whereby the danger and risk consequent on the existing system was averted as far as possible.

The present case is that of an injured employee, and involves the application of the act in respect of automatic couplers, the preliminary question being whether locomotives are required to be equipped with such couplers. And it is not to be successfully denied that they are so required if the words "any car" of the 2d section were intended to embrace, and do embrace, locomotives. But it is said that this cannot be so because locomotives were elsewhere, in terms, required to be equipped with power driving-wheel brakes, and that the rule that the expression of one thing excludes another applies. That, however, is a question of intention, and as there was special reason for requiring locomotives to be equipped with power driving-wheel brakes, if it were also necessary that locomotives should be equipped with automatic couplers, and the word "car" would cover locomotives, then the intention to limit the equipment of locomotives to power driving-wheel brakes, because they were separately mentioned, could not be imputed. Now it was as necessary for the safety of employees in coupling and uncoupling that locomotives should be equipped with automatic couplers as it was that freight and passenger and dining cars should be; perhaps more so, as Judge Thayer suggests, "since engines have occasion to make couplings more frequently."

And manifestly the word "car" was used in its generic sense. There is nothing to indicate that any particular kind of car was meant. Tested by context, subject-matter, and object, "any car" meant all kinds of cars running on the rails, including locomotives. And this view is supported by the dictionary definitions and by many judicial decisions, some of them having been rendered in construction of this act.

The result is that if the locomotive in question was not equipped with automatic couplers, the company failed to comply with the provisions of the act. It appears, however, that this locomotive was in fact equipped with automatic couplers, as well as the dining car; but that the couplers on each, which were of different types, would not couple with each other automatically, by impact, so as to render it unnecessary for men to go between the cars to couple and uncouple.

Nevertheless, the circuit court of appeals was of opinion that it would be an unwarrantable extension of the terms of the law to hold that where the couplers would couple automatically with couplers of their own kind, the couplers must so couple with couplers of different kinds. But we think that what the act plainly forbade was the use of cars which could not be coupled together automatically by impact, by means of the couplers actually used on the cars to be coupled. The object was to protect the lives and limbs of railroad employees by rendering it unnecessary for a man operating the couplers to go between the ends of the cars; and that object would be defeated, not necessarily by the use of automatic couplers of different kinds, but if those different kinds would not automatically couple with each other. The point was that the railroad companies should be compelled, respectively, to adopt devices, whatever they were, which would act so far uniformly as to eliminate the danger consequent on men going between the cars.

If the language used were open to construction, we are constrained to say that the construction put upon the act by the circuit court of appeals was altogether too narrow.

This strictness was thought to be required because the common-law rule as to the assumption of risk was changed by the act, and because the act was penal.

The dogma as to the strict construction of statutes in derogation of the common law only amounts to the recognition of a presumption against an intention to change existing law; and as there is no doubt of that intention here, the extent of the application of the change demands at least no more rigorous construction than would be applied to penal laws. And, as Chief Justice Parker remarked, conceding that statutes in derogation of the common law are to be construed strictly, "They are also to be construed sensibly, and with a view to the object aimed at by the legislature." *Gibson v. Jenney,* 15 Mass. 205.

The primary object of the act was to promote the public welfare by securing the safety of employees and travelers; and it was in that aspect remedial; while for violations a penalty of $100, recoverable in a civil action, was provided for, and in that aspect it was penal. But the design to give relief was more dominant than to inflict punishment, and the act might well be held to fall within the rule applicable to statutes to prevent fraud upon the revenue, and for the collection of customs—that rule not requiring absolute strictness of construction.

Moreover, it is settled that "though penal laws are to be construed strictly, yet the intention of the legislature must govern in the construction of penal as well as other statutes; and they are not to be construed so strictly as to defeat the obvious intention of the legislature." *United States v. Lacher,* 134 U.S. 624, 33 L.Ed. 1080, 10 Sup.Ct.Rep. 625. In that case we cited and quoted from *United States v. Winn,* 3 Sumn. 209, Fed.Cas.No. 16,740, in which Mr. Justice Story, referring to the rule that penal statutes are to be construed strictly, said:

I agree to that rule in its true and sober sense; and that is, that penal statutes are not to be enlarged by implication, or extended to cases not obviously within their words and purport. But where the words are general, and include various classes of persons, I know of no authority which would justify the court in restricting them to one class, or in giving them the narrowest interpretation, where the mischief to be redressed by the statute is equally applicable to all of them. And where a word is used in a statute which has various known significations, I know of no rule that requires the court to adopt one in preference to another, simply because it is more restrained, if the objects of the statute equally apply to the largest and broadest sense of the word. In short, it appears to me that the proper course in all these cases is to search out and follow the true intent of the legislature, and to adopt that sense of the words which harmonizes best with the context, and promotes in the fullest manner the apparent policy and objects of the legislature.

Tested by these principles, we think the view of the circuit court of appeals, which limits the 2d section to merely providing automatic couplers, does not give due effect to the words "coupling automatically by impact, and which can be uncoupled without the necessity of men going between the cars," and cannot be sustained.

We dismiss, as without merit, the suggestion which has been made, that the words "without the necessity of men going between the ends of the cars," which are the test of compliance with § 2, apply only to the act of uncoupling. The phrase literally covers both coupling and uncoupling; and if read, as it should be, with a comma after the word "uncoupled," this becomes entirely clear.

The risk in coupling and uncoupling was the evil sought to be remedied, and that risk was to be obviated by the use of couplers actually coupling automatically. True, no particular design was required, but, whatever the devices used, they were to be effectively interchangeable. Congress was not paltering in a double sense. And its intention is found "in the language actually used, interpreted according to its fair and obvious meaning."

That this was the scope of the statute is confirmed by the circumstances surrounding its enactment, as exhibited in public documents to which we are at liberty to refer. *Church of Holy Trinity v. United States,* 143 U.S. 457, 463, 36 L.Ed. 226, 229.

President Harrison, in his annual messages of 1889, 1890, 1891, and 1892, earnestly urged upon Congress the necessity of legislation to obviate and reduce the loss of life and the injuries due to the prevailing method of coupling and braking.

And he reiterated his recommendation in succeeding messages, saying in that for 1892: "Statistics furnished by the Interstate Commerce Commission show that during the year ending June 30, 1891, there were forty-seven different styles of car couplers reported to be in use, and that during the same period there was 2,660 employees killed and 26,140 injured. Nearly 16 per cent of the deaths occurred in the coupling and uncoupling of cars, and over 36 per cent of the injuries had the same origin."

The Senate report of the first session of the Fifty-second Congress (No. 1049) and the House report of the same session (No. 1678) set out the numerous and increasing casualties due to coupling, the demand for protection, and the necessity of automatic couplers, coupling interchangeably. The difficulties in the case were fully expounded and the result reached to require an automatic coupling by impact so as to render it unnecessary for men to go between the cars; while no particular device or type was adopted, the railroad companies being left free to work out the details for themselves, ample time being given for that purpose. The law gave five years, and that was enlarged, by the Interstate Commerce Commission, as authorized by law, two years, and subsequently seven months, making seven years and seven months in all.

The diligence of counsel has called our attention to changes made in the bill in the course of its passage, and to the debates in the Senate on the report of its committee. 24 Cong.Rec., pt. 2, pp. 1246, 1273 *et seq.* These demonstrate that the difficulty as to interchangeability was fully in the mind of Congress, and was assumed to be met by the language which was used. The essential degree of uniformity was secured by providing that the couplings must couple automatically by impact without the necessity of men going between the ends of the cars.

In the present case the couplings would not work together; Johnson was obliged to go between the cars; and the law was not complied with.

March 2, 1903 (32 Stat. at L. 943, chap. 976), an act in amendment of the act of 1893 was approved, which provided, among other things, that the provisions and requirements of the former act "shall be held to apply to common carriers by railroads in the territories and the district of Columbia, and shall apply in all cases, whether or not the couplers brought together are of the same kind, make, or type;" and "shall be held to apply to all trains, locomotives, tenders, cars, and similar vehicles used on any railroad engaged in interstate commerce."

This act was to take effect September 1st, 1903, and nothing in it was to be held or construed to relieve any common carrier "from any of the provisions, powers, duties, liabilities, or requirements" of the act of 1893, all of which should apply except as specifically amended.

As we have no doubt of the meaning of the prior law, the subsequent legislation cannot be regarded as intended to operate to destroy it. Indeed, the latter act is affirmative and declaratory; and, in effect, only construed and applied the former act. This legislative recognition of the scope of the prior law fortifies, and does not weaken, the conclusion at which we have arrived.

Another ground on which the decision of the circuit court of appeals was rested remains to be noticed. That court held by a majority that, as the dining car was empty and had not actually entered upon its trip, it was not used in moving interstate traffic, and hence was not within the act. The dining car had been constantly used for several years to furnish meals to passengers between San Francisco and Ogden, and for no other purpose. On the day of the accident the eastbound train was so late that it was found that the car could not reach Ogden in time to return on the next westbound train according to intention, and it was therefore dropped off at Promontory, to be picked up by that train as it came along that evening.

The presumption is that it was stocked for the return; and as it was not a new car, or a car just from the repair shop, on its way to its field of labor, it was not "an empty," as that term is sometimes used. Besides, whether cars are empty or loaded, the danger to employees is practically the same, and we agree with the observation of District Judge Shiras, in *Voelker v. Chicago, M. & St. P.R. Co.* 116 Fed. 867, that "it cannot be true that on the eastern trip the provisions of the act of Congress would be binding upon the company, because the cars were loaded, but would not be binding upon the return trip, because the cars are empty."

Counsel urges that the character of the dining car at the time and place of the injury was local only, and could not be changed until the car was actually engaged in interstate movement, or being put into a train for such use, and *Coe v. Errol,* 116 U.S. 517, 29 L.Ed. 715, 6 Sup.Ct.Rep. 475, is cited as supporting that contention. In *Coe v. Errol* it was held that certain logs cut in New Hampshire, and hauled to a river in order that they might be transported to Maine, were subject to taxation in the former state before transportation had begun.

The distinction between merchandise which may become an article of interstate commerce, or may not, and an instrument regularly used in moving interstate commerce, which has stopped temporarily in making its trip between two points in different states, renders this and like cases inapplicable.

Confessedly this dining car was under the control of Congress while in the act of making its interstate journey, and in our judgment it was equally so when waiting for the train to be made up for the next trip. It was being regularly used in the movement of interstate traffic, and so within the law.

The judgment of the Circuit Court of Appeals is reversed; the judgment of the Circuit Court is also reversed, and the cause remanded to that court with instructions to set aside the verdict, and award a new trial.

TRW INC. v. ANDREWS

Supreme Court of the United States, 2001.
534 U.S. 19, 122 S.Ct. 441, 151 L.Ed.2d 339

Justice Ginsburg delivered the opinion of the Court.

This case concerns the running of the two-year statute of limitations governing suits based on the Fair Credit Reporting Act (FCRA or Act), as added, 84 Stat. 1127, and amended, 15 U.S.C. § 1681 *et seq.* (1994 ed. and Supp. V). The time prescription appears in § 1681p, which sets out a general rule and an exception. Generally, an action to enforce any liability created by the Act may be brought "within two years from the date on which the liability arises." The exception covers willful misrepresentation of "any information required under [the Act] to be disclosed to [the plaintiff]": when such a representation is material to a claim under the Act, suit may be brought "within two years after [the plaintiff's] discovery . . . of the misrepresentation."

Section 1681p's exception is not involved in this case; the complaint does not allege misrepresentation of information that the FCRA "require[s] . . . to be disclosed to [the plaintiff]." Plaintiff-respondent Adelaide Andrews nevertheless contends, and the Ninth Circuit held, that § 1681p's generally applicable two-year limitation commenced to run on Andrews' claims only upon her discovery of defendant-petitioner TRW Inc.'s alleged violations of the Act.

We hold that a discovery rule does not govern § 1681p. That section explicitly delineates the exceptional case in which discovery triggers the two-year limitation. We are not at liberty to make Congress' explicit exception the general rule as well.

I

A

Congress enacted the FCRA in 1970 to promote efficiency in the Nation's banking system and to protect consumer privacy. See 15 U.S.C. § 1681(a) (1994 ed.). As relevant here, the Act seeks to accomplish those goals by requiring credit reporting agencies to maintain "reasonable procedures" designed "to assure maximum possible accuracy of the information" contained in credit reports, § 1681e(b), and to "limit the furnishing of [such reports] to" certain statutorily enumerated purposes, § 1681e(a); 15 U.S.C. § 1681b (1994 ed. and Supp. V). The Act creates a private right of action allowing injured consumers to recover "any actual damages" caused by negligent violations and both actual and punitive damages for willful noncompliance. See 15 U.S.C. §§ 1681n, 1681o (1994 ed.).

B

The facts of this case are for the most part undisputed. On June 17, 1993, Adelaide Andrews visited a radiologist's office in Santa Monica, California. She filled out a new patient form listing certain basic information, including her name, birth date, and Social Security number. Andrews handed the form to the office receptionist, one Andrea Andrews (the Impostor), who copied the information and thereafter moved to Las Vegas, Nevada. Once there, the Impostor attempted on numerous occasions to open credit accounts using Andrews' Social Security number and her own last name and address.

On four of those occasions, the company from which the Impostor sought credit requested a repot from TRW. Each time, TRW's computers registered a match between Andrews' Social Security number, last name, and first initial and therefore responded by furnishing her file. TRW thus disclosed Andrews' credit history at the Impostor's request to a bank on July 25, 1994; to a cable television company on September 27, 1994; to a department store on October 28, 1994; and to another credit provider on January 3, 1995. All recipients but the cable company rejected the Impostor's applications for credit.

Andrews did not learn of these disclosures until May 31, 1995, when she sought to refinance her home mortgage and in the process received a copy of her credit report reflecting the Impostor's activity. Andrews concedes that TRW promptly corrected her file upon learning of its mistake. She alleges, however, that the blemishes on her report not only caused her inconvenience and emotional distress, they also forced her to abandon her refinancing efforts and settle for an alternative line of credit on less favorable terms.

On October 21, 1996, almost 17 months after she discovered the Impostor's fraudulent conduct and more than two years after TRW's first two disclosures, Andrews filed suit in the United States District Court for the Central District of California. Her complaint stated two categories of FCRA claims against TRW, only the first of which is relevant here. * * * Those claims alleged that TRW's four disclosures of her information in response to the Impostor's credit applications were improper because TRW failed to verify, predisclosure, that Adelaide Andrews of Santa Monica initiated the requests or was otherwise involved in the underlying transactions. Andrews asserted that by processing requests that matched her profile on Social Security number, last name, and first initial but did not correspond on other key identifiers, notably birth date, address, and first name, TRW had facilitated the Impostor's identity theft. According to Andrews, TRW's verification failure constituted a willful violation of § 1681e(a), which requires credit reporting agencies to maintain "reasonable procedures" to avoid improper disclosures. She sought injunctive relief, punitive damages, and compensation for the "expenditure of time and money, commercial impairment, inconvenience, embarrassment, humiliation and emotional distress" that TRW had allegedly inflicted upon her. * * *

TRW moved for partial summary judgment, arguing, *inter alia*, that the FCRA's statute of limitations had expired on Andrews' claims based on the July 25 and September 27, 1994, disclosures because both occurred more than two years before she brought suit. Andrews countered that her claims as to all four disclosures were timely because the limitations period did not commence until May 31, 1995, the date she learned of TRW's alleged wrongdoing. The District Court, agreeing with TRW that § 1681p does not incorporate a general discovery rule, held that relief stemming from the July and September 1994 disclosures was time bared. *Andrews v. Trans Union Corp.*, 7 F.Supp.2d 1056, 1066–1067 (C.D.Cal.1998).

The Court of Appeals for the Ninth Circuit reversed this ruling, applying what it considered to be the "general federal rule ... that a federal statute of limitations begins to run when a party knows or has reason to know that she was injured." 225 F.3d 1063, 1066 (2000). The court rejected the District Court's conclusion that the text of § 1681p, and in particular the limited exception set forth in that section, precluded judicial attribution of such a rule to the FCRA. "[U]nless Congress has expressly legislated otherwise," the Ninth Circuit declared, "the equitable doctrine of discovery is read into every federal statute of limitations." *Id.*, at 1067 (internal quotation marks omitted). Finding no such express directive, the Court of Appeals held that "none of [Andrews'] injuries were stale when suit was brought." *Id.*, at 1066. Accordingly, the court reinstated Andrews' improper disclosure claims and remanded them for trial.

In holding that § 1681p incorporates a general discovery rule, the Ninth Circuit parted company with four other Circuits; those courts have concluded that a discovery exception other than the one Congress expressed may not be read into the Act. See *Clark v. State Farm Fire & Casualty Ins. Co.*, 54 F.3d 669 (C.A.10 1995); *Rylewicz v. Beaton Servs., Ltd.*, 888 F.2d 1175 (C.A.7 1989); *Houghton v. Insurance Crime Prevention Institute*, 795 F.2d 322 (C.A.3 1986); *Clay v. Equifax, Inc.*, 762 F.2d 952 (C.A.11 1985). We granted certiorari to resolve this conflict, 532 U.S. 902 (2001), and now reverse.

II

The Court of Appeals rested its decision on the premise that all federal statutes of limitations, regardless of context, incorporate a general discovery rule "unless Congress has expressly legislated otherwise." 225 F.3d, at 1067. To the extent such a presumption exists, a matter this case does not oblige us to decide, the Ninth Circuit conspicuously overstated its scope and force.

The Appeals Court principally relied on our decision in *Holmberg v. Armbrecht*, 327 U.S. 392 (1946). See 225 F.3d, at 1067. In that case, we instructed with particularity that "where a plaintiff has been injured by fraud and remains in ignorance of it without any fault or want of diligence or care on his part, the bar of the statute does not begin to run until the fraud is discovered." *Holmberg*, 327 U.S., at 397 (internal quotation marks omitted). *Holmberg* thus stands for the proposition that equity tolls the statute of limitations in cases of fraud or concealment; it does not establish a general presumption applicable across all contexts. The only other cases in which we have recognized a prevailing discovery rule, moreover, were decided in two contexts, latent disease and medical malpractice, "where the cry for [such a] rule is loudest," *Rotella v. Wood*, 528 U.S. 549, 555 (2000). See *United States v. Kubrick*, 444 U.S. 111 (1979); *Urie v. Thompson*, 337 U.S. 163 (1949).

We have also observed that lower federal courts "generally apply a discovery accrual rule when a statute is silent on the issue." *Rotella*, 528

U.S., at 555; see also *Klehr v. A. O. Smith Corp.*, 521 U.S. 179, 191 (1997) (citing *Connors v. Hallmark & Son Coal Co.*, 935 F.2d 336, 342 (C.A.D.C.1991), for the proposition that "federal courts generally apply [a] discovery accrual rule when [the] statute does not call for a different rule"). But we have not adopted that position as our own. And, beyond doubt, we have never endorsed the Ninth Circuit's view that Congress can convey its refusal to adopt a discovery rule only by explicit command, rather than by implication from the structure or text of the particular statute.

The Ninth Circuit thus erred in holding that a generally applied discovery rule controls this case. The FCRA does not govern an area of the law that cries out for application of a discovery rule, nor is the statute "silent on the issue" of when the statute of limitations begins to run. Section 1681p addresses that precise question; the provision reads:

> "An action to enforce any liability created under [the Act] may be brought ... within two years from the date on which the liability arises, except that where a defendant has materially and willfully misrepresented any information required under [the Act] to be disclosed to an individual and the information so misrepresented is material to the establishment of the defendant's liability to that individual under [the Act], the action may be brought at any time within two years after discovery by the individual of the misrepresentation."

We conclude that the text and structure of § 1681p evince Congress' intent to preclude judicial implication of a discovery rule.

"Where Congress explicitly enumerates certain exceptions to a general prohibition, additional exceptions are not to be implied, in the absence of evidence of a contrary legislative intent." *Andrus v. Glover Constr. Co.*, 446 U.S. 608, 616–617 (1980). Congress provided in the FCRA that the two-year statute of limitations runs from "the date on which the liability arises," subject to a single exception for cases involving a defendant's willful misrepresentation of material information. § 1681p. The most natural reading of § 1681p is that Congress implicitly excluded a general discovery rule by explicitly including a more limited one. See *Leatherman v. Tarrant County Narcotics Intelligence and Coordination Unit*, 507 U.S. 163, 168 (1993) ("*Expressio unius est exclusio alterius.*"). We would distort § 1681p's text by converting the exception into the rule. Cf. *United States v. Brockamp*, 519 U.S. 347, 352 (1997) ("explicit listing of exceptions" to running of limitations period considered indicative of Congress' intent to preclude "courts [from] read[ing] other unmentioned, open-ended, 'equitable' exceptions into the statute").

At least equally telling, incorporating a general discovery rule into § 1681p would not merely supplement the explicit exception contrary to Congress' apparent intent; it would in practical effect render that exception entirely superfluous in all but the most unusual circumstances. A consumer will generally not discover the tortious conduct alleged here—the improper disclosure of her credit history to a potential user—until she requests her file from a credit reporting agency. If the agency responds by concealing the offending disclosure, both a generally applicable discovery rule and the misrepresentation exception would operate to toll the statute of limitations until the concealment is revealed. Once triggered, the statute of limitations would run under either for two years from the discovery date. In this paradigmatic setting, then, the misrepresentation exception would have no work to do.

* * *

Andrews advances two additional arguments in defense of the decision below, neither of which we find convincing. She contends, first, that the words "date on which the liability arises"—the phrase Congress used to frame the general rule in § 1681p—"literally expres[s]" a discovery rule because liability does not "arise" until it "present[s] itself" or comes to the attention of the potential plaintiff. Brief for Respondent 13. The dictionary definition of the word "arise" does not compel such a reading; to the contrary, it can be used to support either party's position. See Webster's Third New International Dictionary 117 (1966) (arise defined as "to come into being"; "to come about"; or "to become apparent in such a way as to demand attention"); Black's Law Dictionary 138 (rev. 4th ed. 1968) ("to come into being or notice"). And TRW offers a strong argument that we have in fact construed that word to imply the result Andrews seeks to avoid. See Brief for Petitioner 16–20 (citing, *inter alia*, *McMahon v. United States*, 342 U.S. 25 (1951) (statute of limitations triggered on date "cause of action arises" incorporates injury-occurrence rule)). On balance, we conclude, the phrase "liability arises" is not particularly instructive, much less dispositive of this case.

Similarly unhelpful, in our view, is Andrews' reliance on the legislative history of § 1681p. She observes that early versions of that provision, introduced in both the House and Senate, keyed the start of the limitations period to "the date of the occurrence of the violation." S. 823, 91st Cong., 1st Sess., § 618 (1969); H.R. 16340, 91st Cong., 2d Sess., § 27 (1970); H.R. 14765, 91st Cong., 1st Sess., § 617 (1969). From the disappearance of that language in the final version of § 1681p, Andrews infers a congressional intent to reject the rule that the deleted words would have plainly established.

As TRW notes, however, Congress also heard testimony urging it to enact a statute of limitations that runs from "the date on which the violation is discovered" but declined to do so. Hearings before the Subcommittee on Consumer Affairs of the House Committee on Banking and Currency, 91st Cong., 2d Sess., 188 (1970). In addition, the very change to § 1681p's language on which Andrews relies could be read to refute her position. The misrepresentation exception was added at the same time Congress changed the language "date of the occurrence of the violation" to "liability arises." Compare S. 823, 91st Cong., 1st Sess., § 618 (1969); H.R. 16340, 91st Cong., 2d Sess., § 27 (1970); H.R. 14765, 91st Cong., 1st Sess., § 617 (1969), with H.R. Rep. No. 91–1587, p. 22

(1970). We doubt that Congress, when it inserted a carefully worded exception to the main rule, intended simultaneously to create a general discovery rule that would render that exception superfluous. In sum, the evidence of the early incarnations of § 1681p, like the "liability arises" language on which Congress ultimately settled, fails to convince us that Congress intended *sub silentio* to adopt a general discovery rule in addition to the limited one it expressly provided.

* * *

For the reasons stated, the judgment of the Court of Appeals for the Ninth Circuit is reversed, and the case is remanded for further proceedings consistent with this opinion.

It is so ordered.

JUSTICE SCALIA, with whom JUSTICE THOMAS joins, concurring in the judgment.

As the Court notes, * * * the Court of Appeals based its decision on what it called the "general federal rule ... that a federal statute of limitations begins to run when a party knows or has reason to know that she was injured," 225 F.3d 1063, 1066 (C.A.9 2000). The Court declines to say whether that expression of the governing general rule is correct. * * * ("To the extent such a presumption exists, a matter this case does not oblige us to decide ..."). There is in my view little doubt that it is not, and our reluctance to say so today is inexplicable, given that we held, a mere four years ago, that a statute of limitations which says the period runs from "the date on which the cause of action arose," 29 U.S.C. § 1451(f)(1) (1994 ed.), "incorporates *the standard rule* that the limitations period commences when the plaintiff has a complete and present cause of action," *Bay Area Laundry and Dry Cleaning Pension Trust Fund v. Ferbar Corp. of Cal.*, 522 U.S. 192, 201 (1997) (emphasis added and internal quotation marks omitted).[1]

---

1. This analysis does not, as the Court asserts, *ante*, at 14, n. 6, "ri[p] *Bay Area Laundry* ... from its berth." The question presented on which certiorari was granted in the case was not, as the Court now recharacterizes it, the generalized inquiry "whether a statute of limitations could commence to run on one day while the right to sue ripened on a later day," *ibid.*, but rather (as set forth in somewhat abbreviated form in petitioner Bay Area Laundry's merits brief) the much more precise question, "When does the statute of limitations begin to run on an action under the Multiemployer Pension Plan Amendments Act, 29 U.S.C. § 1381 et seq., to collect overdue employer withdrawal liability payments?" Brief for Petitioner in No. 96–370, O.T. 1997, p. i. (Framing of the question in respondent Ferbar Corporation's merits brief was virtually identical.) The Court's *Bay*

Area Laundry opinion introduced its discussion of the merits as follows:

"[T]he Ninth Circuit's decision conflicts with an earlier decision of the District of Columbia Circuit [which] held that the statute of limitations ... runs from the date the employer misses a scheduled payment, not from the date of complete withdrawal.... The Third and Seventh Circuits have also held that the statute of limitations runs from the failure to make a payment.... We granted certiorari ... to resolve these conflicts." 522 U.S., at 200.

The Court's assertion that we did not answer the question presented, and did not resolve the conflicts—held only that the Ninth Circuit was wrong to say that the limitations period commenced before there was a right of action, and not that the other circuits were right to say that the period commenced upon the failure to make a pay-

Bay Area Laundry quoted approvingly our statement in *Clark v. Iowa City*, 20 Wall. 583, 589 (1875), that "[a]ll statutes of limitation begin to run when the right of action is complete. . . ." This is unquestionably the traditional rule: absent other indication, a statute of limitations begins to run at the time the plaintiff "has the right to apply to the court for relief. . . ." 1 H. Wood, Limitation of Actions § 122a, p. 684 (4th ed. 1916). "That a person entitled to an action has no knowledge of his right to sue, or of the facts out of which his right arises, does not postpone the period of limitation." 2 Wood, *supra*, § 276c(1), at 1411.

The injury-discovery rule applied by the Court of Appeals is bad wine of recent vintage. Other than our recognition of the historical exception for suits based on fraud, *e.g., Bailey v. Glover*, 21 Wall. 342, 347–350 (1875), we have deviated from the traditional rule and imputed an injury-discovery rule to Congress on only one occasion. *Urie v. Thompson*, 337 U.S. 163, 169–171 (1949). We did so there because we could not imagine that legislation as "humane" as the Federal Employers' Liability Act would bar recovery for latent medical injuries. *Id.*, at 170. We repeated this sentiment in *Rotella v. Wood*, 528 U.S. 549, 555 (2000), saying that the "cry for a discovery rule is loudest" in the context of medical-malpractice suits; and we repeat it again today with the assertion that the present case does *not* involve "an area of the law that cries out for application of a discovery rule," *ante*, at 7. These cries, however, are properly directed not to us, but to Congress, whose job it is to decide how "humane" legislation should be—or (to put the point less tendentiously) to strike the balance between remediation of all injuries and a policy of repose. See *Amy v. Watertown (No. 2)*, 130 U.S. 320, 323–324 (1889) ("[T]he cases in which [the statute of limitations may be suspended by causes not mentioned in the statute itself] are very limited in character, and are to be admitted with great caution; otherwise the court would make the law instead of administering it").

Congress has been operating against the background rule recognized in *Bay Area Laundry* for a very long time. When it has wanted us to apply a different rule, such as the injury-discovery rule, it has said so. See, *e.g.*, 18 U.S.C. § 1030(g) (1994 ed., Supp. V)[3] See also, *e.g.*, 15 U.S.C. § 77m (1994 ed., Supp. V);[4] 42 U.S.C. § 9612(d)(2) (1994 ed.).[5] To apply

ment—is as erroneous as it is implausible. *Bay Area Laundry* held that the cause of action arose when "the employer violated an obligation owed the plan," *id.*, at 202, *because* "the standard rule" is that the period begins to run when the plaintiff has a "complete and present cause of action," *id.*, at 201 (internal quotation marks omitted).

3. "No action may be brought under this subsection unless such action is begun within 2 years of the date of the act complained of or the date of the discovery of the damage."

4. "No action shall be maintained to enforce any liability created under section 77k or 77l(a)(2) of this title unless brought within one year after the discovery of the untrue statement or the omission, or after such discovery should have been made by the exercise of reasonable diligence, or, if the action is to enforce a liability created under section 77l(a)(1) of this title, unless brought within one year after the violation upon which it is based."

5. "No claim may be presented under this section . . . unless the claim is presented within 3 years after . . . [t]he date of the

a new background rule to previously enacted legislation would reverse prior congressional judgments; and to display uncertainty regarding the current background rule makes all unspecifying new legislation a roll of the dice. Today's opinion, in clarifying the meaning of 15 U.S.C. § 1681p, casts the meaning of innumerable other limitation periods in doubt.

Because there is nothing in this statute to contradict the rule that a statute of limitations begins to run when the cause of action is complete, I concur in the judgment of the Court.

Notes and Questions

1. All the Justices agreed that the statute in question is unambiguous and should be enforced as written.

2. Does this case reaffirm what you have learned about the process of statutory construction? If you think the answer is clear, how would the Court decide *Riggs*?

4. USE OF CANONS OF CONSTRUCTIONS

Throughout the cases in this chapter, you have observed the use of canons of construction as aids to interpretation of statutes. How many do you recall? For each canon, can you think of an equal and opposite one? Professor Llewellyn has provided a list[o] from which the following excerpt is taken:

THRUST	PARRY
A statute cannot go beyond its text.	To effect its purpose a statute may be implemented beyond its text.
Statutes in derogation of the common law will not be extended by construction.	Such acts will be liberally construed if their nature is remedial.
Statutes are to be read in the light of the common law and a statute affirming a common law rule is to be construed in accordance with the common law.	The common law gives way to a statute which is inconsistent with it and when a statute is designed as a revision of a whole body of law applicable to a given subject it supersedes the common law.
Words and phrases which have received judicial construction before enactment are to be understood according to that construction.	Not if the statute clearly requires them to have a different meaning.
Words are to be interpreted according to the proper grammatical effect of their arrangement within the statute.	Rules of grammar will be disregarded where strict adherence would defeat purpose.

discovery of the loss and its connection with the release in question."

o. Llewellyn, *Remarks on the Theory of Appellate Decision and the Rules or Canons*

About How Statutes Are to Be Construed, 3 Vand. L. Rev. 395, 401 (1950).

Thrust	Parry
Expression of one thing excludes another.	The language may fairly comprehend many different cases where some only are expressly mentioned by way of example.
It is a general rule of construction that where general words follow an enumeration they are to be held as applying only to persons and things of the same general kind or class specifically mentioned (*ejusdem generis*).	General words must operate on something. Further, *ejusdem generis* is only an aid in getting the meaning and does not warrant confining the operations of a statute within narrower limits than were intended.
There is a distinction between words of permission and mandatory words.	Words imparting permission may be read as mandatory and words imparting command may be read as permissive when such construction is made necessary by evident intention or by the rights of the public.

———

As Professor Llewellyn's list effectively illustrates, there are so many maxims relating to statutory interpretation that it seems fruitless to study them, especially when for each maxim there appears to exist a contrary one. Nevertheless, a well trained lawyer must know and be able to employ these canons effectively when advocating a client's position to a court. Some courts may avoid using a canon's label, but may borrow its logic. Knowledge of the canons of statutory construction may also enable lawyers to draft more effective legislation.

Judge Posner, author of the following excerpt, offers some differing views on the canons of statutory construction and interpretation.

THE CANONS OF CONSTRUCTION[p]

A. INTRODUCTION

The canons of statutory construction—for example, one starts with the language of the statute; repeals by implication are not favored; penal statutes are to be construed narrowly and remedial statutes broadly; *expressio unius est exclusio alterius*[25]—occupy a kind of legal *demimonde*. To exaggerate slightly, it has been many years since any legal scholar had a good word to say about any but one or two of the canons, but scholarly opinion—and I include not just the views of professors but the

p. Richard Posner, *Statutory Interpretation—in the Classroom and in the Courtroom*, 50 U. Chi. L. Rev. 800, 805–17 (1983).

25. This term has been described as a "maxim of statutory interpretation meaning that the expression of one thing is the exclusion of another. * * * Under this maxim, if [a] statute specifies one exception to a general rule or assumes to specify the effects of a certain provision, other exceptions or effects are excluded." Black's Law Dictionary 521 (5th ed. 1979).

views expressed in nonjudicial writings of distinguished judges such as Frankfurter and Friendly—has had little impact on the writing of judicial opinions, where the canons seem to be flourishing as vigorously as ever.[26] This persistent gap between scholarly and practical thinking must be due, in part at least, to the lack of systematic attention that statutory interpretation receives in the law schools. The professors drum into their students' heads a distrust of legal formalism, and this has had an effect on opinions. Judicial opinions in America are less formalistic than they once were; courts are less prone to pretend that their conclusions follow by ineluctable logic from premises found in earlier cases, without any leavening of policy or common sense. But judicial opinions continue to pretend far more often than they should that the interpretation of statutes is the mechanical application of well understood interpretive principles—the canons—to legislative materials.

The usual criticism of the canons, forcefully advanced by Professor Llewellyn many years ago, is that for every canon one might bring to bear on a point there is an equal and opposite canon, so that the outcome of the interpretive process depends on the choice between paired opposites—a choice the canons themselves do not illuminate. (You need a canon for choosing between competing canons, and there isn't any.) I think the criticism is correct, but I also think that most of the canons are just plain wrong, and it is that point that I want to develop here.

There is an initial question of what precisely it means to call a canon of statutory construction "wrong." The answer depends on what a canon's function is. There are several possibilities. First, a canon might be part of a code that Congress uses when it writes statutes. Suppose Congress decided that if the meaning of a statute as applied to some problem is plain as a linguistic matter, the statute should be interpreted in accordance with that meaning, even though it is contrary to Congress's actual purpose in enacting the statute. So if Congress grants a tax exemption to "minister[s] of the gospel," rabbis should not be held eligible, and if that makes the exemption unconstitutional under the first amendment because it discriminates against a religious faith, too bad.

I do not think that any of the canons of statutory construction can be defended on the theory that they are keys to deciphering a code. There is no evidence that members of Congress, or their assistants who do the actual drafting, know the code or that if they know, they pay attention to it. Nor, in truth, is there any evidence that they do not; it is remarkable how little research has been done on a question that one might have thought lawyers would regard as fundamental to their

26. For an amusingly dense collocation of canons, with many citations, see *United States v. Scrimgeour*, 636 F.2d 1019, 1022–24 (5th Cir.), *cert. denied*, 454 U.S. 878 (1981). *Compare United States v. Universal C.I.T. Credit Corp.*, 344 U.S. 218, 221 (1952) ("Generalities about statutory construction help us little."), *quoted in Weinberger v. Rossi*, 456 U.S. 25, 28 (1982), *with Weinberger v. Rossi*, 456 U.S. 25, 32 (1982) (a principle that "has been a maxim of statutory construction since" 1804 applies in this case).

enterprise. Probably, though, legislators do not pay attention to it, if only because, as Llewellyn showed, the code is internally inconsistent. We should demand evidence that statutory draftsmen follow the code before we erect a method of interpreting statutes on the improbable assumption that they do.

A second line of defense of the canons is that they, or at least some of them, are common sense guides to interpretation. It is this defense that I shall be questioning at length, by denying that the canons (with two closely related exceptions) have value even as flexible guideposts—rebuttable presumptions—rather than rigid rules. A third line of defense is that even if the canons do not make very good sense, it is better that the judges should feel constrained by some interpretive rules than free to roam at large in a forest of difficult interpretive questions; but I shall argue shortly that the effect of the canons is the opposite of constraining.

There is a fourth line of defense: the canons limit the delegation of legislative power to the courts. The "plain meaning" rule forces the legislature to draft statutes carefully; the rule that repeals by implication are not favored limits the scope of newly enacted statutes; the rule that statutes in derogation of the common law are to be construed strictly narrows the scope of all statutes applied in areas where common law principles would otherwise govern. But of course other canons look in the opposite direction, such as the important canon that remedial statutes are to be construed broadly. And, as noted earlier, two inconsistent canons can usually be found for any specific question of statutory construction. It is therefore unlikely that the canons considered as a whole stand for some general principle of limited government and separation of powers. No doubt one could, by picking and choosing, impose such a principle. But I know of no neutral, nonpolitical basis on which a judge can decide whether the legislature should be forced by some version of strict construction to legislate less or encouraged by some version of loose construction to legislate more. I shall come back to this point, however, in the last part of the paper.

B.   SPECIFIC CANONS

I begin my discussion of specific canons with one that has both a logical priority and an apparent reasonableness that many of the others lack. A milder version of the older, and still frequently invoked, "plain meaning" rule, it holds that in interpreting a statute you should begin, though maybe not end, with the words of the statute. Offered as a description of what judges do, the proposition is false. The judge rarely starts his inquiry with the words of the statute, and often, if the truth be told, he does not look at the words at all. This is notoriously true with regard to the Constitution. More often than not, briefs and judicial opinions dealing with free speech, due process, the right to assistance of counsel, and other constitutional rights do not quote the language of the applicable provision—and not because all concerned know these provisions by heart. The constitutional provisions are in reality the foundations, or perhaps in some cases the pretexts, for the evolution of bodies of case law that are the starting point and usually the ending point of analysis for new cases.

There are many statutes of which this is also true. The one I know best is the Sherman Act. Lawyers and judges do not begin their analyses of a challenged practice by comparing the practice with the language of the Act and, only if they have satisfied themselves that there is some relationship, then proceed to analyze the case law. They start with the case law and may never return to the statutory language—to "restrain trade or commerce" or to "attempt or conspire to monopolize." Even in dealing with statutes that have not generated a huge body of case law, a judge usually begins not with the language of the statute but with some conception of its subject matter and the likely purpose—if only one derived from the name of the statute or the title of the U.S. Code in which it appears. He is right to do so, because it is impossible to make sense of statutory language without some context.

I have thus far assumed that the "start with the words" canon has reference to temporal rather than to logical priority, and that is I think how it is usually meant. But maybe this is being too literal and what really is intended is that the language of a statute be deemed the most important evidence of its meaning—which it normally is—or at least indispensable evidence—which it always is. It is ironic that a principle designed to clarify should be so ambiguous. Of course the words of a statute are always relevant, often decisive, and usually the most important evidence of what the statute was meant to accomplish. I merely object to the proposition that one must always begin with the words, and I am reasonably confident that more often than not the judge—the good judge as well as the bad judge—in fact begins somewhere else.

The "start with the words" canon, like the "plain meaning" canon itself, goes wrong by being unrealistic about how judges read statutes. Another very popular canon, "remedial statutes are to be construed broadly," goes wrong by being unrealistic about legislative objectives. The idea behind this canon is that if the legislature is trying to remedy some ill, it would want the courts to construe the legislation to make it a more rather than a less effective remedy for that ill. This would be a sound working rule if every statute—at least every statute that could fairly be characterized as "remedial" (which I suppose is every regulatory statute that does not prescribe penal sanctions and so comes under another canon, which I discuss later)—were passed because a majority of the legislators wanted to stamp out some practice they considered to be an evil; presumably they would want the courts to construe the statute to advance that objective. But if, as is often true, the statute is a compromise between one group of legislators that holds a simple remedial objective but lacks a majority and another group that has reservations about the objective, a court that construed the statute broadly would upset the compromise that the statute was intended to embody.

Another facet of the same point, which I have discussed elsewhere, is that the absence of effective statutory remedies for violations of statutory commands should not automatically be considered an invitation to judges to create such remedies. The statute may reflect a compromise between those who wanted it to be fully effective in achieving its stated objective and those who wanted a less effective statute; if so, it should be enforced according to that compromise. Both the principle of supplementing weak statutory remedies with strong judicial remedies and the canon that remedial statutes are to be read broadly ignore the role of compromise in the legislative process and, more fundamentally, the role of interest groups, whose clashes blunt the thrust of many legislative initiatives.

The use of postenactment legislative materials to interpret a statute invites a similar objection. Postenactment statements are likely to reflect the current preferences of legislators and of the interest groups that determine or at least influence those preferences, but the current preferences bear no necessary relationship to those of the enacting legislators, who may have been reacting to a different constellation of interest-group pressures. To give effect to the current legislators' preferences is to risk spoiling the deal cut by the earlier legislators—to risk repealing legislation, in whole or in part, without going through the constitutionally prescribed processes for repeal. One cannot assume a continuity of view over successive Congresses.

A court should adhere to the enacting legislature's purposes (so far as those purposes can be discerned) even if it is certain that the current legislature has different purposes and will respond by amending the relevant legislation to reverse the court's interpretation. The court's adherence to the initial compromise will not be futile, for the amending legislation will probably be prospective (that is, applicable only to conduct taking place after the date of amendment), but judicial interpretations of legislation are retrospective (that is, applicable to past conduct at issue in a pending case). Thus if the court were to implement the preferences of the current legislature, it would in effect be repealing the statute earlier than the legislature itself would have repealed it.

And all this assumes that the court can predict the preferences of the current legislature, but of course it cannot. It is one thing to use a committee report to explain the meaning of a statute passed on the committee's recommendation; it is another thing to rely on a committee's report that did not result in legislation to predict how the entire legislature will act if the court does not interpret the existing statute in a particular way. Judges cannot make such predictions with any confidence.

I do not want totally to anathematize the use of postenactment materials to interpret a statute, for such materials may in some cases reflect a disinterested and informed view by a committee that is monitoring the administration of a statute; and I also want to distinguish sharply between postenactment materials and a subsequently enacted statute. Obviously a statute can change the meaning of an earlier statute even if the later statute does not expressly amend the earlier; I shall have something to say in a moment about the canon against implied repeals. But a committee report or a statement on the floor cannot amend an enacted statute, implicitly or explicitly, and rarely will it cast much light on the meaning of the statute.

Another canon that rests on an unrealistic view of the political process is the canon that the interpretation of a statute by the administrative agency that enforces it is entitled to great weight by the courts. There is no reason to expect administrative agency members, appointed and confirmed long after the enactment of the legislation they are enforcing, to display a special fidelity to the original intent of the legislation rather than to the current policies of the Administration and the Congress. They may of course know more than the courts about the legislation, and to the extent they support their interpretation with reasons at least plausibly based on superior knowledge the courts should give that interpretation weight. But the mere fact that it is the current agency interpretation does not entitle it to any particular weight. If the interpretation has persisted through several changes of Administration, that may be a different matter.

Most canons of statutory construction go wrong not because they misconceive the nature of judicial interpretation or of the legislative or political process but because they impute omniscience to Congress. Omniscience is always an unrealistic assumption, and particularly so when one is dealing with the legislative process. The basic reason why statutes are so frequently ambiguous in application is not that they are poorly drafted—though many are—and not that the legislators failed to agree on just what they wanted to accomplish in the statute—though often they do fail—but that a statute necessarily is drafted in advance of, and with imperfect appreciation for the problems that will be encountered in, its application. All this has been explained by Edward Levi in words that I cannot improve on. He points out that the ambiguity of a statute in application—the incompleteness of the statute—

> is not the result of inadequate draftsmanship, as is so frequently urged. Matters are not decided until they have to be. For a legislature perhaps the pressures are such that a bill has to be passed dealing with a certain subject. But the precise effect of the bill is not something upon which the members have to reach agreement. If the legislature were a court, it would not decide the precise effect until a specific fact situation arose demanding an answer. Its first pronouncement would not be expected to fill in the gaps. But since it is not a court, this is even more true. It will not be required to make the determination in any event, but can wait for the court to do so. There is a related and an additional reason for ambiguity. As to what type of situation is the legislature to make a decision? Despite much gospel to the contrary, a legislature is not a fact-finding body. There is no mechanism, as there is with a court, to require the legislature to sift facts and to make a decision about specific situa-

tions. There need be no agreement about what the situation is. The members of the legislative body will be talking about different things; they cannot force each other to accept even a hypothetical set of facts. The result is that even in a non-controversial atmosphere just exactly what has been decided will not be clear.[38]

An example of a canon founded on the assumption of legislative omniscience is the canon that every word of a statute must be given significance; nothing in the statute can be treated as surplusage. No one would suggest that judicial opinions or academic articles contain no surplusage; are these documents less carefully prepared than statutes? There is no evidence for this improbable proposition; what evidence we have, much of it from the statutes themselves, is to the contrary. True, statutory language is in an important sense more compact than the language of judicial opinions and law-review articles. Every word in a statute counts—every word is a constitutive act—whereas much in a judicial opinion will merely be explanatory of its holding, and much in an academic article merely explanatory of its thesis or findings. But it does not follow that statutes are more carefully drafted, or even that greater care assures greater economy of language; a statute that is the product of compromise may contain redundant language as a by-product of the strains of the negotiating process.

Consider now the popular canon that repeals by implication are not favored, and imagine what the idea behind it might be. Maybe it is that whenever Congress enacts a new statute it combs the United States Code for possible inconsistencies with the new statute, and when it spots one, it repeals the inconsistency explicitly. But this would imply legislative omniscience in a particularly uncompromising and clearly unrealistic form, for if Congress could foresee every possible application of a new statute and make provision for it, there would be no need for judicial interpretation at all. Since total foresight is not possible, if some latent inconsistency becomes actual all a court can do is figure out as best it can whether Congress would have wanted to forbid the inconsistent application of the old statute or give less scope to the new one.

An alternative basis for this canon is the idea that if the choice is between giving less scope to the new statute and cutting down the intended scope of the old (because both cannot be enforced fully without conflict), Congress must desire the courts to do the first. But there is no basis for this imputation of congressional purpose, and the opposite inference is if anything more plausible—that the enacting Congress cares more about its statutes than those of previous Congresses.

The canon *expressio unius est exclusio alterius* is also based on the assumption of legislative omniscience, because it would make sense only if all omissions in legislative drafting were deliberate. It seemed dead for a while, but it was resurrected by the Supreme Court a few years ago to provide a basis for refusing to create private remedies for certain statutory violations. Its very recent disparagement by a unanimous

---

38. E. Levi, An Introduction to Legal Reasoning 30–31 (1949) (footnote omitted).

Court puts its future in doubt—or maybe just shows that judicial use of the canons of construction is hopelessly opportunistic. Whether the result in the private-action cases is right or wrong, the use of *expressio unius* is not helpful. If a statute fails to include effective remedies because the opponents were strong enough to prevent their inclusion, the courts should honor the legislative compromise. But if the omission was an oversight, or if Congress thought the courts would provide appropriate remedies for statutory violations as a matter of course, the judges should create the remedies necessary to carry out the legislature's objectives:

> [t]he major premise of the conclusion expressed in a statute, the change of policy that induces the enactment, may not be set out in terms, but it is not an adequate discharge of duty for courts to say: We see what you are driving at, but you have not said it, and therefore we shall go on as before.[45]

My last example of a canon apparently premised on an assumption of legislative omniscience is one that even Judge Friendly, our most trenchant living critic of the canons of statutory construction, has occasionally, though cautiously, invoked: that the reenactment without change of a statute that the courts have interpreted in a particular way may be taken as evidence that the reenactment adopts that construction. Consider Judge Friendly's example of the domestic-relations exception to the diversity jurisdiction of the federal courts. This entirely judge-made exception, although uncertain in scope, is almost as old as the federal courts themselves. The grant of diversity jurisdiction to the federal courts has been reenacted several times since the exception was first recognized, yet neither the text nor legislative history of the successive reenactments has ever referred to it. Can we nevertheless take these reenactments, or at least the most recent, as signifying legislative adoption of the judicially created exception? Probably not. It seems as likely that a majority of the legislators who voted on each reenactment never heard of the exception, which is in fact unknown to all but a small number of specialists in federal jurisdiction and domestic relations, or that they heard of it but had no desire to freeze the existing judicial construction into statute law, being indifferent to whether the courts continued to recognize the exception or decided to abolish it.

I could go on denouncing the canons of statutory construction, but I have discussed the ones that appear most frequently today in judicial decisions and I want to turn now to three canons that have some arguable merit. I have discussed the first of these canons—the canon that penal statutes should be construed narrowly—elsewhere. Here I add only that this canon is bound up with the broader issue of fair notice of potential criminal liability, so that a refusal to interpret criminal statutes narrowly could violate the familiar canon that statutes should, wherever possible, be so interpreted as to be constitutional. This canon rests on the common-sense assumption that the legislators would rather

45. *Johnson v. United States*, 163 Fed. 30, 32 (1st Cir.1908) (Holmes, J.).

not have the courts nullify their effort entirely unless the interpretation necessary to save it would pervert the goals of the legislature in enacting it. It is the *cy pres* doctrine applied to legislation and provides reason enough for interpreting criminal statutes narrowly if, interpreted broadly, they would violate due process.

The next canon is related. It is that statutes should be construed not only to save them from being invalidated but to avoid even raising serious constitutional questions. Judge Friendly has criticized this canon with his customary power. He asks why the legislature should care that its statute raises a constitutional question, so long as the court concludes that it is constitutional. If the court is inclined to hold the statute unconstitutional, then the previous canon on construing to avoid unconstitutionality, which Judge Friendly accepts, comes into play. This criticism is convincing as far as it goes but, as Judge Friendly recognizes, it is incomplete. It leaves out of account the policy—derived from the structure of the Constitution—of avoiding unnecessary constitutional decisions. Applying the canon that constitutional questions are to be avoided wherever possible leaves everything pleasantly vague. Congress can amend the statute if it feels strongly and so precipitate a constitutional controversy that it may lose (not that it must lose, as would be the case if it amended a statute to nullify a construction that was necessary to make the statute constitutional), but if it does not amend the statute a collision with the courts has been averted. And even if the courts were to uphold the statute's constitutionality if forced to grasp the nettle, in the course of doing so they might say something that would cast a constitutional shadow on some other legislation. Construing legislation to avoid constitutional questions, as well as to avoid actual nullification, is thus one of those buffering devices, much discussed by the late Alexander Bickel, by which the frictions created by the institution of judicial review are minimized.[58]

But this does not prove that the canon is a good one. It just shifts the plane of analysis from that of interpreting legislative intent to that of maintaining a proper separation of powers. And I think on this other plane it flops too, so that in the end I agree with Judge Friendly. The Constitution as interpreted in modern cases is extraordinarily far-reaching—a written Constitution in name only. Congress's practical ability to overrule a judicial decision misconstruing one of its statutes, given all the other matters pressing for its attention, is less today than ever before, and probably was never very great. The practical effect of interpreting statutes to avoid raising constitutional questions is therefore to enlarge the already vast reach of constitutional prohibition beyond even the most extravagant modern interpretation of the Constitution—to create a judge-made constitutional "penumbra" that has much the same prohibitory effect as the judge-made (or at least judge-amplified) Constitution itself. And we do not need that.

58. A. Bickel, The Least Dangerous Branch 181 (1962).

If I am right that the canon of narrow construction for penal statutes is really just an aspect of the canon that statutes should be construed to avoid being held unconstitutional, then I am down to just one canon; the rest, I respectfully suggest, should be discarded. But where does this leave us? Might it not be better to subject the judges to the discipline of the canons, even if the canons are in some ultimate sense wrong, than to invite them to approach the task of statutory construction without any standards at all to guide them? I take up that question next. But before doing so I want to raise the question whether the canons, far from imposing a discipline of any sort on judges, do not have the opposite effect—promoting "judicial activism," in the sense of an expansive approach to the power of courts vis-à-vis the other branches of government. Vacuous and inconsistent as they mostly are, the canons do not constrain judicial decision making but they do enable a judge to create the appearance that his decisions are constrained. A standard defense of judicial activism, in the words of a defender, is that it "is, in most instances, not activism at all. Courts do not relish making such hard decisions and certainly do not encourage litigation on social or political problems. But * * * the federal judiciary * * * has the paramount and the continuing duty to uphold the law."[59] By making statutory interpretation seem mechanical rather than creative, the canons conceal, often from the reader of the judicial opinion and sometimes from the writer, the extent to which the judge is making new law in the guise of interpreting a statute or a constitutional provision. You will find more skepticism about the canons of construction in the opinions of practitioners of judicial self-restraint than in the opinions of judicial activists. The judge who recognizes the degree to which he is free rather than constrained in the interpretation of statutes, and who refuses to make a pretense of constraint by parading the canons of construction in his opinions, is less likely to act wilfully than the judge who either mistakes freedom for constraint or has no compunctions about misrepresenting his will as that of the Congress.

Notes and Questions

Judge Posner questions the practice of reading the applicable statute before analyzing legal problems in light of it. He supports the thesis by noting that lawyers and judges do not compare problems to the controlling statutes. He states that "they start at the case law and may never return to the statutory language."

The beginning law student should perhaps take such blanket assertions with the proverbial grain of salt. First, there is ample evidence that lawyers and judges not only read, but pore over, every word in the statutes on which their cases revolve. This practice is clearly shown in the cases in this chapter. Second, most of the statutes that lawyers are called upon to

59. Johnson, *The Role of the Judiciary With Respect to the Other Branches of Government*, 11 Ga. L. Rev. 455, 474 (1977).

interpret have not been previously judicially interpreted. One attempting to look only to case law in such an instance would be lost. Third, Judge Posner cites amorphous or highly specialized areas of the law such as due process, equal protection and antitrust in support of his thesis that reading the statute is unnecessary. The statutory problems with which most lawyers deal are generally much more narrow and technical. The wording of the statute is often determinative of the issue. Finally, to effectively advocate any statutory interpretation, lawyers must know with precision what the statute says. How else can they convey to a judge or administrative tribunal the correctness of their position?

In short, although Judge Posner's proposition may contain some validity for experienced lawyers and judges in a few areas of the law, it is extremely dangerous for novices. Until lawyers have gained absolute expertise regarding any particular statute or regulation, they should read the governing statutes carefully each time they face a legal problem. And since lawyers often take for granted those things that they presume they know, they should reread the controlling statute, frequently to refresh recollection.

C. PROBLEM: THE INTERPRETATION AND CONSTITUTIONALITY OF A CHILD SUPPORT AND SPOUSAL MAINTENANCE STATUTE

Read the following statutes carefully. Frame the issues raised by the problem in statutory terms.

Pursuant to an Arizona Decree of Marital Dissolution, Bob Smith was obligated to pay five hundred dollars per month for child support. His former wife, Mary Smith, pursuant to the statute then in force, filed a petition requesting that the Clerk of the Court issue an order for the assignment of Bob Smith's wages. Specifically, Mary Smith alleged arrearages of three months' duration (fifteen hundred dollars) and requested an order for unpaid installments as well as for currently accruing child support.

The text of Section 25–323.01 of the Arizona Revised Statutes provides as follows:

Ex parte order for assignment of wages

A. If a person obligated to pay child support or spousal maintenance is in arrears for an amount equal to at least one month's child support or spousal maintenance, the person or agency entitled to receive the child support or spousal maintenance may file a verified petition with the clerk of the superior court requesting the clerk to issue an order for assignment for currently accruing child support or spousal maintenance.

B. The petition shall contain a declaration that:

1. The person or agency filing the petition is entitled to receive child support or spousal maintenance.

2. The person obligated to pay child support or spousal maintenance is in arrears for an amount equal to at least one month's child support or spousal maintenance.

3. The name and address of the payor of periodic earnings or other periodic entitlements to monies.

C. The petition need not be verified if filed by the attorney general or county attorney. Following receipt of the petition, the clerk of the superior court, without notice to the person obligated to pay support or maintenance, shall order such person to make an assignment of a portion of such person's periodic earnings or other periodic entitlements to monies without regard to source as is sufficient to pay the amount ordered by the court to the person or agency entitled to receive the child support or spousal maintenance. Such an order shall operate as an assignment and is binding upon any existing or future employer or other payor of the person ordered to pay support or spousal maintenance upon whom a copy of the order is served. The assignment shall be issued for currently accruing child support or spousal maintenance. In those cases in which the payment is made through the court, the support and maintenance records of the clerk of the superior court are prima facie evidence that the person is at least one month in arrears in support under this section.

* * *

E. An assignment order made pursuant to this section does not become binding until fourteen days after service of the order upon an employer or other payor or upon future employers or other future payors. The assignment order shall be served on a person's employer or other payor as provided under the rules of civil procedure, except that an employer or payor, wherever located, may be served by registered mail. Service by registered mail is complete when the mailing is received by the employer or other payor. The employer or other payor shall withhold the amount specified in the assignment from the earnings or other periodic entitlement payable to the person obligated to support and shall transmit such amount to the clerk of the superior court. The employer or other payor may also withhold and retain for application to the employer's or payor's cost of compliance an additional sum not exceeding three dollars for each pay period in which earnings or other funds are withheld.

F. Within ten days of service of an assignment order issued pursuant to this section on an employer or other payor, the person or agency entitled to receive the child support or spousal maintenance shall deliver or mail by registered mail a copy of the assignment order to the person ordered to pay child support or spousal maintenance.

G. A person alleged to be in default may move to quash an assignment order issued under this section and shall file the motion and notice of motion any time after delivery to the person alleged to be in default of notice of the assignment order by the person or agency entitled to receive the child support or spousal maintenance. The person alleged to be in default shall state under oath that at the time the petition was filed the person was not at least one month in arrears for child support or spousal maintenance. The clerk of the court shall set the motion to quash for hearing within thirty days after receipt of the notice of motion. The person alleged to be in default shall mail to the person or agency entitled to receive support at the return address contained in the petition a copy of the motion and notice of motion by mail within five days after receipt of the scheduling of the hearing on the motion.

H. The employer or other payor shall continue to withhold and forward support or spousal maintenance as ordered by the clerk of the superior court until otherwise ordered by the court.

I. An order for assignment may be modified by the court at any time upon petition of either party or the employer or other payor and upon a hearing and showing of change in circumstances which are substantial and continuing.

J. Upon petition to the court and hearing, the court may terminate the order of assignment if all arrearages have been satisfied and if the court deems termination of the assignment order to be in the interest of justice.

* * *

Assume you represent Bob Smith. What issues of statutory construction might you raise? What constitutional issues does the problem raise? Refer to the materials in Chapter III.

In an actual case, a lower court of the State of Arizona declared the statute violative of the United States Constitution. Why? *See* Chapter III, Section C, *supra*. Thereafter the Arizona legislature amended the statute to read as follows:

Ex parte order for assignments

A. If a person obligated to pay child support or spousal maintenance is in arrears for an amount equal to at least one month's child support or spousal maintenance or wishes to implement a voluntary assignment, the person or agency entitled to receive the child support or spousal maintenance or the person obligated to pay support may file a verified petition or request with the clerk of the superior court requesting the clerk to issue an order for assignment for currently accruing child support or spousal maintenance, for unpaid monthly installments which the court has ordered to be paid on any previously established arrearages and, if the petition or request is filed by an agency, for payments on arrearages even if there is no prior order establishing the amount of payments on arrearages.

B. The petition or request shall contain:

1. The name of the person or agency entitled to receive child support or spousal maintenance.

2. A statement that the person obligated to pay child support or spousal maintenance is in arrears for an amount equal to at least one month's child support or spousal maintenance and for unpaid monthly installments to be paid on any arrearages or wishes to implement a voluntary wage assignment.

3. The name and address of the payor of periodic earnings or other periodic entitlements to monies.

C. The petition need not be verified if filed by the attorney general or county attorney. Following receipt of the petition, the clerk of the superior court, without notice to the person obligated to pay support or maintenance, shall order such person to make an assignment of a portion of such person's periodic earnings or other periodic entitlements to monies without regard to source as is sufficient to pay the amount ordered by the court to the person or agency entitled to receive the child support or spousal maintenance. Such an order shall operate as an assignment and is binding upon any existing or future employer or other payor of the person ordered to pay support or spousal maintenance upon whom a copy of the order is served. The assignment shall be issued for currently accruing child support or spousal maintenance and arrearages, if applicable. In those cases in which the payment is made through the court, the support and maintenance records of the clerk of the superior court are prima facie evidence that the person is at least one month in arrears in support under this section. The assignment order shall be accompanied by a written notice in English and Spanish as prescribed in this section.

* * *

E. An assignment order made pursuant to this section does not become binding until thirty-one days after service of a copy of * * * the petition, order and notice upon an employer or other payor or upon future employers or other future payors. The petition, assignment order and notice shall be served on a person's employer or other payor as provided under the rules of civil procedure, except that an employer or payor, wherever located, may be served by registered mail. Service by mail as authorized in this section is complete when the mailing is received by the employer or other payor. The employer or other payor shall withhold the amount specified in the assignment from the earnings, income, entitlements or other monies payable to the person obligated to support and shall transmit such amount to the clerk of the superior court or support payment clearinghouse within ten days after the date the employee is paid. The employer may combine withheld amounts for several employees in a single payment and separately identify the portion of the payment which is attributable to each employee. The employer or other payor may also withhold and retain for application to the employer's or payor's cost of compliance an additional sum not exceeding three dollars for each pay period in which earnings or other funds are withheld.

F. An order of assignment under this section shall be binding upon future employers and other future payors, as an assignment by operation of law, fourteen days after a certified copy of the assignment order is served on such employer or other payor as provided in the rules of civil procedure or by registered mail. Such employer or other payor shall have an opportunity for a hearing by order to show cause proceedings if desired. The filing of a petition for order to show cause or request for hearing by the employer or payor delays implementation of the order of assignment pending a hearing.

G. The order of assignment shall direct the employer or other payor to deliver or mail by registered mail a copy of the petition or request, assignment order and notice to the person ordered to pay child support or spousal maintenance within ten days of service thereof on the employer or other payor. The employer or other payor shall comply with the service requirements of the order. Service by registered mail is complete when the mailing is received by the person ordered to pay child support or spousal maintenance.

H. A person alleged to be in default may move to quash an assignment order issued under this section at any time. If the person requests to have a hearing prior to the assignment order becoming binding on the employer or other payor, the motion to quash or request to stop or modify and notice of such hearing must be filed within ten days after delivery by the person's employer or other payor on such person of the petition or request, assignment order and notice. The person alleged to be in arrears shall state under oath that at the time the petition or request was filed the person was not at least one month in arrears for child support or spousal maintenance or if the amount shown in the petition and order is incorrect or has been modified. The court shall set the motion to quash or request for hearing within ten days after receipt of the motion or request and notice of motion. The person alleged to be in default shall mail to the person or agency entitled to receive support at the return address contained in the petition or request a copy of the motion or request and notice of hearing immediately upon the scheduling of the hearing on the motion or request. If the motion or request and notice of hearing are filed with the court by the person alleged to be in arrears before the date the order of assignment becomes binding on the employer or other payor, the court in its discretion may order the clerk of the court or support payment clearinghouse not to disburse any monies until after the hearing on the motion.

I. The employer or other payor shall continue to withhold and forward support or spousal maintenance as ordered by the clerk of the superior court until otherwise ordered by the court. The employer or other payor shall notify the clerk in writing when the person ordered to pay support or spousal maintenance is no longer employed by the employer or the right to receive earnings, income, entitlements or other monies has been terminated. The employer shall also notify the clerk in writing of the former employee's last known address and the name and address of the former employee's new employer if known. If the employer reemploys the person ordered to pay support within ninety days of termination from employment, the employer is again bound by the order of assignment and is required to perform pursuant to this section. If a payor is again obligated to pay entitlements or monies to the person ordered to pay support within ninety days of the termination of such right, the payor is again bound by the order of assignment and is required to perform as required by this section.

J. An order for assignment may be modified by the court at any time upon petition or request of either party or the employer or other payor and upon a hearing and showing of change in circumstances which are substantial and continuing.

K. Upon petition to the court and hearing, the court may terminate the order of assignment for spousal maintenance if all arrearages have been satisfied and if the court deems termination of the assignment order to be in the interest of justice.

L. Upon petition or request to the court and hearing, the court may terminate the order of assignment for child support if all arrearages have been satisfied, and the person obligated to pay child support is no longer obligated to pay the child support.

* * *

Assume you represent Bob Smith, who has again fallen in arrears on his child support payments. What statutory and constitutional issues are presented under the revised statute?

D. POSTSCRIPT

Years ago, Professors Hart and Sacks warned that there is no consistent, generally accepted way to interpret statutes:

Do not expect anybody's theory of statutory interpretation, whether it is your own or somebody else's, to be an accurate statement of what courts actually do with statutes. The hard truth of the matter is that American courts have no intelligible, generally accepted, and consistently applied theory of statutory interpretation.

When an effort is made to formulate a sound and workable theory, therefore, the most that can be hoped for is that it will have some foundation in experience and in the best practice of the wisest judges, and that it will be well calculated to serve the ultimate purposes of law.[q]

Nevertheless the materials in this chapter should have provided some insights into the problems of statutory construction and a framework for statutory analysis. First, when confronted with a legal problem, the lawyer must determine whether there is a relevant or controlling statute. This task may be simple, as, for example, when the attorney has considerable experience with the specific area of law. Other times, when familiarity is lacking, the process may be time consuming and difficult. Often the search uncovers no provisions directly on point. *See, e.g., Riggs, supra* p. 414.

If a relevant statute is discovered, the next step is to carefully read it, word by word. Note the definitions, qualifications, provisos, exceptions and, above all, possible ambiguities. Does anything within the four corners of the statute, such as the title, preamble, punctuation or headings, suggest its meaning? It has been said, or should have been said, that the three most important rules in the interpretation of statutes are (1) read the statute, (2) read the statute, and (3) read the statute.

Lawyers cannot stop with the first careful reading of a statute. After framing the issue in the precise wording of the statute, they must inquire whether it has been construed by an administrative body or a court. Has there been any commentary on the issue? Is there any relevant legislative history, such as committee hearings, reports, debates, and bills and acts showing additions and deletions to the enactment?

Lawyers also research similar statutes in other jurisdictions and analyze the judicial and administrative opinions construing them.

Statutes play a vital role in the process of law, and there is no easy or mechanical way to deal with them. Predicting how a court will construe or apply a statute is an art developed over time.

---

q. Henry M. Hart, Jr. and Albert M. Sacks, THE LEGAL PROCESS: BASIC PROBLEMS IN THE MAKING AND APPLICATION OF LAW 1169 (1994).

Chapter VI

THE ROLE OF THE COURTS

A. INTRODUCTION

The American court system, with its parallel state and federal court structures, presents a confusing maze to the beginning law student. The process of allocating judicial business between the federal and state systems implicates complex and delicate principles of federalism. Yet this allocation of business between the systems and even within a single system is often the result of patchwork political compromise.

The power to adjudicate a particular type of case, referred to as subject matter jurisdiction, may be concurrent with or exclusive of other courts. To determine whether jurisdiction falls into one classification or the other demands a careful reading of guiding constitutional and statutory provisions. For example, Congress has vested in the United States District Courts exclusive jurisdiction over suits arising under the patent and copyright laws. *See* 28 U.S.C. § 1338. State courts, consequently, may not adjudicate these controversies.

Cases are not cognizable in the federal system unless the Constitution and an implementing statute authorize jurisdiction. Return to Kim's case (Chapter II). A suit against John would fall within the diversity jurisdiction of the federal courts because Kim and John are citizens of different states (provided, of course, that the amount in controversy exceeds $75,000). Diversity cases exceeding the jurisdictional minimum of $75,000 are also cognizable in state courts. Thus the federal and state systems exercise concurrent jurisdiction over these cases. State courts have exclusive jurisdiction of these cases if the amount in controversy is less than $75,000.

Where jurisdiction is concurrent, the plaintiff makes the initial choice of forum, subject to the defendant's statutory right to remove the case from the state to the federal system. The defendant has no corresponding right to remove a case from the federal to the state system.

In addition to subject matter jurisdiction, the court in which the action has been instituted must also meet venue requirements. These requirements are imposed by statute for the convenience of the litigants and witnesses. In federal diversity cases, for example, venue may lie in any judicial district where any defendant resides if all defendants reside in the same state, where the claim arose, or, in limited instances, where the defendants are subject to personal jurisdiction. Venue in *Johnson v. Roscoe* if suit were brought only against John, would be proper in the district of Nevada (where the claim arose) and in the appropriate district of California[a] (defendant's residence). If suit were brought against both John and Curt, venue would lie only in the district of Nevada.

In addition to satisfying subject matter and venue limitations, the forum must be able to assert jurisdiction over the persons or property involved in the litigation. Chapter III traced the development of these jurisdictional concepts from historical origins of territorial sovereignty to modern notions of fairness and justice.

Which courts could properly assert personal jurisdiction over defendant John Roscoe? Traditionally, domicile has always provided a sufficient basis for personal jurisdiction. Kim could therefore bring the action in California. Nevada would be able to assert jurisdiction based upon its nonresident motorist statute, which subjects those involved in accidents within its boundaries to the jurisdiction of its courts. John's presence in Arizona may also give that state a sufficient constitutional basis for the assertion of personal jurisdiction. *See Burnham v. Superior Court,* Chapter III, *supra.*

Once the issues relating to venue and jurisdiction, both subject matter and personal, have been decided, the lawyer must attempt to predict which law will be applied to resolve the controversy or a specific subissue. If only one jurisdiction has had contact with the controversy, only its laws need be examined. If two or more jurisdictions have had some relevant contact with the controversy, however, the lawyer must identify the jurisdiction whose laws will be applied. This process entails an understanding of the subject known as conflict of laws or, more narrowly, choice of law. In Kim's case we have assumed that the law of Nevada, the place where the accident occurred, would govern the substantive issue of liability regardless of the forum in which the action is brought. In other words, Nevada law would govern the defendants' responsibility for their acts and omissions even were the suit instituted in Arizona. With respect to Curt's liability see the *Babcock* line of cases, *supra* Chapter III, Section D, Exercise 3. Yet the forum court normally applies its own procedural rules. Whether the rules are substantive or procedural for these purposes can be difficult to determine. Rules relating to the pleadings, pretrial discovery, and trial procedures are clearly procedural. Other seemingly procedural rules, however, may have such a significant impact on the conduct of the parties or upon the outcome of the litigation that they may be classified as substantive for conflict of law purposes. Of course, these inquiries are academic if the rules of all "interested" states are the same.

    a.   California contains four districts.

Return to Kim's case. Suppose the action had been barred by the Nevada statute of limitations.[b] If suit is commenced in a state that has a longer period of limitations, which limitations period should apply? The subject presents complex and intriguing issues whose resolution not only vitally concerns the parties but also implicates an aspect of federalism.

Should the action be maintained in a federal court, additional principles determine the law to be applied. We shall defer this subject to a later time in your law school studies; for now you may safely assume that in Kim's case federal courts will apply federal procedure and state substantive law to resolve the controversy. Classification problems may arise.

State courts are often called upon to interpret and apply federal law. Indeed, the Supremacy Clause of the United States Constitution obligates state judicial systems to apply relevant federal laws. Therefore, depending on the nature of the issues involved in the lawsuit, a particular case may be governed by a medley of laws—state, federal, and, at times, foreign.

In summary then, the lawyer must thoroughly understand judicial jurisdiction, comprised of the basic elements of subject matter jurisdiction and personal jurisdiction, venue, and the particular conflict of laws principles governing the disposition of the case.

B. THE FEDERAL JUDICIAL SYSTEM

1. THE DISTRICT COURTS[c]

The general court of original jurisdiction in the federal system is the United States District Court. The statutes divide the nation, including the District of Columbia and Puerto Rico, into 91 districts, in each of which there is established a district court. Other courts similarly named are created for the Canal Zone, Guam, the Virgin Islands, and the Northern Mariana Islands. The statutes specify with great particularity the borders of a district, and the places within the district at which court is to be held.

Following the example set in the First Judiciary Act and consistently adhered to since, districts do not—with one insignificant exception—extend across state lines. Thus, a state will constitute at least one judicial district, and many states are divided into two, three, or even, in the case of California, New York, and Texas, four districts. Many districts are further subdivided into divisions, but the divisions are of very little importance. Since 1988 there has been no statutory requirement that an action be commenced in a particular division within a district.

b. The limitations period is the time within which suit must be commenced.

c. The discussion under the headings the District Courts, the Courts of Appeals, and the Supreme Court is quoted from Charles Alan Wright, FEDERAL COURTS 8–13 (6th ed. 2002).

The formation within a state of districts, and of divisions within districts, has not been an entirely rational process. There is no immediately apparent reason, for example, why Mississippi should be divided into two districts, which in turn are subdivided into four and five divisions, while the entire state of Massachusetts, with almost as many district judges, constitutes a single district and single division.

As of 2000, the statute authorizes 651 district judges to sit in the 91 district courts. There were once many districts with only a single judge, but there are no longer any such districts. All districts now have two or more judges, ranging up to the 28 judges authorized for the Southern District of New York. Normally a single judge will sit in a case pending before the district court, and it is the function of the chief judge of the district to apportion the business of the court among the judges in accordance with such rules and orders as the court may have made. There are certain exceptional cases that call for the creation of a statutory three-judge court, made up of at least one circuit judge and the remainder district judges.

In addition, the statutes do not forbid, and some districts follow, the practice of having all the judges of the court sit en banc in important matters. Finally in some districts, on procedural questions and others for which a uniform practice within the district is especially desirable, the judge hearing the case will state in his opinion that he has shown the opinion to the other judges and they concur therein.

The Federal Magistrates Act of 1968 created United States magistrates to assist the district courts. The statute specifies some of the functions that magistrates can perform and allows a district court to assign to the magistrate "such additional duties as are not inconsistent with the Constitution and laws of the United States." The statute has been amended several times since adoption to broaden the duties that can be entrusted to magistrates, and in 1990 the title of those offices was changed to "United States Magistrate Judge."

2. THE COURTS OF APPEALS

The circuit courts of appeals [were created] in 1891, after a century of discontent with the prior structure of the courts.... These courts were renamed by the 1948 Judicial Code, and are now properly known as the United States Court of Appeals for the _____ Circuit.

The work of the courts of appeals is principally appellate, reviewing cases from the district courts, although the courts also have jurisdiction to review orders of many administrative agencies, and to issue original writs in appropriate cases. In the year ended September 30, 1999, 46,931 appeals were filed with the courts of appeals from decisions of the district courts, 1,109 appeals were filed from bankruptcy courts, 3,373 original proceedings were commenced, and 3,280 applications were filed for review of orders of administrative agencies, for a total of 54,693 cases of all types.

There are now 13 courts of appeals, one for the District of Columbia, 11 for numbered circuits that include anywhere from three to ten states and territories, and, created in 1982, the Court of Appeals for the Federal Circuit. Normally cases are heard by a division of the court constituting three judges. The number of judges appointed for each court of appeals ranges from six to twenty-eight, and in addition the Supreme Court justice allotted as circuit justice for the circuit, and other judges or justices designated or assigned, are competent to sit on the court. In particular, the chief judge of the court of appeals may designate and assign a district judge within the circuit to sit as a member of the court of appeals at a specific time, and this power is frequently utilized.

The statute specifies the places within the circuit where the court is to sit during the year, but there is an increasing tendency, with improved methods of transportation, to centralize the work of a particular circuit at one place, and to hold most, or all, of the sessions of the court at that place.

By statute, a majority of the circuit judges of the circuit who are in active service may order a hearing or a rehearing before the court en banc. Prior to 1953 this power was exercised in some circuits, but ignored in others. In that year the Supreme Court held that each circuit should establish a clear procedure for determining when en banc hearings would be had, and cautioned against indiscriminate refusal to order such hearings. That decision has led to more frequent use of the en banc procedure, which has the advantage, in the unusual case to which it is suited, of avoiding conflicts of view within a circuit and promoting finality of decision in the courts of appeals.

* * *

A statute, which seems to state an obvious truth but changed the prior practice when it was first adopted in 1891, provides that no judge shall hear or determine an appeal from the decision of a case or issue tried by him.

The Federal Rules of Appellate Procedure were adopted in 1968 and have been amended several times since. These had the salutary purpose of making procedures in the various courts of appeals largely uniform, rather than leaving appellate procedure, as in the past, to be regulated by rules of each of the courts of appeals. That goal has been made largely illusory by the subsequent adoption of lengthy and inconsistent local rules in each circuit, however.

The last three decades have seen a sudden and sharp increase in the workload of the courts of appeals that poses a major crisis in judicial administration. The number of cases commenced in all of the courts of appeals increased moderately from 2830 in 1950 to 3899 in 1960. By 1970, it was 11,662 and there was a further increase to 26,362 by 1981. By 1992, the total was 47,000, and in 1999, it had risen to 54,693. Congress has provided for additional judgeships, so that there are now 179 judgeships on the 13 courts of appeals compared with 68 in 1960.

The Fifth Circuit, which had grown to 26 judgeships, was split in 1981 after years of discussion, and a new Eleventh Circuit created in the three easternmost states of the former Fifth Circuit. The Ninth Circuit, with 28 judgeships, is now an obvious candidate for a split, but with 46% of its business coming from California it is hard to know how it can be split without taking on a local rather than a national character.

Even without counting the 12 judges who have become judges of the newly-formed Court of Appeals for the Federal Circuit, the number of court-of-appeals judges has increased 128% since 1960, but the number of filings in the courts of appeals has multiplied more than ten times in the same period. In 1960 57.3 cases were filed for each authorized judgeship. In 1999 the number was 305.5. To cope with this vast volume of business the courts have had to restrict or eliminate oral argument in many cases, limit publication of opinions, and adopt other innovations to dispose of more cases more quickly.

3. THE SUPREME COURT

The Supreme Court, alone among the federal courts, is created directly by the Constitution, rather than by choice of Congress. It consists at the present time of the Chief Justice of the United States and eight associate justices.

The Court has not always had a total membership of nine. The First Judiciary Act created a Court with six members. This was increased to seven in 1807, to nine in 1837, and to ten in 1864. An 1866 statute, enacted to prevent Andrew Johnson from making any appointments to the Court, provided that no vacancy should be filled until the number of associate justices was reduced to six, but before enough deaths had occurred to accomplish this object, an 1869 statute was passed setting the size of the Court at nine, where it has since remained. In 1937 President Roosevelt proposed a bill that would have authorized the appointment of an additional justice for each sitting justice over 70 years of age, up to a maximum of 15 justices. The bitter fight that led to the defeat of this "court-packing" plan, as it was regarded, has given the notion of a nine judge Court such sanctity that it is unlikely that the size will again be changed.

The Supreme Court sits in Washington, D.C., in an annual term that begins on the first Monday in October and in recent years has normally recessed in the last week of June or first week of July. Six justices constitute a quorum, and there have been cases in which the Court has been unable to act because of inability to muster six justices who were not, for some reason, disqualified or unwilling to sit on a case. In one such situation Congress has given relief. Where a case comes to the Court on direct appeal from a district court, and there is no quorum, the case may be remitted to the court of appeals for the circuit including the district in which the case arose, and that court may make a final decision. The provision for a quorum of six has led to some criticism in another direction. It means that in some cases a majority of only four justices may reverse a court below, and indeed even hold a statute unconstitutional. There has been a suggestion, never adopted, to prevent such situations by providing for summoning lower court judges to sit with the Supreme Court to make a full bench of nine. The Supreme Court is not authorized to sit in divisions. All the qualified justices participate in each decision of the Court.

The Supreme Court has a limited original jurisdiction, and also exercises appellate jurisdiction, now almost always exercised by the writ of certiorari, over the district courts, the courts of appeals, and the highest courts of the states. In the 1999–2000 Term, the Court disposed of 7,045 cases. In 84 of the cases, the Court disposed of a matter with a full opinion.

There is, of course, no direct review of decisions of the Supreme Court. The late Justice Jackson observed: "We are not final because we are infallible, but we are infallible only because we are final." In some instances, however, decisions of the Supreme Court do not finally resolve a controversy, though they dispose of the particular case. Decisions turning on statutory construction are subject to change in the statute by Congress, and in five instances the Constitution has been amended to overcome Supreme Court decisions.

* * *

SPECIALIZED COURTS

Specialized courts have been created either to exercise jurisdiction in a local geographic area or to handle particular subjects. Courts falling into the former category include the Superior Court of the District of Columbia and the District of Columbia Court of Appeals (not to be confused with the Court of Appeals for the District of Columbia), and courts exercising jurisdiction in the territories. The latter category of courts presently includes the United States Court of Appeals for the Federal Circuit, which has jurisdiction over appeals from the Court of Claims, and the Court of Customs and Patent Appeals.

C. POWER OF THE FEDERAL COURTS TO HEAR CASES

A litigant desiring to commence proceedings in a federal court must find authorization in Article III of the United States Constitution and an implementing statute. Which Article III provisions, excerpted below, might apply to Kim's case (*see* ch. II, *supra*)?

> SECTION 2. The judicial Power shall extend to all Cases, in Law and Equity, arising under this Constitution, the Laws of the United States, and Treaties made, or which shall be made, under their Authority;—to all Cases affecting Ambassadors, other public Ministers and Consuls;—to all Cases of admiralty and maritime Jurisdiction;—to Controversies to which the United States shall be a

Party;—to Controversies between two or more States;—between a State and Citizens of another State;—between Citizens of different States;—between Citizens of the same State claiming Lands under Grants of different States, and between a State, or the Citizens thereof, and foreign States, Citizens or Subjects.

Several federal statutes grant lower federal courts original jurisdiction over particular cases and controversies. Many of them are codified in Title 28 of the United States Code. Two widely used provisions are reprinted below:

§ 1331.

The district courts shall have original jurisdiction of all civil actions arising under the Constitution, laws, or treaties of the United States.

§ 1332.

(a) The district courts shall have original jurisdiction of all civil actions where the matter in controversy exceeds the sum or value of $75,000, exclusive of interest and costs, and is between—

(1) citizens of different States;

(2) citizens of a State and citizens or subjects of a foreign state;

(3) citizens of different States and in which citizens or subjects of a foreign state are additional parties; and

(4) a foreign state, defined in section 1603(a) of this title, as plaintiff and citizens of a State or of different States.

Which statute applies to Kim's case?

In *Strawbridge v. Curtiss,* 7 U.S. (3 Cranch) 267 (1806), the Supreme Court held that for purposes of the diversity statute there must be complete diversity between all plaintiffs and all defendants; thus while Kim, an Arizona citizen, could bring an action against John, a California citizen, in the federal system, joining Curt, an Arizona citizen, as a defendant would destroy federal jurisdiction. What policy reasons support the "complete diversity" doctrine?

A defect in personal jurisdiction may be waived by the parties. A party may submit to the jurisdiction of the court by failing to raise the deficiencies in a timely manner. Not so with subject matter jurisdiction defects! They may be raised at any time during the proceedings. The defect may even be raised *sua sponte*[d] by the tribunal, even on appeal. Parties cannot consensually confer subject matter jurisdiction. Why? Even after the judgment has become final, under certain circumstances the judgment may be collaterally attacked if the court lacked subject matter jurisdiction.[e]

d. On its own motion.

e. For discussion of the concept of collateral attack, see pp. 164–65 *supra.*

It is a principle of first importance that federal courts are courts of limited jurisdiction. This concept was enunciated in the landmark decision of *Marbury v. Madison,* 5 U.S. (1 Cranch) 137 (1803). But *Marbury* did much more than affirm that principle. It granted to the Court the power to inquire into the constitutionality of Acts of Congress and to declare unconstitutional acts to be void. Moreover, it paved the way for executive accountability to the judiciary. But *Marbury* went even further. It expressed the philosophic principle that each citizen who is injured has the right to seek protection and that "one of the first duties of government is to afford that protection." Any analysis of the role of the federal courts in the American legal system must certainly begin by examining the principles of *Marbury.*

Before embarking on the analysis, however, you should appreciate the significant historical background leading to and culminating in the decision.[f]

On January 20, 1801, President John Adams offered the name of John Marshall for approval by the Senate as the fourth Chief Justice of the United States. The President's action followed the resignation of Oliver Ellsworth (who resigned as the third Chief Justice for reasons of health), and an unsuccessful overture to John Jay (the first Chief Justice) who declined the President's appointment on grounds of age and the necessity of sitting on the circuit courts. Marshall was forty-five years old, with twelve years practice but no prior judicial experience, and he was serving as Adams' secretary of state at the time of his appointment to the Court. The Senate approved the appointment and Marshall took the oath of office on February 4, 1801. A strong Federalist, Marshall was already at political odds with Thomas Jefferson who was about to take office as President, and his relationship with Jefferson became more antagonistic as subsequent events began to unfold.

In the presidential election of 1800, Jefferson had received a popular majority over Adams, but Federalist strength among the electors resulted in an electoral-vote tie between Jefferson and Aaron Burr. The election was therefore committed to the House of Representatives. Before the House acted on the presidency, however, the Federalist holdover Congress took a number of actions in an effort to preserve vestiges of party influence during the next administration. Two of these actions had a direct bearing on the federal judiciary.

On February 13, 1801, just nine days after Marshall took office as Chief Justice and four days before Jefferson was declared president by the House, the Federalist Congress adopted the Circuit Courts Act. This act altered the federal judiciary by relieving Supreme Court Justices of circuit duty, reducing the number of Supreme Court Justices from six to five (reportedly to keep Jefferson from appointing a replacement for Mr. Justice Cushing who was ill),

---

f. Van Alstyne, *A Critical Guide to* Marbury v. Madison, 1969 Duke L.J. 1.

and establishing six new circuit courts with sixteen judges all of whom were to be appointed by Adams and quickly approved by Congress before Jefferson took office. On March 2, 1801, two days before the government passed to Jefferson and the Republicans, Senate confirmation of all judicial posts was completed. Virtually all of the appointees were Federalists.

The Circuit Court Act itself, however, was not the immediate source of the legal issue subsequently reviewed in *Marbury v. Madison*. Rather, that issue arose from still another post-election Federalist effort to secure control of certain offices during the anticipated Jefferson administration. Pursuant to an act passed on February 27, 1801, Adams appointed forty-two justices of the peace for the District of Columbia and Alexandria, each to serve for a five-year term as provided by the Act itself. These appointees were all confirmed by the Senate on March 3, 1801, just one day before the national government changed hands. The commissions for these posts were made out in John Marshall's office, as Marshall was still serving as holdover Secretary of State although he had also been Chief Justice for nearly a month, but by midnight of March 3, at least four commissions had not yet been delivered.

Immediately upon assuming office, Jefferson ordered his new Secretary of State, James Madison, to hold up all commissions which had not yet been delivered. One of these was that of William Marbury.

On December 21, 1801, Marbury filed suit in the Supreme Court seeking a writ of mandamus to compel Madison to deliver his commission which, he claimed, Madison had no right to withhold. Marbury was represented by Charles Lee who had served as Attorney General under Adams. Madison received notice, but declined to acknowledge the propriety of the suit even by appearing through counsel. The order to show cause was issued by the Court and the case was set down for argument on the law for the next term. Thus the stage was already set for several important and politically incendiary issues: (1) Was the Secretary of State answerable in court for the conduct of his office? (2) Could the Court countermand a presidential decision respecting subordinate appointments? (3) By what means could any such judicial decision possibly be enforced?

The issue of judicial review came to independent prominence the next year, in 1802, while Marbury's case was still pending, when the Republican Congress debated its own authority to repeal the Circuit Courts Act. There was some apprehension that the Federalist-dominated Supreme Court might presume to declare the proposed act of repeal unconstitutional.

Early in 1802, however, the new Congress overcame its doubts respecting its own authority and that of the Court, and repealed the Circuit Courts Act. To gain time to strengthen Republican control of the national government, Congress also eliminated part of the 1802

Term of the Supreme Court, thus postponing a test of the Repeal Act's constitutionality, of judicial review itself, and of Marbury's case as well. All three matters awaited the Court's determination in 1803.

MARBURY v. MADISON

Supreme Court of the United States, 1803.
5 U.S. (1 Cranch) 137, 2 L.Ed. 60.

At the last term, viz. December term, 1801, William Marbury, Dennis Ramsay, Robert Townsend Hooe, and William Harper, by their counsel, Charles Lee, esq. late attorney general of the United States, severally moved the court for a rule to James Madison, secretary of state of the United States, to show cause why a *mandamus* should not issue commanding him to cause to be delivered to them respectively their several commissions as justices of the peace in the district of Columbia. This motion was supported by affidavits of the following facts; that notice of this motion had been given to Mr. Madison; that Mr. Adams, the late president of the United States, nominated the applicants to the senate for their advice and consent to be appointed justices of the peace of the district of Columbia; that the senate advised and consented to the appointments; that commissions in due form were signed by the said president appointing them justices, & c. and that the seal of the United States was in due form affixed to the said commissions by the secretary of state; that the applicants have requested Mr. Madison to deliver them their said commissions, who has not complied with that request; and that their said commissions are withheld from them; that the applicants have made application to Mr. Madison as secretary of state of the United States at his office, for information whether the commissions were signed and sealed as aforesaid; that explicit and satisfactory information has not been given in answer to that enquiry, either by the secretary of state or any officer in the department of state; that application has been made to the secretary of the Senate for a certificate of the nomination of the applicants, and of the advice and consent of the senate, who has declined giving such a certificate; whereupon a rule was laid to show cause on the 4th day of this term. * * *

* * *

Opinion of the Court [delivered by Chief Justice Marshall].

At the last term on the affidavits then read and filed with the clerk, a rule was granted in this case, requiring the secretary of state to show cause why a *mandamus* should not issue, directing him to deliver to William Marbury his commission as a justice of the peace for the county of Washington, in the district of Columbia.

No cause has been shown, and the present motion is for a *mandamus*. The peculiar delicacy of this case, the novelty of some of its circumstances, and the real difficulty attending the points which occur in it, require a complete exposition of the principles, on which the opinion to be given by the court, is founded.

* * *

In the order in which the court has viewed this subject, the following questions have been considered and decided.

1st. Has the applicant a right to the commission he demands?

2dly. If he has a right, and that right has been violated, do the laws of his country afford him a remedy?

3dly. If they do afford him a remedy, is it a *mandamus* issuing from this court?

The first object of enquiry is,

1st. Has the applicant a right to the commission he demands?

His right originates in an act of congress passed in February 1801, concerning the district of Columbia.

After dividing the district into two counties, the 11th section of this law enacts, "that there shall be appointed in and for each of the said counties, such number of discreet persons to be justices of the peace as the president of the United States shall, from time to time, think expedient, to continue in office for five years.["]

It appears, from the affidavits, that in compliance with this law, a commission for William Marbury as a justice of peace for the county of Washington, was signed by John Adams, then president of the United States; after which the seal of the United States was affixed to it; but the commission has never reached the person for whom it was made out.

In order to determine whether he is entitled to this commission, it becomes necessary to enquire whether he has been appointed to the office. For if he has been appointed, the law continues him in office for five years, and he is entitled to the possession of those evidences of office, which, being completed, became his property.

* * *

It is * * * decidedly the opinion of the court, that when a commission has been signed by the President, the appointment is made; and that the commission is complete, when the seal of the United States has been affixed to it by the secretary of state.

Where an officer is removeable at the will of the executive, the circumstance which completes his appointment is of no concern; because the act is at any time revocable; and the commission may be arrested, if still in the office. But when the officer is not removeable at the will of the executive, the appointment is not revocable, and cannot be annulled. It has conferred legal rights which cannot be resumed.

The discretion of the executive is to be exercised until the appointment has been made. But having once made the appointment, his power over the office is terminated in all cases, where, by law, the officer is not removeable by him. The right to the office is *then* in the person appointed, and he has the absolute, unconditional, power of accepting or rejecting it.

Mr. Marbury, then, since his commission was signed by the President, and sealed by the secretary of state, was appointed; and as the law creating the office, gave the officer a right to hold for five years, independent of the executive, the appointment was not revocable; but vested in the officer legal rights, which are protected by the laws of his country.

To withhold his commission, therefore, is an act deemed by the court not warranted by law, but violative of a vested legal right.

This brings us to the second enquiry; which is,

2dly. If he has a right, and that right has been violated, do the laws of his country afford him a remedy?

The very essence of civil liberty certainly consists in the right of every individual to claim the protection of the laws, whenever he receives an injury. One of the first duties of government is to afford that protection. In Great Britain the king himself is sued in the respectful form of a petition, and he never fails to comply with the judgment of his court.

* * *

The government of the United States has been emphatically termed a government of laws, and not of men. It will certainly cease to deserve this high appellation, if the laws furnish no remedy for the violation of a vested legal right.

If this obloquy is to be cast on the jurisprudence of our country, it must arise from the peculiar character of the case.

It behooves us then to enquire whether there be in its composition any ingredient which shall exempt it from legal investigation, or exclude the injured party from legal redress. In pursuing this enquiry the first question which presents itself, is, whether this can be arranged with the class of cases which come under the description of *damnum absque injuria*—a loss without an injury.

This description of cases never has been considered, and it is believed never can be considered, as comprehending offices of trust, of honor or of profit. The office of justice of peace in the district of Columbia is such an office; it is therefore worthy of the attention and guardianship of the laws. It has received that attention and guardianship. It has been created by special act of congress, and has been secured, so far as the laws can give security to the person appointed to fill it, for five years. It is not then on account of the worthlessness of the thing pursued, that the injured party can be alleged to be without remedy.

Is it in the nature of the transaction? Is the act of delivering or withholding a commission to be considered as a mere political act, belonging to the executive department alone, for the performance of which, entire confidence is placed by our constitution in the supreme executive; and for any misconduct respecting which, the injured individual has no remedy.

That there may be such cases is not to be questioned; but that every act of duty, to be performed in any of the great departments of government, constitutes such a case, is not to be admitted.

* * *

The conclusion from this reasoning is that where the heads of departments are the political or confidential agents of the executive, merely to execute the will of the President, or rather to act in cases in which the executive possesses a constitutional or legal discretion, nothing can be more perfectly clear than that their acts are only politically examinable. But where a specific duty is assigned by law, and individual rights depend upon the performance of that duty, it seems equally clear that the individual who considers himself injured, has a right to resort to the laws of his country for a remedy.

If this be the rule, let us enquire how it applies to the case under the consideration of the court.

That question has been discussed, and the opinion is, that the latest point of time which can be taken as that at which the appointment was complete, and evidenced, was when, after the signature of the president, the seal of the United States was affixed to the commission.

It is then the opinion of the court,

1st. That by signing the commission of Mr. Marbury, the president of the United States appointed him a justice of peace, for the county of Washington in the district of Columbia; and that the seal of the United States, affixed thereto by the secretary of state, is conclusive testimony of the verity of the signature, and of the completion of the appointment; and that the appointment conferred on him a legal right to the office for the space of five years.

2dly. That, having this legal title to the office, he has a consequent right to the commission; a refusal to deliver which is a plain violation of that right, for which the laws of his country afford him a remedy.

It remains to be enquired whether,

3dly. He is entitled to the remedy for which he applies. This depends on,

1st. The nature of the writ applied for, and,

2dly. The power of this court.

1st. The nature of the writ.

* * *

It is true that the *mandamus*, now moved for, is not for the performance of an act expressly enjoined by statute.

It is to deliver a commission; on which subject the acts of congress are silent. This difference is not considered as affecting the case. It has already been stated that the applicant has, to that commission, a vested legal right, of which the executive cannot deprive him. He has been appointed to an office, from which he is not removable at the will of the executive; and being so appointed, he has a right to the commission which the secretary has received from the president for his use. The act of congress does not indeed order the secretary of state to send it to him, but it is placed in his hands for the person entitled to it; and cannot be more lawfully withheld by him, than by any other person.

It was at first doubted whether the action of *detinue* was not a specific legal remedy for the commission which has been withheld from Mr. Marbury; in which case a mandamus would be improper. But this doubt has yielded to the consideration that the judgment in *detinue* is for the thing itself, *or* its value. The value of a public office not to be sold is incapable of being ascertained; and the applicant has a right to the office itself, or to nothing. He will obtain the office by obtaining the commission, or a copy of it from the record.

This, then, is a plain case for a *mandamus*, either to deliver the commission, or a copy of it from the record; and it only remains to be enquired,

Whether it can issue from this court.

The act to establish the judicial courts of the United States authorizes the supreme court "to issue writs of *mandamus*, in cases warranted by the principles and usages of law, to any courts appointed, or persons holding office, under the authority of the United States."

The secretary of state, being a person holding an office under the authority of the United States, is precisely within the letter of the description; and if this court is not authorized to issue a writ of *mandamus* to such an officer, it must be because the law is unconstitutional, and therefore absolutely incapable of conferring the authority, and assigning the duties which its words purport to confer and assign.

The constitution vests the whole judicial power of the United States in one supreme court, and such inferior courts as congress shall, from time to time, ordain and establish. This power is expressly extended to all cases arising under the laws of the United States; and consequently, in some form, may be exercised over the present case; because the right claimed is given by a law of the United States.

In the distribution of this power it is declared that "the supreme court shall have original jurisdiction in all cases affecting ambassadors, other public ministers and consuls, and those in which a state shall be a party. In all other cases, the supreme court shall have appellate jurisdiction."

It has been insisted, at the bar, that as the original grant of jurisdiction, to the supreme and inferior courts, is general, and the clause, assigning original jurisdiction to the supreme court, contains no negative or restrictive words; the power remains to the legislature, to assign original jurisdiction to that court in other cases than those specified in the article which has been recited; provided those cases belong to the judicial power of the United States.

If it had been intended to leave it in the discretion of the legislature to apportion the judicial power between the supreme and inferior courts according to the will of that body, it would certainly have been useless to have proceeded further than to have defined the judicial power, and the tribunals in which it should be vested. The subsequent part of the section is mere surplusage, is entirely without meaning, if such is to be the construction. If congress remains at liberty to give this court appellate jurisdiction, where the constitution has declared their jurisdiction shall be original; and original jurisdiction where the constitution has declared it shall be appellate; the distribution of jurisdiction, made in the constitution, is form without substance.

Affirmative words are often, in their operation, negative of other objects than those affirmed; and in this case, a negative or exclusive sense must be given to them or they have no operation at all.

It cannot be presumed that any clause in the constitution is intended to be without effect; and therefore such a construction is inadmissible, unless the words require it.

When an instrument organizing fundamentally a judicial system, divides it into one supreme, and so many inferior courts as the legislature may ordain and establish; then enumerates its powers, and proceeds so far to distribute them, as to define the jurisdiction of the supreme court by declaring the cases in which it shall take original jurisdiction, and that in others it shall take appellate jurisdiction; the plain import of the words seems to be, that in one class of cases its jurisdiction is original, and not appellate; in the other it is appellate, and not original. If any other construction would render the clause inoperative, that is an additional reason for rejecting such other construction, and for adhering to their obvious meaning.

To enable this court then to issue a *mandamus*, it must be shown to be an exercise of appellate jurisdiction, or to be necessary to enable them to exercise appellate jurisdiction.

It has been stated at the bar that the appellate jurisdiction may be exercised in a variety of forms, and that if it be the will of the legislature that a *mandamus* should be used for that purpose, that will must be obeyed. This is true, yet the jurisdiction must be appellate, not original.

It is the essential criterion of appellate jurisdiction, that it revises and corrects the proceedings in a cause already instituted, and does not create that cause. Although, therefore, a *mandamus* may be directed to courts, yet to issue such a writ to an officer for the delivery of a paper, is in effect the same as to sustain an original action for that paper, and therefore seems not to belong to appellate, but to original jurisdiction.

Neither is it necessary in such a case as this, to enable the court to exercise its appellate jurisdiction.

The authority, therefore, given to the supreme court, by the act establishing the judicial courts of the United States, to issue writs of *mandamus* to public officers, appears not to be warranted by the constitution; and it becomes necessary to enquire whether a jurisdiction, so conferred, can be exercised.

The question, whether an act, repugnant to the constitution, can become the law of the land, is a question deeply interesting to the United States; but, happily, not of an intricacy proportioned to its interest. It seems only necessary to recognize certain principles, supposed to have been long and well established, to decide it.

That the people have an original right to establish, for their future government, such principles as, in their opinion, shall most conduce to their own happiness, is the basis, on which the whole American fabric has been erected. The exercise of this original right is a very great exertion; nor can it, nor ought it to be frequently repeated. The principles, therefore, so established, are deemed fundamental. And as the authority, from which they proceed, is supreme, and can seldom act, they are designed to be permanent.

This original and supreme will organizes the government, and assigns, to different departments, their respective powers. It may either stop here; or establish certain limits not to be transcended by those departments.

The government of the United States is of the latter description. The powers of the legislature are defined, and limited; and that those limits may not be mistaken, or forgotten, the constitution is written. To what purpose are powers limited, and to what purpose is that limitation committed to writing, if these limits may, at any time, be passed by those intended to be restrained? The distinction, between a government with limited and unlimited powers, is abolished, if those limits do not confine the persons on whom they are imposed, and if acts prohibited and acts allowed, are of equal obligation. It is a proposition too plain to be contested, that the constitution controls any legislative act repugnant to it; or, that the legislature may alter the constitution by an ordinary act.

Between these alternatives there is no middle ground. The constitution is either a superior, paramount law, unchangeable by ordinary means, or it is on a level with ordinary legislative acts, and like other acts, is alterable when the legislature shall please to alter it.

If the former part of the alternative be true, then a legislative act contrary to the constitution is not law: if the latter part be true, then written constitutions are absurd attempts, on the part of the people, to limit a power, in its own nature illimitable.

Certainly all those who have framed written constitutions contemplate them as forming the fundamental and paramount law of the nation, and consequently the theory of every such government must be, that an act of the legislature, repugnant to the constitution, is void.

This theory is essentially attached to a written constitution, and is consequently to be considered, by this court, as one of the fundamental principles of our society. It is not therefore to be lost sight of in the further consideration of this subject.

If an act of the legislature, repugnant to the constitution, is void, does it, notwithstanding its invalidity, bind the courts, and oblige them to give it effect? Or, in other words, though it be not law, does it constitute a rule as operative as if it was a law? This would be to overthrow in fact what was established in theory; and would seem, at first view, an absurdity too gross to be insisted on. It shall, however, receive a more attentive consideration.

It is emphatically the province and duty of the judicial department to say what the law is. Those who apply the rule to particular cases, must of necessity expound and interpret that rule. If two laws conflict with each other, the courts must decide on the operation of each.

So if a law be in opposition to the constitution; if both the law and the constitution apply to a particular case, so that the court must either decide that case conformably to the law, disregarding the constitution; or conformably to the constitution, disregarding the law; the court must determine which of these conflicting rules governs the case. This is of the very essence of judicial duty.

If then the courts are to regard the constitution; and the constitution is superior to any ordinary act of the legislature; the constitution, and not such ordinary act, must govern the case to which they both apply.

Those then who controvert the principle that the constitution is to be considered, in court, as a paramount law, are reduced to the necessity of maintaining that courts must close their eyes on the constitution, and see only the law.

This doctrine would subvert the very foundation of all written constitutions. It would declare that an act, which, according to the principles and theory of our government, is entirely void, is yet, in practice, completely obligatory. It would declare, that if the legislature shall do what is expressly forbidden, such act, notwithstanding the express prohibition, is in reality effectual. It would be giving to the legislature a practical and real omnipotence, with the same breath which professes to restrict their powers within narrow limits. It is prescribing limits, and declaring that those limits may be passed at pleasure.

That it thus reduces to nothing what we have deemed the greatest improvement on political institutions—a written constitution—would of itself be sufficient, in America, where written constitutions have been viewed with so much reverence, for rejecting the construction. But the peculiar expressions of the constitution of the United States furnish additional arguments in favour of its rejection.

The judicial power of the United States is extended to all cases arising under the constitution.

Could it be the intention of those who gave this power, to say that, in using it, the constitution should not be looked into? That a case arising under the constitution should be decided without examining the instrument under which it arises?

This is too extravagant to be maintained.

In some cases then, the constitution must be looked into by the judges. And if they can open it at all, what part of it are they forbidden to read, or to obey?

There are many other parts of the constitution which serve to illustrate this subject.

It is declared that "no tax or duty shall be laid on articles exported from any state." Suppose a duty on the export of cotton, of tobacco, or of flour; and a suit instituted to recover it. Ought judgment to be rendered in such a case? Ought the judges to close their eyes on the constitution, and only see the law.

The constitution declares that "no bill of attainder or *ex post facto* law shall be passed."

If, however, such a bill should be passed and a person should be prosecuted under it; must the court condemn to death those victims whom the constitution endeavours to preserve?

"No person," says the constitution, "shall be convicted of treason unless on the testimony of two witnesses to the same overt act, or on confession in open court."

Here the language of the constitution is addressed especially to the courts. It prescribes, directly for them, a rule of evidence not to be departed from. If the legislature should change that rule, and declare *one* witness, or a confession *out* of court, sufficient for conviction, must the constitutional principle yield to the legislative act?

From these, and many other selections which might be made, it is apparent, that the framers of the constitution contemplated that instrument as a rule for the government of *courts*, as well as of the legislature.

Why otherwise does it direct the judges to take an oath to support it? This oath certainly applies, in an especial manner, to their conduct in their official character. How immoral to impose it on them, if they were to be used as the instruments, and the knowing instruments, for violating what they swear to support!

The oath of office, too, imposed by the legislature, is completely demonstrative of the legislative opinion on this subject. It is in these words, "I do solemnly swear that I will administer justice without respect to persons, and do equal right to the poor and to the rich; and that I will faithfully and impartially discharge all the duties incumbent on me as according to the best of my abilities and understanding, agreeably to *the constitution,* and laws of the United States."

Why does a judge swear to discharge his duties agreeably to the constitution of the United States, if that constitution forms no rule for his government? if it is closed upon him, and cannot be inspected by him?

If such be the real state of things, this is worse than solemn mockery. To prescribe, or to take this oath, becomes equally a crime.

It is also not entirely unworthy of observation, that in declaring what shall be the *supreme* law of the land, the *constitution* itself is first mentioned; and not the laws of the United States generally, but those only which shall be made in *pursuance* of the constitution, have that rank.

Thus, the particular phraseology of the constitution of the United States confirms and strengthens the principle, supposed to be essential to all written constitutions, that a law repugnant to the constitution is void; and that *courts*, as well as other departments, are bound by that instrument.

The rule must be discharged.

Notes and Questions

1. It seems obvious that the Court desired to express its view on executive accountability as well as on judicial review. Note the alternatives the Court could have adopted to avoid reaching one or more of these issues. Indeed, consider whether the decision on executive accountability is not pure *dicta. See* Chapter I, *supra.* Among the alternatives open to the Court were the following:

a. classifying the request for mandamus as an exercise of appellate jurisdiction, thus immunizing the jurisdictional statute from any constitutional infirmity. Would this approach have precipitated a confrontation with the executive department?

b. interpreting the statute as not authorizing mandamus in the particular instance, thus rendering academic the question of judicial review;

c. basing the decision on the inappropriateness of mandamus as a remedy because of the revocable nature of the judicial appointment;

d. holding that Marbury did not have a right to the commission until actual delivery. President Jefferson assumed the soundness of this position. Did the Court adequately support its position that Marbury had a right to the commission prior to delivery?

2. Consider the remarkable ingenuity of the opinion, affirming executive and legislative accountability to the judiciary, yet denying relief to Marbury. By refusing to grant any relief, the decision avoided a direct, and perhaps unseemly, confrontation between the President and the Court. Would the President of the United States have disobeyed a judicial order directing delivery of the commission? Recall President Jackson's response to a Supreme Court opinion a few years later: "John Marshall made his

decision: now let him enforce it."[g] Should a court be concerned about the potential of Presidential nullification?

3. Where in the text of the Constitution does the Chief Justice derive the power of judicial review? Note the distinction between the principles of supremacy of the Constitution and of judicial review. The latter principle encompasses the right to disregard acts of Congress that violate the Constitution. The Chief Justice assumed that judicial review followed inevitably from constitutional supremacy. Yet even he conceded that the separation of powers doctrine contemplates the Constitution as a check upon all three branches of government. Did *Marbury* tip the scales too heavily in favor of the judiciary by giving the courts the final word?

4. The Court employed various methods of constitutional construction, from a pure textual analysis to an attempt to divine the intent of the framers. Yet the opinion refers neither to the debates at the constitutional convention nor to other historical evidence, such as the English or state practice prior to ratification, from which such intent could be inferred. Why did the opinion bypass these pages of history? Is it because the historical evidence was not conclusive? *Compare* R. Berger, Congress v. Supreme Court (1969) (finding intent) *with* W. Crosskey, Politics and the Constitution (1953) (finding no intent). Surely it cannot be denied that the Chief Justice was well informed; "(He) had been a part of it all." Beveridge, The Life of John Marshall 479 (1916). *See* The Federalist, no. 78.

5. Do the other departments of government have a role in framing and developing constitutional law? Did *Marbury* recognize this role? Is deference to judicial opinions required by the Constitution? Even in circumstances where the other departments are convinced of the unconstitutionality of the decision? Are there distinctions between the deference due to Supreme Court opinions by states on the one hand, *see Cooper v. Aaron*, 358 U.S. 1 (1958), and by other federal departments on the other? Consider the following Presidential comments on the function of the Supreme Court.

ANDREW JACKSON:

> If the opinion of the Supreme Court covered the whole ground of this act, it ought not to control the coordinate authorities of this Government. The Congress, the Executive, and the Court must each for itself be guided by its own opinion of the Constitution. Each public officer who takes an oath to support the Constitution swears that he will support it as he understands it, and not as it is understood by others. It is as much the duty of the House of Representatives, of the Senate, and of the President to decide upon the constitutionality of any bill or resolution which may be presented to them for passage or approval as it is of the supreme judges when it may be brought before them for judicial decision. The opinion of the judges has no more authority over Congress than the opinion of Congress has over the judges, and on that point the President is independent of both. The authority of the Supreme Court must not, therefore, be permitted to control the Congress or the Executive when acting in their legislative capacities, but to have only such influence as the force of their reasoning may deserve.

g. H. Greeley, 1 THE AMERICAN CONFLICT, A HISTORY OF THE GREAT REBELLION 106 (1864).

2 J. Richardson, Messages and Papers of the Presidents 576, 582 (1896).

ABRAHAM LINCOLN:

I do not forget the position assumed by some that constitutional questions are to be decided by the Supreme Court, nor do I deny that such decisions must be binding in any case upon the parties to a suit as to the object of that suit, while they are also entitled to very high respect and consideration in all parallel cases by all other departments of the Government. And while it is obviously possible that such decision may be erroneous in any given case, still the evil effect following it, being limited to that particular case, with the chance that it may be overruled and never become a precedent for other cases, can better be borne than could the evils of a different practice. At the same time, the candid citizen must confess that if the policy of the Government upon vital questions affecting the whole people is to be irrevocably fixed by decisions of the Supreme Court, the instant they are made in ordinary litigation between parties in personal actions the people will have ceased to be their own rulers, having to that extent practically resigned their Government into the hands of that eminent tribunal. Nor is there in this view any assault upon the court or the judges. It is a duty from which they may not shrink to decide cases properly brought before them, and it is no fault of theirs if others seek to turn their decision to political purposes.

6 J. Richardson, Messages and Papers of the Presidents 5, 9 (1896).

FRANKLIN D. ROOSEVELT:

Manifestly, no one is in a position to give assurance that the proposed act will withstand constitutional tests, for the simple fact that you can get not ten but a thousand differing legal opinions on the subject. But the situation is so urgent and the benefits of the legislation so evident that all doubts should be resolved in favor of the bill, leaving to the courts, in an orderly fashion, the ultimate question of constitutionality. A decision by the Supreme Court relative to this measure would be helpful as indicating, with increasing clarity, the constitutional limits within which this Government must operate. The proposed bill has been carefully drafted by employers and employees working cooperatively. An opportunity should be given to the industry to attempt to work out some of its major problems. I hope your committee will not permit doubts as to constitutionality, however reasonable, to block the suggested legislation.

4 Public Papers and Addresses of Franklin D. Roosevelt 297–98 (1938).

6.   The judiciary's obligation to rule on issues of constitutional law has its limitations, founded in part in the very language of the Constitution. The instrument extends the judicial power only to "cases" and "controversies." Throughout our nation's history, the Court has steadfastly refused to embroil itself in legal disputes not falling within the "case and controversy" limitation. These terms do not lend themselves to litmus-test analysis, though an illustration will aid the focusing process: Congress may refuse to pass a statute because it harbors doubts regarding constitutionality. Or the President, entertaining similar views, may veto a bill that has been passed.

An erroneous reading or understanding of the Constitution *per se* is not a proper subject of judicial review. However, once the statute is enacted, the Court may properly inquire into its constitutionality in connection with an actual case or controversy.

D. LIMITATIONS ON THE POWER OF FEDERAL COURTS TO HEAR CASES

"Sue the bastards" is more than a slogan in contemporary America. It expresses an attitude pervasive in our society affirming the value and function of courts in modern conflict resolution. Society has come to believe that conflicts, ranging from the simple and mundane to those implicating societal norms and human rights, may ultimately be channeled through the judicial process for resolution. *Gideon v. Wainwright,*[h] which launched a movement to provide representation and a full panoply of legal rights by declaring a right to legal representation for indigent defendants in state court felony cases, is representative of that belief. Indeed, the confluence of two ideals—of justice for all parties and of judicial solutions for all problems—has led to the litigation explosion * * *. The effects of this explosion have not been fully seismographed.

Every movement produces its own countervailing forces. The litigation explosion is no exception. Even during the Warren Court era, champions of judicial restraint opposed the Court's entry into areas that previously had not been thought appropriate for judicial resolution. And their arguments for restraint were not unprecedented, for the principle of federal judicial restraint has historical antecedents with threads woven deep into the fabric of the common law. Judicial restraint rests on the essentially political belief that the judicial process cannot be appropriately called upon to ameliorate all of society's ailments and that the extension of the judicial arm into certain areas of controversy creates its own problems. The belief that the judiciary should be limited manifests itself in different ways—variously termed the case and controversy limitation, standing requirements, ripeness, justiciability, mootness, comity, and more recently in the context of federal-state relations, "Our Federalism." The consequence of the application of one or more of these labels to the controversy is the refusal of the federal court to reach the merits of the lawsuit. *See* Michael Berch, *Unchain the Courts—An Essay on the Role of the Federal Courts in the Vindication of Social Rights,* 1976 Ariz. St. L.J. 437, 437–39 (1977).

The remaining materials in this chapter examine doctrines that attempt to contain the litigation explosion by restricting the role of the federal courts in the vindication of constitutional rights. Consider, with respect to each of the doctrines examined, the source of the restriction. Be sure to note whether the restriction is predicated upon (1) the "case" and "controversy" language of Article III or other textual provisions of

h. 372 U.S. 335, 83 S. Ct. 792 (1963), on remand 153 So. 2d 299.

the Constitution, (2) statutory restrictions, or (3) judge-made limitations. Is the basis of the restriction important? It is plain that constitutional restrictions cannot be shunted aside by statute. Any restriction based upon statutory provisions may be abrogated by Congress. The prudential considerations, involving notions that may or may not be rooted in constitutional doctrines, present greater difficulties.

Consider the wisdom of each of the doctrines, especially as applied to the facts of the particular case. Note alternatives that may be open to the litigants or the courts. For example, should the federal court refuse to entertain the controversy, may resort be had to the state court system? Or is the litigant compelled to resort to the political process? The answers to these questions are significant not only to the litigants but to society as well.

1. STANDING

FROTHINGHAM v. MELLON

Supreme Court of the United States, 1923.
262 U.S. 447, 43 S.Ct. 597, 67 L.Ed. 1078.

JUSTICE SUTHERLAND delivered the opinion of the Court.

These cases were argued and will be considered and disposed of together. The first is an original suit in this Court. The other was brought in the Supreme Court of the District of Columbia. That court dismissed the bill and its decree was affirmed by the District Court of Appeals. Thereupon the case was brought here by appeal. Both cases challenge the constitutionality of the Act of November 23, 1921, 42 Stat. 224, c. 135, commonly called the Maternity Act. Briefly, it provides for an initial appropriation and thereafter annual appropriations for a period of five years, to be apportioned among such of the several states as shall accept and comply with its provisions, for the purpose of co-operating with them to reduce maternal and infant mortality and protect the health of mothers and infants. It creates a bureau to administer the act in co-operation with state agencies, which are required to make such reports concerning their operations and expenditures as may be prescribed by the federal bureau. Whenever that bureau shall determine that funds have not been properly expended in respect of any state, payments may be withheld.

It is asserted that these appropriations are for purposes not national, but local to the states, and together with numerous similar appropriations constitute an effective means of inducing the states to yield a portion of their sovereign rights. It is further alleged that the burden of the appropriations provided by this act and similar legislation falls unequally upon the several states, and rests largely upon the industrial states, such as Massachusetts; that the act is a usurpation of power not granted to Congress by the Constitution—an attempted exercise of the power of local self-government reserved to the states by the Tenth Amendment; and that the defendants are proceeding to carry the act into operation. In the *Massachusetts* case it is alleged that the plaintiff's rights and powers as a sovereign state and the rights of its citizens have been invaded and usurped by these expenditures and acts, and that, although the state has not accepted the act, its constitutional rights are infringed by the passage thereof and the imposition upon the state of an illegal and unconstitutional option either to yield to the federal government a part of its reserved rights or lose the share which it would otherwise be entitled to receive of the moneys appropriated. In the *Frothingham* case plaintiff alleges that the effect of the statute will be to take her property, under the guise of taxation, without due process of law.

We have reached the conclusion that the cases must be disposed of for want of jurisdiction, without considering the merits of the constitutional questions.

In the first case, the state of Massachusetts presents no justiciable controversy, either in its own behalf or as the representative of its citizens. The appellant in the second suit has no such interest in the subject-matter, nor is any such injury inflicted or threatened, as will enable her to sue.

* * *

[The] plaintiff [in *Frothingham*] alleges * * * that she is a taxpayer of the United States; and her contention, though not clear, seems to be that the effect of the appropriations complained of will be to increase the burden of future taxation and thereby take her property without due process of law. The right of a taxpayer to enjoin the execution of a federal appropriation act, on the ground that it is invalid and will result in taxation for illegal purposes, has never been passed upon by this court. In cases where it was presented, the question has either been allowed to pass sub silentio or the determination of it expressly withheld. The case last cited came here from the Court of Appeals of the District of Columbia, and that court sustained the right of the plaintiff to sue by treating the case as one directed against the District of Columbia, and therefore subject to the rule, frequently stated by this court, that resident taxpayers may sue to enjoin an illegal use of the moneys of a municipal corporation. The interest of a taxpayer of a municipality in the application of its moneys is direct and immediate and the remedy by injunction to prevent their misuse is not inappropriate. It is upheld by a large number of state cases and is the rule of this court. Nevertheless, there are decisions to the contrary. The reasons which support the extension of the equitable remedy to a single taxpayer in such cases are based upon the peculiar relation of the corporate taxpayer to the corporation, which is not without some resemblance to that subsisting between stockholder and private corporation. But the relation of a taxpayer of the United States to the federal government is very different. His interest in the moneys of the treasury—partly realized from taxation and partly from other sources—is shared with millions of others, is comparatively minute and indeterminable, and the effect upon future taxation, of any payment out of the funds, so remote, fluctuating and uncertain, that no basis is afforded for an appeal to the preventive powers of a court of equity.

The administration of any statute, likely to produce additional taxation to be imposed upon a vast number of taxpayers, the extent of whose several liability is indefinite and constantly changing, is essentially a matter of public and not of individual concern. If one taxpayer may champion and litigate such a cause, then every other taxpayer may do the same, not only in respect of the statute here under review, but also in respect of every other appropriation act and statute whose administration requires the outlay of public money, and whose validity may be questioned. The bare suggestion of such a result, with its attendant inconveniences, goes far to sustain the conclusion which we have reached, that a suit of this character cannot be maintained. It is of much significance that no precedent sustaining the right to maintain suits like this has been called to our attention, although, since the formation of the government, as an examination of the acts of Congress will disclose, a large number of statutes appropriating or involving the expenditure of moneys for nonfederal purposes have been enacted and carried into effect.

The functions of government under our system are apportioned. To the legislative department has been committed the duty of making laws, to the executive the duty of executing them, and to the judiciary the duty of interpreting and applying them in cases properly brought before the courts. The general rule is that neither department may invade the province of the other and neither may control, direct, or restrain the action of the other. We are not now speaking of the merely ministerial duties of officials. We have no power per se to review and annul acts of Congress on the ground that they are unconstitutional. That question may be considered only when the justification for some direct injury suffered or threatened, presenting a justiciable issue, is made to rest upon such an act. Then the power exercised is that of ascertaining and declaring the law applicable to the controversy. It amounts to little more than the negative power to disregard an unconstitutional enactment, which otherwise would stand in the way of the enforcement of a legal right. The party who invokes the power must be able to show, not only that the statute is invalid, but that he has sustained or is immediately in danger of sustaining some direct injury as the result of its enforcement, and not merely that he suffers in some indefinite way in common with people generally. If a case for preventive relief be presented, the court enjoins, in effect, not the execution of the statute, but the acts of the official, the statute notwithstanding. Here the parties plaintiff have no such case. Looking through forms of words to the substance of their complaint, it is merely that officials of the executive department of the government are executing and will execute an act of Congress asserted to be unconstitutional; and this we are asked to prevent. To do so would be, not to decide a judicial controversy, but to assume a position of authority over the governmental acts of another and coequal department, an authority which plainly we do not possess.

No. 24, Original, dismissed.

No. 962 affirmed.

Notes and Questions

1. In *Frothingham,* the Court held that a federal taxpayer lacked standing to challenge the validity of federal expenditures of tax money. The taxpayer in that case alleged that Congress had exceeded the powers delegated to it under Article I of the Constitution and had likewise invaded provinces reserved to the states under the Tenth Amendment. This case stood as a barrier to taxpayer suits in the federal courts for 45 years. Yet even after *Frothingham,* state courts continued to allow taxpayer suits challenging the constitutionality of state tax statutes. Could a state court entertain a suit challenging the constitutionality of a federal tax statute?

2. Standing focuses upon the appropriateness of the petitioning party to appear before the tribunal and raise a particular issue. It does not, by its own force, raise separation of powers problems related to improper judicial interference in areas committed to other branches of the federal government. Yet courts have at times blurred these areas. *See Allen v. Wright,* 468 U.S. 737 (1984).

3. A litigant may be correct regarding the unconstitutionality of the legislative provision, yet be frustrated in judicially challenging the offending act. What other courses of action are open to that litigant? What factors justify foreclosing judicial redress? Consider that in some situations other litigants having proper credentials may be able to bring judicial proceedings. Yet in still others, litigants having the requisite standing may not be found. Who, for example, would have been a more suitable litigant in *Frothingham*? Why the need for standing anyway? In *Baker v. Carr,* reprinted *infra* at 532, the Court focused on the need for the adversary process to illuminate the issues. Is there a correlation between lack of standing, as found in *Frothingham* or in *Sierra Club* (*infra* note 4), and inability to illuminate issues before the Court?

4. In *Sierra Club v. Morton,* 405 U.S. 727 (1972), the organization, known for its dedication to preservation of the environment, brought an action in the federal courts to prevent development of Mineral King Valley into a commercial resort. The complaint charged violations of various congressional statutes. It asserted, without contradiction, that the Sierra Club possessed a special interest in the conservation and sound maintenance of the national parks, game refuges, and forests of the country. The Court, noting that the Club had "failed to allege that it or its members would be affected in any of their activities or pastimes" by the defendant's activities, concluded that it lacked standing. The Court noted that standing is not conferred upon organizations merely having an interest in a problem.

The Court remanded the decision to the lower courts for further proceedings. On remand, an individual having an interest in the preservation of Mineral King Valley intervened in the action. The lower court then reached the merits of the controversy. Do you believe that an individual who occasionally uses a park, game refuge, or forest is able to shed more light on the controversy than the Sierra Club could? Can you fathom why the Sierra Club did not allege that any of its members was specifically injured by the development? Was it merely a mistake in the pleading? A matter of principle? What principle?

Contrast the decision of *United States v. SCRAP*, 412 U.S. 669 (1973), with the opinion in *Sierra Club*. SCRAP, an acronym compromised of the first letters of the last names of law students who formed an unincorporated association whose "primary purpose is to enhance the quality of the human environment for its members, and for all citizens," alleged that its members suffered injury as a result of the failure of the Interstate Commerce Commission to suspend surcharges on freight rates, in violation of its statutory duties. The complaint further elaborated on the injury to its members, as follows:

> [E]ach of its members was caused to pay more for finished products, that each of its members "[u]ses the forests, rivers, streams, mountains, and other natural resources surrounding the Washington Metropolitan area and at his legal residence, for camping, hiking, fishing, sightseeing, and other recreational [and] aesthetic purposes," and that these uses have been adversely affected by the increased freight rates, that each of its members breathes the air within the Washington metropolitan area and the area of his legal residence and that this air has suffered increased pollution caused by modified rate structure, and that each member has been forced to pay increased taxes because of the sums which must be expended to dispose of otherwise reusable waste materials.

Id. at 678.

The Court ruled that SCRAP had the requisite standing.

In light of the policies underlying the standing requirement, are *Sierra Club* and *SCRAP* distinguishable? One commentator has suggested that *Sierra Club* was merely a ruling on a technical pleading matter. Scott, *Standing in the Supreme Court—A Functional Analysis*, 86 Harv. L. Rev. 645, 667 (1973). Other commentators have opined that *Sierra Club* and other cases exemplify the art of judicial legerdemain to avoid or postpone rendering a decision. Should the Court be able to duck its decision–making responsibility in this manner?

Standing in the federal courts is purely a question of federal law. Had *Sierra Club* been permitted to litigate the merits in the state court, would the Supreme Court have been able to review the state court judgment? If not, what is the precedential value of the state court judgment? Should the federal courts dictate standing requirements for plaintiffs seeking to vindicate federal rights in state court systems?

5.   Does *Frothingham* suggest a correlation between standing and the number of persons affected by the alleged unconstitutional governmental action? Should alleged unconstitutional activity by the executive and legislative departments that affects a majority of citizens be subject to judicial review? Consider redress through the political process as an alternative. *See Warth v. Seldin*, 422 U.S. 490 (1975). Although the political process is well

suited to respond to the wishes of the majority, individuals or minority groups may not realistically effectuate political redress.

6. For years scholars have attempted to fathom the unfathomable aspects of the standing requirement. An attempt by Professor Brilmayer notes three interrelated policies underlying the constitutional core of standing:

> [T]he smooth allocation of power among courts over time; the unfairness of holding later litigants to an adverse judgment in which they may not have been properly represented; and the importance of placing control over political processes in the hands of the people most closely involved.

Brilmayer, *The Jurisprudence of Article III: Perspective on the "Case or Controversy" Requirement*, 93 Harv. L. Rev. 297 (1979). These policies may explain some cases. But are the policies to which she alludes applicable to *Sierra Club*? Should these policies apply to proceedings brought by public interest litigants?

7. What is the source of the standing requirement? Cases have recognized that standing may be denied on the basis of the case and controversy requirement contained in Article III, or by reason of prudential considerations. Of what importance is the source of the requirement? Recall that Congress may not interfere where constitutional doctrines are involved. Upon what source does *Frothingham* draw? Consider the position taken in the following article:

> I know no absolute standards for the determination of standing. I do not know whether *Frothingham v. Mellon* is a constitutional decision or a prudential decision. I do not know whether the Court that decided that case would have taken jurisdiction of a taxpayer's action challenging an appropriation as beyond constitutional authority had Congress by statute provided for such an action. But even to say that a statute establishing a mechanism for such a judicial check on the congressional power of appropriation would be upheld is not to say that the Court can properly establish such a check on its own discretion. The question is one of allocation of power between co-ordinate branches of the government. For Congress to grant or acknowledge power over itself is one thing. For the Court to take it is quite another.

Brown, *Quis Custodiet Ipsos Custodes?—The School–Prayer Cases,* 1963 Sup. Ct. Rev. 1, 15–16. To ensure an understanding of the legal process and the proper working relationship of the branches of the government, should not the Court be more specific in designating the sources of its standing decisions? Or should it leave these important considerations to another day—a day, perhaps, when it might be essential to pinpoint the source? Some authorities believe that the Court should not articulate the precise ground upon which its decision rests until a case requires such articulation. Does this belief accord with your understanding of the judicial process at its best? At its worst?

FLAST v. COHEN

Supreme Court of the United States, 1968.
392 U.S. 83, 88 S.Ct. 1942, 20 L.Ed.2d 947.

CHIEF JUSTICE WARREN delivered the opinion of the Court.

In *Frothingham v. Mellon*, 262 U.S. 447, 43 S.Ct. 597, 67 L.Ed. 1078 (1923), this Court ruled that a federal taxpayer is without standing to challenge the constitutionality of a federal statute. That ruling has stood for 45 years as an impenetrable barrier to suits against Acts of Congress brought by individuals who can assert only the interest of federal taxpayers. In this case, we must decide whether the *Frothingham* barrier should be lowered when a taxpayer attacks a federal statute on the ground that it violates the Establishment and Free Exercise Clauses of the First Amendment.

Appellants filed suit in the United States District Court for the Southern District of New York to enjoin the allegedly unconstitutional expenditure of federal funds under Titles I and II of the Elementary and Secondary Education Act of 1965, 79 Stat. 27, 20 U.S.C. §§ 241a *et seq.*, 821 *et seq.* (1964 ed., Supp. II). The complaint alleged that the seven appellants had as a common attribute that "each pay[s] income taxes of the United States," and it is clear from the complaint that the appellants were resting their standing to maintain the action solely on their status as federal taxpayers.[1] The appellees, who are charged by Congress with administering the Elementary and Secondary Education Act of 1965, were sued in their official capacities.

The gravamen of the appellants' complaint was that federal funds appropriated under the Act were being used to finance instruction in reading, arithmetic, and other subjects in religious schools, and to purchase textbooks and other instructional materials for use in such schools. Such expenditures were alleged to be in contravention of the Establishment and Free Exercise Clauses of the First Amendment. Appellants' constitutional attack focused on the statutory criteria which state and local authorities must meet to be eligible for federal grants under the Act. Title I of the Act establishes a program for financial assistance to local educational agencies for the education of low-income families. Federal payments are made to state educational agencies, which pass the payments on in the form of grants to local educational agencies. Under § 205 of the Act, 20 U.S.C. § 241e, a local educational agency wishing to have a plan or program funded by a grant must submit the plan or program to the appropriate state educational agency for approval. The plan or program must be "consistent with such basic criteria as the [appellee United States Commissioner of Education] may establish."

1. The complaint alleged that one of the appellants "has children regularly registered in and attending the elementary or secondary grades in the public schools of New York." However, the District Court did not view that additional allegation as being relevant to the question of standing, and appellants have made no effort to justify their standing on that additional ground.

The specific criterion of that section attacked by the appellants is the requirement

> that, to the extent consistent with the number of educationally deprived children in the school district of the local educational agency who are enrolled in private elementary and secondary schools, such agency has made provision for including special educational services and arrangements (such as dual enrollment, educational radio and television, and mobile educational services and equipment) in which such children can participate * * *. 20 U.S.C. § 241e(a)(2).

Under § 206 of the Act, 20 U.S.C. § 241f, the Commissioner of Education is given broad powers to supervise a State's participation in Title I programs and grants. Title II of the Act establishes a program of federal grants for the acquisition of school library resources, textbooks, and other printed and published instructional materials "for the use of children and teachers in public and private elementary and secondary schools." 20 U.S.C. § 821. A State wishing to participate in the program must submit a plan to the Commissioner for approval, and the plan must

> provide assurance that to the extent consistent with law such library resources, textbooks, and other instructional materials will be provided on an equitable basis for the use of children and teachers in private elementary and secondary schools in the State * * *. 20 U.S.C. § 823(a)(3)(B).

While disclaiming any intent to challenge as unconstitutional all programs under Title I of the Act, the complaint alleges that federal funds have been disbursed under the Act, "with the consent and approval of the [appellees]," and that such funds have been used and will continue to be used to finance "instruction in reading, arithmetic and other subjects and for guidance in religious and sectarian schools" and "the purchase of textbooks and instructional and library materials for use in religious and sectarian schools." Such expenditures of federal tax funds, appellants alleged, violate the First Amendment because "they constitute a law respecting an establishment of religion" and because "they prohibit the free exercise of religion on the part of the [appellants] * * * by reason of the fact that they constitute compulsory taxation for religious purposes." The complaint asked for a declaration that appellees' actions in approving the expenditure of federal funds for the alleged purposes were not authorized by the Act or, in the alternative, that if appellees' actions are deemed within the authority and intent of the Act, "the Act is to that extent unconstitutional and void." The complaint also prayed for an injunction to enjoin appellees from approving any expenditure of federal funds for the allegedly unconstitutional purposes. The complaint further requested that a three-judge court be convened as provided in 28 U.S.C. §§ 2282, 2284.

The Government moved to dismiss the complaint on the ground that appellants lacked standing to maintain the action. District Judge Frankel, who considered the motion, recognized that *Frothingham v. Mellon*, *supra,* provided "powerful" support for the government's position, but he ruled that the standing question was of sufficient substance to warrant the convening of a three-judge court to decide the question. 267 F.Supp. 351 (1967). The three-judge court received briefs and heard arguments limited to the standing question, and the court ruled on the authority of *Frothingham* that appellants lacked standing. Judge Frankel dissented. 271 F.Supp. 1 (1967). From the dismissal of their complaint on that ground, appellants appealed directly to this Court, 28 U.S.C. § 1253, and we noted probable jurisdiction. 389 U.S. 895, 88 S.Ct. 218, 19 L.Ed.2d 212 (1967). For reasons explained at length below, we hold that appellants do have standing as federal taxpayers to maintain this action, and the judgment below must be reversed.

* * *

II.

This Court first faced squarely the question whether a litigant asserting only his status as a taxpayer has standing to maintain a suit in a federal court in *Frothingham v. Mellon, supra,* and that decision must be the starting point for analysis in this case. The taxpayer in *Frothingham* attacked as unconstitutional the Maternity Act of 1921, 42 Stat. 224, which established a federal program of grants to those States which would undertake programs to reduce maternal and infant mortality. The taxpayer alleged that Congress, in enacting the challenged statute, had exceeded the powers delegated to it under Article I of the Constitution and had invaded the legislative province reserved to the several States by the Tenth Amendment. The taxpayer complained that the result of the allegedly unconstitutional enactment would be to increase her future federal tax liability and "thereby take her property without due process of law." 262 U.S., at 486, 43 S.Ct. at 600. The Court noted that a federal taxpayer's "interest in the moneys of the treasury * * * is comparatively minute and indeterminable" and that "the effect upon future taxation, of any payment out of the [Treasury's] funds, * * * [is] remote, fluctuating and uncertain." Id. at 487, 43 S.Ct. at 601. As a result, the Court ruled that the taxpayer had failed to allege the type of "direct injury" necessary to confer standing. *Id.* at 488, 43 S.Ct. at 601.

Although the barrier *Frothingham* erected against federal taxpayer suits has never been breached, the decision has been the source of some confusion and the object of considerable criticism. The confusion has developed as commentators have tried to determine whether *Frothingham* establishes a constitutional bar to taxpayer suits or whether the Court was simply imposing a rule of self-restraint which was not constitutionally compelled.[6] The conflicting viewpoints are reflected in the arguments made to this Court by the parties in this case. The Government has pressed upon us the view that *Frothingham* announced

---

6. The prevailing view of the commentators is that *Frothingham* announced only a nonconstitutional rule of self-restraint.

THE ROLE OF THE COURTS

a constitutional rule, compelled by the Article III limitations on federal court jurisdiction and grounded in considerations of the doctrine of separation of powers. Appellants, however, insist that *Frothingham* expressed no more than a policy of judicial self-restraint which can be disregarded when compelling reasons for assuming jurisdiction over a taxpayer's suit exist. The opinion delivered in *Frothingham* can be read to support either position. The concluding sentence of the opinion states that, to take jurisdiction of the taxpayer's suit, "would be not to decide a judicial controversy, but to assume a position of authority over the governmental acts of another and co-equal department, an authority which plainly we do not possess." 262 U.S. at 489, 43 S.Ct. at 601. Yet the concrete reasons given for denying standing to a federal taxpayer suggest that the Court's holding rests on something less than a constitutional foundation. For example, the Court conceded that standing had previously been conferred on municipal taxpayers to sue in that capacity. However, the Court viewed the interest of a federal taxpayer in total federal tax revenues as "comparatively minute and indeterminable" when measured against a municipal taxpayer's interest in a smaller city treasury. *Id.* at 486–487, 43 S.Ct. at 579–601. This suggests that the petitioner in *Frothingham* was denied standing not because she was a taxpayer but because her tax bill was not large enough. In addition, the Court spoke of the "attendant inconveniences" of entertaining that taxpayer's suit because it might open the door of federal courts to countless such suits "in respect of every other appropriation act and statute whose administration requires the outlay of public money, and whose validity may be questioned." *Id.* at 487, 43 S.Ct. at 601. Such a statement suggests pure policy considerations.

To the extent that *Frothingham* has been viewed as resting on policy considerations, it has been criticized as depending on assumptions not consistent with modern conditions. For example, some commentators have pointed out that a number of corporate taxpayers today have a federal tax liability running into hundreds of millions of dollars, and such taxpayers have a far greater monetary stake in the Federal Treasury than they do in any municipal treasury. To some degree, the fear expressed in *Frothingham* that allowing one taxpayer to sue would inundate the federal courts with countless similar suits has been mitigated by the ready availability of the devices of class actions and joinder under the Federal Rules of Civil Procedure, adopted subsequent to the decision in *Frothingham*. Whatever the merits of the current debate over *Frothingham*, its very existence suggests that we should undertake a fresh examination of the limitations upon standing to sue in a federal court and the application of those limitations to taxpayer suits.

III.

The jurisdiction of federal courts is defined and limited by Article III of the Constitution. In terms relevant to the question for decision in this case, the judicial power of federal courts is constitutionally restricted to "cases" and "controversies." As is so often the situation in constitutional adjudication, those two words have an iceberg quality, containing beneath their surface simplicity submerged complexities which go to the very heart of our constitutional form of government. Embodied in the words "cases" and "controversies" are two complementary but somewhat different limitations. In part those words limit the business of federal courts to questions presented in an adversary context and in a form historically viewed as capable of resolution through the judicial process. And in part those words define the role assigned to the judiciary in a tripartite allocation of power to assure that the federal courts will not intrude into areas committed to the other branches of government. Justiciability is the term of art employed to give expression to this dual limitation placed upon federal courts by the case-and-controversy doctrine.

Justiciability is itself a concept of uncertain meaning and scope. Its reach is illustrated by the various grounds upon which questions sought to be adjudicated in federal courts have been held not to be justiciable. Thus, no justiciable controversy is presented when the parties seek adjudication of only a political question, when the parties are asking for an advisory opinion, when the question sought to be adjudicated has been mooted by subsequent developments, and when there is no standing to maintain the action. Yet it remains true that "[j]usticiability is * * * not a legal concept with a fixed content or susceptible of scientific verification. Its utilization is the resultant of many subtle pressures * * *." *Poe v. Ullman,* 367 U.S. 497, 508, 81 S.Ct. 1752, 1759, 6 L.Ed.2d 989 (1961).

Part of the difficulty in giving precise meaning and form to the concept of justiciability stems from the uncertain historical antecedents of the case-and-controversy doctrine. For example, Mr. Justice Frankfurter twice suggested that historical meaning could be imparted to the concepts of justiciability and case and controversy by reference to the practices of the courts of Westminster when the Constitution was adopted. *Joint Anti–Fascist Refugee Committee v. McGrath,* 341 U.S. 123, 150, 71 S.Ct. 624, 95 L.Ed. 817 (1951) (concurring opinion); *Coleman v. Miller,* 307 U.S. 433, 460, 59 S.Ct. 972, 985, 83 L.Ed. 1385 (1939) (separate opinion). However, the power of English judges to deliver advisory opinions was well established at the time the Constitution was drafted. 3 K. Davis, *Administrative Law Treatise* 127–128 (1958). And it is quite clear that "the oldest and most consistent thread in the federal law of justiciability is that the federal courts will not give advisory opinions." C. Wright, *Federal Courts* 34 (1963). Thus, the implicit policies embodied in Article III, and not history alone, impose the rule against advisory opinions on federal courts. When the federal judicial power is invoked to pass upon the validity of actions by the Legislative and Executive Branches of the Government, the rule against advisory opinions implements the separation of powers prescribed by the Constitution and confines federal courts to the role assigned them by Article III. *See Muskrat v. United States,* 219 U.S. 346, 31 S.Ct. 250, 55 L.Ed. 246 (1911); 3 H. Johnston, *Correspondence and Public Papers of John*

Jay 486–489 (1891) (correspondence between Secretary of State Jefferson and Chief Justice Jay). However, the rule against advisory opinions also recognizes that such suits often "are not pressed before the Court with that clear concreteness provided when a question emerges precisely framed and necessary for decision from a clash of adversary argument exploring every aspect of a multifaced situation embracing conflicting and demanding interests." *United States v. Fruehauf,* 365 U.S. 146, 157, 81 S.Ct. 547, 554, 5 L.Ed.2d 476 (1961). Consequently, the Article III prohibition against advisory opinions reflects the complementary constitutional considerations expressed by the justiciability doctrine: Federal judicial power is limited to those disputes which confine federal courts to a rule consistent with a system of separated powers and which are traditionally thought to be capable of resolution through the judicial process.

Additional uncertainty exists in the doctrine of justiciability because that doctrine has become a blend of constitutional requirements and policy considerations. And a policy limitation is "not always clearly distinguished from the constitutional limitation." *Barrows v. Jackson,* 346 U.S. 249, 255, 73 S.Ct. 1031, 1034, 97 L.Ed. 1586 (1953). For example, in his concurring opinion in *Ashwander v. Tennessee Valley Authority,* 297 U.S. 288, 345–48, 56 S.Ct. 466, 482–83, 80 L.Ed. 688 (1936), Mr. Justice Brandeis listed seven rules developed by this Court "for its own governance" to avoid passing prematurely on constitutional questions. Because the rules operate in "cases confessedly within [the Court's] jurisdiction," *id.* at 346, 56 S.Ct. at 482, they find their source in policy, rather than purely constitutional, considerations. However, several of the cases cited by Mr. Justice Brandeis in illustrating the rules of self-governance articulated purely constitutional grounds for decision. The "many subtle pressures" which cause policy considerations to blend into the constitutional limitations of Article III make the justiciability doctrine one of uncertain and shifting contours.

It is in this context that the standing question presented by this case must be viewed and that the Government's argument on that question must be evaluated. As we understand it, the Government's position is that the constitutional scheme of separation of powers, and the deference owed by the federal judiciary to the other two branches of government within that scheme, present an absolute bar to taxpayer suits challenging the validity of federal spending programs. The Government views such suits as involving no more than the mere disagreement by the taxpayer "with the uses to which tax money is put." According to the Government, the resolution of such disagreements is committed to other branches of the Federal Government and not to the judiciary. Consequently, the Government contends that, under no circumstances, should standing be conferred on federal taxpayers to challenge a federal taxing or spending program.[17] An analysis of the function served by standing limitations compels a rejection of the Government's position.

---

17. The logic of the Government's argument would compel it to concede that a

Standing is an aspect of justiciability and, as such, the problem of standing is surrounded by the same complexities and vagaries that inhere in justiciability. Standing has been called one of "the most amorphous [concepts] in the entire domain of public law." Some of the complexities peculiar to standing problems result because standing "serves, on occasion, as a shorthand expression for all the various elements of justiciability." In addition, there are at work in the standing doctrine the many subtle pressures which tend to cause policy considerations to blend into constitutional limitations.

Despite the complexities and uncertainties, some meaningful form can be given to the jurisdictional limitations placed on federal court power by the concept of standing. The fundamental aspect of standing is that it focuses on the party seeking to get his complaint before a federal court and not on the issues he wishes to have adjudicated. The "gist of the question of standing" is whether the party seeking relief has "alleged such a personal stake in the outcome of the controversy as to assure that concrete adverseness which sharpens the presentation of issues upon which the court so largely depends for illumination of difficult constitutional questions." *Baker v. Carr,* 369 U.S. 186, 204, 82 S.Ct. 691, 703, 7 L.Ed.2d 663 (1962). In other words, when standing is placed in issue in a case, the question is whether the person whose standing is challenged is a proper party to request an adjudication of a particular issue and not whether the issue itself is justiciable. Thus, a party may have standing in a particular case, but the federal court may nevertheless decline to pass on the merits of the case because, for example, it presents a political question. A proper party is demanded so that federal courts will not be asked to decide "ill-defined controversies over constitutional issues," *United Public Workers of America v. Mitchell,* 330 U.S. 75, 90, 67 S.Ct. 556, 564, 91 L.Ed. 754 (1947), or a case which is of "a hypothetical or abstract character," *Aetna Life Insurance Co. of Hartford, Conn. v. Haworth,* 300 U.S. 227, 240, 57 S.Ct. 461, 463, 81 L.Ed. 617 (1937). So stated, the standing requirement is closely related to, although more general than, the rule that federal courts will not entertain friendly suits, *Chicago & Grand Trunk R. Co. v. Wellman, supra,* or those which are feigned or collusive in nature, *United States v. Johnson,* 319 U.S. 302, 63 S.Ct. 1075, 87 L.Ed. 1413 (1943); *Lord v. Veazie,* 8 How. 251, 12 L.Ed. 1067 (1850).

When the emphasis in the standing problem is placed on whether the person invoking a federal court's jurisdiction is a proper party to maintain the action, the weakness of the Government's argument in this

---

taxpayer would lack standing even if Congress engaged in such palpably unconstitutional conduct as providing funds for the construction of churches for particular sects. *See Flast v. Gardner,* D.C., 271 F.Supp. 1, 5 (1967) (dissenting opinion of Frankel, J.). The Government professes not to be bothered by such a result because it contends there might be individuals in society other than taxpayers who could invoke federal judicial power to challenge such unconstitutional appropriations. However, if as we conclude there are circumstances under which a taxpayer will be a proper and appropriate party to seek judicial review of federal statutes, the taxpayer's access to federal courts should not be barred because there might be at large in society a hypothetical plaintiff who might possibly bring such a suit.

case becomes apparent. The question whether a particular person is a proper party to maintain the action does not, by its own force, raise separation of powers problems related to improper judicial interference in areas committed to other branches of the Federal Government. Such problems arise, if at all, only from the substantive issues the individual seeks to have adjudicated. Thus, in terms of Article III limitations on federal court jurisdiction, the question of standing is related only to whether the dispute sought to be adjudicated will be presented in an adversary context and in a form historically viewed as capable of judicial resolution. It is for that reason that the emphasis in standing problems is on whether the party invoking federal court jurisdiction has "a personal stake in the outcome of the controversy," *Baker v. Carr, supra*, 369 U.S. at 204, 82 S.Ct. at 703, and whether the dispute touches upon "the legal relations of parties having adverse legal interests." *Aetna Life Insurance Co. v. Haworth, supra*, 300 U.S. at 240–241, 57 S.Ct. at 464. A taxpayer may or may not have the requisite personal stake in the outcome, depending upon the circumstances of the particular case. Therefore, we find no absolute bar in Article III to suits by federal taxpayers challenging allegedly unconstitutional federal taxing and spending programs. There remains, however, the problem of determining the circumstances under which a federal taxpayer will be deemed to have the personal stake and interest that impart the necessary concrete adverseness to such litigation so that standing can be conferred on the taxpayer *qua* taxpayer consistent with the constitutional limitations of Article III.

IV.

The various rules of standing applied by federal courts have not been developed in the abstract. Rather, they have been fashioned with specific reference to the status asserted by the party whose standing is challenged and to the type of question he wishes to have adjudicated. We have noted that, in deciding the question of standing, it is not relevant that the substantive issues in the litigation might be nonjusticiable. However, our decisions establish that, in ruling on standing, it is both appropriate and necessary to look to the substantive issues for another purpose, namely, to determine whether there is a logical nexus between the status asserted and the claim sought to be adjudicated. For example, standing requirements will vary in First Amendment religion cases depending upon whether the party raises an Establishment Clause claim or a claim under the Free Exercise Clause. *See McGowan v. State of Maryland,* 366 U.S. 420, 429–430, 81 S.Ct. 1101, 1106–1107, 6 L.Ed.2d 393 (1961). Such inquiries into the nexus between the status asserted by the litigant and the claim he presents are essential to assure that he is a proper and appropriate party to invoke federal judicial power. Thus, our point of reference in this case is the standing of individuals who assert only the status of federal taxpayers and who challenge the constitutionality of a federal spending program. Whether such individuals have standing to maintain that form of action turns on whether they can demonstrate the necessary stake as taxpayers in the outcome of the litigation to satisfy Article III requirements.

The nexus demanded of federal taxpayers has two aspects to it. First, the taxpayer must establish a logical link between that status and the type of legislative enactment attacked. Thus, a taxpayer will be a proper party to allege the unconstitutionality only of exercises of congressional power under the taxing and spending clause of Art. I, § 8, of the Constitution. It will not be sufficient to allege an incidental expenditure of tax funds in the administration of an essentially regulatory statute. This requirement is consistent with the limitation imposed upon state-taxpayer standing in federal courts in *Doremus v. Board of Education,* 342 U.S. 429, 72 S.Ct. 394, 96 L.Ed. 475 (1952). Secondly, the taxpayer must establish a nexus between that status and the precise nature of the constitutional infringement alleged. Under this requirement, the taxpayer must show that the challenged enactment exceeds specific constitutional limitations imposed upon the exercise of the congressional taxing and spending power and not simply that the enactment is generally beyond the powers delegated to Congress by Art. I, § 8. When both nexuses are established, the litigant will have shown a taxpayer's stake in the outcome of the controversy and will be a proper and appropriate party to invoke a federal court's jurisdiction.

The taxpayer-appellants in this case have satisfied both nexuses to support their claim of standing under the test we announce today. Their constitutional challenge is made to an exercise by Congress of its power under Art. I, § 8, to spend for the general welfare, and the challenged program involves a substantial expenditure of federal tax funds. In addition, appellants have alleged that the challenged expenditures violate the Establishment and Free Exercise Clauses of the First Amendment. Our history vividly illustrates that one of the specific evils feared by those who drafted the Establishment Clause and fought for its adoption was that the taxing and spending power would be used to favor one religion over another or to support religion in general. James Madison, who is generally recognized as the leading architect of the religion clauses of the First Amendment, observed in his famous Memorial and Remonstrance Against Religious Assessments that "the same authority which can force a citizen to contribute three pence only of his property for the support of any one establishment, may force him to conform to any other establishment in all cases whatsoever." 2 Writings of James Madison 183, 186 (Hunt ed. 1901). The concern of Madison and his supporters was quite clearly that religious liberty ultimately would be the victim if government could employ its taxing and spending powers to aid one religion over another or to aid religion in general. The Establishment Clause was designed as a specific bulwark against such potential abuses of governmental power, and that clause of the First Amendment[25] operates as a specific constitutional limitation upon the

25. Appellants have also alleged that the Elementary and Secondary Education Act of 1965 violates the Free Exercise Clause of the First Amendment. This Court

exercise by Congress of the taxing and spending power conferred by Art. I, § 8.

The allegations of the taxpayer in *Frothingham v. Mellon, supra,* were quite different from those made in this case, and the result in *Frothingham* is consistent with the test of taxpayer standing announced today. The taxpayer in *Frothingham* attacked a federal spending program and she, therefore, established the first nexus required. However, she lacked standing because her constitutional attack was not based on an allegation that Congress, in enacting the Maternity Act of 1921, had breached a specific limitation upon its taxing and spending power. The taxpayer in *Frothingham* alleged essentially that Congress, by enacting the challenged statute, had exceeded the general powers delegated to it by Art. I, § 8, and that Congress had thereby invaded the legislative province reserved to the States by the Tenth Amendment. To be sure, Mrs. Frothingham made the additional allegation that her tax liability would be increased as a result of the allegedly unconstitutional enactment, and she framed that allegation in terms of a deprivation of property without due process of law. However, the Due Process Clause of the Fifth Amendment does not protect taxpayers against increases in tax liability, and the taxpayer in *Frothingham* failed to make any additional claim that the harm she alleged resulted from a breach by Congress of the specific constitutional limitations imposed upon an exercise of the taxing and spending power. In essence, Mrs. Frothingham was attempting to assert the States' interest in their legislative prerogatives and not a federal taxpayer's interest in being free of taxing and spending in contravention of specific constitutional limitations imposed upon Congress' taxing and spending power.

We have noted that the Establishment Clause of the First Amendment does specifically limit the taxing and spending power conferred by Art. I, § 8. Whether the Constitution contains other specific limitations can be determined only in the context of future cases. However, whenever such specific limitations are found, we believe a taxpayer will have a clear stake as a taxpayer in assuring that they are not breached by Congress. Consequently, we hold that a taxpayer will have standing consistent with Article III to invoke federal judicial power when he alleges that congressional action under the taxing and spending clause is in derogation of those constitutional provisions which operate to restrict the exercise of the taxing and spending power. The taxpayer's allegation in such cases would be that his tax money is being extracted and spent in violation of specific constitutional protections against such abuses of

has recognized that the taxing power can be used to infringe the free exercise of religion. *Murdock v. Commonwealth of Pennsylvania,* 319 U.S. 105, 63 S.Ct. 870, 87 L.Ed. 1292 (1943). Since we hold that appellants' Establishment Clause claim is sufficient to establish the nexus between their status and the precise nature of the constitutional infringement alleged, we need not decide whether the Free Exercise claim, standing alone, would be adequate to confer standing in this case. We do note, however, that the challenged tax in *Murdock* operated upon a particular class of taxpayers. When such exercises of the taxing power are challenged, the proper party emphasis in the federal standing doctrine would require that standing be limited to the taxpayers within the affected class.

legislative power. Such an injury is appropriate for judicial redress, and the taxpayer has established the necessary nexus between his status and the nature of the allegedly unconstitutional action to support his claim of standing to secure judicial review. Under such circumstances, we feel confident that the questions will be framed with the necessary specificity, that the issues will be contested with the necessary adverseness and that the litigation will be pursued with the necessary vigor to assure that the constitutional challenge will be made in a form traditionally thought to be capable of judicial resolution. We lack that confidence in cases such as *Frothingham* where a taxpayer seeks to employ a federal court as a forum in which to air his generalized grievances about the conduct of government or the allocation of power in the Federal System.

While we express no view at all on the merits of appellants' claims in this case, their complaint contains sufficient allegations under the criteria we have outlined to give them standing to invoke a federal court's jurisdiction for an adjudication on the merits.

Reversed.

JUSTICE DOUGLAS, concurring.

While I have joined the opinion of the Court, I do not think that the test it lays down is a durable one. I think, therefore, that it will suffer erosion and in time result in the demise of *Frothingham v. Mellon*, 262 U.S. 447, 43 S.Ct. 597, 67 L.Ed. 1078. It would therefore be the part of wisdom, as I see the problem, to be rid of *Frothingham* here and now.

JUSTICE STEWART, concurring.

I join the judgment and opinion of the Court, which I understand to hold only that a federal taxpayer has standing to assert that a specific expenditure of federal funds violates the Establishment Clause of the First Amendment. Because that clause plainly prohibits taxing and spending in aid of religion, every taxpayer can claim a personal constitutional right not to be taxed for the support of a religious institution. The present case is thus readily distinguishable from *Frothingham v. Mellon*, 262 U.S. 447, 43 S.Ct. 597, 67 L.Ed. 1078, where the taxpayer did not rely on an explicit constitutional prohibition but instead questioned the scope of the powers delegated to the national legislature by Article I of the Constitution.

As the Court notes, "one of the specific evils feared by those who drafted the Establishment Clause and fought for its adoption was that the taxing and spending power would be used to favor one religion over another or to support religion in general." Today's decision no more than recognizes that the appellants have a clear stake as taxpayers in assuring that they not be compelled to contribute even "three pence * * * of [their] property for the support of any one establishment." *Ibid*. In concluding that the appellants therefore have standing to sue, we do not undermine the salutary principle, established by *Frothingham* and reaffirmed today, that a taxpayer may not "employ a federal court as a forum in which to air his generalized grievances about the conduct of government or the allocation of power in the Federal System.''

JUSTICE FORTAS, concurring.

I would confine the ruling in this case to the proposition that a taxpayer may maintain a suit to challenge the validity of a federal expenditure on the ground that the expenditure violates the Establishment Clause. As the Court's opinion recites, there is enough in the constitutional history of the Establishment Clause to support the thesis that this Clause includes a *specific* prohibition upon the use of the power to tax to support an establishment of religion. There is no reason to suggest, and no basis in the logic of this decision for implying, that there may be other types of congressional expenditures which may be attacked by a litigant solely on the basis of his status as a taxpayer.

I agree that *Frothingham* does not foreclose today's result. I agree that the congressional powers to tax and spend are limited by the prohibition upon Congress to enact laws ''respecting an establishment of religion.'' This thesis, slender as its basis is, provides a direct ''nexus,'' as the Court puts it, between the use and collection of taxes and the congressional action here. Because of this unique ''nexus,'' in my judgment, it is not far-fetched to recognize that a taxpayer has a special claim to status as a litigant in a case raising the ''establishment'' issue. This special claim is enough, I think, to permit us to allow the suit, coupled, as it is, with the interest which the taxpayer and all other citizens have in the church-state issue. In terms of the structure and basic philosophy of our constitutional government, it would be difficult to point to any issue that has a more intimate, pervasive, and fundamental impact upon the life of the taxpayer—and upon the life of all citizens.

Perhaps the vital interest of a citizen in the establishment issue, without reference to his taxpayer's status, would be acceptable as a basis for this challenge. We need not decide this. But certainly, I believe, we must recognize that our principle of judicial scrutiny of legislative acts which raise important constitutional questions requires that the issue here presented—the separation of state and church—which the Founding Fathers regarded as fundamental to our constitutional system— should be subjected to judicial testing. This is not a question which we, if we are to be faithful to our trust, should consign to limbo, unacknowledged, unresolved, and undecided.

On the other hand, the urgent necessities of this case and the precarious opening through which we find our way to confront it, do not demand that we open the door to a general assault upon exercises of the spending power. The status of taxpayer should not be accepted as a launching pad for an attack upon any target other than legislation affecting the Establishment Clause. See concurring opinion of Stewart, J.

[JUSTICE HARLAN's dissenting opinion is omitted.]

Notes and Questions

1. *Flast* would permit a taxpayer's suit to enjoin the expenditure of federal funds if the taxpayer "establish[ed] a logical link between the taxpayer status and the type of legislative enactment attacked." Thus the suit was proper if the plaintiff taxpayer alleged (1) the unconstitutionality of an exercise of congressional power under the taxing and spending clause, and (2) a nexus between the taxpayer's status and the violation of a specific constitutional limitation. The Court allowed the taxpayer suit upon the establishment of both nexuses. Examine *Frothingham* in light of this test. Clearly, *Frothingham* met the first prong; what about the second?

2. The Court drew from historical insights the fundamental proposition that "one of the specific evils feared by those who drafted the Establishment Clause and fought for its adoption was that the taxing and spending power would be used to favor one religion over another or to support religion in general." Was this proposition a sound reason to lower the standing barriers? If so, why should not any citizen, taxpayer or not, have standing to litigate the separation of church and state issues?

3. Justice Stewart, concurring, understood the majority opinion "to hold only that a federal taxpayer has standing to assert that a specific expenditure of federal funds violates the Establishment Clause of the First Amendment." But the opinion intimated that there may be other specific constitutional restrictions on the taxing and spending powers. Can you think of any?

4. The Court believed that the *Flast* plaintiff would present the legal issues in the proper framework for judicial resolution; it lacked that confidence in *Frothingham*. Why? Do you perceive any difference between the vigor with which *Sierra Club* and *SCRAP* would litigate? Consider Justice Harlan's statement in dissent (not reprinted) that in *Frothingham* the tax statute increased the plaintiff's tax liability (injury in fact) whereas the *Flast* complainant made no similar allegation. Why did Justice Harlan deem that difference of any consequence?

VALLEY FORGE CHRISTIAN COLLEGE v. AMERICANS UNITED FOR SEPARATION OF CHURCH AND STATE

Supreme Court of the United States, 1982.
454 U.S. 464, 102 S.Ct. 752, 70 L.Ed.2d 700.

Justice Rehnquist delivered the opinion of the Court.

I

Article IV, Section 3, Clause 2 of the Constitution vests Congress with the "Power to dispose of and make all needful Rules and Regulations respecting the * * * Property belonging to the United States." Shortly after the termination of hostilities in the Second World War, Congress enacted the Federal Property and Administrative Services Act of 1949, 63 Stat. 377, 40 U.S.C. § 471 *et seq.* (1976 ed. and Supp. III).

The Act was designed, in part, to provide "an economical and efficient system for * * * the disposal of surplus property." 63 Stat. 378, 40 U.S.C. § 471. In furtherance of this policy, federal agencies are directed to maintain adequate inventories of the property under their control and to identify excess property for transfer to other agencies able to use it. See 63 Stat. 384, 40 U.S.C. § 483(b), (c). Property that has outlived its usefulness to the federal government is declared "surplus" and may be transferred to private or other public entities. *See generally* 63 Stat. 385, as amended, 40 U.S.C. § 484.

The Act authorizes the Secretary of Health, Education, and Welfare (now the Secretary of Education) to assume responsibility for disposing of surplus real property "for school, classroom, or other educational use." 63 Stat. 387, as amended, 40 U.S.C. § 484(k)(1). Subject to the disapproval of the Administrator of General Services, the Secretary may sell or lease the property to nonprofit, tax exempt educational institutions for consideration that takes into account "any benefit which has accrued or may accrue to the United States" from the transferee's use of the property. 63 Stat. 387, 40 U.S.C. § 484(k)(1)(A), (C). By regulation, the Secretary has provided for the computation of a "public benefit allowance," which discounts the transfer price of the property "on the basis of benefits to the United States from the use of such property for educational purposes." 34 CFR § 12.9(a) (1980).

The property which spawned this litigation was acquired by the Department of the Army in 1942, as part of a larger tract of approximately 181 acres of land northwest of Philadelphia. The Army built on that land the Valley Forge General Hospital, and for 30 years thereafter, that hospital provided medical care for members of the Armed Forces. In April 1973, as part of a plan to reduce the number of military installations in the United States, the Secretary of Defense proposed to close the hospital, and the General Services Administration declared it to be "surplus property."

The Department of Health, Education, and Welfare (HEW) eventually assumed responsibility for disposing of portions of the property, and in August 1976, it conveyed a 77–acre tract to petitioner, the Valley Forge Christian College. The appraised value of the property at the time of conveyance was $577,500. This appraised value was discounted, however, by the Secretary's computation of a 100% public benefit allowance, which permitted petitioner to acquire the property without making any financial payment for it. The deed from HEW conveyed the land in fee simple with certain conditions subsequent, which required petitioner to use the property for 30 years solely for the educational purposes described in petitioner's application. In that description, petitioner stated its intention to conduct "a program of education * * * meeting the accrediting standards of the State of Pennsylvania, The American Association of Bible Colleges, the Division of Education of the General Council of the Assemblies of God and the Veterans Administration."

Petitioner is a nonprofit educational institution operating under the supervision of a religious order known as the Assemblies of God. By its own description, petitioner's purpose is "to offer systematic training on the collegiate level to men and women for Christian service as either ministers or laymen." App. 34. Its degree programs reflect this orientation by providing courses of study "to train leaders for church related ministries." *Id.* at 102. Faculty members must "have been baptized in the Holy Spirit and be living consistent Christian lives," *id.* at 37, and all members of the college administration must be affiliated with the Assemblies of God, *id.* at 36. In its application for the 77–acre tract, petitioner represented that, if it obtained the property, it would make "additions to its offerings in the arts and humanities," and would strengthen its "psychology" and "counselling" courses to provide services in inner city areas.

In September 1976, respondents Americans United for Separation of Church and State, Inc. (Americans United), and four of its employees, learned of the conveyance through a news release. Two months later, they brought suit in the United States District Court for the Eastern District of Pennsylvania to challenge the conveyance on the ground that it violated the Establishment Clause of the First Amendment.[8] See App. 10. In its amended complaint, Americans United described itself as a nonprofit organization composed of 90,000 "taxpayer members." The complaint asserted that each member "would be deprived of the fair and constitutional use of his (her) tax dollar for constitutional purposes in violation of his (her) rights under the First Amendment of the United States Constitution." *Ibid.* Respondents sought a declaration that the conveyance was null and void, and an order compelling petitioner to transfer the property back to the United States. *Id.* at 11.

On petitioner's motion, the District Court granted summary judgment and dismissed the complaint. App. to Pet. for Cert. A42. The court found that respondents lacked standing to sue as taxpayers under *Flast v. Cohen,* 392 U.S. 83, 88 S.Ct. 1942, 20 L.Ed.2d 947 (1968), and had "failed to allege that they have suffered any actual or concrete injury beyond a generalized grievance common to all taxpayers." App. to Pet. for Cert. A43.

Respondents appealed to the Court of Appeals for the Third Circuit, which reversed the judgment of the District Court by a divided vote. 619 F.2d 252 (1980). All members of the court agreed that respondents lacked standing as taxpayers to challenge the conveyance under *Flast v. Cohen,* since that case extended standing to taxpayers *qua* taxpayers only to challenge congressional exercises of the power to tax and spend conferred by Art. I, § 8, of the Constitution, and this conveyance was authorized by legislation enacted under the authority of the Property Clause, Art. IV, § 3, cl. 2. Notwithstanding this significant factual difference from *Flast,* the majority of the Court of Appeals found that respondents also had standing merely as "citizens," claiming " 'injury in

---

8. "Congress shall make no law respecting an establishment of religion. * * * "

fact' to their shared individuated right to a government that 'shall make no law respecting the establishment of religion.' '' 619 F.2d at 261. In the majority's view, this "citizen standing" was sufficient to satisfy the "case or controversy" requirement of Art. III. One judge, perhaps sensing the doctrinal difficulties with the majority's extension of standing, wrote separately, expressing his view that standing was necessary to satisfy "the need for an available plaintiff," without whom "the Establishment Clause would be rendered virtually unenforceable" by the Judiciary. *Id.* at 267, 268. The dissenting judge expressed the view that respondents' allegations constituted a "generalized grievance * * * too abstract to satisfy the injury in fact component of standing." *Id.* at 269. He therefore concluded that their standing to contest the transfer was barred by this Court's decisions in *Schlesinger v. Reservists Committee to Stop the War,* 418 U.S. 208, 94 S.Ct. 2925, 41 L.Ed.2d 706 (1974), and *United States v. Richardson,* 418 U.S. 166, 94 S.Ct. 2940, 41 L.Ed.2d 678 (1974). 619 F.2d at 270–71.

Because of the unusually broad and novel view of standing to litigate a substantive question in the federal courts adopted by the Court of Appeals, we granted certiorari, 450 U.S. 909, 101 S.Ct. 1345, 67 L.Ed.2d 332 (1981), and we now reverse.

II

Article III of the Constitution limits the "judicial power" of the United States to the resolution of "cases" and "controversies." The constitutional power of federal courts cannot be defined, and indeed has no substance, without reference to the necessity "to adjudge the legal rights of litigants in actual controversies." *Liverpool Steamship Co. v. Commissioners of Emigration,* 113 U.S. 33, 39, 5 S.Ct. 352, 355, 28 L.Ed. 899 (1885). The requirements of Art. III are not satisfied merely because a party requests a court of the United States to declare its legal rights, and has couched that request for forms of relief historically associated with courts of law in terms that have a familiar ring to those trained in the legal process. The judicial power of the United States defined by Art. III is not an unconditioned authority to determine the constitutionality of legislative or executive acts. The power to declare the rights of individuals and to measure the authority of governments, this Court said 90 years ago, "is legitimate only in the last resort, and as a necessity in the determination of real, earnest and vital controversy." *Chicago & Grand Trunk R. Co. v. Wellman,* 143 U.S. 339, 345, 12 S.Ct. 400, 402, 36 L.Ed. 176 (1892). Otherwise, the power "is not judicial * * * in the sense in which judicial power is granted by the Constitution to the courts of the United States." *United States v. Ferreira,* 13 How. 40, 48, 14 L.Ed. 42 (1852).

As an incident to the elaboration of this bedrock requirement, this Court has always required that a litigant have "standing" to challenge the action sought to be adjudicated in the lawsuit. The term "standing" subsumes a blend of constitutional requirements and prudential considerations, *see Warth v. Seldin,* 422 U.S. 490, 498, 95 S.Ct. 2197, 2204, 45

L.Ed.2d 343 (1975), and it has not always been clear in the opinions of this Court whether particular features of the "standing" requirement have been required by Art. III *ex proprio vigore,* or whether they are requirements that the Court itself has erected and which were not compelled by the language of the Constitution. *See Flast v. Cohen,* 392 U.S. at 97, 88 S.Ct. at 1951.

A recent line of decisions, however, has resolved that ambiguity, at least to the following extent: at an irreducible minimum, Art. III requires the party who invokes the court's authority to "show that he personally has suffered some actual or threatened injury as a result of the putatively illegal conduct of the defendant," *Gladstone, Realtors v. Village of Bellwood,* 441 U.S. 91, 99, 99 S.Ct. 1601, 1608, 60 L.Ed.2d 66 (1979), and that the injury "fairly can be traced to the challenged action" and "is likely to be redressed by a favorable decision," *Simon v. Eastern Kentucky Welfare Rights Org.,* 426 U.S. 26, 38, 41, 96 S.Ct. 1917, 1924, 1925, 48 L.Ed.2d 450 (1976). In this manner does Art. III limit the federal judicial power "to those disputes which confine federal courts to a role consistent with a system of separated powers and which are traditionally thought to be capable of resolution through the judicial process." *Flast v. Cohen,* 392 U.S. at 97, 88 S.Ct. at 1951.

The requirement of "actual injury redressable by the court," *Simon,* 426 U.S. at 39, 96 S.Ct. at 1924, serves several of the "implicit policies embodied in Article III," *Flast,* 392 U.S. at 96, 88 S.Ct. at 1950. It tends to assure that the legal questions presented to the court will be resolved, not in the rarified atmosphere of a debating society, but in a concrete factual context conducive to a realistic appreciation of the consequences of judicial action. The "standing" requirement serves other purposes. Because it assures an actual factual setting in which the litigant asserts a claim of injury in fact, a court may decide the case with some confidence that its decision will not pave the way for lawsuits which have some, but not all, of the facts of the case actually decided by the court.

The Art. III aspect of standing also reflects a due regard for the autonomy of those persons likely to be most directly affected by a judicial order. The federal courts have abjured appeals to their authority which would convert the judicial process into "no more than a vehicle for the vindication of the value interests of concerned bystanders." *United States v. SCRAP,* 412 U.S. 669, 687, 93 S.Ct. 2405, 2416, 37 L.Ed.2d 254 (1973). Were the federal courts merely publicly funded forums for the ventilation of public grievances or the refinement of jurisprudential understanding, the concept of "standing" would be quite unnecessary. But the "cases and controversies" language of Art. III forecloses the conversion of courts of the United States into judicial versions of college debating forums. As we said in *Sierra Club v. Morton,* 405 U.S. 727, 740, 92 S.Ct. 1361, 1368, 31 L.Ed.2d 636 (1972):

> The requirement that a party seeking review must allege facts showing that he is himself adversely affected * * * does serve as at least a rough attempt to put the decision as to whether review will

be sought in the hands of those who have a direct stake in the outcome.

The exercise of judicial power, which can so profoundly affect the lives, liberty, and property of those to whom it extends, is therefore restricted to litigants who can show "injury in fact" resulting from the action which they seek to have the Court adjudicate.

The exercise of the judicial power also affects relationships between the coequal arms of the national government. The effect is, of course, most vivid when a federal court declares unconstitutional an act of the Legislative or Executive branch. While the exercise of that "ultimate and supreme function," *Chicago & Grand Trunk R. Co. v. Wellman,* 143 U.S. at 345, 12 S.Ct. at 402, is a formidable means of vindicating individual rights, when employed unwisely or unnecessarily it is also the ultimate threat to the continued effectiveness of the federal courts in performing that role. While the propriety of such action by a federal court has been recognized since *Marbury v. Madison,* 1 Cranch 137, 2 L.Ed. 60 (1803), it has been recognized as a tool of last resort on the part of the federal judiciary throughout its nearly 200 years of existence:

> [R]epeated and essentially head-on confrontations between the life-tenured branch and the representative branches of government will not, in the long run, be beneficial to either. The public confidence essential to the former and the vitality critical to the latter may well erode if we do not exercise self-restraint in the utilization of our power to negative the actions of the other branches. *United States v. Richardson,* 418 U.S. at 188, 94 S.Ct. at 2952 (Powell, J., concurring).

Proper regard for the complex nature of our constitutional structure requires neither that the judicial branch shrink from a confrontation with the other two coequal branches of the federal government, nor that it hospitably accept for adjudication claims of constitutional violation by other branches of government where the claimant has not suffered cognizable injury. Thus this Court has "refrain[ed] from passing upon the constitutionality of an act [of the representative branches] unless obliged to do so in the proper performance of our judicial function, when the question is raised by a party whose interests entitle him to raise it." *Blair v. United States,* 250 U.S. 273, 279, 39 S.Ct. 468, 470, 63 L.Ed. 979 (1919). The importance of this precondition should not be underestimated as a means of "defin[ing] the role assigned to the judiciary in a tripartite allocation of power." *Flast v. Cohen,* 392 U.S. at 95, 88 S.Ct. at 1950.

Beyond the constitutional requirements, the federal judiciary has also adhered to a set of prudential principles that bear on the question of standing. Thus, this Court has held that "the plaintiff generally must assert his own legal rights and interests, and cannot rest his claim to relief on the legal rights or interests of third parties." *Warth v. Seldin,* 422 U.S. at 499, 95 S.Ct. at 2205. In addition, even when the plaintiff has alleged redressable injury sufficient to meet the requirements of Art.

III, the Court has refrained from adjudicating "abstract questions of wide public significance" which amount to "generalized grievances," pervasively shared and most appropriately addressed in the representative branches. *Id.* at 499–500, 95 S.Ct. at 2205–2206. Finally the Court has required that the plaintiff's complaint fall within "the zone of interests to be protected or regulated by the statute or constitutional guarantee in question." *Data Processing Service v. Camp,* 397 U.S. 150, 153, 90 S.Ct. 827, 830, 25 L.Ed.2d 184 (1969).

Merely to articulate these principles is to demonstrate their close relationship to the policies reflected in the Art. III requirement of actual or threatened injury amenable to judicial remedy. But neither the counsels of prudence nor the policies implicit in the "case or controversy" requirement should be mistaken for the rigorous Art. III requirements themselves. Satisfaction of the former cannot substitute for a demonstration of " 'distinct and palpable injury' * * * that is likely to be redressed if the requested relief is granted." *Gladstone, Realtors v. Village of Bellwood,* 441 U.S. at 100, 99 S.Ct. at 1608 (quoting *Warth v. Seldin,* 422 U.S. at 501, 95 S.Ct. at 2206). That requirement states a limitation on judicial power, not merely a factor to be balanced in the weighing of so-called "prudential" considerations.

We need not mince words when we say that the concept of "Art. III standing" has not been defined with complete consistency in all of the various cases decided by this Court which have discussed it, nor when we say that this very fact is probably proof that the concept cannot be reduced to a one-sentence or one-paragraph definition. But of one thing we may be sure: Those who do not possess Art. III standing may not litigate as suitors in the courts of the United States.[13] Art. III, which is every bit as important in its circumscription of the judicial power of the United States as in its granting of that power, is not merely a troublesome hurdle to be overcome if possible so as to reach the "merits" of a lawsuit which a party desires to have adjudicated; it is a part of the basic charter promulgated by the framers of the constitution at Philadelphia in 1787, a charter which created a general government, provided for the interaction between that government and the governments of the several States, and was later amended so as to either enhance or limit its authority with respect to both States and individuals.

13. The dissent takes us to task for "tend[ing] merely to obfuscate, rather than inform, our understanding of the meaning of rights under the law." Were this Court constituted to operate a national classroom on "the meaning of rights" for the benefit of interested litigants, this criticism would carry weight. The teaching of Art. III, however, is that constitutional adjudication is available only on terms prescribed by the Constitution, among which is the requirement of a plaintiff with standing to sue. The dissent asserts that this requirement "overrides no other provision of the Consti- tution," but just as surely the Art. III power of the federal courts does not wax and wane in harmony with a litigant's desire for a "hospitable forum". Art. III obligates a federal court to act only when it is assured of the power to do so, that is, when it is called upon to resolve an actual case or controversy. Then, and only then, may it turn its attention to other constitutional provisions and presume to provide a forum for the adjudication of rights. *See Ashwander v. Tennessee Valley Authority,* 297 U.S. 288, 345, 56 S.Ct. 466, 482, 80 L.Ed. 688 (1936) (Brandeis, J., concurring).

III

The injury alleged by respondents in their amended complaint is the "depriv[ation] of the fair and constitutional use of [their] tax dollar." J.A. 10.[14] As a result, our discussion must begin with *Frothingham v. Mellon,* 262 U.S. 447, 43 S.Ct. 597, 67 L.Ed. 1078 (1923). In that action a taxpayer brought suit challenging the constitutionality of the Maternity Act of 1921, which provided federal funding to the States for the purpose of improving maternal and infant health. The injury she alleged consisted of the burden of taxation in support of an unconstitutional regime, which she characterized as a deprivation of property without due process. "Looking through forms of words to the substance of [the] complaint," the Court concluded that the only "injury" was the fact "that officials of the executive branch of the government are executing and will execute an act of Congress asserted to be unconstitutional." *Id.* at 488, 43 S.Ct. at 601. Any tangible effect of the challenged statute on the plaintiff's tax burden was "remote, fluctuating, and uncertain." *Id.* at 487, 43 S.Ct. at 601. In rejecting this as a cognizable injury sufficient to establish standing, the Court admonished:

> The party who invokes the power [of judicial review] must be able to show not only that the statute is invalid but that he has sustained or is immediately in danger of sustaining some direct injury as the result of its enforcement, and not merely that he suffers in some indefinite way in common with people generally. * * * Here the parties plaintiff have no such case. *Id.* at 488, 43 S.Ct. at 601.

* * *

The Court again visited the problem of taxpayer standing in *Flast v. Cohen,* 392 U.S. 83, 88 S.Ct. 1942, 20 L.Ed.2d 947 (1968). The taxpayer plaintiffs in *Flast* sought to enjoin the expenditure of federal funds under the Elementary and Secondary Education Act of 1965, which they alleged were being used to support religious schools in violation of the Establishment Clause. The Court developed a two-part test to determine whether the plaintiffs had standing to sue. First, because a taxpayer alleges injury only by virtue of his liability for taxes, the Court held that "a taxpayer will be a proper party to allege the unconstitutionality only of exercises of congressional power under the taxing and spending clause of Art. I, § 8, of the Constitution." *Id.* at 102, 88 S.Ct. at 1954. Second, the Court required the taxpayer to "show that the challenged enactment exceeds specific constitutional limitations upon the exercise of the taxing and spending power and not simply that the enactment is generally

---

14. Respondent Americans United has alleged no injury to itself as an organization, distinct from injury to its taxpayer members. As a result, its claim to standing can be no different from those of the members it seeks to represent. The question is whether "its members, or any one of them, are suffering immediate or threatened injury as a result of the challenged action of the sort that would make out a justiciable case had the members themselves brought suit." *Warth v. Seldin,* 422 U.S. at 511, 95 S.Ct. at 2211. *See Simon v. Eastern Kentucky Welfare Rights Org., supra,* 426 U.S. at 40, 96 S.Ct. at 1925; *Sierra Club v. Morton,* 405 U.S. 727, 739–741, 92 S.Ct. 1361, 1368–69, 31 L.Ed.2d 636 (1972).

beyond the powers delegated to Congress by Art. I, § 8." *Id.* at 102–103, 88 S.Ct. at 1954.

The plaintiffs in *Flast* satisfied this test because "[t]heir constitutional challenge [was] made to an exercise by Congress of its power under Art. I, § 8, to spend for the general welfare," *id.* at 103, 88 S.Ct. at 1954, and because the Establishment Clause, on which plaintiffs' complaint rested, "operates as a specific constitutional limitation upon the exercise by Congress of the taxing and spending power conferred by Art. I, § 8," *id.* at 104, 88 S.Ct. at 1954. The Court distinguished *Frothingham v. Mellon,* on the ground that Mrs. Frothingham had relied, not on a specific limitation on the power to tax and spend, but on a more general claim based on the Due Process Clause. *Id.* at 105, 88 S.Ct. at 1955. Thus, the Court reaffirmed that the "case or controversy" aspect of standing is unsatisfied "where a taxpayer seeks to employ a federal court as a forum in which to air his generalized grievances about the conduct of government or the allocation of power in the Federal System." *Id.* at 106, 88 S.Ct. at 1956.

Unlike the plaintiffs in *Flast,* respondents fail the first prong of the test for taxpayer standing. Their claim is deficient in two respects. First, the source of their complaint is not a congressional action, but a decision by HEW to transfer a parcel of federal property. *Flast* limited taxpayer standing to challenges directed "only [at] exercises of congressional power." *Id.* at 102, 88 S.Ct. at 1954. *See Schlesinger v. Reservists Committee to Stop the War,* 418 U.S. 208, 228, 94 S.Ct. 2925, 2935, 41 L.Ed.2d 706 (1974) (denying standing because the taxpayer plaintiffs "did not challenge an enactment under Art. I, § 8, but rather the action of the Executive Branch").

Second, and perhaps redundantly, the property transfer about which respondents complain was not an exercise of authority conferred by the taxing and spending clause of Art. I, § 8. The authorizing legislation, the Federal Property and Administrative Services Act of 1949, was an evident exercise of Congress' power under the Property Clause, Art. IV, § 3, cl. 2. Respondents do not dispute this conclusion, *see* Brief for Respondents 10, and it is decisive of any claim of taxpayer standing under the *Flast* precedent.

Any doubt that once might have existed concerning the rigor with which the *Flast* exception to the *Frothingham* principle ought to be applied should have been erased by this Court's recent decisions in *United States v. Richardson,* 418 U.S. 166, 94 S.Ct. 2940, 41 L.Ed.2d 678 (1974), and *Schlesinger v. Reservists Committee to Stop the War,* 418 U.S. 208, 94 S.Ct. 2925, 41 L.Ed.2d 706 (1974). In *Richardson,* the question was whether the plaintiff had standing as a federal taxpayer to argue that legislation which permitted the Central Intelligence Agency to withhold from the public detailed information about its expenditures violated the Accounts Clause of the Constitution.[18] We rejected plaintiff's

18. U.S. Const., Art. I, § 9, cl. 7 ("[A]nd a regular Statement and Account of the

claim of standing because "his challenge [was] not addressed to the taxing or spending power, but to the statutes regulating the CIA." 418 U.S. at 175, 94 S.Ct. at 2945. The "mere recital" of those claims "demonstrate[d] how far he [fell] short of the standing criteria of *Flast* and how neatly he [fell] within the *Frothingham* holding left undisturbed." *Id.* at 174–175, 94 S.Ct. at 2945.

* * *

Respondents, therefore, are plainly without standing to sue as taxpayers. The Court of Appeals apparently reached the same conclusion. It remains to be seen whether respondents have alleged any other basis for standing to bring this suit.

IV

Although the Court of Appeals properly doubted respondents' ability to establish standing solely on the basis of their taxpayer status, it considered their allegations of taxpayer injury to be "essentially an assumed role." 619 F.2d at 261.

> Plaintiffs have no reason to expect, nor perhaps do they care about, any personal tax saving that might result should they prevail. The crux of the interest at stake, the plaintiffs argue, is found in the Establishment Clause, not in the supposed loss of money as such. As a matter of primary identity, therefore, the plaintiffs are not so much taxpayers as separationists * * *. *Ibid.*

In the court's view, respondents had established standing by virtue of an " 'injury in fact' to their shared individuated right to a government that 'shall make no law respecting the establishment of religion.' " *Ibid.* The court distinguished this "injury" from "the question of 'citizen standing' as such." *Id.* at 262. Although citizens generally could not establish standing simply by claiming an interest in governmental observance of the Constitution, respondents had "set forth instead a particular and concrete injury" to a "personal constitutional right." *Id.* at 265.

The Court of Appeals was surely correct in recognizing that the Art. III requirements of standing are not satisfied by "the abstract injury in nonobservance of the Constitution asserted by * * * citizens." *Schlesinger v. Reservists Committee to Stop the War,* 418 U.S. at 223, n. 13, 94 S.Ct. at 2933, n. 13. This Court repeatedly has rejected claims of standing predicated on " 'the right, possessed by every citizen, to require that the Government be administered according to law * * *.' *Fairchild v. Hughes,* 258 U.S. 126, 129 [42 S.Ct. 274, 275, 66 L.Ed. 499] [1922]." *Baker v. Carr,* 369 U.S. 186, 208, 82 S.Ct. 691, 705, 7 L.Ed.2d 663 (1962). *See Schlesinger v. Reservists Committee to Stop the War,* 418 U.S. at 216–222, 94 S.Ct. at 2929–2932; *Laird v. Tatum,* 408 U.S. 1, 92 S.Ct. 2318, 33 L.Ed.2d 154 (1972); *Ex parte Levitt,* 302 U.S. 633, 58 S.Ct. 1, 82

Receipts and Expenditures of all public Money shall be published from time to time").

L.Ed. 493 (1937). Such claims amount to little more than attempts "to employ a federal court as a forum in which to air * * * generalized grievances about the conduct of government." *Flast v. Cohen*, 392 U.S. at 106, 88 S.Ct. at 1956.

In finding that respondents had alleged something more than "the generalized interest of all citizens in constitutional governance," *Schlesinger*, 418 U.S. at 217, 94 S.Ct. at 2930, the Court of Appeals relied on factual differences which we do not think amount to legal distinctions. The court decided that respondents' claim differed from those in *Schlesinger* and *Richardson*, which were predicated, respectively, on the Incompatibility and Accounts Clauses, because "it is at the very least arguable that the Establishment Clause creates in each citizen a 'personal constitutional right' to a government that does not establish religion." 619 F.2d at 265 (footnote omitted). The court found it unnecessary to determine whether this "arguable" proposition was correct, since it judged the mere allegation of a legal right sufficient to confer standing.

This reasoning process merely disguises, we think with a rather thin veil, the inconsistency of the court's results with our decisions in *Schlesinger* and *Richardson*. The plaintiffs in those cases plainly asserted a "personal right" to have the government act in accordance with their views of the Constitution; indeed, we see no barrier to the *assertion* of such claims with respect to any constitutional provision. But assertion of a right to a particular kind of government conduct, which the government has violated by acting differently, cannot alone satisfy the requirements of Art. III without draining those requirements of meaning.

Nor can *Schlesinger* and *Richardson* be distinguished on the ground that the Incompatibility and Accounts Clauses are in some way less "fundamental" than the Establishment Clause. Each establishes a norm of conduct which the federal government is bound to honor—to no greater or lesser extent than any other inscribed in the Constitution. To the extent the Court of Appeals relied on a view of standing under which the Art. III burdens diminish as the "importance" of the claim on the merits increases, we reject that notion. The requirement of standing "focuses on the party seeking to get his complaint before a federal court and not on the issues he wishes to have adjudicated." *Flast v. Cohen*, 392 U.S. at 99, 88 S.Ct. at 1952. Moreover, we know of no principled basis on which to create a hierarchy of constitutional values or a complementary "sliding scale" of standing which might permit respondents to invoke the judicial power of the United States.[20] "The proposition that all

20. The dissent is premised on a revisionist reading of our precedents which leads to the conclusion that the Art. III requirement of standing is satisfied by any taxpayer who contends "that the federal government has exceeded the bounds of the law in allocating its largesse." "The concept of taxpayer injury necessarily recognizes the continuing stake of the taxpayer in the disposition of the Treasury to which he has contributed his taxes, and his right to have those funds put to lawful uses." On this novel understanding, the dissent reads cases such as *Frothingham* and *Flast* as decisions on the merits of the taxpayers' claims. *Frothingham* is explained as a hold-

constitutional provisions are enforceable by any citizen simply because citizens are the ultimate beneficiaries of those provisions has no boundaries." *Schlesinger v. Reservists Committee to Stop the War,* 418 U.S. at 227, 94 S.Ct. at 2935.

The complaint in this case shares a common deficiency with those in *Schlesinger* and *Richardson.* Although they claim that the Constitution has been violated, they claim nothing else. They fail to identify any personal injury suffered by the plaintiffs *as a consequence* of the alleged constitutional error, other than the psychological consequence presumably produced by observation of conduct with which one disagrees. That is not an injury sufficient to confer standing under Art. III, even though the disagreement is phrased in constitutional terms. It is evident that respondents are firmly committed to the constitutional principle of separation of church and State, but standing is not measured by the intensity of the litigant's interest or the fervor of his advocacy. "[T]hat concrete adverseness which sharpens the presentation of issues," *Baker v. Carr,* 369 U.S. at 204, 82 S.Ct. at 703, is the anticipated consequence of proceedings commenced by one who has been injured in fact; it is not a permissible substitute for the showing of injury itself.

In reaching this conclusion, we do not retreat from our earlier holdings that standing may be predicated on noneconomic injury. *See, e.g., United States v. SCRAP,* 412 U.S. at 686–88, 93 S.Ct. at 2415–2416; *Data Processing Service v. Camp,* 397 U.S. at 153–154, 90 S.Ct. at 829–30. We simply cannot see that respondents have alleged an *injury of any* kind, economic or otherwise, sufficient to confer standing. Respondents

ing that a taxpayer ordinarily has no legal right to challenge congressional expenditures. The dissent divines from *Flast* the holding that a taxpayer *does* have an enforceable right "to challenge a federal bestowal of largesse" for religious purposes. This right extends to "the Government as a whole, regardless of which branch is at work in a particular instance," and regardless of whether the challenged action was an exercise of the spending power.

However appealing this reconstruction of precedent may be, it bears little resemblance to the cases on which it purports to rest. *Frothingham* and *Flast* were decisions that plainly turned on *standing,* and just as plainly they rejected any notion that the Art. III requirement of direct injury is satisfied by a taxpayer who contends "that the federal government has exceeded the bounds of the law in allocating its largesse." Moreover, although the dissent's view may lead to a result satisfying to many in this case, it is not evident how its substitution of "legal interest," for "standing" enhances "our understanding of the meaning of rights under law." Logically, the dissent must shoulder the burden of explaining why taxpayers with standing have no "legal interest" in congressional expendi-

tures except when it is possible to allege a violation of the Establishment Clause: yet it does not attempt to do so.

Nor does the dissent's interpretation of standing adequately explain cases such as *Schlesinger* and *Richardson.* According to the dissent, the taxpayer plaintiffs in those cases lacked standing, not because they failed to challenge an exercise of the spending power, but because they did not complain of "the distribution of government largesse." And yet if the standing of a taxpayer is established by his "continuing stake * * * in the disposition of the Treasury to which he has contributed his taxes," it would seem to follow that he can assert a right to examine the budget of the CIA, as in *Richardson, see* 418 U.S. at 211, 94 S.Ct. at 2927, and a right to argue that members of Congress cannot claim reserve pay from the government, as in *Schlesinger, see* 418 U.S. at 211, 94 S.Ct. at 2927. Of course, both claims have been rejected, precisely because Art. III requires a demonstration of redressable injury that is not satisfied by a claim that tax monies have been spent unlawfully.

complain of a transfer of property located in Chester County, Pennsylvania. The named plaintiffs reside in Maryland and Virginia, their organizational headquarters are located in Washington, D.C. They learned of the transfer through a news release. Their claim that the government has violated the Establishment Clause does not provide a special license to roam the country in search of governmental wrongdoing and to reveal their discoveries in federal court. The federal courts were simply not constituted as ombudsmen of the general welfare.

V

The Court of Appeals in this case ignored unambiguous limitations on taxpayer and citizen standing. It appears to have done so out of the conviction that enforcement of the Establishment Clause demands special exceptions from the requirement that a plaintiff allege " 'distinct and palpable injury to himself,' * * * that is likely to be redressed if the requested relief is granted." *Gladstone, Realtors v. Village of Bellwood,* 441 U.S. at 100, 99 S.Ct. at 1608 (quoting *Warth v. Seldin,* 422 U.S. at 501, 95 S.Ct. at 2206). The court derived precedential comfort from *Flast v. Cohen:* "The underlying justification for according standing in *Flast* it seems, was the implicit recognition that the Establishment Clause does create in every citizen a personal constitutional right, such that any citizen, including taxpayers, may contest under that clause the constitutionality of federal expenditures." 619 F.2d at 262. The concurring opinion was even more direct. In its view, "statutes alleged to violate the Establishment Clause may not have an individual impact sufficient to confer standing in the traditional sense." *Id.* at 268. To satisfy "the need for an available plaintiff," *id.,* at 267, and thereby to assure a basis for judicial review, respondents should be granted standing because, "as a practical matter, no one is better suited to bring this lawsuit and thus vindicate the freedoms embodied in the Establishment Clause," *id.* at 266.

Implicit in the foregoing is the philosophy that the business of the federal courts is correcting constitutional errors, and that "cases and controversies" are at best merely convenient vehicles for doing so and at worst nuisances that may be dispensed with when they become obstacles to that transcendent endeavor. This philosophy has no place in our constitutional scheme. It does not become more palatable when the underlying merits concern the Establishment Clause. Respondents' claim of standing implicitly rests on the presumption that violations of the Establishment Clause typically will not cause injury sufficient to confer standing under the "traditional" view of Art. III. But "[t]he assumption that if respondents have no standing to sue, no one would have standing, is not a reason to find standing." *Schlesinger v. Reservists Committee to Stop the War,* 418 U.S. at 227, 94 S.Ct. at 2935. This view would convert standing into a requirement that must be observed only when satisfied. Moreover, we are unwilling to assume that injured parties are nonexistent simply because they have not joined respondents in their suit. The law of averages is not a substitute for standing.

Were we to accept respondents' claim of standing in this case, there would be no principled basis for confining our exception to litigants relying on the Establishment Clause. Ultimately, that exception derives from the idea that the judicial power requires nothing more for its invocation than important issues and able litigants. The existence of injured parties who might not wish to bring suit becomes irrelevant. Because we are unwilling to countenance such a departure from the limits on judicial power contained in Art. III, the judgment of the Court of Appeals is reversed.

It is so ordered.

JUSTICE BRENNAN, with whom JUSTICE MARSHALL and JUSTICE BLACKMUN join, dissenting.

* * *

III

Blind to history, the Court attempts to distinguish this case from *Flast* by wrenching snippets of language from our opinions, and by perfunctorily applying that language under color of the first prong of *Flast*'s two-part nexus test. The tortuous distinctions thus produced are specious, at best: at worst, they are pernicious to our constitutional heritage.

First, the Court finds this case different from *Flast* because here the "source of [plaintiff's] complaint is not a *congressional* action, but a decision by HEW to transfer a parcel of federal property." This attempt at distinction cannot withstand scrutiny. *Flast* involved a challenge to the actions of the Commissioner of Education, and other officials of HEW, in disbursing funds under the Elementary and Secondary Education Act of 1965 to "religious and sectarian" schools. Plaintiffs disclaimed "any intention to challenge all programs under * * * the Act." *Flast,* at 87, 88 S.Ct. at 1946. Rather, they claimed that defendant-administrators' approval of such expenditures was not authorized by the Act, or alternatively, to the extent the expenditure was authorized, the Act was "unconstitutional and void." *Ibid.* In the present case, respondents challenge HEW's grant of property pursuant to the Federal Property and Administrative Services Act of 1949, seeking to enjoin HEW "from making a grant of this and other property to the [defendant] so long as such grant will violate the Establishment Clause." App. 12. It may be that the Court is concerned with the adequacy of respondents' pleading; respondents have not, in so many words, asked for a declaration that the "Federal Property and Administrative Services Act is unconstitutional and void to the extent that it authorizes HEW's actions." I would not construe their complaint so narrowly.

More fundamentally, no clear division can be drawn in this context between actions of the legislative branch and those of the executive branch. To be sure, the First Amendment is phrased as a restriction on Congress' legislative authority; this is only natural since the Constitution assigns the authority to legislate and appropriate only to the Congress. But it is difficult to conceive of an expenditure for which the last governmental actor, either implementing directly the legislative will, or acting within the scope of legislatively delegated authority, is not an Executive Branch official. The First Amendment binds the Government as a whole, regardless of which branch is at work in a particular instance.

The Court's second purported distinction between this case and *Flast* is equally unavailing. The majority finds it "decisive" that the Federal Property and Administrative Services Act of 1949 "was an evident exercise of Congress' power under the Property Clause, Art. IV, § 3, cl. 2," while the government action in *Flast* was taken under the Art. I, § 8. The Court relies on *United States v. Richardson,* 418 U.S. 166, 94 S.Ct. 2940, 41 L.Ed.2d 678 (1974), and *Schlesinger v. Reservists Committee to Stop the War,* 418 U.S. 208, 94 S.Ct. 2925, 41 L.Ed.2d 706 (1974), to support the distinction between the two clauses, noting that those cases involved alleged deviations from the requirements of Art. I, § 9, cl. 7, and Art. I, § 6, cl. 2, respectively. The standing defect in each case was *not,* however, the failure to allege a violation of the Spending Clause; rather, the taxpayers in those cases had not complained of the distribution of government largesse, and thus failed to meet the essential requirement of taxpayer standing recognized in *Doremus.*

It can make no constitutional difference in the case before us whether the donation to the defendant here was in the form of a cash grant to build a facility, *see Tilton v. Richardson,* 403 U.S. 672, 91 S.Ct. 2091, 29 L.Ed.2d 790 (1971), or in the nature of a gift of property including a facility already built. That this is a meaningless distinction is illustrated by *Tilton.* In that case, taxpayers were afforded standing to object to the fact that the Government had not received adequate assurance that if the property that it financed for use as an educational facility was later converted to religious uses, it would receive full value for the property, as the Constitution requires. The complaint here is precisely that, although the property at issue is actually being used for a sectarian purpose, the government has not received, nor demanded, full value payment. Whether undertaken pursuant to the Property Clause or the Spending Clause, the breach of the Establishment Clause, and the relationship of the taxpayer to that breach, is precisely the same.

JUSTICE STEVENS, dissenting.

In Parts I, II, and III of his dissenting opinion, Justice Brennan demonstrates that respondent taxpayers have standing to mount an Establishment Clause challenge against the Federal Government's transfer of property worth $1,300,000 to the Assembly of God. For the Court to hold that plaintiffs' standing depends on whether the Government's transfer was an exercise of its power to spend money, on the one hand, or its power to dispose of tangible property, on the other, is to trivialize the standing doctrine.

510 THE ROLE OF THE COURTS Ch. 6

One cannot read the Court's opinion and the concurring opinions of Justice Stewart and Justice Fortas in *Flast v. Cohen,* 392 U.S. 83, 88 S.Ct. 1942, 20 L.Ed.2d 947, without forming the firm conclusion that the plaintiffs' invocation of the Establishment Clause was of decisive importance in resolving the standing issue in that case. Justice Fortas made this point directly:

> I agree that the congressional powers to tax and spend are limited by the prohibition upon Congress to enact laws "respecting an establishment of religion." This thesis, slender as its basis is, provides a direct "nexus," as the Court puts it, between the use and collection of taxes and the congressional action here. Because of this unique "nexus," in my judgment, it is not far-fetched to recognize that a taxpayer has a special claim to status as a litigant in a case raising the "establishment" issue. This special claim is enough, I think, to permit us to allow the suit, coupled, as it is, with the interest which the taxpayer and all other citizens have in the church-state issue. In terms of the structure and basic philosophy of our constitutional government, it would be difficult to point to any issue that has a more intimate, pervasive, and fundamental impact upon the life of the taxpayer—and upon the life of all citizens.
>
> Perhaps the vital interest of a citizen in the establishment issue, without reference to his taxpayer's status, would be acceptable as a basis for this challenge. We need not decide this. But certainly, I believe, we must recognize that our principle of judicial scrutiny of legislative acts which raise important constitutional questions requires that the issue here presented—the separation of state and church—which the Founding Fathers regarded as fundamental to our constitutional system—should be subjected to judicial testing. This is not a question which we, if we are to be faithful to our trust, should consign to limbo, unacknowledged, unresolved, and undecided.
>
> On the other hand, the urgent necessities of this case and the precarious opening through which we find our way to confront it, do not demand that we open the door to a general assault upon exercises of the spending power. The status of taxpayer should not be accepted as a launching pad for an attack upon any target other than legislation affecting the Establishment Clause. *Id.* at 115–16, 88 S.Ct. at 1960–61.

Today the Court holds, in effect, that the Judiciary has no greater role in enforcing the Establishment Clause than in enforcing other "norm[s] of conduct which the federal government is bound to honor," such as the Accounts Clause, *United States v. Richardson,* 418 U.S. 166, 94 S.Ct. 2940, 41 L.Ed.2d 678, and the Incompatibility Clause, *Schlesinger v. Reservists Committee to Stop the War,* 418 U.S. 208, 94 S.Ct. 2925, 41 L.Ed.2d 706. Ironically, however, its decision rests on the premise that the difference between a disposition of funds pursuant to the Spending Clause and a disposition of realty pursuant to the Property

Clause is of fundamental jurisprudential significance. With all due respect, I am persuaded that the essential holding of *Flast v. Cohen* attaches special importance to the Establishment Clause and does not permit the drawing of a tenuous distinction between the Spending Clause and the Property Clause.

For this reason, and for the reasons stated in Parts I, II, and III of Justice Brennan's opinion, I would affirm the judgment of the Court of Appeals.

Notes and Questions

1. In *Valley Forge*, the plaintiffs, an organization dedicated to the separation of church and state and four of its members, brought suit to enjoin a transfer of a seventy-seven acre tract by the Department of Health, Education and Welfare to Valley Forge Christian College. Undoubtedly guided by *Flast*, the complainant alleged that each member "would be deprived of the fair and constitutional use of his/her tax dollar for constitutional purposes in violation of his/her rights under the First Amendment of the United States Constitution." The Supreme Court held that the complainants lacked the requisite standing to commence judicial proceedings. The Court noted two deficiencies regarding the taxpayer status. First, the "source of their complaint is not a congressional action, but a decision by HEW to transfer a parcel of federal property. * * * Second, and perhaps redundantly, the property transfer about which respondents [plaintiffs] complain was not an exercise of authority conferred by the taxing and spending clause of Article I, Sec. 8 * * * [but] an evident exercise of Congress' power under the Property Clause, Art. IV, Sec. 3 cl. 2 * * *." Are you persuaded by these distinctions?

2. The Court drew support from two post-*Flast* cases, *Schlesinger v. Reservists Committee to Stop the War,* 418 U.S. 208 (1974), and *United States v. Richardson,* 418 U.S. 166 (1974). In *Richardson,* the Court denied a federal taxpayer standing to assert the unconstitutionality of legislation permitting the Central Intelligence Agency to withhold receipts and expenditures from the public, in violation of Article I, Sec. 9, cl. 7 (requiring a "regular Statement and Account of the Receipts and Expenditures of all public Money"). In *Schlesinger* the Court denied a federal taxpayer and citizen standing to challenge the military reserves membership of members of Congress as inconsistent with the Incompatibility Clause of Article I, Sec. 6, cl. 2 (specifying that "no Person holding any Office under the United States, shall be a Member of either House during his continuance in Office").

3. In *Valley Forge*, the Court slammed the door on an expansive reading of *Flast*. As Justice Stevens noted in dissent, the Court distinguished between cases brought pursuant to the Taxing and Spending Clause on the one hand and the Property Clause on the other. Is that distinction justifiable? *Flast* suggested that there might be other limitations on the spending power that would give a taxpayer the requisite standing. Does this suggestion survive *Valley Forge?*

COMMENTARY ON STANDING IN CRIMINAL CASES

In *Alderman v. United States,* 394 U.S. 165 (1969), the United States engaged in electronic surveillance that might have violated the petitioners' Fourth Amendment rights and tainted their convictions. (See the discussion of the exclusionary rule in the *Wolf* and *Mapp* cases, *supra* pp. 344–63 Vacating the judgments of conviction, the Supreme Court remanded the cases for further hearings, findings, and conclusions. The Court held (1) that a defendant whose incriminating conversations were overheard by illegal eavesdropping had standing to object; (2) that a defendant whose premises were "bugged" likewise had standing to suppress evidence obtained as a fruit of illegal surveillance of those premises, even if he were not present and did not participate in the overheard conversations; but (3) that codefendants and coconspirators who suffered no intrusion upon their conversations or premises lacked standing to object to the admission of evidence obtained as a fruit of the illegal practices.

Suppose, after *Alderman,* that the authorities unlawfully "bug" a telephone conversation between "A" and "B," and obtain information implicating "A", "B," "C," and "D" in a criminal conspiracy. Suppose further that the call was made from "C's" office where the bug was planted. Under the Court's ruling, "A," "B," and "C" would prevail on a motion to suppress; "D" would lack standing.

The *Alderman* opinion states in pertinent part:

> The rule is stated in *Jones v. United States,* 362 U.S. 257, 261 (1960):
>
>> In order to qualify as a "person aggrieved by an unlawful search and seizure" one must have been a victim of a search or seizure, one against whom the search was directed, as distinguished from one who claims prejudice only through the use of evidence gathered as a consequence of a search or seizure directed at someone else. * * *
>
>> Ordinarily, then, it is entirely proper to require of one who seeks to challenge the legality of a search as the basis for suppressing relevant evidence that he allege, and if the allegation be disputed that he establish, that he himself was the victim of an invasion of privacy.
>
> * * *
>
> We adhere to * * * the general rule that Fourth Amendment rights are personal rights which, like some other constitutional rights, may not be vicariously asserted. * * * There is no necessity to exclude evidence against one defendant in order to protect the rights of another. No rights of the victim of an illegal search are at stake when the evidence is offered against some other party. The victim can and very probably will object for himself when and if it becomes important for him to do so.

What petitioners appear to assert is an independent constitutional right of their own to exclude relevant and probative evidence because it was seized from another in violation of the Fourth Amendment. But we think there is a substantial difference for constitutional purposes between preventing the incrimination of a defendant through the very evidence illegally seized from him and suppressing evidence on the motion of a party who cannot claim this predicate for exclusion.

* * *

Of course, Congress or state legislatures may extend the exclusionary rule and provide that illegally seized evidence is inadmissible against anyone for any purpose. But for constitutional purposes, we are not now inclined to expand the existing rule that unlawful wiretapping or eavesdropping, whether deliberate or negligent, can produce nothing usable against the person aggrieved by the invasion.

* * *

394 U.S. at 173–75.

Justice Fortas, concurring in part and dissenting in part, observed that the Fourth Amendment generally prohibits unreasonable searches and seizures[i] and that strong arguments can be advanced for the idea "that any defendant against whom illegally acquired evidence is offered, whether or not it was obtained in violation of his right to privacy, may have the evidence excluded." Recognizing that this would be contrary to many decisions, he urged that, at the least, standing should be extended to one who was a target of the investigation. "Such a person," he stated, "is surely 'the victim of an invasion of privacy' * * * even though it is not his property that was searched or seized." In this view, Justice Fortas was joined by Justice Douglas.

Consider, now, the question of standing in the context of a violation of the Fifth Amendment's privilege against self-incrimination. Suppose that police officers obtained admissions from Smith during a stationhouse interrogation without giving him his *Miranda*[j] warnings, and that he has not only implicated himself but named Jones as his partner in the criminal venture. Acting on this lead, the police investigate Jones and obtain evidence of his involvement. Can Jones rely on the violation of Smith's rights to exclude evidence traceable to the unlawful interrogation of Smith? The Supreme Court's consistent answer has been "no." Only the person subjected to testimonial compulsion has standing to rely on the privilege.

---

i. The Fourth Amendment provides as follows: "The right of the people to be secured in their persons, houses, papers, and effects, against unreasonable searches and seizures, shall not be violated, and no Warrants shall issue, but upon probable cause, supported by Oath or affirmation, and particularly describing the place to be searched, and the persons or things to be seized."

j. *Miranda v. Arizona*, 384 U.S. 436 (1966).

2. MOOTNESS

DeFUNIS v. ODEGAARD

Supreme Court of the United States, 1974.
416 U.S. 312, 94 S.Ct. 1704, 40 L.Ed.2d 164.

PER CURIAM.

In 1971 the petitioner Marco DeFunis, Jr., applied for admission as a first-year student at the University of Washington Law School, a state-operated institution. The size of the incoming first-year class was to be limited to 150 persons, and the Law School received some 1,600 applications for these 150 places. DeFunis was eventually notified that he had been denied admission. He thereupon commenced this suit in a Washington trial court, contending that the procedures and criteria employed by the Law School Admissions Committee invidiously discriminated against him on account of his race in violation of the Equal Protection Clause of the Fourteenth Amendment to the United States Constitution.

DeFunis brought the suit on behalf of himself alone, and not as the representative of any class, against the various respondents, who are officers, faculty members, and members of the Board of Regents of the University of Washington. He asked the trial court to issue a mandatory injunction commanding the respondents to admit him as a member of the first-year class entering in September 1971, on the ground that the Law School admissions policy had resulted in the unconstitutional denial of his application for admission. The trial court agreed with his claim and granted the requested relief. DeFunis was, accordingly, admitted to the Law School and began his legal studies there in the fall of 1971. On appeal, the Washington Supreme Court reversed the judgment of the trial court and held that the Law School admissions policy did not violate the Constitution. By this time DeFunis was in his second year at the Law School.

He then petitioned this Court for a writ of certiorari, and Mr. Justice Douglas, as Circuit Justice, stayed the judgment of the Washington Supreme Court pending the "final disposition of the case by this Court." By virtue of this stay, DeFunis has remained in law school, and was in the first term of his third and final year when this Court first considered his certiorari petition in the fall of 1973. Because of our concern that DeFunis' third-year standing in the Law School might have rendered this case moot, we requested the parties to brief the question of mootness before we acted on the petition. In response, both sides contended that the case was not moot. The respondents indicated that, if the decision of the Washington Supreme Court were permitted to stand, the petitioner could complete the term for which he was then enrolled but would have to apply to the faculty for permission to continue in the school before he could register for another term.

We granted the petition for certiorari on November 19, 1973. 414 U.S. 1038, 94 S.Ct. 538, 38 L.Ed.2d 329. The case was in due course orally argued on February 26, 1974.

In response to questions raised from the bench during the oral argument, counsel for the petitioner has informed the Court that De-Funis has now registered "for his final quarter in law school." Counsel for the respondents have made clear that the Law School will not in any way seek to abrogate this registration. In light of DeFunis' recent registration for the last quarter of his final law school year, and the Law School's assurance that his registration is fully effective, the insistent question again arises whether this case is not moot, and to that question we now turn.

The starting point for analysis is the familiar proposition that "federal courts are without power to decide questions that cannot affect the rights of litigants in the case before them." *North Carolina v. Rice,* 404 U.S. 244, 246, 92 S.Ct. 402, 404, 30 L.Ed.2d 413 (1971). The inability of the federal judiciary "to review moot cases derives from the requirement of Art. III of the Constitution under which the exercise of judicial power depends upon the existence of a case or controversy." Although as a matter of Washington state law it appears that this case would be saved from mootness by "the great public interest in the continuing issues raised by this appeal," 82 Wash.2d 11, 23 n. 6, 507 P.2d 1169, 1177 n. 6 (1973), the fact remains that under Art. III "[e]ven in cases arising in the state courts, the question of mootness is a federal one which a federal court must resolve before it assumes jurisdiction." *North Carolina v. Rice,* 404 U.S. at 246, 92 S.Ct. at 404.

The respondents have represented that, without regard to the ultimate resolution of the issues in this case, DeFunis will remain a student in the Law School for the duration of any term in which he has already enrolled. Since he has now registered for his final term, it is evident that he will be given an opportunity to complete all academic and other requirements for graduation, and, if he does so, will receive his diploma regardless of any decision this Court might reach on the merits of this case. In short, all parties agree that DeFunis is now entitled to complete his legal studies at the University of Washington and to receive his degree from that institution. A determination by this Court of the legal issues tendered by the parties is no longer necessary to compel that result, and could not serve to prevent it. DeFunis did not cast his suit as a class action, and the only remedy he requested was an injunction commanding his admission to the Law School. He was not only accorded that remedy, but he now has also been irrevocably admitted to the final term of the final year of the Law School course. The controversy between the parties has thus clearly ceased to be "definite and concrete" and no longer "touch[es] the legal relations of parties having adverse legal interests." *Aetna Life Ins. Co. v. Haworth,* 300 U.S. 227, 240–41, 57 S.Ct. 461, 464, 81 L.Ed. 617 (1937).

It matters not that these circumstances partially stem from a policy decision on the part of the respondent Law School authorities. The respondents, through their counsel, the Attorney General of the State, have professionally represented that in no event will the status of DeFunis now be affected by any view this Court might express on the merits of this controversy. And it has been the settled practice of the Court, in contexts no less significant, fully to accept representations such as these as parameters for decision.

There is a line of decisions in this Court standing for the proposition that the "voluntary cessation of allegedly illegal conduct does not deprive the tribunal of power to hear and determine the case, *i.e.*, does not make the case moot." These decisions and the doctrine they reflect would be quite relevant if the question of mootness here had arisen by reason of a unilateral change in the *admissions procedures* of the Law School. For it was the admissions procedures that were the target of this litigation, and a voluntary cessation of the admissions practices complained of could make this case moot only if it could be said with assurance "that 'there is no reasonable expectation that the wrong will be repeated.' " *United States v. W. T. Grant Co.*, 345 U.S. at 633, 73 S.Ct. at 897. Otherwise, "[t]he defendant is free to return to his old ways," *id.* at 632, 73 S.Ct. at 897, and this fact would be enough to prevent mootness because of the "public interest in having the legality of the practices settled." *Ibid.* But mootness in the present case depends not at all upon a "voluntary cessation" of the admissions practices that were the subject of this litigation. It depends, instead, upon the simple fact that DeFunis is now in the final quarter of the final year of his course of study, and the settled and unchallenged policy of the Law School to permit him to complete the term for which he is now enrolled.

It might also be suggested that this case presents a question that is "capable of repetition, yet evading review," and is thus amenable to federal adjudication even though it might otherwise be considered moot. But DeFunis will never again be required to run the gantlet of the Law School's admission process, and so the question is certainly not "capable of repetition" so far as he is concerned. Moreover, just because this particular case did not reach the Court until the eve of the petitioner's graduation from Law School, it hardly follows that the issue he raises will in the future evade review. If the admissions procedures of the Law School remain unchanged, there is no reason to suppose that a subsequent case attacking those procedures will not come with relative speed to this Court, now that the Supreme Court of Washington has spoken. This case, therefore, in no way presents the exceptional situation in which the *Southern Pacific Terminal* doctrine might permit a departure from "[t]he usual rule in federal cases * * * that an actual controversy must exist at stages of appellate or certiorari review, and not simply at the date the action is initiated." *Roe v. Wade*, [410 U.S.] at 125, 93 S.Ct. at 712; *United States v. Munsingwear, Inc.*, 340 U.S. 36, 71 S.Ct. 104, 95 L.Ed. 36 (1950).

Because the petitioner will complete his law school studies at the end of the term for which he has now registered regardless of any decision this Court might reach on the merits of this litigation, we conclude that the Court cannot, consistently with the limitations of Art. III of the Constitution, consider the substantive constitutional issues tendered by the parties. Accordingly, the judgment of the Supreme Court of Washington is vacated, and the cause is remanded for such proceedings as by that court may be deemed appropriate.

It is so ordered.

Vacated and remanded.

[The dissenting opinion of Justice Douglas is omitted.]

* * *

JUSTICE BRENNAN, with whom JUSTICE DOUGLAS, JUSTICE WHITE, and JUSTICE MARSHALL concur, dissenting.

I respectfully dissent. Many weeks of the school term remain, and petitioner may not receive his degree despite respondents' assurances that petitioner will be allowed to complete this term's schooling regardless of our decision. Any number of unexpected events—illness, economic necessity, even academic failure—might prevent his graduation at the end of the term. Were that misfortune to befall, and were petitioner required to register for yet another term, the prospect that he would again face the hurdle of the admissions policy is real, not fanciful; for respondents warn that "Mr. DeFunis would have to take some appropriate action to request continued admission for the remainder of his law school education, and *some discretionary action by the University on such request would have to be taken.*" Respondents' Memorandum on the Question of Mootness 3–4 (emphasis supplied). Thus, respondents' assurances have not dissipated the possibility that petitioner might once again have to run the gantlet of the University's allegedly unlawful admissions policy. The Court therefore proceeds on an erroneous premise in resting its mootness holding on a supposed inability to render any judgment that may affect one way or the other petitioner's completion of his law studies. For surely if we were to reverse the Washington Supreme Court, we could insure that, if for some reason petitioner did not graduate this spring, he would be entitled to re-enrollment at a later time on the same basis as others who have not faced the hurdle of the University's allegedly unlawful admissions policy.

In these circumstances, and because the University's position implies no concession that its admissions policy is unlawful, this controversy falls squarely within the Court's long line of decisions holding that the "[m]ere voluntary cessation of allegedly illegal conduct does not moot a case." *United States v. Concentrated Phosphate Export Assn.,* 393 U.S. 199, 203, 89 S.Ct. 361, 364, 21 L.Ed.2d 344 (1968). Since respondents' voluntary representation to this Court is only that they will permit petitioner to complete this term's studies, respondents have not borne the "heavy burden," *United States v. Concentrated Phosphate Export Assn.,* 393 U.S. at 203, 89 S.Ct. at 364, of demonstrating that there was not even a "mere possibility" that petitioner would once again be subject to the challenged admissions policy. *United States v. W. T. Grant Co.,* 345 U.S. at 633, 73 S.Ct. at 898. On the contrary, respondents have positioned themselves so as to be "free to return to [their] old ways." *Id.* at 632, 73 S.Ct. at 897.

I can thus find no justification for the Court's straining to rid itself of this dispute. While we must be vigilant to require that litigants maintain a personal stake in the outcome of a controversy to assure that "the questions will be framed with the necessary specificity, that the issues will be contested with the necessary adverseness and that the litigation will be pursued with the necessary vigor to assure that the constitutional challenge will be made in a form traditionally thought to be capable of judicial resolution," *Flast v. Cohen,* 392 U.S. 83, 106, 88 S.Ct. 1942, 1955, 20 L.Ed.2d 947 (1968), there is no want of an adversary contest in this case. Indeed, the Court concedes that, if petitioner has lost his stake in this controversy, he did so only when he registered for the spring term. But appellant took that action only after the case had been fully litigated in the state courts, briefs had been filed in this Court, and oral argument had been heard. The case is thus ripe for decision on a fully developed factual record with sharply defined and fully canvassed legal issues. *Cf. Sibron v. New York,* 392 U.S. 40, 57, 88 S.Ct. 1889, 1899, 20 L.Ed.2d 917 (1968).

Moreover, in endeavoring to dispose of this case as moot, the Court clearly disserves the public interest. The constitutional issues which are avoided today concern vast numbers of people, organizations, and colleges and universities, as evidenced by the filing of twenty-six *amicus curiae* briefs. Few constitutional questions in recent history have stirred as much debate, and they will not disappear. They must inevitably return to the federal courts and ultimately again to this Court. *Cf. Richardson v. Wright,* 405 U.S. 208, 212, 92 S.Ct. 788, 791, 31 L.Ed.2d 151 (1972) (dissenting opinion). Because avoidance of repetitious litigation serves the public interest, that inevitability counsels against mootness determinations, as here, not compelled by the record. Although the Court should, of course, avoid unnecessary decisions of constitutional questions, we should not transform principles of avoidance of constitutional decisions into devices for side-stepping resolution of difficult cases. *Cf. Cohens v. Virginia,* 6 Wheat. 264, 404–405, 5 L.Ed. 257 (1821) (Marshall, C.J.).

On what appears in this case, I would find that there is an extant controversy and decide the merits of the very important constitutional questions presented.

Notes and Questions

1. What is the justification for the mootness doctrine? Is it based upon constitutional or prudential considerations? What is the time frame for ascertaining whether a case is moot? The time the lawsuit is filed? When the case is heard? At the time of the appeal? Assume DeFunis died one day before the Court would have announced its decision. What then?

2. What is the rationale for deciding cases that present issues "capable of repetition, yet evading review"? *Roe v. Wade,* 410 U.S. 113 (1973) (abortion). Why didn't this exception apply to *DeFunis*? Would a class action have saved the case from mootness? A class action is a suit in which a

representative party brings proceedings on behalf of members similarly situated. If the representative's claim becomes moot, may the case still receive judicial attention? *See Sosna v. Iowa*, 419 U.S. 393 (1975) (affirmative answer).

3. The Washington Supreme Court held that the law school admissions policy did not violate the Constitution. The Supreme Court of the United States vacated the state court judgment and remanded for such proceedings as that court deemed appropriate. What should the state court have done? Does the original state supreme court opinion have any precedential value in Washington?

4. Another exception to the mootness principle is the proposition that "voluntary cessation of allegedly illegal conduct so as to deprive the tribunal of power to hear and determine the case" is not effective. The majority and dissent discussed this exception in light of the facts of *DeFunis*. Which side presented the more cogent argument?

5. Justice Douglas, dissenting, wrote a separate opinion in which he reached the merits of the controversy. Was his approach a sound one? Are such "advisory opinions" helpful? Constitutional? Suppose a judge decided instead to write a law review article. Are there any differences?

6. In a 1997 case, after discussing mootness, standing, abstention, and the "case-or-controversy" requirement, the Court examined and recommended another procedure that the parties might have invoked to obtain a faster, more efficient resolution of their case—or at least one that would not consume the efforts of the nation's highest court and might forestall a decision on a constitutional issue—that is, certification of the controlling question to the state's supreme court. *See Arizonans for Official English v. Arizona*, 520 U.S. 43, 117 S. Ct. 1055 (1997).[k] By a vote of 9–0, the Court ultimately determined that the case was moot. Given that disposition, should the Court have addressed the other issues?

LANE v. WILLIAMS

Supreme Court of the United States, 1982.
455 U.S. 624, 102 S.Ct. 1322, 71 L.Ed.2d 508.

JUSTICE STEVENS delivered the opinion of the Court.

In 1975, respondents pleaded guilty in Illinois state court to a charge of burglary, an offense punishable at that time by imprisonment for an indeterminate term of years and a mandatory three year parole term. We granted certiorari to consider whether the failure of the trial court to advise respondents of that mandatory parole requirement before accepting their guilty pleas deprived them of due process of law. We are unable to reach that question, however, because we find that respondents' claims for relief are moot.

I

On March 11, 1975 respondent Lawrence Williams appeared in Illinois state court and pleaded guilty to a single count of burglary.

k. Co-author Rebecca White Berch served as lead counsel for the State of Ari- zona while serving as the state's solicitor general.

Before accepting the guilty plea, the trial judge elicited Williams' understanding of the terms of a plea agreement, in which his attorney and the prosecutor had agreed that Williams would receive an indeterminate sentence of from one to two years in prison in exchange for pleading guilty. The judge informed Williams that he would impose the bargained sentence, and advised him of both the nature of the charge against him and the constitutional rights that he would waive by pleading guilty. After the prosecutor established a factual basis for the plea, Williams indicated that he understood his rights and wished to plead guilty.

At the time that Williams pleaded guilty, Illinois law required every indeterminate sentence for certain felonies, including burglary, to include a special parole term in addition to the term of imprisonment. During the plea acceptance hearing, neither the trial judge, the prosecutor, nor defense counsel informed Williams that his negotiated sentence included a mandatory parole term of three years.

Williams was discharged from prison on May 20, 1976 and released on parole. On March 3, 1977 he was arrested for reasons that do not appear in the record and, on March 16, 1977, he was returned to prison as a parole violator. While in custody, Williams filed a petition for a writ of *habeas corpus* in the United States District Court for the Northern District of Illinois. He alleged that he "was not informed" that a mandatory parole term had attached to his sentence until two months before his discharge from prison and that "his present incarceration is therefore in violation of the Due Process Clause of the 14th Amendment to the U. S. Constitution." App. 12. Williams' petition did not ask the federal court to set aside his conviction and allow him to plead anew. It requested an order "freeing him from the present control" of the warden and from "all future liability" under his original sentence.

On January 4, 1978 the District Court found that Williams' guilty plea had been induced unfairly in violation of the Due Process Clause of the Fourteenth Amendment and ordered Williams released from custody. *United States ex rel. Williams v. Morris,* 447 F.Supp. 95 (N.D.Ill.1978). The court expressly "opted for specific performance" of the plea bargain "rather than nullification of the guilty plea." *Id.* at 101. The relief granted was precisely what Williams had requested.

Williams was not, however, immediately released from custody. The District Court entered a stay to give the State an opportunity to file a motion for reconsideration. Before that stay was lifted, Williams was released from prison on a special six month "supervisory release term." The District Court subsequently denied the State's motion to reconsider and the State appealed. While that appeal was pending, Williams' six month release term expired and he was released from the custody of the Illinois Department of Corrections.

The facts concerning respondent Southall are similar. Pursuant to a plea bargain with the prosecutor that was accepted in advance by an Illinois trial court, Southall pleaded guilty to a single charge of burglary and was sentenced to prison for a minimum period of one year and a maximum period not to exceed three years. The transcript of the plea acceptance proceeding contains no statement by the prosecutor, Southall's public defender, or the trial judge that the bargained and imposed sentence included the mandatory three year parole term. Like respondent Williams, Southall completed his sentence, was released on parole, and later declared a parole violator. While reincarcerated, he filed a petition for *habeas corpus* in federal court, seeking his "immediate release." App. 65. His case was consolidated in the District Court with that of respondent Williams.

The District Court found "Southall's situation to be factually indistinguishable from Williams'." 447 F.Supp. at 102. The court thus granted Southall's petition for a writ of *habeas corpus*. The State filed an appeal from that decision, but discharged Southall in compliance with the decision of the District Court.

The Court of Appeals reversed on the ground that respondents had failed to exhaust an available state remedy. 594 F.2d 614 (C.A.7 1979). Before reaching that decision, however, the court requested the parties to submit supplemental briefs on the issue of mootness. The court concluded that the cases were not moot. It noted that Southall's mandatory parole term extended beyond the date of its decision and thus could be reinstated. While Williams' parole term had expired, the court concluded that the controversy was still alive because "there remain collateral consequences which might have lingering effects since [Williams was] found guilty of [a] violatio[n] of the mandatory parole"; that violation "would remain upon [his] recor[d] with various possible adverse consequences." *Id.* at 615.[7] Moreover, the court found the issue to be capable of repetition yet evading review; "[i]t is obvious that because of the short terms often remaining in the mandatory parole terms that the same issue may be expected to be raised as to other petitioners similarly situated with doubtful expectations of resolution." *Ibid.*

After the Court of Appeals had rendered its decision, respondent Southall was discharged from the custody of the Illinois Department of Corrections. On remand, the District Court concluded that, as a result of an intervening decision of the Illinois Supreme Court, exhaustion of state remedies would be futile. 483 F.Supp. 775 (1980). The court again entered judgment for respondents; since they had already been released from custody, the court simply entered an order "declaring void the mandatory parole term[s]." App. 39. The Court of Appeals affirmed that decision, 633 F.2d 71 (1980), and we granted the State's petition for certiorari. *Sub nom. Franzen v. Williams*, 452 U.S. 914, 101 S.Ct. 3047, 69 L.Ed.2d 417.

II

Respondents claim that their constitutional rights were violated when the trial court accepted their guilty pleas without informing them

7. The court did not identify these collateral effects or adverse consequences. It found the situation "similar in principle," however, to that considered in *Carafas v. LaVallee*, 391 U.S. 234, 88 S.Ct. 1556, 20 L.Ed.2d 554.

of the mandatory parole requirement. Assuming, for the sake of argument, that the court's failure to advise respondents of this consequence rendered their guilty pleas void, respondents could seek to remedy this error in two quite different ways. They might ask the District Court to set aside their convictions and give them an opportunity to plead anew; in that event, they might either plead not guilty and stand trial or they might try to negotiate a different plea bargain properly armed with the information that any sentence they received would include a special parole term. Alternatively, they could seek relief in the nature of "specific enforcement" of the plea agreement as they understood it; in that event, the elimination of the mandatory parole term from their sentences would remove any possible harmful consequence from the trial court's incomplete advice.

If respondents had sought the opportunity to plead anew, this case would not be moot. Such relief would free respondents from all consequences flowing from their convictions, as well as subject them to reconviction with a possibly greater sentence. *Cf. North Carolina v. Pearce,* 395 U.S. 711, 89 S.Ct. 2072, 23 L.Ed.2d 656. Thus, a live controversy would remain to determine whether a constitutional violation in fact had occurred and whether respondents were entitled to the relief that they sought.

Since respondents had completed their previously imposed sentences, however, they did not seek the opportunity to plead anew. Rather, they sought to remedy the alleged constitutional violation by removing the consequence that gave rise to the constitutional harm. In the course of their attack, that consequence expired of its own accord. Respondents are no longer subject to any direct restraint as a result of the parole term. They may not be imprisoned on the lesser showing needed to establish a parole violation than to prove a criminal offense. Their liberty or freedom of movement is not in any way curtailed by a parole term that has expired.

Since respondents elected only to attack their sentences, and since those sentences expired during the course of these proceedings, this case is moot. "Nullification of a conviction may have important benefits for a defendant * * * but urging in a *habeas corpus* proceeding the correction of a sentence already served is another matter." *North Carolina v. Rice,* 404 U.S. 244, 248, 92 S.Ct. 402, 405, 30 L.Ed.2d 413.

The Court of Appeals, relying on *Carafas v. LaVallee,* 391 U.S. 234, 88 S.Ct. 1556, 20 L.Ed.2d 554, concluded that respondents' parole violations had sufficient "collateral effects" to warrant an exercise of federal habeas corpus relief. In *Carafas* we held that an attack on a criminal conviction was not rendered moot by the fact that the underlying sentence had expired. On the basis of New York law, we noted that "[i]n consequence of [the petitioner's] conviction, he cannot engage in certain businesses; he cannot serve as an official of a labor union for a specified period of time; he cannot vote in any election held in New York State; he cannot serve as a juror." 391 U.S. at 237, 88 S.Ct. at 1559 (footnotes omitted). These substantial civil penalties were sufficient to ensure that the litigant had "a substantial stake in the judgment of conviction which survives the satisfaction of the sentence imposed on him." *Ibid.* (quoting *Fiswick v. United States,* 329 U.S. 211, 222, 67 S.Ct. 224, 230, 91 L.Ed. 196). In *Sibron v. New York,* 392 U.S. 40, 57, 88 S.Ct. 1889, 1899, 20 L.Ed.2d 917, we stated that "a criminal case is moot only if it is shown that there is no possibility that any collateral legal consequences will be imposed on the basis of the challenged conviction."

The doctrine of *Carafas* and *Sibron* is not applicable in this case. No civil disabilities such as those present in *Carafas* result from a finding that an individual has violated parole. At most, certain non-statutory consequences may occur; employment prospects, or the sentence imposed in a future criminal proceeding, could be affected. *Cf. People v. Halterman,* 45 Ill.App.3d 605, 608, 4 Ill.Dec. 271, 359 N.E.2d 1223 (1977).[13] The discretionary decisions that are made by an employer or a sentencing judge, however, are not governed by the mere presence or absence of a recorded violation of parole; these decisions may take into consideration, and are more directly influenced by, the underlying conduct that formed the basis for the parole violation. Any disabilities that flow from whatever respondents did to evoke revocation of parole are not removed—or even affected—by a District Court order that simply recites that their parole terms are "void."[14]

Respondents have never attacked, on either substantive or procedural grounds, the finding that they violated the terms of their parole. Respondent Williams simply sought an order "freeing him from the present control" of the warden and from "all future liability" under his original sentence; Southall sought his "immediate release" from custody. Through the mere passage of time, respondents have obtained all the relief that they sought. In these circumstances, no live controversy remains.

13. In his dissenting opinion, Justice Marshall argues that this case is not moot because a possibility exists under state law that respondents' parole violations may be considered in a subsequent parole determination. This "collateral consequence" is insufficient to bring this case within the doctrine of *Carafas.* That case concerned existing civil disabilities; as a result of the petitioner's conviction, he was presently barred from holding certain offices, voting in state elections, and serving as a juror. This case involves no such disability. The parole violations that remain a part of respondents' records cannot affect a subsequent parole determination unless respondents again violate state law, are returned to prison, and become eligible for parole. Respondents themselves are able—and indeed required by law—to prevent such a possibility from occurring. Moreover, the existence of a prior parole violation does not render an individual ineligible for parole under Illinois law. It is simply one factor, among many, that may be considered by the parole authority in determining whether there is a substantial risk that the parole candidate will not conform to reasonable conditions of parole.

Collateral review of a final judgment is not an endeavor to be undertaken lightly. It is not warranted absent a showing that the complainant suffers actual harm from the judgment that he seeks to avoid.

14. The District Court's order did not require the warden to expunge or make any change in any portion of respondents' records. Nor have respondents ever requested such relief.

The Court of Appeals also held that this case was not moot because it was "capable of repetition, yet evading review." *Southern Pacific Terminal Co. v. ICC,* 219 U.S. 498, 515, 31 S.Ct. 279, 283, 55 L.Ed. 310. That doctrine, however, is applicable only when there is "a reasonable expectation that the same complaining party would be subjected to the same action again." *Weinstein v. Bradford,* 423 U.S. 147, 149, 96 S.Ct. 347, 348, 46 L.Ed.2d 350; *Murphy v. Hunt,* 455 U.S. 478, 482, 102 S.Ct. 1181, 1183, 71 L.Ed.2d 353. Respondents are now acutely aware of the fact that a criminal sentence in Illinois will include a special parole term; any future guilty plea will not be open to the same constitutional attack. The possibility that other persons may litigate a similar claim does not save this case from mootness.

The judgment of the Court of Appeals is vacated. The case should be dismissed as moot.

It is so ordered.

JUSTICE MARSHALL, with whom JUSTICE BRENNAN and JUSTICE BLACKMUN join, dissenting.

The majority announces today that this case is moot because, in its view, no collateral consequences flow from respondents' parole revocations, which were based on findings that respondents had violated the conditions of parole terms declared void by the courts below. I dissent from this holding because I believe it is contrary to this Court's precedents and because it ignores the fact that the State of Illinois does attach collateral consequences to parole revocations, a fact recognized both in the State's brief to the Court of Appeals on the issue of mootness and in state court decisions in analogous cases.

I

The majority recognizes that in habeas corpus challenges to criminal convictions, the case "is moot only if it is shown that there is no possibility that any collateral legal consequences will be imposed on the basis of the challenged conviction." *Sibron v. New York,* 392 U.S. 40, 57, 88 S.Ct. 1889, 1899, 20 L.Ed.2d 917 (1968). This Court has consistently refused to canvass state law to ascertain "the actual existence of specific collateral consequences," and has presumed that such consequences exist. *Id.* at 55, 88 S.Ct. at 1898 (discussing *United States v. Morgan,* 346 U.S. 502, 74 S.Ct. 247, 98 L.Ed. 248 (1954), and *Pollard v. United States,* 352 U.S. 354, 77 S.Ct. 481, 1 L.Ed.2d 393 (1957)). *See also Carafas v. LaVallee,* 391 U.S. 234, 237–38, 88 S.Ct. 1556, 1559, 20 L.Ed.2d 554 (1968).

Today, the majority finds the *Carafas* doctrine inapplicable, arguing that because respondents did not seek to set aside their convictions, their situation is analogous to that of a defendant who seeks *habeas corpus* review to correct a sentence already served. *See North Carolina v. Rice,* 404 U.S. 244, 92 S.Ct. 402, 30 L.Ed.2d 413 (1971) (per curiam). Had respondents served the allegedly void mandatory parole term without incident, I might agree that *North Carolina v. Rice* controls and join the majority's conclusion that the consequence of the constitutional violation "expired of its own accord." Here, however, respondents were found to have violated the conditions of their parole. Therefore, unlike the situation in *North Carolina v. Rice,* respondents seek more than a mere reduction in sentence after the sentence has been completed: they seek to have the parole term declared void, or expunged, in order to avoid the future consequences that attach to parole violations. If collateral consequences do attach to parole violations, both the State and respondents have a live interest in this Court's review of the lower courts' holdings that the alleged constitutional violations rendered the guilty pleas void and that respondents were entitled to specific performance of the pleas, in the form of a declaration that the mandatory parole terms were void and should be expunged.

The existence of a live controversy in this case turns on whether collateral consequences attach to parole violations. Because this determination involves a difficult question of state law, I believe that the doctrine of *Sibron* and *Carafas* should be applied. This doctrine avoids placing a federal court in the awkward position of determining questions of state law not directly before it. By presuming the existence of collateral consequences, federal courts are not required to predict the manner in which a State may use convictions or parole violations in future proceedings. An erroneous determination that collateral consequences do not attach not only injures the individuals challenging the constitutionality of the guilty pleas, but also hinders the State's ability to use these violations in future proceedings. Today's opinion is an unfortunate example of such an erroneous interpretation.

II

The majority's decision is apparently based on a cursory examination of Illinois statutes. Finding no statutory civil disabilities, the majority glibly dismisses nonstatutory consequences as "discretionary decisions" that would remain whether or not the parole terms were declared void or expunged. This reasoning has no basis in Illinois law and appears to derive from nothing more than judicial intuition.

Several collateral consequences attach to parole violations under Illinois law. First, a sentencing judge may consider parole violations in aggravation of sentence. The majority makes the unwarranted assumption that declaring void the parole term upon which a violation is based has no effect because a sentencing judge would consider the conduct underlying the violation, and not the violation itself, in deciding whether to enhance a sentence. However, as the majority recognizes, there is no way for this Court to determine the basis for respondents' parole revocation. Under Illinois law, the Prisoner Review Board is given substantial discretion in setting conditions of parole. *See* Ill.Rev.Stat., ch. 38, ¶ 1003–3–7 (Supp.1980). Conditions of parole may prohibit conduct that is otherwise innocent and may affirmatively require the parolee to engage in specified work or rehabilitation programs. Parole may be revoked upon a finding that the parolee has violated *any* of these parole conditions. *See* Ill.Rev.Stat., ch. 38, ¶ 1003–3–9 (Supp.1980); Prisoner Review Board, State of Illinois, Rules Governing Parole 9–10, 13–16 (1979); Ill. Register 144, 162–166 (1979). Therefore, conduct giving rise to a parole violation may be completely innocuous but for the fact that it was prohibited or required as a condition of parole, and it may be entirely irrelevant to a sentencing decision once the parole term is declared void.

Moreover, it is not clear under Illinois law whether a sentencing judge would consider the conduct underlying a parole violation, even if the conduct is not otherwise innocent, where the parole term itself is declared void. In a similar context, the Illinois appellate courts have held that trial courts may not consider a reversed conviction in aggravation of sentence, even where the court, in remanding for a new trial, noted that the evidence was sufficient to support the verdict beyond a reasonable doubt and the matter was never retried. *See, e.g., People v. Chellew,* 20 Ill.App.3d 963, 313 N.E.2d 284 (1974). *Cf. People v. Wunnenberg,* 87 Ill.App.3d 32, 34, 42 Ill.Dec. 606, 608, 409 N.E.2d 101, 103 (1980). The Illinois courts have also held that review of probation revocation is not rendered moot merely because the defendant has served his entire sentence. *See People v. Halterman,* 45 Ill.App.3d 605, 608, 4 Ill.Dec. 271, 274, 359 N.E.2d 1223, 1225 (1977) (challenge to probation revocation not moot because "the fact that the defendant has had his probation revoked might be submitted to another judge for his consideration in sentencing the defendant if he has the misfortune of again being convicted of some crime"). These cases do not conclusively demonstrate that a judge would not consider the conduct underlying the violation of a void parole term in aggravation of sentence. However, they cast serious doubt on the validity of the majority's assumption to the contrary. Furthermore, the State argued to the Court of Appeals that the case was not moot because the State "is deeply interested in whether or not it can use the parole violation status of [respondents] for sentencing purposes should they ever again come into contact with the criminal justice system." Additional Memorandum for Appellants in Nos. 78–1321, 78–1322, 78–1323, 78–1380 in the United States Court of Appeals for the Seventh Circuit (Mem. to Court of Appeals) 5. This argument at least implies that the State would not use this status for sentencing purposes after a court had declared the parole terms void.

Second, the majority completely overlooks an important collateral consequence that attaches to parole violations should the respondents ever have the misfortune of returning to prison. Under these rules, parole may be denied simply on the basis of a prior parole violation; the conduct underlying the parole violation is apparently irrelevant unless it falls within one of the other criteria listed in that section. We have no reason to assume that the conduct underlying respondents' violations would fall within one of the other factors, or that the Prisoner Review Board would deny parole based on a parole violation notwithstanding the fact that the parole term had been declared void. In fact, the State argued to the Court of Appeals that the case was not moot because respondents "still have a substantial stake in ensuring that their parole terms are, indeed, expunged," because the parole violations would be burdensome if respondents were ever again considered for parole. Mem. to Court of Appeals 5. *See also United States ex rel. Howell v. Wolff,* No. 78 C 951 (ND Ill. August 9, 1978) (unpublished opinion of Judge Leighton, reprinted in App. to Mem. to Court of Appeals) (finding case not moot due to potential burden on future parole decision from parole-violation status).

III

Today's decision, in which the majority undertakes a cursory and misleading examination of state law, starkly demonstrates the wisdom of applying the doctrine of *Carafas* and *Sibron* to the determination whether a State attaches collateral consequences to parole violations. I would apply that doctrine, presume the existence of collateral consequences, and reach the merits of this case. Even if the doctrine of *Carafas* and *Sibron* does not apply, an examination of state law reveals that the majority is wrong in concluding that actual collateral consequences do not attach under state law; there are sufficient collateral consequences flowing from parole-violation status that both the State and the respondents have a live interest in this Court's resolution of the constitutional question. Therefore, I dissent from the majority's conclusion that this case is moot.

Notes and Questions

1. Consider the relationship between the pleadings and the doctrine of mootness. Had respondents requested that the convictions be vacated and that they be granted the opportunity to plead anew, the case would not have been moot. Respondents did not request this relief. Why? What relief did they request? The two opinions differed in their characterization of respondents' requests for relief. Which opinion presented the more accurate portrayal?

2. After *Lane,* is the test "that there is no possibility that any collateral legal consequences will be imposed on the basis of the challenged conviction" still good law? Did the dissent not convincingly show the possibility of collateral legal consequences, or at least demonstrate that the possibility had not been rebutted? Do you concur with the dissent that such consequences should be presumed?

3. What policies does the mootness doctrine serve? Should the doctrine be reexamined in light of parties' wishes to have the Court decide the issues? Are you disturbed that these cases became moot only after the federal court decisions had been rendered? Did appellate proceedings merely keep the cases alive for the purpose of rendering them moot? What end was served by vacating the court of appeals decision? What precedential effect, if any, does the lower court opinion have?

4. What did Justice Stevens mean by his statement that "we are unable to reach (the constitutional question presented) * * * because we find that respondents' claims for relief are moot"? Did the Court lack the

discretion under these circumstances to render a decision? Suppose the petitioner deliberately delayed proceedings until the case became moot? Would such tactics be a factor the Court might consider? Suppose the prison authorities freed the prisoner immediately before the decision? If there were no collateral consequences as in *Carafas,* would such voluntary action be permitted to frustrate judicial review? Should it? *See Ex parte Yerger,* 75 U.S. (8 Wall.) 85 (1868).

3. RIPENESS

UNITED PUBLIC WORKERS v. MITCHELL

Supreme Court of the United States, 1947.
330 U.S. 75, 67 S.Ct. 556, 91 L.Ed. 754.

JUSTICE REED delivered the opinion of the Court.

* * *

The present appellants sought an injunction before a statutory three judge district court of the District of Columbia against appellees, members of the United States Civil Service Commission, to prohibit them from enforcing against petitioners the provisions of the second sentence of § 9(a) of the Hatch Act for the reason that the sentence is repugnant to the Constitution of the United States. A declaratory judgment of the unconstitutionality of the sentence was also sought. The sentence referred to reads, "No officer or employee in the executive branch of the Federal Government * * * shall take any active part in political management or in political campaigns."

[The Act imposes a penalty of dismissal from employment for its violation. The Act also provides that activities theretofore forbidden to civil service employees by the civil service rules shall be deemed to be within its prohibitions for all federal employees. The relevant part of the applicable Civil Service Rule, 5 C.F.R., Cum.Supp. § 1.1 reads:

"Persons who by the provisions of the rules in this chapter are in the competitive classified service, while retaining the right to vote as they please and to express their opinion on all political subjects, shall take no active part in political management or in political campaigns."]

Various individual employees of the federal executive civil service and the United Public Workers of America, a labor union with these and other executive employees as members, as a representative of all its members, joined in the suit. It is alleged that the individuals desire to engage in acts of political management and in political campaigns. * * * From the affidavits it is plain, and we so assume, that these activities will be carried on completely outside of the hours of employment. Appellants challenge the second sentence of § 9(a) as unconstitutional for various reasons. * * *

None of the appellants, except George P. Poole, has violated the provisions of the Hatch Act. They wish to act contrary to its provisions and those of § 1 of the Civil Service Rules and desire a declaration of the legally permissible limits of regulation. Defendants moved to dismiss the complaint for lack of a justiciable case or controversy. The District Court determined that each of these individual appellants had an interest in their claimed privilege of engaging in political activities, sufficient to give them a right to maintain this suit. *United Federal Workers of America (C.I.O.) v. Mitchell,* D.C., 56 F.Supp. 621, 624. The District Court further determined that the questioned provision of the Hatch Act was valid and that the complaint therefore failed to state a cause of action. It accordingly dismissed the complaint and granted summary judgment to defendants. * * *

Second. At the threshold of consideration, we are called upon to decide whether the complaint states a controversy cognizable in this Court. We defer consideration of the cause of action of Mr. Poole until section *Three* of this opinion. The other individual employees have elaborated the grounds of their objection in individual affidavits for use in the hearing on the summary judgment. We select as an example one that contains the essential averments of all the others and print below the portions with significance in this suit.[18] Nothing similar to the fourth paragraph of the printed affidavit is contained in the other affidavits. The assumed controversy between affiant and the Civil Service Commis-

18. "At this time, when the fate of the entire world is in the balance, I believe it is not only proper but an obligation for all citizens to participate actively in the making of the vital political decisions on which the success of the war and the permanence of the peace to follow so largely depend. For the purpose of participating in the making of these decisions it is my earnest desire to engage actively in political management and political campaigns. I wish to engage in such activity upon my own time, as a private citizen.

"I wish to engage in such activities on behalf of those candidates for public office who I believe will best serve the needs of this country and with the object of persuading others of the correctness of my judgments and of electing the candidates of my choice. This objective I wish to pursue by all proper means such as engaging in discussion, by speeches to conventions, rallies and other assemblages, by publicizing my views in letters and articles for publication in newspapers and other periodicals, by aiding in the campaign of candidates for political office by posting banners and posters in public places, by distributing leaflets, by 'ringing doorbells', by addressing campaign literature, and by doing any and all acts of like character reasonably designed to assist in the election of candidates I favor.

"I desire to engage in these activities freely, openly, and without concealment. However, I understand that the second sen-

tence of Section 9(a) of the Hatch Act and the Rules of the C.S.C. provide that if I engage in this activity, the Civil Service Commission will order that I be dismissed from federal employment. Such deprivation of my job in the federal government would be a source of immediate and serious financial loss and other injury to me.

"At the last Congressional election I was very much interested in the outcome of the campaign and offered to help the party of my choice by being a watcher at the polls. I obtained a watcher's certificate but I was advised that there might be some question of my right to use the certificate and retain my federal employment. Therefore, on November 1, 1943, the day before the election, I called the regional office of the Civil Service Commission in Philadelphia and spoke to a person who gave his name as * * *. Mr. * * * stated that if I used my watcher's certificate, the Civil Service Commission would see that I was dismissed from my job at the * * * for violation of the Hatch Act. I, therefore, did not use the certificate as I had intended.

"I believe that Congress may not constitutionally abridge my right to engage in the political activities mentioned above. However, unless the courts prevent the Civil Service Commission from enforcing this unconstitutional law, I will be unable freely to exercise my rights as a citizen." [Identifying words omitted.]

sion as to affiant's right to act as watcher at the polls on November 2, 1943, had long been moot when this complaint was filed. We do not therefore treat this allegation separately. The affidavits it will be noticed, follow the generality of purpose expressed by the complaint. * * * They declare a desire to act contrary to the rule against political activity but not that the rule has been violated. In this respect, we think they differ from the type of threat adjudicated in *Railway Mail Association v. Corsi*, 326 U.S. 88, 65 S.Ct. 1483, 89 L.Ed. 2072. In that case, the refusal to admit an applicant to membership in a labor union on account of race was involved. Admission had been refused. 326 U.S. at 93, note 10, 65 S.Ct. at 1487, 89 L.Ed. 2072. Definite action had also been taken in *Hill v. Florida*, 325 U.S. 538. In the *Hill* case an injunction had been sought and allowed against Hill and the union forbidding Hill from acting as the business agent of the union and the union from further functioning as a union until it complied with the state law. The threats which menaced the affiants of these affidavits in the case now being considered are closer to a general threat by officials to enforce those laws which they are charged to administer, compare *Watson v. Buck,* 313 U.S. 387, 400, 61 S.Ct. 962, 966, 85 L.Ed. 1416, than they are to the direct threat of punishment against a named organization for a completed act that made the *Mail Association* and the *Hill* cases justiciable.

As is well known, the federal courts established pursuant to Article III of the Constitution do not render advisory opinions. For adjudication of constitutional issues, "concrete legal issues, presented in actual cases, not abstractions" are requisite. This is as true of declaratory judgments as any other field. These appellants seem clearly to seek advisory opinions upon broad claims of rights protected by the First, Fifth, Ninth and Tenth Amendments to the Constitution. As these appellants are classified employees, they have a right superior to the generality of citizens, compare *Fairchild v. Hughes,* 258 U.S. 126, 42 S.Ct. 274, 66 L.Ed. 499, but the facts of their personal interest in their civil rights, of the general threat of possible interference with those rights by the Civil Service Commission under its rules, if specified things are done by appellants, does not make a justiciable case or controversy. Appellants want to engage in "political management and political campaigns," to persuade others to follow appellants' views by discussion, speeches, articles and other acts reasonably designed to secure the selection of appellants' political choices. Such generality of objection is really an attack on the political expediency of the Hatch Act, not the presentation of legal issues. It is beyond the competence of courts to render such a decision. *State of Texas v. Interstate Commerce Commission,* 258 U.S. 158, 162, 42 S.Ct. 261, 262, 66 L.Ed. 531.

The power of courts, and ultimately of this Court to pass upon the constitutionality of acts of Congress arises only when the interests of litigants require the use of this judicial authority for their protection against actual interference. A hypothetical threat is not enough. We can only speculate as to the kinds of political activity the appellants desire to engage in or as to the contents of their proposed public statements or the circumstances of their publication. It would not accord with judicial responsibility to adjudge, in a matter involving constitutionality, between the freedom of the individual and the requirements of public order except when definite rights appear upon the one side and definite prejudicial interferences upon the other.

The Constitution allots the nation's judicial power to the federal courts. Unless these courts respect the limits of that unique authority, they intrude upon powers vested in the legislative or executive branches. * * * Should the courts seek to expand their power so as to bring under their jurisdiction ill-defined controversies over constitutional issues, they would become the organ of political theories. Such abuse of judicial power would properly meet rebuke and restriction from other branches. * * * No threat of interference by the Commission with rights of these appellants appears beyond that implied by the existence of the law and the regulations. * * * These reasons lead us to conclude that the determination of the trial court, that the individual appellants, other than Poole, could maintain this action, was erroneous.

Third. The appellant Poole does present by the complaint and affidavit matters appropriate for judicial determination. The affidavits filed by appellees confirm that Poole has been charged by the Commission with political activity and a proposed order for his removal from his position adopted subject to his right under Commission procedure to reply to the charges and to present further evidence in refutation. We proceed to consider the controversy over constitutional power at issue between Poole and the Commission as defined by the charge and preliminary finding upon one side and the admissions of Poole's affidavit upon the other. Our determination is limited to those facts. This proceeding so limited meets the requirements of defined rights and a definite threat to interfere with a possessor of the menaced rights by a penalty for an act done in violation of the claimed restraint.

Because we conclude hereinafter that the prohibition of § 9 of the Hatch Act and Civil Service Rule 1 * * * [is] valid, it is unnecessary to consider, [as this is a declaratory judgment action,] whether or not this appellant sufficiently alleges that an irreparable injury to him would result from his removal from his position. Nor need we inquire whether or not a court of equity would enforce by injunction any judgment declaring rights. Since Poole admits that he violated the rule against political activity and that removal from office is therefore mandatory under the act, there is no question as to the exhaustion of administrative remedies. The act provides no administrative or statutory review for the order of the Civil Service Commission. *Compare Stark v. Wickard,* 321 U.S. 288, 306–10, 64 S.Ct. 559, 569–71, 88 L.Ed. 733; *Macauley v. Waterman S. S. Corporation,* 327 U.S. 540, 66 S.Ct. 712. As no prior proceeding, offering an effective remedy or otherwise, is pending in the courts, there is no problem of judicial discretion as to whether to take cognizance of this case. *Brillhart v. Excess Insurance Co.,* 316 U.S. 491, 496–497, dissent at page 500, 62 S.Ct. 1173, 1176, dissent at page 1178, 86 L.Ed. 1620; *Larson v. General Motors Corporation,* 2 Cir., 134 F.2d

450, 453. Under such circumstances, we see no reason why a declaratory judgment action, even though constitutional issues are involved, does not lie. *See* Rules of Civil Procedure, Rule 57. *Steele v. Louisville & Nashville Railroad Co.,* 323 U.S. 192, 197, 207, 65 S.Ct. 226, 229, 234, 89 L.Ed. 173; *Tunstall v. Brotherhood of Locomotive Firemen & Enginemen,* 323 U.S. 210, 212, *et seq.,* 65 S.Ct. 235, 236, 89 L.Ed. 187. * * *

[The Court held that Poole had violated the Act, and that the Act as applied to him was valid.]

Notes and Questions

1. Is the ripeness doctrine based upon constitutional or prudential considerations? What additional allegations would have rendered the case ripe for adjudication? Do the mootness and ripeness doctrines derive from a common nucleus of policy considerations? Or are there substantial differences in the policy considerations underlying the doctrines?

2. The Court ultimately reached certain of the constitutional issues in the case involving appellant Poole. Does this render the opinion regarding the remaining litigants more or less understandable? Why?

3. Note the dilemma facing potential litigants. If the case becomes stale, even after the proceedings have been instituted, mootness aborts it. *See* p. 513, *supra.* This is what happened to the controversy respecting the affiant's right to act as a watcher at the polls. At the other extreme, litigants who jump the gun are subject to dismissal under the ripeness doctrine. What should the litigant do? Violate the statute and be dismissed from employment? Or in other statutory schemes be subject to criminal prosecution? Is this a sensible solution? We will return to these issues shortly in our discussion of federalism. *See infra* Chapter 6, Section 5.

4. THE POLITICAL QUESTION DOCTRINE

BAKER v. CARR

Supreme Court of the United States, 1962.
369 U.S. 186, 82 S.Ct. 691, 7 L.Ed.2d 663.

JUSTICE BRENNAN delivered the opinion of the Court.

This civil action was brought under 42 U.S.C. §§ 1983 and 1988 to redress the alleged deprivation of federal constitutional rights. The complaint, alleging that by means of a 1901 statute of Tennessee apportioning the members of the General Assembly among the State's 95 counties, "these plaintiffs and others similarly situated, are denied the equal protection of the laws accorded them by the Fourteenth Amendment to the Constitution of the United States by virtue of the debasement of their votes," was dismissed by a three-judge court convened under 28 U.S.C. § 2281 in the Middle District of Tennessee. The court held that it lacked jurisdiction of the subject matter and also that no claim was stated upon which relief could be granted. 179 F.Supp. 824. We noted probable jurisdiction of the appeal. * * * We hold that the dismissal was error, and remand the cause to the District Court for trial and further proceedings consistent with this opinion.

* * *

Tennessee's standard for allocating legislative representation among her counties is the total number of qualified voters resident in the respective counties, subject only to minor qualifications. Decennial reapportionment in compliance with the constitutional scheme was effected by the General Assembly each decade from 1871 to 1901. * * *

Between 1901 and 1961, Tennessee has experienced substantial growth and redistribution of her population. * * * It is primarily the continued application of the 1901 Apportionment Act to this shifted and enlarged voting population which gives rise to the present controversy.

* * * The complaint concludes that "these plaintiffs and others similarly situated, are denied the equal protection of the laws accorded them by the Fourteenth Amendment to the Constitution of the United States by virtue of the debasement of their votes." They seek a declaration that the 1901 statute is unconstitutional and an injunction restraining the appellees from acting to conduct any further elections under it. They also pray that unless and until the General Assembly enacts a valid reapportionment, the District Court should either decree a reapportionment by mathematical application of the Tennessee constitutional formulae to the most recent Federal Census figures, or direct the appellees to conduct legislative elections, primary and general, at large. They also pray for such other and further relief as may be appropriate.

* * *

IV.

JUSTICIABILITY.

* * * We hold that this challenge to an apportionment presents no nonjusticiable "political question." * * *

Of course the mere fact that the suit seeks protection of a political right does not mean it presents a political question. Such an objection "is little more than a play upon words." *Nixon v. Herndon,* 273 U.S. 536, 540, 47 S.Ct. 446, 71 L.Ed. 759. Rather, it is argued that apportionment cases, whatever the actual wording of the complaint, can involve no federal constitutional right except one resting on the guaranty of a republican form of government,[30] and that complaints based on that clause have been held to present political questions which are nonjusticiable.

We hold that the claim pleaded here neither rests upon nor implicates the Guaranty Clause and that its justiciability is therefore not

---

30. "The United States shall guarantee to every State in this Union a Republican Form of Government, and shall protect each of them against Invasion; and on Application of the Legislature, or of the Executive (when the Legislature cannot be convened) against domestic Violence." U.S.Const., Art. IV, § 4.

foreclosed by our decisions of cases involving that clause. The District Court misinterpreted *Colegrove v. Green* and other decisions of this Court on which it relied. Appellants' claim that they are being denied equal protection is justiciable, and if "discrimination is sufficiently shown, the right to relief under the equal protection clause is not diminished by the fact that the discrimination relates to political rights." *Snowden v. Hughes,* 321 U.S. 1, 11, 64 S.Ct. 397, 402, 88 L.Ed. 497. To show why we reject the argument based on the Guaranty Clause, we must examine the authorities under it. But because there appears to be some uncertainty as to why those cases did present political questions, and specifically as to whether this apportionment case is like those cases, we deem it necessary first to consider the contours of the "political question" doctrine.

* * * [I]n the Guaranty Clause cases and in the other "political question" cases, it is the relationship between the judiciary and the coordinate branches of the Federal Government, and not the federal judiciary's relationship to the States, which gives rise to the "political question."

We have said that "In determining whether a question falls within [the political question] category, the appropriateness under our system of government of attributing finality to the action of the political departments and also the lack of satisfactory criteria for a judicial determination are dominant considerations." *Coleman v. Miller,* 307 U.S. 433, 454–55, 59 S.Ct. 972, 982, 83 L.Ed. 1385. The nonjusticiability of a political question is primarily a function of the separation of powers. Much confusion results from the capacity of the "political question" label to obscure the need for case-by-case inquiry. Deciding whether a matter has in any measure been committed by the Constitution to another branch of government, or whether the action of that branch exceeds whatever authority has been committed, is itself a delicate exercise in constitutional interpretation, and is a responsibility of this Court as ultimate interpreter of the Constitution. * * *

Foreign relations: There are sweeping statements to the effect that all questions touching foreign relations are political questions. Not only does resolution of such issues frequently turn on standards that defy judicial application, or involve the exercise of a discretion demonstrably committed to the executive or legislature; but many such questions uniquely demand single-voiced statement of the Government's views. Yet it is error to suppose that every case or controversy which touches foreign relations lies beyond judicial cognizance. Our cases in this field seem invariably to show a discriminating analysis of the particular question posed, in terms of the history of its management by the political branches, of its susceptibility to judicial handling in the light of its nature and posture in the specific case, and of the possible consequences of judicial action. For example, though a court will not ordinarily inquire whether a treaty has been terminated, since on that question "governmental action * * * must be regarded as of controlling importance," if there has been no conclusive "governmental action" then a court can construe a treaty and may find it provides the answer. * * * Though a court will not undertake to construe a treaty in a manner inconsistent with a subsequent federal statute, no similar hesitancy obtains if the asserted clash is with state law. * * *

While recognition of foreign governments so strongly defies judicial treatment that without executive recognition a foreign state has been called "a republic of whose existence we know nothing," and the judiciary ordinarily follows the executive as to which nation has sovereignty over disputed territory, once sovereignty over an area is politically determined and declared, courts may examine the resulting status and decide independently whether a statute applies to that area. Similarly, recognition of belligerency abroad is an executive responsibility, but if the executive proclamations fall short of an explicit answer, a court may construe them seeking, for example, to determine whether the situation is such that statutes designed to assure American neutrality have become operative. *The Three Friends,* 166 U.S. 1, 63, 66, 17 S.Ct. 495, 502, 503, 41 L.Ed. 897. Still again, though it is the executive that determines a person's status as representative of a foreign government, *Ex parte Hitz,* 111 U.S. 766, 4 S.Ct. 698, 28 L.Ed. 592, the executive's statements will be construed where necessary to determine the court's jurisdiction, *In re Baiz,* 135 U.S. 403, 10 S.Ct. 854, 34 L.Ed. 222. Similar judicial action in the absence of a recognizedly authoritative executive declaration occurs in cases involving the immunity from seizure of vessels owned by friendly foreign governments. *Compare Ex parte Peru,* 318 U.S. 578, 63 S.Ct. 793, 87 L.Ed. 1014, *with Mexico v. Hoffman,* 324 U.S. 30, 34–35, 65 S.Ct. 530, 532, 89 L.Ed. 729.

Dates of duration of hostilities: Though it has been stated broadly that "the power which declared the necessity is the power to declare its cessation, and what the cessation requires," *Commercial Trust Co. v. Miller,* 262 U.S. 51, 57, 43 S.Ct. 486, 488, 489, 67 L.Ed. 858, here too analysis reveals isolable reasons for the presence of political questions, underlying this Court's refusal to review the political departments' determination of when or whether a war has ended. Dominant is the need for finality in the political determination, for emergency's nature demands "A prompt and unhesitating obedience," *Martin v. Mott,* 12 Wheat. 19, 30, 6 L.Ed. 537 (calling up of militia). Moreover, "the cessation of hostilities does not necessarily end the war power. It was stated in *Hamilton v. Kentucky Distilleries & W. Co.,* 251 U.S. 146, 161, 40 S.Ct. 106, 110, 64 L.Ed. 194, that the war power includes the power 'to remedy the evils which have arisen from its rise and progress' and continues during that emergency. *Stewart v. Kahn,* 11 Wall. 493, 507, 20 L.Ed. 176." *Fleming v. Mohawk Wrecking Co.,* 331 U.S. 111, 116, 67 S.Ct. 1129, 1132, 91 L.Ed. 1375. But deference rests on reason, not habit. The question in a particular case may not seriously implicate considerations of finality—e.g., a public program of importance (rent control) yet not central to the emergency effort. Further, clearly definable criteria for decision may be available. In such case the political question barrier falls away: "[A] Court is not at liberty to shut its eyes to an obvious mistake, when the validity of the law depends upon the truth of what is declared. * * * [It can] inquire whether the exigency still existed upon which the continued operation of the law depended." *Chastleton Corp. v. Sinclair,* 264 U.S. 543, 547–548, 44 S.Ct. 405, 406, 68 L.Ed. 841. *Compare Woods v. Miller Co.,* 333 U.S. 138, 68 S.Ct. 421, 92 L.Ed. 596. On the other hand, even in private litigation which directly implicates no feature of separation of powers, lack of judicially discoverable standards and the drive for even-handed application may impel reference to the political departments' determination of dates of hostilities' beginning and ending. *The Protector,* 12 Wall. 700, 20 L.Ed. 463.

Validity of enactments: In *Coleman v. Miller,* * * * this Court held that the questions of how long a proposed amendment to the Federal Constitution remained open to ratification, and what effect a prior rejection had on a subsequent ratification, were committed to congressional resolution and involved criteria of decision that necessarily escaped the judicial grasp. Similar considerations apply to the enacting process: "The respect due to coequal and independent departments," and the need for finality and certainty about the status of a statute contribute to judicial reluctance to inquire whether, as passed, it complied with all requisite formalities. *Field v. Clark,* 143 U.S. 649, 672, 676–677, 12 S.Ct. 495, 497, 499, 36 L.Ed. 294; *see Leser v. Garnett,* 258 U.S. 130, 137, 42 S.Ct. 217, 218, 66 L.Ed. 505. But it is not true that courts will never delve into a legislature's records upon such a quest: If the enrolled statute lacks an effective date, a court will not hesitate to seek it in the legislative journals in order to preserve the enactment. *Gardner v. The Collector,* 6 Wall. 499, 18 L.Ed. 890. The political question doctrine, a tool for maintenance of governmental order, will not be so applied as to promote only disorder.

The status of Indian tribes: This Court's deference to the political departments in determining whether Indians are recognized as a tribe, while it reflects familiar attributes of political questions, *United States v. Holliday,* 3 Wall. 407, 419, 18 L.Ed. 182, also has a unique element in that "the relation of the Indians to the United States is marked by peculiar and cardinal distinctions which exist nowhere else. * * * [The Indians are] domestic dependent nations * * * in a state of pupilage. Their relation to the United States resembles that of a ward to his guardian." *The Cherokee Nation v. Georgia,* 5 Pet. 1, 16, 17, 8 L.Ed. 25. Yet, here too, there is no blanket rule. * * *

It is apparent that several formulations which vary slightly according to the settings in which the questions arise may describe a political question, although each has one or more elements which identify it as essentially a function of the separation of powers. Prominent on the surface of any case held to involve a political question is found a textually demonstrable constitutional commitment of the issue to a coordinate political department; or a lack of judicially discoverable and manageable standards for resolving it; or the impossibility of deciding without an initial policy determination of a kind clearly for nonjudicial discretion; or the impossibility of a court's undertaking independent resolution without expressing lack of the respect due coordinate branches of government; or an unusual need for unquestioning adherence to a political decision already made; or the potentiality of embarrassment from multifarious pronouncements by various departments on one question.

Unless one of these formulations is inextricable from the case at bar, there should be no dismissal for nonjusticiability on the ground of a political question's presence. The doctrine of which we treat is one of "political questions," not one of "political cases." The courts cannot reject as "no law suit" a bona fide controversy as to whether some action denominated "political" exceeds constitutional authority. The cases we have reviewed show the necessity for discriminating inquiry into the precise facts and posture of the particular case, and the impossibility of resolution by any semantic cataloguing.

But it is argued that this case shares the characteristics of decisions that constitute a category not yet considered, cases concerning the Constitution's guaranty, in Art. IV, § 4, of a republican form of government. A conclusion as to whether the case at bar does present a political question cannot be confidently reached until we have considered those cases with special care. We shall discover that Guaranty Clause claims involve those elements which define a "political question," and for that reason and no other, they are nonjusticiable. In particular, we shall discover that the nonjusticiability of such claims has nothing to do with their touching upon matters of state governmental organization.

Republican form of government: Luther v. Borden, 7 How. 1, 12 L.Ed. 581, though in form simply an action for damages for trespass was, as Daniel Webster said in opening the argument for the defense, "an unusual case." The defendants, admitting an otherwise tortious breaking and entering, sought to justify their action on the ground that they were agents of the established lawful government of Rhode Island, which State was then under martial law to defend itself from active insurrection; that the plaintiff was engaged in that insurrection; and that they entered under orders to arrest the plaintiff. The case arose "out of the unfortunate political differences which agitated the people of Rhode Island in 1841 and 1842," 7 How. at 34, and which had resulted in a situation wherein two groups laid competing claims to recognition as the lawful government. The plaintiff's right to recover depended upon which of the two groups was entitled to such recognition; but the lower court's refusal to receive evidence or hear argument on that issue, its charge to the jury that the earlier established or "charter" government was lawful, and the verdict for the defendants, were affirmed upon appeal to this Court.

Chief Justice Taney's opinion for the Court reasoned as follows: (1) If a court were to hold the defendants' acts unjustified because the charter government had no legal existence during the period in question, it would follow that all of that government's actions—laws enacted, taxes collected, salaries paid, accounts settled, sentences passed—were of no effect; and that "the officers who carried their decisions into operation [were] answerable as trespassers, if not in some cases as criminals." There was, of course, no room for application of any doctrine of *de facto* status to uphold prior acts of an officer not authorized *de jure*, for such would have defeated the plaintiff's very action. A decision for the plaintiff would inevitably have produced some significant measure of chaos, a consequence to be avoided if it could be done without abnegation of the judicial duty to uphold the Constitution.

(2) No state court had recognized as a judicial responsibility settlement of the issue of the locus of state governmental authority. Indeed, the courts of Rhode Island had in several cases held that "it rested with the political power to decide whether the charter government had been displaced or not," and that that department had acknowledged no change.

(3) Since "[t]he question relates, altogether, to the constitution and laws of [the] * * * State," the courts of the United States had to follow the state courts' decisions unless there was a federal constitutional ground for overturning them.

(4) No provision of the Constitution could be or had been invoked for this purpose except Art. IV, § 4, the Guaranty Clause. Having already noted the absence of standards whereby the choice between governments could be made by a court acting independently, Chief Justice Taney now found further textual and practical reasons for concluding that, if any department of the United States was empowered by the Guaranty Clause to resolve the issue, it was not the judiciary * * *.

Clearly, several factors were thought by the Court in *Luther* to make the question there "political": the commitment to the other branches of the decision as to which is the lawful state government; the unambiguous action by the President, in recognizing the charter government as the lawful authority; the need for finality in the executive's decision; and the lack of criteria by which a court could determine which form of government was republican.[48]

But the only significance that *Luther* could have for our immediate purposes is in its holding that the Guaranty Clause is not a repository of judicially manageable standards which a court could utilize independently in order to identify a State's lawful government. The Court has since refused to resort to the Guaranty Clause—which alone had been invoked for the purpose—as the source of a constitutional standard for invalidat-

---

48. Even though the Court wrote of unrestrained legislative and executive authority under this Guaranty, thus making its enforcement a political question, the Court plainly implied that the political question barrier was no absolute: "Unquestionably a military government, established as the permanent government of the State, would not be a republican government, and it would be the duty of Congress to overthrow it." 7 How. at 45. Of course, it does not necessarily follow that if Congress did not act, the Court would. For while the judiciary might be able to decide the limits of the meaning of "republican form," and thus the factor of lack of criteria might fall away, there would remain other possible barriers to decision because of primary commitment to another branch, which would have to be considered in the particular fact setting presented.

ing state action. *See* * * * *Pacific States Tel. & T. Co. v. Oregon,* 223 U.S. 118, 32 S.Ct. 224, 56 L.Ed. 377 (claim that initiative and referendum negated republican government held nonjusticiable) * * *.

Just as the Court has consistently held that a challenge to state action based on the Guaranty Clause presents no justiciable question so has it held, and for the same reasons, that challenges to congressional action on the ground of inconsistency with that clause present no justiciable question. * * * *Georgia v. Stanton,* 6 Wall. 50, 18 L.Ed. 721. * * *

* * *

We come, finally, to the ultimate inquiry whether our precedents as to what constitutes a nonjusticiable "political question" bring the case before us under the umbrella of that doctrine. A natural beginning is to note whether any of the common characteristics which we have been able to identify and label descriptively are present. We find none: The question here is the consistency of state action with the Federal Constitution. We have no question decided, or to be decided, by a political branch of government coequal with this Court. Nor do we risk embarrassment of our government abroad, or grave disturbance at home if we take issue with Tennessee as to the constitutionality of her action here challenged. Nor need the appellants, in order to succeed in this action, ask the Court to enter upon policy determinations for which judicially manageable standards are lacking. Judicial standards under the Equal Protection Clause are well developed and familiar, and it has been open to courts since the enactment of the Fourteenth Amendment to determine, if on the particular facts they must, that a discrimination reflects *no* policy, but simply arbitrary and capricious action.

This case does, in one sense, involve the allocation of political power within a State, and the appellants might conceivably have added a claim under the Guaranty Clause. Of course, as we have seen, any reliance on that clause would be futile. But because any reliance on the Guaranty Clause could not have succeeded it does not follow that appellants may not be heard on the equal protection claim which in fact they tender. True, it must be clear that the Fourteenth Amendment claim is not so enmeshed with those political question elements which render Guaranty Clause claims nonjusticiable as actually to present a political question itself. But we have found that not to be the case here.

In this connection special attention is due *Pacific States Tel. & T. Co. v. Oregon,* 223 U.S. 118, 32 S.Ct. 224, 56 L.Ed. 377. In that case a corporation tax statute enacted by the initiative was attacked ostensibly on three grounds: (1) due process; (2) equal protection; and (3) the Guaranty Clause. But it was clear that the first two grounds were invoked solely in aid of the contention that the tax was invalid by reason of its passage * * *.

The due process and equal protection claims were held nonjusticiable in *Pacific States* not because they happened to be joined with a

Guaranty Clause claim, or because they sought to place before the Court a subject matter which might conceivably have been dealt with through the Guaranty Clause, but because the Court believed that they were invoked merely in verbal aid of the resolution of issues which, in its view, entailed political questions. * * *

We conclude then that the nonjusticiability of claims resting on the Guaranty Clause which arises from their embodiment of questions that were thought "political," can have no bearing upon the justiciability of the equal protection claim presented in this case. Finally, we emphasize that it is the involvement in Guaranty Clause claims of the elements thought to define "political questions," and no other feature, which could render them nonjusticiable. Specifically, we have said that such claims are not held nonjusticiable because they touch matters of state governmental organization. * * *

* * *

We conclude that the complaint's allegations of a denial of equal protection present a justiciable constitutional cause of action upon which appellants are entitled to a trial and a decision. The right asserted is within the reach of judicial protection under the Fourteenth Amendment.

The judgment of the District Court is reversed and the cause is remanded for further proceedings consistent with this opinion.

JUSTICE WHITTAKER did not participate in the decision of this case.

* * *

[The concurring opinions of Justices Douglas, Clark, and Stewart, are omitted.]

JUSTICE FRANKFURTER, whom JUSTICE HARLAN joins, dissenting.

The Court today reverses a uniform course of decision established by a dozen cases, including one by which the very claim now sustained was unanimously rejected only five years ago. The impressive body of rulings thus cast aside reflected the equally uniform course of our political history regarding the relationship between population and legislative representation—a wholly different matter from denial of the franchise to individuals because of race, color, religion or sex. Such a massive repudiation of the experience of our whole past in asserting destructively novel judicial power demands a detailed analysis of the role of this Court in our constitutional scheme. Disregard of inherent limits in the effective exercise of the Court's "judicial Power" not only presages the futility of judicial intervention in the essentially political conflict of forces by which the relation between population and representation has time out of mind been and now is determined. It may well impair the Court's position as the ultimate organ of "the supreme Law of the Land" in that vast range of legal problems, often strongly entangled in popular feeling, on which this Court must pronounce. The Court's authority—possessed of neither the purse nor the sword—ultimately rests on sustained public confidence in its moral sanction. Such feeling must be nourished by the Court's complete detachment, in fact and in appearance, from political entanglements and by abstention from injecting itself into the clash of political forces in political settlements.

* * *

I.

In sustaining appellants' claim, based on the Fourteenth Amendment, that the District Court may entertain this suit, this Court's uniform course of decision over the years is overruled or disregarded. Explicitly it begins with *Colegrove v. Green,* * * * decided in 1946, but its roots run deep in the Court's historic adjudicatory process.

Colegrove held that a federal court should not entertain an action for declaratory and injunctive relief to adjudicate the constitutionality, under the Equal Protection Clause and other federal constitutional and statutory provisions, of a state statute establishing the respective districts for the State's election of Representatives to the Congress. Two opinions were written by the four Justices who composed the majority of the seven sitting members of the Court. Both opinions joining in the result in *Colegrove v. Green* agreed that considerations were controlling which dictated denial of jurisdiction though not in the strict sense of want of power. While the two opinions show a divergence of view regarding some of these considerations, there are important points of concurrence. Both opinions demonstrate a predominant concern, first, with avoiding federal judicial involvement in matters traditionally left to legislative policy making; second, with respect to the difficulty—in view of the nature of the problems of apportionment and its history in this country—of drawing on or devising judicial standards for judgment, as opposed to legislative determinations, of the part which mere numerical equality among voters should play as a criterion for the allocation of political power; and, third, with problems of finding appropriate modes of relief—particularly, the problem of resolving the essentially political issue of the relative merits of at-large elections and elections held in districts of unequal population.

The broad applicability of these considerations—summarized in the loose shorthand phrase, "political question"—in cases involving a State's apportionment of voting power among its numerous localities has led the Court, since 1946, to recognize their controlling effect in a variety of situations. (In all these cases decision was by a full Court.) The "political question" principle as applied in *Colegrove* has found wide application commensurate with its function as "one of the rules basic to the federal system and this Court's appropriate place within that structure." *Rescue Army v. Municipal Court,* 331 U.S. 549, 570, 67 S.Ct. 1409, 1420, 91 L.Ed. 1666.

* * *

II.

The *Colegrove* doctrine, in the form in which repeated decisions have settled it, was not an innovation. It represents long judicial thought and experience. From its earliest opinions this Court has consistently recognized a class of controversies which do not lend themselves to judicial standards and judicial remedies. To classify the various instances as "political questions" is rather a form of stating this conclusion than revealing of analysis.

* * *

The Court has been particularly unwilling to intervene in matters concerning the structure and organization of the political institutions of the States. The abstention from judicial entry into such areas has been greater even than that which marks the Court's ordinary approach to issues of state power challenged under broad federal guarantees. "We should be very reluctant to decide that we had jurisdiction in such a case, and thus in an action of this nature to supervise and review the political administration of a state government by its own officials and through its own courts. The jurisdiction of this court would only exist in case there had been * * * such plain and substantial departure from the fundamental principles upon which our government is based that it could with truth and propriety be said that if the judgment were suffered to remain, the party aggrieved would be deprived of his life, liberty or property in violation of the provisions of the Federal Constitution." *Wilson v. North Carolina,* 169 U.S. 586, 596, 18 S.Ct. 435, 439, 42 L.Ed. 865. *See Taylor and Marshall v. Beckham (No. 1),* 178 U.S. 548, 20 S.Ct. 890, 44 L.Ed. 1187; *Walton v. House of Representatives,* 265 U.S. 487, 44 S.Ct. 628, 68 L.Ed. 1115; *Snowden v. Hughes,* 321 U.S. 1, 64 S.Ct. 397, 88 L.Ed. 497. *Cf. In re Sawyer,* 124 U.S. 200, 220–21, 8 S.Ct. 482, 492–493, 31 L.Ed. 402.

Where, however, state law has made particular federal questions determinative of relations within the structure of state government, not in challenge of it, the Court has resolved such narrow, legally defined questions in proper proceedings. *See Boyd v. Nebraska ex rel. Thayer,* 143 U.S. 135, 12 S.Ct. 375, 36 L.Ed. 103. In such instances there is no conflict between state policy and the exercise of federal judicial power.

* * * The cases involving Negro disfranchisement are no exception to the principle of avoiding federal judicial intervention into matters of state government in the absence of an explicit and clear constitutional imperative. For here the controlling command of Supreme Law is plain and unequivocal. An end of discrimination against the Negro was the compelling motive of the Civil War Amendments. The Fifteenth expresses this in terms, and it is no less true of the Equal Protection Clause of the Fourteenth. *Slaughter-House Cases,* 16 Wall. 36, 67–72, 21 L.Ed. 394; *Strauder v. West Virginia,* 100 U.S. 303, 306–307, 25 L.Ed. 664; *Nixon v. Herndon,* 273 U.S. 536, 541, 47 S.Ct. 446, 447, 71 L.Ed. 759. Thus the Court, in cases involving discrimination against the Negro's right to vote, has recognized not only the action at law for damages, but, in appropriate circumstances, the extraordinary remedy of declaratory or injunctive relief. *Schnell v. Davis,* 336 U.S. 933, 69 S.Ct. 749, 93 L.Ed. 1093; *Terry v. Adams,* 345 U.S. 461, 73 S.Ct. 809, 97 L.Ed. 1152. Injunctions in these cases, it should be noted, would not have restrained state-wide general elections.

* * *

The influence of these converging considerations—the caution not to undertake decision where standards meet for judicial judgment are lacking, the reluctance to interfere with matters of state government in the absence of an unquestionable and effectively enforceable mandate, the unwillingness to make courts arbiters of the broad issues of political organization historically committed to other institutions and for whose adjustment the judicial process is ill-adapted—has been decisive of the settled line of cases, reaching back more than a century, which holds that Art. IV, § 4, of the Constitution, guaranteeing to the States "a Republican Form of Government," is not enforceable through the courts. *E.g., O'Neill v. Leamer,* 239 U.S. 244, 36 S.Ct. 54, 60 L.Ed. 249; *Mountain Timber Co. v. Washington,* 243 U.S. 219, 37 S.Ct. 260, 61 L.Ed. 685; *Cochran v. Board of Education,* 281 U.S. 370, 50 S.Ct. 335, 74 L.Ed. 913; *Highland Farms Dairy, Inc. v. Agnew,* 300 U.S. 608, 57 S.Ct. 549, 81 L.Ed. 835. Claims resting on this specific guarantee of the Constitution have been held nonjusticiable which challenged state distribution of powers between the legislative and judicial branches, *Ohio ex rel. Bryant v. Akron Metropolitan Park District,* 281 U.S. 74, 50 S.Ct. 228, 74 L.Ed. 710, state delegation of power to municipalities, *Kiernan v. Portland, Oregon,* 223 U.S. 151, 32 S.Ct. 231, 56 L.Ed. 386, state adoption of the referendum as a legislative institution, *Ohio ex rel. Davis v. Hildebrant,* 241 U.S. 565, 569, 36 S.Ct. 708, 710, 60 L.Ed. 1172, and state restriction upon the power of state constitutional amendment, *Marshall v. Dye,* 231 U.S. 250, 256–57, 34 S.Ct. 92, 93–94, 58 L.Ed. 206. The subject was fully considered in *Pacific States Telephone & Telegraph Co. v. Oregon,* 223 U.S. 118, 32 S.Ct. 224, 56 L.Ed. 377, in which the Court dismissed for want of jurisdiction a writ of error attacking a state license-tax statute enacted by the initiative, on the claim that this mode of legislation was inconsistent with a Republican Form of Government and violated the Equal Protection Clause and other federal guarantees. After noting " * * * the ruinous destruction of legislative authority in matters purely political which would necessarily be occasioned by giving sanction to the doctrine which underlies and would be necessarily involved in sustaining the propositions contended for," the Court said:

> [The] essentially political nature [of this claim] is at once made manifest by understanding that the assault which the contention here advanced makes it [*sic*] not on the tax as a tax, but on the State as a State. It is addressed to the framework and political character of the government by which the statute levying the tax was passed. It is the government, the political entity, which (reducing the case to its essence) is called to the bar of this court, not for the purpose of

testing judicially some exercise of power assailed, on the ground that its exertion has injuriously affected the rights of an individual because of repugnancy to some constitutional limitation, but to demand of the State that it establish its right to exist as a State, republican in form. Id. at 150–151, 32 S.Ct. at 231.

The starting point of the doctrine applied in these cases is, of course, *Luther v. Borden,* 7 How. 1, 12 L.Ed. 581.

* * *

III.

The present case involves all of the elements that have made the Guarantee Clause cases non-justiciable. It is, in effect, a Guarantee Clause claim masquerading under a different label. But it cannot make the case more fit for judicial action that appellants invoke the Fourteenth Amendment rather than Art. IV, § 4, where, in fact, the gist of their complaint is the same—unless it can be found that the Fourteenth Amendment speaks with greater particularity to their situation. We have been admonished to avoid "the tyranny of labels." *Snyder v. Massachusetts,* 291 U.S. 97, 114, 54 S.Ct. 330, 335, 78 L.Ed. 674. Art. IV, § 4, is not committed by express constitutional terms to Congress. It is the nature of the controversies arising under it, nothing else, which has made it judicially unenforceable. Of course, if a controversy falls within judicial power, it depends "on how he [the plaintiff] casts his action," *Pan American Petroleum Corp. v. Superior Court,* 366 U.S. 656, 662, 81 S.Ct. 1303, 1307, 6 L.Ed.2d 584, whether he brings himself within a jurisdictional statute. But where judicial competence is wanting, it cannot be created by invoking one clause of the Constitution rather than another. When what was essentially a Guarantee Clause claim was sought to be laid, as well, under the Equal Protection Clause in *Pacific States Telephone & Telegraph Co. v. Oregon,* the Court had no difficulty in "dispelling any mere confusion resulting from forms of expression and considering the substance of things * * *." 223 U.S. at 140, 32 S.Ct. at 227, 56 L.Ed. 377.

Here appellants attack "the State as a State," precisely as it was perceived to be attacked in the *Pacific States* case, *id.* at 150, 32 S.Ct. at 231. Their complaint is that the basis of representation of the Tennessee Legislature hurts them. They assert that "a minority now rules in Tennessee," that the apportionment statute results in a "distortion of the constitutional system," that the General Assembly is no longer "a body representative of the people of the State of Tennessee," all "contrary to the basic principle of representative government * * *." Accepting appellants' own formulation of the issue, one can know this handsaw from a hawk. Such a claim would be nonjusticiable not merely under Art. IV, § 4, but under any clause of the Constitution, by virtue of the very fact that a federal court is not a forum for political debate. *Massachusetts v. Mellon, supra.*

But appellants, of course, do not rest on this claim *simpliciter*. In invoking the Equal Protection Clause, they assert that the distortion of representative government complained of is produced by systematic discrimination against them, by way of "a debasement of their votes * * *." Does this characterization, with due regard for the facts from which it is derived, add anything to appellants' case?

At first blush, this charge of discrimination based on legislative underrepresentation is given the appearance of a more private, less impersonal claim, than the assertion that the frame of government is askew. Appellants appear as representatives of a class that is prejudiced as a class, in contradistinction to the polity in its entirety. However, the discrimination relied on is the deprivation of what appellants conceive to be their proportionate share of political influence. This, of course, is the practical effect of any allocation of power within the institutions of government. Hardly any distribution of political authority that could be assailed as rendering government nonrepublican would fail similarly to operate to the prejudice of some groups, and to the advantage of others, within the body politic. It would be ingenuous not to see, or consciously blind to deny, that the real battle over the initiative and referendum, or over a delegation of power to local rather than state-wide authority, is the battle between forces whose influence is disparate among the various organs of government to whom power may be given. No shift of power but works a corresponding shift in political influence among the groups composing a society.

What, then, is this question of legislative apportionment? Appellants invoke the right to vote and to have their votes counted. But they are permitted to vote and their votes are counted. They go to the polls, they cast their ballots, they send their representatives to the state councils. Their complaint is simply that the representatives are not sufficiently numerous or powerful—in short, that Tennessee has adopted a basis of representation with which they are dissatisfied. Talk of "debasement" or "dilution" is circular talk. One cannot speak of "debasement" or "dilution" of the value of a vote until there is first defined a standard of reference as to what a vote should be worth. What is actually asked of the Court in this case is to choose among competing bases of representation—ultimately, really, among competing theories of political philosophy—in order to establish an appropriate frame of government for the State of Tennessee and thereby for all the States of the Union.

In such a matter, abstract analogies which ignore the facts of history deal in unrealities; they betray reason. This is not a case in which a State has, through a device however oblique and sophisticated, denied Negroes or Jews or redheaded persons a vote, or given them only a third or a sixth of a vote. That was *Gomillion v. Lightfoot,* 364 U.S. 339, 81 S.Ct. 125, 5 L.Ed.2d 110. What Tennessee illustrates is an old and still widespread method of representation—representation by local geographical division, only in part respective of population—in preference to others, others, forsooth, more appealing. Appellants contest this choice and seek to make this Court the arbiter of the disagreement. They would make the Equal Protection Clause the charter of adjudication, asserting that the equality which it guarantees comports, if not the assurance of equal weight to every voter's vote, at least the basic conception that representation ought to be proportionate to population, a standard by reference to which the reasonableness of apportionment plans may be judged.

To find such a political conception legally enforceable in the broad and unspecific guarantee of equal protection is to rewrite the Constitution. *See Luther v. Borden, supra.* Certainly, "equal protection" is no more secure a foundation for judicial judgment of the permissibility of varying forms of representative government than is "Republican Form." Indeed since "equal protection of the laws" can only mean an equality of persons standing in the same relation to whatever governmental action is challenged, the determination whether treatment is equal presupposes a determination concerning the nature of the relationship. This, with respect to apportionment, means an inquiry into the theoretic base of representation in an acceptably republican state. For a court could not determine the equal-protection issue without in fact first determining the Republican–Form issue, simply because what is reasonable for equal-protection purposes will depend upon what frame of government, basically, is allowed. To divorce "equal protection" from "Republican Form" is to talk about half a question.

* * *

Manifestly, the Equal Protection Clause supplies no clearer guide for judicial examination of apportionment methods than would the Guarantee Clause itself. Apportionment, by its character, is a subject of extraordinary complexity, involving—even after the fundamental theoretical issues concerning what is to be represented in a representative legislature have been fought out or compromised—considerations of geography, demography, electoral convenience, economic and social cohesions or divergencies among particular local groups, communications, the practical effects of political institutions like the lobby and the city machine, ancient traditions and ties of settled usage, respect for proven incumbents of long experience and senior status, mathematical mechanics, censuses compiling relevant data, and a host of others.

* * *

Although the District Court had jurisdiction in the very restricted sense of power to determine whether it could adjudicate the claim, the case is of that class of political controversy which, by the nature of its subject, is unfit for federal judicial action. The judgment of the District Court, in dismissing the complaint for failure to state a claim on which relief can be granted, should therefore be affirmed.

[The dissent of Justice Harlan is omitted.]

Notes and Questions

1. Is the political question doctrine based upon constitutional or prudential considerations? Does this doctrine differ fundamentally from standing, mootness, and ripeness? In what ways?

2. Is the doctrine a wise exercise of judicial restraint? Should the Court have entered the fray and decided the reapportionment issue? What problems did the lower courts face in implementing the decision? Does the balance between federal and state interests (federalism) suggest that federal courts should exercise judicial restraint?

3. Professor Scharf has suggested three rationales for the political question doctrine: the "opportunistic" theory, focusing on the Court's instinct for survival; the "cognitive" rationale, examining the absence of judicially discoverable standards to govern the cases; and the "normative" rationale, eschewing a rule of law to govern all situations and leaving matters to discretionary factors or further insights. Scharf, *Judicial Review and the Political Question: A Functional Analysis,* 75 Yale L.J. 517 (1966). Consider Henkin, *Is there a Political Question Doctrine?*, 85 Yale L.J. 597 (1976).

4. Are national political parties and their nominating conventions subject to regulation by the courts or only by Congress? This question was expressly left open in *Cousins v. Wigoda*, 419 U.S. 477 (1975). How would you answer this question in light of *Baker v. Carr*?

5. Does the political question doctrine foreclose judicial review of the constitutionality of a war? *See Mora v. McNamara,* 389 U.S. 934 (1967) (certiorari denied). Would your answer depend on the manner in which the case reached the court system? Suppose the Court had held the Vietnam War unconstitutional. What would have happened? Does your answer depend upon the date of the decision? Why? *See Goldwater v. Carter,* 444 U.S. 996 (1979) (dismissal of a suit by several members of the Congress seeking to have the Court declare that the president's unilateral notice of termination of the mutual defense treaty with the Republic of China, pursuant to a termination clause in the treaty, was ineffective absent congressional approval).

The furthest potential extension of the political question doctrine, refusal to question the propriety of executive action in any case, was soundly rejected by the Court in *Marbury v. Madison. See supra* p. 464.

6. In *Bush v. Palm Beach County Canvassing Board*, 531 U.S. 70 (2000) (per curiam), and *Bush v. Gore*, 531 U.S. 98 (2000) (per curiam), the Court decided sensitive questions relating to the presidential election of 2000 without even a reference to the political question doctrine. Was it so clear that the doctrine did not apply?

5. FEDERALISM

Introductory Note

Federalism is a doctrine that restrains federal courts from adjudicating constitutional challenges to state action under circumstances in which the federal action is deemed inappropriate and an improper intrusion on the rights of the states to enforce their own laws in their own courts. The cases in this section explore the delicate balance between federal and state interests.

YOUNGER v. HARRIS

Supreme Court of the United States, 1971.
401 U.S. 37, 91 S.Ct. 746, 27 L.Ed.2d 669.

JUSTICE BLACK delivered the opinion of the Court.

Appellee, John Harris, Jr., was indicted in a California state court, charged with violation of the California Penal Code §§ 11400 and 11401, known as the California Criminal Syndicalism Act * * *. He then filed a complaint in the Federal District Court, asking that court to enjoin the appellant, Younger, the District Attorney of Los Angeles County, from prosecuting him, and alleging that the prosecution and even the presence of the Act inhibited him in the exercise of his rights of free speech and press, rights guaranteed him by the First and Fourteenth Amendments. Appellees Jim Dan and Diane Hirsch intervened as plaintiffs in the suit, claiming that the prosecution of Harris would inhibit them as members of the Progressive Labor Party from peacefully advocating the program of their party, which was to replace capitalism with socialism and to abolish the profit system of production in this country. Appellee Farrell Broslawsky, an instructor in history at Los Angeles Valley College, also intervened claiming that the prosecution of Harris made him uncertain as to whether he could teach about the doctrines of Karl Marx or read from the Communist Manifesto as part of his classwork. All claimed that unless the United States court restrained the state prosecution of Harris each would suffer immediate and irreparable injury. A three-judge Federal District Court, convened pursuant to 28 U.S.C. § 2284, held that it had jurisdiction and power to restrain the District Attorney from prosecuting, held that the State's Criminal Syndicalism Act was void for vagueness and overbreadth in violation of the First and Fourteenth Amendments, and accordingly restrained the District Attorney from "further prosecution of the currently pending action against plaintiff Harris for alleged violation of the Act." 281 F.Supp. 507, 517 (1968).

The case is before us on appeal by the State's District Attorney Younger, pursuant to 28 U.S.C. § 1253. In his notice of appeal and his jurisdictional statement appellant presented two questions: (1) whether the decision of this Court in *Whitney v. California,* 274 U.S. 357, 47 S.Ct. 641, 71 L.Ed. 1095, holding California's law constitutional in 1927 was binding on the District Court and (2) whether the State's law is constitutional on its face. In this Court the brief for the State of California, filed at our request, also argues that only Harris, who was indicted, has standing to challenge the State's law, and that issuance of the injunction was a violation of a longstanding judicial policy and of 28 U.S.C. § 2283, which provides:

> A court of the United States may not grant an injunction to stay proceedings in a State court except as expressly authorized by Act of Congress, or where necessary in aid of its jurisdiction, or to protect or effectuate its judgments.

See, e.g., Atlantic Coast Line R. Co. v. Engineers, 398 U.S. 281, 285–86, 90 S.Ct. 1739, 1742–43, 26 L.Ed.2d 234 (1970). Without regard to the questions raised about *Whitney v. California, supra,* since overruled by *Brandenburg v. Ohio*, 395 U.S. 444, 89 S.Ct. 1827, 23 L.Ed.2d 430 (1969), or the constitutionality of the state law, we have concluded that the judgment of the District Court, enjoining appellant Younger from prosecuting under these California statutes, must be reversed as a violation of the national policy forbidding federal courts to stay or enjoin pending state court proceedings except under special circumstances.[2] We express no view about the circumstances under which federal courts may act when there is no prosecution pending in state courts at the time the federal proceeding is begun.

I

Appellee Harris has been indicted, and was actually being prosecuted by California for a violation of its Criminal Syndicalism Act at the time this suit was filed. He thus has an acute, live controversy with the State and its prosecutor. But none of the other parties plaintiff in the District Court, Dan, Hirsch, or Broslawsky, has such a controversy. None has been indicted, arrested, or even threatened by the prosecutor. About these three the three-judge court said:

> Plaintiffs Dan and Hirsch allege that they are members of the Progressive Labor Party, which advocates change in industrial ownership and political change, and that they feel inhibited in advocating the program of their political party through peaceful, nonviolent means, because of the presence of the Act "on the books," and because of the pending criminal prosecution against Harris. Plaintiff Broslawsky is a history instructor, and he alleges that he is uncertain as to whether his normal practice of teaching his students about the doctrines of Karl Marx and reading from the Communist Manifesto and other revolutionary works may subject him to prosecution for violation of the Act. 281 F.Supp. at 509.

2. Appellees did not explicitly ask for a declaratory judgment in their complaint. They did, however, ask the District Court to grant "such other and further relief as to the Court may seem just and proper," and the District Court in fact granted a declaratory judgment. For the reasons stated in our opinion today in *Samuels v. Mackell*, 401 U.S. 66, 91 S.Ct. 764, 27 L.Ed.2d 688, we hold that declaratory relief is also improper when a prosecution involving the challenged statute is pending in state court at the time the federal suit is initiated.

Whatever right Harris, who is being prosecuted under the state syndicalism law may have, Dan, Hirsch, and Broslawsky cannot share it with
him. If these three had alleged that they would be prosecuted for the
conduct they planned to engage in, and if the District Court had found
this allegation to be true—either on the admission of the State's district
attorney or on any other evidence—then a genuine controversy might be
said to exist. But here appellees Dan, Hirsch, and Broslawsky do not
claim that they have ever been threatened with prosecution, that a
prosecution is likely, or even that a prosecution is remotely possible.
They claim the right to bring this suit solely because, in the language of
their complaint, they "feel inhibited." We do not think this allegation,
even if true, is sufficient to bring the equitable jurisdiction of the federal
courts into play to enjoin a pending state prosecution. A federal lawsuit
to stop a prosecution in a state court is a serious matter. And persons
having no fears of state prosecution except those that are imaginary or
speculative, are not to be accepted as appropriate plaintiffs in such cases.
See *Golden v. Zwickler,* 394 U.S. 103, 89 S.Ct. 956, 22 L.Ed.2d 113
(1969). Since Harris is actually being prosecuted under the challenged
laws, however, we proceed with him as a proper party.

II

Since the beginning of this country's history Congress has, subject
to few exceptions, manifested a desire to permit state courts to try state
cases free from interference by federal courts. In 1793 an Act uncondi-
tionally provided: "[N]or shall a writ of injunction be granted to stay
proceedings in any court of a state * * *." 1 Stat. 335, c. 22, § 5. A
comparison of the 1793 Act with 28 U.S.C. § 2283, its present-day
successor, graphically illustrates how few and minor have been the
exceptions granted from the flat, prohibitory language of the old Act.
During all this lapse of years from 1793 to 1970 the statutory exceptions
to the 1793 congressional enactment have been only three: (1) "except as
expressly authorized by Act of Congress"; (2) "where necessary in aid of
its jurisdiction"; and (3) "to protect or effectuate its judgments." In
addition, a judicial exception to the longstanding policy evidenced by the
statute has been made where a person about to be prosecuted in a state
court can show that he will, if the proceeding in the state court is not
enjoined, suffer irreparable damages. See *Ex parte Young,* 209 U.S. 123,
28 S.Ct. 441, 52 L.Ed. 714 (1908).

The precise reasons for this longstanding public policy against
federal court interference with state court proceedings have never been
specifically identified but the primary sources of the policy are plain. One
is the basic doctrine of equity jurisprudence that courts of equity should
not act, and particularly should not act to restrain a criminal prosecution, when the moving party has an adequate remedy at law and will not
suffer irreparable injury if denied equitable relief. The doctrine may
originally have grown out of circumstances peculiar to the English
judicial system and not applicable in this country, but its fundamental
purpose of restraining equity jurisdiction within narrow limits is equally

important under our Constitution, in order to prevent erosion of the role of the jury and avoid a duplication of legal proceedings and legal sanctions where a single suit would be adequate to protect the rights asserted. This underlying reason for restraining courts of equity from interfering with criminal prosecutions is reinforced by an even more vital consideration, the notion of "comity," that is, a proper respect for state functions, a recognition of the fact that the entire country is made up of a Union of separate state governments, and a continuance of the belief that the National Government will fare best if the States and their institutions are left free to perform their separate functions in their separate ways. This, perhaps for lack of a better and clearer way to describe it, is referred to by many as "Our Federalism," and one familiar with the profound debates that ushered our Federal Constitution into existence is bound to respect those who remain loyal to the ideals and dreams of "Our Federalism." The concept does not mean blind deference to "States' Rights" any more than it means centralization of control over every important issue in our National Government and its courts. The Framers rejected both these courses. What the concept does represent is a system in which there is sensitivity to the legitimate interests of both State and National Governments, and in which the National Government, anxious though it may be to vindicate and protect federal rights and federal interests, always endeavors to do so in ways that will not unduly interfere with the legitimate activities of the States. It should never be forgotten that this slogan, "Our Federalism," born in the early struggling days of our Union of States, occupies a highly important place in our Nation's history and its future.

This brief discussion should be enough to suggest some of the reasons why it has been perfectly natural for our cases to repeat time and time again that the normal thing to do when federal courts are asked to enjoin pending proceedings in state courts is not to issue such injunctions. In *Fenner v. Boykin,* 271 U.S. 240, 46 S.Ct. 492, 70 L.Ed. 927 (1926), suit had been brought in the Federal District Court seeking to enjoin state prosecutions under a recently enacted state law that allegedly interfered with the free flow of interstate commerce. The Court, in a unanimous opinion made clear that such a suit, even with respect to state criminal proceedings not yet formally instituted, could be proper only under very special circumstances:

> *Ex parte Young,* 209 U.S. 123, 28 S.Ct. 441, 52 L.Ed. 714, and following cases have established the doctrine that, when absolutely necessary for protection of constitutional rights, courts of the United States have power to enjoin state officers from instituting criminal actions. But this may not be done, except under extraordinary circumstances, where the danger of irreparable loss is both great and immediate. Ordinarily, there should be no interference with such officers; primarily, they are charged with the duty of prosecuting offenders against the laws of the state, and must decide when and how this is to be done. The accused should first set up and rely upon his defense in the state courts, even though this involves a

challenge of the validity of some statute, unless it plainly appears that this course would not afford adequate protection. *Id.* at 243–244, 46 S.Ct. at 493.

These principles, made clear in the *Fenner* case, have been repeatedly followed and reaffirmed in other cases involving threatened prosecutions. *See, e.g., Spielman Motor Sales Co. v. Dodge,* 295 U.S. 89, 55 S.Ct. 678, 79 L.Ed. 1322 (1935); *Beal v. Missouri Pac. R. Co.,* 312 U.S. 45, 61 S.Ct. 418, 85 L.Ed. 577 (1941); *Watson v. Buck,* 313 U.S. 387, 61 S.Ct. 962, 85 L.Ed. 1416 (1941); *Williams v. Miller,* 317 U.S. 599, 63 S.Ct. 258, 87 L.Ed. 489 (1942); *Douglas v. City of Jeannette,* 319 U.S. 157, 63 S.Ct. 877, 87 L.Ed. 1324 (1943).

In all of these cases the Court stressed the importance of showing irreparable injury, the traditional prerequisite to obtaining an injunction. In addition, however, the Court also made clear that in view of the fundamental policy against federal interference with state criminal prosecutions, even irreparable injury is insufficient unless it is "both great and immediate." *Fenner, supra.* Certain types of injury, in particular, the cost, anxiety, and inconvenience of having to defend against a single criminal prosecution, could not by themselves be considered "irreparable" in the special legal sense of that term. Instead, the threat to the plaintiff's federally protected rights must be one that cannot be eliminated by his defense against a single criminal prosecution. *See, e.g., Ex parte Young,* 209 U.S. at 145–147, 28 S.Ct. at 447–49. Thus, in the *Buck* case, 313 U.S. at 400, 61 S.Ct. at 966, we stressed:

> Federal injunctions against state criminal statutes, either in their entirety or with respect to their separate and distinct prohibitions, are not to be granted as a matter of course, even if such statutes are unconstitutional. "No citizen or member of the community is immune from prosecution, in good faith, for his alleged criminal acts. The imminence of such a prosecution even though alleged to be unauthorized and hence unlawful is not alone ground for relief in equity which exerts its extraordinary powers only to prevent irreparable injury to the plaintiff who seeks its aid." *Beal v. Missouri Pacific Railroad Corp.,* 312 U.S. 45, 49, 61 S.Ct. 418, 420, 85 L.Ed. 577.

And similarly, in *Douglas, supra,* we made clear, after reaffirming this rule, that:

> It does not appear from the record that petitioners have been threatened with any injury other than that incidental to every criminal proceeding brought lawfully and in good faith * * *. 319 U.S. at 164, 63 S.Ct. at 881.

This is where the law stood when the Court decided *Dombrowski v. Pfister,* 380 U.S. 479, 85 S.Ct. 1116, 14 L.Ed.2d 22 (1965), and held that an injunction against the enforcement of certain state criminal statutes could properly issue under the circumstances presented in that case. In *Dombrowski,* unlike many of the earlier cases denying injunctions, the complaint made substantial allegations that:

the threats to enforce the statutes against appellants are not made with any expectation of securing valid convictions, but rather are part of a plan to employ arrests, seizures, and threats of prosecution under color of the statutes to harass appellants and discourage them and their supporters from asserting and attempting to vindicate the constitutional rights of Negro citizens of Louisiana, 380 U.S. at 482, 85 S.Ct. at 1118–1119.

The appellants in *Dombrowski* had offered to prove that their offices had been raided and all their files and records seized pursuant to search and arrest warrants that were later summarily vacated by a state judge for lack of probable cause. They also offered to prove that despite the state court order quashing the warrants and suppressing the evidence seized, the prosecutor was continuing to threaten to initiate new prosecutions of appellants under the same statutes, was holding public hearings at which photostatic copies of the illegally seized documents were being used, and was threatening to use other copies of the illegally seized documents to obtain grand jury indictments against the appellants on charges of violating the same statutes. These circumstances, as viewed by the Court sufficiently establish the kind of irreparable injury, above and beyond that associated with the defense of a single prosecution brought in good faith, that had always been considered sufficient to justify federal intervention. *See, e.g., Beal,* 312 U.S. at 50, 61 S.Ct. at 421. Indeed, after quoting the Court's statement in *Douglas* concerning the very restricted circumstances under which an injunction could be justified, the Court in *Dombrowski* went on to say:

> But the allegations in this complaint depict a situation in which defense of the State's criminal prosecution will not assure adequate vindication of constitutional rights. They suggest that a substantial loss of or impairment of freedoms of expression will occur if appellants must await the state court's disposition and ultimate review in this Court of any adverse determination. These allegations, if true, clearly show irreparable injury. 380 U.S. at 485–86, 85 S.Ct. at 1120.

And the Court made clear that even under these circumstances the District Court issuing the injunction would have continuing power to lift it at any time and remit the plaintiffs to the state courts if circumstances warranted. 380 U.S. at 491, 492, 85 S.Ct. at 1123, 1124. Similarly, in *Cameron v. Johnson,* 390 U.S. 611, 88 S.Ct. 1335, 20 L.Ed.2d 182 (1968), a divided Court denied an injunction after finding that the record did not establish the necessary bad faith and harassment; the dissenting Justices themselves stressed the very limited role to be allowed for federal injunctions against state criminal prosecutions and differed with the Court only on the question whether the particular facts of that case were sufficient to show that the prosecution was brought in bad faith.

It is against the background of these principles that we must judge the propriety of an injunction under the circumstances of the present case. Here a proceeding was already pending in the state court, affording Harris an opportunity to raise his constitutional claims. There is no suggestion that this single prosecution against Harris is brought in bad faith or is only one of a series of repeated prosecutions to which he will be subjected. In other words, the injury that Harris faces is solely "that incidental to every criminal proceeding brought lawfully and in good faith," *Douglas, supra,* and therefore under the settled doctrine we have already described he is not entitled to equitable relief "even if such statutes are unconstitutional," *Buck, supra.*

The District Court, however, thought that the *Dombrowski* decision substantially broadened the availability of injunctions against state criminal prosecutions and that under that decision the federal courts may give equitable relief, without regard to any showing of bad faith or harassment, whenever a state statute is found "on its face" to be vague or overly broad, in violation of the First Amendment. We recognize that there are some statements in the *Dombrowski* opinion that would seem to support this argument. But, as we have already seen, such statements were unnecessary to the decision of that case, because the Court found that the plaintiffs had alleged a basis for equitable relief under the long-established standards. In addition, we do not regard the reasons adduced to support this position as sufficient to justify such a substantial departure from the established doctrines regarding the availability of injunctive relief. It is undoubtedly true, as the Court stated in *Dombrowski,* that "[a] criminal prosecution under a statute regulating expression usually involves imponderables and contingencies that themselves may inhibit the full exercise of First Amendment freedoms." 380 U.S. at 486, 85 S.Ct. at 1120. But this sort of "chilling effect," as the Court called it, should not by itself justify federal intervention. In the first place, the chilling effect cannot be satisfactorily eliminated by federal injunctive relief. In *Dombrowski* itself the Court stated that the injunction to be issued there could be lifted if the State obtained an "acceptable limiting construction" from the state courts. The Court then made clear that once this was done, prosecutions could then be brought for conduct occurring before the narrowing construction was made, and proper convictions could stand so long as the defendants were not deprived of fair warning. 380 U.S. at 491 n. 7, 85 S.Ct. at 1123. The kind of relief granted in *Dombrowski* thus does not effectively eliminate uncertainty as to the coverage of the state statute and leaves most citizens with virtually the same doubts as before regarding the danger that their conduct might eventually be subjected to criminal sanctions. The chilling effect can, of course, be eliminated by an injunction that would prohibit any prosecution whatever for conduct occurring prior to a satisfactory rewriting of the statute. But the States would then be stripped of all power to prosecute even the socially dangerous and constitutionally unprotected conduct that had been covered by the statute, until a new statute could be passed by the state legislature and approved by the federal courts in potentially lengthy trial and appellate proceedings. Thus, in *Dombrowski* itself the Court carefully reaffirmed the principle that even in the direct prosecution in the State's own courts, a valid narrowing construction can be applied to conduct occurring prior to the date when the narrowing construction was made, in the absence of fair warning problems.

Moreover, the existence of a "chilling effect," even in the area of First Amendment rights, has never been considered a sufficient basis, in and of itself, for prohibiting state action. Where a statute does not directly abridge free speech, but—while regulating a subject within the State's power—tends to have the incidental effect of inhibiting First Amendment rights, it is well settled that the statute can be upheld if the effect on speech is minor in relation to the need for control of the conduct and the lack of alternative means for doing so. Just as the incidental "chilling effect" of such statutes does not automatically render them unconstitutional, so the chilling effect that admittedly can result from the very existence of certain laws on the statute books does not in itself justify prohibiting the State from carrying out the important and necessary task of enforcing these laws against socially harmful conduct that the State believes in good faith to be punishable under its laws and the Constitution.

Beyond all this is another, more basic consideration. Procedures for testing the constitutionality of a statute "on its face" in the manner apparently contemplated by *Dombrowski,* and for then enjoining all action to enforce the statute until the State can obtain court approval for a modified version, are fundamentally at odds with the function of the federal courts in our constitutional plan. The power and duty of the judiciary to declare laws unconstitutional is in the final analysis derived from its responsibility for resolving concrete disputes brought before the courts for decision; a statute apparently governing a dispute cannot be applied by judges, consistently with their obligations under the Supremacy Clause, when such an application of the statute would conflict with the Constitution. *Marbury v. Madison,* 5 U.S. (1 Cranch) 137, 2 L.Ed. 60 (1803). But this vital responsibility, broad as it is, does not amount to an unlimited power to survey the statute books and pass judgment on laws before the courts are called upon to enforce them. Ever since the Constitutional Convention rejected a proposal for having members of the Supreme Court render advice concerning pending legislation it has been clear that, even when suits of this kind involve a "case or controversy" sufficient to satisfy the requirements of Article III of the Constitution, the task of analyzing a proposed statute, pinpointing its deficiencies, and requiring correction of these deficiencies before the statute is put into effect, is rarely if ever an appropriate task for the judiciary. The combination of the relative remoteness of the controversy, the impact on the legislative process of the relief sought, and above all the speculative and amorphous nature of the required line-by-line analysis of detailed statutes, ordinarily results in a kind of case that is wholly unsatisfactory for deciding constitutional questions, whichever way they might be decided. In light of this fundamental conception of the Framers as to the proper place of the federal courts in the governmental processes of passing and enforcing laws, it can seldom be appropriate for these courts to exercise any such power of prior approval or veto over the legislative process.

For these reasons, fundamental not only to our federal system but also to the basic functions of the Judicial Branch of the National Government under our Constitution, we hold that the *Dombrowski* decision should not be regarded as having upset the settled doctrines that have always confined very narrowly the availability of injunctive relief against state criminal prosecutions. We do not think that opinion stands for the proposition that a federal court can properly enjoin enforcement of a statute solely on the basis of a showing that the statute "on its face" abridges First Amendment rights. There may, of course, be extraordinary circumstances in which the necessary irreparable injury can be shown even in the absence of the usual prerequisites of bad faith and harassment. For example, as long ago as the *Buck* case, *surpa,* we indicated:

> It is of course conceivable that a statute might be flagrantly and patently violative of express constitutional prohibitions in every clause, sentence and paragraph, and in whatever manner and against whomever an effort might be made to apply it. 313 U.S. at 402, 61 S.Ct. at 967.

Other unusual situations calling for federal intervention might also arise, but there is no point in our attempting now to specify what they might be. It is sufficient for purposes of the present case to hold, as we do, that the possible unconstitutionality of a statute "on its face" does not in itself justify an injunction against good-faith attempts to enforce it, and that appellee Harris has failed to make any showing of bad faith, harassment, or any other unusual circumstance that would call for equitable relief. Because our holding rests on the absence of the factors necessary under equitable principles to justify federal intervention, we have no occasion to consider whether 28 U.S.C. § 2283, which prohibits an injunction against state court proceedings "except as expressly authorized by Act of Congress" would in and of itself be controlling under the circumstances of this case.

The judgment of the District Court is reversed, and the case is remanded for further proceedings not inconsistent with this opinion.

Reversed.

JUSTICE BRENNAN, with whom JUSTICE WHITE and JUSTICE MARSHALL join, concurring in the result.

I agree that the judgment of the District Court should be reversed. Appellee Harris had been indicted for violations of the California Criminal Syndicalism Act before he sued in federal court. He has not alleged that the prosecution was brought in bad faith to harass him. His constitutional contentions may be adequately adjudicated in the state criminal proceeding, and federal intervention at his instance was therefore improper.

JUSTICE STEWART, with whom JUSTICE HARLAN joins, concurring.

The questions the Court decides today are important ones. Perhaps as important, however, is a recognition of the areas into which today's holdings do not necessarily extend. In all of these cases, the Court deals only with the proper policy to be followed by a federal court when asked to intervene by injunction or declaratory judgment in a criminal prosecution which is contemporaneously pending in a state court.

The Court confines itself to deciding the policy considerations that in our federal system must prevail when federal courts are asked to interfere with pending state prosecutions. Within this area, we hold that a federal court must not, save in exceptional and extremely limited circumstances, intervene by way of either injunction or declaration in an existing state criminal prosecution. Such circumstances exist only when there is a threat of irreparable injury "both great and immediate." A threat of this nature might be shown if the state criminal statute in question were patently and flagrantly unconstitutional on its face, *Younger v. Harris,* 401 U.S. at 53–54, 91 S.Ct. at 755; *cf. Evers v. Dwyer,* 358 U.S. 202, 79 S.Ct. 178, 3 L.Ed.2d 222, or if there has been bad faith and harassment—official lawlessness—in a statute's enforcement, *Younger v. Harris,* 401 U.S. at 47–49, 91 S.Ct. at 752–53. In such circumstances the reasons of policy for deferring to state adjudication are outweighed by the injury flowing from the very bringing of the state proceedings, by the perversion of the very process that is supposed to provide vindication, and by the need for speedy and effective action to protect federal rights. *Cf. Georgia v. Rachel,* 384 U.S. 780, 86 S.Ct. 1783, 16 L.Ed.2d 925.

Notes and Questions

1. Why did the Court elect not to analyze the statutory grounds for nonintervention? The anti-injunction statute, 28 U.S.C. § 2283, provides as follows: "A court of the United States may not grant an injunction to stay proceedings in a State Court except as expressly authorized by Act of Congress, or where necessary in aid of its jurisdiction, or to protect or effectuate its judgments." Recall the materials in Chapter V. What are the key words and phrases in the statute upon which the *Younger* defendant would rely? In *Mitchum v. Foster,* 407 U.S. 225 (1972), the Court held that suits under the Civil Rights Act[k] fall within the "expressly authorized" exception to the statutory bar.

2. Note the different plaintiffs in *Younger.* Why would a lawyer choose to represent these different interests rather than to bring the action on behalf of just one of them? Could joint representation by the same attorney present conflict of interest problems? *See supra* p. 77.

---

k. The Civil Rights Act provides, in pertinent part, as follows: Every person who, under color of any statute, ordinance, regulation, custom, or usage, of any State or Territory or the District of Columbia, subjects, or causes to be subjected, any citizen of the United States or other persons within the jurisdiction thereof to the deprivation of any rights, privileges or immunities secured by the Constitution and laws, shall be liable to the person injured in an action at law, suit in equity, or other proper proceedings for redress. For purposes of this section, any Act of Congress applicable exclusively to the District of Columbia shall be considered to be a statute of the District of Columbia. 42 U.S.C. § 1983.

3. What happened to *Dombrowski*? Did that case contain the seeds of its own destruction? Did Justice Black fairly treat the "chilling effect" language of *Dombrowski*?

4. Consider the Court's statement that federal injunctive relief is justified only upon a showing of bad faith, harassment, or "other unusual circumstances that would call for equitable relief." What does the quoted passage mean? Unconstitutionality on its face is not sufficient, unless perhaps the statute is "flagrantly and patently violative of express constitutional prohibitions in every clause, sentence and paragraph and in whatever manner and against whomever an effort might be made to apply it." Can you conceive of any such flagrant situation?

5. May the parties avoid citing *Younger* in order to obtain a judicial pronouncement? Consider the following passage from *Sosna v. Iowa,* 419 U.S. 393, 396 (1975):

> Our request that the parties address themselves to *Younger v. Harris,* 401 U.S. 37, 27 L.Ed.2d 669, 91 S.Ct. 746 (1971), and related cases, indicated our concern as to whether either this Court or the District Court should reach the merits of the constitutional issue presented by the parties in light of appellant Sosna's failure to appeal the adverse ruling of the State District Court through the state appellate network. In response to our request, both parties urged that we reach the merits of appellant's constitutional attack on Iowa's durational residency requirement.

> In this posture of the case, and in the absence of a disagreement between the parties, we have no occasion to consider whether any consequences adverse to appellant resulted from her first obtaining an adjudication of her claim on the merits in the Iowa state court and only then commencing this action in the United States District Court.

STEFFEL v. THOMPSON

Supreme Court of the United States, 1974.
415 U.S. 452, 94 S.Ct. 1209, 39 L.Ed.2d 505.

JUSTICE BRENNAN delivered the opinion of the Court.

When a state criminal proceeding under a disputed state criminal statute is pending against a federal plaintiff at the time his federal complaint is filed, *Younger v. Harris,* 401 U.S. 37, 91 S.Ct. 746, 27 L.Ed.2d 669 (1971), and *Samuels v. Mackell,* 401 U.S. 66, 91 S.Ct. 764, 27 L.Ed.2d 688 (1971), held, respectively, that, unless bad-faith enforcement or other special circumstances are demonstrated, principles of equity, comity, and federalism preclude issuance of a federal injunction restraining enforcement of the criminal statute and, in all but unusual circumstances, a declaratory judgment upon the constitutionality of the statute. This case presents the important question reserved in *Samuels v. Mackell, id.* at 73–74, 91 S.Ct. at 768–69, whether declaratory relief is precluded when a state prosecution has been threatened, but is not pending, and a showing of bad-faith enforcement or other special circumstances has not been made.

Petitioner, and others, filed a complaint in the District Court for the Northern District of Georgia, invoking the Civil Rights Act of 1871, 42 U.S.C. § 1983, and its jurisdictional implementation, 28 U.S.C. § 1343. The complaint requested a declaratory judgment pursuant to 28 U.S.C. §§ 2201–2202, that Ga.Code Ann. § 26–1503 (1972) was being applied in violation of petitioner's First and Fourteenth Amendment rights, and an injunction restraining respondents the Solicitor of the Civil and Criminal Court of DeKalb County, the chief of the DeKalb County Police, the owner of the North DeKalb Shopping Center, and the manager of that shopping center from enforcing the statute so as to interfere with petitioner's constitutionally protected activities.

The parties stipulated to the relevant facts: On October 8, 1970, while petitioner and other individuals were distributing handbills protesting American involvement in Vietnam on an exterior sidewalk of the North DeKalb Shopping Center, shopping center employees asked them to stop handbilling and leave. They declined to do so, and police officers were summoned. The officers told them that they would be arrested if they did not stop handbilling. The group then left to avoid arrest. Two days later petitioner and a companion returned to the shopping center and again began handbilling. The manager of the center called the police, and petitioner and his companion were once again told that failure to stop their handbilling would result in their arrests. Petitioner left to avoid arrest. His companion stayed, however, continued handbilling, and was arrested and subsequently arraigned on a charge of criminal trespass in violation of § 26–1503. Petitioner alleged in his complaint that, although he desired to return to the shopping center to distribute handbills, he had not done so because of his concern that he, too, would be arrested for violation of § 26–1503; the parties stipulated that, if petitioner returned and refused upon request to stop handbilling, a warrant would be sworn out and he might be arrested and charged with a violation of the Georgia statute.

After hearing, the District Court denied all relief and dismissed the action, finding that "no meaningful contention can be made that the state has [acted] or will in the future act in bad faith," and therefore "the rudiments of an active controversy between the parties * * * [are] lacking." 334 F.Supp. 1386, 1389–90 (1971). Petitioner appealed only from the denial of declaratory relief.[6] The Court of Appeals for the Fifth Circuit, one judge concurring in the result, affirmed the District Court's judgment refusing declaratory relief. *Becker v. Thompson,* 459 F.2d 919 (1972). The court recognized that the holdings of *Younger v. Harris,* 401 U.S. 37, 91 S.Ct. 746, 27 L.Ed.2d 669 (1971), and *Samuels v. Mackell,* 401 U.S. 66, 91 S.Ct. 764, 27 L.Ed.2d 688 (1971), were expressly limited to situations where state prosecutions were pending when the federal action commenced, but was of the view that *Younger v. Harris* "made it clear beyond peradventure that irreparable injury must be measured by

6. Petitioner's notice of appeal challenged the denial of both injunctive and declaratory relief. However, in his appellate brief, he abandoned his appeal from denial of injunctive relief. *Becker v. Thompson,* 459 F.2d 919, 921 (C.A.5 1972).

bad faith harassment and such test must be applied to a request for injunctive relief against *threatened* state court criminal prosecution" as well as against a pending prosecution; and, furthermore, since the opinion in *Samuels v. Mackell* reasoned that declaratory relief would normally disrupt the state criminal justice system in the manner of injunctive relief, it followed that "the same test of bad faith harassment is prerequisite * * * for declaratory relief in a threatened prosecution." 459 F.2d at 922. A petition for rehearing en banc was denied, three judges dissenting. 463 F.2d 1338 (Cir.1972).

We granted certiorari, 410 U.S. 953, 93 S.Ct. 1424, 35 L.Ed.2d 686 (1973), and now reverse.

I

At the threshold we must consider whether petitioner presents an "actual controversy," a requirement imposed by Art. III of the Constitution and the express terms of the Federal Declaratory Judgment Act, 28 U.S.C. § 2201.[9]

Unlike three of the appellees in *Younger v. Harris,* 401 U.S. at 41, 91 S.Ct. at 749, petitioner has alleged threats of prosecution that cannot be characterized as "imaginary or speculative," *id.* at 42, 91 S.Ct. at 749. He has been twice warned to stop handbilling that he claims is constitutionally protected and has been told by the police that if he again handbills at the shopping center and disobeys a warning to stop he will likely be prosecuted. The prosecution of petitioner's handbilling companion is ample demonstration that petitioner's concern with arrest has not been "chimerical," *Poe v. Ullman,* 367 U.S. 497, 508, 81 S.Ct. 1752, 1758–59, 6 L.Ed.2d 989 (1961). In these circumstances, it is not necessary that petitioner first expose himself to actual arrest or prosecution to be entitled to challenge a statute that he claims deters the exercise of his constitutional rights. *See, e.g., Epperson v. Arkansas,* 393 U.S. 97, 89 S.Ct. 266, 21 L.Ed.2d 228 (1968). Moreover, petitioner's challenge is to those specific provisions of state law which have provided the basis for threats of criminal prosecution against him.

Nonetheless, there remains a question as to the *continuing* existence of a live and acute controversy that must be resolved on the remand we order today. In *Golden v. Zwickler,* 394 U.S. 103, 89 S.Ct. 956, 22 L.Ed.2d 113 (1969), the appellee sought a declaratory judgment that a state criminal statute prohibiting the distribution of anonymous election-campaign literature was unconstitutional. The appellee's complaint

---

9. Section 2201 provides:

"In a case of actual controversy within its jurisdiction, except with respect to Federal taxes, any court of the United States, upon the filing of an appropriate pleading, may declare the rights and other legal relations of any interested party seeking such declaration, whether or not further relief is or could be sought. Any such declaration shall have the force and effect of a final judgment or decree and shall be reviewable as such."

Section 2202 further provides:

"Further necessary or proper relief based on a declaratory judgment or decree may be granted, after reasonable notice and hearing, against any adverse party whose rights have been determined by such judgment."

had expressed a desire to distribute handbills during the forthcoming re-election campaign of a Congressman, but it was later learned that the Congressman had retired from the House of Representatives to become a New York Supreme Court Justice. In that circumstance, we found no extant controversy, since the record revealed that appellee's sole target of distribution had been the Congressman and there was no immediate prospect of the Congressman's again becoming a candidate for public office. Here, petitioner's complaint indicates that his handbilling activities were directed "against the war in Vietnam and the United States' foreign policy in Southeast Asia." Since we cannot ignore the recent developments reducing the Nation's involvement in that part of the world, it will be for the District Court on remand to determine if subsequent events have so altered petitioner's desire to engage in handbilling at the shopping center that it can no longer be said that this case presents "a substantial controversy, between parties having adverse legal interests, of sufficient immediacy and reality to warrant the issuance of a declaratory judgment." *Maryland Casualty Co. v. Pacific Coal & Oil Co.*, 312 U.S. 270, 273, 61 S.Ct. 510, 512, 85 L.Ed. 826 (1941); *see Zwickler v. Koota*, 389 U.S. 241, 244 n. 3, 88 S.Ct. 391, 393, 19 L.Ed.2d 444 (1967).

II

We now turn to the question of whether the District Court and the Court of Appeals correctly found petitioner's request for declaratory relief inappropriate.

Sensitive to principles of equity, comity, and federalism, we recognized in *Younger v. Harris, supra,* that federal courts should ordinarily refrain from enjoining ongoing state criminal prosecutions. We were cognizant that a pending state proceeding, in all but unusual cases, would provide the federal plaintiff with the necessary vehicle for vindicating his constitutional rights, and, in that circumstance, the restraining of an ongoing prosecution would entail an unseemly failure to give effect to the principle that state courts have the solemn responsibility, equally with the federal courts "to guard, enforce, and protect every right granted or secured by the constitution of the United States. * * *" *Robb v. Connolly*, 111 U.S. 624, 637, 4 S.Ct. 544, 551, 28 L.Ed. 542 (1884). In *Samuels v. Mackell, supra,* the Court also found that the same principles ordinarily would be flouted by issuance of a federal declaratory judgment when a state proceeding was pending, since the intrusive effect of declaratory relief "will result in precisely the same interference with and disruption of state proceedings that the long-standing policy limiting injunctions was designed to avoid." 401 U.S. at 72, 91 S.Ct. at 767.[11] We therefore held in *Samuels* that, "in cases where the state criminal prosecution was begun prior to the federal suit, the same equitable

---

11. The Court noted that under 28 U.S.C. § 2202 a declaratory judgment might serve as the basis for issuance of a later injunction to give effect to the declaratory judgment, *see* n. 9, *supra,* and that a declaratory judgment might have a res judicata effect on the pending state proceeding. 401 U.S. at 72, 91 S.Ct. at 767–68.

principles relevant to the propriety of an injunction must be taken into consideration by federal district courts in determining whether to issue a declaratory judgment. * * * " *Id.* at 73, 91 S.Ct. at 768.

Neither *Younger* nor *Samuels,* however, decided the question whether federal intervention might be permissible in the absence of a pending state prosecution. In *Younger,* the Court said:

> We express no view about the circumstances under which federal courts may act when there is no prosecution pending in state courts at the time the federal proceeding is begun. 401 U.S. at 41, 91 S.Ct. at 749.

See also id. at 55, 91 S.Ct. at 757 (Stewart and Harlan, JJ., concurring); *id.* at 57, 91 S.Ct. at 756 (Brennan, White, and Marshall, JJ., concurring). Similarly, in *Samuels v. Mackell,* the Court stated:

> We, of course, express no views on the propriety of declaratory relief when no state proceeding is pending at the time the federal suit is begun. 401 U.S. at 73–74, 91 S.Ct. at 768.

See also id. at 55, 91 S.Ct. at 757 (Stewart and Harlan, JJ., concurring); *id.* at 75–76, 91 S.Ct. at 756 (Brennan, White, and Marshall, JJ., concurring).

These reservations anticipated the Court's recognition that the relevant principles of equity, comity, and federalism "have little force in the absence of a pending state proceeding." *Lake Carriers' Assn. v. MacMullan,* 406 U.S. 498, 509, 92 S.Ct. 1749, 1757, 32 L.Ed.2d 257 (1972). When no state criminal proceeding is pending at the time the federal complaint is filed, federal intervention does not result in duplicative legal proceedings or disruption of the state criminal justice system; nor can federal intervention, in that circumstance, be interpreted as reflecting negatively upon the state court's ability to enforce constitutional principles. In addition, while a pending state prosecution provides the federal plaintiff with a concrete opportunity to vindicate his constitutional rights, a refusal on the part of the federal courts to intervene when no state proceeding is pending may place the hapless plaintiff between the Scylla of intentionally flouting state law and the Charybdis of forgoing what he believes to be constitutionally protected activity in order to avoid becoming enmeshed in a criminal proceeding. *Cf. Dombrowski v. Pfister,* 380 U.S. 479, 490, 85 S.Ct. 1116, 1123, 14 L.Ed.2d 22 (1965).

When no state proceeding is pending and thus considerations of equity, comity, and federalism have little vitality, the propriety of granting federal declaratory relief may properly be considered independently of a request for injunctive relief. Here, the Court of Appeals held that, because injunctive relief would not be appropriate since petitioner failed to demonstrate irreparable injury—a traditional prerequisite to injunctive relief, *e.g., Dombrowski v. Pfister, supra*—it followed that declaratory relief was also inappropriate. Even if the Court of Appeals correctly viewed injunctive relief as inappropriate—a question we need not reach today since petitioner has abandoned his request for that remedy, *see* n. 6 *supra*—the court erred in treating the requests for injunctive and declaratory relief as a single issue. "[W]hen no state prosecution is pending and the only question is whether declaratory relief is appropriate[,] * * * the congressional scheme that makes the federal courts the primary guardians of constitutional rights, and the express congressional authorization of declaratory relief, afforded because it is a less harsh and abrasive remedy than the injunction, become the factors of primary significance." *Perez v. Ledesma*, 401 U.S. 82, 104, 91 S.Ct. 674, 686, 27 L.Ed.2d 701 (1971) (separate opinion of Brennan, J.).

The subject matter jurisdiction of the lower federal courts was greatly expanded in the wake of the Civil War. A pervasive sense of nationalism led to enactment of the Civil Rights Act of 1871, 17 Stat. 13, empowering the lower federal courts to determine the constitutionality of actions, taken by persons under color of state law, allegedly depriving other individuals of rights guaranteed by the Constitution and federal law, *see* 42 U.S.C. § 1983, 28 U.S.C. § 1343(3).[13] Four years later, in the Judiciary Act of March 3, 1875, 18 Stat. 470, Congress conferred upon the lower federal courts, for but the second time in their nearly century-old history, general federal-question jurisdiction subject only to a jurisdictional-amount requirement, see 28 U.S.C. § 1331. With this latter enactment, the lower federal courts "ceased to be restricted tribunals of fair dealing between citizens of different states and became the *primary* and powerful reliances for vindicating every right given by the Constitution, the laws, and treaties of the United States." F. Frankfurter & J. Landis, *The Business of the Supreme Court* 65 (1928) (emphasis added). These two statutes, together with the Court's decision in *Ex parte Young*, 209 U.S. 123, 28 S.Ct. 441, 52 L.Ed. 714 (1908)—holding that state officials who threaten to enforce an unconstitutional state statute may be enjoined by a federal court of equity and that a federal court may, in appropriate circumstances, enjoin future state criminal prosecutions under the unconstitutional Act—have "established the modern framework for federal protection of constitutional rights from state interference." *Perez v. Ledesma*, 401 U.S. at 107, 91 S.Ct. at 688 (separate opinion of Brennan, J.).

A "storm of controversy" raged in the wake of *Ex parte Young*, focusing principally on the power of a single federal judge to grant *ex parte* interlocutory injunctions against the enforcement of state statutes. This uproar was only partially quelled by Congress' passage of legislation, 36 Stat. 557, requiring the convening of a three-judge district court before a preliminary injunction against enforcement of a state statute could issue, and providing for direct appeal to this Court from a decision

---

13. "Sensitiveness to 'states' rights,' fear of rivalry with state courts and respect for state sentiment, were swept aside by the great impulse of national feeling born of the Civil War. Nationalism was triumphant; in national administration was sought its vin-dication. The new exertions of federal power were no longer trusted to the enforcement of state agencies." F. Frankfurter & J. Landis, *The Business of the Supreme Court* 64 (1928).

granting or denying such relief. *See* 28 U.S.C. §§ 2281, 1253. From a State's viewpoint the granting of injunctive relief—even by these courts of special dignity—"rather clumsily" crippled state enforcement of its statutes pending further review, *see* H.R.Rep. No. 288, 70th Cong., 1st Sess., 2 (1928); H.R.Rep.No. 94, 71st Cong., 2d Sess., 2 (1929); H.R.Rep. No. 627, 72d Cong., 1st Sess., 2 (1932). Furthermore, plaintiffs were dissatisfied with this method of testing the constitutionality of state statutes, since it placed upon them the burden of demonstrating the traditional prerequisites to equitable relief—most importantly, irreparable injury. *See, e.g., Fenner v. Boykin,* 271 U.S. 240, 243, 46 S.Ct. 492, 493, 70 L.Ed. 927 (1926).

To dispel these difficulties, Congress in 1934 enacted the Declaratory Judgment Act, 28 U.S.C. §§ 2201–2202. That Congress plainly intended declaratory relief to act as an alternative to the strong medicine of the injunction and to be utilized to test the constitutionality of state criminal statutes in cases where injunctive relief would be unavailable is amply evidenced by the legislative history of the Act, traced in full detail in *Perez v. Ledesma,* 401 U.S. at 111–115, 91 S.Ct. at 690–692 (separate opinion of Brennan, J.). The highlights of that history, particularly pertinent to our inquiry today, emphasize that:

> [I]n 1934, without expanding or reducing the subject matter jurisdiction of the federal courts, or in any way diminishing the continuing vitality of *Ex parte Young* with respect to federal injunctions, Congress empowered the federal courts to grant a new remedy, the declaratory judgment. * * *
>
> The express purpose of the Federal Declaratory Judgment Act was to provide a milder alternative to the injunction remedy. * * * Of particular significance on the question before us, the Senate report [S.Rep. No. 1005, 73d Cong., 2d Sess. (1934)] makes it even clearer that the declaratory judgment was designed to be available to test state criminal statutes in circumstances where an injunction would not be appropriate.
>
> * * *

Much of the hostility to federal injunctions referred to in the Senate report was hostility to their use against state officials seeking to enforce state regulatory statutes carrying criminal sanctions; this was the strong feeling that produced the Three–Judge Court Act in 1910, the Johnson Act of 1934, 28 U.S.C. § 1342, and the Tax Injunction Act of 1937, 28 U.S.C. § 1341. The Federal Declaratory Judgment Act was intended to provide an alternative to injunctions against state officials, except where there was a federal policy against federal adjudication of the class of litigation altogether. * * * Moreover, the Senate report's clear implication that declaratory relief would have been appropriate in *Pierce v. Society of Sisters,* 268 U.S. 510, 45 S.Ct. 571, 69 L.Ed. 1070 (1925), and *Village of Euclid v. Ambler Realty Co.,* 272 U.S. 365, 47 S.Ct. 114, 71 L.Ed. 303 (1926), both cases involving federal adjudication of the constitutionality of a state statute carrying criminal penalties, and the report's quotation from *Terrace v. Thompson,* which also involved anticipatory federal adjudication of the constitutionality of a state criminal statute, make it plain that Congress anticipated that the declaratory judgment procedure would be used by the federal courts to test the constitutionality of state criminal statutes. 401 U.S. at 111–112, 115, 91 S.Ct. at 690–92.

It was this history that formed the backdrop to our decision in *Zwickler v. Koota,* 389 U.S. 241, 88 S.Ct. 391, 19 L.Ed.2d 444 (1967), where a state criminal statute was attacked on grounds of unconstitutional overbreadth and no state prosecution was pending against the federal plaintiff. There, we found error in a three-judge district court's considering, as a single question, the propriety of granting injunctive and declaratory relief. Although we noted that injunctive relief might well be unavailable under principles of equity jurisprudence canvassed in *Douglas v. City of Jeannette,* 319 U.S. 157, 63 S.Ct. 877, 87 L.Ed. 1324 (1943), we held that "a federal district court has the duty to decide the appropriateness and the merits of the declaratory request irrespective of its conclusion as to the propriety of the issuance of the injunction." 389 U.S. at 254, 88 S.Ct. at 399. Only one year ago, we reaffirmed the *Zwickler v. Koota* holding in *Roe v. Wade,* 410 U.S. 113, 93 S.Ct. 705, 35 L.Ed.2d 147 (1973), and *Doe v. Bolton,* 410 U.S. 179, 93 S.Ct. 739, 35 L.Ed.2d 201 (1973). In those two cases, we declined to decide whether the District Courts had properly denied to the federal plaintiffs, against whom no prosecutions were pending, injunctive relief restraining enforcement of the Texas and Georgia criminal abortion statutes; instead, we affirmed the issuance of declaratory judgments of unconstitutionality, anticipating that these would be given effect by state authorities. We said:

> The Court has recognized that *different considerations* enter into a federal court's decision as to declaratory relief, on the one hand, and injunctive relief, on the other. *Zwickler v. Koota,* 389 U.S. 241, 252–255, 88 S.Ct. 391, 397–399, 19 L.Ed.2d 444 (1967); *Dombrowski v. Pfister,* 380 U.S. 479, 85 S.Ct. 1116, 14 L.Ed.2d 22 (1965). *Roe v. Wade, supra,* 410 U.S., at 166, 93 S.Ct., at 733 (emphasis added). *See Doe v. Bolton,* 410 U.S. at 201, 93 S.Ct. at 752.

The "different considerations" entering into a decision whether to grant declaratory relief have their origins in the preceding historical summary. First, as Congress recognized in 1934, a declaratory judgment will have a less intrusive effect on the administration of state criminal laws. As was observed in *Perez v. Ledesma,* 401 U.S. at 124–126, 91 S.Ct. at 696–697 (separate opinion of Brennan, J.):

> Of course, a favorable declaratory judgment may nevertheless be valuable to the plaintiff though it cannot make even an unconstitutional statute disappear. A state statute may be declared unconstitutional *in toto*—that is, incapable of having constitutional applications; or it may be declared unconstitutionally vague or overbroad—

that is, incapable of being constitutionally applied to the full extent of its purport. In either case, a federal declaration of unconstitutionality reflects the opinion of the federal court that the statute cannot be fully enforced. If a declaration of total unconstitutionality is affirmed by this Court, it follows that this Court stands ready to reverse any conviction under the statute. If a declaration of partial unconstitutionality is affirmed by this Court, the implication is that this Court will overturn particular applications of the statute, but that if the statute is narrowly construed by the state courts it will not be incapable of constitutional applications. Accordingly, the declaration does not necessarily bar prosecutions under the statute, as a broad injunction would. Thus, where the highest court of a State has had an opportunity to give a statute regulating expression a narrowing or clarifying construction but has failed to do so, and later a federal court declares the statute unconstitutionally vague or overbroad, it may well be open to a state prosecutor, after the federal court decision, to bring a prosecution under the statute if he reasonably believes that the defendant's conduct is not constitutionally protected and that the state courts may give the statute a construction so as to yield a constitutionally valid conviction. Even where a declaration of unconstitutionality is not reviewed by this Court, the declaration may still be able to cut down the deterrent effect of an unconstitutional state statute. The persuasive force of the court's opinion and judgment may lead state prosecutors, courts, and legislators to reconsider their respective responsibilities toward the statute. Enforcement policies or judicial construction may be changed, or the legislature may repeal the statute and start anew. Finally, the federal court judgment may have some *res judicata* effect, though this point is not free from difficulty and the governing rules remain to be developed with a view to the proper workings of a federal system. What is clear, however, is that even though a declaratory judgment has "the force and effect of a final judgment," 28 U.S.C. § 2201, it is a much milder form of relief than an injunction. Though it may be persuasive, it is not ultimately coercive; noncompliance with it may be inappropriate, but is not contempt. (Footnote omitted.)

Second, engrafting upon the Declaratory Judgment Act a requirement that all of the traditional equitable prerequisites to the issuance of an injunction be satisfied before the issuance of a declaratory judgment is considered would defy Congress' intent to make declaratory relief available in cases where an injunction would be inappropriate.

Were the law to be that a plaintiff could not obtain a declaratory judgment that a local ordinance was unconstitutional when no state prosecution is pending unless he could allege and prove circumstances justifying a federal injunction of an existing state prosecution, the Federal Declaratory Judgment Act would have been *pro tanto* repealed. *Wulp v. Corcoran*, 454 F.2d 826, 832 (C.A.1 1972) (Coffin, J.).

See Perez v. Ledesma, 401 U.S. at 116, 91 S.Ct. at 692–693 (separate opinion of Brennan, J.). Thus, the Court of Appeals was in error when it ruled that a failure to demonstrate irreparable injury—a traditional prerequisite to injunctive relief, having no equivalent in the law of declaratory judgments, precluded the granting of declaratory relief.

The only occasions where this Court has disregarded these "different considerations" and found that a preclusion of injunctive relief inevitably led to a denial of declaratory relief have been cases in which principles of federalism militated altogether against federal intervention in a class of adjudications. *See Great Lakes Dredge & Dock Co. v. Huffman,* 319 U.S. 293, 63 S.Ct. 1070, 87 L.Ed. 1407 (1943) (federal policy against interfering with the enforcement of state tax laws); *Samuels v. Mackell,* 401 U.S. 66, 91 S.Ct. 764, 27 L.Ed.2d 688 (1971). In the instant case, principles of federalism not only do not preclude federal intervention, they compel it. Requiring the federal courts totally to step aside when no state criminal prosecution is pending against the federal plaintiff would turn federalism on its head. When federal claims are premised on 42 U.S.C. § 1983 and 28 U.S.C. § 1343(3)—as they are here—we have not required exhaustion of state judicial or administrative remedies, recognizing the paramount role Congress has assigned to the federal courts to protect constitutional rights. *See, e.g., McNeese v. Board of Education,* 373 U.S. 668, 83 S.Ct. 1433, 10 L.Ed.2d 622 (1963); *Monroe v. Pape,* 365 U.S. 167, 81 S.Ct. 473, 5 L.Ed.2d 492 (1961). But exhaustion of state remedies is precisely what would be required if both federal injunctive and declaratory relief were unavailable in a case where no state prosecution had been commenced.

III

Respondents, however, relying principally upon our decision in *Cameron v. Johnson,* 390 U.S. 611, 88 S.Ct. 1335, 20 L.Ed.2d 182 (1968), argue that, although it may be appropriate to issue a declaratory judgment when no state criminal proceeding is pending and the attack is upon the *facial validity* of a state criminal statute, such a step would be improper where, as here, the attack is merely upon the constitutionality of the statute as applied, since the State's interest in unencumbered enforcement of its laws outweighs the minimal federal interest in protecting the constitutional rights of only a single individual. We reject the argument.

In *Cameron v. Johnson,* the appellants sought a declaratory judgment that a Mississippi anti-picketing law was an overly broad and vague regulation of protected expression and an injunction restraining *pending* prosecutions against them for violations of the statute. We agreed with the District Court that the statute was not overly broad or vague and that nothing in the record supported appellants' assertion that they were being prosecuted in bad faith. In that circumstance, we held that "[t]he mere possibility of erroneous application of the statute does not amount 'to the irreparable injury necessary to justify a disruption of orderly state proceedings.' * * * The issue of guilt or innocence is for the state court at the criminal trial; the State was not required to prove appellants guilty in the federal proceeding to escape the finding that the State had no expectation of securing valid convictions." *Id.* at 621, 88 S.Ct. at 1341. Our holding in *Cameron* was thus that the state courts in which prosecutions were already pending would have to be given the first opportunity to correct any misapplication of the state criminal laws; *Cameron* is plainly not authority for the proposition that, in the absence of a pending state proceeding, a federal plaintiff may not seek a declaratory judgment that the state statute is being applied in violation of his constitutional rights.

Indeed, the State's concern with potential interference in the administration of its criminal laws is of lesser dimension when an attack is made upon the constitutionality of a state statute as applied. A declaratory judgment of a lower federal court that a state statute is invalid *in toto*—and therefore incapable of any valid application—or is overbroad or vague—and therefore no person can properly be convicted under the statute until it is given a narrowing or clarifying construction, *see, e.g., United States v. Thirty-Seven Photographs,* 402 U.S. 363, 369, 91 S.Ct. 1400, 1404–1405, 28 L.Ed.2d 822 (1971); *Gooding v. Wilson,* 405 U.S. 518, 520, 92 S.Ct. 1103, 1105, 31 L.Ed.2d 408 (1972)—will likely have a more significant potential for disruption of state enforcement policies than a declaration specifying a limited number of impermissible applications of the statute. While the federal interest may be greater when a state statute is attacked on its face, since there exists the potential for eliminating any broad-ranging deterrent effect on would-be actors, *see Dombrowski v. Pfister,* 380 U.S. 479, 85 S.Ct. 1116, 14 L.Ed.2d 22 (1965), we do not find this consideration controlling. The solitary individual who suffers a deprivation of his constitutional rights is no less deserving of redress than one who suffers together with others.[21]

We therefore hold that, regardless of whether injunctive relief may be appropriate, federal declaratory relief is not precluded when no state prosecution is pending and a federal plaintiff demonstrates a genuine threat of enforcement of a disputed state criminal statute, whether an attack is made on the constitutionality of the statute on its face or as applied. The judgment of the Court of Appeals is reversed, and the case is remanded for further proceedings consistent with this opinion.

It is so ordered.

Reversed and remanded.

JUSTICE STEWART, with whom THE CHIEF JUSTICE joins, concurring.

21. Abstention, a question "entirely separate from the question of granting declaratory or injunctive relief," *Lake Carriers' Assn. v. MacMullan,* 406 U.S. 498, 509 n. 13, 92 S.Ct. 1749, 1756, 32 L.Ed.2d 257 (1972), might be more appropriate when a challenge is made to the state statute as applied, rather than upon its face, since the reach of an uncertain state statute might, in that circumstance, be more susceptible of a limiting or clarifying construction that would avoid the federal constitutional question. *Cf. Zwickler v. Koota,* 389 U.S. at 249–52, 254, 88 S.Ct. at 396–98, 399; *Baggett v. Bullitt,* 377 U.S. 360, 375–78, 84 S.Ct. 1316, 1324–1326, 12 L.Ed.2d 377 (1964).

While joining the opinion of the Court, I add a word by way of emphasis.

Our decision today must not be understood as authorizing the invocation of federal declaratory judgment jurisdiction by a person who thinks a state criminal law is unconstitutional, even if he genuinely feels "chilled" in his freedom of action by the law's existence, and even if he honestly entertains the subjective belief that he may now or in the future be prosecuted under it.

As the Court stated in *Younger v. Harris,* 401 U.S. 37, 52, 91 S.Ct. 746, 754, 27 L.Ed.2d 669:

> The power and duty of the judiciary to declare laws unconstitutional is in the final analysis derived from its responsibility for resolving concrete disputes brought before the courts for decision * * *.

See also Boyle v. Landry, 401 U.S. 77, 80–81, 91 S.Ct. 758, 759–760, 27 L.Ed.2d 696.

The petitioner in this case has succeeded in objectively showing that the threat of imminent arrest, corroborated by the actual arrest of his companion, has created an actual concrete controversy between himself and the agents of the State. He has, therefore, demonstrated "a genuine threat of enforcement of a disputed state criminal statute * * *." Cases where such a "genuine threat" can be demonstrated will, I think, be exceedingly rare.

JUSTICE WHITE, concurring.

I offer the following few words in light of Mr. Justice Rehnquist's concurrence in which he discusses the impact on a pending federal action of a later filed criminal prosecution against the federal plaintiff, whether a federal court may enjoin a state criminal prosecution under a statute the federal court has earlier declared unconstitutional at the suit of the defendant now being prosecuted, and the question whether that declaratory judgment is res judicata in such a later filed state criminal action.

It should be noted, first, that his views on these issues are neither expressly nor impliedly embraced by the Court's opinion filed today. Second, my own tentative views on these questions are somewhat contrary to my Brother's.

At this writing at least, I would anticipate that a final declaratory judgment entered by a federal court holding particular conduct of the federal plaintiff to be immune on federal constitutional grounds from prosecution under state law should be accorded res judicata effect in any later prosecution of that very conduct. There would also, I think, be additional circumstances in which the federal judgment should be considered as more than a mere precedent bearing on the issue before the state court.

Neither can I at this stage agree that the federal court, having rendered a declaratory judgment in favor of the plaintiff, could not enjoin a later state prosecution for conduct that the federal court has declared immune. The Declaratory Judgment Act itself provides that a "declaration shall have the force and effect of a final judgment or decree," 28 U.S.C. § 2201; eminent authority anticipated that declaratory judgments would be res judicata. E. Borchard, Declaratory Judgments 10–11 (2d ed. 1941); and there is every reason for not reducing declaratory judgments to mere advisory opinions. *Toucey v. New York Life Insurance Co.,* 314 U.S. 118, 62 S.Ct. 139, 86 L.Ed. 100 (1941), once expressed the view that 28 U.S.C. § 2283 forbade injunctions against relitigation in state courts of federally decided issues, but the section was then amended to overrule that case, the consequence being that "[i]t is clear that the Toucey rule is gone, and that to protect or effectuate its judgment a federal court may enjoin relitigation in the state court." C. Wright, *Federal Courts* 180 (2d ed. 1970). I see no more reason here to hold that the federal plaintiff must always rely solely on his plea of res judicata in the state courts. The statute provides for "[f]urther necessary or proper relief * * * against any adverse party whose rights have been determined by such judgment," 28 U.S.C. § 2202, and it would not seem improper to enjoin local prosecutors who refuse to observe adverse federal judgments.

Finally, I would think that a federal suit challenging a state criminal statute on federal constitutional grounds could be sufficiently far along so that ordinary consideration of economy would warrant refusal to dismiss the federal case solely because a state prosecution has subsequently been filed and the federal question may be litigated there.

Justice Rehnquist, with whom The Chief Justice joins, concurring.

I concur in the opinion of the Court. Although my reading of the legislative history of the Declaratory Judgment Act of 1934 suggests that its primary purpose was to enable persons to obtain a definition of their rights before an actual injury had occurred, rather than to palliate any controversy arising from *Ex parte Young,* 209 U.S. 123, 28 S.Ct. 441, 52 L.Ed. 714 (1908), Congress apparently was aware at the time it passed the Act that persons threatened with state criminal prosecutions might choose to forgo the offending conduct and instead seek a federal declaration of their rights. Use of the declaratory judgment procedure in the circumstances presented by this case seems consistent with that congressional expectation.

If this case were the Court's first opportunity to deal with this area of law, I would be content to let the matter rest there. But, as our cases abundantly illustrate, this area of law is in constant litigation, and it is an area through which our decisions have traced a path that may accurately be described as sinuous. Attempting to accommodate the principles of the new declaratory judgment procedure with other more established principles—in particular a proper regard for the relationship between the independent state and federal judiciary systems—this Court has acted both to advance and to limit the Act. Because the opinion today may possibly be read by resourceful counsel as commencing a new and less restrictive curve in this path of adjudication, I feel it is important to emphasize what the opinion does and does not say.

To begin with, it seems appropriate to restate the obvious: the Court's decision today deals only with declaratory relief and with threatened prosecutions. The case provides no authority for the granting of any injunctive relief nor does it provide authority for the granting of any relief at all when prosecutions are pending. The Court quite properly leaves for another day whether the granting of a declaratory judgment by a federal court will have any subsequent res judicata effect or will perhaps support the issuance of a later federal injunction. But since possible resolutions of those issues would substantially undercut the principles of federalism reaffirmed in *Younger v. Harris,* 401 U.S. 37, 91 S.Ct. 746, 27 L.Ed.2d 669 (1971), and preserved by the decision today, I feel it appropriate to add a few remarks.

First, the legislative history of the Declaratory Judgment Act and the Court's opinion in this case both recognize that the declaratory judgment procedure is an alternative to pursuit of the arguably illegal activity. There is nothing in the Act's history to suggest that Congress intended to provide persons wishing to violate state laws with a federal shield behind which they could carry on their contemplated conduct. Thus I do not believe that a federal plaintiff in a declaratory judgment action can avoid, by the mere filing of a complaint, the principles so firmly expressed in *Samuels, supra.* The plaintiff who continues to violate a state statute after the filing of his federal complaint does so both at the risk of state prosecution and at the risk of dismissal of his federal lawsuit. For any arrest prior to resolution of the federal action would constitute a pending prosecution and bar declaratory relief under the principles of *Samuels.*

Second, I do not believe that today's decision can properly be raised to support the issuance of a federal injunction based upon a favorable declaratory judgment. The Court's description of declaratory relief as " 'a milder alternative to the injunction remedy,' " having a "less intrusive effect on the administration of state criminal laws" than an injunction, indicates to me critical distinctions which make declaratory relief appropriate where injunctive relief would not be. It would all but totally obscure these important distinctions if a successful application for declaratory relief came to be regarded, not as the conclusion of a lawsuit, but as a giant step toward obtaining an injunction against a subsequent criminal prosecution. The availability of injunctive relief must be considered with an eye toward the important policies of federalism which this Court has often recognized.

If the rationale of cases such as *Younger* and *Samuels* turned in any way upon the relative ease with which a federal district court could reach a conclusion about the constitutionality of a challenged state statute, a preexisting judgment declaring the statute unconstitutional as applied to a particular plaintiff would, of course, be a factor favoring the issuance of an injunction as "further relief" under the Declaratory

Judgment Act. But, except for statutes that are " 'flagrantly and patently violative of express constitutional prohibitions in every clause, sentence and paragraph * * *,' " *Younger v. Harris, supra,* at 53, 91 S.Ct. at 755, the rationale of those cases has no such basis. Their direction that federal courts not interfere with state prosecutions does not vary depending on the closeness of the constitutional issue or on the degree of confidence which the federal court possesses in the correctness of its conclusions on the constitutional point. Those decisions instead depend upon considerations relevant to the harmonious operation of separate federal and state court systems, with a special regard for the State's interest in enforcing its own criminal laws, considerations which are as relevant in guiding the action of a federal court which has previously issued a declaratory judgment as they are in guiding the action of one which has not. While the result may be that injunctive relief is not available as "further relief" under the Declaratory Judgment Act in this particular class of cases whereas it would be in similar cases not involving considerations of federalism, this would be no more a *pro tanto* repeal of that provision of the Declaratory Judgment Act than was *Younger* a *pro tanto* repeal of the All Writs Act, 28 U.S.C. § 1651.

A declaratory judgment is simply a statement of rights, not a binding order supplemented by continuing sanctions. State authorities may choose to be guided by the judgment of a lower federal court, but they are not compelled to follow the decision by threat of contempt or other penalties. If the federal plaintiff pursues the conduct for which he was previously threatened with arrest and is in fact arrested, he may not return the controversy to federal court, although he may, of course, raise the federal declaratory judgment in the state court for whatever value it may prove to have.[3] In any event, the defendant at that point is able to present his case for full consideration by a state court charged, as are the federal courts, to preserve the defendant's constitutional rights. Federal interference with this process would involve precisely the same concerns discussed in *Younger* and recited in the Court's opinion in this case.

Third, attempts to circumvent *Younger* by claiming that enforcement of a statute declared unconstitutional by a federal court is *per se* evidence of bad faith should not find support in the Court's decision in this case. As the Court notes, quoting my Brother Brennan's separate opinion in *Perez v. Ledesma,* 401 U.S. 82, 125, 91 S.Ct. 674, 697, 27 L.Ed.2d 701:

> The persuasive force of the [federal] court's opinion and judgment *may* lead state prosecutors, courts, and legislators to reconsider their respective responsibilities toward the statute. Enforcement

3. The Court's opinion notes that the possible res judicata effect of a federal declaratory judgment in a subsequent state court prosecution is a question " 'not free from difficulty.' " I express no opinion on that issue here. However, I do note that the federal decision would not be accorded the *stare decisis* effect in state court that it would have in a subsequent proceeding within the same federal jurisdiction. Although the state court would not be compelled to follow the federal holding, the opinion might, of course, be viewed as highly persuasive.

policies or judicial construction *may* be changed, or the legislature *may* repeal the statute and start anew. (Emphasis added.)

This language clearly recognizes that continued belief in the constitutionality of the statute by state prosecutorial officials would not commonly be indicative of bad faith and that such allegations, in the absence of highly unusual circumstances, would not justify a federal court's departure from the general principles of restraint discussed in *Younger*.

If the declaratory judgment remains, as I think the Declaratory Judgment Act intended, a simple declaration of rights without more, it will not be used merely as a dramatic tactical maneuver on the part of any state defendant seeking extended delays. Nor will it force state officials to try cases time after time, first in the federal courts and then in the state courts. I do not believe Congress desired such unnecessary results, and I do not think that today's decision should be read to sanction them. Rather the Act, and the decision, stand for the sensible proposition that both a potential state defendant, threatened with prosecution but not charged, and the State itself, confronted by a possible violation of its criminal laws, may benefit from a procedure which provides for a declaration of rights without activation of the criminal process. If the federal court finds that the threatened prosecution would depend upon a statute it judges unconstitutional, the State may decide to forgo prosecution of similar conduct in the future, believing the judgment persuasive. Should the state prosecutors not find the decision persuasive enough to justify forbearance, the successful federal plaintiff will at least be able to bolster his allegations of unconstitutionality in the state trial with a decision of the federal district court in the immediate locality. The state courts may find the reasoning convincing even though the prosecutors did not. Finally, of course, the state legislature may decide, on the basis of the federal decision, that the statute would be better amended or repealed. All these possible avenues of relief would be reached voluntarily by the States and would be completely consistent with the concepts of federalism discussed above. Other more intrusive forms of relief should not be routinely available.

These considerations should prove highly significant in reaching future decisions based upon the decision rendered today. For the present it is enough to say, as the Court does, that petitioner, if he successfully establishes the existence of a continuing controversy on remand, may maintain an action for a declaratory judgment in the District Court.

Notes and Questions

1. Are considerations governing the issuance of injunctive relief after state prosecutions have begun different from those where the prosecution has not yet commenced? Why?

2. In the *Steffel* situation the litigant must also avoid commencing proceedings too early. Why? With *Younger* restricting intervention in state court proceedings on the one hand and the ripeness doctrine requiring an

actual controversy between the litigants on the other hand, is *Steffel* of much significance? *Steffel* eventually limited the relief sought to a declaratory judgment. Yet the Court had previously announced that the principles of *Younger* ordinarily apply even to suits for declaratory relief. *See Samuels v. Mackell,* 401 U.S. 66 (1971).

3. Suppose the litigant institutes a federal action before the commencement of state court proceedings. Note the inapplicability of the statutory and judicial bar. Assume that during the pendency of the federal proceedings the state issues an indictment. Do the *Younger* principles then apply? Reconsider your answer after reading the following case.

HICKS v. MIRANDA

Supreme Court of the United States, 1975.
422 U.S. 332, 95 S.Ct. 2281, 45 L.Ed.2d 223.

Justice White delivered the opinion of the Court.

This case poses issues under *Younger v. Harris,* 401 U.S. 37, 91 S.Ct. 746, 27 L.Ed.2d 669 (1971), *Samuels v. Mackell,* 401 U.S. 66, 91 S.Ct. 764, 27 L.Ed.2d 688 (1971), and related cases, as well as the preliminary question as to our jurisdiction of this direct appeal from a judgment of a three-judge District Court.

I

On November 23 and 24, 1973, pursuant to four separate warrants issued seriatim, the police seized four copies of the film "Deep Throat," each of which had been shown at the Pussycat Theatre in Buena Park, Orange County, Cal. On November 26 an eight-count criminal misdemeanor charge was filed in the Orange County Municipal Court against two employees of the theater, each film seized being the subject matter of two counts in the complaint. Also on November 26, the Superior Court of Orange County ordered appellees to show cause why "Deep Throat" should not be declared obscene, an immediate hearing being available to appellees, who appeared that day, objected on state-law grounds to the court's jurisdiction to conduct such a proceeding, purported to "reserve" all federal questions, and refused further to participate. Thereupon, on November 27 the Superior Court held a hearing, viewed the film, took evidence, and then declared the movie to be obscene and ordered seized all copies of it that might be found at the theater. This judgment and order were not appealed by appellees.

Instead, on November 29, they filed this suit in the District Court against appellants—four police officers of Buena Park and the District Attorney and Assistant District Attorney of Orange County. The complaint recited the seizures and the proceedings in the Superior Court, stated that the action was for an injunction against the enforcement of the California obscenity statute, and prayed for judgment declaring the obscenity statute unconstitutional, and for an injunction ordering the return of all copies of the film, but permitting one of the films to be duplicated before its return.

A temporary restraining order was requested and denied, the District Judge finding the proof of irreparable injury to be lacking and an insufficient likelihood of prevailing on the merits to warrant an injunction. He requested the convening of a three-judge court, however, to consider the constitutionality of the statute. Such a court was then designated on January 8, 1974.

Service of the complaint was completed on January 14, 1974, and answers and motions to dismiss, as well as a motion for summary judgment, were filed by appellants. Appellees moved for a preliminary injunction. None of the motions was granted and no hearings held, all of the issues being ordered submitted on briefs and affidavits. The Attorney General of California also appeared and urged the District Court to follow *People v. Enskat,* 33 Cal.App.3d 900, 109 Cal.Rptr. 433 (1973), *hearing denied* Oct. 24, 1973, which, after *Miller v. California,* 413 U.S. 15, 93 S.Ct. 2607, 37 L.Ed.2d 419 (1973) (*Miller I*), had upheld the California obscenity statute.

Meanwhile, on January 15, the criminal complaint pending in the Municipal Court had been amended by naming appellees as additional parties defendant and by adding four conspiracy counts, one relating to each of the seized films. Also, on motions of the defendants in that case, two of the films were ordered suppressed on the ground that the two search warrants for seizing "Deep Throat" last issued, one on November 23 and the other on November 24, did not sufficiently allege that the films to be seized under those warrants differed from each other and from the films previously seized, the final two seizures being said to be invalid multiple seizures. Immediately after this order, which was later appealed and reversed, the defense and the prosecution stipulated that for purposes of the trial, which was expected to be forthcoming, the four prints of the film would be considered identical and only one copy would have to be proved at trial.

On June 4, 1974, the three-judge court issued its judgment and opinion declaring the California obscenity statute to be unconstitutional for failure to satisfy the requirements of *Miller I* and ordering appellants to return to appellees all copies of "Deep Throat" which had been seized as well as to refrain from making any additional seizures. Appellants' claim that *Younger v. Harris,* 401 U.S. 37, 91 S.Ct. 746, 27 L.Ed.2d 669 (1971), and *Samuels v. Mackell,* 401 U.S. 66, 91 S.Ct. 764, 27 L.Ed.2d 688 (1971), required dismissal of the case was rejected, the court holding that no criminal charges were pending in the state court against appellees and that in any event the pattern of search warrants and seizures demonstrated bad faith and harassment on the part of the authorities, all of which relieved the court from the strictures of *Younger v. Harris, supra,* and its related cases.

Appellants filed various motions for rehearing, to amend the judgment, and for relief from judgment, also later calling the court's attention to two developments they considered important: First, the dismissal on July 25, 1974, "for want of a substantial federal question" of the appeal in *Miller v. California,* 418 U.S. 915, 94 S.Ct. 3206, 41 L.Ed.2d 1158 (*Miller II*), from a judgment of the Superior Court, Appellate Department, Orange County, California, sustaining the constitutionality of the very California obscenity statute which the District Court had declared unconstitutional; second, the reversal by the Superior Court, Appellate Department, of the suppression order which had been issued in the criminal case pending in the Municipal Court, the *per curiam* reversal citing *Aday v. Superior Court,* 55 Cal.2d 789, 13 Cal.Rptr. 415, 362 P.2d 47 (1961), and saying the "requisite prompt adversary determination of obscenity under *Heller v. New York* * * * has been held."

On September 30, the three-judge court denied appellants' motions, reaffirmed its June 4 *Younger v. Harris* ruling and, after concluding it was not bound by the dismissal of *Miller II,* adhered to its judgment that the California statute was invalid under the Federal Constitution. In response to appellants' claim that they were without power to comply with the June 4 injunction, the films being in the possession of the Municipal Court, the court amended the injunctive portion of its order so as to read as follows:

> The defendants shall in good faith petition the Municipal Court of the North Orange County Judicial District to return to the plaintiffs three of the four film prints seized from the plaintiffs on November 23 and 24, 1973, in the City of Buena Park.

Appeals were taken to this Court from both the judgment of June 4 and the amended judgment of September 30. We postponed further consideration of our jurisdiction to the consideration of the merits of the case. 419 U.S. 1018, 95 S.Ct. 491, 42 L.Ed.2d 291 (1974).

* * *

III

The District Court committed error in reaching the merits of this case despite the appellants' insistence that it be dismissed under *Younger v. Harris,* 401 U.S. 37, 91 S.Ct. 746, 27 L.Ed.2d 669 (1971), and *Samuels v. Mackell,* 401 U.S. 66, 91 S.Ct. 764, 27 L.Ed.2d 688 (1971). When they filed their federal complaint, no state criminal proceedings were pending against appellees by name; but two employees of the theater had been charged and four copies of "Deep Throat" belonging to appellees had been seized, were being held, and had been declared to be obscene and seizable by the Superior Court. Appellees had a substantial stake in the state proceedings, so much so that they sought federal relief, demanding that the state statute be declared void and their films be returned to them. Obviously, their interests and those of their employees were intertwined; and, as we have pointed out, the federal action sought to interfere with the pending state prosecution. Absent a clear showing that appellees, whose lawyers also represented their employees, could not seek the return of their property in the state proceedings and see to it that their federal claims were presented there, the requirements of *Younger v. Harris* could not be avoided on the ground that no criminal prosecution was pending against appellees on the date the federal complaint was filed. The rule in *Younger v. Harris* is designed to "permit state courts to try state cases free from interference by federal courts," *id.*, 401 U.S. at 43, 91 S.Ct. at 750, particularly where the party to the federal case may fully litigate his claim before the state court. Plainly, "[t]he same comity considerations apply," *Allee v. Medrano*, 416 U.S. 802, 831, 94 S.Ct. 2191, 2208, 40 L.Ed.2d 566 (Burger, C.J., concurring), where the interference is sought by some, such as appellees, not parties to the state case.

What is more, on the day following the completion of service of the complaint, appellees were charged along with their employees in Municipal Court. Neither *Steffel v. Thompson*, 415 U.S. 452, 94 S.Ct. 1209, 39 L.Ed.2d 505 (1974), nor any other case in this Court has held that for *Younger v. Harris* to apply, the state criminal proceedings must be pending on the day the federal case is filed. Indeed, the issue has been left open; and we now hold that where state criminal proceedings are begun against the federal plaintiffs after the federal complaint is filed but before any proceedings of substance on the merits have taken place in the federal court, the principles of *Younger v. Harris* should apply in full force. Here, appellees were charged on January 15, prior to answering the federal case and prior to any proceedings whatsoever before the three-judge court. Unless we are to trivialize the principles of *Younger v. Harris*, the federal complaint should have been dismissed on the appellants' motion absent satisfactory proof of those extraordinary circumstances calling into play one of the limited exceptions to the rule of *Younger v. Harris* and related cases.

The District Court concluded that extraordinary circumstances had been shown in the form of official harassment and bad faith, but this was also error. The relevant findings of the District Court were vague and conclusory. There were references to the "pattern of seizure" and to "the evidence brought to light by the petition for rehearing"; and the unexplicated conclusion was then drawn that "regardless of the nature of any judicial proceeding," the police were bent on banishing "Deep Throat" from Buena Park. Yet each step in the pattern of seizures condemned by the District Court was authorized by judicial warrant or order; and the District Court did not purport to invalidate any of the four warrants, in any way to question the propriety of the proceedings in the Superior Court, or even to mention the reversal of the suppression order in the Appellate Department of that court. Absent at least some effort by the District Court to impeach the entitlement of the prosecuting officials to rely on repeated judicial authorization for their conduct, we cannot agree that bad faith and harassment were made out. Indeed, such conclusion would not necessarily follow even if it were shown that the state courts were in error on some one or more issues of state or federal law.

In the last analysis, it seems to us that the District Court's judgment rests almost entirely on its conclusion that the California obscenity statute was unconstitutional and unenforceable. But even assuming that the District Court was correct in its conclusion, the statute had not been so condemned in November 1973, and the District Court was not entitled to infer official bad faith merely because it—the District Court—disagreed with *People v. Enskat.* Otherwise, bad faith and harassment would be present in every case in which a state statute is ruled unconstitutional, and the rule of *Younger v. Harris* would be swallowed up by its exception. The District Court should have dismissed the complaint before it and we accordingly reverse its judgment.

So ordered.

Judgment reversed.

[The concurring opinion of Chief Justice Burger is omitted.]

JUSTICE STEWART, with whom JUSTICE DOUGLAS, JUSTICE BRENNAN, and JUSTICE MARSHALL join, dissenting.

There are many aspects of the Court's opinion that seem to me open to serious challenge. This dissent, however, is directed only to Part III of the opinion, which holds that "[t]he District Court committed error in reaching the merits of this case despite the appellants' insistence that it be dismissed under *Younger v. Harris* * * * and *Samuels v. Mackell.* * * * *"

In *Steffel v. Thompson,* 415 U.S. 452, 94 S.Ct. 1209, 39 L.Ed.2d 505, the Court unanimously held that the principles of equity, comity, and federalism embodied in *Younger v. Harris,* 401 U.S. 37, 91 S.Ct. 746, 27 L.Ed.2d 669, and *Samuels v. Mackell,* 401 U.S. 66, 91 S.Ct. 764, 27 L.Ed.2d 688, do not preclude a federal district court from entertaining an action to declare unconstitutional a state criminal statute when a state criminal prosecution is threatened but not pending at the time the federal complaint is filed. Today the Court holds that the *Steffel* decision is inoperative if a state criminal charge is filed at any point after the commencement of the federal action "before any proceedings of substance on the merits have taken place in the federal court." Any other rule, says the Court, would "trivialize" the principles of *Younger v. Harris.* I think this ruling "trivializes" *Steffel,* decided just last Term, and is inconsistent with those same principles of equity, comity, and federalism.[1]

1. There is the additional difficulty that the precise meaning of the rule the Court today adopts is a good deal less than apparent. What are "proceedings of substance on the merits"? Presumably, the proceedings must be both "on the merits" and "of substance." Does this mean, then, that months of discovery activity would be insufficient, if no question on the merits is presented to the court during that time? What proceedings "on the merits" are sufficient is also unclear. An application for a temporary restraining order or a preliminary injunction requires the court to make an assessment about the likelihood of success on the merits. Indeed, in this case, appellees filed an application for a temporary restraining order along with six supporting affidavits on November 29, 1973. Appellants responded on December 3, 1973, with six affidavits of their own as well as additional documents. On December 28, 1973, Judge Lydick denied the request for a temporary restraining order, in part because appellees "have failed totally to make that showing of * * * likelihood of prevailing on the merits needed to justify the issuance of a temporary restraining order." These proceedings the Court says implicitly, were not sufficient to satisfy the test it announces. Why that

There is, to be sure, something unseemly about having the applicability of the *Younger* doctrine turn solely on the outcome of a race to the courthouse. The rule the Court adopts today, however, does not eliminate that race; it merely permits the State to leave the mark later, run a shorter course, and arrive first at the finish line. This rule seems to me to result from a failure to evaluate the state and federal interests as of the time the state prosecution was commenced.

As of the time when its jurisdiction is invoked in a *Steffel* situation, a federal court is called upon to vindicate federal constitutional rights when no other remedy is available to the federal plaintiff. The Court has recognized that at this point in the proceedings no substantial state interests counsel the federal court to stay its hand. Thus, in *Lake Carriers' Assn. v. MacMullan,* 406 U.S. 498, 92 S.Ct. 1749, 32 L.Ed.2d 257, we noted that "considerations of equity practice and comity in our federal system * * * have little force in the absence of a pending state proceeding." *Id.* at 509. And in *Steffel,* a unanimous Court explained the balance of interests this way:

> When no state criminal proceeding is pending at the time the federal complaint is filed, federal intervention does not result in duplicative legal proceedings or disruption of the state criminal justice system; nor can federal intervention, in that circumstance, be interpreted as reflecting negatively upon the state court's ability to enforce constitutional principles. In addition, while a pending state prosecution provides the federal plaintiff with a concrete opportunity to vindicate his constitutional rights, a refusal on the part of the federal courts to intervene when no state proceeding is pending may place the hapless plaintiff between the Scylla of intentionally flouting state law and the Charybdis of forgoing what he believes to be constitutionally protected activity in order to avoid becoming enmeshed in a criminal proceeding. 415 U.S. at 462, 94 S.Ct. at 1217.

Consequently, we concluded that "[r]equiring the federal courts totally to step aside when no state criminal prosecution is pending against the federal plaintiff would turn federalism on its head." *Id.* at 472, 94 S.Ct. at 1222. In such circumstances, "the opportunity for adjudication of constitutional rights in a federal forum, as authorized by the Declaratory Judgment Act, becomes paramount." *Ellis v. Dyson,* 421 U.S. 426, 432, 95 S.Ct. 1691, 1695, 44 L.Ed.2d 274. *See also Huffman v. Pursue, Ltd.,* 420 U.S. 592, 602–603, 95 S.Ct. 1200, 1207, 43 L.Ed.2d 482.

The duty of the federal courts to adjudicate and vindicate federal constitutional rights is, of course, shared with state courts, but there can be no doubt that the federal courts are "the primary and powerful reliances for vindicating every right given by the Constitution, the laws, and treaties of the United States." F. Frankfurter & J. Landis, *The Business of the Supreme Court: A Study in the Federal Judicial System* 65 (1927). The statute under which this action was brought, 42 U.S.C. § 1983, established in our law "the role of the Federal Government as a

should be, even in terms of the Court's
holding is a mystery.

guarantor of basic federal rights against state power." Indeed, "[t]he very purpose of § 1983 was to interpose the federal courts between the States and the people." And this central interest of a federal court as guarantor of constitutional rights is fully implicated from the moment its jurisdiction is invoked. How, then, does the subsequent filing of a state criminal charge change the situation from one in which the federal court's dismissal of the action under *Younger* principles "would turn federalism on its head" to one in which *failure* to dismiss would "trivialize" those same principles?

A State has a vital interest in the enforcement of its criminal law, and this Court has said time and again that it will sanction little federal interference with that important state function. But there is nothing in our decision in *Steffel* that requires a State to stay its hand during the pendency of the federal litigation. If, in the interest of efficiency, the State wishes to refrain from actively prosecuting the criminal charge pending the outcome of the federal declaratory judgment suit, it may, of course, do so. But no decision of this Court requires it to make that choice.

The Court today, however, goes much further than simply recognizing the right of the State to proceed with the orderly administration of its criminal law; it ousts the federal courts from their historic role as the "primary reliances" for vindicating constitutional freedoms. This is no less offensive to "Our Federalism" than the federal injunction restraining pending state criminal proceedings condemned in *Younger v. Harris.* The concept of federalism requires "sensitivity to the legitimate interest of *both* State and National Governments." 401 U.S. at 44, 91 S.Ct. at 750 (emphasis added). *Younger v. Harris* and its companion cases reflect the principles that the federal judiciary must refrain from interfering with the legitimate functioning of state courts. But surely the converse is a principle no less valid.

The Court's new rule creates a reality which few state prosecutors can be expected to ignore. It is an open invitation to state officials to institute state proceedings in order to defeat federal jurisdiction. One need not impugn the motives of state officials to suppose that they would rather prosecute a criminal suit in state court than defend a civil case in a federal forum. Today's opinion virtually instructs state officials to answer federal complaints with state indictments. Today, the State must file a criminal charge to secure dismissal of the federal litigation; perhaps tomorrow an action "akin to a criminal proceeding" will serve the purpose, see *Huffman v. Pursue, Ltd.,* 95 S.Ct. 1200, 43 L.Ed.2d 482; and the day may not be far off when any state civil action will do.

The doctrine of *Younger v. Harris* reflects an accommodation of competing interests. The rule announced today distorts that balance beyond recognition.

Notes and Questions

1. Do you agree with the Court's rationale?

2. Note the federal plaintiff's dilemma. If the plaintiff proceeds too early, the case may be dismissed for lack of ripeness. If the action is timely, it may be aborted by the filing of criminal charges by the state. Indeed, the federal action may actually precipitate such action. How would you proceed in these circumstances, assuming, of course, a desire to litigate the constitutional claim in a federal court? *See Doran v. Salem Inn, Inc.,* 422 U.S. 922 (1975).

3. What does the Court mean by "proceedings of substance on the merits"? Why was the test not satisfied in *Hicks?*

TRAINOR v. HERNANDEZ

Supreme Court of the United States, 1977.
431 U.S. 434, 97 S.Ct. 1911, 52 L.Ed.2d 486.

JUSTICE WHITE delivered the opinion of the Court.

The Illinois Department of Public Aid (IDPA) filed a lawsuit in the Circuit Court of Cook County, Ill., on October 30, 1974, against appellees Juan and Maria Hernandez, alleging that they had fraudulently concealed assets while applying for and receiving public assistance. Such conduct is a crime under Illinois law, Ill.Rev.Stat., c. 23, § 11–21 (1973). The IDPA, however, proceeded civilly and sought only return of the money alleged to have been wrongfully received. The IDPA simultaneously instituted an attachment proceeding against appellees' property. Pursuant to the Illinois Attachment Act, Ill.Rev.Stat., c. 11 (1973) (Act), the IDPA filed an affidavit setting forth the nature and amount of the underlying claim and alleging that the appellees had obtained money from the IDPA by fraud. The writ of attachment was issued automatically by the clerk of the court upon receipt of this affidavit. The writ was then given to the sheriff who executed it, on November 5, 1974, on money belonging to appellees in a credit union. Appellees received notice of the attachment, freezing their money in the credit union, on November 8, 1974, when they received the writ, the complaint, and the affidavit in support of the writ. The writ indicated a return date for the attachment proceeding of November 18, 1974. Appellees appeared in court on November 18, 1974, and were informed that the matter would be continued until December 19, 1974. Appellees never filed an answer either to the attachment or to the underlying complaint. They did not seek a prompt hearing, nor did they attempt to quash the attachment on the ground that the procedures surrounding its issuance rendered it and the Act unconstitutional. Instead appellees filed the instant lawsuit in the United States District Court for the Northern District of Illinois on December 2, 1974, seeking, *inter alia,* return of the attached money. The federal complaint alleged that the appellees' property had been attached pursuant to the Act and that the Act was unconstitutional in that it provided for the deprivation of debtors' property without due process of law. Appellees as plaintiffs sought to represent a class of those "who have had or may have their property attached without notice or hearing upon the creditor's mere allegation of fraudulent conduct pursuant to the Illinois Attachment Act." App. 6–7. They named as defendants appellants Trainor and O'Malley, officials of the IDPA, and sought declaration of a defendant class made up of all the court clerks in the Circuit Courts of Illinois, and of another defendant class of all sheriffs in Illinois. They sought an injunction against Trainor and O'Malley forbidding them to seek attachments under the Act and an injunction against the clerks and sheriffs forbidding them to issue or serve writs of attachment under the Act. Appellees also sought preliminary relief in the form of an order directing the Sheriff of Cook County to release the property which had been attached. Finally, appellees sought the convening of a three-judge court pursuant to 28 U.S.C. § 2284.

The District Court declined to rule on the request for preliminary relief because the parties had agreed that one-half of the money in the credit union would be returned. A three-judge court was convened. It certified the suit as a plaintiff and defendant class action as appellees had requested. App. 63. In an opinion dated December 19, 1975, almost one year after the return date of the attachment in state court, it declined to dismiss the case under the doctrine of *Younger v. Harris*, 401 U.S. 37, 91 S.Ct. 746, 27 L.Ed.2d 669 (1971), and *Huffman v. Pursue, Ltd.*, 420 U.S. 592, 95 S.Ct. 1200, 43 L.Ed.2d 482 (1975), stating:

> In *Huffman*, the State of Ohio proceeded under a statute which gave an exclusive right of action to the state. By contrast, the Illinois Attachment Act provides a cause of action for any person, public or private. It is mere happenstance that the State of Illinois was the petitioner in this attachment proceeding. It is likewise coincidental that the pending state proceedings may arguably be quasi-criminal in nature; under the Illinois Attachment Act, they need not be. These major distinctions preclude this Court from extending the principles of *Younger*, based on considerations of equity, comity and federalism, beyond the quasi-criminal situation set forth in *Huffman*. *Hernandez v. Danaher*, 405 F.Supp. 757, 760 (1975).

Proceeding to the merits, it held §§ 1, 2, 2a, 6, 8, 10, and 14 of the Act to be "on [their face] patently violative of the due process clause of the Fourteenth Amendment to the United States Constitution." 405 F.Supp., at 762. It ordered the clerk of the court and the Sheriff of Cook County to return to appellees the rest of their attached property; it enjoined all clerks and all sheriffs from issuing or serving attachment writs pursuant to the Act and ordered them to release any currently held attached property to its owner; and it enjoined appellants Trainor and O'Malley from authorizing applications for attachment writs pursuant to the Act. App. 65–66. Appellants appealed to this Court under 28 U.S.C. § 1253, claiming that under *Younger* and *Huffman* principles the District Court should have dismissed the suit without passing on the constitutionality of the Act and that the Act is in any event constitutional. Since we agree with appellants that *Younger* and *Huffman* principles do apply here, we do not reach their second claim.

Because our federal and state legal systems have overlapping jurisdiction and responsibilities, we have frequently inquired into the proper role of a federal court, in a case pending before it and otherwise within its jurisdiction, when litigation between the same parties and raising the same issues is or apparently soon will be pending in a state court. More precisely, when a suit is filed in a federal court challenging the constitutionality of a state law under the Federal Constitution and seeking to have state officers enjoined from enforcing it, should the federal court proceed to judgment when it appears that the State has already instituted proceedings in the state court to enforce the challenged statute against the federal plaintiff and the latter could tender and have his federal claims decided in the state court?

Younger v. Harris, supra, and *Samuels v. Mackell,* 401 U.S. 66, 91 S.Ct. 764, 27 L.Ed.2d 688 (1971), addressed these questions where the already pending state proceeding was a criminal prosecution and the federal plaintiff sought to invalidate the statute under which the state prosecution was brought. In these circumstances, the Court ruled that the Federal District Court should issue neither a declaratory judgment nor an injunction but should dismiss the case. The first justification the Court gave for this rule was simply the "basic doctrine of equity jurisprudence that courts of equity should not act, and particularly should not act to restrain a criminal prosecution, when the moving party has an adequate remedy at law and will not suffer irreparable injury if denied equitable relief." *Younger v. Harris, supra,* 401 U.S. at 43–44, 91 S.Ct. at 750.

Beyond the accepted rule that equity will ordinarily not enjoin the prosecution of a crime, however, the Court voiced a "more vital consideration," 401 U.S. at 44, 91 S.Ct. at 750, namely, that in a Union where both the States and the Federal Government are sovereign entities, there are basic concerns of federalism which counsel against interference by federal courts, through injunctions or otherwise, with legitimate state functions, particularly with the operation of state courts. Relying on cases that declared that courts of equity should give "scrupulous regard [to] the rightful independence of state governments," *Beal v. Missouri Pacific R. Corp.,* 312 U.S. 45, 50, 61 S.Ct. 418, 421, 85 L.Ed. 577 (1941), the Court held, that in this intergovernmental context, the two classic preconditions for the exercise of equity jurisdiction assumed new dimensions. Although the existence of an adequate remedy at law barring equitable relief normally would be determined by inquiring into the remedies available in the federal rather than in the state courts, *Great Lakes Co. v. Huffman,* 319 U.S. 293, 297, 63 S.Ct. 1070, 1072, 87 L.Ed. 1407 (1943), here the inquiry was to be broadened to focus on the remedies available in the pending state proceeding. " 'The accused should first set up and rely upon his defense in the state courts, even though this involves a challenge of the validity of some statute, unless it plainly appears that this course would not afford adequate protection.' "

Younger v. Harris, 401 U.S. at 45, 91 S.Ct. at 751 quoting *Fenner v. Boykin,* 271 U.S. 240, 243–244, 46 S.Ct. 492, 493, 70 L.Ed. 927 (1926). Dismissal of the federal suit "naturally presupposes the opportunity to raise and have timely decided by a competent state tribunal the federal issues involved." *Gibson v. Berryhill,* 411 U.S. 564, 577, 93 S.Ct. 1689, 1697, 36 L.Ed.2d 488 (1973). "The policy of equitable restraint * * * is founded on the premise that ordinarily a pending state prosecution provides the accused a fair and sufficient opportunity for vindication of federal constitutional rights." *Kugler v. Helfant,* 421 U.S. 117, 124, 95 S.Ct. 1524, 1531, 44 L.Ed.2d 15 (1975).

The Court also concluded that the other precondition for equitable relief—irreparable injury—would not be satisfied unless the threatened injury was both great and immediate. The burden of conducting a defense in the criminal prosecution was not sufficient to warrant interference by the federal courts with legitimate state efforts to enforce state laws; only extraordinary circumstances would suffice.[7] As the Court later explained, to restrain a state proceeding that afforded an adequate vehicle for vindicating the federal plaintiff's constitutional rights "would entail an unseemly failure to give effect to the principle that state courts have the solemn responsibility equally with the federal courts" to safeguard constitutional rights and would "reflec[t] negatively upon the state court's ability" to do so. *Steffel v. Thompson,* 415 U.S. 452, 460–461, 462, 94 S.Ct. 1209, 1216–1217, 39 L.Ed.2d 505 (1974). The State would be prevented not only from "effectuating its substantive policies,

---

7. *See Kugler v. Helfant,* 421 U.S. 117, 124–125, 95 S.Ct. 1524, 1530–31, 44 L.Ed.2d 15 (1975):

"Although the cost, anxiety, and inconvenience of having to defend against a single criminal prosecution alone do not constitute 'irreparable injury' in the 'special legal sense of that term,' [*Younger v. Harris,* 401 U.S.] at 46, 91 S.Ct. at 751, the Court in *Younger* left room for federal equitable intervention in a state criminal trial where there is a showing of 'bad faith' or 'harassment' by state officials responsible for the prosecution, *id.* at 54, 91 S.Ct. at 755, where the state law to be applied in the criminal proceeding is 'flagrantly and patently violative of express constitutional prohibitions,'*id.* at 53, 91 S.Ct. at 755, or where there exist other 'extraordinary circumstances in which the necessary irreparable injury can be shown even in the absence of the usual prerequisites of bad faith and harassment.' *Ibid.* In the companion case of *Perez v. Ledesma,* 401 U.S. 82, 91 S.Ct. 674, 27 L.Ed.2d 701, the Court explained that '[o]nly in cases of proven harassment or prosecutions undertaken by state officials in bad faith without hope of obtaining a valid conviction and perhaps in other extraordinary circumstances where irreparable injury can be shown is federal injunctive relief against pending state prosecutions appropriate.' *Id.* at 85, 91 S.Ct. at 677. *See Mitchum v. Foster,* 407 U.S. 225, 230–231, 92 S.Ct. 2151, 2156, 32 L.Ed.2d 705.

"The policy of equitable restraint expressed in *Younger v. Harris,* in short, is founded on the premise that ordinarily a pending state prosecution provides the accused a fair and sufficient opportunity for vindication of federal constitutional rights. *See Steffel v. Thompson,* 415 U.S. 452, 460, 94 S.Ct. 1209, 1216, 39 L.Ed.2d 505. Only if 'extraordinary circumstances' render the state court incapable of fairly and fully adjudicating the federal issues before it, can there be any relaxation of the deference to be accorded to the state criminal process. The very nature of 'extraordinary circumstances,' of course, makes it impossible to anticipate and define every situation that might create a sufficient threat of such great, immediate, and irreparable injury as to warrant intervention in state criminal proceedings. [Footnote omitted.] But whatever else is required, such circumstances must be 'extraordinary' in the sense of creating an extraordinarily pressing need for immediate federal equitable relief, not merely in the sense of presenting a highly unusual factual situation."

but also from continuing to perform the separate function of providing a forum competent to vindicate any constitutional objections interposed against those policies." *Huffman v. Pursue, Ltd.,* 420 U.S. at 604, 95 S.Ct. at 1208.

Huffman involved the propriety of a federal injunction against the execution of a judgment entered in a pending state-court suit brought by the State to enforce a nuisance statute. Although the state suit was a civil rather than a criminal proceeding, *Younger* principles were held to require dismissal of the federal suit. Noting that the State was a party to the nuisance proceeding and that the nuisance statute was "in aid of and closely related to criminal statutes," the Court concluded that a federal injunction would be "an offense to the State's interest in the nuisance litigation [which] is likely to be every bit as great as it would be were this a criminal proceeding." 420 U.S. at 604, 95 S.Ct. at 1208. Thus, while the traditional maxim that equity will not enjoin a criminal prosecution strictly speaking did not apply to the nuisance proceeding in *Huffman,* the " 'more vital consideration' " of comity, *id.* at 601, 95 S.Ct. at 1208, quoting *Younger v. Harris,* 401 U.S. at 44, 91 S.Ct. at 750, counseled restraint as strongly in the context of the pending state civil enforcement action as in the context of a pending criminal proceeding. In these circumstances, it was proper that the federal court stay its hand.

We have recently applied the analysis of *Huffman* to proceedings similar to state civil enforcement actions—judicial contempt proceedings. *Juidice v. Vail,* 430 U.S. 327, 97 S.Ct. 1211, 51 L.Ed.2d 376 (1977). The Court again stressed the "more vital consideration" of comity underlying the *Younger* doctrine and held that the state interest in vindicating the regular operation of its judicial system through the contempt process— whether that process was labeled civil, criminal, or quasi-criminal—was sufficiently important to preclude federal injunctive relief unless *Younger* standards were met.

These cases control here. An action against appellees was pending in state court when they filed their federal suit. The state action was a suit by the State to recover from appellees welfare payments that allegedly had been fraudulently obtained. The writ of attachment issued as part of that action. The District Court thought that *Younger* policies were irrelevant because suits to recover money and writs of attachment were available to private parties as well as the State; it was only because of the coincidence that the State was a party that the suit was "arguably" in aid of the criminal law. But the fact remains that the State was a party to the suit in its role of administering its public-assistance programs. Both the suit and the accompanying writ of attachment were brought to vindicate important state policies such as safeguarding the fiscal integrity of those programs. The state authorities also had the option of vindicating these policies through criminal prosecutions. Although, as in *Juidice,* the State's interest here is "[p]erhaps * * * not quite as important as is the State's interest in the enforcement of its criminal laws * * * or even its interest in the maintenance of a quasi-criminal proceeding * * *," 430 U.S. at 335, 97 S.Ct. at 1217, the principles of *Younger* and *Huffman* are broad enough to apply to interference by a federal court with an ongoing civil enforcement action such as this, brought by the State in its sovereign capacity.

For a federal court to proceed with its case rather than to remit appellees to their remedies in a pending state enforcement suit would confront the State with a choice of engaging in duplicative litigation, thereby risking a temporary federal injunction, or of interrupting its enforcement proceedings pending decision of the federal court at some unknown time in the future. It would also foreclose the opportunity of the state court to construe the challenged statute in the face of the actual federal constitutional challenges that would also be pending for decision before it, a privilege not wholly shared by the federal courts. Of course, in the case before us the state statute was invalidated and a federal injunction prohibited state officers from using or enforcing the attachment statute for any purpose. The eviscerating impact on many state enforcement actions is readily apparent. This disruption of suits by the State in its sovereign capacity, when combined with the negative reflection on the State's ability to adjudicate federal claims that occurs whenever a federal court enjoins a pending state proceeding, leads us to the conclusion that the interests of comity and federalism on which *Younger* and *Samuels v. Mackell* primarily rest apply in full force here. The pendency of the state-court action called for restraint by the federal court and for the dismissal of appellees' complaint unless extraordinary circumstances were present warranting federal interference or unless their state remedies were inadequate to litigate their federal due process claim.

No extraordinary circumstances warranting equitable relief were present here. There is no suggestion that the pending state action was brought in bad faith or for the purpose of harassing appellees. It is urged that this case comes within the exception that we said in *Younger* might exist where a state statute is " 'flagrantly and patently violative of express constitutional prohibitions in every clause, sentence and paragraph, and in whatever manner and against whomever an effort might be made to apply it.' " 401 U.S. at 53–54, 91 S.Ct. at 755, quoting *Watson v. Buck*, 313 U.S. 387, 402, 61 S.Ct. 962, 967, 85 L.Ed. 1416 (1941). Even if such a finding was made below, which we doubt (*see supra*, at 439 (1916)), it would not have been warranted in light of our cases. *Compare North Georgia Finishing, Inc. v. Di–Chem, Inc.*, 419 U.S. 601, 95 S.Ct. 719, 42 L.Ed.2d 751 (1975), *with Mitchell v. W. T. Grant Co.*, 416 U.S. 600, 94 S.Ct. 1895, 40 L.Ed.2d 406 (1974).

As for whether appellees could have presented their federal due process challenge to the attachment statute in the pending state proceeding, that question, if presented below, was not addressed by the District Court, which placed its rejection of *Younger* and *Huffman* on broader grounds. The issue is heavily laden with local law, and we do not rule on it here in the first instance.

The grounds on which the District Court refused to apply the principles of *Younger* and *Huffman* were infirm; it was therefore error, on those grounds, to entertain the action on behalf of either the named or the unnamed plaintiffs and to reach the issue of the constitutionality of the Illinois attachment statute.

The judgment is therefore reversed, and the case is remanded to the District Court for further proceedings consistent with this opinion.

It is so ordered.

JUSTICE STEWART substantially agrees with the views expressed in the dissenting opinions of JUSTICE BRENNAN and JUSTICE STEVENS. Accordingly, he respectfully dissents from the opinion and judgment of the Court.

JUSTICE BLACKMUN, concurring.

I join the Court's opinion and write only to stress that the substantiality of the State's interest in its proceeding has been an important factor in abstention cases under *Younger v. Harris,* 401 U.S. 37, 91 S.Ct. 746, 27 L.Ed.2d 669 (1971), from the beginning. In discussing comity, the Court in *Younger* clearly indicated that both federal and state interests had to be taken into account:

> The concept does not mean blind deference to "States' Rights" any more than it means centralization of control over every important issue in our National Government and its courts. The Framers rejected both these courses. What the concept does represent is a system in which there is sensitivity to the legitimate interests of both State and National Governments, and in which the National Government, anxious though it may be to vindicate and protect federal rights and federal interests, always endeavors to do so in ways that will not unduly interfere with the legitimate activities of the States. *Id.* at 44, 91 S.Ct. at 751.

Consistently with this requirement of balancing the federal and state interests, the Court in previous *Younger* cases has imposed a requirement that the State must show that it has an important interest to vindicate in its own courts before the federal court must refrain from exercising otherwise proper federal jurisdiction. In *Younger* itself, the Court relied on the State's vital concern in the administration of its criminal laws. In *Huffman v. Pursue, Ltd.,* 420 U.S. 592, 95 S.Ct. 1200, 43 L.Ed.2d 482 (1975), the Court stressed the fact that it dealt with a quasi-criminal state proceeding to which the State was a party. The proceeding was both in aid of and closely related to criminal statutes. Thus, the State's underlying policy interest in the litigation was deemed to be as great as the interest found in *Younger*. Similarly, in *Juidice v. Vail,* 430 U.S. 327, 97 S.Ct. 1211, 51 L.Ed.2d 376 (1977), the Court found that the State's interest in its contempt procedures was substantial.

In cases where the State's interest has been more attenuated, the Court has refused to order *Younger* abstention. Thus, in *Steffel v. Thompson,* 415 U.S. 452, 94 S.Ct. 1209, 39 L.Ed.2d 505 (1974), in which a state prosecution was merely threatened, the federal court was free to reach the merits of the claim for a declaratory judgment. *Id.* at 462, 94 S.Ct. at 1217. In such a case, "the opportunity for adjudication of constitutional rights in a federal forum, as authorized by the Declaratory Judgment Act, becomes paramount." *Ellis v. Dyson,* 421 U.S. 426, 432, 95 S.Ct. 1691, 1695, 44 L.Ed.2d 274 (1975). See generally Kanowitz, Deciding Federal Law Issues in Civil Proceedings: State Versus Federal Trial Courts, 3 Hastings Const.L.Q. 141 (1976).

Application of these principles to the instant case leads me to agree with the Court's order reversing and remanding the case. Like the Court, I am satisfied that a state proceeding was pending. I, too, find significant the fact that the State was a party in its sovereign capacity to both the state suit and the federal suit. *Ante,* at 1918. Here, I emphasize the importance of the fact that the state interest in the pending state proceeding was substantial. In my view, the fact that the State had the option of proceeding either civilly or criminally to impose sanctions for a fraudulent concealment of assets while one applies for and receives public assistance demonstrates that the underlying state interest is of the same order of importance as the interests in *Younger* and *Huffman.* The propriety of abstention should not depend on the State's choice to vindicate its interests by a less drastic, and perhaps more lenient, route. In addition, as the Court notes, the state court proceeding played an important role in safeguarding the fiscal integrity of the public assistance programs. Since the benefits of the recovery of fraudulently obtained funds are enjoyed by all the taxpayers of the State, it is reasonable to recognize a distinction between the State's status as creditor and the status of private parties using the same procedures.

For me, the existence of the foregoing factors brings this case squarely within the Court's prior *Younger* abstention rulings.

JUSTICE BRENNAN, with whom JUSTICE MARSHALL joins, dissenting.

The Court continues on, to me, the wholly improper course of extending *Younger* principles to deny a federal forum to plaintiffs invoking 42 U.S.C. § 1983 for the decision of meritorious federal constitutional claims when a *civil* action that might entertain such claims is pending in a state court. Because I am of the view that the decision patently disregards Congress' purpose in enacting § 1983—to open federal courts to the decision of such claims without regard to the pendency of such state civil actions—and because the decision indefensibly departs from prior decisions of this Court, I respectfully dissent.

* * *

III

Even assuming, *arguendo,* the applicability of *Younger* principles, I agree with the District Court that the Illinois Attachment Act falls within one of the established exceptions to those principles. As an example of an "extraordinary circumstance" that might justify federal-court intervention, *Younger* referred to a statute that " 'might be flagrantly and patently violative of express constitutional prohibitions in every clause, sentence and paragraph, and in whatever manner and against whomever an effort might be made to apply it.' '' 401 U.S. at 53–54, 91 S.Ct. at 755, quoting *Watson v. Buck,* 313 U.S. 387, 402, 61 S.Ct. 962, 967, 85 L.Ed. 1416 (1941). Explicitly relying on this exception to *Younger,* the District Court held that the Illinois Act is "patently and flagrantly violative of the constitution." 405 F.Supp. at 760. The Court holds that this finding is insufficient to bring this case within the *Younger* exception because that exception "might exist where a state statute is 'flagrantly and patently violative of express constitutional prohibitions in every clause, sentence and paragraph, and in whatever manner and against whomever an effort might be made to apply it.' 401 U.S. at 53–54, 91 S.Ct. at 755, quoting *Watson v. Buck,* 313 U.S. 387, 402, 61 S.Ct. 962, 967, 85 L.Ed. 1416 (1941). Even if such a finding was made below, which we doubt * * *, it would not have been warranted in light of our cases." I disagree.

Obviously, a requirement that the *Watson v. Buck* formulation must be literally satisfied renders the exception meaningless, and, as my Brother Stevens demonstrates, elevates to a literalistic definitional status what was obviously meant only to be illustrative and nonexhaustive. The human mind does not possess a clairvoyance that can foresee whether "every clause, sentence and paragraph" of a statute will be unconstitutional "in whatever manner and against whomever an effort might be made to apply it." The only sensible construction of the test is to treat the "every clause, etc.," wording as redundant, at least when decisions of this Court make clear that the challenged statute is "patently and flagrantly violative of the Constitution." I thought that the Court had decided as much in *Kugler v. Helfant,* 421 U.S. 117, 124, 95 S.Ct. 1524, 1530, 44 L.Ed.2d 15 (1975), in stating that "*Younger* left room for federal equitable intervention in a state criminal trial *where the state law to be applied in the criminal proceeding is 'flagrantly and patently violative of express constitutional prohibitions.'*" (Emphasis supplied.)

Clearly the Illinois Attachment Act is "flagrantly and patently violative of express constitutional prohibitions" under the relevant decisions of this Court. *North Georgia Finishing, Inc. v. Di–Chem, Inc.,* 419 U.S. 601, 95 S.Ct. 719, 42 L.Ed.2d 751 (1975), struck down a Georgia garnishment statute that permitted the issuance of a writ of garnishment by the court clerk upon the filing of an affidavit containing only conclusory allegations, and under which there was "no provision for an early hearing at which the creditor would be required to demonstrate at least probable cause for the garnishment." *Id.* at 607, 95 S.Ct. at 723. The Illinois Attachment Act is constitutionally indistinguishable from the Georgia statute struck down in *North Georgia Finishing.* As in that case, the affidavit filed here contained only conclusory allegations, which in this case were taken from a preprinted form requiring only that the affiant fill in the names of the persons whose property he wished to attach. Upon the filing of this form affidavit, the court clerk issued the writ of attachment as a matter of course. Far from requiring an "early hearing" at which to challenge the validity of the attachment, the Illinois Act provided that the party seeking the attachment could unilaterally set the return date of the writ at any time from 10 to 60 days from the date of its execution. Ill.Rev.Stat., c. 11, § 6 (1973). And, as this case demonstrates, the 60–day interval does not necessarily represent the outer limit for the actual hearing date, for the Illinois court here was willing to grant a 30–day continuance beyond the date provided in the writ of attachment, even though appellees appeared in court on the proper date and wished to go forward with the hearing at that time.

No one could seriously contend that the Illinois Act even remotely resembles that sustained in *Mitchell v. W.T. Grant Co.,* 416 U.S. 600, 94 S.Ct. 1895, 40 L.Ed.2d 406 (1974), and thus falls within the exception to *Sniadach v. Family Finance Corp.,* 395 U.S. 337, 89 S.Ct. 1820, 23 L.Ed.2d 349 (1969), *Fuentes v. Shevin,* 407 U.S. 67, 92 S.Ct. 1983, 32 L.Ed.2d 556 (1972), and *North Georgia Finishing, supra,* carved out by that case. *W.T. Grant* upheld a Louisiana sequestration statute under which a writ of sequestration was issued only after the filing of an affidavit in which " 'the grounds relied upon for the issuance of the writ clearly appear[ed] from specific facts,' " 416 U.S. at 605, 94 S.Ct. at 1899. The showing of grounds for the issuance of the writ was made before a judge rather than a court clerk, *id.* at 606, 94 S.Ct. at 1899, and the debtor was entitled "immediately [to] have a full hearing on the matter of possession following the execution of the writ," *id.* at 610, 94 S.Ct. at 1901. None of those procedural safeguards is provided by the Illinois Act. The three-judge District Court unanimously and correctly concluded that the Act "is on its face patently violative of the due process clause of the Fourteenth Amendment." 405 F.Supp. at 762.

The Court gives only bare citations to *North Georgia Finishing* and *W.T. Grant,* and declines to discuss or analyze them in even the most cursory manner. These decisions so clearly support the District Court's holding under any sensible construction of the *Younger* exception that the Court's silence, and its insistence upon compliance with the literal wording of *Watson v. Buck,* only confirms my conviction that the Court is determined to extend to "state *civil* proceedings generally the holding of *Younger,*" *Huffman v. Pursue, Ltd.,* 420 U.S. at 613, 95 S.Ct. at 1212, and to give its exceptions the narrowest possible reach. I respectfully dissent.

JUSTICE STEVENS, dissenting.

Today the Court adds four new complexities to a doctrine that has bewildered other federal courts for several years. First, the Court finds a meaningful difference between a state procedure which is "patently and flagrantly violative of the Constitution" and one that is "flagrantly and patently violative of express constitutional prohibitions in every clause, sentence and paragraph, and in whatever manner and against whomever an effort might be made to apply it." Second, the Court holds that an unconstitutional collection procedure may be used by a state agency, though not by others, because there is "a distinction between the State's status as creditor and the status of private parties using the same procedures." Third, the Court's application of the abstention doctrine in this case provides even greater protection to a State when it is proceeding as an ordinary creditor than the statutory protection mandated by Congress for the State in its capacity as a tax collector. Fourth, without disagreeing with the District Court's conclusion that the Illinois attachment procedure is unconstitutional, the Court remands in order to enable the District Court to decide whether that invalid procedure provides an adequate remedy for the vindication of appellees' federal rights. A comment on each of these complexities may shed light on the character of the abstention doctrine as now viewed by the Court.

I

The District Court found the Illinois attachment procedure "patently and flagrantly violative of the constitution." *Hernandez v. Danaher,* 405 F.Supp. 757, 760 (N.D.Ill.1975). This Court, on the other hand, writes:

> "It is urged that this case comes within the exception that we said in *Younger* might exist where a state statute is 'flagrantly and patently violative of express constitutional prohibitions in every clause, sentence and paragraph, and in whatever manner and against whomever an effort might be made to apply it.' 401 U.S., at 53–54, 91 S.Ct. 755, quoting *Watson v. Buck,* 313 U.S. 387, 402, 61 S.Ct. 962, 967, 85 L.Ed. 1416 (1941). Even if such a finding was made below, *which we doubt * * *,* it would not have been warranted in light of our cases." *Ante,* at 1920 (emphasis added).

Since there is no doubt whatsoever as to what the District Court actually said, this Court's expression of doubt can only refer to its uncertainty as to whether a finding that the crux of the statute is patently and flagrantly unconstitutional is sufficient to satisfy the requirement that the statute be patently and flagrantly unconstitutional "in every clause, sentence and paragraph * * *." It is, therefore, appropriate to consider what is left of this exception to the *Younger* doctrine after today's decision.

The source of this exception is the passage Mr. Justice Black had written some years earlier in *Watson v. Buck,* 313 U.S. 387, 402, 61 S.Ct. 962, 967, 85 L.Ed. 1416, a case which involved a complicated state antitrust Act. On the basis of its conclusion that certain sections were unconstitutional, a three-judge District Court had enjoined enforcement of the entire Act. This Court reversed, holding: first, that the invalidity of a part of a statute would not justify an injunction against the entire Act; and second, that in any event the eight sections in question were valid.

In his explanation of the first branch of the Court's holding, Mr. Justice Black pointed out that there are few, if any, statutes that are totally unconstitutional in every part. Since *Watson* involved a new statute which had not been construed by any state court, and since such construction might have affected its constitutionality, Mr. Justice Black's comment emphasized the point that an untried state statute should not be invalidated by a federal court before the state court has an opportunity to construe it. This consideration is not present in a case involving an attack on a state statute that has been in use for more than a century. Nothing in *Watson* implies that a limited injunction against an invalid portion of a statute of long standing would be improper.

When he wrote the Court's opinion in *Younger v. Harris,* 401 U.S. 37, 91 S.Ct. 746, 27 L.Ed.2d 669, Mr. Justice Black quoted the foregoing excerpt from the *Watson* case as an example of a situation in which it would be appropriate for a federal court to enjoin a pending state criminal prosecution. He did not, however, imply that his earlier language rigidly defined the boundaries of one kind of exception from the equitable rationale underlying the *Younger* decision itself.

Today the Court seems to be saying that the "patently and flagrantly unconstitutional" exception to *Younger*-type abstention is unavailable whenever a statute has a legitimate title, or a legitimate severability clause, or some other equally innocuous provision. If this is a fair reading of the Court's opinion, the Court has given Mr. Justice Black's illustrative language definitional significance. In effect, this treatment preserves an illusion of flexibility in the application of a *Younger*-type abstention, but it actually eliminates one of the exceptions from the doctrine. For the typical constitutional attack on a statute focuses on one, or a few, objectionable features. Although, as Mr. Justice Black indicated in *Watson,* it is conceivable that there are some totally unconstitutional statutes, the possibility is quite remote. More importantly, the Court has never explained why all sections of any statute must be considered invalid in order to justify an injunction against a portion that is itself flagrantly unconstitutional. Even if this Court finds the constitutional issue less clear than did the District Court, I do not understand what governmental interest is served by refusing to address the merits at this stage of the proceedings.

II

The Court explicitly does not decide "whether *Younger* principles apply to all civil litigation." Its holding in this case therefore rests squarely on the fact that the State, rather than some other litigant, is the creditor that invoked the Illinois attachment procedure. This rationale cannot be tenable unless principles of federalism require greater deference to the State's interest in collecting its own claims than to its interest in providing a forum for other creditors in the community. It would seem rather obvious to me that the amount of money involved in any particular dispute is a matter of far less concern to the sovereign than the integrity of its own procedures. Consequently, the fact that a State is a party to a pending proceeding should make it *less* objectionable to have the constitutional issue adjudicated in a federal forum than if only private litigants were involved. I therefore find it hard to accept the

Court's contrary evaluation as a principled application of the majestic language in Mr. Justice Black's *Younger* opinion.

The dissent's discussion of the third and fourth "complexities" is omitted.

Notes and Questions

1. Consider the substantive issue involved in *Trainor*. How would you have ruled on the constitutionality of the attachment statute? *See supra* Chapter III, Section C. Note the majority opinion's reference to *Di–Chem* and *Mitchell*. They were cited for the proposition that the state statute could not be considered "flagrantly and patently violative of express constitutional prohibitions in every clause, sentence and paragraph, and in whatever manner and against whomever an effort might be made to apply it." Does this test make any sense?

2. The Court held that the principles of *Younger* were broad enough to prevent interference with ongoing civil enforcement actions brought by the state in its sovereign capacity. Should *Trainor* be read to extend to all civil proceedings? Why? Can traditional civil suits be distinguished from criminal proceedings for purposes of the *Younger* rule and its underlying policies?

3. Do the principles of *Younger* apply to noncriminal administrative proceedings? In *Middlesex County Ethics Committee v. Garden State Bar Association,* 457 U.S. 423 (1982), the Court refused, on *Younger* principles, to interfere with an attorney disciplinary proceeding challenged on First Amendment grounds. The federal claimant had not charged the local ethics committee with bad faith in the conduct of the proceedings. *See also Rizzo v. Goode,* 423 U.S. 362 (1976).

4. In light of the opinions of the Justices in *Trainor,* how should a state court rule on the constitutionality of the Illinois statute? Additional sources may be found in the Second Exercise in Synthesis, Chapter III, Section C.

E. POSTSCRIPT

A Legal Method and Process book published in the first decade of the 21st century could not go to press without noting the Supreme Court's role in the presidential election of 2000 and, in particular, alluding to the viability of several of the doctrines discussed in this chapter to the issues presented to the Court. *See Bush v. Palm Beach County Canvassing Bd.,* 531 U.S. 70, 121 S. Ct. 471 (2000) (per curiam); *Bush v. Gore,* 531 U.S. 98, 121 S. Ct. 525 (2000) (per curiam). Only time will tell whether these cases will have continuing precedential value in other areas or whether they will be confined to the context of an impasse in a presidential election. We do know that the Court was willing to decide politically charged issues without discussion of the political question doctrine in either case. Why? And, without any reference to his standing, the Court permitted George W. Bush to raise claims that a partial recount ordered by the Florida Supreme Court lacked adequate standards to protect Florida voters' constitutional rights. And what happened to the doctrine of federalism and the deference to state court interpretations of state law?

We have now examined various doctrines restricting the jurisdictional fabric of the federal courts in the resolution of constitutional disputes. Standing, mootness, ripeness, the political question doctrine, concepts of federalism, separation of powers, and the case and controversy requirement are the major threads. Yet, whatever doctrine is employed to justify dismissal of a case, each opinion imparts fresh insights into the Court's view of its role in conflict resolution. Perhaps, for the beginning law student, a grasp of this role is of greater significance than a clear perception of each of the threads. These doctrines will be further isolated and analyzed in courses on federal courts and constitutional law.

Index

References are to Pages

LEGAL METHOD
See Case Law; Case Method of Law Study.

LEGAL PRINCIPLES
Identification of, 93–94.

LEGAL REASONING
    See also Case Law; Logic.
Analogy, rule of, 59–60.
Custom, effect of, 62–63.
Distinguishing cases, 57–59.
Dynamic quality of law, 57.
History, effect of, 61–63.
Logic, role of, 61.
Philosophy, force of, 61–63.
Social welfare in creation of law, 63–64.

LEGISLATION
    See Statutes.
Drafting of, 371–372.

LEVI, DEAN EDWARD
Introduction to Legal Reasoning, 57.
Statutory application, 442–443.

LINCOLN, ABRAHAM
On the Supreme Court, 475.

LLEWELLYN, KARL
Statutes and canons of construction, 436–437.
Synthesis, 148–150.
The Bramble Bush,
    Case method, notes on, 30–32.
    Legal reasoning, 57–59.
    Student responsibility, 149 Note 12.

LOGIC
    See also Case Law; Legal Reasoning.
Use of, 59–61.

McKELWAY, ST. CLAIR
Attempts to evade service, 103–105.

MISDEMEANORS
See Criminal Justice System.

MOOTNESS
See Federal Court System, Limitations of Powers.

MOTIONS
See Pleading and Motions.

NEGOTIATIONS
Settlement of dispute, 95, 106–107.

NEWMAN, FRANK C. & SURREY, STANLEY S.
Statutory interpretation, sources of, 421.

NOTICE
See Due Process Clause.

OLIPHANT, HERMAN
Legal reasoning, 67–69.

PATTERSON, EDWIN W.
Case method, 24–30.

PERJURY
See Ethics, Legal; Facts of the Case.

PETTY OFFENSES
    See Criminal Justice System.
Defined, 298.

PLEADINGS AND MOTIONS
    See also Criminal Justice System.
Answer, 107–110.
Complaint, 101–102.
Mootness, related to, 527 Note 1.
Motions,
    Directed verdict, 143–144.
    Post-trial, 146, 303.
    Summary judgment, 113–114.
    To dismiss, pre-answer, 108–109.
Service of Process, 103–105.
Summons, 102–103, 106.

POLITICAL QUESTIONS
See Federal Court System, Limitations of Powers.

POSNER, RICHARD A.
Statutory construction, 437–447.

PRECEDENTS
See Case Law.

PRETRIAL CONFERENCE
Purposes and benefits, 119–120.

PRIVILEGES AND IMMUNITIES CLAUSE
Rights of citizens, 171.

PROCEDURE
See Discovery; Pleadings and Motions; Pretrial Conference; Trial.

REPLEVIN
See Due Process Clause.

RES JUDICATA
See Case Law.

RIPENESS
See Federal Court System, Limitations of Powers.

ROOSEVELT, FRANKLIN D.
On Supreme Court, 475.

SANDALOW, TERRENCE
Thinking like a lawyer, 32–34.

SCALIA, ANTONIN
Statutory interpretation, 413.

SEIZURE OF PROPERTY
As notice of jurisdiction, 99, 156, 163–164, 165 Note 7.
In rem jurisdiction, 150–163.
Notice and right to hearing, 218–261.
Quasi in rem jurisdiction, 186–209.

WARRANTS
See Fourth Amendment.

WORLD TRADE CENTER
Governmental searches and seizures, 369.

WRIGHT, CHARLES ALAN
Federal Courts, 456–460.

†

0–314–26002–1

90000

9 780314 260024